Presbyterian and Reformed Churches

Presbyterian and Reformed Churches
A Global History

James Edward McGoldrick

with
Richard Clark Reed

and
Thomas Hugh Spence Jr.

Reformation Heritage Books
Grand Rapids, Michigan

Presbyterian and Reformed Churches
© 2012 by James Edward McGoldrick

Reformation Heritage Books
2965 Leonard St. NE
Grand Rapids, MI 49525
616-977-0889 / Fax 616-285-3246
orders@heritagebooks.org
www.heritagebooks.org

Printed in the United States of America
12 13 14 15 16 17/10 9 8 7 6 5 4 3 2 1

Library of Congress Cataloging-in-Publication Data

McGoldrick, James Edward.
  Presbyterian and Reformed churches : a global history / by James Edward McGoldrick with Richard Clark Reed and Thomas Hugh Spence, Jr.
    p. cm.
  Rev. ed. of: History of the Presbyterian churches of the world / by R.C. Reed. Includes bibliographical references and index.
  ISBN 978-1-60178-162-8 (hardcover : alk. paper) 1. Presbyterian Church—History. 2. Reformed churches—History. I. Reed, R. C. (Richard Clark), 1851-1925. II. Spence, Thomas Hugh, 1899-1986. III. Reed, R. C. (Richard Clark) , 1851-1925. History of the Presbyterian churches of the world. IV. Title.
  BX8931.3.M36 2012
  285.09—dc23
                            2012004982

For additional Reformed literature, both new and used, request a free book list from Reformation Heritage Books at the above regular or e-mail address.

Contents

Preface

In 1905 Richard Clark Reed (1851–1925), then professor of church history at Columbia Theological Seminary, produced his *History of the Presbyterian Churches of the World*. Westminster Press published the book, and it soon became a widely read survey of Presbyterian and Reformed growth around the globe.

Reed followed his father into the ministry of the Presbyterian Church in the United States after study at King College and Union Theological Seminary in Virginia. The future historian was pastor of congregations in Tennessee, Virginia, and North Carolina before he joined the faculty of Columbia Theological Seminary in 1898. In addition to his pastoral and professorial labors, Reed was associate editor of the *Presbyterian Quarterly* and the *Presbyterian Standard* and moderator of the General Assembly of his church in 1892. He wrote *The Gospel as Taught by Calvin, A Historical Sketch of the Presbyterian Church in the United States,* and *What Is the Kingdom of God?,* as well as his major history of Presbyterianism and numerous articles.

As his publications indicate, Reed was an active churchman. While a professor at the seminary in Columbia, South Carolina, he decried the higher critical approach to the Old Testament popular in some American institutions. Reed warned that the influence of critical hypotheses about the composition of the Bible would lead to a loss of confidence in its divine authority. As a contributor to the *Presbyterian Standard*, the professor vigorously defended the historic Reformed commitment to the supremacy of Scripture and opposed the contentions of Charles Darwin, which he found incompatible with the teaching of Christianity.

Reed demonstrated his conservative posture further by resisting the Federal Council of Churches because that body engaged in political activities that, in his judgment, violated necessary separation of church and state. Reed opposed forming a council of Reformed churches because he feared it would lead to a union of denominations that lacked doctrinal homogeneity. When the General Assembly of his own church decided to allow a woman to address that body in 1920, Reed cast the only vote against it.

In his *History of the Presbyterian Churches of the World*, Reed provided a substantial survey in a readable style as a textbook for colleges and seminaries. He treated no era or church body in detail, and his coverage of events ended at the opening of the twentieth century. Although individual Presbyterian and Reformed groups have produced their own denominational histories, and compendia of information have appeared in historical dictionaries, no work comparable in scope to Reed's history has appeared in print since publication of his work.

Thomas Hugh Spence Jr. (1899–1986), a Presbyterian minister and at one time director of the Presbyterian Historical Foundation in Montreat, North Carolina, composed a manuscript that covers most of the same ground as Reed but more thoroughly. Spence's work, however, remains unpublished, despite the wealth of information it contains. With the permission of Mrs. Maria Elizabeth Thomas, Spence's daughter, I have made extensive use of his material in this revision and expansion of the pioneer work of Reed, so I have included Thomas Hugh Spence Jr., along with Reed, as one of the authors of the book. Thanks to the kindness of Mrs. Thomas and the encouragement of my colleague Dr. Morton H. Smith, who brought the Spence manuscript to my attention, it became possible to proceed with this project to provide a lucid, up-to-date history for Presbyterian and Reformed believers of all nations.

When Reed chose the title for his book, he explained the term *Presbyterian* signified those churches that subscribe to that form of connectional polity, even though some of them refer to themselves as Reformed rather than Presbyterian. In this new version of the history, I have followed Reed's practice but have altered the title to be more evidently descriptive.

In general the description of events follows the same order the original author designed. At the end of each chapter I have added suggestions for further reading. In some cases it was necessary to add or delete material, but the book as revised remains, up to the twentieth century, in large part the accomplishment of Richard Clark Reed, a tribute to his enduring relevance as a church historian.

The scope of this book takes the history through the twentieth century. The few references to developments since then are incidental and intended only to provide logical and chronological connections. In historiographical terms, the period since the year 2000 is one of current events, the history of which remains to be written when scholars have the opportunity to assess their effects.

Although the objective of this study is to give due recognition to the numerous Presbyterian and Reformed bodies around the world, the constraints of time and space made it necessary to be less than all-inclusive. In some cases this was because the Reformed presence in some countries is so small as to be almost negligible in influence, while in other cases the number of denominations and subgroups is so large that it became necessary to be selective. In the matter of statistics, I have relied on three major sources, but, to my dismay, they often do not agree, and sometimes the discrepancies are astonishing. Readers who consult these resources will readily see the problem. In almost all accounts, the statistics are therefore, at best, estimates.

Special thanks are due to the many authors from whose works I have gleaned useful information and to Linda Rudolph, who typed the manuscript and encouraged me as I progressed with this project. For her patience, diligence, and cheerful disposition I shall always be grateful. Thanks are due to Annette Gysen, who edited the manuscript and made helpful suggestions for improving it.

James Edward McGoldrick
Taylors, South Carolina

ONE

Introduction to Presbyterian History

Presbyterian history may be said to have originated in the New Testament, when the apostles of Christ organized a form of church government that placed authority over the congregations in the hands of elders. This was not an innovation but a continuation of the pattern that had prevailed in Jewish synagogues for many years. In the New Testament the terms *pastor*, *elder*, and *bishop* are used interchangeably, as, for example, when Peter admonished church leaders: "The elders who are among you I exhort, I who am a fellow elder and a witness of the sufferings of Christ.... Shepherd [pastor] the flock of God which is among you, serving as overseers [bishops] (1 Peter 5:1–2 NKJV).

Presbyters, or elders, were bishops in apostolic times, and there was a plurality of them in each congregation. Some elders concentrated on teaching the Word of God while others exercised governing oversight, but all were equal in authority and ruled together. Presbyterianism is, then, a form of church polity found in the New Testament. Any church body that implements this pattern may be called Presbyterian regardless of its doctrinal principles, although most churches that fit this description have espoused to some degree the position known as Calvinism or Reformed theology.

The Church of the Second Century

According to the church father Ignatius of Antioch (d. ca. 111), a gradation of authority among elders began to appear early in the second century. It then became common to regard only one elder in each congregation as the bishop and to acknowledge his precedence over the others. Gradually the distinction became pronounced, and by the end of the second century, bishops had gained superiority over elders. In this way the church moved from its original Presbyterian polity toward episcopacy (rule by bishops, from the Greek term *episcopos*, which means overseer).

The movement toward episcopacy was not uniform throughout the church, since it progressed more rapidly in some areas than in others. Traces of the older form of government lingered in some regions into the fifth century. Episcopacy was at first parochial, not diocesan. Each congregation, such as that at Smyrna or Philadelphia, had its own bishop, elders, and deacons. Although information about ecclesiastical developments in this early era is scant, it appears that elders and deacons then functioned much as they do in modern Presbyterian churches, and bishops operated in ways comparable to pastors today.

The Movement toward the Papacy

The evolution in church government can be traced with approximate accuracy only in outlines, but there is reason to believe it began when one elder in each congregation acquired the position of permanent moderator in the session of presbyters. The one who held that office would, as a matter of course, be noted because of his gifts for leadership and force of character, which would make him chief spokesman for his church in his relations with other congregations. As heresies and other disorders affected the Christian community, his position grew in influence and authority.

It is a well-attested fact that nothing contributed so much to the rise of authoritative bishops as the demand for speedy, stringent discipline to suppress developing disorders. As the church father and famous Bible scholar Jerome (340–420) explained, "Before factions were introduced...by the devil, churches were governed by a council of presbyters; but as soon as each man began to consider those whom he had baptized as belonging to himself and not to Christ, it was decided throughout the world that one elected from among the elders should be placed over the rest, so that the care of the church should devolve on him, and the seeds of schism be removed."

The motive that prompted departure from scriptural simplicity was the belief that, for the preservation of sound doctrine and good order, it was necessary to concentrate authority in a few hands, that discipline might be more effectively administered. This motive continued, along with less worthy ones, until parochial episcopacy changed into diocesan rule, and that into the papacy. Municipal bishops gained ascendancy over rural ones and patriarchal bishops over them. Eventually the patriarch of Rome gained preeminence over all.

The Extinction of Presbyterianism

The exaltation of bishops, of course, diminished the influence of elders. As the latter ceased to be bishops in name, they ceased to be overseers in practice and were reduced to the role of servants to the bishops, who deputed them to preach and administer the sacraments. This development occurred concurrent with belief in the sacerdotal character of the ministry, and in keeping with this, it became a custom to regard pastors as priests. In this connection, the sacramental role of priests took precedence over the ministry of preaching. Eventually clergymen came to regard their function as hearing confessions, prescribing penances, and celebrating masses. Not only did the office of ruling elder fade away, that of teaching elder also declined in influence. So-called priests usurped the functions of the one Mediator (1 Timothy 2:5–6) and claimed almost exclusive control over the means of grace. When almost all traces of biblical eldership disappeared, little of apostolic Presbyterianism remained.

Church Polity and the Protestant Reformers

By the time Protestantism made its debut in the sixteenth century, the medieval church had developed an extensive hierarchy over which the pope presided in a regal manner. Late medieval efforts to restrict the pontiff's prerogatives through occasional general councils had been only slightly successful, so the ecclesiastical monarchy appeared to be firmly entrenched. When the work of reformation began with the labors of Martin Luther (1483–1546), he and his coworkers did not at first give great attention to church polity, for their initial concern was to correct false teaching about sin and salvation. Protestants extolled the authority of the Bible, but it did not yet occur to them that Scripture had a message for them about the visible form of Christ's kingdom of grace. They therefore left church government to develop under the influence of the circumstances in which they lived.

The State of the Church in England

When Protestant influences appeared in England early in the sixteenth century, the monarchy resisted changes in doctrine or polity, as Henry VIII (r. 1509–1547) defended traditional Catholic teachings. Even after the king broke with Rome and assumed rule over his church, he opposed the Protestants and maintained the episcopate, which then became subservient to the Crown rather than the pope. The government of the church remained

hierarchical, with the king as supreme head and the archbishops and bishops as royal servants who held their positions at the king's pleasure.

The death of Henry VIII allowed Protestants to assert themselves vigorously because Edward VI (r. 1547–1553), the new monarch, embraced the
Reformation. He and his religious advisors, however, remained committed
to an episcopal system to administer the church. At that point the Church
of England set for itself a difficult task. Having renounced the papacy in
favor of Scripture as the supreme authority, Anglican scholars tried to show
that the government of the church was derived from the Word of God.
Thereafter, for many years learned Anglicans published academic treatises
to verify their ecclesiastical structure, while sometimes godless rulers controlled the state church and used it to sanctify their policies. Like popes of
the Middle Ages, monarchs of England claimed preeminence in church
and state. Any reform in church government would have entailed major
political consequences, and many strong Protestants feared the loss of royal
patronage would damage their cause. They therefore endorsed a form of
polity for which no higher warrant could be found than political expediency.

Luther and Germany

The challenge to Roman Catholicism that brought the Reformation to
England originated in Germany, when Martin Luther decried the financial
abuses connected with the sale of indulgences. It proceeded from that point
to subject the entire structure of the medieval church to scrutiny under the
searchlight of Scripture. In his 1520 *Address to the Christian Nobility*, Luther
denied the sacerdotal character of the clergy when he asserted there is but
one spiritual estate of which all genuine Christians are members, whether
they are pastors or laymen. He proclaimed the universal priesthood of
believers and insisted ordained ministers are but servants of their people.
In addition, Luther contended God's people have the right to choose their
pastors and to participate with them in matters of church discipline.

Luther's position was a radical contrast with centuries of tradition, and
even some of his most zealous supporters recoiled from implementing the
changes in polity it would have required. The Reformer himself allowed the
circumstances of the time to deter him from pursuing drastic alterations in
polity, since he judged the German people too ignorant to discharge the
duties of self-government in the church.

Between 1524 and 1525, Germany was engulfed in a Peasants' War that
brought massive loss of life and property before civil authorities suppressed

it. Some of the rebels cited Luther's teaching about universal priesthood as inspiration for the uprising, but the Reformer denounced the insurgents and called the princes to crush them, which they were already resolved to do, with or without Luther's approval. One consequence of this tragedy was that Luther lost all confidence in common people and turned even more than before to the rulers of the German churches, in which evangelical princes exerted decisive authority. A 1555 formal agreement among the rulers affirmed their right to determine the religion of their territories, Catholic or Lutheran. What Luther expected to be benevolent leadership, however, eventually became authoritarian control over religion, but Luther was dead by then.

The early German Reformers were occupied primarily with proclaiming salvation by grace alone, and they did not attach great importance to any particular form of church government. They would have accepted the traditional episcopate, had the bishops embraced the evangelical faith. In their Augsburg Confession of Faith (1530), Lutheran leaders affirmed: "Our meaning is not to have rule taken from the bishops; but this one thing only is required at their hands, that they would permit the Gospel to be purely taught, and that they would relax a few observances which cannot be held without sin."

When Sweden adopted the Lutheran faith as an act of state, it left the episcopate in place, while in Denmark the king appointed superintendents who performed episcopal functions. Most German states put the management of church affairs in the hands of consistories, courts composed of clergymen and civil jurists subject to the princes. Undergirding the Lutheran approach to ecclesiastical polity was the belief that Scripture does not mandate a specific pattern, so Christians have the option to adopt whichever one is suitable to the needs of their particular situation. Lutheran churches today continue to operate with a variety of forms.

A Presbyterian Experiment in Hesse

Consonant with the elastic ecclesiology of the Lutheran Reformers, there was an effort in the German state of Hesse to adopt a generally Presbyterian polity. There Prince Philip (1504–1567), a champion of the Reformation, under the influence of Francis Lambert (1487–1530), his chief religious advisor, sought to strengthen the Protestant cause by all available means. Guided by Lambert, a converted Franciscan friar, a synod met at Homburg in 1525 to draft a charter for the government of the church in the principality of Hesse. That document called for congregations to elect their own pastors and to exercise discipline over their members. There was to be a synod of pastors and delegates from each local church to meet yearly to consider issues submitted by the congregations. This proposal, at least in purpose, approximated the New Testament model that became the pattern of later Presbyterianism, and it agreed with Luther's early teaching, but the great Reformer opposed the scheme as impracticable in the circumstances of the time. The plan did not take effect.

Zwingli and German Switzerland

Concurrent with the work of Luther in Germany, Ulrich Zwingli (1484–1531) led the Reformation in Zurich. Although the two Reformers had much in common, they disagreed about some doctrines and labored independently of each other. Zwingli, even more than Luther, resolved to apply biblical patterns to all of life, but unlike the Wittenberg Reformer, he regarded the Old Testament as an authoritative model for church-state relations. He therefore had no conception of the church as an entity distinct from civil authority with its own structure of government. He favored an ecclesiocracy, in which church and state were one and the laws of the land regulated religious life. For example, Zwingli awarded the power of excommunication from the church to the civil magistrates. The council that governed the state selected pastors for the congregations.

Although some Reformers in German Switzerland advised giving the members some role in church polity, the magistrates retained their authority, and other Protestant cantons in general observed the same practice. While it is customary among historians to cite Zwingli's work as initiating the Reformed branch of the Protestant faith, his union of church and state was far removed from the Presbyterian pattern that became standard in Reformed churches around the world.

Early Presbyterianism

It is evident the first generation of Protestant Reformers concentrated on maintaining purity in doctrine and restoring biblical patterns in worship. They did not pursue the restoration of New Testament polity with the same fervor. This was, in the case of the Lutherans, a matter of exercising options, and for Zurich a simple adherence to Old Testament precedents.

Some Reformers were willing to accept almost any plan, while others left the matter to be decided by the exigencies of the future. To them church government was among the *adiaphora*, things indifferent because they were unrelated to the ministry of Word and sacraments. Credit for restoring church polity to the level it merits belongs to Martin Bucer (1491–1551) of Strasbourg and to John Calvin (1509–1564) of Geneva. Bucer, once a Dominican friar, was converted to the evangelical faith through the witness of Luther when the Wittenberg professor presented an outline of his theology at Heidelberg in 1518. Bucer arrived in Strasbourg in 1523, and soon the city council adopted the Reformation, as Protestant preachers worked to implement changes mandated by their allegiance to the gospel. Strasbourg was a comparatively tolerant community to which refugees from persecution in Catholic lands fled for safety.

Bucer had considerable influence as an evangelical theologian and churchman who strove relentlessly to promote unity within Protestant ranks. He failed to bring Luther and Zwingli together after their dispute about the real presence of Christ in the Eucharist, but he was able to unite the Protestants of South Germany into fellowship with the Lutherans. In church government Bucer introduced the office of *wardens*, officials selected from prominent Strasbourg families with the approval of the city council. He found the basis for wardens in the office of elders in the New Testament. Bucer distinguished between teaching and ruling elders, as most modern Presbyterians do. In developing his pattern for church order in Strasbourg, Bucer set an example that was to influence Calvin and the church in Geneva and, indirectly, Reformed churches around the world. Bucer and Calvin met in 1539 and became close friends.

Bucer's influence upon Calvin was substantial, both in doctrine and practice. The future Reformer of Geneva spent three years in Strasbourg, where he became acquainted with Bucer's teaching about offices of ministry, church order, discipline, and education. While residing there Calvin was pastor of a congregation in which Lutheran influence was prominent, but he did not accept German indifference toward forms of church government. On the contrary, Calvin came to believe early it is of paramount importance to distinguish clearly between church and society at large and that the church, not civil authorities, must administer discipline over its members. In his view the power of the Reformed faith could not be effective in vigorous evangelism without a clearly defined independent ecclesiastical organization. The kingdom of Christ, while not of this world, is nevertheless in this world and is here for the purpose of conquest. It must therefore have visible shape, and in order to have this, its limits and powers must be clearly demarcated. Calvin went to the Bible for his model, but, unlike Zwingli, he resorted to the New Testament alone for guidance in this area.

So important was ecclesiology, the doctrine of the church, that Calvin devoted about five hundred pages of his *Institutes of the Christian Religion* (1559) to that subject. Once he discovered the principles of correct polity in the New Testament, the Reformer resolved to implement them consistently, an effort that involved him in years of conflict with city magistrates who resisted any diminution of their authority over religion. Calvin's desire to free the church from state control initiated a struggle that lasted fifteen years, a period during which he was sometimes in danger because of the animosity his proposals provoked.

Despite the hardships he endured, Calvin's teaching prevailed. Great was his service as a theologian, but no less great was his contribution as a churchman. In restoring the New Testament rule by elders, he gave the laity a half-share in the government of the church. One effect of this was to bring pastors and people together to discredit the idea of a sacerdotal clergy spiritually superior to ordinary Christians. A second effect was to encourage people to demand the right to govern themselves and thereby initiate resistance to tyrannies.

Calvin's influence was due not only to the system of doctrine he composed but also to the republican form of government he implemented in the church. Wherever his teaching gained acceptance, people began to demand their rights as *citizens*, not *subjects*, of the state. He did not advocate democracy in the modern usage of that term, yet the freest nations of the contemporary world are still those in which his teaching has the deepest roots.

SUGGESTED ADDITIONAL READINGS >>

Barrett, David R., ed. *World Christian Encyclopedia.* Oxford: Oxford University Press, 1982.

Bauswein, Jean-Jacques and Lukas Vischer, eds. *The Reformed Family Worldwide.* Grand Rapids: Eerdmans, 1999.

Benedetto, Robert with Darrell L. Guder and Donald K. McKim. *Historical Dictionary of Reformed Churches.* Lanham, Md.: Scarecrow Press, 1991.

Clark, Gordon H. *What Do Presbyterians Believe?* Philadelphia: Presbyterian and Reformed, 1965.

Glover, Robert Hall and J. Herbert Kane. *The Progress of World-Wide Missions.* Rev. ed. New York: Harper & Row, 1960.

Goddard, Burton, ed. *The Encyclopedia of Modern Christian Missions.* Camden, N.J.: Nelson, 1967.

Hillerbrand, Hans J., ed. *Encyclopedia of Protestantism.* 4 vols. New York: Routledge, 2004.

Jackson, Samuel Macauley, ed. *The New Schaff-Herzog Encyclopedia of Religious Knowledge.* 13 vols. Reprint, Grand Rapids: Baker, 1977.

Kane, J. Herbert. *A Concise History of the Christian World Mission.* Rev. ed. Grand Rapids: Baker, 1982.

Latourette, Kenneth S. *Christianity in a Revolutionary Age.* 4 vols. Grand Rapids: Zondervan, 1962. Reprinted 1969.

———. *A History of the Expansion of Christianity.* 7 vols. New York: Harper & Row, 1943.

Leitch, Addison H. *A Layman's Guide to Presbyterian Beliefs.* Grand Rapids: Zondervan, 1967.

Lingle, Walter. *Presbyterians: Their History and Beliefs.* Richmond, Va.: John Knox, 1944.

Loetscher, Lefferts A., ed. *Twentieth Century Encyclopedia of Religious Knowledge.* 2 vols. Grand Rapids: Baker, 1977.

Lucas, Sean Michael. *On Being Presbyterian: Our Beliefs, Practices, and Stories.* Phillipsburg, N.J.: P&R, 2006.

McKim, Donald K. and David F. Wright, eds. *Encyclopedia of the Reformed Faith.* Louisville, Ky.: Westminster/John Knox, 1992.

Moreau, A. Scott with Harold Netland and Charles Van Engen, eds. *Evangelical Dictionary of World Missions.* Grand Rapids: Baker, 2000.

Reed, R. C. *History of the Presbyterian Churches of the World.* Philadelphia: Westminster, 1905.

Smith, Ebgbert Watson. *The Creed of Presbyterians.* Rev. ed. Richmond, Va.: John Knox, 1941.

Thiessen, John Caldwell. *A Survey of World Missions.* Chicago: InterVarsity, 1955.

Tucker, Ruth A. *From Jerusalem to Irian Jaya: A Biographical History of Christian Missions.* Grand Rapids: Zondervan, 1983.

TWO

Switzerland

With all due regard for the contributions of Martin Bucer, in terms of lasting influence, the reform in Geneva provided the nursery for the development of modern Presbyterianism. France furnished the man (Calvin), but Switzerland supplied the home.

Geneva

Until 1648, the region around Lake Geneva was, like the rest of Switzerland, a nominal part of the Holy Roman Empire. Actually it was a loose confederation of autonomous cantons. The Catholic Church there was subject ultimately to the pope and immediately to its bishops. Conditions among the Swiss clergymen were poor, in that numerous priests maintained concubines in violation of canon law, and the bishops fined them for that practice but did not try to terminate it. Mountainous terrain divided the people into regions remote from one another, so communications were slow. Each province had its own traditions, so strong cantonal identity was more pronounced than nationality. Should nonconformity in religion appear, the papacy would have much difficulty suppressing it, and that happened in French-speaking Switzerland when William Farel (1489–1565) began preaching in several cities. This fearless Frenchman pursued his work with fervor to the point of arousing powerful backlashes against his contentions.

Farel first appeared in Geneva in 1532. He found the city a place of lax morals and much anxiety because its liberty was in jeopardy as the Duke of Savoy conspired to subdue it to his rule. Bern, which had embraced the Protestant faith earlier, was eager to promote the Reformation in Geneva, so Bernese authorities sent Farel there to initiate the effort. By the end of 1533, he had gained enough supporters to form a congregation. After his attacks on Catholic monasticism and a debate with a Dominican scholar, a riot erupted, and Reformed zealots seized a monastery chapel for their own place of worship. Since Protestant Bern was Geneva's only reliable ally against Savoy, the city government allowed the reform to proceed. In this way the success of Protestantism was linked to the preservation of Geneva's independence. By this time the Catholic bishop had fled and joined Savoy to prepare an attack on the city. When Farel and his associate Pierre Viret (1511–1571) triumphed in various debates with Catholic spokesmen, more people adhered to their cause. Violent assaults upon Catholic church buildings occurred, and in May 1536 the government declared Geneva a Protestant city. Support from Bern enabled it to withstand Savoy and to retain its independence as a free city.

Because political action as much as religious fervor had ended Catholic rule, the city was still not committed earnestly to the gospel. There was urgent need to organize a Reformed church there, but that was a task beyond the talents of Farel, and he soon recruited John Calvin to lead that endeavor.

Enter John Calvin

Calvin arrived in Geneva in 1536 with no intention to remain there, for he was not there as an emissary of the Reformed faith but as a transient. When Farel learned of Calvin's presence, he sought to recruit the learned Frenchman to assist in the work of reformation, a task Calvin was not disposed to undertake. However, despite efforts to refuse Farel's request, Calvin relented when his comrade uttered a curse upon him much in the manner of some biblical prophets. The "dreadful imprecation" frightened the sensitive scholar and led him to comply with Farel's demand. Calvin then joined the staff of the church, though at first he was engaged as a lecturer rather than a minister. To Farel belongs a twofold credit, since he recognized Calvin's abilities and persuaded him to pursue them in the service of Geneva. In his old age, when Farel walked from his home in Neuchatel to visit the dying Calvin, he could temper his grief with the knowledge God had used him to cement a tie that led to great achievements for the cause of Christ in Geneva and beyond.

As coworkers, Farel and Calvin sought restoration of biblical doctrines in order to effect a reformation of morals and manners in a city notorious for vice. The preachers proclaimed the law of God and expected people to obey it, and they promised to do so. Calvin prepared a confession of faith, and the city government required all residents to subscribe by oath to accept it. Those who refused to do so had to leave Geneva.

Opposition to the stern innovations the Reformed preachers introduced was strong. Even before Calvin arrived in Geneva, there were plots to murder Farel, Viret, and other ministers, and a servant girl accused of serving them poisoned soup had been executed. The pastors survived, although Viret became very sick.

Although the magistrates adopted the Protestant Reformation officially, establishment of a biblical church required organization and education of the populace. To his dismay, Calvin soon learned that many residents had so little comprehension of the gospel that they thought reform could be achieved merely by removing idols and other symbols of the old religion from municipal life. The vigor with which the ministers promoted changes then irritated even some of the city rulers, especially when the Reformers demanded freedom for the church to administer its own affairs and to discipline its members. Most magistrates deeply resented any efforts to deprive the government of its authority over the church, and the issue came to a head in 1538, when the pastors refused to administer the Lord's Supper because they perceived there was still flagrant immorality within the church. The civil authorities then ordered Calvin, Farel, and some other ministers to leave the city after only two years of labor there. Farel went to Neuchatel, where he remained until his death. Calvin moved to Zurich and then to Basel before he settled in Strasbourg, where he was a pastor until 1541. There he married Idelette de Bure (1505–1549), a widow of an Anabaptist who had accepted the Reformed faith.

Calvin's sojourn in Strasbourg was highly productive, as he taught theology and wrote some of his most enduringly influential treatises. There he revised and enlarged his *Institutes on the Christian Religion*, authored a commentary of the epistle to the Romans, prepared a psalter, and wrote an essay about the Eucharist. One of Protestantism's most important documents came from his pen at this time as *A Reply to Sadoleto* (1539).

Jacopo Sadoleto (1477–1547) was a cardinal and bishop of Carpentras who, when he learned Geneva had expelled Calvin, wrote to the Genevans in a cordial, diplomatic manner, seeking to convince them to return to the Roman fold. Calvin soon issued a rebuttal since there was no scholar of repute in Geneva then to perform that service. Sadoleto, a fine scholar, was a conciliatory apologist for Catholicism who had thwarted Protestant efforts within his own diocese, and he was known to oppose persecution of religious dissidents. His appeal to Geneva was in general an eloquent affirmation of traditional Catholicism with little reference to Scripture. Calvin's response, which arrived in Geneva September 1, 1539, made a favorable impression because of the skill with which he defended the Protestant position. This allowed supporters of Farel and Calvin who regretted the expulsion of 1538 to strengthen their influence, and after some tumultuous dissension, the party supportive of the Reformers gained control of the government and petitioned them to return. Calvin did so with great reluctance and spent the rest of his life there.

During the time of Calvin's absence (1538–1541), Geneva had experienced much disorder. Of the four magistrates in office at the time Farel and Calvin were banished, one was killed while seeking to escape arrest, one was beheaded, and the others fled into exile. Calvin agreed to return only with the condition that the people submit to discipline as members of the church. Soon the government ratified Ecclesiastical Ordinances, which an assembly of citizens endorsed by vote. This marked such a decisive victory for the Reformation that some historians cite it as the birthday of modern Presbyterianism.

Church and State in Geneva

A republican structure was already in place in Geneva long before the Protestant Reformers arrived. A General Council composed of all male citizens over twenty-one years of age had primary authority in matters of state, and it assembled in St. Peter's Church when criers announced meetings by blowing trumpets in the streets. The council elected four magistrates with the title of syndics, and they in turn appointed the Lesser Council, a body of twenty-five. There were two other councils, one of two hundred members, the other of sixty. The latter handled routine matters of government and was an influence for stability, since meetings of the General Council often became disorderly as factions asserted their particular interests. Relations among these levels of authority were not clearly defined, but the power of each council was in inverse ratio to its size. For example, the General Council could not consider an issue until the Council of 200 debated it first, and only after the Council of 60 had done so. At the top of the ladder stood the Lesser Council, which initiated all legislation. Geneva was, in practice, an oligarchy.

Calvin had no desire to organize a church entirely separate from the state, and he could not foresee a situation in which church and state might be hostile to each other. His reliance upon the Old Testament led him to seek a Christian state in which the civil and religious authorities would have distinct spheres of operation, each supporting the other in the discharge but not in the legislation of its God-given duties. Mutual cooperation for the glory of God and the benefit of the people was Calvin's ideal. This concern meant the church would place the policies of the state under its scrutiny, lest the magistrates enact immoral or heretical measures. Calvin took a personal interest in advising the rulers to be sure the laws of the community would concur with the laws of God revealed in Scripture.

The Ecclesiastical Ordinances (1541)
Perhaps the best way to describe the character of the ordinances that regulated church-state relations in Geneva is to transcribe a few of the most important articles. The civil authorities prefaced the adoption of these provisions with the following declaration:

> In the name of the most mighty God, we syndics, with the Great and Small Councils of Geneva, with our people assembled by sound of the trumpet, and the great bell, following our ancient customs, having considered that it is a thing worthy of commendation above all other that the doctrine of the holy gospel of our Lord God be conserved well in purity, and the Christian Church maintained accordingly, also that youth in time to come be well and faithfully instructed, and the hospital be ordered in good state for the sustentation of the poor, the which cannot be except there be established a certain rule and manner to live, by the which every state may understand the duty of his office. For this cause it seemed good to us that the spiritual government, such as God hath showed unto us and instituted by his word, be brought into good form, to have place and to be observed by us, and we have ordained and established to follow and to keep in our own town and territory the ecclesiastical polity following, which is taken out of the gospel of Jesus Christ:
>
> Church Officers.—First of all, there are four orders of officers, which our Lord hath instituted for the government of his Church, that is to say, pastors, doctors, elders, otherwise named commissioners for the seniory, and fourthly deacons. If we will have a church well ordered and kept in the purity, we must observe this form of government.
>
> 1. As concerning pastors, which the Scriptures name sometime watchmen, and sometime ministers, their offices are to declare the word of God, to teach, to admonish, to exhort, to prove as well publicly as privately, to minister sacraments, and to do brotherly correction with the elders, or commissioners.

2. The proper office of doctors is to teach the faithful with sound doctrine to the end that the purity of the gospel be not corrupted by ignorance, or wicked opinions; nevertheless, according as things be disposed in these days, we do comprehend them under this title, to be aides and instruments to conserve the doctrine of God, so that the church be not desolate for fault of pastors and ministers, but to use a word more intelligible we shall call them the order of scholars.

3. The office of the elders is to take heed and to watch of the demeanor and behavior of all and every of the people, to admonish lovingly those which they see fall, or lead a dissolute life, or if it be needful to make the report, or to do brotherly correction, and that shall be commonly done by the company that shall be thereto appointed.

4. There hath been always two sundry kinds or sorts of officers in the ancient Church, the one were deputies to receive, to deliver and to conserve the goods of the poor, as well daily alms, as possessions, stipends and pensions; the other to feed and oversee the sick, and to minister the portion of the poor.

When Geneva adopted these ordinances, it established a pattern for the administration of the church, which, with some modifications, remains in effect in today's Presbyterian churches. Modern Presbyterians have discarded the office of *doctor* because of their belief that pastors and teachers in the New Testament held the same office. It is likely that Calvin intended the doctors to educate candidates for the ministry. Such professors were chosen by men already in the ministry. Approval required action by the city government, and the candidates were subject to church discipline.

The deacons had two principal responsibilities. Some of them cared for the hospital and public health in general, while others ministered to the poor, the widows, and the orphans. Geneva had a rather elaborate social welfare program maintained in part to serve the many refugees who had fled there to escape persecution in Catholic regions.

Election and Appointment of Church Officers

A company of pastors examined candidates for the ministry and recommended to the Lesser Council those the pastors approved. If candidates satisfied the council, they were invited to preach before the people, who would then vote. If the decision were positive, the man would be inducted into office after subscribing to a comprehensive oath of loyalty to the city and its institutions.

The Reformed church chose its elders from among members of the various city councils, two from the Lesser Council, four from the Council of 60, six from the Council of 200. All nominations originated with the Lesser Council in conference with the pastors, and approval of nominees required concurrence from the Council of 200. Elders thus chosen swore to be faithful to the duties of their office and to be loyal to the city. Elders were placed on probation for one year before they could be confirmed in office. The Lesser Council chose the deacons in much the same manner.

The Consistory

The only ecclesiastical court in Geneva was the Consistory, composed of the pastors of the city and twelve elders chosen by the Council of 200. Elders were to oversee the populace and to meet each Thursday with the ministers to consider church matters and to find remedies for any disorders that might occur. Should the Consistory conclude that a church member was deserving of censure, the Lesser Council would summon him to appear before the Consistory. If the offense were one that merited only admonition, the Consistory would dispose of the matter. If the issue involved a grave offense, the Consistory could decide for excommunication, but it had to report its finding to the council. The Consistory resembled a local church session, but a presbytery as well. It issued rules for behavior and disciplined violators. Among the prohibitions it enacted were adultery, playing cards, visiting taverns, attending theaters, and public criticism of ministers.

As an adjunct to the Consistory there was a commission of visitors who toured the parishes once a year to inquire about the fidelity of ministers. The magistrates appointed two of these visitors, and the Venerable Company of Pastors chose the other two. The commissioners reported any serious failures on the part of pastors to the Lesser Council. As a rule the pastors appreciated the accountability this imposed.

Church-State Conflicts

Although the government of the church in Geneva was Calvin's design, he did not enjoy exemption from the constraints of jealous civil authorities. Conflicts between church and state were common, as the Lesser Council sometimes claimed the right to negate decisions of the Consistory in cases of excommunication. Calvin struggled fifteen years before he was able to emancipate the church from the interference of the civil powers. His great achievement was the assertion of some fundamental principles that became and remain features of Presbyterian polity. In this regard he sought a church distinct from the state, if not independent of it. He revived the New Testament offices of elder and deacon, and he placed church government in the hands of teaching and ruling elders. He organized a means to preserve the unity of the church by placing the parishes under the discipline of one court. These measures are constituent elements of Presbyterianism, and it is proper therefore to cite Geneva as the mother church of modern Presbyterian bodies.

While it is well to hail Calvin's accomplishments, an objective examination of the ecclesiastical establishment in Geneva requires the admission that not all was well there. Church and state were too closely aligned, joined in an unholy, and in the end, unhappy wedlock. Lordship belonged to the state, the church being the weaker partner. The harmful consequences became evident after Calvin's death, when his powerful presence could no longer defend the rights of the church. Thereafter the Lesser Council often intruded into church affairs, as the structure of the Ecclesiastical Ordinances permitted. On occasions the magistrates overturned decisions of the Consistory, either to lighten penalties for offenses or to make them more severe.

A notorious incident in which the Lesser Council acted as the final authority was the trial and execution of the convicted Spanish Anabaptist heretic, Michael Servetus (1511–1553). Prosecution and execution in Geneva followed the same condemnation in Catholic territory from which Servetus had escaped. His offense was a militant denial of the Trinity, which he expressed in two books, *The Errors of the Trinity* (1532) and *The Restitutes of the Christian Religion* (1553). The title of the second work shows the author's intention to attack Calvin, whom he viewed as the destroyer of Christianity. The Roman Church had for centuries regarded heresy as the worst of crimes because it destroyed souls, and that church expected civil rulers to suppress false doctrine and to remove those who persisted in teaching it. Calvin and other Reformers failed to perceive the fallacy in that policy and so approved the prosecution of Servetus. Calvin believed the accused heretic deserved death and so charged him before a civil court.

Why Servetus went to Geneva remains a mystery. His previous attacks upon Calvin's doctrine and personal insults about the Reformer's character almost assured a hostile reception there, but it is likely Calvin's enemies lured the heretic to Geneva in the hope of creating an incident that would embarrass, and perhaps discredit, the despised pastor. Since Calvin's opponents, whom he called Libertines, still had substantial influence with the

Lesser Council, they had some reason to expect success against him. Civil law in Geneva prescribed death for denial of the Trinity, but the Ecclesiastical Ordinances called only for banishment. Since the trial was in a civil court, the criminal code applied, and death by burning occurred in October 1553. Although Calvin consented to the decision, he asked the court to execute Servetus by decapitation because he thought burning a cruel method. The magistrates rejected his appeal.

Attempts to excuse Calvin's role in this tragedy have not been successful, but some mitigating factors merit consideration. Calvin was not, at the time of the trial, a citizen of the republic and so could not vote in the public assembly or hold any political office. Proceedings against the accused heretic were in a court where the Reformer had no authority to pass judgment or to impose the sentence. Other Swiss cities expressed approval, and even Philip Melanchthon (1497–1560), Luther's rather irenic colleague and successor at Wittenberg, consented to the execution. Such endorsements confirmed Calvin in his opinion and greatly enhanced his prestige in Geneva.

In the sixteenth century few religious leaders favored broad toleration of diverse beliefs. Only adherents to the so-called Radical Reformation—Anabaptists, Rationalists, and Spiritualists—sought full freedom of religion, and they had a vested interest in doing so, since both Catholic and Protestant authorities viewed them as subversives.

After all factors are considered, it is wrong to say Calvin executed Servetus, but his complicity in that event is evident. He lacked a clear perception of the proper relation between things that belong to Caesar and those that belong to God.

Authoritarian Rule

Calvin and his coadjutors had slight respect for the rights of conscience. They left nothing to its decision but tried by a rigid discipline, covering all areas of life, including minute details of conduct, to constrain everyone to live by the rules they prescribed. Proclamations, published with sound of trumpet, laid down injunctions and prohibitions and imposed severe penalties for violations. For example,

> No manner of person…shall wear any chains of gold or silver; but those who have been accustomed to wear them, shall put them off and wear them no more,…upon pain of three score shillings for every time…. No woman may wear more than two rings on her fingers, except on the day of her marriage, she may wear more and on the

day after, upon pain of three score shillings each time. No manner of persons, making…banquets or feasts, shall have above three courses or services to the said feasts, and to every course or service, not above four dishes…upon pain of three score shillings for each time, fruit excepted.*

All such proclamations—and there were many of them—were issued with the authority of the syndics and the city councils. They were civil, not ecclesiastical, enactments. The state sought to make upright living the ultimate aim of its endeavors since the city had adopted the Reformed faith, and the citizens took an oath to live according to God's law. Many residents, however, did not support this policy, and some who did at first grew weary of it eventually. The majority, however, stood with Calvin, as the state used its machinery to require subscription to orthodoxy and to compel the living of holy lives. Although the severe discipline was easily abused and unrest inevitable, on the surface, at least, Geneva was a city transformed from its old addiction to vice into one famed for the virtue of its people.

Calvin and his coworkers believed in the power of God's Word to change lives radically, so they required church attendance and participation in Christian education. Accordingly, an ordinance required that

> all persons shall send their children to the catechism to be instructed,…upon pain of three shillings, when they shall be found absent. No manner of person…[shall] swear by the name of God, under pain the first time to kiss the ground; the second time to kiss the ground and pay three shillings; the third time to pay forty shillings and three days in prison; the fourth time to be banished from the town a year and a day.

These declarations were civil, not ecclesiastical, enactments, which show while the state held the church in its embrace, the state in the end, not the church, had the preeminent authority. It made the upright behavior of the citizens its highest concern, and it reserved the right to set requirements that had no biblical basis. When Geneva adopted the Reformed faith, the citizens swore to obey divine law, but some of the enactments had little, if any, correspondence with God's law. Some people objected to this rigor, but most of them stood with Calvin, who used the machinery of the state to make people profess orthodoxy and to live holy lives, as the state defined holiness.

---

*"The Laws and Statutes of Geneva," quoted in Francis Gribble, *Geneva* (London: Adam and Charles Black, 1908), 25–26.

Geneva as a Center of Learning

A learned ministry has been a fundamental feature of Presbyterianism since the Reformation, and the precedent came from Geneva, where an academy opened in 1559 under the direction of Theodore Beza (1519–1565) as rector. Calvin had sought a public institute of higher learning for several years, and eventually the government provided funds. Calvin then recruited the finest scholars and teachers available, some from Bern, Beza among them.

Born in the village of Vezelay in Burgundy, Beza came from a genteel and learned family, and from childhood he displayed great intelligence and scholarly aptitude. An uncle arranged for the youth to study at Orleans with Melchior Wolmar (1497–1561), an outstanding scholar in the Greek language who taught Calvin also. Beza began these studies at age nine and lived with the Wolmar family at Orleans and later at Bourges. By then Wolmar had become interested in the teachings of Martin Luther, which had begun to attract attention in France. Exposure to evangelical principles early in life left a lasting impression upon Beza, who, at the same time, learned about much corruption within the Catholic Church. He was not, at that point, however, inclined to break with his church, and by his uncle's design, he began to study law at the University of Orleans, from which he graduated in 1559. The study of law was not his major interest, although he excelled in his classes, and he turned to classical literature, in the manner of contemporary humanists, when he moved to Paris. Subsidies arranged by his uncle allowed Beza to pursue his interests, and soon publication of some Latin poems brought him acclaim, a satisfaction tempered by serious illness, which threatened to take his life.

While recuperating Beza resolved to leave the Roman Church and to embrace publicly the doctrine of the Reformation he had learned from Wolmar. He left Paris for Geneva in October 1548, and there he completed the transition from humanist scholar to Protestant theologian. In 1549, in response to an invitation from Pierre Viret, he became a professor of Greek at the Protestant Academy of Lausanne, where he lectured on the New Testament, preached often, and helped to prepare a French version of the psalter. When Geneva called him to teach, Beza accepted, much to the dismay of Viret and others at Lausanne, and he remained in Geneva for the rest of his life.

Soon after beginning his work at the academy, Beza became pastor of one of Geneva's congregations. He served with great distinction in both positions, as he and Calvin labored as partners with mutual affection and respect. When Calvin died, his friend became the chief pastor in Geneva, presided at the funeral, and wrote the first biography of Calvin.

Under Beza's direction, the theology school at the academy became the most renowned center of Reformed scholarship in Europe, and students came to it from many lands. Prominent among them was Scotland's John Knox, who referred fondly to Geneva as "the most perfect school of Christ that ever was on earth since the days of the Apostles." The academy did not restrict its focus to the preparation of ministers, but with public funds, it provided education for all ages and levels of society. As constituted, the new school had two divisions: a *college*, which was a primary school of seven grades open to all youths; and a *scholia publica*, an advanced institute that presented instruction in theological subjects. By 1564, some three hundred students had attended, and graduates carried the faith to France, England, Scotland, and elsewhere, and English Puritans soon brought it to America. Eventually the academy became the University of Geneva.

The Decline of the Reformed Faith in French Switzerland

After Calvin's death in 1564, his church lapsed under increasing civil control until it lost all semblance of autonomy and became an agency of the state. The Venerable Company of Pastors lost authority over the academy, and in the eighteenth century the state officially renounced the Reformed confession of faith. As the union of church and state sapped the church's spiritual vitality, the state set standards for the ordination of ministers without regard to their beliefs, part of a process of decline that had begun much earlier. Geneva then became a graphic example of the consequences that ensue when the church depends upon the state for support. The long-term effects of the Ecclesiastical Ordinances, or the perversion thereof, left the established church Reformed in name only. In 1849 some evangelical Protestants seceded from the state church and formed the Free Evangelical Church of Geneva, but few people supported it. Similar developments ruined the Reformed witness in Neuchatel, where Farel labored, and in Lausanne, the site of Viret's ministry. Across Switzerland Reformed churches lost authority to state governments, and rationalism infected their ministries. Free churches survived but with little public support.

During the interval between the Reformation and the secession of 1849, the Swiss universities, founded upon Protestant principles, succumbed to the inroads of a rationalistic worldview that came with the so-called *Enlightenment* of the eighteenth century. This was a time when it became fashionable for intellectuals to exalt human reason to the highest eminence and to predict that science would unlock all the mysteries of life. Although few of the trendsetters in thought espoused atheism, the biblical doctrines of creation and providence fell into disfavor, as deism fascinated the minds of scholars who delighted in ridiculing Christian beliefs. As one modern author summarized the new outlook, it featured a worldview in which "the fervor of the reformers seemed to be constructing a new religion of which reason was God, Newton's ideas the Bible, Voltaire and others the prophets. The *Philosophes* attempted to offer the spiritual leadership of which, they believed, the Church was no longer capable. [They]…put forth a huge propaganda,…all full of serious reason and witty mockery."*

As rationalism took root in the universities, it permeated the theological faculties as well as other academic departments, and most pastors educated there imbibed the skeptical ideas and allowed them to shape the character of their ministries in the state churches. There was a pronounced tendency among them to reject miracles as incompatible with science and reason and to deny the validity of special revelation in verbal form. These theologians and pastors allowed the philosophers and scientists to set the academic agenda, and then they adjusted the claims of religion to satisfy the requirements of *reason* as the skeptics understood them. Traditional Christian beliefs were all subject to revision or elimination, and only those that supported the ethical concerns of the deists were to be retained. Religion was useful only to the extent that it provided support for the contentions of the rationalists. They thought, for example, belief in some kind of deity and in judgment after death was essential for public morality.

The Loss of a Legacy

A review of Presbyterian history in Switzerland leads not to an account of healthy development but to one of distressing degeneracy. The noble labors of Farel, Calvin, Viret, Beza, and others failed to achieve permanent results worthy of their illustrious names. Four centuries later, in the cantons of Geneva, Neuchatel, and Vaud, churches no longer adhere to the principles that were the inspiration for the Reformers' ministries. The Free churches remain weak and must struggle against the secularism that has become almost omnipresent in the land. The Free Church of Geneva still

---

*Frederick Artz, *The Enlightenment in France* (Kent, Ohio: Kent State University Press, 1968), 32–33.

maintains its independence, but those in Vaud and Neuchatel reunited with the state churches in 1943 and 1966 respectively. Swiss churches are tied to their particular cantons, so a national church body has not appeared. Early in the twentieth century Reformed churches in Basel and Geneva gained some autonomy from civil control, but those in Bern, Vaud, and Zurich remain subject to their cantonal governments. By 1980 Roman Catholicism had become the majority religion in Switzerland, claiming 47.6 percent of the population to 44.3 percent for Protestants and 8.1 percent for other religions. Even in Geneva Catholics now outnumber Protestants, although church attendance for both groups is very low.

Swiss Protestants of the Reformation eagerly asserted their beliefs in the form of confessions and catechisms. The First Helvetic Confession (1536), the Second Helvetic Confession (1566), Calvin's Catechism (1537), and the Formula of Consensus (1675) are all powerful declarations of Reformed dogma, but by the nineteenth century they had lost their significance for most members of the state churches. A resurgence of Christian fervor and evangelism known as *Le Reveil* did occur in the eighteenth century and extended into the following one, but it was not consistently Reformed in character.

In the period after the defeat of Napoleon and the French efforts to impose the anti-Christian ideas of their revolution (1789–1815) on all of Europe, some Swiss evangelicals reacted against the rationalism that had infected their churches. By then, the Venerable Company of Pastors in Geneva had prohibited the preaching of such historic Reformed doctrines as original sin, election, and the deity of Christ. The company removed Calvin's Catechism and replaced it with one of a rationalist slant. Leaders of the *Reveil* complained and organized the Evangelical Theological Seminary in Geneva, where J. H. Merle d'Aubigne (1794–1872) became a professor. He helped to establish the Free Church of Geneva and became famous as author of the comprehensive *History of the Reformation in the Sixteenth Century*. Despite his great reputation, the church Merle d'Aubigne helped to found did not prosper. Evangelical influence did spread, however, to France, the Netherlands, Belgium, Hungary, and Italy.

In addition to Merle d'Aubigne, Cesar H. A. Malan (1787–1864) and François S. R. L. Gaussen (1790–1863), scholars of great ability strove to preserve biblical Christianity in Switzerland. Their publications, like Merle d'Aubigne's, gave the Reformed faith some academic respectability and provided education for men who otherwise would have studied at the liberal universities. Alexander R. Vinet (1797–1847), poet, theologian, and champion of the separation of church and state, helped to organize the Free Church in the canton of Vaud, while noteworthy Bible commentator Frederic L. Godet (1812–1900) taught in Neuchatel at the seminary of the Evangelical Free Church. Only a few Swiss congregations, however, remained loyal to their heritage, while other Christians there met the challenge of deism by espousing a broadly evangelical message without the distinctive principles that had been fundamental to the Reformed faith since the sixteenth century.

In the twentieth century Switzerland witnessed the appearance of another reaction against modern revisionist approaches to Christianity, when the neo-orthodox movement made its debut within the established liberal churches. Karl Barth (1886–1968) and Emil Brunner (1889–1966) were the major spokesmen for this school of theological thought.

Neo-orthodoxy was the most influential theological movement to appear between the two world wars, and Barth was its pioneer. Born in Basel, he obtained his higher education at the universities of Bern, Berlin, Marburg, and Tubingen, but he never earned a doctoral degree. Following his father into the ministry, Barth became an assistant pastor in Geneva, where he preached from what had been Calvin's pulpit. From 1911 to 1921 he was pastor at Safenwill. During this phase of his life, Barth underwent developments in his thinking that carried him from the pietism he had received from his parents to modern liberalism and eventually to a religious type of socialism. In 1916, however, he broke with the liberal religion he had learned from his former professors such as Adolf Harnack at Berlin and Wilhelm Hermann at Marburg. The rupture with liberalism occurred when, as a pastor, Barth encountered much difficulty in preaching because his ministerial education had given him no vital message to proclaim. He said of his mentors, "I could no longer follow either their ethics and dogmatics or their understanding of the Bible and history." Barth had begun assailing the god of liberalism as an idol, and he resolved to make a fresh study of Scripture without presuppositions dictated by modern scholarship.

Thereafter Barth contended that mankind's knowledge of God comes exclusively from divine revelation—the *Word of God*. In 1919 he published the first edition of his commentary on the Epistle to the Romans, a work in which he rejected the teaching of his professors and portrayed God as the *Wholly Other*, known only by His self-disclosure. In 1921 the University of Göttingen, where the faculty of theology was Lutheran, employed Barth as a "Calvinist" scholar. In that position he revised his work on Romans until six editions appeared, each one showing important changes in his thinking. These alterations have led to diverse interpretations of his views, but some themes remained constant throughout his writing.

The capstone of Barth's academic career came with the publication of his *Church Dogmatics* (1932–1967), a massive treatise covering a wide spectrum of theological subjects. It shows the author's renunciation of liberalism did not include a rejection of the liberal critical theories about the nature of Holy Scripture. On the contrary, he regarded the Bible as a fallible, but still primary, witness to the Living Word of God—Jesus Christ. God speaks through the Bible despite the errors it contains. Because Scripture is a human document, it must be fallible, but the Holy Spirit uses it to communicate God's Word, and the work of the Spirit transcends the errors of human authors.

A second area of thought that remained constant in Barth's teaching is his view of election, in which he accused Augustine and Calvin of treating the doctrine in an abstract manner. Barth contended Christ is *both* the *electing God* and the *elected man*, and election is universal in scope. The task of the church is to proclaim that God has chosen everyone, and Christ alone is a rejected reprobate. Barth held that election and reprobation do not proceed from eternal divine decrees, so only people who reject their election could be lost. Human, not divine, choice is ultimate in salvation. This is a form of Arminian soteriology all Reformed confessions of faith reject.

Despite his deviations from historic Christianity and Reformed confessional beliefs, Karl Barth deserves recognition for his resolute stand against the Nazis and against timid Christians who did not oppose them. Barth helped to found the Confessing Church as a rebuke to the established Lutheran and Reformed bodies that failed to condemn the state's official ideology. In 1934 the dissident body issued the Declaration of Barmen, of which Barth was the principal author. Soon the Nazis forced him to leave Germany, where he had been lecturing at the University of Bonn, and go to Basel, where he joined the faculty of the university. His account of this era appears in his book *The German Church Struggle*.

Second only to Barth as a spokesman for neo-orthodoxy in Switzerland was Emil Brunner, a native of Winterthur, who studied at the universities of Zurich and Berlin, as well as at Union Theological Seminary in New York. In 1913 he received the doctor of theology from Zurich, and he became a professor there in 1924. Prior to obtaining his doctorate, he was a pastor in Glarus, and while there he began to question the liberal theology he had acquired when he was a university student. Brunner read Barth's work on Romans with much appreciation and soon became a vigorous disciple of the Safenwill pastor. Publication of *Die Mystic und das Wort* (1924) established Brunner's reputation as a critic of liberal religion, as in that work he analyzed and refuted the theology of Friedrich Schleiermacher (1768–1874), once a minister in the German Reformed church and a professor at the University of Berlin. Schleiermacher was the most influential early exponent of a critical approach to the Bible and a rejection of confessional Christianity in favor of a religion based upon emotions. He maintained that the historic doctrines of the faith were always open to revision, as human experience might dictate.

Brunner's critique of modern liberalism made him duly famous, as his influence spread to the United Kingdom and the United States, where his books appeared in English translations. He lectured at Princeton Theological Seminary in 1938 to 1939, and for a few years was a professor at the Christian University in Tokyo. Broad intellectual interests led him to write about ethics, psychology, and philosophy as well as theology.

Like Barth, Brunner regarded himself as a theologian of the Word of God, and he contended that divine revelation transcends human knowledge and reason. He, however, rejected the traditional belief in the Bible as that revelation, a belief he scorned as static orthodoxy. For Brunner revelation comes through a dialectical process, so truth is not objective but personal, acquired through encounters with God. Revelation is not a disclosure of facts from or about God, but God's disclosure of Himself. Brunner said he found contradictions in the Bible, for example, in its teachings about final judgment as contrasted with its assurance of universal salvation. He maintained that Scripture is, therefore, not a reliable guide to the future.

Disagreements about the connection between Scripture and divine revelation led eventually to dissension between Brunner and Barth. The appearance of Brunner's *The Mediator* (1927) and *The Divine Imperative* (1932) caused Barth to issue strong criticisms and to produce an attack in print. Barth accused Brunner of conceiving of revelation apart from Christ, and the dispute between the two reached its peak during the period of the church struggle in Germany.

Although the two fathers of neo-orthodoxy disagreed about the validity of general (natural) revelation, which Barth denied but Brunner affirmed, they maintained practically the same attitude toward the Bible. They believed God speaks through Scripture, but His voice must be distinguished from many "incidental noises" within it.* Since all writers of the Bible were fallible humans, they could not produce an inerrant book. Brunner used as an illustration an old Enrico Caruso record now scratched and warped. The great tenor's voice is there, but there are other sounds as well. Readers of the Bible then must discern the voice of God when He chooses to communicate with them through it, and they must not allow "incidental noises," such as the static of an old record, to mislead them. How to distinguish between the voice of God and the human "static" these theologians did not make clear. Brunner admitted that the authors of Scripture claimed to receive infallible revelation, but he rejected their claims as mistaken.

With regard to the doctrine of salvation, Brunner rejected the virgin birth of Christ and derided the historic Reformed position on election and reprobation as almost blasphemous. He viewed faith as a native human ability to choose God. In the *ordo salutis* he placed decision before regeneration in the manner of ancient semi-Pelagians and modern Arminians.

Despite the term *neo-orthodoxy*, the movement by that name made major concessions to liberalism by conceding the fallibility of Scripture and by departing from the confessions in matters crucial to the Reformed faith. There has been no powerful resurgence of biblical Christianity in Switzerland, so that land is now a mission field for emissaries of Christ and heirs of the Reformers to reclaim through vigorous evangelism and church planting. Perhaps the beginning of such an effort is underway. In 1948 American missionary Francis Schaeffer (1912–1984) went to Switzerland as an appointee of the Independent Board for Presbyterian Foreign Missions, and in 1955 he founded L'Abri, a study center in the Alps to which thousands of intellectuals have gone for instruction. Schaeffer's numerous writings have extended the influence of L'Abri far beyond Switzerland, but so far it appears the effects of his ministry have been greater outside that country than within it.

Protestant Ecumenism in Switzerland

Geneva, once a stronghold of Reformed orthodoxy, in the nineteenth century became the headquarters of the Pan-Presbyterian Alliance, an international body that promoted cooperation among Reformed churches without requiring adherence to any precise doctrinal position. It, for example, received the Cumberland Presbyterian Church from the United States into membership

---

*H. Emil Brunner, *Our Faith*, trans. John W. Rilling (London: SCM Press, 1949), 19–20.

in 1884, even though that denomination was frankly Arminian in its teachings. The alliance published a number of organs to promote its ideals and programs, the first being *The Catholic Presbyterian* (1879–1883). Next came *The Presbyterian Register* (1886–1948), followed by *The Reformed and Presbyterian World*, which became *The Presbyterian World* in 1949.

As Protestant ecumenism became popular in Europe and America, the alliance became ever more inclusive, and even churches with congregational polity were welcome to affiliate. In 1970 the International Congregational Union merged with the alliance, and the united bodies formed the World Alliance of Reformed Churches. Switzerland had become the nucleus of nonconfessional religion that continued to identify itself as the Reformed faith, while in practice ignoring the historic beliefs and practices of that honorable Reformation tradition.

SUGGESTED ADDITIONAL READINGS >>

Bainton, Roland H. *The Travail of Religious Liberty*. New York: Harper & Brothers, 1951.

Barth, Karl. *The German Church Conflict*. Translated by P. T. A. Parker. Richmond, Va.: John Knox, 1965.

———. *The Great Invitation*. Translated by Harold Knight. Philadelphia: Westminster, 1955.

———. *A Shorter Commentary on Romans*. Richmond, Va.: John Knox, 1959.

Brunner, H. Emil. *Our Faith*. Translated by John Riling. London: SCM, 1949.

Calvin, John. *A New Compend of Calvin's Institutes*. Edited by Hugh T. Kerr. Louisville, Ky.: Westminster/John Knox, 1989.

Casalis, Georges. *Portrait of Karl Barth*. Translated by Robert McAfee Brown. Garden City, N.Y.: Doubleday, 1963.

Clark, Gordon H. *Karl Barth's Theological Method*. Philadelphia: Presbyterian and Reformed, 1963.

George, Timothy. *Theology of the Reformers*. Nashville: Broadman, 1988.

Klooster, Fred H. *The Significance of Barth's Theology*. Grand Rapids: Baker, 1961.

Leonard, Emile G. *A History of Protestantism*. Vol. 1. Edited by H. H. Rowley. Translated by Joyce M. H. Reid. Indianapolis: Bobbs-Merrill, 1968.

Lindsay, Thomas M. *A History of the Reformation*. Vol. 2. New York: Charles Scribner's Sons, 1907.

McGoldrick, James Edward. "John Calvin—Erudite Educator." *Mid-America Journal of Theology* 21 (2010): 121–32.

———. "John Calvin and the Missionary Mandate." *Banner of Truth* no. 563–64 (August–September 2010): 11–25.

———. "Calvin and Luther: Comrades in Christ." In *Tributes to John Calvin*, ed. David W. Hall (Phillipsburg, N.J.: P&R, 2010), 166–86.

McNeill, John T. *The History and Character of Calvinism.* Oxford: Oxford University Press, 1954.

Merle d'Aubigne, J. H. *A History of the Reformation in Europe in the Time of Calvin.* 4 vols. Reprint, Harrisonburg, Va.: Sprinkle Publications, 2000.

Monter, William. *Calvin's Geneva.* New York: John Wiley & Sons, 1967.

Reardon, Bernard M. G. *Religious Thought in the Reformation.* London: Longman Group, 1981.

Reid, W. Stanford, ed. *John Calvin: His Influence in the Western World.* Grand Rapids: Zondervan, 1982.

Reville, Jean. *Liberal Christianity: Its Origin, Nature, and Mission.* Translated by Victor Leuliette. New York: G. P. Putnam's Sons, 1903.

Schaff, Philip. *History of the Christian Church.* 3rd ed. Vol. 8. Grand Rapids: Eerdmans, 1976. Reprint of 1910 edition.

Stephens, W. P. *Theology of Huldrych Zwingli.* Oxford: Clarendon, 1986.

———. *Zwingli: An Introduction to His Thought.* Oxford: Clarendon, 1994.

Walker, Williston W. *John Calvin, the Organizer of Reformed Protestantism.* New York: Schocken Books, 1969. Reprint of 1906 edition.

Wendel, Francois. *Calvin: Origins and Development of His Religious Thought.* Translated by Philip Mairet. Durham, N.C.: Labyrinth, 1963.

Williams, George H. *The Radical Reformation.* 3rd ed. Kirksville, Mo.: Sixteenth Century Journal Publishers, 1992.

Zwingli, Ulrich. *Selected Works.* Edited by Samuel Macauley Jackson. Philadelphia: University of Pennsylvania Press, 1972.

THREE

France

Relations between the papacy and the kingdom of France had been irregular during the Middle Ages. At times Frankish monarchs had rescued beleaguered popes from the clutches of their enemies, but conflicts between Rome and Paris were common and sometimes bitter. During the period when the Vatican operated in Avignon rather than Rome (1309–1377), the pontiffs were all Frenchmen subject to much royal influence. French prelates dominated the College of Cardinals and thereby controlled the election of popes. The perceived subservience of the papacy to the crown of France, of course, aggravated other rulers and contributed to a serious loss of prestige for the Vatican, while at the same time the French monarchy grew stronger and became ever more assertive in its dealings with Rome.

In the face of mounting criticism from several sources, Pope Gregory XI (r. 1370–1378) returned to Rome in 1377, but he died soon thereafter, and the church experienced perhaps the greatest crisis of her history to that point in time. Angry Italians practically forced the cardinals to choose a pope of their nationality, after decades of French pontiffs. The intimidated French cardinals eventually declared the election invalid and chose one of their own number, whom they installed in Avignon. Rival popes then reigned in Italy and France, and soon a third contender appeared in Pisa after a council of the church tried unsuccessfully to restore order by removing the current rivals. Although the later Council of Constance (1414–1417) did establish a unified papacy, the damage to the church at large could not be repaired quickly or entirely.

The role of the French hierarchy in the divisive ecclesiastical conflicts reflects the great strength of the crown in its dealings with the Catholic Church. In 1438 King Charles VII (r. 1422–1461) asserted the liberties of the Gallican church when he obtained the Pragmatic Sanction of Bourges, by which the Vatican relinquished its right to collect some revenues in

France, a decision prompted by many protests against papal avarice. This agreement reaffirmed an earlier one by which King Louis IX (r. 1226–1270) had gained royal control over the selection of bishops, and it asserted the supremacy of general councils of the church, as the Council of Basel (1431–1449) had decreed. In effect, the Pragmatic Sanction gave the king the means to supervise the French church, which he promised to protect. Although the pope still, in principle, claimed the highest authority, the kings maintained their prerogatives until the French Revolution, which began in 1789 and soon thereafter abolished the monarchy. In some ways an ambiguous tension between church and state continued until 1906, when the Republic imposed an official separation of the two. As the Middle Ages came to an end, the cause of national monarchy was well advanced in France, so the temporal authority of the papacy declined, as even French clerics looked to the king as their sovereign.

Religious Nonconformity

The Albigenses

While the crown was gaining recognition throughout the state and the papacy was losing prestige and influence, religious sects of diverse character further weakened the Catholic Church. In southern France the Cathars, a dualist cult perhaps related to the Bogomils of eastern Europe, gained a substantial following.

The Catholic Church condemned the Cathar doctrine as heresy, but it was, in fact, a belief entirely contrary to the Christian tradition, that is, a different religion. Since the region around Albi was a center of strength for the sect, it became a practice to call its adherents Albigenses. The low view of the Vatican common at the time made many people receptive to alien religious ideas, which ignorant priests were not competent to refute. Even some nobles joined the Cathars, and their support made it difficult for Catholic authorities to suppress the movement. The challenge from this sect led Pope Gregory IX (r. 1227–1241) to create the Inquisition and to call for secular rulers to execute the nonconformists by burning.

The methodical work of the papal inquisitors diminished the Albigenses, but it required a large military crusade to crush them. Pope Innocent III (r. 1198–1216) summoned the forces that destroyed Catharism as an organized religion and thereby rid France of an anti-Trinitarian, dualist religion, one so bizarre it appears to have promulgated doctrines such as the reincarnation of souls. The surprising strength of the Albigenses and the support they obtained from some aristocrats show that the papal church in France faced serious challenges to its authority.

The Waldenses

A less radical but ultimately more significant challenge to Rome came from the Poor Men of Lyons, a movement within Catholicism to revive the practice of preaching while returning in some measure to the simplicity of the early church. The Poor Men became known as Waldenses because their founder was Peter Waldo (d. ca. 1216), a merchant from Lyons, who renounced his wealth and adopted poverty as a means to conform to the example of Jesus. He often applied biblical injunctions literally in his desire to follow Christ. To satisfy his thirst for knowledge of Scripture, Waldo paid two scholars to render the New Testament into Provencal, his native tongue.

Waldo's actions did not violate the canons of the Roman Church. He was neither a monk nor a priest, but a devout layman who sought the approval of his church, and soon his sincerity attracted disciples who shared his zeal. The Poor Men had no desire to alter the doctrines of their church, but they stressed personal piety and good works in imitation of Jesus and the apostles. The bishops might not have objected to the Waldenses, had the zealots not assumed the right to preach. In 1179 a delegation from the movement arrived in Rome during meetings of the Third Lateran Council and asked Pope Alexander III (r. 1159–1181) to approve their ministry, and they gave the pontiff a copy of their Bible translation. Alexander and the council acknowledged the right of the Poor Men to pursue the life of evangelical perfection, but they would not grant permission for them to preach.

Denial of their request led the Waldenses to defy church authorities, and as a consequence, they incurred the charge of heresy followed by excommunication. Innocent III enticed some of them to return to the Roman Church, where he allowed them to form a religious order of Poor Catholics. The others proceeded to subject Catholic dogmas to scrutiny in the light of Scripture, and in that way they came to espouse teachings that, in the judgment of Rome, justified the accusation of heresy.

Exclusion from the Catholic Church forced the Poor Men to establish their own congregations, and soon such bodies appeared across France and spread into Italy, Germany, Switzerland, and elsewhere. The Waldenses were the only medieval nonconformist church that would survive into modern times, and a Waldensian Church remains in Italy, despite savage persecution in previous centuries.

Surviving evidence about the teachings of the Waldenses shows they had little interest in systematic expressions of doctrine, but the generally Christian character of their beliefs is clear, and efforts to connect them with the Cathars have been libelous. They were Trinitarians who gradually elevated the Bible to the status of supreme authority. Their view of the Christian life was at least semi-monastic, especially because they extolled poverty as the foremost virtue. After Waldo died, his church departed farther from Roman teachings than he had been willing to go, and by the fifteenth century, considerable deviation from medieval orthodoxy was evident, as the sect discarded its original monastic character. By then some pastors in the movement had adopted a symbolic understanding of the Eucharist, and they declared people could be saved without the sacraments.

By the early sixteenth century, the doctrines of the Waldenses contrasted rather sharply with those of that body as Waldo had founded it. To some extent they began to correspond to Protestant beliefs as proclaimed by Luther and other Reformers. Perhaps they were attracted to the Protestant position because both groups shared a strong disdain for the papacy and a deep love for the Bible. Soon after Protestant literature reached the Waldenses in Italy and France, their leaders contacted the Reformers who had broken with Rome. William Farel met a delegation of Waldenses in Switzerland, and from that contact many members of the sect came to favor joining the Reformed church. In 1532, at a meeting in Chanforan, Italy, in the presence of Farel, the assembly voted to embrace the Protestant cause. At that point the Waldenses abandoned all remnants of medieval Catholicism and adopted Reformed theology. This aroused the anger of Catholic authorities even more than before, and they moved to suppress the accused heretics with renewed energy. Not until 1848 would the Italian Kingdom of Piedmont-Sardinia grant legal toleration to the Waldense church. The papacy did not endorse toleration for the Waldenses until 1929, when Pope Pius XI (r. 1922–1939) signed the Lateran Treaty with the government of Benito Mussolini.

During the era of persecution, some Italian Waldenses fled to Uruguay and Argentina and founded churches there. Until 1965 the congregations in that region were part of their mother church in Italy, but in that year they organized their own synod though they remained in fraternal relation with the parent body.

During Waldo's life and for some time thereafter, the Waldenses maintained an episcopal form of church government, but association with the Reformed leaders led them to adopt a synodical pattern comparable to the typical Presbyterian form. This entitles them to inclusion in the history of Presbyterian churches.*

The Role of the Monarchy

When Francis I (r. 1515–1547) became king, he assumed rule over a powerful nation, one in which the Roman Catholic Church enjoyed the status of the established religion, despite the challenges from the Cathars and the Waldenses. The king remained loyal to that faith, even while he exercised much control over church affairs. Francis was a highly cultured person who surrounded himself with artists and scholars, patronizing the Renaissance in France. Some of the protégés who lived by his subsidies had doubts about some principles and practices of the medieval church, but the king maintained a generally indulgent attitude toward such people. He would not, however, tolerate overt attacks upon his church, for he believed the unity of the state required uniformity in religion. The king did not oppose reforms in the church, so long as they left dogmas and royal prerogatives undisturbed. With his beloved sister Margaret, Francis sought to elevate French culture at home and to raise the nation's prestige abroad.

Margaret d'Angouleme, queen of Navarre (r. 1527–1549), was an intelligent and learned patron of art and scholarship and a talented author in the manner of Renaissance writers. When the Protestant challenge appeared, she advised her brother to avoid repressive measures, but he spurned that counsel and began persecuting religious dissidents. Margaret responded by granting asylum to refugees at her kingdom in the Pyrenees. Among her guests were Jacques Lefevre d'Etaples (ca. 1460–1536), a humanist critic of abuses and ignorance among Catholic priests, and John Calvin, who fled from France when Francis I initiated the burning of Protestants. Eventually Queen Margaret embraced some of the doctrines of the Reformers, but she remained within the Roman Church. Her *Mirror of a Sinful Soul* (1531) is a spiritual autobiography as well as a fine specimen of Renaissance literature. Like some other humanist scholars, Margaret was not willing to disrupt the unity of her church, even though it had become corrupt in doctrine and practice.

Although his sister encouraged the Reformers, Francis and other leaders resolved to destroy them. The royal reaction to Protestantism was due in part to zealous but insensitive actions by the evangelicals themselves. Too often

---

*For a succinct examination of the Cathars and Waldenses, see James Edward McGoldrick, *Baptist Successionism* (Lanham, Md.: Scarecrow Press, 1994), a work that refutes the claim that these and other sects were medieval Baptists.

their fervor exceeded common sense; for example, they posted placards in public places, even in the king's bedchamber, to denounce the Mass as an abomination. The angry king ordered the burning of suspected culprits.

Though a convinced Catholic, Francis I was at times pragmatic in his policy where religion was involved. His chief competitor for power in Europe was the Holy Roman Emperor Charles V (r. 1519–1556), a fellow Catholic monarch who was king of Spain as well as emperor. Charles faced the challenge of Protestantism in Germany, where Martin Luther protested against false doctrine and financial corruption in the church. When some German princes adopted Luther's teaching, Francis began to court them as potential allies against Emperor Charles. The king of France at one point even apologized for his brutality toward his own Protestant subjects, whom he portrayed falsely as fanatical Anabaptists opposed to Luther's theology.

Francis's attempts to placate German Lutheran princes did not lead him to tolerate the evangelical faith in France, and continued persecution led Calvin to defend the Protestants against the charge of sedition. In 1536 Calvin, writing in exile, addressed the first edition of his *Institutes of the Christian Religion* to Francis in the hope of persuading him to end the repression. That appeal left the monarch unmoved, and about that time he aided the pope in launching a cruel offensive against the Waldenses. A Reformed congregation had been established by then at Meux, but the execution of fourteen of its members soon terminated its ministry.

While the government sought to rid France of Reformed believers, Calvin encouraged them by sending them printed Bibles and other literature and by writing letters of advice. Once he was settled in Geneva, Calvin dispatched newly educated missionaries to France, about 120 of them between 1555 and 1564. Conversions of Frenchmen from all classes of society strengthened the Reformed church, especially because substantial numbers of them were from the nobility and the bourgeoisie.

Francis I died in 1547, and his son succeeded him as Henry II (r. 1547–1559). Like his father, the new ruler despised and persecuted Protestants. Henry's wife was Catherine de Medici, niece of Pope Clement VII (r. 1523–1534). The king and queen resolved to combat heresy, but their efforts were, in the end, unavailing.

In 1547 the Parlement of Paris, the major royal law court, created the Burning Chamber for efficient disposing of heretics, and at the same time the court condemned the French translation of the Bible Robert Estienne (1503–1559) had printed. In 1551 the king issued the Edict of

Chateaubriand to restrict the presses as part of an effort to thwart the dissemination of objectionable literature. The year 1553 brought a decree from the Parlement of Paris for the execution of five young preachers educated in Lausanne who had returned to their homeland as missionaries of the Reformed church.

The Organization of the Reformed Church

While royal opposition continued, believers organized a French Reformed church on both a local and a national scale. Jean le Macon (ca. 1533–1572), known as La Riviere, became pastor of the first formally organized Reformed church in Paris in 1555. That body elected elders and deacons, and soon a consistory was functioning. In rapid order more congregations appeared across France, and by 1562 the Reformed leader Admiral Gaspar de Coligny (1519–1572) reported that 2,150 local churches were operating, many with pastors educated in Geneva.

Soon after the organization of the local church in Paris, Protestants, advised by Calvin, formed their first National Synod, which adopted the Confession of La Rochelle, because the synod met in that city. It produced a Book of Discipline during the same sessions. Before long, provincial synods were in operation, while later arrangements introduced the colloquy, a type of presbytery, and provided that the general (national) synod be composed of commissioners from the provincial synods. A Presbyterian system of polity was then in place.

Religion and Politics

Henry II died in 1559 as a result of wounds incurred during a joust at the marriage of his daughter Elizabeth to Philip II of Spain (r. 1556–1598). His eldest son came to the throne as Francis II (r. 1559–1560), a sickly young man under the domination of his mother, Catherine de Medici, the Queen Regent. She made political power and the stability of the state her priority and so wished to avoid sectarian strife, although she hated Protestantism. Catherine faced a threatening situation as the aristocracy became divided over religion, with the Duke of Guise leading a fanatical Catholic faction and the noble family of Bourbon, for the most part, supporting the Protestant cause. By this time about 1.5 million Frenchmen had adhered to the Reformed faith, and through vigorous evangelism, the Protestants were gaining converts rapidly. Queen Catherine assumed the posture of a *politique*, one who pursues whatever course of action is politically advantageous, regardless of the effect upon religion. Her attitude angered the Guise party, and Francis, Duke of Guise, became leader of an effort to control the throne to assure continuing Catholic domination of the kingdom.

Fear of the Guises caused leaders of the House of Bourbon, that is, Antoine of Navarre (d. 1562) and Louis, Prince of Condé (d. 1569), to unite with Admiral Coligny in defense of the Protestant faith, although political interests were, in some incidents, at last as important as religious ones. As tensions increased, the Prince of Condé tried to capture the king in order to keep him from the control of the Guise faction. This Conspiracy of Amboise failed and led to the execution of some of the participants. Condé was sentenced to death, but the demise of Francis II in December 1560 spared him.

When the next son of the late Francis I became monarch as Charles IX (r. 1560–1574), his mother, Catherine, continued as regent since her son was but ten years old. Protestants, known as Huguenots for reasons not at all clear, were resorting to militant measures provoked by reprisals that followed the Conspiracy of Amboise. Since she wanted peace, the regent relaxed some of the anti-Protestant policies and released Condé from prison, while she granted limited toleration to the Huguenots.

To further her scheme, Catherine arranged the Colloquy of Poissy in 1561 so that Catholic and Reformed leaders could discuss the issues that divided them. The Catholic Cardinal of Lorraine presided, and Beza led the Reformed delegation. Since the regent did not guarantee the safety of Calvin, he did not attend. By that time the French edition of his *Institutes* had appeared, and large numbers of Huguenot pastors had studied in Geneva, so the queen held Calvin responsible for the dissension that wracked France. Calvin had, however, opposed the Protestants' resort to violence there, and he did not approve of the conspiracy to kidnap Francis II. The Colloquy, which met in a nunnery at Poissy, was a grand occasion with much fanfare, but it accomplished nothing, since neither side would concede.

Despite the failure at Poissy, Catherine issued the Edict of St. Germain, a grant of limited freedom to the Protestants that amounted to legal recognition of their church. The law required Huguenots to worship outside the cities and to return all church buildings they had occupied inside of them. Beza, Coligny, and Calvin urged their people to accept the terms, but the ensuing peace lasted only six weeks. When the Duke of Guise massacred a congregation worshiping in a barn at Vassy, the Protestants replied with armed insurrection, thereby initiating a conflict that would last thirty years.

Civil War

Since the Huguenots were about only 10 percent of the population, their cause appeared hopeless, even though perhaps half of the nobles supported it. Condé died in battle, but his forces inflicted heavy losses upon their enemies, and at one point Protestant troops from Hesse and the Palatinate in Germany joined the Huguenots. Condé's death put command of his army under Coligny, who proved to be an able military leader. The war continued through several phases with periods of truce between them, while Queen Catherine tried to reconcile the warring factions. The Protestants might have gained her support because she feared the Guises so much, but they failed to seek such an arrangement, and the Guise party secured control of the government.

Catherine de Medici persisted in seeking ways to thwart the powerful Guises, and that desire, at times, worked to the advantage of the Protestants. Her most ambitious effort led to a marriage and to a massacre. The queen arranged a marriage for her daughter, Margaret of Valois, to Henry, Prince of Navarre, a Bourbon and heir to the royal crown of Navarre, a kingdom in the Pyrenees Mountains. The wedding was set for August 8, 1572, and both Catholic and Protestant nobles attended at Catherine's invitation. Henry of Navarre became nominal head of the Bourbons at Condé's death, but Coligny was their actual leader. The queen, at that point, tried to pacify the admiral by inviting him to reside in Paris where he had access to King Charles IX. To Coligny this appeared to be an expression of goodwill, but the queen soon regretted giving him an opportunity to influence the monarch, so she conspired with Guise to kill Coligny. The first attempt only wounded the admiral, so the queen and the duke struck at the wedding festival, the feast of St. Bartholomew. Assassins murdered Coligny and about three hundred other Protestants in Paris, and thousands more fell as victims elsewhere. Pope Gregory XIII (r. 1572–1585) rejoiced to learn of the slaughter and struck a medallion to commemorate the occasion. Approximately twenty thousand people perished in the massacre.

Protestant Successes and Failures

Truth, crushed to earth, showed surprising vitality in rising again, for the Protestant flame was far from extinguished. Despite grave losses, the Huguenots endured, with Henry Bourbon of Navarre as their leader. He had survived the St. Bartholomew's Day Massacre by pretending to renounce his Huguenot religion, and for some time, he was practically a prisoner at the royal court. He emerged as the clear leader of the Protestant cause in the

War of the Three Henrys (1585–1589). Henry III (r. 1574–1589) was king by then, while Henry Guise led the Catholic party and Henry of Navarre commanded the Protestants. Guise formed a militant Catholic League and gained support from Spain. He then forced the uncooperative king to leave Paris, and the angry Henry responded by arranging to have Guise murdered. Soon, however, a fanatical monk killed the king, whose death without children left Henry of Navarre heir to the throne. Although he had clear title to the crown, Henry Bourbon knew Catholic France would not accept a Protestant monarch, so to avoid more bloodshed, he embraced Catholicism and soon granted freedom of religion to all Frenchmen. In his decision to become Catholic, Henry IV (r. 1589–1610) displayed a *politique* disposition comparable to that of Catherine de Medici. A persistent tradition holds that he justified his decision by saying "Paris is well worth a Mass." Some Huguenots, of course, denounced his perfunctory adoption of Catholicism, although they soon learned he still had their interests at heart.

The so-called Wars of Religion had cost France dearly, and the Protestants suffered the loss of many congregations during that struggle. By 1598 they had only 760 local churches, but the same year brought them official toleration when the king promulgated the Edict of Nantes, a landmark in the history of civil liberties.

Henry IV was a pragmatic monarch but not one devoid of principles. He had lived among the Valois royalty, where he showed shrewdness and learned the art of political survival, so he understood that peace and stability could not be achieved unless toleration of religious diversity became national policy. The Edict of Nantes allowed Protestants to worship freely outside Paris, while France remained officially a Catholic nation. Huguenots could, however, attend universities, hold public offices, and assemble without fear of persecution. The law allowed them to govern and fortify those towns already in their possession, a remarkable concession that created almost a state within the state and caused trouble for later kings.

Although war-weary people, Catholic and Protestant, welcomed the new policy, diehards in both camps were critical. Extremists within the Catholic League hated Protestants to such an extent they viewed the edict as treason against the true church. Huguenot militants, on the other hand, detested the provision in the law that recognized Catholicism as the national religion. The pope was appalled by the grant of rights to Protestants, but the edict actually aided the Roman Church by including freedom for Catholics to celebrate masses in areas where Huguenot power had prevented them from celebrating the rite for some time. Clement VIII would not have granted absolution to Henry IV had he not agreed to reinstate Catholic worship inside Protestant towns. To the pope's dismay, the royal government gave a financial subsidy to the Reformed church, which allowed it to establish several schools, including theological seminaries at Montauban and Samur.

Once it seemed to be secure in its rights, the French Reformed church held national synods regularly and applied ecclesiastical discipline faithfully, especially in cases where church members failed to live in accord with their professions of faith. The synod sometimes published lists of deposed ministers and elders with warnings to the congregations to avoid such men.

Protestant Fortunes under Louis XIII

When Henry IV fell victim to assassination in 1610, his nine-year-old son succeeded him as Louis XIII (r. 1610–1643), and the child's mother, Marie de Medici (ca. 1573–1642) became Queen Regent. She at first showed some favor toward the Reformed church, to which the government paid enlarged subsidies. Trouble lay ahead, nevertheless, because the queen installed Armand-Jean du Plessis (1585–1642) as her chief minister. Better known as Cardinal Richelieu, he sought to eliminate all obstacles to royal absolutism, and the semi-autonomous Huguenot towns stood in his way. Richelieu required the National Synod to meet in the presence of a royal commissioner to insure it transacted only ecclesiastical business. The cardinal asserted his intention to break the power of the Protestants while at the same time compelling the feudal aristocrats to submit to the king's authority. His policy provoked a Huguenot uprising, one that brought defeat to the rebels. In 1628 Richelieu launched an attack against La Rochelle, the Protestant stronghold on the west coast. When it fell to government forces, the political power of the Huguenots collapsed. The cardinal was, however, magnanimous in victory in that he confirmed the religious rights of the Protestants, along with the civil liberties they had gained from Henry IV. From the fall of La Rochelle to the death of Richelieu and Louis XIII, both in the same year, there was peace in the kingdom.

Repression under Louis XIV

Richelieu carefully planned for France's future by training his own successor. Giulio Mazzarini (1602–1661) became chief minister to the next king, Louis XIV (r. 1643–1715), who inherited the throne at age four. In a remarkable repetition of events, his mother, Anne of Austria (d. 1666), assumed the regency, while Cardinal Mazarin directed affairs of state. The policy toward the Reformed church remained in place for the time being, as Mazarin expressed some appreciation for the Protestants, especially because they did not support an uprising of disgruntled nobles known as the *Fronde*. In 1660, however, the situation began to change when the government decreed that the National Synod could convene only when the crown authorized meetings. Thereafter the provincial synods were to administer affairs of the Reformed church without any national convocations. There would be no national meetings until 1872.

When Mazarin died in 1661, the position of the Huguenots became precarious. The king's one-time mistress who had become his wife, Madame de Maintenon (1635–1719), often influenced his decisions and may have been behind the change of policy toward his Protestant subjects. Louis began a calculated effort to demoralize the Huguenots by depriving them of all the patronage and favors preceding rulers had granted them. The king was an extreme egotist who could not understand why anyone would disagree with him, especially about religion. He expressed this attitude when he said France must have *un roi, une loi, une foi*—one king, one law, one faith. Complaints from Reformed believers aroused the king's anger, and persecution was the consequence.

Before taking punitive measures against the dissidents, Louis XIV tried bribery to entice some of them to adhere to the Roman Church. Many of the leading Protestants were noblemen to whom the king offered lucrative positions in the government. He excluded from office any who declined his offer. Such people could no longer sit in the courts or parlements, administer finances, or practice law or medicine. Although some Huguenots succumbed to the pressure, the vast majority remained steadfast in their faith. The frustrated king responded with repressive enactments. He forbade Protestant pastors to seek converts from Catholicism, and he ordered the destruction of any chapel that received former Catholics into its membership. Ministers of offending congregations were subject to banishment from the nation. The monarch sent troops into Protestant areas and billeted them in the people's homes; soldiers often treated the people brutally. At the same time Catholic clerics made energetic efforts to convince the dissidents to join the Church of Rome. When Protestants refused, priests sometimes urged soldiers to even greater cruelties in dealing with them. Such atrocities persuaded many persecuted people to leave France, but the king forbade them to flee. About 250 thousand left anyway. Refugees apprehended in flight were sometimes impressed into slavery in the galleys of French ships. Some Protestants who could neither leave nor endure the persecution complied with Louis's demand and professed to accept his religion, although such conversions seldom indicated a genuine change of heart.

In order to provide a legal basis for the changes he initiated, Louis XIV directed his attorneys to draft the Edict of Fontainebleau, which abrogated the Edict of Nantes. As of October 1685 when the new law took effect, the Reformed faith became a *religio illicita*—an illegal religion. The law called for the demolition of Protestant church buildings and prohibited all non-Catholic religious assemblies. All ministers were to leave the country within two weeks. All Protestant schools had to close, and all parents were to present their children to Catholic priests for baptism. The law made it a crime for a minister to remain in France or for a layman to leave it.

The Church of the Desert

Although persecution damaged the French Reformed church, it did not destroy it. Many believers remained loyal to God by meeting in secret, while their pastors served at great risk. Huguenots referred to their illegal assemblies as the Church of the Desert, while Lausanne became the site of a refugee settlement where the Reformed church educated pastors to serve the underground congregations in France. Deprived of both the means and legal right to worship, many turned to the hills and mountain fastnesses, where they kept the faith far from the centers in which it had been publicly and widely exercised. Others continued their secret devotions without benefit of religious assemblies.

The Museum of the Society of French Protestantism in Paris has preserved various memorials of these stirring and hazardous times. A miniature New Testament, called a "rat Bible" because it was designed for concealment in a woman's headdress, finds a place in these collections. These include a specially made stool with a secret receptacle for a large Bible, contrived in such a fashion as to lead no one to suspect that it provided such a place of concealment.

Another relic of that era is the desert pulpit. When the Huguenots met for worship at some selected mountain rendezvous, they frequently provided a portable pulpit for the use of their minister. Different elders assumed the custody of various parts of the pulpit and, upon receiving notice of a service, would gather and erect the platform for that particular occasion. The meeting being ended, they divided it among themselves for retention against the next such gathering.

The exodus of refugees deprived France of some of its most talented and industrious citizens, since many Huguenots were skilled craftsmen or successful merchants. Upon leaving their homeland, large numbers went to England, Switzerland, the Netherlands, and several German states that received them gladly. Some of the exiles joined the armed forces of those countries and fought against the imperialism of Louis XIV, as he sought to impose his hegemony upon Europe.

The Cevennes Mountains furnished a convenient hiding place for people who could not escape to a greater distance, but the persecutors followed them there and murdered several pastors. These atrocities enraged the victims of repression to the point that they became defiant in the face of danger, and some displayed a spirit of fanaticism that claimed the gift of prophecy and the ability to speak in ecstatic tongues like modern charismatics. These would-be prophets denounced the Church of Rome and called its priests agents of Satan, while they predicted the downfall of that "Babylon." Angry mobs of Protestants attacked the home of Abbé du Chayla, leader of a mission seeking to convert them to Roman beliefs. The abbé had arrested some Protestants, and incensed peasants insisted he release them. When he refused, the mob killed him and his collaborators. This violence had been inspired by the declarations of men who claimed to be prophets speaking for God. The government responded by sending troops into that region of Languedoc, an action that initiated the war of the Camisards, a name derived from a native-style shirt many of the Protestants wore.

The ensuing conflict brought atrocities on both sides, but the rebels were hopelessly outnumbered, and their heroism was not sufficient to defeat the king's forces. After three years of combat the royal army triumphed, but military victory did not bring the elimination of the Reformed faith, even though Louis XIV declared his country free of Protestant heresy.

Revival and Transition

The year 1715 brought the reign and life of Louis XIV to an end, and he died maintaining the delusion that the Reformed faith had perished before his own demise. Just ten days prior to the king's decease, however, Reformed pastors and elders met near Nimes, where they formed the Synod of the Desert. Under the capable leadership of Pastor Antoine Court (1696–1760), they laid plans to reorganize and energize the Huguenot congregations.

Eventually a total of eight such synods convened, the last in 1763. All meetings were clandestine, because the government was still hostile. The results of these efforts gratified the Protestants greatly. Within a few years, hundreds of congregations were flourishing, although they still had to meet in secret. About 120 parishes in Languedoc and more in Dauphiné numbered all told about two hundred thousand members.

The government of the new monarch Louis XV (r. 1715–1774) continued the policy of persecution, so Protestant church services were sometimes disrupted by police raids. Prison still awaited female heretics, while males had to endure slavery in the galleys. Antoine Court, like Calvin before him, fled from France. He settled in Lausanne, where he educated ministers for service in France. From his home in Switzerland, Court conducted regular correspondence with his oppressed brethren, and through his efforts Reformed scholars went to France to teach future pastors by conducting classes in remote, inconspicuous places. Meanwhile the growth of the *religio illicita* continued, to the frustration of the ruling authorities, who began to doubt the wisdom of continuing the repression. In the second half of the eighteenth century, they relaxed their efforts to expunge the Reformed faith, so Huguenots began to meet for worship during daylight hours, which they had not dared to do before.

Protestants did not yet enjoy official toleration, but their cause received important support when Voltaire came to their aid. Francois Marie Arouet (1694–1778), better known as Voltaire, was a brilliant writer and critical thinker who found the government's policy toward nonconformity reprehensible. His public complaints led to imprisonment for a brief time, after which he went to England, a much freer society. By the decade of the 1730s, Voltaire had won a reputation as a skillful author. He returned to France eventually but lived close to the Swiss border and moved to Geneva when he deemed it unsafe to remain in his homeland. Although he despised Christianity and promoted deism and a rationalist worldview, Voltaire came to the defense of a persecuted Protestant family, and thereby he indirectly aided the Reformed church as it sought freedom.

Voltaire's involvement with the Huguenots came as part of his campaign to obtain freedom of religion for everyone. Since he doubted that any system of belief was correct, he saw no reason to suppress any one of them. In 1762 Roman Catholic authorities accused a Protestant named Jean Calas of killing his son in order to prevent him from converting to Catholicism. Torture did not convince the father to confess, so the authorities executed him by strangling. Voltaire met the widow of Calas and resolved to exonerate her husband, and in 1763 he published a *Treatise on Tolerance,* in which he called for a fresh investigation into the charges against Calas. Two years later a court reversed the earlier verdict, a decision that elicited broad public approval.

A generation after the Calas Affair, the Marquis de Lafayette (1757–1834), who had been inspired with the spirit of liberty while helping the Americans gain their independence, initiated an effort to recognize the right of dissent in France, and a formal edict of toleration crowned his endeavor with success in 1787. The Catholic clergy protested granting rights that properly pertained only to the true church to heretics. Underlying this contention was the belief that adherents to error should have no rights.

Revolution and *Reveil*

The year 1789 is never to be forgotten. The gorgeous extravagance of Louis XIV, the wasteful prodigality of his feeble successors, and the rapacity of a luxurious and profligate priesthood had brought the nation to the verge of ruin. The public coffers were empty, and the government was at the end of its resources. One-third of the landed property was owned by the church, and this was largely exempt from taxation. The oppressed people had carried the double burden of state and church until they could bear it no longer. The Huguenots' thrift and energy would have stood the nation in good stead at this critical time. Perhaps this crisis would never have come had not this substantial element of the population been driven out of the country. The moral stamina of the Calvinists was needed even more than their financial help. Had the Reformed Church been permitted a normal development, not only would she have furnished in her own membership a powerful conservative force to withstand the evil influences that brought such sorrow and disaster during the period of revolution, but her great rival, the papal church, might have kept herself from such a career of shame.

In the nation's dire extremity, the king summoned the Estates-General, an assembly composed of representatives of all the estates of the realm, the nobles, the clergy, and the common people, the first such convocation in 175 years. So long as king, clergy, and nobles could indulge themselves in the wildest excess of luxury, they did not concern themselves about the under crust. The delegates of the third estate, as the commons were called, outnumbered the representatives from both the other orders. To prevent their exercising an absolute authority, the nobles and clergy proposed that each estate should vote separately and that no measure should carry without receiving the votes of two estates. They hoped by combining to control the assembly, but the third estate demanded that the assembly should vote as individuals, and the majority carry the day. They succeeded after a protracted struggle in enforcing their demand, and that put them in complete control. They had some able and fearless leaders. One of these, Talleyrand Périgord, came over to them from the ranks of the clergy. It was on his motion that the Estates-General, after discussing various methods for raising money, finally decided to confiscate the property of the church. By this act it put the equivalent of 40 million dollars of annual income into the state's treasury. The clergy opposed, as a matter of course, but to no avail. The assembly proceeded to divide the church into dioceses and parishes, decreed that the people had a right to call their own bishops and pastors, and set aside a modest salary for them out of the revenues of the confiscated property. The state had served the church long enough; now the church must serve the state. The clergy were required to take an oath to the new constitution. The pope forbade their doing this, and many refused and some left the country.

The sentiments of justice and humanity that seem to have animated the Estates-General in the early part of its movements gave place, by and by, to impracticable theories of government. The people, so long oppressed and their rights ignored, were intoxicated with the idea of power and taxed their wits for novel ways to exercise it. In September 1792, the revolutionary National Assembly declared France a republic. In January of the next year it beheaded the king and inaugurated the "Reign of Terror." Christianity was abolished. The calendar was changed, and the birthday of the republic, September 23, 1792, was selected to mark the beginning of a new era. The Sabbath was abrogated, and a week of ten days was substituted for a week of seven days. For eighteen months not a church in France opened its doors to worshipers. In Notre Dame, Paris, the Goddess of Reason was enthroned in the person of a profligate woman, dressed in the classic costume of ancient Greece. France reveled in atheism and blood and gave the world proof that only a little while would be required for unrestrained wickedness to make a hell of earth. By 1795 the land began to awaken from its horrible nightmare, and the churches opened again. From this date the Huguenot church, having survived two centuries of strenuous endeavor to exterminate it, has enjoyed freedom of worship.

During the rule of Napoleon (1749–1815), the Reformed Church, like every other institution, felt the weight of his iron hand. He tampered with its government and shaped it to suit his peculiar notions. His special concern was to see that its national unity was destroyed. Rather than emasculate the Reformed Church, Napoleon suffered final defeat at the hands of Britain and Prussia in 1815, an event that coincided in time with a revival among Protestants.

The *Reveil*, or Awakening, that originated in Geneva about 1815 spread into France through the preaching of zealous evangelists such as Henry Pyt (1796–1835) and Felix Neff (1798–1820) and through the distribution of Christian literature. For several decades of the nineteenth century, Protestant churches in France benefited from this resurgence of piety and fervor. Two brothers, Adolphe (1802–1856) and Frédéric Monod (1794–1863) were prominent leaders in the *Reveil*, and Adolphe was one of the Reformed Church's greatest preachers and a skillful author. Opposition to the conservative theology of the Monod brothers from within Reformed circles shows that even there the rationalism of the era had made considerable inroads. By the time the Monods began their ministries, the French Reformed Church was already divided over issues of doctrine, and it no longer had any national structure, due to the policies of Napoleon I. The Confession of 1559 no longer held the church together.

The strength of opposition to the awakening led Frederic Monad to lead a secession that produced the Union of Free Evangelical Churches of France, which renounced all concessions to the rationalism of the age and sought to preserve the historic character of the Huguenot faith. This movement was not, however, consistently Reformed in theology, as a broader evangelical belief characterized adherents to the Free Church. By the end of the nineteenth century, this denomination had only four thousand members. The older, more liberal churches with Reformed roots had dwindled to about eight hundred thousand communicants.

State control and surveillance of the churches did not end in 1815 with the fall of Napoleon, but continued until 1906, as events at midcentury demonstrated. While Napoleon III ruled (1852–1870), the government legislated the recreation of the consistory but not the National Synod of the traditional Reformed Church. The same law established a Central Council of the Reformed Churches of France, with headquarters in Paris. This agency was to be an intermediary between church and state. When the council tried to legislate for the church, the state restricted such activities. While Protestant churches grappled with intrusions of state authority, the Roman Catholic Church regained some of the strength it had lost in the revolution of 1789–1815.

The Modern Era

In 1871, following the defeat of the country in the Franco-Prussia War, France granted the Reformed Church the right to reconstitute the National Synod, which met the next year. That convocation, however, soon became the site of contention between the liberal and the evangelical parties, with the latter a majority at the time. The synod adopted a brief confession of faith, one that did not include the distinctively Reformed features of the historic declaration of 1559. This was evidence that the church of the Huguenot heritage was becoming satisfied with a broadly evangelical theology rather than the doctrine for which its founders had bled and died. Some commissioners present at the Synod of 1872 protested the adoption of any statement of belief.

Distinguished among members of that synod was Francois Pierre Guillaume Guizot (1787–1874), who supported the conservative position. He had held several political offices, including that of France's premier from 1840 to 1848. Guizot became duly famous as a historian, so his reputation gave enhanced credibility to the evangelical party within the Reformed Church, but difficult days lay ahead for advocates of orthodoxy.

Although the government allowed Reformed Protestants to convene a National Synod, the state continued into the early twentieth century to subject their church to its control. After the Franco-Prussian War, the German government closed the Lutheran seminary in Strasbourg, but France allowed the formation of a Protestant school of theology in Paris, one with a combined Lutheran and Reformed faculty. Auguste Sabatier (1839–1901), one of the original professors, became a prominent leader in the liberal wing of the Reformed church. The composite character of the seminary in Paris and the eminence of Sabatier reflected the growing ascendancy of theological liberalism in French Protestantism.

The year 1906 was a turning point in French church history, because at that time Catholicism lost its position as the state religion, and the government terminated its financial subsidies to all churches. This was due in part to the leftward drift of the nation in general and the political posture of the Roman Church in particular. A sensational trial for treason had condemned Captain Alfred Dreyfus (1859–1935) to imprisonment on Devil's Island on the charge he had aided the Germans by disclosing military secrets. Dreyfus was a Jew, and the high command of the army, where anti-Semitism was present, chose to make him a scapegoat to protect the real culprits. Leading Catholic clerics were among the most vitriolic accusers of Dreyfus.

A court in 1899 pardoned the captain, but exoneration and restoration did not come until 1906. As a consequence of the Dreyfus Affair, the Catholic hierarchy and religious orders of the church lost much credibility, and the state deprived the church of its favored position. Thereafter no ecclesiastical body would enjoy the status of the national religion.

While the disestablishment of Catholicism freed the Protestant churches from state control, the Reformed community suffered from grow-ing dissension within. Three movements emerged, each displaying a specific theological character and an individual posture on the issues that divided them. The Union of Evangelical Free Churches was a conservative, but not strictly Reformed, association. Liberals formed the Union of Reformed Churches, while the National Union of Reformed Churches tried to medi-ate between the other two groups. Mediation was not successful, and the National Union merged with the liberal body in 1912.

World War I exacted a heavy toll from the Reformed churches in France, especially in areas overrun by German armies. Many pastors were conscripted into military service, and numerous church buildings were destroyed. The financial condition of many congregations was desperate. A small infusion of strength did, however, occur after the war, when the Reformed churches of Alsace and Lorraine became part of France but retained their own synodical structure. France had lost Alsace and Lorraine in the Franco-Prussian War.

In 1924 Gaston Doumergue (1863–1937) became president of France, the first Protestant head of state since Henry IV abjured that faith in 1593. In 1938 Reformed pastor Marc Boegner (1881–1970) presided over an assembly of delegates from the Reformed Church, the Evangelical Free Churches, the Evangelical Methodist Church, and the Congregational Free Churches that united those bodies as the Reformed Church of France. It adopted a minimal statement of faith consistent with the liberal persuasion of the delegates. About forty of the more conservative congregations, most of them in the southern part of the country, declined to enter the general union. They then formed the Independent Evangelical Reformed Churches of France and founded a theological seminary at Aix-en-Provence in 1940, the professors of which subscribed to the Confession of La Rochelle (1593). During World War II the school enrolled about ninety students.

Liberal theology, which dominated Protestant circles in the nine-teenth century, continued to do so into the twentieth century until the rise of neo-orthodoxy and the teachings of Barth challenged some of its extreme tenets. Auguste Lecerf (1872–1943), who had helped to establish the Calvinistic Society in 1926, became a professor on the University of Paris faculty of theology, where he helped to initiate a French component of neo-orthodoxy known as neo-Calvinism.

The Second World War brought severe trials to the Reformed churches in France. When French forces surrendered to the Germans, the victors divided the country into occupied and unoccupied sectors, with the Vichy Republic, a puppet regime, in charge of the unoccupied zone. The division of the nation hindered communications among the churches, and there were no truly representative meetings of the National Synod between 1939 and 1943. Church buildings suffered great damage during the war, and there was an acute shortage of pastors.

Some Protestants sought relief from their hardships through ecumenical endeavors such as the Taizé Community founded in 1940 by Roger Schutz (b. 1915), a theological graduate of the University of Lausanne. Taizé, in the city of that name, introduced features of monasticism, and the community welcomed and received a number of Roman Catholic members. Adherents adopted the traditional vows of monks to practice poverty, chastity, and obedience. In 1956 the Taizé Press began publishing Verbum Caro, a theological journal. The involvement of Protestants who professed the Reformed faith in this ecumenical effort is clear evidence that the doctrines of the Protestant Reformation no longer held sway in France, except in a small minority of churches that remained faithful to their heritage. In 1965 the Reformed National Synod approved the ordination of women pastors. In the closing part of the twentieth century, the Independent Evangelical Reformed Church of France could claim only twelve thousand members in forty-nine congregations and five mission stations.

Reformed Journalism

Numerous periodicals have marked the course of the French church since the early nineteenth century. The *Archives du Christianisme au dixneuvième siècle* (Archives of Christianity in the nineteenth century), beginning in 1818 and closing fifty years later, was the first of these. Frédéric Monod was long associated with this conservative paper.

Pioneer among the liberal periodicals was the *Annales Protestant* (Protestant annals), conducted by Charles Coquerel (1797–1851) and circulated in undated issues for barely a single year during 1819 to 1910. Of similar sympathies was Samuel Vincent's *Mélanges de Religion* (Blending of religion) (1820–1824).

The periodical *Le Semeur* (The sower), dealing with affairs of religion, politics, and philosophy, originated in 1831 and ceased publication in 1850. The weekly *L'Espérance* (Hope), an important paper begun in Geneva but soon moved to Paris, ran from 1838 until 1866. Influential among liberal publications of the same era was *Le Lien* (Link) (1841–1870).

Following the close of the *Archives du Christianisme*, a successor appeared in 1869 under the title of *L'Eglise Libre* (The free church) (1869). Another weekly in the orthodox field, *Le Christianisme au XIXe siècle* (Christianity in the nineteenth century), entered the picture in 1872, continuing as a journal of importance into the 1900s with an appropriate revision of title. In 1886 the liberals launched *Evangile et Liberté* (Gospel and freedom) upon a lengthy career.

Later publications of Reformed interest include *Foi et Vie* (Faith and life) (1897); *Pour la Vérité* (For the truth) (1935), issued by the Evangelical Free Church; *Christe et France—Sur le Roc* (Christ and France—on the rock) of the Reformed Evangelical churches; along with *Réformé* (Reform) (1945). The bilingual *Messager Évangélique* (Gospel message), earlier a Lutheran paper, later came to serve the Reformed Church of Alsace and Lorraine as well as that of the Augsburg Confession (Lutheran).

Strasbourg was the source of liberal journals, particularly concerned with critical approaches to the study of the Bible and collectively known as the *Strasbourg Review*. The most significant of these was *Revue de Théologie et de Philosophie Chrétienne* (Review of theology and Christian philosophy) (1854–1926), an able journal of the type indicated, circulated from Paris during the greater part of its prolonged career.

Etudes Théologiques et Religieuses (Religious and theological studies) appeared at Montpellier in 1926, later to come under the sponsorship of the Protestant theological staffs of Montpellier and Paris in collaboration with that of Strasbourg. In 1941 the more conservative *Etudes Évangéliques* (Evangelical studies) published at Aix-en-Provence, entered the arena of reviews. The Calvinistic Society established *La Revue Réformée* (The Reformed journal).

Baird, Henry Martyn. *History of the Rise of the Huguenots of France.* 2 vols. Edmonton, Alberta: Still Waters Revival Books. Reprint of 1895 edition.

Beick, William. *Absolutism and Society in Seventeenth Century France.* Cambridge: Cambridge University Press, 1985.

Benedict, Philip. *Rouen during the Wars of Religion.* Cambridge: Cambridge University Press, 1981.

Brooke, Rosalind and Christopher. *Popular Religion in the Middle Ages.* London: Thames and Hudson, 1984.

Carr, John Lawrence. *Life in France under Louis XIV.* New York: Capricorn, 1970.

Curtis, S. A. *Educating the Faithful: Schooling and Society in Nineteenth-Century France.* DeKalb: Northern Illinois State University Press, 2000.

Dansette, Adrien. *Religious History of Modern France.* 2 vols. New York: Herder & Herder, 1961.

Diefendorf, Barbara B. *Beneath the Cross: Catholics and Huguenots in Sixteenth-Century Paris.* Oxford: Oxford University Press, 1991.

Eire, Carlos. *War against the Idols: Worship from Erasmus to Calvin.* Cambridge: Cambridge University Press, 1989.

Foote, William Henry. *The Huguenots; or, Reformed French Church.* Harrisonburg, Va.: Sprinkle Publications, 2002. Reprint of 1870 edition.

Golden, Richard M., ed. *Church, State, and Society under the Bourbon Kings.* Lawrence, Kans.: Coronado, 1982.

Gray, Janet G. *The French Huguenots: Anatomy of Courage.* Grand Rapids: Baker, 1981.

Greengrass, Mark. *The French Reformation.* Oxford: Blackwell, 1987.

Holt, M. P. *The French Wars of Religion, 1562–1629.* Cambridge: Cambridge University Press, 1995.

Kingdon, Robert M. *Geneva and the Coming of the Wars of Religion.* Geneva: Droz, 1956.

———. *Geneva and the Consolidation of the French Protestant Movement.* Geneva: Droz, 1967.

McManners, John T. *The French Revolution and the Church.* Westport, Conn.: Greenwood, 1982. Reprint of 1969 edition.

Merle d'Aubigne, J. H. *History of the Reformation in Europe in the Time of Calvin.* 4 vols. Reprint, Harrisonburg, Va.: Sprinkle Publications, 2000.

Ozment, Steven. *The Age of Reform, 1250–1550.* New Haven, Conn.: Yale University Press, 1980.

Rothrock, George A. *The Huguenots: A Biography of a Minority.* Chicago: Nelson-Hall, 1979.

Sutherland, N. M. *The Huguenot Struggle for Recognition.* New Haven, Conn.: Yale University Press, 1980.

Van Kley, Dale K. *The Religious Origins of the French Revolution.* New Haven, Conn.: Yale University Press, 1996.

Van Stam, F. P. *The Controversy over the Theology of Samur, 1635–1650.* Amsterdam: APA-Holland University Press, 1988.

FOUR

The Netherlands

By the opening of the sixteenth century, the Low Countries of northwestern Europe were among the most prosperous and cultured parts of the continent. Although these countries were subject to the rule of reactionary Spain, Renaissance humanism had become an influential force among their artists and scholars, whom the wealthy middle classes often patronized. Holy Roman Emperor Charles V (r. 1519–1556) was born in the region, and though he taxed the people heavily, he allowed the nobles to exercise their traditional feudal privileges without much interference from the crown. The emperor despised heresy and made occasional efforts to suppress it in the Netherlands, but he did not pursue a consistent, systematic program to destroy nonconformity in religion. When Charles relinquished his throne as king of Spain in 1556, however, he asked Philip II, his son, to wage a relentless campaign to eliminate Protestantism in his Netherland provinces, a task Philip undertook with vigor.

King Philip II (r. 1556–1598) was a stern, resolute monarch bent upon securing royal authority throughout the vast Spanish empire, so he disliked the divided political structure of the Low Countries, where often uncooperative aristocrats governed the provinces. Like his father, Philip considered religious uniformity essential for the political security of his realm, so he wanted bishops who functioned as instruments of the crown.

In order to cement direct rule over the Netherlands, Philip resolved to strip the nobles of their traditional autonomy and to place the church under the supervision of Spanish bishops known for their opposition to Protestantism. To enforce his program the king dispatched royal governors and generals with battle-hardened troops to the region and authorized the Spanish Inquisition to deal with heretics. Philip appointed his sister Margaret of Parma (1522–1556) as governor, a woman whose chief spiritual advisor was Ignatius Loyola (1491–1556), founder of the Society of Jesus, a new religious order that became the vanguard of the Counter-Reformation. To finance the changes he desired to impose, the king resorted to additional heavy taxation, a policy that aroused Catholics as well as Protestants. Economic and political factors provoked resistance to Spain, and Protestantism infused it with spiritual energy and dedication. The history of the Reformation in the Netherlands is therefore the story of a struggle not only against religious despotism but against political tyranny also. The courage, endurance, and persistence of the Netherlanders in this conflict constitute a saga of heroic proportions. Although at times it appeared they might be exterminated, it never appeared they would be subjugated. They knew how to suffer and how to meet death on the battlefield, at the stake, and by starvation in times of siege, but refused to learn to accept defeat.

The Eighty Years' War (1568–1648)

As Holy Roman emperor, Charles V had to face the Lutheran challenge in Germany; as Charles I (r. 1516–1556), king of Spain, he confronted a growing Protestant presence in the Low Countries. Charles, however, retired from political life in 1556 after his efforts to destroy heresy in Germany had failed. Frustrated and weary, he could no longer bear the burdens of monarchy, so he returned to Spain to live among monks, there to end his life a drunken sot.

Philip II appeared ready and able to prosecute the war against the Protestants in an organized manner, and he viewed his political ambitions and religious duties as fully harmonious, if not identical. The king decreed death for recalcitrant heretics—burning for men and burying women alive. Philip was determined to transform the Netherlands so the region in religion and government would conform to the pattern of Spain. He employed bishops who were skillful theologians equipped to refute heretics, and he ordered his Council of State in the Low Countries to impose political union and religious uniformity.

Rigorous absolutism led some nobles to refuse to implement the directives of the council and the Inquisition and to appeal for toleration of diversity in religion. Philip responded by ordering enforcement of the decrees of the Council of Trent (1545–1563), the official Roman Catholic proclamations to rebut Protestant teachings. This caused evangelical believers to undertake armed resistance, and many liberal-minded Catholics sympathized with them. Persecution not only inflamed the Protestants' zeal, it increased the number of conversions to their cause. Gradually, aristocratic opposition to royal absolutism, religious dissent, and economic grievances combined to oppose the Spaniards. Reformed preachers evangelized vigorously and aroused the populace against the king, who responded by sending the Duke of Alva to place the land under military rule.

Alva governed through a Council of Troubles, which Netherlanders called a Council of Blood. There were many executions and many more imprisonments. About sixty thousand Protestants fled from the southern to the northern provinces, carrying their faith with them, when Alva conducted a *reconquista* to impose Tridentine Catholicism and to cement royal authority. In one three-month period there were 180 executions, and some of the victims perished for the crime of attending Protestant funeral services. In 1573 Philip said, "I would rather lose the Low Countries than reign over them, if they ceased to be Catholic."

William of Orange

When it became evident that Spain would not grant toleration, William of Orange (1533–1584), a leading nobleman, went to the Rhineland to enlist support for the rebels, but the first army he took to the Netherlands did not succeed. Orange, who had worked in the court of Charles V and had been reared a Catholic, became first a Lutheran and later a Calvinist. Unlike most religious partisans of that era, however, he favored freedom of religion and made that one of his objectives in leading the resistance. Realizing Spanish forces were poorly financed, he urged people to withhold taxes. In general, supporters of the prince of Orange were less libertarian than their leader, and when they conquered towns, they would impose their religion. It is clear they did not share William's dream for a united Netherlands with freedom for all.

The barbarities of the Inquisition and brutal Spanish policy on one hand and the intolerance of the Calvinists on the other made Catholic-Protestant collaboration impossible to maintain, and the Spaniards were able to recruit many Catholics in the Low Countries by making concessions to their political and economic interests. When Alexander Farnese (1542–1592) became governor in 1578, he enlisted the support of the Walloons, southern nobles, by promising to respect their traditional liberties in exchange for their aid against the rebels.

Spanish-Walloon collaboration created a crisis for the resistance, and soon Flanders and Brabant fell to royal forces. After Philip II promised twenty-five thousand pieces of gold and a title of nobility to an assassin, in

1584 a bounty hunter murdered William of Orange, whom the king condemned for advocating "liberty of conscience, which we hold to be nothing but veritable confusion in religion." Farnese was on the verge of victory when Philip withdrew some forces for war against France, and soon the Rhine River became the dividing line in the Low Countries, as the seven northern provinces declared independence and became the Dutch Republic. After 1590 Spain made no energetic efforts to retake the north. The Peace of Westphalia ended the Eighty Years' War and ratified the independence of the United Provinces of the Netherlands in 1648. The Spaniards almost eliminated Protestantism in the south, while the Dutch in the north dealt harshly with Roman Catholics who remained there.

Formation of the Dutch Reformed Church

The murder of William of Orange was only the most conspicuous act of persecution Dutch Protestants had to endure. As early as 1523 two Augustinian friars attracted to the teachings of Luther suffered death by burning at Brussels. To the consternation of Charles V and Philip II, however, the regents they appointed to govern the Low Countries did not always demonstrate great zeal to extirpate heresy, so Protestant doctrines spread rather broadly. When the Duke of Alva assumed command of military affairs, repression of dissidents increased greatly, but it was already too late to destroy Protestantism, even by overwhelming force.

As was the case elsewhere in Europe, Luther's teaching was the first expression of evangelical theology to appear in the Netherlands, but Huguenot influence from France arrived soon thereafter, and most Protestants thereby followed the lead of Geneva rather than Wittenberg. The effort to organize a Reformed church began in the southern provinces in 1566, when Protestant leaders met in secret at Antwerp to plan for the future. By that time many nobles had joined the evangelical movement, a factor that encouraged Reformed believers to take bold measures in public preaching. The excitement this aroused led mobs to attack Roman Catholic houses of worship to destroy idols and other religious artifacts. The frenzied throngs made a hideous wreck of the cathedral in Antwerp, destroying its priceless collection of art. The predictable Catholic reaction was outrage, and many Romanists who shared the Calvinists' disdain for Spanish tyranny were repelled by what seemed to them nothing less than sacrilegious vandalism. This event may have convinced Philip II to dispatch Alva to the Netherlands. It is ironic that Philip's troops plundered Antwerp far more mercilessly than had the angry Protestants who attacked its cathedral, as soldiers stole from helpless victims of both religions and did not spare Catholic churches in their lust for loot. Thousands of people perished because of the Spanish Fury, as it became known.

As of 1579 in the Treaty of Utrecht, Spain practically conceded the right of the Dutch people to be independent, although plots to resubjugate them continued. Out of the bloody turmoil of the period, the Calvinists of the seven northern provinces organized their own republic and their own church.

One of the most influential figures in the formation of the Dutch Reformed Church was Guido de Brés (d. 1567), a French-speaking Walloon who founded several congregations. He had been a Roman Catholic but was converted through personal study of the Bible and had fled to England to escape persecution. King Edward VI (r. 1547–1553) received him warmly in England, but De Brés eventually returned to his homeland as an evangelist and church planter. A period of study in Geneva caused him to adopt Calvin's version of the Protestant faith. While he ministered in Valenciennes, Catholic forces besieged the town and took him prisoner. Death by hanging ended his career, as he prayed publicly for the authorities who were executing him.

De Brés made his mark as a theologian as well as a preacher and martyr. In 1559 he composed the Belgic Confession of Faith (first published in 1561), for which the Huguenot Confession of La Rochelle was the model. Calvin read the document and advised a few changes, which the author readily accepted. The Belgic Confession along with the Heidelberg Catechism (1563)* soon became an official declaration of faith for the Dutch Reformed Church.

Presbyterian Polity

When the Duke of Alva unleashed his troops against them, many Netherlanders fled for refuge into the German city of Wesel, near the border. There they convened a synod in 1568, and that body ratified the adoption of the confession and catechism and established a framework for church government. The synod made provision for pastors, teachers, elders, and deacons. A later synod at Emden confirmed the action of Wesel and required ministers to subscribe to the standards of doctrine, and it authorized creation

---

*See chapter 5, under "Germany," for an explanation of the origins of the Heidelberg Catechism.

of a consistory to govern each congregation. Classes were to do the work of presbyteries and should meet quarterly, or at least semiannually. In these synods the Reformed church constructed a practical form of order that would be implemented in the Netherlands as soon as conditions there would permit. The provinces of Holland and Zealand were the first to put the plan into operation. The first synod to meet on native soil convened at Dort in 1574, and the first National Synod met there in 1578. That assembly completed the program for church order by defining four courts of the church—consistories, classes, and provincial and national synods, the last to meet triennially.

Relation of Church and State

At the time of the Reformation, very few of the religious groups that separated from Rome sought full separation of church and state, and those that did so sought thereby to protect themselves from hostile civil authorities. Dutch Calvinists were unexceptional in their expectation that the government of the United Provinces would maintain a supportive posture toward their church. When they held their first national synod, however, the Reformed churches did so without the consent of civil authorities, and they declared the church had the right to administer its own affairs. There was a consensus among Reformed leaders that the church and the state should be cooperative partners in serving God by maintaining the true religion. The church should advise the state about spiritual and moral matters, and the state should use its power to protect the church and enforce its moral prescriptions. Like the French Reformed Church, the Reformed Church of the Netherlands in its confession of faith affirmed the obligation of civil magistrates to "remove and prevent all idolatry and false worship, that the kingdom of Antichrist may thus be destroyed, and the kingdom of Christ promoted" (Belgic Confession, Art. 36). The Protestant Reformers then, like the papacy, expected the rulers to suppress false teaching, by force if necessary. They, of course, disagreed with Rome about what constituted heresy.

Although there was broad agreement among religious leaders of that era regarding the role of the state in religion, not everyone concurred. Luther, for example, had warned against the use of compulsion in matters of conscience, and Anabaptists sought separation of church and state because they feared repression from both institutions. Even among Calvinists there was some reluctance to enforce conformity in religion. William of Orange was especially noteworthy for his desire to extend freedom of worship even to Catholics and Anabaptists. He saw the struggle against Spain as a campaign for freedom from tyranny, so he opposed giving any church the means to persecute dissidents. He was not alone in this conviction, for even some Dutch magistrates resisted making the state an instrument to enforce the polities of the church. In a shortsighted manner, however, leaders of the Reformed Church thought they could preserve an autonomous church while depending on the state for protection and support. Instead, the civil authorities exercised substantial control over ecclesiastical affairs and for some time did not allow the convening of National Synods but insisted that each provincial synod be the highest court in the Dutch Reformed Church. By seeking the aid of the state, the church subjected itself unwittingly to civil supervision.

Reformed Learning

Consistent with the belief that sound learning is essential for the spiritual as well as the social and economic health of the nation, Dutch Protestants vigorously promoted education for all levels of the populace. They argued that the Church of Rome had failed to provide adequate instruction for common people who needed the knowledge of God's Word obtained through personal study. The Reformers saw Protestantism as a revival of the pure doctrines of the gospel, so they moved with dispatch to create schools that would educate people in the faith. Like other Calvinists, they stressed the necessity for a learned ministry, and they resolved to make learning available for laymen as well.

The first Protestant effort in the Netherlands to establish a Christian university occurred when, in 1574, William of Orange granted to the city of Leyden authority to create such an institution. This was a reward to Leyden for its defense against Spanish assaults during a siege that lasted almost a year and brought the people to the verge of starvation. The new university became known as the Bastion of Liberty, and much of the funding for it came from the confiscation of the Abbey of Egmont.

From its inception the University of Leyden maintained academic excellence, and its professors and graduates became duly famous for their scholarship. The official constitution of the new university took place on February 5, 1575, after which there was a parade of military units through the city. Figures from classical times, such as Plato, Aristotle, Cicero, and Virgil, were portrayed in costume, as the officials conducted great pageantry to mark the occasion. The procession ended at the Cloister of St. Barbara, which had been assigned to the university. A huge banquet closed the proceedings in the city, which only weeks before had been the site of famine and almost indescribable suffering.

In 1586 the University of Franeker opened its doors as the second Dutch institution of higher learning, and in the seventeenth century three more universities appeared. The Dutch Republic had become the fountainhead of learning for Reformed Christendom. Although they achieved fame for scholarship in many fields, these universities gave preeminence to theology, especially Leyden, the theologians of which became world renowned.

The Challenge of Arminianism

The oldest and most distinguished university of the Netherlands at Leyden, founded upon Calvinist principles, soon, however, became the scene of the first organized challenge to the doctrines of the Reformed faith to arise within its own ranks. This occurred when Jacob Arminius (1559–1609), a pastor in the Dutch Reformed Church who had studied in Geneva, became a professor there. Sometime before joining the faculty, Arminius had begun to doubt some features of the Reformed doctrine of sin and salvation. While still a pastor in Amsterdam, he expressed ideas contrary to the Belgic Confession, although he did not publish his views. Other Reformed scholars at the university, especially Franciscus Gomarus (1563–1641), resisted the proposal to employ Arminius, but the university did so nevertheless, even though there was substantial reason to question his doctrine. Leyden conferred the doctor of divinity upon the new professor, despite his deviations from the official teachings of his church.

Soon after beginning his professorial duties, Arminius encountered strong criticism from Gomarus, who accused him of heterodoxy and of improperly teaching the New Testament, a subject the academic senate had awarded to Gomarus. The validity of the first complaint became evident in February 1604, when Arminius expounded his understanding of predestination. A serious dispute was underway, aggravated by strong personality conflict between the two contenders. Not only Gomarus, but also numerous pastors, called Arminius a Pelagian, a charge that associated his teaching with an ancient heresy refuted by Augustine of Hippo in the fifth century. Many concerned church leaders called for a national synod to resolve the controversy, and Arminius and his principal academic supporter, Johannes Uitenbogaert (1557–1644), agreed that was the best way to settle the quarrel, but Arminius died before a synod could be convened.

The university paid a pension to his widow and children. Thereafter Uitenbogaert, Simon Episcopius (1583–1643), and forty-two other ministers drafted a Remonstrance in five articles, each of them a complaint against an aspect of Calvinist soteriology.

The teaching of Arminius was not strictly Pelagian, for he did not deny the necessity for preceding grace before sinners could believe the gospel and embrace Christ as savior. He did, however, reject total depravity as an accurate description of the human condition because of the fall of Adam and Eve. In the manner of semi-Pelagians, Arminius held that Christ died for everyone, and God bestows His grace universally. The human response to grace is strictly a volitional act in which the choice of the will is ultimate. Since humans are not depraved, they have the ability either to accept or reject the offer of the gospel. Arminius suggested, but did not assert, that because freewill choice is ultimate, redeemed sinners, subsequent to conversion, may renounce Christ and be lost. When these ideas gained a considerable following, Prince Maurice, a supporter of the orthodox Reformed party, practically compelled the States-General to summon a synod to settle the issues.

The Synod of Dort (1618–1619)

When the synod assembled in the city of Dort, the participants included invited representatives from England, Scotland, Switzerland, and several German states—102 representatives from the various Reformed churches. Calvinists controlled the body and did not seat any avowed Remonstrants (Arminians), while Simon Episcopius and thirteen others appeared there to answer the charge of heresy brought against their doctrine.

After several months in session, the synod reaffirmed the Belgic Confession and the Heidelberg Catechism and published its own rebuttal of the five articles the Arminians had presented. The five points of Calvinism, as stated in the Canons of Dort, then became the recognized summary of Reformed teaching about sin and salvation.

After the decision at Dort, the Dutch government forbade the Remonstrants to preach or publish their views. Arminians had to vacate offices they held in the Dutch Reformed Church, and civil rulers banished their leaders from the republic. By 1626, however, they were allowed to return and establish a Remonstrant Seminary in Amsterdam, an institution that became an effective means to spread Arminian doctrine through much of Europe. In the eighteenth century, that teaching gained much acceptance in England through the work of John and Charles Wesley, whose Methodist church was the only major Protestant denomination to adopt Arminian theology officially. English Methodists exhibited much evangelical fervor, however, while many of their Dutch counterparts lapsed into rationalism and therefore promulgated liberal theology.

The Netherlands as a Place of Refuge

Although no country in Europe extended full freedom of religion in the seventeenth century, the Netherlands was perhaps the most liberal. The republic received Protestant refugees such as Huguenots from France, Puritans from England, and Covenanters from Scotland. The Dutch allowed foreigners to establish their own congregations, and in some cases, they provided buildings in which the strangers could worship. Dutch universities welcomed students from abroad and thereby educated numerous pastors to serve in their homelands when conditions allowed them to return. Reformed theology as taught in those universities exerted great influence upon students from England and Scotland especially, and the confessional statements of the churches in those countries reflect Dutch teaching.

The Rise of Rationalism

The effect of the Synod of Dort was to draw more closely the bond between church and state. The synod was called by the state, its meetings were supervised by delegates from the state, it asked and obtained the approval of the state for all its proceedings, and it expected the state to enforce its decisions against the Remonstrants. From this time forth the church was in bondage to the state. It derived its support from the public purse and took its law largely from the secular power. It gave birth to many great and noble spirits, such as Wilhelmus á Brakel, Gisbertus Voetius, Herman Witsius, and Alexander Comrie, leaders of the Dutch Further Reformation, a powerful spiritual movement that had its course from the early seventeenth till the mid-eighteenth century. It did much to promote sound learning, and for a time exhibited a fair measure of zeal in the maintenance and promotion of a high type of piety, yet the freshness and buoyancy of its young life felt the deadening effect of this unhappy union.

This condition continued until the French Revolution, when the Dutch Republic became a part of the empire of France. The bond between church and state was severed, and for a few years the church was thrown on her own resources and permitted to go her own way. At the fall of Napoleon, the Netherlands was transformed into a kingdom, with William I (r. 1815–1844) on the throne. He laid a strong hand on the church, throwing rigid restrictions around the administration of its courts and decreeing that none of its resolutions should be promulgated without his approval.

The Dutch attachment to liberty, although praiseworthy in some ways, in the end had a detrimental effect upon the national church because that body became ever more subject to state authority. University professors in particular soon became enamored with ideas contrary to Christian doctrine, ideas that arose in connection with scientific inquiries that began in the era of the Reformation and gained broad acceptance with intellectuals in the eighteenth century—the so-called Enlightenment. To win approval of the academic community, scholars in many disciplines, including theology, subjected the Christian faith to the judgments of human reason. Many were willing to make concessions and adjustments in order to accommodate the contentions of what they perceived to be a scientific worldview.

Since pastors of the Dutch Reformed Church studied in the universities, they were exposed to teachings critical of orthodoxy, and like the philosophers and scientists, many of them dismissed the historic doctrines of their church and preached a social message focused on humanity and its earthly needs rather than upon God and the urgency of preparing for eternity. In doing this, ministers violated their ordination vows, but the Reformed Church hesitated to take disciplinary action against them. Orthodox believers who protested about departures from the faith on the part of their ministers found no encouragement from their synods. Often pastors subscribed formally to the doctrinal standards but reserved the right to decide for themselves which articles in the confession were in accord with the Word of God. In the name of liberty, they denied the faith but remained pastors nevertheless, and the support of state officials for the rights of the liberals made it impossible for believers to obtain redress. By the early nineteenth century, some frustrated orthodox ministers concluded they could not be faithful to Christ while remaining in the national church. Their only recourse was to leave it.

Long before orthodox believers entertained the prospect of leaving the *Hervormde Kerk* (national church), prominent Dutch scholars had been advocating revisionist conceptions of the Christian faith. Hugo Grotius (1583–1645), for example, a distinguished jurist and political theoretician, endorsed the Arminian position on sin and salvation and then proceeded to promote a broad view of Christianity that would minimize confessional declarations and emphasize traditional doctrines about which all Christians could agree. His book *The Truth of the Christian Religion* (1622) was an eloquent and influential assertion of his proposals, one that enjoyed approval from anti-Calvinist elements in the nation. Grotius eventually went beyond espousing a vague ecumenicity and began denying fundamental tenets of the faith. This became clear when he rejected the penal substitutionary character of Jesus' atoning sacrifice. According to Grotius, Christ died to show God's willingness to forgive while at the same time to demonstrate the seriousness of humanity's offenses against its Creator.

Concurrent with the work of Grotius was the career of René Descartes (1596–1650), a philosopher, mathematician, and scientist reared a Roman Catholic and educated by Jesuits. His *Discourse on Method* (1637) and his *Meditations on Philosophy* (1641) indicate he saw no conflict between his philosophical position and his inherited religion. Descartes was offended when Catholic and Protestant scholars rejected his ideas and accused him of heresy. The reaction was due in part to his insistence that people should believe nothing that has not been proven. The Cartesian method called for doubt toward any knowledge not obtained through sense perception, but full confidence in knowledge perceived through reason. He built his own system on a foundation of doubt, that is, an unwillingness to believe anything until it had been proven. Many of Descartes's critics understood his position to be entire skepticism, but he did not contend certainty is impossible, only that it could not occur without verification. Once he was convinced of a certainty, he used that truth to prove even the existence of God. He argued that God is the perfect being, and man's idea of perfect being must arise from God placing that concept in the human mind.

The major error of Descartes, the one that aroused opposition among theologians, was his exaltation of reason, rather than revelation, to the summit of authority. Although he may not have intended to denigrate revelation, that was the effect of his teaching, and soon philosophers began to construct their systems on reason alone with no regard for revelation. In the Netherlands some Protestant scholars, enamored with Descartes's rationalism, concluded they could reinterpret Christian doctrine in such a way as to dispense with those beliefs they deemed incompatible with reason. Descartes's connection with the papal church did not deter them from adopting his method and carrying it to lengths he did not intend. At the same time the Arminian Grotius was encouraging defections from Reformed theology, Descartes was prompting scholars in many fields to devalue divine revelation in favor of reason, as a type of religious humanism supplanted biblical Christianity in academic circles.

The Secession of 1834

In 1816 King William I imposed a number of changes on the Dutch Reformed Church, including a new form of government in which civil authorities selected the commissioners to sit in the National Synod. The state had subjected the highest court of the national church to its control, and the king appointed the president of each provincial synod as well. A government minister of public worship administered ecclesiastical affairs for the crown. The authoritarian character of church polity after 1816 made it almost impossible to protest effectively when theologians and ministers taught contrary to the historic doctrines of the church, introduced innovations in public worship, or neglected duties such as the catechetical instruction of the young. The efforts of Isaac da Costa (1798–1860) and Guillaume Groen van Prinsterer (1801–1876) show, nevertheless, that orthodox believers made great efforts to resist corruptions and tried to reclaim their church for biblical Christianity.

Isaac da Costa, of Portuguese-Jewish descent, had come under the influence of Willem Bilderdijk (1756–1831), a poet of strong Calvinistic convictions, who wanted to restore the biblical faith and practice of the Reformed church at the time of the *Reveil*. He led Da Costa to Christ, and like his mentor, Da Costa scorned the secular humanism that was infecting the church. He was both a physician and a poet, a man of great learning and deep devotion that drew people to Bible studies he conducted. In 1823 he produced a booklet titled *Bezwaren tegen den geest der eeuw* (Objections against the spirit of the age), an essay that assailed the drift of the nation away from its biblical heritage. His critics responded with venom and ridicule. Government officials denounced him as an obscurant disturber of the peace, and church leaders were especially offended because of his complaints about their dereliction.

Guillaume Groen van Prinsterer was a lawyer and historian who served in the royal cabinet. He remained within the *Hervormde Kerk* until his death, but a strong attachment to orthodoxy made him sympathetic toward critics of the church who suffered persecution for their efforts to preserve its historic character. Groen had once approved of the liberal trends leading church and society away from Christianity, but the witness of Swiss historian J. H. Merle d'Aubigne had led him to embrace the Reformed faith wholeheartedly. The influence of Bilderdijk, too, was a factor in his conversion. When some orthodox believers decided loyalty to Christ required leaving the national church, Groen disagreed, but he defended their right to do so and protested against measures to repress them.

The *Afscheiding* (Secession) occurred in 1834, when Hendrik de Cock (1801–1842) and a number of other conservative ministers led their congregations out of the *Hervormde Kerk* after exhausting all legal or church orderly means to restore orthodoxy within it. De Cock, a pastor in Ulrum, Groningen, educated in theological liberalism, at first showed little interest in the distinctive beliefs of the Reformed faith. He was a pastor eight years before he read the Canons of Dort and was unacquainted with Calvin's *Institutes of the Christian Religion,* until a friend loaned him a copy. Once he learned the truth, however, De Cock embraced it heartily and preached it zealously, to the consternation of fellow ministers who viewed his position as untenable and likely to disturb the peace of the church.

De Cock's fervor and outspoken criticism of infidelity led church authorities to censure, suspend, and eventually depose him from the ministry. Civil magistrates used the power of the state against him and his supporters, some of whom had to endure persecution at the hands of their neighbors. It is ironic that a nation that had fought to gain freedom of religion harassed and abused some of its own citizens who asserted that right by dissenting from the established order for reasons of conscience. De Cock spent three months in prison, and he and his people were subjected to heavy fines. The government forbade Seceders to hold religious services, even in private homes, if more than twenty persons were present, unless the state had given permission for such assemblies. Such policies remained in effect until William II ascended the throne in 1844 and relaxed many of the restrictions imposed on the Seceders and their congregations.

Secession from the national church in 1834 led to formation of the Christian Reformed Church in 1869, a body independent of the state, but one that adhered faithfully to the Reformed faith as expressed in the Belgic Confession, Heidelberg Catechism, and Canons of Dort. The Christian Reformed Church adhered to the Presbyterian form of church government as set forth in the historic Church Order of Dort. Another distinctive was the exclusive use of the Psalms as the content of worship song, together with the New Testament canticles and metrical versions of the Ten Commandments, the Lord's Prayer, and the Apostles' Creed.

This church established a theological seminary at Kampen, and later, the Theological University at Apeldoorn. Today the Christian Reformed Churches (the name adopted in 1947) has about seventy-five thousand adherents in 183 congregations. Its missionary outreach has extended to Indonesia, South Africa, and Botswana, and church-planting efforts have been active in Belgium as well as in the homeland. After World War II, members emigrating to Canada and the United States were instrumental in establishing a sister denomination known as the Free Reformed Churches of North America.

The *Doleantie* of 1892

Despite the membership losses incurred by the *Afscheiding*, the Dutch Reformed Church continued to move away from the historic Reformed faith as declared in its confessions. It released ministers from the obligation to subscribe to any creed or confession, providing they affirmed "the spirit and essence" of the faith. This was even less exacting than the rule of 1816, which required pastors to accept the standards in "so far as" they accorded with Scripture. The result of this practice was an elastic Protestantism that tolerated a wide spectrum of beliefs, and even no particular belief at all.

Only a minority of orthodox believers joined the secession of 1834, so those who remained within the national church had to contend with continuing defections from the Reformed faith. The University of Groningen became a source of great controversy when some of its scholars rejected the hypostatic union of Christ as the God-man. The Groningen theology and other versions of liberalism excited an orthodox reaction, the leader of which was Abraham Kuyper (1837–1920), a graduate of the University of Leyden, who once espoused the modern critical approach to the Bible and had expressed disdain for historic Christian beliefs such as the bodily resurrection of Christ.

Kuyper was a brilliant scholar with an almost encyclopedic breadth of knowledge. After receiving the doctor of theology, he became pastor of the Reformed church at Beesd, Gelderland, where he served three years. During that time some of his own parishioners challenged his shallow preaching and urged him to consider the state of his soul. One of them gave him Calvin's *Institutes,* which he promised to read for the first time. While he read, members of his church prayed for their pastor's conversion, and God heard their prayers. Kuyper then understood the gospel and began proclaiming it eagerly. Soon he received a call to join the pastoral staff of the large Cathedral Church of St. Martin in Utrecht, and there he organized orthodox pastors and elders for a concerted effort to reform the national church. Kuyper's eloquence and academic prestige assured him a hearing, and the vigor with which he contended for the faith put liberals on notice that they had a formidable adversary.

The endeavor to restore biblical truth to a position of centrality in church and society led Kuyper to found Christian newspapers and to organize a Reformed political movement known as the Anti-Revolutionary Party, the focus of which was to combat the secularist ideas of the French Revolution. His own experience at the University of Leyden convinced him that the work of reformation required a genuinely Christian institution of higher learning, where scholars would interpret all disciplines and all of life within the framework of a biblical worldview. Against enormous odds he founded the Free University of Amsterdam for that purpose.

Kuyper maintained that theological liberalism was a religious expression of a secular humanist worldview to which Calvinism was the only adequate rebuttal. He saw the matter as a collision between competing authorities, as liberalism made man supreme, the proper point of reference from which to judge life and the world. Since this is antithetical to biblical teaching, Christians must resist it. For Kuyper, modernism-liberalism was not only an anti-Christian system of theology but also a godless worldview made popular by the influence of the French Revolution. He cited the rise of socialism and nihilism and a growing rejection of Christian moral values as evidences to support his contention.

By about 1885 Kuyper came to believe restoration of orthodoxy within the Dutch Reformed Church was not attainable. His best efforts had failed to turn the tide against unbelief, so he and a substantial number of Reformed Church ministers, elders, and church members renounced the authority of the National Synod, a move that aroused the animosity of the state authorities as well as synodical leaders. Like the seceders of 1834, Kuyper stressed the claim that the orthodox party was the real Reformed Church, loyal to the historic confessions of the national church. The national church had forsaken God's Word and was Reformed in name only. The experience of separation from apostasy was a painful one, and Kuyper's movement became known as the *Doleantie*, a Latin term signifying sorrow or mourning. A large majority of churchgoers in Amsterdam supported Kuyper's movement, but the National Synod deposed Kuyper and other leaders of this secession.

Although the churches of the *Doleantie* were preserving the Reformed faith, court decisions awarded their buildings to the National Church. The departure of congregations continued nevertheless, as about two hundred local churches and 170 thousand members withdrew to form a new body that took the historic name from the National Church. Before 1816, the National Church was called the *Nederduits Gereformeerde Kerk*. King William reorganized it in 1816 as the *Nederlands Hervormde Kerk*. The new church adopted the older name and began as the *Nederduits Gereformeerde Kerken* (*Dolerende*), in English, the Protesting Dutch Reformed Churches.

Some orthodox believers remained within the Dutch Reformed Church, convinced separation was wrong, but members of the Christian Reformed Church soon realized the commonality between their denomination and the *Doleerende Kerken*, and most of them supported the merger of the two bodies, an event that occurred in 1892. The united body became the *Gereformeerde Kerken in Nederland* (Reformed Churches in the Netherlands). It returned to the polity of the Reformation and required officers to subscribe to the Three Forms of Unity: the Belgic Confession, Heidelberg Catechism, and the Canons of Dort. A small group of congregations refrained from joining the merger and continued as the *Christelijk Gereformeerde Kerk* (Christian Reformed Church).

Twentieth-Century Developments

Some Christian Reformed congregations then did not participate in the merger and have retained their distinct identity to the present. The united church depended upon the Free University of Amsterdam and Kampen Theological Seminary for the education of its pastors, while in 1909 the *Gereformeerde Kerken* began publishing a weekly organ titled *De Waarheid* (The truth). Two years earlier a number of independent congregations followed the lead of G. H. Kersten (1882–1948) and established their own denomination, the Reformed Congregations in the Netherlands, with a seminary in Rotterdam. The daughter denomination in North America is the Netherlands Reformed Congregations.

Recurrent theological controversies have punctuated the history of the Reformed bodies in the Netherlands from the Reformation to the present. Within the *Gereformeerde Kerken,* a dispute in the 1920s led to another division when Johannes G. Geelkerken (1879–1960) of Amsterdam questioned the historicity of Genesis 2 and 3. The synod suspended him for three months, but he withdrew and led a few congregations out of that church. This faction united with the national church in 1946.

World War II inflicted great hardship on all Dutch churches during the German occupation of the country. Many church buildings were destroyed, and some pastors died while in prison for opposing the Nazi regime and its anti-Semitic policy. The year 1944 brought another division in the ranks of Reformed believers, when Klaas Schilder (1890–1952) protested some decisions of the synod of the *Gereformeerde Kerken*. Schilder was then a professor at the theological school in Kampen and editor of *De Reformatie* (The Reformation), an influential organ of his church. His complaint pertained to some resolutions of a doctrinal nature that the synod had adopted in 1942. The controverted issues included the subjects of common grace, the covenant of grace, the union of Christ's two natures, and the relation of baptism to regeneration. When the synod summoned him to appear, Schilder refused, and that court suspended him for disobedience and later deposed him from the ministry. The outcome was a schism, as a substantial number of congregations left the *Gereformeerde Kerken* to form the Reformed Churches Liberated. About one hundred thousand members supported this body, which organized its own seminary at Kampen, an institution that developed into a university competing with the older school in the same city. The Liberated Churches soon began missionary works in Indonesia, South Africa, Brazil, Ukraine, and Congo. The daughter denomination of the Liberated Churches in Canada is called the Canadian Reformed Churches.

Noteworthy Modern Theologians

Although the Netherlands is a small country, it has exerted great influence in many areas, including theology. Among the many distinguished scholars in this discipline, four examples are worthy of inclusion in this survey.

Contemporary with Kuyper was Herman Bavinck (1854–1921), a minister of the *Gereformeerde Kerken*, who had served the Christian Reformed Church prior to the merger of 1892. Bavinck, who earned a doctorate at the University of Leyden, was professor of theology at the seminary in Kampen from 1882 to 1902, when he joined the faculty of the Free University. By then he had already gained a fine reputation for scholarship through publication of his *Reformed Dogmatics*, a four-volume systematic theology that expounds Reformed beliefs while engaging post-Reformation developments in theological writing. Along with Kuyper, Bavinck helped to give the Free University an international reputation as a center of Reformed learning.

Hendrik Kraemer (1888–1965) was a neo-orthodox theologian, a champion of ecumenicity, and, for sixteen years, a missionary of the Netherlands Bible Society in Indonesia. Concurrent with his work of translating the Bible and Christian literature, Kraemer developed a theology of missions that related Christianity to other religions. In 1937 he moved to Leyden to become a professor at the university there. His most famous publication is *The Christian Message in a Non-Christian World* (1938), which he prepared for use at the World Missionary Conference in Tambaram, India. This work shows the author's attachment to the dialectical theology of neo-orthodox exponents such as Barth and Brunner. When the World Council of Churches opened an ecumenical institute in Bossy, Switzerland, Kraemer became its first director. Although he was a member of the liberal Dutch Reformed Church, he insisted Christianity is the only religion derived from divine revelation, and *The Christian Message* is a warning against syncretism in religion.

Another celebrated ecumenist from the Netherlands was Willem Adolf Visser 't Hooft (1900–1985). A doctor of theology educated at the University of Leyden, 't Hooft served the YMCA, the World Student Christian Federation, and the World Council of Churches, of which he was general secretary from 1938 to 1966. He edited the *Ecumenical Review* (1948–1966) and was a prolific author of books such as *The Kingship of Christ* (1947), *No Other Name: The Choice between Syncretism and Christian Universalism* (1974), and *The Genesis and Formation of the World Council of Churches* (1982).

The foremost Reformed theologian of the Netherlands in the twentieth century was Gerrit Cornelis Berkouwer (1903–1996), a graduate of the Free University of Amsterdam, where he studied the works of Kuyper and Bavinck. Berkouwer was a pastor before he became a professor of theology at his alma mater in 1940. He was a very influential figure in church affairs, serving as president of the General Synod of the *Gereformeerde Kerken* during the trying years of 1943 to 1945. While he was in that office, his opposition to Schilder helped to produce the schism that led to the formation of the Reformed Churches Liberated in 1944. Berkouwer described that conflict in his last book, an autobiography published in 1990.

Berkouwer was a popular professor, and some of his graduate students became distinguished theologians in their own right. His own thinking about doctrinal matters was in general conservative in his early years, but during the 1950s he reconsidered the historic Reformed position and altered his own views in a somewhat liberal direction. The change became evident in his writings, especially as he dealt with subjects such as the authority of Scripture and original sin. His magnum opus is the eighteen-volume *Studies in Dogmatics* (1952–1976). In addition he produced *Karl Barth* (1936), *Conflict with Rome* (1948), and *The Triumph of Grace in the Theology of Karl Barth* (1954). An observer at Vatican Council II in 1962, he wrote *The Second Vatican Council and the New Catholicism* in 1965. Translations of many of his books have made Berkouwer an influential theologian around the world.

Recent Developments in Church Order

In 1945, while the Netherlands celebrated the end of World War II, the *Hervormde Kerk* met in Amsterdam to reconstitute itself, and the civil government did not interfere. The assembly disbanded the prewar polity and created a new General Synod elected by the constituents of the church rather than being chosen by the state. A new book of church order was authorized, and a committee charged to prepare it finished its task in 1950, when the General Synod adopted it. The Dutch Reformed Church thus gained independence from the state and consolidated several agencies, bringing them under closer church supervision. The new church order did not include a requirement for subscription to the Three Forms of Unity.

Membership in the *Hervormde Kerk* has been declining since the nineteenth century, due in part to advancing secularism in Dutch society, but separations too have taken a heavy toll, as orthodox groups have found it necessary to leave in order to preserve their doctrinal integrity. By 1976 only 23.6 percent of the population identified with the old national church, although it was still the largest ostensibly Reformed body in the nation.

The *Gereformeerde Kerken*, the second largest denomination, also lost ground, especially after the Second World War, when theological liberalism and ecumenism gained acceptance within its ranks. In 1967 that church decided to relegate the Three Forms of Unity to the status of historical documents rather than expressions of faith to which its officers must subscribe. Liberalism became evident in the faculties at the Free University of Amsterdam and the Theological University at Kampen. In 1971 the *Gereformeerde Kerken* joined the World Council of Churches and then engaged in discussions and cooperative endeavors with the *Hervormde Kerk*. In 2004 the *Hervormde Kerk* and the *Gereformeerde Kerken*, along with the Evangelical Lutheran Church, joined in forming the *Protestantse Kerk in Nederland*, a decidedly liberal, ecumenical body. About 125 conservative congregations refused to join the united Protestant denomination. These dissidents formed the Restored Reformed Church and established fraternal relations with the Continuing Christian Reformed Church organized in 1892. The main organ of the old national church is the *Nederlands Theologisch Tydschrift,* and that of the smaller denomination is the *Gereformeerde Theologisch Tydschrift.*

SUGGESTED ADDITIONAL READINGS >>

Bangs, Carl. *Arminius: A Study in the Dutch Reformation.* Nashville: Abingdon, 1971.

Berkouwer, G. C. *A Half-Century of Theology.* Translated and edited by Lewis B. Smedes. Grand Rapids: Eerdmans, 1977.

Duke, Alastair C. *Reform and Revolt in the Low Countries.* London: Hambledon, 1990.

Geyl, Pieter. *The Revolt of the Netherlands.* London: Ernest Benn, 1966. Reprint of 1932 edition.

Haley, K. H. D. *The Dutch in the Seventeenth Century.* London: Thames and Hudson, 1972.

Harrison, A.W. *Arminianism.* London: Duckworth, 1937.

Langley, McKendree R. *The Practice of Political Spirituality.* Jordan Station, Ontario: Paideia, 1984.

Latourette, Kenneth S. *Christianity in a Revolutionary Age.* Vols. 2 and 3. Grand Rapids: Zondervan, 1969. Reprint of 1959 edition.

Mackay, James Hutton. *Religious Thought in Holland during the Nineteenth Century.* London: Hodder & Stoughton, 1911.

McGoldrick, James Edward. "Claiming Every Inch: The Worldview of Abraham Kuyper." In *A Christian Worldview: Essays from a Reformed Perspective,* 31–45. Taylors, S.C.: Presbyterian Press, 2008.

———. *God's Renaissance Man: The Life and Work of Abraham Kuyper.* Darlington, U.K.: Evangelical Press, 2000.

Motley, John Lothrop. *The Rise of the Dutch Republic.* 3 vols. New York: John D. Morris, 1901.

Pettegree, Andrew. *Emden and the Dutch Revolt.* Oxford: Clarendon, 1992.

Praamsma, Louis. *The Church in the Twentieth Century.* St. Catharines, Ontario: Paideia, 1981.

————. *Let God Be King: Reflections on the Life and Times of Abraham Kuyper.* Jordan Station, Ontario: Paideia, 1985.

Rowen, H. H., ed. *The Low Countries in Early Modern Times.* New York: Walker, 1972.

Sprunger, Keith L. *Dutch Puritanism: A History of English and Scottish Churches in the Netherlands in the Sixteenth and Seventeenth Centuries.* Leiden: E. J. Brill, 1982.

Ten Zythoff, Gerrit J. *Sources of Secession.* Grand Rapids: Eerdmans, 1987.

Vanderlaan, Eldred. *Protestant Modernism in Holland.* Oxford: Oxford University Press, 1924.

Vlekke, Bernard H. *Evolution of the Dutch Nation.* New York: Roy, 1945.

Wedgwood, C. V. *William the Silent.* New York: W. W. Norton, 1968. Reprint of 1944 edition.

Wilson, Charles. *The Dutch Republic.* New York: McGraw-Hill, 1968.

FIVE

Central and Eastern Europe

By the late Middle Ages most of Germany and eastern Europe lay within the borders of the Holy Roman Empire, a loose confederation of states without ethnic, linguistic, and economic unity. The imperial crown, though elective in principle, was in the hands of the Habsburg dynasty centered in Austria. Germans, Italians, Slavs, Hungarians, and others populated a vast territory that had no capital city, no uniform coinage or system of taxation, and no efficient federal government. Every prince, almost a king in his own castle, jealously guarded his autonomy against any moves to transform the empire into a nation-state. Religion was the one factor that almost all peoples of the empire had in common, although some Jews and Muslims lived within the structure, and in some areas the Eastern Orthodox Church had a following. The German Hapsburgs presided over this polyglot edifice until 1806, when Napoleon Bonaparte subdued the German principalities and compelled the Holy Roman emperor to relinquish that title and to rule thereafter as emperor of Austria.

Nonconformity in the Holy Roman Empire

In the fourteenth and fifteenth centuries, the appearance of movements critical of the Roman Catholic Church challenged papal supremacy and thereby disrupted the religious unity of the empire. In Bohemia John Hus (1372–1415) and Jerome of Prague (ca. 1370–1416) led protests against moral corruptions and financial abuses of the hierarchy while denying the traditional claim that Catholicism with the pope as its head was the true church of Christ. They did not reject the large body of Catholic doctrine that had accumulated across the centuries, but they contended the true church is the body of God's elect and should not be confused with the visible organization subject to Rome. Moreover, they insisted the eucharistic cup as well as the bread belonged to the laity as well as the clergy.

The Roman Church had for some time followed the teaching of Thomas Aquinas (ca. 1225–1274) known as *concomitance,* which holds that Christ is whole and entire in each of the eucharistic elements, and therefore those who receive the bread alone receive both the body and blood of Christ.

Hussite Resistance

Although neither Hus nor Jerome espoused all of the doctrines that became characteristic of the later Protestant Reformers, their challenge to papal supremacy prepared the way for others to deny it and to call boldly for a return to New Testament teachings. Some Hussites went well beyond the protests of their leaders and eventually espoused doctrines comparable to those of the sixteenth-century Protestants. Papal and imperial hostility caused the Hussites great suffering, but the dissidents' resolve enabled them to withstand military assaults and to survive even after their forces were defeated in battle.

Frustrated in their efforts to crush the Hussites, the pope and emperor agreed to conciliate them if possible, and for that purpose they invited them to the Council of Basel in 1431, which the Hussites attended after the emperor assured their safety. The council had a broad agenda dealing with various proposals for church reform, as well as seeking reunion with the Greek Orthodox Church, from which Rome had been alienated since 1054. In January 1433 delegates arrived from Bohemia to present the Hussite demands. Basel eventually agreed to allow the Bohemians to serve the Eucharist in both species to the laity and to allow them to conduct church services in their native tongue rather than in Latin. These concessions (and a few more) satisfied some of the dissidents, but others remained unreconciled to Catholicism. A policy of divide and conquer proved successful, as Emperor Sigismund (1410–1437) enlisted cooperative Bohemians to support him in suppressing the stubborn Taborites, so called because they maintained a fortress on Mount Tabor.

The United Brethren

After the crushing of the Taborites, the less militant Calixtines, so called because of their demand that the *calyx* (eucharistic cup) be restored to the laity, lost much of their earlier fervor and adjusted to being part of the Catholic Church. God, however, preserved a remnant eager for the truth, and about the middle of the fifteenth century, an evangelical party appeared in Bohemia and took the name *Unitas Fratorum*—United Brethren, soon to be known as Bohemian Brethren. Many nobles joined them, and by the opening of the next century, the Brethren had about two hundred thousand members organized in a roughly Presbyterian form of church polity and affirming evangelical doctrines. This development made the soil of Bohemia fertile ground for planting the seeds of Protestant principles when Martin Luther and others discovered the gospel and began proclaiming it widely.

Luther's Influence

Soon after Luther began assailing the errors of Rome, his teachings reached Bohemia, carried there by students from the University of Wittenberg and through distribution of the German Reformer's writings. Leaders of the Bohemian Brethren consulted with Luther and in 1536 presented him with their confession of faith. He recommended some changes and then published the document with his own laudatory preface. When Germany exploded in domestic warfare between Catholic and Protestant states, the Bohemian Brethren supported the Lutheran side in defiance of their own Catholic king. They suffered terribly for this, as the monarch took vengeance upon them. Their church survived, nevertheless, and grew numerically after the war ended in 1555. Since the next ruler was much less hostile, the Bohemian Brethren enjoyed a period of peace.

Reformed Influence

In the second half of the sixteenth century, Reformed Protestants from Switzerland began missionary endeavors in Bohemia and enjoyed considerable success with the non-German population of that country. By the early seventeenth century, about four-fifths of the people there claimed to be Protestants, and the majority of them were Reformed. They were sufficiently strong to convince Emperor Rudolf II (r. 1576–1612) to grant them full political and religious rights, and that included his permission for them to form a consistory at Prague and to exert control of the university in that city. This favorable arrangement did not, however, last long. When Matthias (r. 1612–1619) succeeded Rudolf, violations of the *Letter of Majesty*, by which Rudolf had made concessions to the Protestants, began to occur. In 1617 Ferdinand of Styria convinced the nobles to acknowledge his right to succeed when the childless Matthias died. In this way a zealot for the Counter-Reformation became ruler in Bohemia and later Holy Roman emperor as Ferdinand II (r. 1619–1637).

Once Ferdinand's intentions became evident, Protestant nobles determined to oppose him. They threw two of the monarch's agents out of a castle window to express their defiance, so the *Defenestration of Prague* initiated a devastating conflict that came to be known as the Thirty Years' War (1618–1648). The rebels deposed Ferdinand as king of Bohemia and awarded that crown to the Calvinist Prince Elector Frederick III (r. 1610–1632) of the German state of Palatine.

Frederick III expected broad support from Protestant states, but that did not occur, while imperial and Spanish forces came to the aid of the emperor, who defeated the rebels at White Mountain in 1620. Ferdinand II then confiscated the Protestants' properties and employed the Jesuits to reimpose Catholicism in Bohemia and Moravia. The emperor beheaded twenty-five rebellious nobles and enslaved thousands of Protestants to work in his silver mines, where many died because of maltreatment. Peasants, too, suffered great brutality, as Ferdinand's depredations reduced the population by two-thirds and almost eliminated any evidence of a Protestant presence in the land. A comparable repression occurred in Austria at the same time. The Palatinate soon fell to Spanish forces, and Frederick III lost his lands, his title going to Maximilian I, Duke of Bavaria (r. 1598–1622), who had supported the emperor by leading the Catholic League of German princes.

Toleration in Habsburg Lands

The details of the Thirty Years' War belong to the political and military history of this era and are beyond the scope of this book. It is important to note, however, that freedom for Protestants in the Habsburg Empire did not become a reality until Joseph II (r. 1765–1790) issued an edict of toleration in 1781. This emperor was a rationalist disciple of the French philosophers who, like Voltaire and others, opposed persecution of religious dissidents. Joseph aspired to rule as an enlightened despot, but he had the misfortune of ruling an empire in which vested interests did all they could to thwart his humane politics. Since the reign of Charles V (r. 1519–1556), the Habsburg dynasty had been a champion of Catholicism. Joseph II practiced that religion but favored toleration of other faiths, such as Lutheran, Reformed, and Greek Orthodox, all of which had adherents within his domain. This monarch had a favorable attitude even toward Jews, to whom he granted remission of some discriminatory taxes and the right to worship in private.

In his efforts to implement reforms across his empire, Joseph faced stern opposition from the hierarchy of the Catholic Church, some institutes of which he sought to subject to the crown. The ruler deeply disliked religious orders such as the Jesuits, and to combat their influence he closed six hundred monasteries. He closed several seminaries too because they taught future priests to make enactment of papal programs their priority. As an alternative, this would-be enlightened despot created seminaries of his own to educate priests disposed to put the needs of their parishioners before the interests of the Vatican. He paid the salaries of such clergymen and thereby made them almost employees of the state. In some respects Joseph's ecclesiastical reforms prefigured those of the French Revolution. Even a visit from Pope Pius VI (r. 1774–1799) in 1782 could not convince this ruler to rescind his policies.

Because he offended both the church hierarchy and the feudal nobility, Joseph II encountered implacable resistance. He died in 1790 a sad, defeated man who considered himself a failure. His brother succeeded him as Leopold II (r. 1790–1792), and, succumbing to various pressures, he repealed some of Joseph's most progressive decrees. Leopold did, however, allow his brother's policy toward religion to remain largely in place, but the law still prohibited adherents of one religion to seek converts from another.

Public worship of the Reformed pattern began in Austria in 1781, after the imperial edict of toleration took effect. At that time a number of foreigners residing in Vienna met together, adopted the Second Helvetic Confession as their creedal standard, and initiated services with Karl Wilhelm Hilchenbach, a minister attached to the Dutch embassy, as preacher. Civil authorities permitted erection of a Reformed chapel in 1784, but with the provision that there be no spire and the entrance not be evident from the street. They relaxed the second stipulation when Henriette von Nassau-Weilburg, wife of Archduke Charles, began attending worship in the building.

Reformed leaders founded a seminary in Vienna in 1821. A law known as the *Protestantpatent* of 1861 extended official recognition to Protestantism but reserved for the emperor control over appointment of church officials and the right to veto decisions of the evangelical synod. A Society for the History of Protestants in Austria was formed in 1880, and in 1887 the government sanctioned the erection of chapels with spires and street-level entrances. The number of Protestants in Austria grew substantially into the early twentieth century, but World War I led to the dissolution of the Habsburg Empire, and most of the Protestants found themselves assigned to the new Republic of Hungary. In 1922 the Reformed theological school aligned with the University of Vienna.

Hungary and Transylvania

From 1867 to 1918 the centerpiece of the Habsburg Empire was the Dual Monarchy, a reform of Francis Joseph (r. 1848–1916) to placate the assertive and progressive Magyars, who dominated the Hungarian portion of the empire. Because of this arrangement Francis Joseph was emperor of Austria and king of Hungary, and a bicameral parliament administered the entire Habsburg domain.

Protestantism began in Hungary when students from Wittenberg carried Luther's teachings to their homeland, and by the middle of the sixteenth century there was an organized church there, one that adopted the Augsburg Confession of Faith. Among early zealots for Luther's doctrine was Matthias Devay (ca. 1500–1545), who studied at Wittenberg prior to becoming an evangelist in his native land. Devay, however, went to Basel in 1537 and there embraced the Swiss view of the sacraments, which he then proclaimed to his countrymen and thereby initiated a move toward the Reformed faith. Although Devay's change of doctrine irritated Luther, his fellow Hungarians accepted it readily.

Peter Melius (1515–1572) also was a Lutheran who turned to Calvinism and became an influential figure in the development of the Hungarian Reformed Church. The effective leadership of Melius brought him recognition as the Calvin of Hungary. The first Hungarian language edition of the New Testament appeared in 1541, the work of John Sylvester (1504–1560). A complete Bible in the Magyar tongue was not available until 1590.

Next to Hungary in the eastern part of the Habsburg Empire was Transylvania, another region receptive to the Protestant Reformation. It was a province separate from Hungary with its own dynasty of rulers subject to the emperor in Vienna. Lutheranism penetrated this region and enjoyed a substantial following, but agents of Reformed theology arrived soon thereafter, and considerable tension between the two schools of thought became evident, the Saxon Germans in the region preferring Luther's position, while the Magyars favored Calvin's doctrine. This did not necessitate a hostile rupture, since the two Reformers in question maintained a cordial, fraternal relationship with each other. Their disciples, nevertheless, related poorly to one another. In April 1564 the two parties met in a synod and were unable to reach agreement, so separate Lutheran and Reformed churches emerged, both receiving government recognition. Calvinist scholars from the University of Heidelberg advised Reformed leaders in both Hungary and Transylvania and recommended they adopt the Heidelberg Catechism as a manual for instruction in doctrine, and that instrument quickly gained acceptance across a wide area. A synod meeting at Debreczin in 1567 completed the organization of the Reformed church by adopting the Second Helvetic Confession and a book of church order and discipline. At that point the church was under almost complete clerical supervision, so it had not yet adopted Calvin's pattern of polity.

Trials and Triumphs

Although Protestants were able to establish their presence in parts of the Habsburg Empire, Catholic rulers in Vienna remained opposed to them. Conditions were better for non-Catholics in Transylvania than in Hungary proper because native princes in Transylvania were generally tolerant toward diversity in religion. In Hungary a different attitude prevailed, especially after the Jesuits arrived and introduced their characteristic militancy in dealing with alleged heretics. Rudolf II (r. 1576–1612), who had been educated in Spain, shared the Jesuits' severe disdain for all forms of Protestantism. His efforts to impose religious uniformity included the conquest of Transylvania and a vigorous persecution of Protestants. The strength of reaction against his repressions forced Rudolf, as king of Hungary, to grant religious freedom by an enactment in 1606, but the Protestants' gain was an ephemeral one, and sectarian divisions among them weakened their cause at the very time their survival depended upon unity. The Jesuits, meanwhile, continued to plot for a resumption of persecution, which began after Ferdinand II (r. 1619–1637) ascended to the throne of Austria and Hungary. Thereafter Protestants suffered varying degrees of violence for over a century, and their numbers diminished sharply.

In 1674 there was an especially cruel attack upon the evangelicals. Many pastors were executed, while others escaped by defecting to Catholicism. Enslavement in the galleys or confinement to dungeons was the fate of others. A law enacted in 1731 required all public officials to invoke the Virgin Mary and other Catholic saints when they assumed their positions, a measure that effectively barred Protestants from places in government service. This policy of discrimination remained in force until 1781, when Joseph II issued a decree of toleration that eliminated the religious oath for officeholders and allowed Protestants to erect church buildings.

During the 1840s the parliament moved somewhat hesitantly toward freedom, at least for "accepted religions." In 1881 a national synod of the Reformed Church of Debreczin created an executive and administrative body known as the General Convent composed of the bishops and curators of the church together with twenty-eight others, members elected from various districts of the denomination. The General Synod became the highest court of the church.

A Reformed home mission association began operations in 1892, and the Christian Missionary Society commenced its work as the foreign missionary arm of the church in 1903. By that time a vigorous social service ministry was functioning, much of it under the direction of deaconesses. When the Treaty of Trianon officially ended Hungary's participation in World War I, the victors partitioned the country in such a manner that large numbers of Reformed believers were assigned to the jurisdiction of Romania, Czechoslovakia, and Yugoslavia, moves that reduced the numbers of Reformed congregations in Hungary proper by almost one thousand. Because of these imposed political arrangements, separate Reformed churches developed their own organizations in Slovakia and Russo-Carpathia. The ethnic composition of these bodies was still largely Hungarian, especially in Slovakia.

Despite the changes due to defeat in the First World War, the Hungarian Reformed Church enjoyed substantial growth in the period between 1921 and 1941. It erected fifty-six new church buildings, and the number of congregations in Budapest rose from eight to twenty-two. In 1941 Hungary entered World War II as an ally of Germany and the Axis powers, another conflict that brought defeat and hardship to the country and its churches. Adolf Hitler controlled Hungarian affairs until the Soviets occupied the country near the end of the war. By 1948 a Communist government was in control subject to dictation from Josef Stalin and the Kremlin.

The Reformed Church in Hungary early came to terms with the Red rulers by signing an agreement by which the state promised to continue the subsidies that it had been paying to the churches since 1868, but on a decreasing scale. Reductions in the subsidies were to be at a rate of 25 percent every five years until 1968, when they were to end. The state did not, however, impose the full amount of the decreases at first. The government assumed full control of education, long a prerogative of the churches, as a policy of indoctrinating the youth in Communist ideology. The state did allow seminaries and a few other distinctively religious schools to continue under church auspices. The Roman Catholic Church, rather than the Protestant bodies, was most prominent in its opposition to the officially atheistic regime, as Joseph Cardinal Mindszenty (1892–1975) led an effort to preserve freedom for his own church.

To the discredit of the Reformed Church, it cooperated with state programs as the price to pay for a limited degree of liberty. It usually endorsed peace proposals of Communist origin and often criticized the stern resistance of the Western nations to the propaganda and policies of the Soviet bloc. In 1960 the General Synod of the Reformed Church issued its official approval of the social and economic order then in place, and by a unanimous vote declared:

> We affirm…that we regard our popular-democratic state and its government as the authority ordained by God, and we gladly and voluntarily contribute our service to its work for the progress of the Hungarian people. We approve the building of socialism and we offer anew our prayers and work toward its final realization.

The above affirmation of confidence in the Red regime appeared four years after forces from the Soviet Union brutally suppressed protests that became a revolt in Budapest, as many thousands of people demanded freedom. The synod meeting in 1960 roundly condemned the uprising and censured ministers who had supported it, while leaders of the church made public declarations of loyalty to the state.

The organization of the Hungarian Reformed Church features a modified version of Presbyterianism in that the church has bishops. These officials do not, however, function in an authoritative role comparable to churches that have a formal episcopate. Each Hungarian bishop is a pastor of a particular local congregation and holds the status of "first among equals" in relations with other pastors. The church has traditional presbyteries and district and provincial synods, with the General Synod as its highest court. By the end of the twentieth century, 20 percent of Hungarians claimed affiliation with the Hungarian Reformed Church. There were about eleven hundred congregations and three theological schools.

A new era began in Hungary in 1989 when the Communist government lost power. Free elections brought a constitutional guarantee of religious freedom, and the state restored many properties the former rulers had confiscated from the churches. The Hungarian Reformed Church and other bodies have launched substantial missionary and educational projects since regaining their liberty.

The Czech and Slovak Republics

Although the victors in World War I created a new Republic of Czechoslovakia, that state was an artificial construct from its birth, one that did not comply with the wishes of the nationalities concerned. When the Soviet Bloc in Eastern Europe gained its freedom after 1989, the Czechs and Slovaks agreed to dissolve the political arrangement imposed upon them in 1919. Since 1918 the Lutheran and Reformed churches in the Czech-speaking area had operated as the United Evangelical Church of the Czech Brethren, an affiliate of the World Alliance of Reformed Churches. The merger that produced this denomination included about 34,000 Lutherans and 126,000 Reformed believers. Converts from Catholicism were rather considerable and so enlarged the membership. In 1919 the Jan Hus Faculty of Theology opened in Prague, with professors drawn from both of the constituent denominations. Eventually the General Synod of the United Evangelical Church adopted both the Augsburg and the Second Helvetic Confessions.

As in most of Eastern Europe, Communists gained political control in Czechoslovakia after the Second World War, and the churches lost much freedom as a consequence. In a manner comparable to the Hungarians, Czech Protestants for the most part complied with demands from the state and publicly endorsed the Red regime and its socialist programs. Noteworthy among church leaders who acted as an agent for state interests was Josef Hromadka (1889–1969), a respected scholar and churchman, who made numerous pronouncements favorable to the government. As president of the Christian Peace Conference, he had many opportunities to promote socialist causes and to encourage his church to endorse them. He was not entirely uncritical toward the Red rulers, and eventually he resigned from the Peace Conference when he was accused of putting the interests of his own nation above those of that organization.

The Communist regime in Czechoslovakia was not the most repressive in Eastern Europe, and because it allowed development of some groups unacceptable to the Kremlin, Soviet and other Warsaw Pact forces occupied that country in 1968. Even that display of power did not, however, intimidate the advocates of freedom, and after the crisis passed, Czech authorities returned to a policy of leniency toward dissenters. In 1980 the state allowed distribution of 120 thousand copies of a new Czech language translation of the Bible. Publication of the united church's monthly magazine *Brotherhood* continued without government interference.

The Slovak portion of Czechoslovakia became the home of the Reformed Christian Church of Slovakia after World War I. It was a body with a large Hungarian component, and it operated a seminary in Bratislava, and a college, designed primarily for the education of teachers, opened in 1935.

Although a large number of Czechs were Protestants in the seventeenth century, by 1781, when Emperor Joseph II adopted a policy of official toleration, only about one hundred thousand any longer claimed Lutheran or Reformed identity. The forces of the Counter-Reformation had succeeded in crippling the evangelical movement, reducing its membership to a very small minority of the population. Imperial policy after 1781 did allow Reformed congregations to operate in conjunction with a consistory in Vienna, which thereby preserved a Presbyterian form of polity. In most cases rural churches depended upon Hungarian and Slovak pastors. The small Czech Reformed Church joined the World Alliance of Reformed Churches in 1877.

When Soviet Bloc forces occupied Czechoslovakia in 1968, many Reformed pastors lost their positions and their licenses to minister because they had supported efforts to initiate liberal reforms. After the fall of Communism, the Reformed Church gained new vitality and assumed the lead in several social service projects. Its theological school affiliated with Charles University in Prague. Fewer than 5 percent of the Czech people now claim to be Protestants, most of them Reformed. The formal dissolution of Czechoslovakia occurred in 1993, when the Czech and Slovak Republics were inaugurated. In Slovakia about 120 thousand people now identify with the Czech Reformed Church, a body with a synodical structure and seven presbyteries.

Romania and Yugoslavia

At the end of World War I Transylvania became part of Romania, a move that incorporated many ethnic Hungarians into a culture dominated by the Romanian Orthodox Church. The Reformed believers were thus a small but vigorous minority that demonstrated considerable strength in the era between world wars. During the time when the Axis powers controlled the region (1940–1944), Transylvania was restored to Hungarian control, only to return to Romania in the closing part of the Second World War. Four decades of Communist rule followed, and persecution became the plight of serious Christians. Pastors who refused to implement state dictates were

imprisoned and some were executed. Officials of various churches sometimes collaborated with the Red regime in order to preserve a limited
freedom to conduct their work.

Despite cruel repression, the Reformed church survived, and after the
collapse of Communism, it displayed surprising energy in erecting new
church buildings and engaging in extensive social service, especially caring
for orphans. Much to the dismay of Reformed leaders, the non-Communist
government rejected the church's request to operate religious schools, and
it did not cooperate in returning church properties confiscated during
the era of dictatorship. About 700 thousand people claim membership in
the Reformed church, a denomination with two districts and a synodical
arrangement to administer its affairs.

The existence of a Reformed church in Yugoslavia is due largely to
the assignment of Hungarian territory to that new nation in the settlement after the First World War. This church adopted the same governing
pattern as in Hungary, with bishops exercising leadership but not authoritarian control. A synod is the highest church court, and a synodical council
administers ecclesiastical affairs between meetings of the synod. Unlike
Hungary, the state in Yugoslavia provided no support for the Reformed
church, most of whose members were very poor. Very limited income has
been a problem from the start of this church. During the Communist era
the state regulated church affairs so as to exclude its participation in politics, but there was no repression of religion comparable to that in Romania,
except when religious leaders criticized the regime in public.

An acute shortage of ministers and funds to pay them plagued the
Reformed church badly, so in 1983 the synod authorized laymen to perform
ministerial functions after they had completed correspondence courses of
study prescribed by the synod. These lay preachers teach the congregations
and administer the sacraments, as well-educated, ordained clergymen do in
other lands.

The post-Communist period has been one of great instability in Yugoslavia, as ethnic groups such as Ruthenians, Croats, and Macedonians have
seceded from the confederation and created new republics of their own.
Only Serbia and Montenegro remain joined in the state of Yugoslavia, and
the future of their relationship is in doubt. Like Czechoslovakia, Yugoslavia
was a creation of the peacemakers in 1919, one that gave little attention to
the desires of the nationalities compressed together in an artificial political
arrangement. This state of affairs has inevitably affected the churches as,

for example, when the Reformed Christian Church in Croatia declared its autonomy. Only seventeen thousand people in what remains of Yugoslavia regard themselves as Reformed Protestants.

Germany

In the land of Luther, Protestants who bear his name have outnumbered all others since the Reformation. In three areas of the country, however, Calvinism gained a following of substantial strength. These were East Friesland, the lower Rhine Valley, and the Palatinate. John á Lasco (1499–1560) was a dynamic leader of the Reformed movement in East Friesland until 1548, when a decree of Holy Roman Emperor Charles V forced him to leave. The city of Emden produced such a volume of Calvinist literature that it became known as the "Geneva of the North." Eventually the Evangelical Reformed Church of Northwest Germany came into being, as about one hundred congregations affiliated in response to a directive from Prussian King William I (r. 1861–1888), who became emperor of Germany in 1871. This body adopted a representative polity and joined the World Alliance of Reformed Churches.

The Rhine River flows from Germany into the Low Countries, and the establishment of a Reformed church in the Rhine Valley was due mainly to the arrival there of refugees from persecution in the Netherlands, beginning in 1545. The town of Wesel was a center for such temporary settlers who, in 1564, adopted the Heidelberg Catechism and thereby signified their adherence to the Calvinist faith. Adoption of the Presbyterian church order came at a meeting in Wesel in 1568. The Dutch refugees organized the Classis of Cleves in 1572, and comparable courts, frequently called synods, appeared in Julich (1572) and Berg (1579). A German congregation aligned with the Dutch organization at Wesel in 1579, and others did the same soon thereafter. When persecution of Protestants in the Netherlands moderated, most of the Dutch Reformed believers returned to their homeland. By then the German portion of the church was strong enough to sustain itself, while remaining connected with the Dutch body until 1610.

In the lower part of northwest Germany, the National Church of Lippe, founded in 1648, became the major Reformed denomination, and it eventually acquired the status of a *Landeskirche,* a territorial church approved by the state. It is still operating under that arrangement with its own Presbyterian form of polity. The character of this body is rather unusual in that its membership is both Reformed and Lutheran. About four-fifths of the congregations are Reformed, one-fifth Lutheran. It is organized into six classes (presbyteries), five of which are Reformed, one Lutheran.

The success of Calvinism in the Palatinate was due in part to the Religious Peace of Augsburg, which ended a Catholic-Protestant war in 1555, when both sides were exhausted and longed for an end to hostilities. The work of the princes, the settlement provided that each ruler would determine the policy toward religion in his state, whether it would be Catholic or Lutheran. Soon the Prince Elector Frederick III (r. 1559–1576), ruler of Palatine, extended the provisions of the treaty to the Calvinists in his state and became a Calvinist himself.

Frederick III, a generous patron of the Reformed church, subsidized a theological school to promote Calvinism, and he employed the distinguished scholars Zacharias Ursinus (1534–1583) and Kaspar Olevianus (1536–1587) to compose a statement of Reformed doctrine for use in the parishes of his principality. The Heidelberg Catechism was the fruit of their labor. Reformed scholars in Heidelberg, with the prince's encouragement, produced an impressive body of theological literature and thereby contributed much to the credibility of the Reformed faith.

The death of Frederick III brought a setback to the cause of Calvinism in the Palatinate because his successor, Ludwig VI (d. 1583), was a convinced and intolerant Lutheran with a strong dislike for Reformed teachings. This became obvious when he refused to allow a Reformed minister to officiate at the funeral of his father, the late prince. When Ludwig passed from the scene, his successors favored Calvinism, so the Reformed church recovered its favored standing. From 1618 to 1648 Germany was engulfed in the horrors of the Thirty Years' War, one of the most destructive conflicts in history. When the Peace of Westphalia ended it, the Reformed churches gained recognition as legal religious bodies alongside the Roman Catholic and Lutheran churches.

In the early eighteenth century, large numbers of Germans migrated to America and took the German Reformed faith with them. While this did much to encourage the growth of Calvinism in the New World, it depleted the ranks of Reformed believers in their homeland. This occurred about the same time that new challenges were arising in Europe that would weaken the Christian community as a whole and from which the Reformed churches could not isolate themselves. Rationalism as a worldview was fascinating intellectuals in many countries, as it contested long-held Christian beliefs that the churches in general seemed incompetent to defend. All

Christian bodies, as a consequence, suffered losses, first among intellectuals, but eventually among common people too.

In addition to the appearance of anti-Christian philosophy, there was a growing tendency for civil authorities to impose their will upon state churches dependent upon them for financial support. This became particularly apparent in the Kingdom of Prussia, where Frederick William III (r. 1797–1840) imposed a consolidation of the Lutheran and Reformed churches of his nation in 1817, a date chosen because it coincided with the three hundredth anniversary of Luther posting the Ninety-Five Theses at Wittenberg. Although this Prussian Union allowed each congregation to continue its traditional practices and to affirm its own confession of faith, the arrangement worked to the disadvantage of the Reformed church. Soon most of the German states in which both Protestant denominations operated followed the lead of Prussia, which is evidence that rationalism had diminished concern for doctrinal exactitude, while a growing indifference toward biblical truth was spreading across Europe. Frederick William III was a deeply religious man, but his grasp of theology was poor, and at times he violated the terms of the Prussian Union by trying to impose uniformity upon local congregations. Some rigorously orthodox Lutherans refused to join the union and maintained the Evangelical Lutheran Church in Prussia, which gained state recognition under the next monarch in 1845. Staunch Calvinists also resented royal dictation to the churches and resisted the union where they could.

A number of Calvinists responded to the royal policy by starting separate churches both in Prussia and in other states that had imposed union. The Reformed Church of Betheim and East Friesland was one such endeavor, and the Prussian-based Evangelical Free Church of Germany was another, although the latter did not organize until 1860. A celebration of the four hundredth anniversary of the birth of Ulrich Zwingli, which met in Marburg in 1884, launched an effort to revive the Reformed movement by creating the *Reformierter Bund für Deutschland* (Reformed Alliance for Germany), which was not a denomination but rather an organization to promote Reformed teachings in various church bodies. The *Bund* published the *Reformierter Kirchenzeitung* (Reformed church newspaper), which J. N. Ogilvie, missionary and leader in the Church of Scotland, hailed as the "soul of Presbyterianism of Germany."

The long-established pattern of state churches in Europe, including Germany, had the effect of emasculating those churches of vitality and making them vulnerable to alien influences they were not prepared to resist. In the twentieth century this became distressingly evident in Germany, when some church leaders succumbed to Nazi pressures and allowed themselves to become agents of an anti-Christian regime. Subservience toward the state led them to surround Hitler and the Nazi Party with an aura of religious sanctity, even when the government began ruthless persecution of Jews. Resistance to the regime in power was generally feeble, with only a few church leaders taking a bold stand against the evil policy. A few Reformed believers joined with some Lutherans and members of other denominations to condemn the godless state by issuing the Barmen Declaration in 1934, a manifesto that Christ alone is head of the church. The leading figure from Reformed ranks who participated in this protest against tyranny was Swiss theologian Karl Barth.

In the 1840s a number of Lutheran, Reformed, and other religious bodies drew together in a federation known as the Evangelical Church of Germany. The Reformed Churches of Lippe and Northwest Germany were among the founding members. The united body has an elaborate organization but little authority. Its synod meets once a year, and a council of twelve members administers church business between synods. The composite character of this church reflects a lack of concern for doctrinal purity, so its adherence to Reformed standards is only nominal.

The Soviet conquest of East Germany in 1945 led to the division of the country into Communist and non-Communist republics. East Germany was predominantly Protestant at the time of the Russian occupation and creation of the German Democratic Republic, a satellite of the Soviet Union. There were five territorial churches with Lutheran and Reformed constituents in East Germany at the end of World War II, each of which had connections with comparable churches in West Germany. The East German regime in 1968 compelled the churches under its authority to sever those connections, and membership in the churches of the East declined greatly during the era of Communist rule. By 1976 fewer than twenty-five thousand people in East Germany claimed membership in Reformed churches. Lutherans were substantially more numerous, although they too incurred large losses.

Conclusion

By the end of the twentieth century, East and West Germany had reunited as the Cold War between the Soviet Bloc and the Western nations came to an end, and churches separated by the Iron Curtain were able to restore relations with one another. The ecclesiastical picture that emerged was not, however, an encouraging one. Many church bodies with roots in the Protestant Reformation remained, but in a badly weakened condition. Most of those that professed to be Reformed had long before discarded the historic doctrines of their forefathers while preserving in some degree the polity of Presbyterianism. A survey of a few examples is in order.

The Evangelical-Reformed Church originated in the former Kingdom of Hanover, which Prussia absorbed, and in 1882 the king allowed Reformed congregations to establish their own ecclesiastical organization to which local Reformed churches in the surrounding region, some of them of Huguenot origin, adhered. In 1988 the Evangelical-Reformed Church of Bavaria merged with this denomination. The merged body has about two hundred thousand members in 142 congregations spread across Germany. It does not adhere strictly to any historic Reformed confession, so laxity in doctrine prevails. The Evangelical-Reformed Church is prominent in social service projects and maintains membership in the World Alliance of Reformed Churches and in the World Council of Churches.

The Reformed Alliance in Germany came into being in 1884 as an effort to stimulate the growth of Reformed ministries and thereby to arrest their decline and losses to Lutheranism. The German Alliance is affiliated with the World Alliance of Reformed Churches and is now deeply involved in the ecumenical movement. Members of the German Alliance include the Church of Lippe, the Evangelical-Reformed Church, and some smaller bodies.

In the north German state of Brandenburg is the Evangelical-Reformed Council of Berlin-Brandenburg, a denomination of two consistories, one French Reformed, the other German Reformed. The French presence is due to the flight of Huguenots into Brandenburg after King Louis XIV in 1684 deprived his Protestant subjects of their freedom. The two consistories together comprise the United Synod of the Evangelical-Reformed Congregations in Berlin-Brandenburg, which has a membership of only about twenty-two hundred. Its affirmation of the Heidelberg Catechism and the Gallican Confession is only perfunctory.

The Evangelical Church in the Rhineland is a denomination of about 1.1 million communicant members within a united church formed in 1817, when the king of Prussia sponsored a union of Lutheran and Reformed congregations. Since local churches could retain their own confessions of faith, some continued to endorse the Heidelberg Catechism, and to that many have added the anti-Nazi Declaration of Barmen from 1934, but as with most other German churches, there is no firm commitment to a confessional position.

Another area where Reformed congregations have retained their identity within a united-church structure is Sachsen-Anhalt in east Germany. The union of 1817 did not entirely blur the distinctions between Lutherans and Calvinists there, and about the time of the union, the king of Prussia appointed a professor of Reformed theology to the faculty at the University of Halle. The Evangelical Church of the Church-Province of Sachsen, a denomination of about a half million members, maintains numerous ecumenical connections and does not require subscription to any historic confession, although it does in principle endorse the Heidelberg Catechism, the Barmen Declaration, and the ancient creeds.

The lack of spiritual vitality among German churches of Reformation origin is evident in the very low attendance at services of worship. Except for the independent *Freikirchen* (Free Churches), which are not numerous, the traditional denominations all appear to be in decline. Pastors as a rule obtain their education in universities where secular humanism prevails and informs the teaching of all disciplines, including theology. This situation has prompted some American denominations, the Presbyterian Church in America among them, to send missionaries to Germany as well as to other European nations where the situation is comparable.

SUGGESTED ADDITIONAL READINGS >>

Barth, Karl. *Protestant Theology in the Nineteenth Century.* Valley Forge, Pa.: Judson, 1973.

Bauhofer, Janos G. *History of the Protestant Church in Hungary.* Harrisonburg, Va.: Sprinkle Publications, 2001. Reprint of 1854 edition.

Bigler, Robert M. *The Politics of German Protestantism: The Rise of the Protestant Church Elite in Prussia, 1576–1612.* Berkeley: University of California Press, 1972.

Bryce, James. *The Holy Roman Empire.* Reprint, New York: Schocken Books, 1961.

Budgen, Victor. *On Fire for God: The Story of John Hus.* Darlington, U.K.: Evangelical Press, 1983.

Capek, D., ed. *Fellowship of Service: Life and Work of Protestant Churches in Czechoslovakia.* Prague: Ecumenical Council of Churches, 1961.

Dusicza, Ferenc. *History of the Reformed Church in Hungary*. Budapest: Edito Calvin, 1999.

Evans, R. J. W. *The Making of the Habsburg Monarchy, 1550–1700*. Oxford: Oxford University Press, 1979.

———. *Rudolf II and His World: A Study in Intellectual History, 1576–1612*. Rev. ed. Oxford: Oxford University Press, 1984.

Johnston, W. M. *The Austrian Mind: An Intellectual and Social History, 1848–1938*. Berkeley: University of California Press, 1972.

Kadar, I. *The Church in Storm Time*. Budapest: Bibliotheca, 1957.

———. *Five Years of Hungarian Protestantism, 1945–1950*. Budapest: Hungarian Church Press, 1950.

Lortz, Josef. *The Reformation in Germany*. 2 vols. New York: Herder & Herder, 1968.

Moeller, Bernard. *Imperial Cities and the Reformation*. Translated by H. C. E. Midelfort and M. U. Edwards. Philadelphia: Fortress, 1972.

Murdock, Graeme. *Calvinism on the Frontier, 1600–1660: International Calvinism and the Reformed Church in Hungary and Transylvania*. Oxford: Clarendon, 2000.

Otter, Jin. *The Witness of Czech Protestantism*. Prague: Evangelical Church of Czech Brethren, 1970.

Ozment, Steven. *The Reformation in the Cities*. New Haven, Conn.: Yale University Press, 1975.

Prestwich, Menna, ed. *International Calvinism, 1541–1715*. Oxford: Clarendon, 1985.

Raitt, Jill, ed. *Shapers of Religious Traditions in Germany, Switzerland, and Poland, 1560–1600*. New Haven, Conn.: Yale University Press, 1981.

Revesz, Imre, ed. *History of the Hungarian Reformed Church*. Translated by George Knight. Washington, D.C.: Hungarian Federation of America, 1956.

Roubiczek, Paul and Joseph Kalmer. *Warrior of God: The Story of John Hus*. London: Nicholson & Watson, 1947.

Spinka, Matthew. *The Church in a Communist Society: A Study in J. L. Hromadka's Theological Politics*. Hartford, Conn.: Hartford Seminary Press, 1964.

———. *John Hus: A Biography*. Hamden, Conn.: Archon Books, 1966. Reprint of 1941 edition.

Tonkin, John. *The Church and the Secular Order in Reformation Thought*. New York: Columbia University Press, 1971.

Wedgwood, C.V. *The Thirty Years War*. London: Pimlico, 1997. Reprint of 1938 edition.

Welch, Claude. *Protestant Thought in the Nineteenth Century.* New Haven, Conn.: Yale University Press, 1972.

Zeman, Jarold K. *The Hussite Movement and the Reformation in Bohemia and Slovakia, 1350–1650.* Ann Arbor: University of Michigan Press, 1977.

SIX

Elsewhere in Europe

The prominence of the Reformed faith in nations such as France, Switzerland, the Netherlands, and Germany contrasts sharply with its lack of success in other parts of Europe. It is nevertheless appropriate to recognize efforts of valiant Reformed believers in places where their endeavors did not produce impressive results, and Scandanavia is a place to start.

Scandinavia

The Lutheran movement has long been dominant in Scandinavia, where the Reformed faith has barely any following, but when Charlotte Amalie from the Landgraviate of Hesse-Cassel became engaged to the prince who would become Danish King Christian V in 1667, the agreement provided that a Reformed pastor would reside in Copenhagen to minister to her spiritual needs. After becoming queen, Charlotte Amalie staunchly maintained her Calvinist faith and as a consequence was not actually crowned. In 1684, the king, to the consternation of strict Lutherans, granted freedom of worship to non-Lutherans and allowed persecuted Huguenots from France to settle in his nation. Jean de la Placette (1639–1718) was the first Huguenot pastor to arrive in Denmark, and in 1688 the queen laid the cornerstone for the first Reformed church building. Before long, four Reformed congregations were functioning, but due to economic difficulties, only two survived. There has been no appreciable growth of the Reformed church in Denmark since then.

In Norway a small body of Reformed believers established four congregations in 1877 after they withdrew from the state Lutheran Church. The only Reformed organization in Sweden originated as the French Reformed Church of Stockholm, founded by Huguenots in the late seventeenth century.

Poland

The Reformed faith enjoyed a bit more success in Poland, at least for a while. John á Lasco (1499–1560), the country's most distinguished Protestant leader, was a staunch Calvinist whose introduction to Protestant beliefs came through contacts with Lutherans. He spent three years in England during the reign of Protestant King Edward VI (r. 1547–1553), but when Mary Tudor (r. 1553–1558) ascended the throne, Lasco fled to avoid persecution and returned to his native Poland, where he strove unsuccessfully to unite Lutherans and Calvinists. When his aspiration for a united Protestant church failed, he worked to create a Reformed church in which Calvinist doctrine and Presbyterian polity would prevail. Against great odds he was able to lead Calvinism to some considerable but short-lived gains. For a while the Protestant cause seemed promising, even though the throne remained firmly Catholic. Rebellious nobles failed to place a Protestant on the Polish throne, and when the monarch extended some concessions in the matter of religious freedom, the Protestants had no incentive to support rebellion against him. The landed nobles eventually abandoned their struggle against the crown, and most returned to the Catholic Church in order to avoid being excluded from royal appointments and favors.

Reformed theology and church order never became well established in Poland, due in part to the influence of the Jesuits in the Counter-Reformation. A small Reformed Evangelical Church in Poland continues, with its principal congregations in Warsaw and Lodz. Its membership is only about four thousand people organized in a Presbyterian form of polity and asserting formal but not obligatory adherence to the Second Helvetic Confession and the creeds of the ancient church.

Greece

The Greek Evangelical Church, with a Reformed character, came into being in 1885 through the efforts of Presbyterians from America. Samuel R. Houston (1806–1887) and George W. Leyburn (1809–1875) had labored in Greece as agents of the Presbyterian Church (U.S.A.) serving with the American Board of Commissioners for Foreign Missions since the 1830s. Thornton R. Sampson (1852–1915) followed them but came as an appointee of the Presbyterian Church in the United States (South). The British and Foreign Bible Society dispatched native Greek Michael Demetrius Kalopothakes (1825–1911), who was quite influential in the work of the Evangelical Church, for which he incurred much hostility from Greek

Orthodox clerics. The first synod of the Evangelical Church convened in 1885, with but three congregations participating. The first church building had been erected in 1871. The growth of the Reformed movement has been very slow, and the country remains overwhelmingly Greek Orthodox. During the 1970s Greece was subject to a military dictatorship that treated nonconformist religions badly. The return of free elections brought new opportunities to the Evangelical Church, but its efforts have met with little success, perhaps because Protestant principles are so foreign to the culture of the country. The Evangelical Church has recently initiated missionary work in Albania, where most of the populace is Muslim. The church continues to operate with a Presbyterian polity, and its statement of faith is a modified version of the Westminster Confession. It is a member of the World Alliance of Reformed Churches and the World Council of Churches. Its membership barely exceeds five thousand.

Spain

Although the Reformation entered Spain at an early date and enjoyed some appreciation, countervailing factors, chief among them the efficiency of the Inquisition, were able to eliminate almost all traces of Protestantism by about 1570, and it would not be until the nineteenth century that another concerted effort at establishing a Reformed presence would occur. In 1871 the formation of the Christian Church in Spain followed the union of two earlier organizations, both of them Presbyterian. One was the work of the Spanish Evangelical Society founded in Edinburgh in 1855, while the second was a group in Madrid that had originated in Switzerland. The United Presbyterians of Scotland and the Irish Presbyterians gave substantial support to this effort, and the Irish contribution made possible the creation of a theological school to educate pastors for service in Spain.

Part of the reason Protestants were able to minister in a generally hostile environment in Spain was because of British possession of Gibraltar, out of which evangelists could operate. After a long period of repression, which included arrests, imprisonments, and expulsions, the Spanish government bowed to international pressures in 1868 and granted freedom of religion as a constitutional right. Thereafter the Protestant body that adopted the name Spanish Reformed Church operated legally alongside the older Christian Church in Spain. Efforts to unite the two failed, and in 1880 another version of Protestantism appeared in the form of the Spanish Reformed Episcopal Church, which adopted the Anglican liturgy. In 1890 a merger of several congregations led to the adoption of a new name, the Spanish Evangelical Church, to replace the Christian Church in Spain. Through times of trial and considerable persecution, the Protestant cause endured. In incremental steps the various governments in Madrid extended freedom to non-Catholics, but it was not until 1980 that full liberty of belief and practice became a fixture in state policy. By the end of the twentieth century, the Spanish Evangelical Church was the major Reformed body in the country. It has about ten thousand members and subscribes in principle to the Heidelberg Catechism, the Second Helvetic Confession, and the creeds of the ancient church. It is affiliated with the World Council of Churches and the World Alliance of Reformed Churches. The generally lax attitude toward doctrine that now prevails in the Evangelical Church allowed it in 1955 to admit into membership the Methodist Church of Catalonia, a group with non-Reformed roots and teachings.

Portugal

Next to Spain is Portugal, in which Protestantism made even less headway. Portuguese in the sixteenth century had almost no contact with the teachings of Luther and Calvin. Far from the centers of Protestant activity and subject to the Inquisition and the presence of the Jesuits, Portugal was almost isolated. The effective introduction of Protestantism would not occur until the twentieth century. The Presbyterian Church in Brazil initiated missionary work in Portugal in 1910, an endeavor that faced stern opposition from church and state, but a few congregations developed nevertheless. It was not until 1952 that the Evangelical Presbyterian Church of Portugal came into being as an organized denomination. The first congregation of that name began its ministry in Lisbon in 1871, and the first effort at forming a presbytery was in 1940. A movement to establish Congregational churches developed parallel to the Presbyterian effort, and the organization of 1952 included most of the Congregational assemblies as members of the Presbyterian synod. Membership in the combined body was only 1,350 in 1999, and two even smaller Presbyterian groups claimed a total of five congregations.

Italy

Another European nation in which Protestantism has made little headway is Italy, where the Waldenses have maintained a nonconformist presence since the twelfth century. In the late Middle Ages, contacts between the

Waldenses and the Hussites of Bohemia strengthened both movements, and in the sixteenth century a substantial group of Waldenses adhered to the Reformed faith through the efforts of Farel, the friend and collaborator of Calvin.

Through most of their history, the Waldenses were victims of persecution, as the Roman Catholic Church and various civil governments tried to destroy them. Although those dissidents who lived in French territory suffered terribly too, their ordeal did not last so long as that of their brethren in Italy. Not until the mid-nineteenth century did they obtain legal toleration there. The Dukes of Piedmont and Savoy had for a long time suppressed the Waldenses, as a massacre in 1655 attests. When the French king Louis XIV revoked the Edict of Nantes and thereby deprived his Protestant subjects of their freedom, the rulers in Piedmont and Savoy demanded that the Waldenses renounce their faith or suffer banishment. This led refugees to flee into the Cottian Alps between Italy and France, there to maintain a precarious existence as a church in hiding.

Persecution in the domain ruled by the House of Savoy ended in 1848, when King Charles Albert (r. 1831–1849) granted a constitution that provided for freedom of religion. This encouraged church-planting endeavors, and soon Waldense congregations were operating in Florence, and then Turin not long after that. Gradually the rest of Italy extended toleration, and by 1883 the Waldenses had formed a mission organization with its headquarters in Rome. Various Protestant groups outside Italy hastened to give aid to the Waldenses, and they established their own school of theology at Torre Pellice in 1855 but moved it to Florence in 1860. Peace and freedom brought a substantial increase in the number of Waldenses in the Cottian Alps, so many migrated to other parts of Italy and Europe, some to South Africa, Uruguay, and Argentina.

The Waldensian Church, as organized, created only one court, a General Synod, to meet annually. Two laymen from each congregation, the professors from the theological school at Florence, and delegates from the mission stations are eligible to vote. Although this is not a strictly Presbyterian arrangement, the official statement of faith that the Waldenses adopted is the thoroughly Reformed Confession of La Rochelle, a Huguenot affirmation from 1571.

Full freedom of religion for the Waldenses became a reality throughout Italy in 1929, when the Vatican signed the Lateran Treaty with the Fascist government of Benito Mussolini. By terms of this agreement the state promised to favor Catholicism while assuring the rights of other religions. After the fall of Mussolini, the post-World War II republican government ratified full religious liberty for all Italians.

Although the Waldenses since the sixteenth century have subscribed in principle to the tenets of the Reformed faith, in the twentieth century they gradually abandoned it. Their modern disregard for Reformed theology is evident in the integration of their church with the Italian Methodists in 1975, a combination that has produced the Waldensian Evangelical Church, a body of about twenty-eight thousand members that has extensive connections with the current ecumenical movement.

Belgium

Although the Dutch Republic secured independence from Spain by the Treaty of Westphalia (1648), the southern provinces of the Low Countries remained subject to Madrid. After King Philip II abandoned hope of regaining the northern provinces, he and his successors relentlessly pursued Protestants in the south, with the result that the Reformed presence there was reduced to a tiny minority. Philip had allowed nonconformists two years to embrace Catholicism or to leave the country. Belgium, therefore, became almost totally Catholic. Not until 1781, when Spain no longer ruled the area, did religious freedom became a fact there, but by then there were very few Protestants to enjoy their new liberty.

The defeat of Napoleon in 1815 brought major geopolitical changes across Europe, as the powers that defeated him redrew the map of the continent. At the Congress of Vienna (1814–1815), the victors transferred the southern Netherlands to the newly created kingdom of the Netherlands ruled by the House of Orange. This was an unhappy union, one in which disagreement about religion was a prominent factor between the Protestant north and the Catholic south. In 1830 the Belgians revolted against Dutch rule, and with British support, they obtained international recognition as an independent constitutional monarchy. Soon thereafter, seven Protestant congregations formed the Union of Evangelical Churches in Belgium, a body that adopted a generally Presbyterian polity but not a Reformed statement of doctrine.

Parallel to the creation of the Union, Bible societies emerged first in Brussels and began distributing the Scriptures in large quantities. This effort received considerable support from the famous British and Foreign Bible Society, and soon an upsurge of interest in Reformed theology occurred with the result that a church developed, one that adopted the historic Belgic Confession from 1561.

In the era after the Second World War, the Union of Evangelical Churches discarded any attachment to the Reformed faith and merged with the Belgian Conference of the United Methodist Church to become the Protestant Church of Belgium. Soon this body merged with the Belgian sector of the Reformed Churches of the Netherlands (*Gereformeerde Kerken*) and formed the United Protestant Church of Belgium, a denomination of about forty thousand members in about one hundred congregations organized in a Presbyterian form of government, but with no commitment to Reformed theology.

SUGGESTED ADDITIONAL READINGS >>

Andersson, Ingvar. *History of Sweden*. New York: Praeger, 1956.

Butler, C. M. *The Reformation in Sweden*. New York: A. D. F. Randolph, 1883.

Callahan, William J. *Church, Politics, and Society in Spain, 1750–1874*. Cambridge, Mass.: Harvard University Press, 1984.

Chanu, Pierre, ed. *The Reformation*. New York: St. Martin's, 1986.

Dunkley, E. H. *The Reformation in Denmark*. London: SPCK, 1948.

Elton, G. R., ed. *New Cambridge Modern History*. 2nd ed. Vol. 2. Cambridge: Cambridge University Press, 1990.

Garstein, Oskar. *Rome and the Counter-Reformation in Scandinavia*. 4 vols. Leiden, Netherlands: E. J. Brill, 1963–1992.

Greengrass, Mark. *The European Reformation*. London: Addison Wesley, Longman, 1998.

Grell, Ole Peter. *The Scandinavian Reformation: From Evangelical Movement to Institutionalisation of Reform*. Cambridge: Cambridge University Press,1995.

Hillerbrand, Hans J. *The World of the Reformation*. New York: Charles Scribner's Sons, 1973.

Huntford, Roland. *The New Totalitarians*. New York: Stein and Day, 1972.

Jensen, De Lamar. *Reformation Europe*. 2nd ed. Lexington, Mass.: D. C. Heath, 1992.

Jones, R. Tudur. *The Great Reformation*. Downers Grove, Ill.: InterVarsity, 1985.

Lannon, Frances. *Privilege, Persecution, and Prophecy: The Catholic Church in Spain, 1875–1975*. Oxford: Clarendon, 1987.

Lindsay, Thomas M. *A History of the Reformation.* Vol. 2. New York: Charles Scribner's Sons, 1907.

Livermore, Harold. *A History of Spain.* New York: Grove Press, 1958.

Musteikis, Antanas. *The Reformation in Lithuania.* Boulder, Colo.: Distributed by Columbia University Press, 1988.

Polland, A. F. *The Jesuits in Poland.* New York: Haskell House, 1971. Reprint of 1892 edition.

Raitt, Jill, ed. *Shapers of Religious Traditions in Germany, Switzerland, and Poland.* New Haven, Conn.: Yale University Press, 1981.

Ramet, Pedro, ed. *Christianity: Protestantism and Politics in Eastern Europe: The Communist and Post-Communist Eras.* Durham, N.C.: Duke University Press, 1992.

Roberts, Michael. *The Early Vasas: A History of Sweden, 1523–1611.* Reprint, Cambridge, U.K.: Cambridge University Press, 1986.

Sanchez, Jose. *Reform and Reaction: The Politico-Religious Background of the Spanish Civil War.* Chapel Hill: University of North Carolina Press, 1964.

———. *The Spanish Civil War as a Religious Tragedy.* Notre Dame, Ind.: University of Notre Dame Press, 1987.

Solberg, Richard W. *God and Caesar in East Germany.* New York: Macmillan, 1961.

SEVEN

Scotland

By the late fifteenth century, influences from the Renaissance were becoming evident in Scotland's political and social matters, and the machinery of national monarchy was gradually taking shape despite the resistance of often rebellious barons. The country was relatively poor, so its royal court did not compare favorably with those of Spain or France, or even with that of England. The Crown relied upon the commercial class for support, while maintaining fine relations with the Catholic Church. James IV (r. 1488–1513) aspired to be a Renaissance prince and seemed committed to governing justly and efficiently, but the Highlands and some lesser islands were unruly and troublesome for the king.

As an expression of his interest in learning, James IV founded King's College, Aberdeen, and his son established St. Leonard's College in the town of St. Andrews. In both institutions the techniques of humanist scholarship were soon apparent. A Royal College of Surgeons opened in Edinburgh in 1505, and the printing industry appeared soon thereafter. Both St. Leonard's College and the printing press were to become important instruments of the Protestant Reformers.

Relations between Scotland and England were often contentious, and when England fought France, the Scots sometimes allied with the French. In 1513, however, the English won a smashing victory at the Battle of Flodden Field, where James Stuart, the king, and most of his leading nobles perished in combat with the forces of England's King Henry VIII (r. 1509–1547).

Although the loss to England was costly and humiliating, Scotland recovered during the reign of James V (r. 1513–1542), who ascended the throne as a child and left government in the hands of his mother Margaret, the Queen Regent, until he reached age sixteen. James V was a strong ruler and firm military leader who ably suppressed uncooperative barons while maintaining fine relations with Parliament. This allowed the monarch to extend his authority into resistant areas where he greatly improved the administration of justice and thereby enhanced his own popularity.

By the time James V took charge of government, the Protestant Reformation had begun on the Continent, so Catholic clerics urged him to keep Scotland free of heretical ideas. Some nobles who otherwise might have opposed the expansion of royal authority supported the king as the best means to hold Protestantism at bay. James continued the traditional alliance with France and married a French duchess, thereby declaring his resolution to remain Roman Catholic. When the king died in 1542, he left a baby daughter to rule his still Catholic kingdom.

Arrival of Luther's Teaching

The first forceful challenge to the Roman Catholic Church in Scotland occurred when Lollards from England carried the doctrines of John Wyclif to the northern kingdom early in the fifteenth century. Due to a lack of surviving evidence, the extent of Lollard activity is unclear, but burnings of accused heretics did occur, sometimes in retaliation, when Lollards exposed corruption within the church. It appears that James Resby, an English priest who had become a disciple of Wyclif, was the first Lollard martyr in Scotland, his execution occurring at Perth in 1407. In 1410 Hussites in Bohemia published four letters by a Scottish Lollard named Quentin Folkhyrde, which is evidence that the Lollards had international connections, and in 1416 the University of St. Andrews required all master of arts students to denounce Lollardy and promise to defend Catholicism.

Even though insufficient evidence leaves Scottish Lollardy wrapped in clouds of obscurity, it is clear Catholic authorities perceived it to be a serious threat, especially because the Lollard Bible circulated widely there in hand-copied editions. At the least it is certain that Lollardy in Scotland, as in England, prepared the country for the advent of Protestantism.

The initial discovery of Luther's writings in Scotland occurred about the same time they appeared in England. By then, William Tyndale's translation of the New Testament became available. In 1525, the Scottish parliament banned the German Reformer's works.

Patrick Hamilton (d. 1528) was the first noteworthy Scotsman to espouse Luther's teachings. This son of a nobleman, related to the royal family, had become titular abbot of a monastery at age thirteen as part of an arrangement that imposed no monastic duties upon him but provided funds for his education as he prepared for a career as a high-ranking cleric.

With the income from his ecclesiastical position, Patrick Hamilton went to the University of Paris, from which he received the master of arts in 1520.

While in Paris, Hamilton became acquainted with Catholic humanist scholars who decried ignorance and corruption among the clergy of their own church, and at the same time he learned about Luther's teachings, which had spread to Paris from Wittenberg. It appears Hamilton found Catholic humanism attractive, because he moved to the University of Louvain, where Desiderius Erasmus (1466–1536), the foremost humanist scholar of that era, was teaching. At Louvain Hamilton distinguished himself in the classical languages and Platonic philosophy. His mastery of Greek equipped him to read the New Testament in the critically prepared edition Erasmus had produced in 1516. The fine education Hamilton obtained on the Continent prepared him well for the role of a reformer at home, and he returned there in 1523 and joined the faculty of arts at St. Andrews University.

Hamilton did not at first promote Lutheran ideas at his university but stressed the need to improve education by adopting the scholarly methods of the humanists. In the manner of Erasmus and others, he decried moral evils and abusive ecclesiastical practices, while leaving Catholic dogmas unchallenged. It is clear he had not yet embraced beliefs the Roman Church regarded heretical. Hamilton's criticisms of the clergy and other members of the faculty, however, provoked a backlash, as those he indicted for ignorance and corruption tried to deflect his accusations by calling him a Lutheran heretic. Even though the charge was unjust, it was a convenient means to silence an embarrassing critic. The effect of this contrivance was to lead Hamilton to consider Luther's position seriously and to leave Scotland before his enemies could seize him. He arrived in Wittenberg in May 1527, where Luther and Melanchthon received him warmly.

After a brief stay with the German Reformers, Hamilton, who had become a convinced evangelical, joined the faculty at the new University of Marburg, and while in that position he wrote a treatise about justification through faith alone. This work, the first theological writing by a Scottish Protestant, became known as *Patrick's Places*, an English translation of which became available in 1532. This doctrinal work expounds Luther's understanding of law and gospel with emphasis upon justification *sola fide*, which the Wittenberg theologian considered the article by which the church would stand or fall.

Late in 1527 Patrick Hamilton returned to Scotland and preached boldly while enjoying the protection of some of his powerful relatives, but Catholic authorities were determined to stop him. Archbishop James Beaton eventually seized Hamilton after luring him to a meeting with the promise he would discuss Hamilton's proposals for reform. After a trial for heresy and his refusal to recant, execution by burning took place outside the gate of St. Andrews University on February 29, 1528.

While death removed Hamilton from the scene, his teachings continued to spread, and within a dozen years of the execution a number of prominent citizens and officials of Edinburgh, Leith, Ayr, Perth, St. Andrews, and Dundee had embraced the evangelical faith, and some of them, like Hamilton, gave their lives as martyrs for it. The earliest Scottish Protestants were then Lutherans, but Reformed teachings from the Continent, building on the Lutheran foundation, erected the structure of Calvin's theology, which rather quickly gained acceptance.

George Wishart and the Reformed Faith

The principal agent of Reformed influence in Scotland was George Wishart (ca. 1513–1546), who had fled to the Continent after being accused of heresy for promoting the study of the Greek New Testament. He had received his education at the University of Cambridge, and there he became a zealous adherent to Reformed theology, at first in the form espoused by Ulrich Zwingli at Zurich.

In 1543 Wishart returned to Scotland and took with him the First Helvetic Confession of Faith (1536), a systematic declaration of Protestant doctrine that expresses specific rejoinders to the perceived errors of the Roman Church. At first Wishart enjoyed protection from a few powerful barons and was able to preach freely for about two years. Eventually, however, David Cardinal Beaton arrested him. The execution of this Reformer was especially gruesome, as Beaton erected a gallows outside his palace, and through a window he and his friends watched with glee as the body of his victim dangled from a rope. After the cardinal tired of the spectacle, he ordered the burning of Wishart's remains.

The Reformer's death did not, however, terminate his influence, for the First Helvetic Confession quickly became the most widely accepted doctrinal standard among Scotland's Protestants. This statement declared the civil authorities were bound to defend the true religion and to command the citizens to accept it. Since the monarch was still Roman Catholic, this assertion had revolutionary implications. Beaton had expected Wishart's execution to cripple the Reformation, but it had the opposite effect. Protestant supporters of the late Reformer killed the cardinal and threw his body through the same window where he had watched Wishart strangle to death. The conspirators who dispatched Beaton then took refuge in St. Andrews Castle, and John Knox, who was not part of the plot, joined them.

Enter John Knox

The Reformer who, more than any other, would shape the contours of Scottish Protestantism was John Knox (ca. 1514–1572), a priest until his study of the works of Augustine of Hippo led him to question some doctrines and practices of the medieval church. Soon he became a disciple of Wishart and then leader of the Protestants just at the time the Roman Catholics were preparing a counterattack upon the occupants of St. Andrews Castle. With the aid of French warships, which bombarded the ramparts from the sea, government forces besieged the castle and took the defenders prisoners. For the next nineteen months Knox and others were galley slaves forced to row a French vessel.

After his release in 1549, Knox went to England, where Protestant King Edward VI (r. 1547–1553) welcomed him, and remained from 1549–1554, when the next monarch, Mary I (r. 1553–1558), initiated a vicious persecution of Protestants. While he was in England, Knox was a royal chaplain and could have become an Anglican bishop, an honor he declined.

Fleeing Mary's wrath, Knox went to Frankfort, Germany, and from there to Geneva, where he became an eager student of Calvin and remained eighteen months in what he called "the most perfect school of Christ on earth since the apostles." While he was in Geneva, Protestant nobles at home formed the Lords of the Congregation of Jesus Christ and signed the first Scottish Covenant, by which they pledged to reform the kingdom. At the urging of the Lords, Knox returned to Scotland in 1559 and almost immediately preached against the papacy in a manner that aroused mobs to attack priests and Catholic church buildings.

Scotland was then under the rule of Mary Guise (r. 1515–1560), the French mother of Mary Stuart, who would be queen of Scots from 1542 to 1568, when her enemies forced her to leave the country. As Queen Regent, Mary Guise failed to suppress rebellious Protestant nobles, even though she had French aid, and by her death in 1560 the Protestant cause seemed impregnable.

During the time of religious strife in her homeland, Mary Stuart was living in France, where she married the man who would become King Francis II, but his death in 1561 left Mary a widow at age eighteen. Since the French government had no further use for her, Mary reluctantly returned to Scotland, where she encountered stern Protestant resistance to her own sincere Catholic faith. Before arriving there, Mary as queen promised to remove French troops and to renounce her claim to the throne of England, where her Protestant relative Elizabeth I (r. 1558–1603) reigned. About the same time, the parliament of Scotland officially renounced papal authority, and soon thereafter it established the Church of Scotland, a national Protestant institution.

Not long after her arrival in Edinburgh, the Queen of Scots received a visit from an ambassador of the King of Kings, John Knox, who feared Mary's intentions since she brought two Catholic priests with her from France to celebrate Mass in her chapel. To Knox, celebration of the Mass was abominable idolatry. He responded to the queen with a thunderous sermon in which he denounced her religion from the pulpit of St. Giles Church, Edinburgh. Mary then summoned him to appear before her and proceeded to lecture him about his duties as a subject to his sovereign. To the queen's face Knox replied, "I call Rome a harlot; for that church is altogether polluted with all kinds of spiritual fornication, as well in doctrine as in manners." Just as he had agitated opposition to the preceding Queen Regent, the Reformer defied the new ruler.

Mary Stuart was not a skillful leader, and her lack of discretion enabled Knox to inflame public opinion against her. She contracted two very damaging marriages, the first to her English cousin Lord Darnley, a vain, weak, and profligate man. After making himself odious to Mary by participating in the murder of her secretary and paramour, Darnley too fell victim to assassination as part of a plot in which his wife appears to have been involved. Three months after the killings she married James Bothwell, whom many people believed was the major agent in the killing of Darnley. Soon there was a public outcry against the queen, and Protestant nobles forced her to leave her infant son in their custody, whom they reared in their religion. When it became evident that Mary had little hope of remaining Scotland's queen, she fled to England, where her cousin Elizabeth was not pleased to see her. Since Mary had previously claimed that she was the rightful heir to the crown of England, Elizabeth placed her under surveillance, at times in a condition of house arrest. Mary, nevertheless, became the center of a plot to overthrow the Protestant monarch and the Church of England, an effort that failed and ended in the execution of Mary Stuart.

Establishment of the Reformed Religion

When Parliament abolished papal jurisdiction in 1560, it banned the Mass and stipulated penalties for anyone who promoted Romanism. The first offense led to a fine, the second to banishment, and the third death. The state did not, however, inflict the death penalty, and not one priest or Catholic died for his religion. At the same time Parliament repudiated papal authority, it adopted the Scots Confession of Faith, the principal author of which was Knox.

The Church of Scotland held its first General Assembly at the end of 1560, and forty men, only six of them ministers, participated. This body adopted the Book of Discipline as the basis for the operation of the church in a Presbyterian structure, with elders and deacons elected to one-year terms, a measure intended to prevent development of an ecclesiastical tyranny, as the Reformers perceived the Catholic system to be.

The Book of Discipline divided Scotland into ten districts for administration with national, provincial, and local church courts, the last being congregational sessions. Since pastors were few in number, the Discipline called for readers to convene congregations for the public reading of Scripture in that time of prevailing illiteracy. Readers often exhorted the people, and some became pastors after improving their own learning. *Superintendents* were temporary officials, pastors who served both their own parishes and others to which they traveled on a circuit. Every established congregation was to maintain a school to teach Latin grammar and catechism. High schools and additional universities came next, with a view toward obtaining learned ministers for the church.

Church-State Relations

While Mary Stuart was still in Scotland, the Catholic faction viewed her as the best means to negate Protestant gains, but when she left in 1567, Parliament declared the Reformed religion to be "the only true and holy Kirk within this realm." Scotland was officially Protestant, but the relationship of church and state remained to be defined.

Mary Stuart's son James VI (r. 1567–1625) remained in Scotland under the regency that proposed to control church properties and to appoint bishops over the church. Some greedy nobles sought to appropriate to themselves revenues of the old Catholic bishoprics, since the Church of Scotland did not have bishops per se. The Book of Discipline specified that such funds be used to support church schools and for the relief of the poor. In 1572 the Convention of Leith met to decide this matter, and it appointed nominal bishops who were to surrender episcopal revenues to the lords who appointed them. These *Tulchan Bishops* were often objects of ridicule, and the very arrangement that created them foreshadowed severe conflicts between church and state (*tulchan* was a stuffed calfskin placed by the side of a cow who had lost her calf in order to make her give milk). Stormy days lay ahead, as Scots struggled to achieve a viable church polity and to protect their church from domination by the state.

Exit John Knox

Knox seldom did things by halves. In many respects he was less prudent, and distinctly less diplomatic, than Calvin, rather resembling Luther in the unrestrained sweep of his imagination and resultant unfettered action. Knox exemplifies this attitude in his most vivid literary work, the *First Blast of the Trumpet against the Monstrous Regiment of Women*, published in 1558. The basic position of the writer was that generally held in his age, but the book seems to have drawn forth such pronounced and sustained counter-blasts as to deter the author from his professed purpose of indulging in two further such sallies. It created a furor, the like of which even Knox had not anticipated, though his preface shows that he was prepared for some considerable commotion in the wake of its appearance.

Mary of Lorraine, regent of Scotland, and Mary Tudor, queen of England, were the likely targets of the *First Blast*. But the latter very inconsiderately—at least from Knox's standpoint—died soon after its publication, leaving Elizabeth as her successor to the English throne. As a result, Elizabeth was regarded as the inevitable object of the work's strident strictures. This naturally aroused her wrath. The ensuing situation even provoked Calvin's displeasure when he discovered that a present, in the form of a copy of his recently issued commentary on Isaiah, had been rejected by Queen Elizabeth because of her erroneous assumption that the author had, in some way, been party to Knox's denunciation of the rule of women.

Knox provided posterity with a lively record of Scottish reform, and his part in the establishment of the new order. This he accomplished by writing *The Historie of the Reformation of the Church of Scotland*, which he produced during the years 1560 to 1566. The *Historie* has received a much more favorable acclaim than that from time to time so violently bestowed upon his *First Blast of the Trumpet*. It is vigorous, informing, and not devoid of levity, for Knox had a good sense of humor—too good, say his critics, and even some of his friends join in this appraisal, citing remarks in his account of the slaying of Cardinal Beaton in substantiation of their judgment.

There may have been dull moments in his life, but these were not for long. When Knox himself failed to provide excitement, his foes took care that it was not lacking. Even when his tempestuously constructive career was nearing its end, the knowledge of his approaching departure was not enough for his enemies, one of whom tried to assassinate him as he sat in his Edinburgh home. The assailant's bullet, however, went somewhat wide of its mark; but the attempt, coupled with certain other considerations, led to Knox's withdrawal or, more accurately, being withdrawn by his friends, from the demonstrated hazards of Edinburgh to the relative seclusion of St. Andrews, fifty miles away. Here he preached during the twilight time of his ministry at the same center where he first stood to proclaim the evangel. During these days and under such severely restricted circumstances a St. Andrews student by the name of James Melville described him as "lyk to ding that pulpit blads, and fly out of it!"

It was not fitting that this first citizen should die elsewhere than in Edinburgh, center of his multiplied associates, scene of his strenuous labors, and field of much of his ministry. After his return from St. Andrews in August 1572, he preached, although with weakened voice, in a small space partitioned in St. Giles that he might be better heard by the congregation.

With the approaching end, his mind and spirit turned toward Geneva, as he called for certain of Calvin's sermons to be read to him. As the sand was sinking low in his glass, he listened to 1 Corinthians 15, followed by that passage whereon he described himself as having first cast his anchor—John 17. On November 24, 1572, his earthly activities came to a close, set safe beyond the reach of controversy and eternally impervious to the vicissitudes that characterized his mortal career.

No one familiar with the Reformer and his manifold activities would contend that he was free from faults, and it is not to be understood that every Scotsman is an unrestrained admirer of John Knox. Such a scholar as Andrew Lang and other lights of varying degrees of learning have found much to question in the man and his methods.

Knox had come upon the scene as the defender of the Reformer Wishart. Before long, he was defending the evangelical position from which he was soon to carry the fight to the offensive in proclaiming the principles of justification through faith and the ready access of the believer to his Lord.

His work consisted in much more than denunciation. The fact that a number of the dramatic episodes of a far-from-humdrum life focused upon controversy has tended to draw attention from the positive aspects of his message and from the constructive nature of his accomplishments. He was instrumental in providing his people with a constitution for their church that included plans for the education of children, but he did much more. It was he who gave them a vision of the Scotland that was to be and how such a nation, by the grace of God, might be fashioned in the years to come.

Role of Andrew Melville

The death of Knox left the leadership of Scotland's Protestants in the hands of Andrew Melville (1545–1622). An excellent scholar who had studied with Beza in Geneva, Melville was principal at the universities in Glasgow, Aberdeen, and St. Andrews and became famous as the one who revised the Book of Discipline so as to make Presbyterian polity the pattern of government for the Church of Scotland.

James VI despised the Presbyterian system and desired episcopacy with bishops he could control, but Melville showed that the New Testament uses the terms *bishop* and *elder* interchangeably, and on that basis he prepared a statement of polity, which the General Assembly adopted in 1580. This document declared the office of authoritarian bishops unlawful because it is without warrant in Scripture. Melville was emphatic in asserting the independence of the church in spiritual matters, by which he set the stage for a confrontation with the king.

James VI took personal charge of government when he was but twelve years old and susceptible to flattery and poor advice. He appointed one of his favorites to be archbishop of Glasgow, but the Church of Scotland would not accept him and pronounced the archbishop-designate excommunicated. The king's Privy Council dutifully declared that action null and void, and when Melville decried royal interference with the church, the Privy Council accused him of treason, and he fled to England. In 1584 the subservient parliament deprived the church of all autonomy and awarded the crown full authority over it, an action that prompted Melville to return in order to lead the opposition to the monarch. Not until 1592 did Parliament restore the rights of the church, including its conformity to Presbyterian polity. In a shortsighted manner, Melville and other church leaders assumed they could enjoy ecclesiastical freedom while calling the state to assist and maintain the discipline of the church and to apply civil penalties to its errant members. Subsequent events would demonstrate the serious error in this judgment.

Policy of James VI and I

This duplicitous monarch on one hand professed allegiance to the Reformed faith, while on the other he tried to reduce the church to a department of the state. He seems to have been a theoretical Calvinist, that is, one who espoused the doctrines of the Reformation but lived in a licentious manner that contradicted his own religious profession. Assuming he held his throne by divine right, James dictated to the church and expected obedience to his commands. Melville, however, boldly informed him Christ alone is head of the church, and the earthly king is Jesus' subject. Undeterred, James appointed three bishops and seated them as spiritual lords in Parliament, which is evidence of his fondness for the Church of England, of which he became head when he succeeded Elizabeth I as ruler of the southern British kingdom in 1603.

James VI of Scotland became James I of England (r. 1603–1625) because Elizabeth I died without heirs, and so the Stuart dynasty would thereafter rule two kingdoms concurrently. James at first enjoyed a royal welcome from his English subjects, particularly from the Puritans, who hoped he would support their call for further reforms in the Anglican Church, of which James had become supreme governor. James had a reputation for being a Calvinist, even an amateur theologian of some learning, and it soon became clear that he enjoyed England to the point he returned to Scotland only once, in 1618. The Puritans would learn quickly that their Scottish monarch was no friend, for he aspired to unite the two kingdoms and impose the Anglican polity and liturgy in both lands.

Tension between the new king and his Puritan subjects became severe when James convened a conference to which he invited nine Anglican bishops, seven deans, and two other ministers of the Church of England to meet with four Puritans to discuss the issues and proposals of those who sought additional reforms in the church. In disposing of the request for a Presbyterian polity, James curtly dismissed the matter with the remark that presbytery "agrees with monarchy as God with the devil." The delighted bishops hailed the king's wisdom as comparable to that of Solomon, and the king told his opponents he would compel them to submit to the rule of bishops and accept the Anglican liturgy, or he would "harry them out of the land."

James intended to do in Scotland what he was doing in England, and to demonstrate his resolution, the monarch imprisoned Melville for four years and then banished him for life. The king visited Scotland in 1618 to impose his scheme for church government, and the Church of Scotland was compelled to endure episcopacy for a time. Three bishops consecrated in London took charge of ecclesiastical affairs, as an assembly in Perth adopted articles that imposed observance of the Anglican Church calendar and the rites of confirmation, kneeling to receive the Eucharist, private baptism of children in their homes, and other practices to which Scottish Protestants objected strenuously. Parliament ratified these measures in 1621, thereby adding civil to ecclesiastical sanction. The action of Parliament occurred in spite of resistance from participants at Perth who voted against the articles. James had bribed some of the majority at that assembly to support his program, and knowledge of that made many Scots even more determined to resist the king.

Charles I

The accession of a new king in 1625 did not bring substantial changes in church-state relations, since Charles I (r. 1625–1649) continued the policies of his father. He espoused the theory of divine-right monarchy and resolved to subject Scottish Presbyterians and English Puritans to royal supremacy in church as well as state. The new king's principal advisors were Charles Wentworth, Earl of Stratford, and William Laud, Archbishop of Canterbury, who conspired with him to make the Crown independent of Parliament and supreme in church affairs.

Unlike James I, who, at least in principle, professed to be a Calvinist, Charles I was an Arminian, as was Archbishop Laud, and together they promoted liturgical uniformity as the soul of religion. Laud inspired two other bishops to compose the Book of Common Prayer and Administration of the Sacraments and Other Parts of Divine Service for the Use of the Church of Scotland. The Book of Common Prayer is an episcopal compilation, mitigated here and there by the insertion of Presbyterian terminology. At points it savors of Roman Catholicism. Fortified by the inclusion of an appropriate proclamation from King Charles, its compilers and their allies committed the volume to the clergy for use and commended it to the laity for acceptance or, at least, acquiescence.

Certain writers of anti-Presbyterian bias have accused some of the Scots ministers of inflaming the minds of their parishioners against the Book of Common Prayer even before its official inauguration in the North Country. One would find it difficult to refute this thesis. For example: "Forbear in any case," wrote the good Samuel Rutherford, "to hear the reading of the new fatherless Service-book, full of gross heresies, popish and superstitious errors, without any warrant of Christ, tending to the overthrow of preaching."*

After having set Easter of 1637 for its initiation, those in charge of such arrangements postponed their effort until July 23. With a large and representative congregation gathered in St. Giles, the dean of Edinburgh began the service. No sooner had he opened the Book of Common Prayer, according to a report obviously unfriendly to the Presbyterian party, "but a number of the meaner sort (many of them being Women)" raised "an hideous noise and hubbub." The bishop of the city, in an effort to allay these protestations, entered the pulpit, thus presenting an unintended, though self-defined, target for a stool, which was directed at his head. A benevolent bystander diverted the unconventional missile from its intended objective.

Consistent tradition, though not every historian, attributes this specific unpleasantry to an otherwise undistinguished woman by the name of Jenny Geddes, who is reputed to have added interrogatory protest to her deed in the Scots equivalent of "False thief, wouldst thou say Mass in my ear?" Thus she has come to be numbered among the Presbyterian heroes, or heroines, through the generally dubious procedure of disturbing a service of public worship. More stools followed this woman's, all directed toward the offending ecclesiastics.

The officials having cleared the church of the most turbulent of the objectors, the dean proceeded to read the service, not, however, apart from what must have been rather annoying intrusions, in that the ejectees shouted, rapped at the doors, threw stones in through the windows, and voiced their displeasure at the prevailing status of affairs with cries of "A Pape, a Pape, Antichrist, pull him down."

The liturgy fared slightly better at the next church to St. Giles, though, even there "noise and tumult accompanied the reading, while at Greyfriars, only the initial portion of the service could be completed before the officiating clergyman bowed before tactics similar to those in the other two

---

*Samuel Rutherford, *Letters of the Rev. Samuel Rutherford* (Edinburgh: Oliphant, Anderson, and Ferrier, 1881), 45.

churches. While such unseemly conduct can scarcely be condoned, it can be understood by anyone acquainted with the Scots and the tensions of the times. Not all antiroyal demonstrations were spontaneous. Some were the work of careful planning by zealous Calvinists and supportive noblemen.

Rise of the Covenanters

The strength of resistance to the changes Charles and Laud tried to impose infuriated the monarch and made him stubborn, and his refusal to negotiate led the Scots to organize and to pledge to one another they would maintain the Reformed faith and restore Presbyterianism. At a meeting in Greyfriars Churchyard, Edinburgh, on March 1, 1638, nobles, gentry men, merchants, peasants, and ministers renewed the National Covenant James I had accepted in 1580. This event initiated what has become known as the Second Scottish Reformation. James I had promised allegiance to the Church of Scotland as constituted in the Book of Discipline, but that king was devoid of sincerity and secretly taught his son to despise Presbyterianism and to plan overthrowing it as soon as feasible.

Because Charles I lacked adequate forces to compel obedience to his will, he agreed to call a meeting of the General Assembly and one of Parliament to seek peace and order for the kingdom. The ruler dispatched the Marquis of Hamilton to be his spokesman, and through him hoped to control assembly proceedings.

The covenant of 1580 renewed in 1638 condemned popery and a list of errors it cited in detail, and it also cited various acts of Parliament that had affirmed the evangelical faith. Alexander Henderson (1583–1646), a village pastor, composed the final section of the document, which declares the resolution of the signers to support the true religion as set forth in the Scots Confession of 1560 and to live in a godly manner, rendering all due respect to their earthly king. Their first loyalty would, however, be to the King of Kings.

In December 1638, with Henderson as moderator, the General Assembly abolished the episcopate and expelled bishops then in office. The Church of Scotland was to return to the polity for which Melville had striven valiantly. The General Assembly nullified all previous acts that had approved prelacy, and it denounced the Articles of Perth and the imposed Anglican liturgy. The king responded with outrage and decided for war against the Scots.

War within the Kingdom

When Charles I resorted to arms, Scottish forces entered England, and when the opposing sides met near the border, the Scots raised a blue banner on which was the statement "For Christ's Crown and Covenant." The intimidated king decided at that point not to engage his rebellious subjects but to seek aid from the English Parliament, which refused to fund a war. Charles then turned to wealthy bishops, who responded with generous donations. The king's tensions with the English Parliament nevertheless ruined his prospects in Scotland. With money raised from his prelates, he again marched against the Scots, only once more to lose his nerve and not fight. Another appeal to England's Parliament was fruitless, and this Long Parliament, as it became known, remained in place for twenty years, during which it eliminated Charles I, Laud, Wentworth, and the established Church of England as it had been organized since Henry VIII.

Charles could not subdue the Scots, because he faced defiance in his own legislature at the same time. War between the king and Parliament erupted in England in 1642, and both sides courted support from Scotland. As the price for their aid, the Scots obtained the adherence of the English Parliament to the Solemn League and Covenant of 1638, by which both kingdoms pledged to reform church and society in those lands and in Ireland. This entailed elimination of popery and prelacy and affirmation of Christ's kingship over all. Implementation of this agreement would have produced not only an official embrace of Reformed theology but adoption of Presbyterian polity as well. The Scots had been reluctant to take arms against their earthly king, but his behavior convinced them that loyalty to the King of Kings required it.

The Westminster Assembly (1643–1648)

On June 12, 1643, in defiance of the king, the English Parliament summoned an assembly to reform the liturgy and government of the Church of England and to promote unity with the Scottish Presbyterians and Reformed churches on the Continent. This effort to continue the reformation that royal interference had arrested met at Westminster Abbey on July 1, with William Twisse (ca. 1580–1646), a learned minister, presiding over a gathering of Puritans opposed to Charles I and Archbishop Laud. Parliament created this assembly to advise it about ecclesiastical affairs, with revision of the Thirty-Nine Articles of Religion as the chief objective, but soon Parliament ordered consideration of church polity as well. The General

Assembly of the Church of Scotland sent commissioners after Parliament and the Westminster Assembly subscribed to the Solemn League and Covenant. The influence of the Scots was decisive, even though they were present only in an advisory capacity. Soon the assembly agreed to draft a new confession, catechism, and directory for worship and to reform church government, although polity was a divisive issue among the various Protestants—Presbyterians, Episcopalians, and Independents.

The proceedings of the Westminster Assembly included long periods of prayer as well as impassioned sermons and scholarly discussions. Robert Baillie (1599–1662), professor of divinity at the University of Glasgow, kept a careful record of the sessions that describes times of fervent prayer and fasting. There was practically unanimous agreement to purge England of Pelagian, Arminian, and Roman Catholic teachings, and the commissioners saw themselves as agents of Providence to accomplish that task. By this time the works of Calvin and Beza were available in English translations, and Calvin's *Institutes of the Christian Religion* had become a textbook at Oxford and Cambridge Universities.

In addition to Robert Baillie, the Scots present at Westminster were ministers Alexander Henderson (1583–1646); Robert Douglas (1594–1674); Samuel Rutherford (1600–1661); and George Gillespie (1613–1648), and ruling elders John, Earl of Cassilis (1595–1688), later Duke of Lauderdale; and Sir Archibald Johnston (1611–1663), Lord Wariston.

Documents of the Assembly

The Directory for Public Worship provided for the conducting of church services, administration of the sacraments, and burial of the dead. Expository preaching was to be the central feature of worship, which was to be subject to the Puritan regulative principle. The Form of Government specified the offices of pastor, doctor (teacher), elder, and deacon, and it called for the creation of congregational, regional, provincial, and national convocations. Ordination was to be by act of presbytery after careful examination of the candidates. Parliament approved this procedure in July 1645.

The Westminster Confession of Faith, the Larger Catechism, and the Shorter Catechism expound and apply the doctrines of the Reformed faith, and Parliament ratified these documents in March 1648. A fuller consideration of the Westminster Standards appears in the section of this book that deals with Presbyterianism in England.

Scots in England's Civil War

Although Scottish Protestants contested their king's right to rule in an abusive manner, they did not desire abolition of the monarchy but a restriction of its powers so as to protect their church and their own liberties. In the English Parliament, however, where the Independents became the dominant faction, there was an increasing determination to eliminate the king. The Puritan army, especially after Oliver Cromwell (1599–1658) became its leader, resolved to remove Charles I, who had surrendered to the Scots, who then remanded him to the English.

A broad spectrum of Puritans and Baptists supported Cromwell, and some of them did not accept Presbyterian teaching about church polity. The crafty king exploited this difference among his enemies and convinced his fellow Scots to rally to his side with an attack upon England. As an inducement he led the Scots to believe he would accept a Presbyterian establishment in both kingdoms. In August 1648, however, Cromwell's forces defeated the Scots, and he quickly purged Parliament of its Presbyterian members, an event since known as Pride's Purge because Colonel Pride's soldiers barred the doors so Presbyterian members could not enter. This left only ninety members of Parliament, a remnant of that body thereafter dubbed the Rump Parliament, a term that signifies the members left sitting after the expulsion of the Presbyterians and their supporters.

Parliament, as Cromwell reconstituted it, represented chiefly the army, and the government of England became a military despotism. When the House of Lords would not agree to the execution of King Charles I, the Commons decreed it anyway, clear evidence the traditional separation of powers among Crown, Lords, and Commons no longer existed. Commons formally abolished both the monarchy and the House of Lords and declared England a commonwealth. A new law granted toleration to all religious bodies except Catholics and Episcopalians, a measure that enjoyed little public support, and Ireland and Scotland became hotbeds of resistance where strong factions sought restoration of the monarchy in the person of Charles II, son of the executed king.

Cromwell subdued Ireland in 1649, and Scotland the next year. The Scots had accepted Charles II because he had signed the National Covenant, but their embrace of another Stuart provoked Cromwell to attack, and victory made him ruler of Scotland, while Charles II escaped. After subduing the Scots, Cromwell governed in an authoritarian manner, even to the point he sold some prisoners to be slaves in New England. He did, nevertheless, protect Scotland against Roman Catholic plots to gain power, and he allowed Presbyterians and other Protestants to worship freely. Since Cromwell forbade prelacy, most Scots were pleased to that extent, although they resented English domination.

Until his death in 1658, Cromwell ruled Scotland with a despotism that brooked no opposition, but it was authoritarian rule in the interest of righteousness. He molested no minister who devoted himself to his proper work of building the kingdom of Christ, and fair-minded Scots admitted that, while his rule was contrary to their desires, it was honest and, for the most part, just. Religion flourished as at no time since the Reformation.

Restoration of the Monarchy (1660)

The death of Oliver Cromwell left his son Richard as successor in the role of Lord Protector, but he was only a pale shadow of his father, and events soon demonstrated that it was the elder Cromwell's strength that held the Commonwealth together. Richard had the good sense to realize his own inability and resigned after a few months in office. Army leaders then took charge of the government and summoned the Rump Parliament into session, but complaints from that body led the military leaders to dismiss it. The angry public demanded an end to military rule, and General George Monk, commander of the troops in Scotland, compelled Parliament to disband after calling for new elections. The new legislature quickly invited Charles II to take the throne. Since the new king had subscribed to the National Covenant, the Scots rejoiced about the restoration, but it soon became evident that though Charles had no scruples in signing the National Covenant, he was certainly not supportive of it.

Although Charles II was an ungodly person, he took a serious interest in religious affairs, but in ways contrary to the interests of Presbyterians and Independents. His objective was to reinstate the episcopate, so he conspired with ousted bishops to restore their authority and their revenues, and they in turn supported his scheme to become absolute ruler over church and state. To accomplish this, the monarch and his prelates had to destroy Presbyterianism, and at first they appeared to be successful. A supine Parliament accepted the royal proposals and abrogated the Solemn League and Covenant. Soon thereafter Charles declared the reestablishment of the episcopate and consecrated four Scottish bishops, who then consecrated ten more.

The king ordered all pastors installed during the Commonwealth era to submit to the bishops or lose their positions. The demoralized Presbyterians seemed incapable at the moment of raising effective resistance, but about four hundred of them resigned their parishes rather than comply with the king's demand, and many of their congregations went with them. The government used troops to compel attendance at official churches and imposed fines and imprisonment upon dissidents. This policy led many believers to meet in secret for worship, while the bishops urged the Crown to apply ever more stringent measures to eliminate Presbyterianism.

The Killing Time in Scotland

With the return of episcopacy, James Sharp (1618–1679) became archbishop of St. Andrews and primate of Scotland in 1661. A former Presbyterian, Sharp demonstrated great disdain for his old church and did what he could to make conditions harsh for non-Episcopalians. Parliament enacted a law against *conventicles,* or unofficial religious meetings, and it decreed death for ministers who officiated at such gatherings. Public reaction was intense; angry dissidents slew Archbishop Sharp, to which the government responded with more repression. One feature of the official reaction was to impose a special tax to pay troops who enforced laws against nonconformity.

The regime of Charles II established a High Commission, which acted like the Spanish Inquisition by applying torture to obtain compliance with the king's policy. In 1666 the beleaguered Scots rose in revolt at Rullion Green on the Pentland Hills, but the king's professional army had little trouble defeating the untrained rebels. Ten prisoners were then executed for treason while royal soldiers committed unspeakable atrocities against their defeated foes, even women and children. Outspoken Covenanters suffered the most.

Among people who participated in the persecution of Presbyterians were a number of fellow Scotsmen who had defected to the royal side after renouncing the Reformed faith. Prominent among them was the Duke of Lauderdale, who had sat in the Westminster Assembly as an elder from the Church of Scotland. After becoming an Episcopalian, Lauderdale obtained a civil position as secretary of state, and he and James Sharp were leaders of the cruel repression of their former comrades. Presbyterians' efforts to protect themselves included posting armed guards at places of their clandestine meetings. A battle at Bothwell Bridge cost the rebels four hundred men killed and about twelve hundred taken prisoners. Presbyterians thereafter referred to this era of suffering for their faith as the *Killing Time.* Only a minority of the populace participated in armed resistance, and most of those who did so were of the lower socioeconomic class. Noblemen no longer led the opposition to the king.

Once Charles II believed he would triumph in Scotland, he issued an indulgence by which he promised limited toleration for private Presbyterian services, if the pastors refrained from political agitation. Many discouraged dissidents accepted the king's terms, but others regarded that a surrender to evil and resolved to continue the struggle. One faction followed Richard Cameron (ca. 1648–1680), a master of arts from the University of St. Andrews, who was a vigorous preacher at secret services. By 1678 Cameron had become spokesman for people eager to defy the government in political as well as religious matters. In June 1680, he and his followers issued the Sanquhar Declaration, by which they repudiated the king and resolved to overthrow his tyranny. The government declared Cameron a traitor and put a price on his head, and within a month of the declaration royal troops had killed him and many of his followers. To make him an object lesson, the enemies severed Cameron's head and hands and displayed them at Netherbow Port, but his death inspired further resistance, as he acquired the status of a martyr. The cause for which Richard Cameron lost his life survived, even though some Covenanters eventually disclaimed the Sanquhar Declaration.

Reign of James VII

Upon the death of Charles II, his brother succeeded him as James VII (r. 1684–1688) in Scotland, James II in England. Since the new king was a Roman Catholic, he might have cared little which version of the Protestant faith prevailed in Scotland. James, however, like his predecessor, viewed the episcopate as a means to further royal authority, so he despised Presbyterianism. Most Scots and Englishmen expected their new monarch to keep his religion a private affair, and since he was fifty-two years old, they assumed he would produce no heirs, and both kingdoms would have a Protestant ruler in the near future. Much to their irritation, James began demonstrating the seriousness of his attachment to Catholicism when he began extending favors to his coreligionists, actions that aroused resentment in both of his kingdoms. By ignoring the Anti-Popery Laws, James alienated a broad spectrum of Protestants, which led many of his subjects to fear a Catholic restoration was his actual goal. Continuing persecution of Covenanters confirmed that suspicion in the minds of many people. In 1688, when James sired a son and presented his subjects with the prospect of a Catholic dynasty, most Protestants concluded his continuing reign was intolerable.

When he realized his position was in jeopardy, James tried to placate his critics by revoking some of the more objectionable measures he had imposed, but it was too late to save his crown. He had unwittingly united his people in opposition to their ruler, as Anglicans and dissenters, Whigs and Tories, agreed the king had to go. Devoid of adequate support, James fled to France to become a guest of King Louis XIV, with whom he had been conspiring to make his rule absolute and to reimpose Catholicism. He never relinquished his claim to be divine-right monarch of Scotland and England, but retrieval of his crown was not possible. The ouster of James VII and II became known as the Glorious Revolution (1688–1689), a bloodless change of monarchs that upheld the rule of law against a tyrant.

Reign of William III and Mary II

Once they had agreed to depose James, the leaders of the Whig and Tory political factions contacted William of Orange, stadtholder of the Netherlands and husband of Mary Stuart, Protestant daughter of James, and offered to make him and her joint rulers of England. A convention of elected representatives issued a formal invitation, and William III and Mary II (r. 1689–1702) assumed the crowns of England, much to the acclaim of the nation. A small faction of diehard zealots for divine-right monarchy refused to accept the change and thereafter was known as Jacobites, to signify their allegiance to the deposed James Stuart.

William III had already established a reputation for being a champion of Protestantism and liberty against the aggressions of Louis XIV (1643–1715) and Catholic France. His staunch Protestant faith suited most of his new subjects in Britain, and his cordiality toward Presbyterians pleased the Scots especially. The Glorious Revolution made William and Mary monarchs of England, but not of Scotland. To settle that matter the Scots asked William to convene a convention there as had occurred in England, and it formally invited William and Mary to become Scotland's monarchs. There was resistance, nevertheless, when a substantial number of Scottish Jacobites raised a military force to resist them. By trickery and forcefulness William defeated his opponents, but his brutal policy, especially against the clan Macdonald of Glencoe, engendered a stubbornness that made it difficult to govern. To pacify Scotland the king made concessions to the advantage of the Presbyterians, whose Reformed theology he already espoused. Like his great-grandfather William the Silent (1533–1584), he favored broad toleration in religion, and he was well disposed toward Presbyterian church polity.

The year 1690 brought the Revolution Settlement, by which the Presbyterian church was once more established by law in Scotland, and all previous measures against it were repealed. Surviving ministers deposed in 1662 regained their positions, and the Church of Scotland affirmed the Westminster Confession of Faith and Presbyterian polity. The Scottish Parliament ratified the decision of the church and in doing so relinquished some civil authority over ecclesiastical affairs. Enactments against the strictest Presbyterians, however, remained in effect, even those that condemned the National Covenant and the Solemn League and Covenant. This new policy of toleration was then a pragmatic concession rather than a national reaffirmation of Reformed principles. The Revolution Settlement allowed pastors installed by Episcopal prelates to remain in their parishes, even though they were not loyal Presbyterians. Many of them made only a perfunctory subscription to the Westminster Standards, and their "Moderate" Party later caused a major dilution of Reformed theology in the Church of Scotland. Moderates emphasized scholarship and the ethical components of Christianity rather than seeking conversion of lost sinners and instructing believers in the historic doctrines of the Reformed faith.

Covenanters' Response

Although the settlement of 1690 brought relief to persecuted Presbyterians, the stricter adherents among them were not satisfied. On principle the Cameronians, adherents to the principles of Richard Cameron, decried the settlement because it was an act of the state, which, they contended, had no right to regulate such matters. Some Covenanters appealed to the General Assembly, but that body was not disposed to deal with issues of principle. Only three Covenanter ministers joined the established church of the Glorious Revolution. Because the Covenanters in general regarded the settlement as sinful, they continued to maintain their united societies of dissenting congregations until 1743, when they organized the Reformed Presbytery as a formal body that renounced the role of the state in matters of religion. In 1761 the Reformed Presbytery issued an elaborate statement of objections to the Revolution Settlement, which at the same time declared Presbyterian polity to be the revealed will of God. Before long some presbyteries that had entered the established church withdrew to join the Covenanters, who had remained aloof from it. Most Scottish Presbyterians, however, supported William III's policy as expedient because it brought peace to the land.

Ecclesiastical Divisions

The last member of the Stuart dynasty came to the throne when Queen Anne assumed the rule in 1702. True to her heritage, she meddled in affairs of the Scottish church, as became evident after the Act of Union merged England and Scotland to become the United Kingdom of Great Britain in 1707. During the early years of Anne's reign (1702–1714), the parliaments of England and Scotland often quarreled, and some Scots desired to separate succession to their throne from that of England. The union of 1707 was a compromise to prevent that from occurring, a decision that sent sixteen peers and forty-five members of Commons from Scotland to sit in the British Parliament at Westminster. This agreement left the Church of Scotland in place with its Westminster Confession of Faith and Presbyterian polity. Within five years, however, the national parliament, despite vociferous protests from Scotland, imposed upon the Scottish church one of the most damaging arrangements in its history.

During the Middle Ages landowners often endowed churches and monasteries and appointed the clerics who served there. This practice of *patronage* led to abuses such as when priests or abbots took income from the position but employed vicars to perform the duties prescribed. The Protestant Reformers proposed to correct this corruption by eliminating patronage and placing election of pastors in the power of the congregations. Landowners were, in most cases, insistent upon retaining their prerogatives, since they provided facilities for the churches and paid subsidies for pastors' salaries. Nominees were sometimes acceptable to the congregations, but when they were not, dissensions arose. In 1649 Parliament abolished patronage, and the General Assembly of the Church of Scotland authorized congregations to choose their own ministers. In 1662, however, an act of rescission nullified the law of 1649, but in 1690 the Presbyterians once more obtained the termination of patronage. The issue remained a contentious one, and disputes about clerical appointments were common.

In 1712, Parliament once more restored patronage, and sponsors of the legislation, it is clear, intended thereby to promote an Episcopal resurgence in Scotland. Tensions between patrons and congregations were often severe, as local churches protested the appointment of unacceptable pastors. Although the General Assembly deplored the return of patronage, and presbyteries sometimes refused to install appointees, the Moderate faction within the Church of Scotland accepted the practice because it appeared to favor the liberal theology that segment of the church espoused. The

Evangelical faction opposed it strongly, although some people of that persuasion submitted to it.

The matter of patronage provoked a crisis in 1733, when Ebenezer Erskine (1680–1754), pastor at Portmoak near Kinross, a great preacher, protested patronage as an intolerable evil and demanded reform. Many laymen and ministers supported him, as he petitioned his presbytery for a redress of grievances. Presbytery submitted the matter to the General Assembly, but the church's highest court refused to consider the case. Erskine had preached against the Act of Patronage before the Synod of Perth and Stirling in 1732, and the next year the General Assembly rebuked him, as the synod had done the year before. When he and three other ministers protested the censure, the General Assembly removed them from their positions and declared their pulpits vacant.

The four deprived ministers responded by forming the Associate Presbytery at the end of 1733. Erskine defiantly continued preaching in his church until 1740, when the Church of Scotland closed its building. Undeterred, he gathered a large number of supporters and formed a new congregation. Erskine and his comrades William Wilson (1690–1741), Alexander Moncrief (1695–1761), and James Fisher (1697–1775) created the Associate Presbytery, which at first conducted religious services only and did not assume judicial authority, since the members still hoped for the reform of the Church of Scotland, against which they issued protests about corruption and violations of Presbyterian polity. In 1735 the Associate Presbytery despaired of reform and seceded officially. Efforts at reconciliation failed, and the Church of Scotland formally deposed the offending ministers in 1740. Within two years, however, the Associate Presbytery had twenty affiliated congregations.

Formation of the Relief Church

The problem of patronage continued to plague the Church of Scotland, as congregations protested the imposition of unfit pastors. When presbyteries cooperated with patrons, unhappy church members sometimes became belligerent. Thomas Gillespie (1708–1774), pastor at Carnock and a leading evangelistic preacher, resisted an order from the General Assembly to install a minister chosen by a patron in Dunfermline Presbytery over the protests of the congregation. The General Assembly deposed Gillespie, who then formed another congregation to which he ministered until his death. When the General Assembly moved to depose Gillespie, fifty-six commissioners voted to do so, but 102 abstained, a factor that led Gillespie to believe the deposition was unlawful.

In 1761 Gillespie, with Thomas Boston of Jedburgh and Thomas Colier of Colinsburgh, formed a presbytery, as they said, "for the relief of Christians oppressed in their Christian privilege" to free them from the evil of patronage and the Moderate Party that favored it. The Relief Church or Synod was a champion of religious liberty and the right of congregations to choose their own pastors. The leaders of this movement were not Covenanters, and they maintained open communion with believers in other bodies, a policy some conservatives decried.

Upon leaving the Church of Scotland, many congregations aligned with the Relief Church, and by 1772 that body had two presbyteries. By 1807 it had grown to sixty local churches with thirty-six thousand members. To the Relief Church belongs the distinction of being the first Reformed denomination in Scotland to organize a foreign missions program, and it was vigorous in planting churches at home as well. Likewise to its credit, this church denounced British participation in the African slave trade. It departed from the Presbyterian tradition of exclusive psalmody by authorizing use of hymns, and the songs of Isaac Watts, John Newton, and Philip Doddridge became quite popular in Relief Church congregations.

The formal secession of the Relief Church from the Church of Scotland occurred at a time when William Robertson (1729–1793) was the dominant ecclesiastical politician in the established church, where he led the Moderate Party and was a champion for the cause of patronage, perhaps because his first clerical appointment came by that means. Robertson was a brilliant scholar and author of numerous distinguished books of history, so his reputation enhanced the influence of the faction he led for twenty-eight years. Robertson's role in the General Assembly helped provoke the secession of the Relief Church.

In 1762 William Robertson became principal at the University of Edinburgh, a position of much influence, which enabled him to further the drift of his church from its Reformed roots. Two friends and fellow scholars he most admired were Edward Gibbon (1737–1794), a celebrated historian, and the philosopher David Hume (1711–1776), both of whom were hostile to the Christian faith. During the era when, as a representative of his university, Robertson dominated the General Assembly, he supported rigorous enforcement of the patronage laws, even to the point of calling the government to use force to assure compliance.

An Evangelical Revival

Despite the damaging effects of the patronage disputes and the spread of liberal theology in the Church of Scotland, an evangelical resurgence within that body occurred early in the nineteenth century. Among the divinely chosen agents to accomplish this impressive spiritual vitality was Andrew Mitchell Thomson (1779–1831), editor of the *Edinburgh Christian Instructor* and noted pastor in the capital city. As champion of the Evangelical Party, Thomson led an effort to preserve the historic Reformed faith and to restore the character of his church. From his pulpit and on the pages of his newspaper, he decried infidelity in doctrine and practice, much to the chagrin of the Moderates, who watched in dismay as he built the Evangelical Party into a majority for awhile within the General Assembly. Moderates denounced the *Instructor* as an organ of divisiveness, and they especially despised Thomson's repeated attacks upon patronage.

In addition to his work as a pastor, journalist, and exponent of orthodoxy, Thomson helped to form the Edinburgh Bible Society, was an active voice in the Anti-Slavery Society, and founder of a school for poor children. Leaders in the Relief Church appreciated his defense of the faith, and they sometimes contributed essays to his newspaper.

A second, and now better known, leader of the Evangelical cause was Thomas Chalmers (1780–1847), a highly learned graduate of the University of St. Andrews, who became a distinguished theologian, churchman, social reformer, and author of twenty-five volumes of published works. After twelve years as minister at Kilmany, he became pastor of the renowned Tron Church in Glasgow. In 1823 St. Andrews made him professor of moral philosophy, and five years later he became professor of divinity at Edinburgh. Chalmers finished his academic career at New College, Edinburgh, after he led a secession from the Church of Scotland that produced the Free Church of Scotland in 1843. A powerful conversion during a time of serious illness had transformed Chalmers from an ordinary cleric into a dynamic evangelist and staunch defender of the Reformed faith. He maintained keen interest in issues such as relief for the poor, and for a long time he espoused the church-state alliance because it gave national support to Christianity. Like many others, Chalmers thought the state owed protection and support to the church, while it should refrain from exerting control over ecclesiastical affairs. His leadership brought substantial credibility to the Evangelical cause, as the rapid growth of the Free Church attests.

One of the most beneficial aspects of the Evangelical revival was energetic mission work at home and abroad. The Church of Scotland initiated an extension program that established two hundred chapels across the land, and parallel to that was a concerted effort to spread the gospel to foreign lands, a cause dear to the heart of Chalmers, whose teaching inspired Alexander Duff (1806–1878) to dedicate his life for service in India.

A native of the Highlands educated at the University of St. Andrews, Duff's decision to become a missionary occurred while he was attending classes with Professor Chalmers. Like his mentor, Duff was brilliant and became highly learned. His reputation as a zealous educator in his own right led the Church of Scotland to commission him as its first missionary to India, to which he sailed in 1829. Prior to the assignment of Duff, the Church of Scotland had relied on voluntary circles within it to conduct foreign missions.

William Carey (1761–1834), the pioneer Baptist missionary, and some other Protestants had preceded Duff to India, and when he arrived, he encountered difficulties with both the natives and some Roman Catholic missionaries already there. To that point there had been little fruit to reward the labors of missionaries in India, so some church officials and others questioned the value of their work. Duff perceptively proposed a new approach to the Indians, one that featured emphasis on Christian higher education to rebut Hinduism and to protect native Christians who might succumb to an agnostic Western science that sometimes assailed the teachings of Scripture. Duff held firmly to the unity of truth and so maintained Christians have nothing to fear from scientific inquiry. His scheme of education promoted the integration of biblical teachings and scholarly investigations in the physical sciences, all instruction to be in the English language. Requiring students to learn English would, he contended, encourage them to explore Christian literature abundantly available only in that tongue. Duff believed this method would lead to many more conversions than overt attacks upon Hindu doctrines could achieve. In other words, he was convinced genuine scholarship would discredit Hinduism in the minds of intellectuals educated in Christian colleges. Converts obtained in that way would then be well prepared to evangelize their own people.

The first college organized in accord with Duff's plan opened in Calcutta, a center of European activity. Wealthy Hindus, eager to promote the economic progress of their children, enrolled them in the college where Duff was a professor. When some students embraced Christ, there was an unfavorable reaction, but the excellent quality of instruction continued to draw students, some of whom became effective Protestant leaders.

By the time Duff went to India, British policy there had developed from a sense of stewardship toward colonial peoples, and British administrators supported the use of English as the language of instruction. Duff advocated education for women as well as men, and that too became British policy, although it ran contrary to centuries of Indian tradition. Careers in the Indian Civil Service awaited competent graduates of such colleges, a factor that further enhanced the popularity of attending them.

Duff ended his service in India in 1863 to become a lecturer in missiology at colleges in Edinburgh, Aberdeen, and Glasgow. When the Disruption (secession) of 1843 occurred, Duff aligned with the Free Church, as did most of his missionary colleagues in India. Both the Church of Scotland and the Free Church made India the focus of their foreign ministries, a fact that must have brought delight to Duff as he watched his projects flourish in that land. His endeavors had produced a college, hospital, and medical school in Calcutta, institutions for which he raised funds for the rest of his life.

Creation of the Free Church of Scotland

In 1834 the General Assembly of the Church of Scotland agreed to stop imposing pastors upon unwilling congregations through the process of patronage. It forbade presbyteries to install ministers in opposition to the desires of local churches. A civil court, however, declared that action illegal, so patrons retained their power, and the Church of Scotland, rather than accept unpleasant consequences, submitted to the judicial decision. This led a large number of ministers and elders to renounce the inappropriate role of civil government in church affairs and to seek only private funds for their ministries. On May 18, 1843, 470 pastors and their supporters withdrew from the Church of Scotland to form the Free Church of Scotland, and within four years seven hundred congregations had adhered to that body. Generous donations from zealous members funded both the current operations and a church-planting outreach. Chalmers, by then a professor at the University of Edinburgh, led the secession and left his academic post to teach at New College, an institution affiliated with the Free Church. By the end of the nineteenth century, the new denomination had over a thousand congregations.

Although the practice of patronage was the most conspicuous cause of the Disruption of 1843, long-standing doctrinal issues also were involved in the secession. The Moderate Party, largely indifferent to historic theology, had supported patronage while leading the Church of Scotland away from its Reformation heritage, as the role of William Robertson illustrates well. It is rather ironic that Chalmers and other Free Church leaders continued to favor a church established by law, if they could achieve that status for their own denomination. They failed to realize state control is an inevitable corollary of state support.

In addition to Chalmers and Duff, other eminent Scotsmen joined the Free Church. One of them, Robert Candlish (1806–1873), pastor of St. George's Church, Edinburgh, had been a prominent leader of the Evangelical Party in the years preceding the Disruption. A preacher of powerful eloquence, he led his Edinburgh congregation in vigorous evangelism and church extension. Candlish was second only to Chalmers in the Free Church, of which he was moderator in 1861. New College employed him as principal in 1862, and his commentaries on Genesis, 1 John, and Ephesians received wide acclaim, as did his *Life in the Risen Saviour* and *The Two Great Commandments*.

Another Free Church preacher of great renown was Thomas Guthrie (1803–1873), a University of Edinburgh graduate, who served Old Greyfriars and St. John's Church in Edinburgh but had to leave the pastorate for several years due to poor health. During that period he was not inactive but instead founded the Ragged Schools, institutions to educate poor children and to provide them with food, clothing, and training that would enable them to find employment. His social concern extended to dealing with alcoholism as well. Many of Guthrie's vividly pictorial sermons appeared in print, and the topics he addressed often expressed his concern for the material as well as the spiritual needs of Scotland's people. Foreign missions was another cause dear to his heart.

Divided Presbyterianism

The exodus of the Free Church both injured and inspired the Church of Scotland. The new competition stimulated the established church to organize home and foreign missions, and the loss of income due to the secession prompted an increase in voluntary contributions. Patronage ended finally in 1874.

The Disruption of 1843 was the largest and most costly schism the Church of Scotland had to endure. At one point in the eighteenth century there were seven Presbyterian bodies in the kingdom. The Covenanters still rejected state control, while demanding the government maintain the principles of the National Covenant and protect the true faith. The Reformed Presbyterian Church (Cameronians) claimed liberty for itself but denied other religious bodies were entitled to it. Covenanters acknowledged no distinction between civil right and moral right and often called for a renewal of the National Covenant and the Solemn League and Covenant.

In 1863 the Reformed Presbyterian Synod became embroiled in a dispute about voting in civil elections. The Synod recommended that its members abstain because voting required an oath of allegiance to the Crown, but it threatened no disciplinary action against members who did vote. Three ministers and a few supporters renounced the action of the Synod and separated from it.

As the nineteenth century neared its close, there was yet another division among Presbyterians of Scotland. In 1893 a small group left the Free Church to form the Presbytery of Scotland, which later became the Free Presbyterian Church of Scotland. The founders of this body were Donald Macfarlane (1834–1926) and Donald Macdonald (1825–1901), both ministers, and Alexander Macfarlane, a ruling elder. The reason for this schism was a decision by the General Assembly of the Free Church to relax the required subscription to the Westminster Confession of Faith, an action the dissidents believed would encourage theological liberalism. Acceptance of hymn singing rather than exclusive psalmody and use of musical instruments in services of worship were other issues in dispute.

In addition to the founders, James S. Sinclair (1868–1921), a pastor in Glasgow, was another leader in the Free Presbyterian Church. He founded the *Free Presbyterian Magazine* in 1896 and was for many years its editor, and, through that organ, the principal voice of his church. Donald Beaton (1872–1953) was the next editor, one who enjoyed a reputation for theological scholarship and was the author of books on church history and biography.

The Free Presbyterian Church, which advocated strict observance of the Sabbath, found most of its following in the north, although it established congregations in Edinburgh and Glasgow as well. Free Presbyterian missionaries carried the faith to Canada, Australia, Palestine, and Rhodesia.

Presbyterian Ecumenism

A pronounced aversion to compromise when serious matters were at stake has been a prominent characteristic of Scottish Presbyterians throughout their history. Their desire for unity has been, nevertheless, genuine, and at times they have achieved union and reunion of their individual church bodies.

In 1820 two factions of Erskine's church merged to form the United Secession Church, a denomination of 280 congregations formerly aligned with either the Associate Synod or the General Associate Synod. Cooperation among members of both bodies in Bible societies, missionary projects, and other religious causes convinced them they belonged together, and people in the two churches petitioned their respective synods to consider union. All but a small minority agreed. When the official merger occurred, it was with the understanding the United Secession Church would not endorse any policy that would approve of compulsion in matters of religion. Two outstanding theologians from the United Secession Church were John Brown (1784–1858) and John Dick (1764–1833), whose published writings continue to attract readers.

The year 1847 brought union between the United Secession Church and the Relief Church to form the United Presbyterian Church of 518 congregations. By then both groups had diluted their Calvinism, so the new church did not require its officers to subscribe to the Westminster Standards, although the United Presbyterian Church was generally evangelical in character and vigorous in missionary endeavors.

In 1876 the Free Church and the Reformed Presbyterian Church (larger synod) united, although twelve congregations of the latter remained aloof. The new church allowed its members to subscribe to the concept of the National Covenant, but it did not endorse that document per se.

A large ecclesiastical union resulted from the merger of the Free Church with the United Presbyterian Church in 1900, a union made possible by the drift of both denominations away from the historic doctrines of the Reformed faith. The United Free Church had, at that time, over five hundred thousand members in about fifteen hundred congregations, and it supported 396 missionaries. The broadly evangelical character of this church is evident in the latitude of interpretation it allowed with regard to the Westminster Standards. By action of its General Assembly, the United Free Church declared it was at liberty to alter its doctrinal position so as not to be bound by its own confession of faith. This church became in practice a nonconfessional body in which conservatives and liberals could function so long as they refrained from attacking one another. Seldom did the United Free Church give serious attention to alleged heresy within its ranks. The major exception was when George Adam Smith (1856–1942), professor of

Old Testament at the United Free Church College in Glasgow, published *Modern Criticism and the Preaching of the Old Testament*, a work that led some readers to charge Smith had denied the inspiration and authority of the Bible. The General Assembly, however, sustained the recommendation of the professor's college not to prosecute him, a decision that opened the door for further and more radical authors to promote liberal ideas. Robert Rainy (1826–1906), for example, first moderator of the United Free Church, maintained an indulgent attitude toward advocates of the higher criticism of Scripture and aided in suppressing the charge against George Adam Smith. An erudite scholar himself, Rainy must have understood the conflict between higher criticism and full acceptance of the Bible as the Word of God. He was a vigorous exponent of the view that the church had the right to alter its teachings at any time.

Illustrative of the elastic character of the United Free Church is the work of James Orr (1844–1913), a staunch conservative evangelical, but not a Calvinist. His book *The Christian View of God and the World* (1893) made him famous as a Christian apologist who stressed acceptance of the cardinal doctrines as he perceived them. He did not support strict subscription to the Westminster Standards, but Orr was nevertheless an effective critic of liberal theologians such as Albrecht Ritschl (1822–1889) and Adolf Harnack (1851–1930), German scholars of great renown. In the controversy surrounding Smith, Orr upheld the overall reliability of Scripture but would not affirm its inerrancy. His book *The Virgin Birth of Christ* is a powerful defense of that doctrine, and eventually Orr contributed to *The Fundamentals*, a series of books published in America to rebut theological liberalism and to assert historic Christian beliefs in a credible, scholarly manner.

Beginning in 1909 leaders of the United Free Church met with their counterparts in the Church of Scotland to discuss possible reunion. The status of the Church of Scotland as the body established by law was a major obstacle since the United Free Church espoused ecclesiastical independence from the state, but a parliamentary enactment in 1921 allowed the Church of Scotland practical autonomy and thereby removed the principal barrier to merger. In May 1929 the General Assembly of the United Free Church adopted the Plan of Union, with only thirty-nine congregations voting against it. Opposition to the union did, however, develop, and a United Free Church Continuing emerged. With about fourteen thousand members, the Continuing Church maintained a generally evangelical posture but became increasingly liberal with the passage of time. It was the first Presbyterian body in Scotland to ordain a female to the ministry and, in 1960, the first to elect a woman moderator of its General Assembly.

Modern Developments

Division, union, and reunion have punctuated Scotland's ecclesiastical history. Many fine Christians left the Church of Scotland in the Disruption of 1843, but many others remained within it in the hope of restoring its historic character. Among the latter, Norman MacLeod (1812–1872) was one of the most prominent. This graduate of the University of Edinburgh studied with Thomas Chalmers, whose teaching made a deep impression upon him. While serving the Barony Church, Glasgow, MacLeod became famous as a preacher and a chaplain to Queen Victoria, while his tireless efforts to aid poor people of industrial Glasgow gained national attention. He designed church services specifically for impoverished people and helped to create banks from which they could obtain loans, and he established schools for their benefit. MacLeod's theological position was warmly evangelical, but he did not adhere to Reformed doctrine as affirmed in the Westminster Confession of Faith. Foreign missions were of great concern to him, especially in India, for which he raised substantial support. A man of amazing energy, MacLeod edited the *Edinburgh Christian Magazine* and a periodical named *Good Works*.

When Thomas Chalmers left the Church of Scotland, James Robertson (1803–1860) emerged as the most dynamic leader of the establishment. Educated at the University of Aberdeen, which awarded him the doctor of divinity degree in 1843, Robertson became professor of church history at Edinburgh in 1844, but his contributions to that field of study were few. He acquired his reputation as a churchman by leading rapid extension programs and by promoting mission work in India. Robertson, like other leaders in the Church of Scotland, did not adhere strictly to the Westminster Standards and preferred to be known as a moderate in doctrine.

In 1874 the British Parliament, in a move long overdue, abolished the law of patronage, which had been a plague on the Church of Scotland since 1712. Between these dates the Associate, the Relief, and the Free Churches had seceded from it in large part because of that dispute, and repeal went far toward laying a basis for the return of these groups and that of their successors. Additional encouragement toward reunion came in 1921, when Parliament, in effect, freed the Church of Scotland to legislate her own affairs without state interference.

In the midst of her own troubles with dissension and losses due to secessions, the Church of Scotland became an active participant in ecumenical affairs, as affection for its Calvinistic heritage waned. The movement in this direction became evident in 1910, when Edinburgh was the site for the meeting of the World Missionary Conference, a broadly Protestant gathering of many denominations. The work of this assembly led to formation of the International Missionary Council, the parent of several ecumenical agencies that ignored the distinctive of Reformed theology, while emphasizing social services as perhaps the foremost ministry the churches could render to the world. Toward the end of the twentieth century, the focus of ecumenists turned to interfaith, as well as interdenominational relations, with the Church of Scotland deeply involved.

A quasi-monastic revival occurred within the Church of Scotland in 1938, when George F. MacLeod (1895–1991) established the Iona Community on the island of that name, the site of an ancient monastery founded by Columba (ca. 521–597) in 563. Under MacLeod's leadership, a group of clerics and laymen rebuilt the medieval Benedictine monastery that had fallen into ruin. Their purpose was to provide a place to prepare ministers for service in industrial towns and to promote communal living among professing Christians. Many ministers from Iona became industrial workers themselves in the belief that would enhance their understanding of, and relations with, workers in factories. In 1951 the Church of Scotland adopted the Iona Community as one of its official ministries, and Iona soon embraced Roman Catholics as well as Protestants of various denominations. The movement has spread into several urban areas, where Columban houses attract adherents. Members of these communities follow a liturgy comparable to that of traditional Catholic monasteries. By the end of the twentieth century, about thirty-five hundred persons, clerics and lay people, were members of the Iona Community.

The Recent and Contemporary Situation

By 1956 the Church of Scotland had a communicant membership of 1,320,091. By 1981 that had declined to 938,930, while presently fewer than 500,000 Scots adhere to the national church in a country with a population of over five million. The church has lost contact with a large portion of the nation, and its ecumenical endeavors appear to be signs of weakness rather than strength. Although observers of the ecclesiastical scene have offered diverse, and sometimes conflicting, explanations for the decline, it is obvious that the church is no longer the vibrant force it was in the era of the Protestant Reformation. Some leaders of the establishment have been frank in admitting the losses are due to a lack of confidence in Scripture and a consequent decline in evangelistic and missionary fervor. They know the nineteenth century began with a spiritual awakening in Scotland but ended in discouragement because of large losses in the national church.

Presbyterian denominations other than the Church of Scotland have also experienced declension. Between 1929, when it refused to join the merger with the national church, and 1956, the United Free Church Continuing enjoyed considerable growth, but since 1956 the opposite has occurred. Active participation in social causes and ecumenical affairs plus ordination of women ministers and elders have become standard practices in the denomination, which has about seventy congregations and seven thousand members.

The Free Presbyterian Church of Scotland convened its first presbytery in 1893, when it declared separation from the Free Church of Scotland after that body announced it had the right to decide which of the historic Reformed doctrines it would espouse. The Free Presbyterian Church, on the contrary, affirms the Westminster Standards and the inerrancy of Scripture. It does not employ musical instruments in services of worship, and congregations sing only the Psalms. In line with earlier Covenanters, this body upholds the kingship of Christ over the nations and holds the state responsible to support and protect the true religion. The church's outreach extends to Africa, Australia, and New Zealand, where there are affiliated congregations, and its missionaries labor in Kenya and Zimbabwe. This denomination suffered secession in 1989 because of a dispute about Christian liberty. As a consequence a group of ministers and elders formed the Associated Presbyterian Churches of Scotland, now a body of fewer than a thousand members in about ten congregations with mission works in Romania, Hong Kong, and various Mediterranean sites.

Toward the end of the twentieth century, the Free Church of Scotland was divided over a discipline case involving a prominent minister. This resulted in two bodies claiming to be the Free Church of Scotland, the smaller body of which is commonly identified as the Free Church of Scotland (Continuing). The membership of the Continuing Church is about two thousand. The church has started a small seminary (Free Church Seminary) to train its own men, along with others, for the ministry. The Free Church (Continuing) publishes a monthly magazine called the *Free Church Witness.*

The land where Presbyterianism was once the faith of almost the entire population is now but a shadow of its former self. Although orthodox believers remain, even within liberal denominations, and some local churches are dynamic in proclaiming the doctrines of the Reformation, Scotland as a whole is in a retrograde spiritual condition.

SUGGESTED ADDITIONAL READINGS >>

Black, C. Stewart. *The Scottish Church*. Glasgow: William MacLellan, 1952.

Bowle, John. *Charles the First*. Boston: Little, Brown, 1975.

Brown, Stewart J. *Thomas Chalmers and the Godly Commonwealth in Scotland*. Oxford: Oxford University Press, 1982.

Burleigh, John H. S. A. *Church History of Scotland*. London: B.T. Batsford, 1960.

Calderwood, David. *The History of the Kirk of Scotland*. 4 vols. Edinburgh: The Woodrow Society, 1842.

Cameron, Alexander, ed. *Patrick Hamilton; First Scottish Martyr of the Reformation*. Edinburgh: Scottish Reformation Society, 1929.

Cameron, Nigel M. de S., et al., eds. *Dictionary of Scottish Church History and Theology*. Downers Grove, Ill.: InterVarsity, 1993.

Coffin, Robert P.T. *Laud: Storm Center of Stuart England*. New York: Bretano's, 1930.

Cowan, Ian B. *The Scottish Reformation: Church and Society in Sixteenth Century Scotland*. New York: St. Martin's, 1982.

Davie, George E. *The Scottish Enlightenment*. Edinburgh: Polygon, 1991.

Donaldson, Gordon T. *The Faith of the Scots*. London: B. T. Batsford, 1990.

———. *Scottish Church History*. Edinburgh: Scottish Academic, 1985.

Drummond, Andrew and James Bulloch. *The Scottish Church, 1688–1843, the Age of the Moderates*. Edinburgh: St. Andrew, 1973.

Fawcett, Arthur. *The Cambuslang Revival: The Scottish Evangelical Revival of the Eighteenth Century*. Edinburgh: Banner of Truth, 1971.

Fleming, David Hay. *The Reformation in Scotland*. London: Hodder & Stoughton, 1910.

Fraser, Antonia. *Mary, Queen of Scots*. New York: Delacorte, 1969.

Greaves, Richard L. *Theology and Revolution in the Scottish Reformation*. Grand Rapids: Eerdmans, 1980.

Hamilton, Ian. *The Erosion of Calvinist Orthodoxy: Seceders and Subscription in Scottish Presbyterianism.* Edinburgh: Rutherford House, 1990.

Johnson, Dale W. and James Edward McGoldrick. "Prophet in Scotland: The Self-Image of John Knox." *Calvin Theological Journal* 33 (1998): 76–86.

Kirk, James. *The Church in the Highlands.* Edinburgh: Scottish Church History Society, 1998.

Kyle, Richard G. *The Mind of John Knox.* Lawrence, Kans.: Coronado, 1984.

Kyle, Richard G. and Dale W. Johnson. *John Knox: An Introduction to His Life and Works.* Eugene, Ore.: Wipf and Stock, 2009.

Lee, Maurice Jr. *Great Britain's Solomon: James I in His Three Kingdoms.* Urbana: University of Illinois Press, 1990.

Leith, John H. *Assembly at Westminster: Reformed Theology in the Making.* Richmond, Va.: John Knox, 1973.

Linklater, Eric. *The Royal House of Scotland.* London: Macmillan, 1970.

MacGregor, Geddes. *The Thundering Scot: A Portrait of John Knox.* Philadelphia: Westminster, 1958.

Mackie, J. D. *A History of Scotland.* Baltimore: Penguin, 1964.

McEwen, James S. *The Faith of John Knox.* Richmond, Va.: John Knox, 1961.

McGoldrick, James Edward. *Luther's Scottish Connection.* 2nd ed. Birmingham, Ala.: Solid Ground Christian Books, 2008.

———. "Patrick Hamilton, Luther's Scottish Disciple." *Sixteenth Century Journal* 17 (1986): 81–88.

McIntosh, John R. *Theology and Church in Enlightenment Scotland: The Popular Party, 1740–1800.* Linton, Scotland: Tuckwell, 1998.

Piggin, Stuart and John Roxborough. *The St. Andrews Seven: The Finest Flowering of Missionary Zeal in Scottish History.* Edinburgh: Banner of Truth, 1985.

Reid, W. Stanford. *Trumpeter of God: A Biography of John Knox.* Grand Rapids: Baker, 1982. Reprint of 1974 edition.

Roxborough, John. *Thomas Chalmers and the Mission of the Church.* Wellington, New Zealand: Presbyterian Historical Society, 1980.

Stevenson, David. *The Covenanters: The National Covenant and Scotland.* Edinburgh: Saltire Society, 1988.

Vos, Johannes G. *The Scottish Covenanters.* Edinburgh: Blue Banner Productions, 1988. Reprint of 1940 edition.

Wedgwood, C. V. *A Coffin for King Charles.* New York: Time Inc., 1966.

———. *The King's Peace, 1637–1641.* New York: Macmillan, 1956.

Willson, David Harris. *King James VI & I.* Oxford: Oxford University Press, 1967. Reprint of 1956 edition.

Wormaid, Jenny. *Court, Kirk, and Community: Scotland 1470–1625.* London: Edward Arnold, 1981.

Wright, Ronald Selby. *Fathers of the Kirk: Some Leaders of the Church in Scotland from the Reformation to the Reunion.* Oxford: Oxford University Press, 1966.

EIGHT

Ireland

Although tradition regards St. Patrick (ca. 389–461) as the pioneer Christian missionary to Ireland, it appears there were some believers there prior to his ministry. Pope Celestine I (r. 422–432) dispatched Palladius (fl. 430) as the first bishop to Ireland in 431, shortly before Patrick arrived there. Palladius established three congregations before leaving for Scotland or Britain, where he died soon thereafter. Legends about him and Patrick abound, and separating fact from fiction sometimes is not possible.

Whatever the truth about Palladius may be, Patrick enjoys and deserves recognition as the apostle to Ireland, although chroniclers may have exaggerated the extent of his success. Patrick's method was to found monasteries, not only as places of retreat for religious devotions but as sites from which evangelists would go to seek converts across the land. Irish Christianity was organized around a series of monastic houses, the abbots of which functioned as bishops did on the Continent. Clerics who bore the title *bishop* had sacramental duties rather than administrative authority over the churches. This Celtic version of Christianity distinguished itself from the typical Roman practice, which led to conflicts between the two orders. Only slowly did Irish monks submit to papal jurisdiction, although Patrick gained the approval of Pope Celestine I and of Germanus of Auxerre (ca. 378–448) for his mission to Ireland, as Palladius had also. Germanus had gone from Gaul to Britain to combat Pelagian heresy, which originated with the teaching of Pelagius (ca. 360–420), a monk from the British Isles who earned stern opposition from Augustine, bishop of Hippo (354–430). Church leaders in Britain had been unable to refute Pelagianism effectively and so appealed to ecclesiastical authorities in Gaul to send defenders of the faith. When Germanus arrived in Britain, his mission was to seek the conversion of pagans and to refute the doctrine of Pelagius. Germanus consecrated Patrick a bishop whose work in Ireland closely resembled his own ministry in Britain. It is evident that some version of the Christian faith was present in Ireland even before Palladius and Patrick arrived, but paucity of evidence leaves the matter enveloped in obscurity. Hagiography and history are tightly intertwined.

Irish monasteries gradually became centers of learning, and by Patrick's day, the more prominent among them dominated the administration of church affairs. Missionaries from such centers then spread the faith across Ireland and eventually to the Highlands of Scotland, where they evangelized the Picts. Columba (d. 597) was the most famous of them, his labors earning for him recognition as the apostle to Scotland. Conflict between Celtic and Roman liturgical practices continued to about the middle of the eighth century, when the Roman mode triumphed over its rival. By then most of Ireland professed the Christian faith, although paganism had not disappeared.

The ministry of Patrick merits some attention in a history of the Reformed faith because his doctrine of salvation appears to have been akin to that of the Protestant Reformers of the sixteenth century. Only two of Patrick's writings have survived, neither of which is rich in detail about his theology, but his *Confession* relates a conversion in which he extolled the efficacy of God's grace and made no reference to his own merit gained by good works. In Patrick's own words,

> The Lord opened my awareness of my unbelief so that I might...
> remember my faults and turn with all my heart to the Lord my God,
> who had regard for my lowly estate and took pity on my youth and
> ignorance and watched over me even before I knew Him and before
> I learned sense or could distinguish between good and evil, and who
> comforted me as a father might his son.
>
> Before I was humbled [by grace], I was like a stone lying in deep
> mud; He that is mighty came, and in His mercy lifted me up, and
> indeed, raised me up and placed me on the top of the wall; and so
> I ought to shout out aloud to render some thanks to the Lord for
> His great benefits here and forever, benefits which the human will
> cannot assess.[*]

Although Patrick's *Confession* is not a systematic statement of doctrine, its references to the sovereignty of saving grace demonstrate clearly that he was not a Pelagian. It is probable, moreover, that Patrick espoused the

---

[*]St. Patrick, *His Writings and Muirchu's Life*, ed. and trans. A. B. E. Hood (Totowa, N.J.: Rowman and Littlefield, 1978), 41.

Augustinian teaching about salvation *sola gratia,* as would Protestants a millennium later. In ecclesiology the apostle to Ireland was not Reformed, but his soteriology appears to have been compatible with that of Calvin, Knox, and historic Presbyterianism, although Roman Catholics, Episcopalians, and Baptists have all claimed him as one of their own.

English Rule in Ireland

The political situation in Ireland during the early Middle Ages was one of tribal divisions in which elected kings were but chieftains. The more powerful ones allied with lesser rulers, but there was nothing comparable to national monarchy. The Vikings invaded Ireland in 795, and their brutality led many chieftains to see the wisdom of consolidating their strength, and by the opening of the eleventh century Brian Boru (d. 1014), king of Dal Cais in the western part of the isle, declared himself king of the Irish after defeating a number of tribal lords.

By the time Boru asserted his kingship, the Vikings had adopted Christianity, and ecclesiastical relations with Rome had introduced reforms that produced an Irish episcopate under the primacy of the archbishop of Armagh. National monarchy and the Roman pattern of church government were then developing concurrently, as religious influences from Europe spread widely. Ireland appeared to be emerging as a state in its own right comparable to others in Western Europe, but an Anglo-Norman invasion terminated that development and plunged the country into a long era of violence and oppression.

The only English pope, Adrian IV (r. 1154–1159), urged English King Henry II (r. 1154–1189) in 1155 to pacify turbulent Ireland and thereby to protect the Roman Church there. It is ironic that the Irish remained loyal to Catholicism, even though the pope encouraged English domination of the Emerald Isle. Norman barons from England initiated the assault, ostensibly to restore order and to promote the prosperity of religion. Henry II, however, saw control of Ireland as a strategic asset because that would prevent it from falling under Spanish or French domination, which would then menace England's security. He did not foresee centuries of animosity and recurrent rebellions as the Irish chafed under English rule.

Irish resentment was due both to the presence of foreign governors and to the policies of repression those rules imposed. An Irish parliament convened in 1279, but natives were not allowed to participate, and the use of French and English as the language of debate there insulted the people, whose native tongue was Gaelic. Laws prohibited intermarriage between colonizers and natives, as the government endeavored to eradicate the culture of a people the conquerors regarded as their inferiors. Anglo-Normans resolutely refused to be assimilated into Irish civilization as the Vikings had been earlier. This posture and the policies it inspired established a legacy of hatred that became especially pronounced when the Protestant Reformation triumphed in England and Scotland and the Reformers aspired to claim Ireland too for their faith.

Arrival of Protestantism

The Anglican version of the Protestant faith preceded Presbyterianism in Ireland by almost a century. During the era of the Tudor Dynasty (1485–1603), the English presence in Ireland expanded gradually, and when England embraced Protestantism officially in the reign of Edward VI (1547–1553), the national Church of England took advantage of the opportunity to enlarge its role in Ireland. Following his renunciation of papal authority in 1534, Henry VIII (r. 1509–1547) had attempted to subject the Irish Catholic Church to his own authority, but stern opposition confronted him. His son Edward VI decreed the initiation of Protestant services in the English language, but that too encountered strong resistance. Queen Mary I (r. 1553–1558), a zealous Catholic, deliberately rescinded the religious measures of her predecessor. English policy during the reign of Elizabeth I (r. 1558–1603) sought to extirpate the Irish language and to promote Protestant interests in the Emerald Isle, but the effect was to make the Irish more stubborn in their allegiance to Rome. English confiscations of Roman Catholic Church properties provoked several violent uprisings, as the papacy and Catholic Spain encouraged the rebels, and it required a large military presence to maintain English authority in Ireland. Despite deep resentment among Irish Catholics and occasional disturbances, England was nevertheless able to establish her rule over all of Ireland by the time Elizabeth I died in 1603. By then many thousands of Catholics had become casualties in the resistance, and English colonists had seized six hundred thousand acres of land.

Because the papacy and Catholic rulers on the Continent had been plotting to overthrow England's government and Protestant church, Elizabeth's policy had been to outlaw Catholicism in Ireland and to require attendance at Anglican worship. The Catholic response was defiance orchestrated by Jesuit priests, papal agents of the Counter-Reformation. In many places angry Catholics removed Anglican pastors and restored their own services. Retaliatory measures provoked only more uprisings.

The government of James I (1603–1625) continued the program of repression in Ireland with additional seizures of Catholic properties, especially in the northern part of the island, where the crown sold lands to English speculators and Scottish settlers. The influx of Scots then established Protestant dominance in the northern counties of Ulster. Although English authorities improved conditions of life for their Irish subjects by bringing order and English law to the land, antiforeign and anti-Protestant resentment remained pronounced.

An Irish parliament convened in 1615, with some Catholics holding seats in the lower house, while the upper house remained almost entirely Protestant. The government required all holders of public office to subscribe to the Oath of Supremacy, which declared the English monarch head of the church, a measure that effectively excluded Roman Catholics and, of course, intensified native hostility toward the English Crown.

The Church of Ireland, an extension of the Church of England, was the established religion supported by taxes that all residents of Ireland were required to pay. Its doctrinal position was categorically Protestant, as the Irish Articles (1615) attest in their affirmation of Calvinist soteriology and covenant theology.

The Coming of Presbyterianism

Conditions in Ulster were quite favorable for the introduction of the Presbyterian faith when Scots began migrating there at the urging of King James I. The monarch, a Scottish Stuart himself, subscribed at least in principle to Reformed theology, but he despised Presbyterian ecclesiology, which hailed Christ as the only head of the church. This monarch ruled Scotland as well as England, and was known as James VI (1567–1625) in his northern kingdom. The king's intention was to impose episcopacy in the English manner upon his native land, so he viewed Presbyterians as so many obstacles to be overcome. To escape the repressive policies of their king, many Scots found the lure of cheap land in Ireland irresistible, and to James their departure was good riddance. Thus he put an inducement in front of and a goad behind them.

In addition to the prospect of greater freedom and inexpensive land, Scottish Presbyterians enjoyed the benevolent disposition of James Ussher (1581–1656), a primatial archbishop of Armagh, a convinced Calvinist of

Puritan proclivities. Ussher, a graduate of Trinity College, Dublin, had studied there with Walter Travers (1548–1635), whose teaching and example had left him with an enduringly favorable impression of Presbyterians. Robert Echlin (1576–1635), Protestant bishop of Down, also received the Presbyterians kindly, and both Irish prelates were glad to have Presbyterian preachers to assist in providing ministries to the people of Ulster.

Of course, not all Scots who moved to northern Ireland were devout Christians. Many of them, and some from England too, were contentious, unruly, and irreligious. Such people were in urgent need of a Christian ministry, and godly Scots were eager to reach them. To help meet the spiritual needs of the new arrivals, the bishops of Ulster opened their pulpits to Presbyterian preachers and allowed them to conduct worship services in the manner of the Church of Scotland without Episcopal ordination. Presbyterian pastors then received tithes and administered church discipline much as they would have done in their native land.

Edward Brice (1569–1636) was the first Scottish preacher to settle in Ulster, where in 1613 he became pastor in Broadisland, and many others soon followed him, although the first decade of their work in Ireland brought little fruit to encourage them. In 1625, however, a dramatic change occurred in connection with the preaching of James Glendinning (1583–ca. 1663), a graduate of the University of St. Andrews, whose manner of ministry excited great emotional response, which at times expressed itself in very peculiar ways. Glendinning preached the law of God with great zeal, and the Lord brought throngs of people to deep conviction of sin, sometimes expressed in agonizing contrition accompanied by remarkable physical manifestations. Glendinning was very effective in denouncing evil but not adept at proclaiming the gospel of forgiveness. Other preachers, realizing his deficiency, came to the aid of Glendinning with their proclamations of grace and salvation. These associations of Scottish pastors led eventually to monthly meetings in Antrim in which ministers encouraged one another and laid the foundation for a Presbyterian structure.

The success of the Presbyterian pastors had the effect of eventually leading Bishop Echlin to reconsider his support for their labors. Perhaps because of jealousy, he aroused other Anglican clerics to oppose them, once it became clear the Scots intended to remain Presbyterian and would not bow to episcopal authority. In 1632 Echlin removed a number of Scottish ministers from Church of Ireland pulpits and began harassing them, especially those who insisted Presbyterian polity is the divine prescription for

Christ's church. To facilitate his efforts to silence such preachers, the bishop appealed to King Charles I and William Laud, archbishop of Canterbury, both of whom sought to make the Crown supreme in church and state. As in Scotland, so in Ireland, Presbyterians endured persecution at the hands of an autocratic monarchy, and even the intercession of godly and genial Archbishop Ussher could not secure their liberty.

Repression in Ireland convinced some Presbyterians to migrate to America, but their ship *Eagle Wing* encountered severe weather that forced it to return, whereupon many of the passengers fled to Scotland to avoid arrest. In 1639 the government ordered subscription to the Black Oath, whereby people not only had to swear allegiance to the king but also were required to repudiate the Scottish covenants. As a result, many more Presbyterians left Ulster for Scotland.

Persecution of Presbyterians in Ulster

Armed with the Black Oath, Thomas Wentworth (1593–1641), an agent of Archbishop Laud and lord deputy for Ireland, initiated cruel persecution against nonconforming Scots. Many lost their homes and suffered imprisonment as Wentworth sought to rid the province of Presbyterians. The policy of repression would not succeed, and in the end, the king, the archbishop, and the lord deputy all lost their heads to the executioner's ax in the anti-Stuart turbulence of English politics at the mid-seventeenth century.

Even more devastating than government oppression was the suffering the Scots of Ulster experienced when, in 1641, Irish Catholics rose in revolt against the foreigners who had taken their lands. Agitated by their priests and with encouragement from the papal ambassador in Ireland, the Catholics perpetrated many atrocities, sparing no one, neither women nor children. Perceived enemies were subjected to burnings, mutilation of their bodies, even being buried alive. Episcopalians and Presbyterians alike experienced the wrath of Irish peasants, although most Presbyterian ministers had fled to Scotland to evade the repressions of Wentworth before the uprising began. As Catholic nobles led the rebels to attack town after town, Pope Urban VIII (r. 1623–1644) threatened to excommunicate any Catholics who refused to support the revolt. Unburied corpses rotted in the streets, giving rise to diseases that worsened the death toll. There is no agreement about the number of casualties, but a conservative estimate puts it at forty thousand. These killings aroused Puritans throughout the British

Isles to blame Charles I, and the rebels' claim that the king supported their cause seemed to confirm Puritan suspicions toward the Crown.

The defeat of the Irish rebels, when it occurred, was the work of Scottish legions under the command of General Robert Munro (d. ca. 1680), who led the first contingent of three thousand soldiers, and then of the Earl of Leven, who brought seven thousand more. The troops went to Ireland under terms of an agreement between the English and Scottish parliaments, and because their pay and supplies were not forthcoming, they had to live off the land. In some cases their behavior was no better than that of the insurgents they went to subdue, but godly chaplains who accompanied them conducted a vigorous ministry among the soldiers, and as a consequence Presbyterianism began to flourish. The first Irish presbytery developed from within the army when, at the urging of their chaplains, the soldiers elected ruling elders and organized sessions. When the number of functioning sessions reached four, their representatives formed a presbytery on June 10, 1642. Whereas they had once served within the Church of Ireland, Presbyterian pastors thereafter ministered under the auspices of their own ecclesiastical polity, as the Presbyterian Church in Ireland came into being at Carrickfergus, a little north of Belfast. The Church of Scotland responded quickly to appeals from Ireland for pastors to serve the growing number of Presbyterian congregations in several counties. Some army chaplains remained in Ireland to preach after their regiments returned to Scotland. While it was eager to help in Ireland, the Church of Scotland had no surplus of ministers, so those who served in Ireland did so on a temporary basis. The Presbyterian Church in Ireland would therefore have to produce pastors of its own, a daunting responsibility at that time.

Civil War in England

As suppression of the rebels in Ireland was nearing completion, England erupted in war between King Charles I and the Puritan-dominated Long Parliament. In defiance of the monarch, Parliament dissolved the established church and expelled its bishops from the House of Lords. A few months later, Parliament summoned the Westminster Assembly to advise it on matters of religion and to propose a church polity agreeable to Scripture, that is, a church government comparable to that of the Church of Scotland and continental Reformed bodies. When Parliament sought Scottish aid in the struggle against Royalist forces, the Scots complied on the condition that the English endorse the Solemn League and Covenant. This agreement bound both kingdoms to maintain the Reformed faith, including the Presbyterian form of church government. The Scots and English furthermore agreed to bring Ireland also into conformity with this arrangement, and soon Scottish pastors appeared in Ireland to promulgate the Solemn League and Covenant and to persuade people to sign the document as the charter of their newly born liberty. Among Protestants there was much enthusiasm for this, especially among the more than thirty Presbyterian pastors residing in Ulster, ministers Parliament allowed to collect tithes for their support.

Despite the cooperation between Scots and Englishmen, relations between them were not always cordial, and in the end, the decision to execute Charles I caused a rupture between them. By order of Parliament the monarch was beheaded on January 30, 1649, an action Presbyterians in all three kingdoms opposed. In fact, it required expulsion of the Presbyterian members of the English Parliament to obtain the agreement to dispatch the king.

Scottish Presbyterians soon invited Charles Stuart, son of the late monarch, to become their king as Charles II (r. 1649–1685), while their coreligionists in Ireland condemned the killing of Charles I and sent an emphatic protest to the English Parliament. The now famous poet John Milton composed Parliament's reply to the Irish complaint. England minus the king had become a commonwealth with a unicameral legislature under the domination of Puritans determined to prevent the return of monarchy. This Rump Parliament demanded the Irish submit to an oath known as the Engagement, by which they would repudiate the House of Stuart and affirm allegiance to the Commonwealth. On the grounds that Charles II had a hereditary right and because monarchy, with proper restrictions, was the best form of government, Presbyterian pastors refused to swear the oath. Their loyalty to the king cost the Scots-Irish dearly because he, in the end, demonstrated hatred for Presbyterianism and sought to make his rule absolute. Those who supported Charles II faced imprisonment, so to evade that punishment, some Presbyterians fled to Scotland.

Oliver Cromwell's Protectorate
Although Irish Presbyterians suffered because of their loyalty to King Charles II, the duration of their tribulation was short. Oliver Cromwell (1599–1658), leader of the Independent Puritans and hero of the victory over Charles I, assumed the title Lord Protector, and with the aid of the

army abolished the Rump Parliament in 1653 and took supreme authority into his own hands. The Protector had reason to suspect the Presbyterians of Scotland and Ireland because of their loyalty to the Stuart monarch, but he chose to be magnanimous toward those people, with whom he shared a fervent attachment to the Reformed faith, even though he disagreed with their church polity. The Presbyterian Church in Ireland then flourished under his government, the Protector being glad for the spiritual ministry that church provided for the Irish people. The number of presbyteries in Ireland soon increased from one to five, the number of pastors from twenty-four to seventy.

The Stuart Restoration (1660)

At Cromwell's death in 1658 his title passed to his son Richard (1626–1712), who soon demonstrated inability to govern and wisely chose to resign. By that time the English nation had tired of authoritarian military rule, and a groundswell of opinion called for a return to monarchy. The Rump Parliament reconvened but soon became divided against itself, and army leaders forced it to disband. At that point General George Monck (1608–1670), commander of forces in Scotland, took soldiers to London, where he required the Rump to reassemble and then to dissolve itself. When the parliamentarians refused, he restored its Presbyterian members purged in 1648, and that parliament ordered new elections and then disbanded as well. The newly elected legislature summoned a convention that promptly asked Charles II to assume the crown of England as he had done earlier in Scotland. The new king of England ruled there from 1660 to 1685. Much to their dismay, for Presbyterians this restoration they supported would bring a return to repression of their faith.

Once he felt secure, Charles II demonstrated deep hostility toward his Presbyterian subjects in all three British kingdoms. An Anglican by persuasion, Charles, like his late father, restored episcopacy and required the Book of Common Prayer be used in all church services. The new king decreed episcopal ordination mandatory for all members of the clergy. Sixty ministers in Ulster who refused to comply with that demand lost their positions, while only seven pastors met the requirement of the Act of Uniformity (1662) by submitting to the bishops for ordination. Once the new law took effect, no one could preach legally without a license from a bishop, and Jeremy Taylor (1613–1667), bishop of Down, denying the validity of the Presbyterian ministry, expelled thirty-six pastors, as other prelates did likewise.

Presbyterian services of worship continued clandestinely, and some public officials ignored them, but the expulsions had cost the Protestants of Ulster two-thirds of their clerics. Moreover, royal policy required all subjects to promise never to bear arms against the king and to renounce the Solemn League and Covenant as impious and illegal. The effects of the Act of Uniformity fell first upon Ireland and a year later upon England, where the ejection of nonconforming pastors deprived far more men of their ministries and livelihoods.

Despite the wishes of the king, it became clear by 1668 that few officials were zealous to prosecute dissenting ministers in Ireland, and informal religious bodies began to erect chapels. Within twenty years, Presbyterians were once again conducting public worship, constructing buildings, and functioning as organized bodies, even though the law against nonconformity was still in place. The good will or benign indifference of magistrates had rendered the king's policy ineffective during the years between 1662 and 1685. In the latter year Irish Protestantism received a new infusion of strength when Huguenots arrived in Ulster after fleeing persecution in France, where Louis XIV (1638–1715) had deprived them of their freedom of religion.

Reign of James II

Upon the death of Charles II, the crowns of Scotland and England passed to his brother James II (r. 1685–1688), an ardent Catholic ruling over two decidedly Protestant kingdoms. James's major interest in Ireland, it soon became clear, was to restore Catholic control, and his principal agent in this effort was his brother-in-law the Earl of Clarendon. Clarendon became lord lieutenant for Ireland, while the Earl of Tyrconnel received command of royal military forces there. James needed Irish support for his pro-Catholic polities, as he collided with the majority of Englishmen who desired to preserve the Protestant ascendancy both at home and in the Emerald Isle. The king's officers purged the army in Ireland of Protestants, as the crown appointed Catholics to judgeships and various political offices. Irish Protestants promptly responded by supporting efforts to overthrow the ruler.

At first the repressive measures of Clarendon and Tyrconnel affected only the Episcopalians in Ireland, because the king sought the aid of nonconformist Protestants as well as Catholics. Although James II despised Presbyterianism, he allowed ministers of that body much freedom in the hope of obtaining their support against the Anglican establishment. The

Presbyterians, however, had no reason to trust the king, and they knew his program could lead to Roman Catholic domination throughout Ireland. They understood the royal leniency toward them was not an expression of good will, and they realized, if Catholicism triumphed, the evils they had endured for dissenting from episcopacy would be light in comparison with the trials their new masters would inflict upon them.

Siege of Londonderry

At the end of 1688 an anonymous letter, found on a street near Belfast and addressed to the Earl of Mount Alexander, warned that a massacre of Protestants would occur on December 9. Soon copies of the letter circulated through Belfast, and Protestants who could remember the bloodbath of 1641 prepared for combat. The Earl of Tyrconnel had by then become lord lieutenant for Ireland, and his hatred for Protestants was notorious. Reports that royal troops were assembling seemed to confirm the warning in the letter, so Protestants in the towns of Enniskillen and Londonderry prepared their defenses to withstand a siege that, in Londonderry, became legendary in Irish history.

When royal forces arrived before the gates of Londonderry and demanded admittance, the Episcopal bishop of the city advised municipal leaders to grant them entry, since it was the duty of Christian subjects to obey their king. Presbyterian Pastor James Gordon, however, urged resistance, and his admonition prevailed. For 105 days the citizens of Londonderry endured terrible privations due to bombardments aggravated by disease and hunger. The Royalist army had left for Ireland the same week William of Orange arrived in England to take the throne James II had been forced to vacate in the Glorious Revolution. Despite the deaths of thousands of defenders, the city withstood the assaults, even though the ousted James II brought French troops to aid the attackers. A British fleet broke through the barricade on the Foyle River in June 1689 and thereby ended the siege. Although there are conflicting accounts of the battle and the atrocities royal forces committed, it is clear the Protestant cause triumphed, and the siege became a fixture in the memories of those whose forefathers waged the successful and heroic defense.

Ireland and the Glorious Revolution (1688–1689)

The coming of William III and Mary II, as joint rulers, brought Protestant monarchs to England and Scotland, sovereigns who favored the Reformed faith, so Ulster Presbyterians rejoiced. In fact, the change of dynasties occurred while the siege of Londonderry was in progress. William, an effective ruler, sent aid to the beleaguered Protestants and soon appeared in Ireland to lead his troops. The decisive victory came at the Battle of the Boyne River, July 1, 1690, which destroyed the hope of James II to regain his lost throne and dealt a heavy blow to Roman Catholic aspirations in Ulster. Although the triumphant king was lenient toward defeated rebels, Irish Protestants were not so inclined. Their control of Ireland's parliament enabled them to enact anti-Catholic laws to exclude Romanists from public office, and one such act required that a Catholic's estate, at his death, be divided equally among his heirs. If one child became a Protestant, the entire estate would go to him or her. Because of this, Catholic land holdings became smaller and smaller, to the impoverishment of the owners. Other laws excluded Catholics from teaching in schools and forbade them to marry Protestants. These and other penal measures made life miserable for Irish Catholics and thereby assured their ceaseless hostility toward their Protestant rulers and governors, who added insult to injury by requiring them to pay tithes to the established Church of Ireland.

Although the Protestants had triumphed in Ireland, it was the Episcopalians rather than the Presbyterians who enjoyed most of the benefits of the victory. The Anglican Church of Ireland remained the religion established by law, and members of that body dominated local governments. Presbyterians still had no legal standing, despite the king's call for toleration. He appreciated the heroic sacrifices Presbyterians had made in defense of Londonderry and Enniskillen, but the Irish House of Lords, through its Committee for Religion, proposed no freedom for Presbyterians unless they conformed to the Test Act the English Parliament had passed in 1673. This required reception of the Eucharist in an Anglican service as a condition for holding public office. While the obvious intention behind this was to exclude Catholics, it pertained to nonconformist Protestants as well. The desire to apply this legislation originated among Episcopal bishops who sat in the Irish House of Lords. William III, however, refused to sanction the action of the Irish Lords, and he rewarded the Presbyterian loyalists with financial subsidies and worked to thwart the discriminations for which the Episcopalians were responsible. By the time King William died in 1702, nine presbyteries and three synods were operating in Ireland, as the Presbyterian church flourished in the face of opposition from prelates eager for dominance over religion.

Ireland during the Reign of Anne

The death of their grateful patron left Irish Presbyterians vulnerable when the last of the Stuarts ascended the throne as Queen Anne in 1702, who reigned until 1714. The new monarch, in rather typical Stuart fashion, soon displayed her hostility toward Presbyterianism, perhaps because she saw the bishops as staunch supporters of the Crown and exponents of divine-right monarchy, while she perceived Presbyterians to be adherents to limited government. At the urging of the bishop of Londonderry, Queen Anne awarded control of the royal subsidies for Irish Presbyterians to the lord lieutenant, who soon ended the grants entirely. A further grievance occurred in 1704 with the application of the Test Act to Ireland, a measure William III had prevented. Few Presbyterians complied with this despised law, and some who held public offices lost them, but the prelates' expectation that the law would lead many dissenters to conform to the Church of Ireland was not fulfilled. In Londonderry alone ten of the twelve aldermen vacated their offices rather than compromise their faith. A similar development occurred in Belfast. At one point, in 1709, officials of the Church of Ireland, aided by justices of the peace, arrested members of a presbytery in session on the charge of convening an illegal assembly. In several Ulster towns angry Episcopalians sealed the doors of Presbyterian meeting houses and accused their pastors of sympathy for the ousted James II. Fines and imprisonments were the lot of some stubborn Presbyterians, whose cause continued to prosper, to the frustration of their enemies.

Cruel discriminations led some Presbyterians to consider migrating to America. As early as 1681 a call from the colony of Maryland asked for a minster, and the Presbytery of Lagan sent Francis Mackemie (ca. 1658–1708), a graduate of the University of Glasgow, to the New World, where he organized the Presbytery of Philadelphia in 1706. About that time some twelve thousand Ulster Scots were going to America each year, so a major Presbyterian presence was developing there. Episcopal animosity did not then efface Presbyterianism in Ireland, but, contrary to the wishes of Irish prelates, it promoted the growth of the "sect" in the New World. One of the greatest achievements of the Presbyterian Church in Ireland was to establish a strong core of Reformed believers in America, which the persecuting policy of the government in England and Ireland had encouraged.

Dilution of the Reformed Faith

Early in the eighteenth century Scots-Irish Presbyterians became embroiled in theological controversies when the ancient heresy Arianism gained the acceptance of some of their ministers. The first sign of trouble appeared when, in 1702, the church deposed Thomas Emlyn, pastor of Wood Street Presbyterian Church, Dublin, for denying the essential, eternal deity of Christ, the major error of Arian doctrine. The Synod of Ulster responded to the Arian challenge by requiring all ministers and candidates for licensure to preach to subscribe to the Westminster Confession of Faith, an unequivocally Trinitarian statement.

In 1705 John Abernathy (1680–1740), a pastor in Antrim, led in the formation of the Belfast Society, a club of intellectuals, many of them clerics, interested to advance scholarship and culture through research, publication, and discussion of a broad spectrum of ideas. In 1719 Abernathy delivered a lecture titled "Religious Obedience Founded on Personal Persuasion" to the society, a presentation destined to agitate Presbyterian circles for many years. Members of the Belfast Society received Abernathy's lecture enthusiastically because they regarded requiring subscription to any creed a violation of personal freedom. Within the Presbyterian Church, leaders of a liberal disposition soon began demanding an end to subscription.

The issue over subscription became especially troublesome when, in 1719, Samuel Haliday, a candidate for installation in a Belfast congregation, refused to endorse the Westminster Confession and as an alternative presented his own statement to the presbytery. That body accepted Haliday's document and installed him over the protests of a minority that then appealed the matter to the Synod of Ulster. That court rebuked the majority that had accepted the disputed confession, but it took no action to remedy the situation.

In 1721 the General Synod of the Presbyterian Church asked all officers to subscribe to the Westminster Confession, but members of the Belfast Society complained and resisted even a synodal declaration of faith in the essential deity of Christ, as they contended against all tests of orthodoxy. A large majority of those present at the General Synod signed the Westminster Confession, but some who refused became a party of nonsubscribers. Efforts to confine this faction to the Presbytery of Antrim failed, and a majority of ruling elders led the General Synod in 1722 to expel the nonsubscribers.

After 1725 efforts to maintain subscription within the Presbyterian Church declined in frequency and vigor as part of a general laxity in doctrine, which, by mid-eighteenth century, allowed the infiltration of Arminian ideas into Presbyterian circles, as Wesleyan influences became prominent in the British Isles.

Arrival of the Secession Church from Scotland

Infidelity within the Presbyterian Church in Ireland continued, as Arian and Socinian ideas fascinated intellectuals attracted to rationalism-deism as a worldview. Most Presbyterian pastors imbibed some measure of that philosophy while pursuing their ministerial education in Scotland. Drawing pastors from Scotland or those educated in Scottish universities exposed Irish congregations to liberal systems of thought prevalent there, so in 1742, a group of Reformed believers in Lylehill near Belfast asked for recognition from the Associate Presbytery of Scotland, the Secession Church of Ebenezer Erskine, and Isaac Patton (1725–1814) went to Lylehill as pastor of the first Secession congregation on Irish soil.

Most Irish Presbyterian pastors resented the Seceders' intrusion, and some made unfounded accusations about them, even raising questions about the Seceders' orthodoxy. Thomas Clark (1720–1792), a spokesman for the Associate Presbytery of Glasgow, answered the charges and in the process indicted the Presbyterian Church in Ireland for allowing teaching of false doctrine within its own ranks. The Associate Church grew rapidly in Ireland, and by 1750 it had its own organized presbytery. There were about fifty congregations by 1800 and almost triple that number by 1840, when there was a union between the Associate Church and the Presbyterian Church in Ireland.

The presence and vigor of the Associate Church prompted many ministers of the Presbyterian Church in Ireland to maintain strict orthodoxy in their own preaching and to guard their own denomination against further deviations in doctrine. In some areas of the country, preachers of the Secession Church provided a gospel ministry no longer available in older Presbyterian congregations, while in other places Secession church plants introduced gospel preaching for the first time. The Associate Church was the salt that preserved Presbyterianism in Ireland from putrefaction, as the older body was becoming ever more lax about its adherence to the Reformed faith.

Political Presbyterians

At this time the Sunday school movement was beginning to make itself felt within the ranks of the Presbyterians of Ulster. Though not regarded with appreciation by many of them, these schools increased both in enrollment and in influence from about 1775.

Among the tragic episodes of Irish history—and their number, if not legion, is all too great—was that of the rise and fall of the United Irishmen, a society formed in October of 1791. Theodore Wolfe Tone (1763–1798), who was a Protestant, was the chief promoter and moving spirit of the organization. The landlord-tenant system of that day was such as to call for basic changes in the interests of justice, and this situation proved a powerful factor in attracting Irishmen of various backgrounds and different faiths to the movement. Among these were many Presbyterians.

Within the course of several years, however, the United Irishmen concentrated their energies upon securing absolute political independence from England, and its leaders reconstituted the organization in 1795 as a secret society with revolution toward this end as their objective. Tone and his associates entered into negotiations with France for the provision of military aid in prospect of such a projected uprising. French influence and arms became directly involved in the undertaking, though neither proved of any determining moment as events developed.

Some of the ministers of the Synod of Ulster and many of its communicants, along with others, took part in the activities of the society, though without the blessing of the governing bodies of their respective organizations. The endeavors of the United Irishmen finally culminated in a series of unsuccessful attacks upon several towns and cities of Ireland. The civil and military authorities effectively crushed the uprising and then imposed severe, and at times excessive, penalties upon the insurrectionists.

These authorities compelled three ministers of the Presbyterian Church in Ireland to emigrate to the wilds of America, so vividly depicted by a fellow countryman by the name of Goldsmith in his poem "Deserted Village." They imprisoned a Presbyterian clergyman, William Steel Dickson (1744–1824), at Fort George in Scotland for almost three years on the indictment of having served as a general in the forces of the United Irishmen. The diversity of religious attachment of members of this order is illustrated by the fact that among Dickson's nineteen fellow prisoners were four Roman Catholics, five Presbyterians, and ten Anglicans.

The most stringent penalty inflicted upon a Presbyterian minister in connection with the movement was the hanging of James Porter (1753–1798), also of the Synod of Ulster. This took place on July 2, 1798, after his trial by court martial. The charge against Porter was that of implication through being present on an occasion when the royal mails were robbed, but it appears that his determining offense lay in having published a series of effectively sarcastic articles depicting the conditions prevailing with respect to the tenancy of lands. These sketches presented one of the civil dignitaries of the day in a decidedly unfavorable light. This official was the very man who was in a position to save Porter from the gallows but who declined to do so, despite the entreaties of a number of persons, including his own daughter.

Several picturesque and insidious organizations came upon the scene about this time. Among them was a Protestant group known as the Peep of Day Boys who devoted themselves to several types of nefariousness, but specialized in driving Roman Catholics from their homes, a pastime at which they proved to be adept. The rival Defenders, made up of Roman Catholics, regardless of the implication of the name of their society, were not all averse to taking the offensive when such strategy fitted into their plans and indulged in murder on more than one occasion.

On September 21, 1795, representatives of these opposing forces clashed in an outright battle—a massacre according to certain historians sympathetic to the losers—at a place called the Diamond in County Armagh. The outnumbered Peep of Day Boys emerged victorious, reputedly killing forty-eight of the Defenders without the loss of a single life. On the following day a number of Protestants organized the Orange Society, which has played such a sustained role in the unfolding of Protestantism and, by way of incidence, Presbyterianism. Considering the background, it is not surprising that the early Orangemen were not altogether exemplary in their individual conduct and in that of the society at its beginning. Anglicans were dominant in the organization in the earliest days, but many Presbyterians soon entered the Orange ranks.

The Ministry of Henry Cooke

At a time of great need in the history of Ireland, God provided assistance through the work of Henry Cooke (1788–1868), a brilliant, articulate defender of the faith and zealous preacher of the gospel, educated at the University of Glasgow. Born in the county of Londonderry, Cooke

came from a family descended from English Puritans, a family that emigrated to County Down early in the seventeenth century. At home and in
school he learned the doctrines of strict Presbyterianism, from which he
never deviated.

Cooke's first pastoral ministry began when he was but twenty years
old, a parish at Duneane, County Antrim, where he remained only two
years. After being tutor to the children of farmer Alexander Brown near
Ballymena for a brief period, Cooke returned to pastoral service by accept-
ing a call to the church at Donegore in the Templepatrick Presbytery, a
congregation that had recently rejected the candidacy of Henry Montgomery (1788–1865), who would eventually become the major critic of
Cooke's efforts to defend orthodoxy. His orthodox party within the Synod
of Ulster became known as Old Lights, while the liberal faction known
as New Lights sought toleration for a broad spectrum of doctrinal views.
The congregation at Donegore staunchly rejected the New Light position
Montgomery espoused vigorously.

For a brief time his church allowed Cooke leave to further his education in Dublin, and while there he preached in several churches where his
stout orthodoxy and fervent evangelism were welcome. Much to the chagrin of believers in Donegore, Cooke accepted a call to Killyleagh in 1818,
and it was there he became prominent as leader of the Old Lights.

Cooke's reputation as defender of the Reformed faith was due in part
to his stern opposition to Arian-Unitarian doctrine as proclaimed by John
Smethurst, who traveled across Ireland to promote his anti-Trinitarian view
of God. Cooke responded to Smethurst's challenge to historic Christianity,
confronting him at several sites where Smethurst had gone to lecture, and
public acclamations for his endeavors convinced Cooke God had called
him to be a guardian of the Trinitarian faith.

Although Unitarian doctrine had only a small number of adherents in
Ireland, Cooke surmised correctly that it had the potential to inflict much
damage on Christianity in general and on his own church in particular.
Both within and outside the Presbyterian Church in Ireland, some intellectuals accepted an Arian view of Christ, one that regarded him as the Son
of God but not God the Son, more than human but less than divine. To
Cooke and the Old Lights that belief was but a less overt form of Unitarianism to be resisted at all costs. An occasion for such resistance occurred
in 1821, when the Belfast Academical Institution appointed an Arian as
professor of biblical languages. The institution already had a reputation

for encouraging liberal ideas, so confessional Presbyterians did not want it to become a theological college preparing men for the ministry in their church. Many ministerial students nevertheless enrolled there, rather than travel to Scotland. When Cooke and other conservatives complained about the teaching at the school, there was little initial support for their position, and that led Cooke to organize a concerted effort to expose and combat the errors of Arian-Unitarian theology.

When he became moderator of the synod in 1824, Cooke acquired an advantageous position from which to prosecute his case against the Belfast Institution, but still there was little readiness to accept his charges against the faculty. He turned therefore to deal with pastors who readily admitted their Arian beliefs, among them the distinguished and eloquent Henry Montgomery. A synodal meeting in 1827 became the occasion for a confrontation with Montgomery, whose appeals for liberty of conscience fell on deaf ears. The body overwhelmingly affirmed its commitment to Trinitarian doctrine. When it became clear that the Old Lights intended to reject all candidates for the ministry who maintained Arian beliefs, Montgomery and others withdrew from the Synod of Ulster and created the Remonstrant Synod, so named after their remonstrance against the decisions of the Ulster Synod failed to win acceptance. Seventeen congregations formed the new body of Non-Subscribing Presbyterians.

One beneficial effect of this dispute, from the conservative point of view, was the consolidation of doctrinal orthodoxy within the Presbyterian Church in Ireland, which became evident when, in 1836, the church required all of its officers to subscribe to the Westminster Confession of Faith. This action led to reunion with the Secession Church, which formed the General Assembly of the Presbyterian Church in Ireland, a denomination of 433 congregations.

Once the Presbyterian Church in Ireland settled the controversies about doctrine, vigorous missionary work began in India, and church extension projects flourished at home, while there were special efforts to evangelize Jews. Theological colleges opened in Londonderry and Belfast, and the church founded several orphanages. When instrumental music appeared in the churches, protracted debates ensued, which ended with an agreement that each congregation would be free to decide its own policy about the practice. All things considered, by the opening of the twentieth century, the Presbyterian Church in Ireland seemed orthodox, vigorous, and healthy.

Non-Subscribing Presbyterians

The rise of anticonfessional and Arian beliefs among Irish Presbyterians had become especially evident at First Presbyterian Church, Belfast, in the first half of the eighteenth century. When Samuel Haliday became pastor there in 1720, he refused to endorse the Westminster Confession, although he did not object publicly to its theology but rather argued against making a human document binding upon pastors or churches. When some members of First Presbyterian Church formed a second Presbyterian congregation in Belfast, they too objected to the historic confession, but a faction within that body withdrew to form a third congregation, one that embraced the confession heartily.

Pastor William Bruce, who served the First Presbyterian Church from 1812–1868, was avowedly Unitarian in theology and Arminian in his understanding of sin and salvation, as was his successor, John Scott Porter, minister there until 1880, as that congregation continued to be the center of anti-Reformed teaching in Presbyterian ranks. Bruce was instrumental in the first effort to organize the Association of Non-Subscribing Presbyterians, which came into being in 1835. That association became progressively more liberal through the nineteenth century, and in 1910 that body joined with other nonorthodox congregations, some of them frankly Unitarian, to form the Non-Subscribing Presbyterian Church of Ireland. A succession of pastors at First Presbyterian Church, Belfast, were leaders in the new denomination that maintained accommodation to modern culture was essential for the survival of the church at large. In this way Non-Subscribing congregations retained Presbyterian polity while discarding Reformed theology.

Presbyterian Education in Ireland

The years 1846 to 1847 brought great suffering to Ireland due to the failure of the potato crop, a victim of fungus. The population fell from about eight million to 6.5 million, as people died from famine or disease or left the country, many going to America. Membership in the Presbyterian Church in Ireland, which, in 1840, had stood at about 185 thousand, had fallen to 122,790 by 1864.

Despite the hardships of that time, Presbyterians continued their ministries and took measures to educate their own pastors, rather than depend upon English or Scottish universities to do so. In 1841 the Synod of Ulster withdrew approval from the Belfast Academical Institution because of the

Arian persuasion of some professors there, and in 1847 Presbyterians created a theological college in Belfast. J. H. Merle d'Aubigne, a renowned church historian from Geneva, delivered the major address at the opening ceremony, and church members in general rejoiced to have their own school. Soon a second school of theology opened, this one due to a legacy from Martha Marie Magee of Dublin, who left twenty thousand pounds for the creation of a college to include a department of theology. Magee College in Londonderry began classes in 1865.

Financial support for ministers from the British government, the so-called *Regium Donum,* or Royal Subsidy, ended in 1869, when Parliament disestablished the Church of Ireland. This measure, designed to placate Catholics, forced to support a church they did not attend, inflicted hardship upon Protestant beneficiaries of the royal favor. The Irish Church Act, however, provided payments of lump sums to assist churches through the transition to full self-support, and the Presbyterian college at Belfast received 39,500 pounds, while other church agencies received varying sums of money. In 1881 the British government authorized the Presbyterian colleges in Belfast and Londonderry to grant the bachelor of divinity and doctor of divinity degrees.

Twentieth-Century Developments in the Presbyterian Church in Ireland

Anti-British resentment in Erie, the largest part of Ireland, where the Catholic population was dominant, grew steadily through the nineteenth century, and Protestant endeavors to evangelize Catholics increased the tensions greatly. Irish nationalism and Catholic religion were almost indistinguishable, even though some noteworthy Protestants supported the nationalist movement. The general poverty of the Catholic Irish when compared with the relative prosperity of Ulster Protestants added fuel to the flames of discontent, as did the effects of the famine of 1846 to 1847, which were more devastating in Erie than in Ulster.

In northern Ireland the Presbyterian Church in Ireland continued to prosper as the twentieth century progressed, and a vigorous missionary program extended its influence overseas, for example, into China, India, Southeast Asia, and several parts of Africa. Theological liberalism, however, affected the Presbyterian Church in Ireland to some extent and produced a decline in zeal comparable to that in other countries of the British Isles. The Presbyterian Church in Ireland joined the World Presbyterian Alliance in 1870, and by the opening of the twentieth century, 307,863 people held membership in the denomination. The church began ordaining women elders in 1926 and received them as ministers for the first time in 1976.

Social reform has been a prominent emphasis within the Presbyterian Church in Ireland for some time. A *Programme for Social Reform* adopted by the General Assembly in 1921 called for welfare state policies in the government, while the church itself maintained several orphanages, youth hostels, clinics for alcoholics and drug addicts, and homes for elderly indigent people. A Presbyterian Housing Association received financial aid from the government in a church-state partnership. Even in Erie (now the Republic of Ireland), Presbyterian agencies receive state aid for their services.

After creating the General Assembly in 1840, the Presbyterian Church in Ireland adopted an ecclesiastical structure of a bureaucratic character in which central offices administer programs of the church. Church House in Belfast became the headquarters, and there the General Assembly meets annually. In 1948 the Presbyterian Church in Ireland became a charter member of the World Council of Churches.

Relations between the Presbyterian Church in Ireland and the Roman Catholic Church changed substantially in the twentieth century. When Pope John XXIII (r. 1958–1963) summoned Vatican Council II in 1962, he initiated dramatic changes within his own church, among them a new attitude and posture toward non-Roman religious bodies. The traditional appellation "Protestant heretics," in use since the Reformation of the sixteenth century, was to disappear, and "separated brethren" would take its place. Once it became clear this marked a genuine change of policy and not just an improvement in ecclesiastical manners, Irish Presbyterians responded positively. A striking evidence of the new interchurch relationship occurred in 1963, when the General Assembly of the Presbyterian Church in Ireland stood to honor John XXIII when the commissioners learned that he had died.

Vatican Council II, true to the wish of its convener, issued a Decree of Ecumenism that called for dialogue with non-Roman churches and cooperation with them, even though the council did not rescind the claim that Roman Catholicism is the only true church. The conciliar affirmation of religious liberty impressed Protestants, especially in Ireland, where conflicts were deep-seated and sometimes expressed themselves in violence. The General Assembly of the Presbyterian Church in Ireland received the Decree on Ecumenism gladly at its meeting in 1965, and it issued a statement of regret for unkind pronouncements about Catholicism made in the past. Conferences between Catholic and Presbyterian leaders became increasingly frequent, and publications to which both contributed began to appear.

In addition to cordial relations with Roman Catholics, the Presbyterian Church in Ireland has moved toward greater cooperation with other Protestant bodies such as the Methodist Church in Ireland and the Anglican Church of Ireland. The matter of episcopacy in the Church of Ireland has, however, prevented serious consideration of union between that denomination and the Presbyterian Church in Ireland.

The Reformed Presbyterian Church of Ireland

In addition to the larger body represented by the General Assembly, the four separate Presbyterian churches in Ireland are the Reformed, the Non-Subscribing, the Evangelical, and the Free.

David Houston (1633–1696) introduced Reformed Presbyterian principles into Ulster. He was a native Scot who shuttled back and forth between these two lands. An avowed advocate and protagonist of the Covenants and Covenanting, his activities proved painfully disconcerting to the more staid clergy of the Presbyterian Church in Ireland. After receiving regular ordination, the Presbytery of Route deposed Houston in 1687, and he formally joined the Covenanters five years later.

Matthew Lynn (1731–1800), or Lynd, was the first regular minister of this branch of Presbyterianism in Ulster. William Martin (1733–1808) labored in a similar capacity for the Reformed Presbyterians in the same area. A Reformed presbytery founded in 1763 had become extinct by 1779, in large part due to the removal of its ministers, including Lynn and Martin, to America.

The Covenanters put forth another, and this time successful, effort for the establishment of a presbytery in 1792, during a period in which William Stavely (1743–1825) proved to be a leading spirit in its affairs. Though the entire church numbered but eighteen congregations in 1810, these were so widely scattered as to make it difficult for their representatives to assemble for presbytery meetings. In that year, therefore, the presbytery divided itself into four presbyteries subordinate to a synod, which first met in 1811. The early nineteenth-century controversies relating to the *Regium Donum* within the Synod of Ulster and among the Seceders tended to swell the ranks of the Reformed Presbyterians, since these Covenanters rejected the idea of any government subsidy for their organization.

The Reformed Presbyterians of Ireland established a missionary society in 1823 that soon began work near home among those of Covenanting connections in Liverpool and across the Atlantic in New Brunswick and Nova Scotia. Reorganized under the auspices of the synod in 1828, the society set forth its objective as "the spread of the Gospel, and particularly of the doctrines of the Reformation" at home and in foreign lands.

In December 1830, *The Covenanter* began a long career as the literary organ of the church. A series of articles dealing with the civil magistrate and published in that paper proved to be such strong meat that members of the Eastern Presbytery entered a protest, and with certain other sympathizers, organized the independent Eastern Reformed Presbyterian Synod on October 18, 1842. This synod continued to function until 1902, when it voted to enter the General Assembly of the Presbyterian Church in Ireland, only to discover that half of its congregations preferred the fellowship of the older Covenanter Synod.

Up to the middle of the nineteenth century, ministerial candidates of the church made the short journey to Scotland for the completion of their education. In 1854 the synod elected two professors of divinity, James Dick (1799–1880) and Thomas Houston, thus establishing its own theological seminary in north Ireland.

The Reformed Presbyterian Church was among the beneficiaries of revival in 1859, as its communicant membership rose from 4,050 to 4,450 in two years. The Irish Covenanters commissioned their first missionary in conjunction with the Reformed Presbyterians of Scotland in 1871 and reported forty-eight hundred members about 1880.

The Reformed Presbyterians of Ireland have shown less inclination toward ecclesiastical association with the Roman Catholic Church than has the General Assembly of the Presbyterian Church in Ireland. In adopting the report of its Committee on Protestantism, the Synod of 1974 held, "the increasing fraternization of some Protestant leaders with the Papacy can only be regarded as a cynical betrayal of Protestantism and a repudiation of a heritage which our fathers counted dear." At the same time the synod continued: "The very Gospel which we proclaim stands as an insuperable barrier between us and the Papacy, yet that same Gospel is the only hope of individual Roman Catholics, and we must take it to them lovingly and humbly."

The Irish and Scottish Reformed Presbyterian churches maintain close contacts. The two synods merged their official periodicals in January 1967 as the *Covenanter Witness of Scotland and Ireland*, thus illustrating the practical strength of these ties. By 1974 the two churches were engaged in a series of conferences looking toward closer cooperation, and perhaps some type of union involving them. One suggestion in this connection contemplated the erection of a General Assembly including the synods, with each of the two presently existing courts continuing to care for matters of a domestic nature within their respective territories.

The Reformed Presbyterians of Ireland moved their theological hall, long located in downtown Belfast, to the Cameron House on Lisburn Road, which had become the center of the church's general operations. Classes began at the new site with the opening of the 1971–1972 sessions of that seminary. Another important development of the 1970s occurred at its meeting in 1974, when the synod of the Reformed Presbyterian Church acted to grant full autonomy to its small Reformed Presbytery in Australia, a body that consisted of three ministers and two congregations.

The Reformed Presbyterian Church has remained staunchly confessional in its doctrine, the Westminster Standards holding preeminence as its official statement of faith. In the tradition of the Scottish Covenanters, it continues to maintain insistence on Christ's right to sovereign rule over all creation, a right civil government is obliged to recognize. This church opposes abortion, homosexuality, pornography, and other immoral practices, and it protests violations of the Sabbath and the practices of gambling and consumption of alcoholic beverages. Reformed Presbyterians lament the policy in the United Kingdom of not requiring moral or religious qualifications for holding public office. These and other perceived evils they attribute to the failure of the state to acknowledge the reign of Christ, in the judgment of Reformed Presbyterians, a grave national sin. Members of this church do not, as a rule, participate in secular politics.

The Reformed Presbyterian Church does not engage in interchurch relations with the Catholic Church or with liberal Protestants but restricts such contacts to other Reformed bodies that share its doctrinal position. It is a member of the International Conference of Reformed Churches, and its ministers serve with the Scripture Gift Mission, Christian Witness to Israel, and the Evangelical Fellowship of Ireland. Missionaries of this denomination have served in Australia, Canada, Cyprus, Syria, Lebanon, France, and the Republic of Ireland. Thirty-seven congregations with about

3,100 members comprise this church. Its publications include the *Reformed Theological Journal*, issued annually, and the *Covenanter Witness*, a monthly magazine. Although a few congregations minister in Erie, most are in rural parts of Ulster.

The Evangelical Presbyterian Church in Ireland

The Irish Evangelical Church originated in 1927 following protests against the teachings of several of the professors in the Theological College of the Presbyterian Church in Ireland, with special reference to views thus set forth by J. E. Davey (1890–1942), a member of the college faculty. W. J. Grier (b. 1902), a student in the institution, and James Hunter (1863–1942), a Presbyterian minister, were active in pressing such charges, with the latter circulating a series of leaflets in this connection during 1926. The protestors formed the Presbyterian Bible Standards League in the interests of their cause.

The matter reached its climax with Hunter's presentation of formal charges against Professor Davey before the Presbytery of Belfast in 1926. These charges alleged that Davey denied the imputation of Christ's righteousness to the believer; that he held a position contrary to the Scriptures with respect to "the absolute perfection of our Lord's character," that "he taught views contrary to the Word of God and the Westminster Confession" regarding the "inspiration, infallibility, and Divine authority of the Holy Scriptures"; and that he "held and taught that the doctrine of the Trinity is not taught in the word of God." The presbytery cleared the accused of the first charge by finding him not guilty, and of the others on Davey's plea of justification. On appeal to the General Assembly, that court dismissed the appeal from the findings of the presbytery.

In July 1927, following these actions, Hunter withdrew from Belfast Presbytery, thereby severing his connection with the Presbyterian Church in Ireland. Others joined him and on October 15 of that year, they convened to form a new organization to be known as the Irish Evangelical Church.

The Irish Evangelical, the monthly magazine of the newly constituted body, began publication with the issue of June 1928. As of March 1964, the denomination changed its title to the Evangelical Presbyterian Church, and *The Irish Evangelical* became *The Evangelical Presbyterian* in June of that year.

The experience of this church with confessional statements is an unusual one. Eight articles of faith served in this respect at the beginning.

When it became apparent that these were inadequate, the church adopted the Westminster Larger and Shorter Catechisms. Still later it added the Westminster Confession of Faith to its official creed. With the passage of time the body moved more and more toward a Calvinist position in theology, as is indicated by the foregoing sequence and confirmed by the statement of its historian.

The Evangelical Presbyterian Church is closely affiliated with the Free Church of Scotland, through which it conducts its foreign missionary work and to whose theological college it looks for the training of its ministers. Its first foreign missionary was a physician who, in 1937, sailed for Peru, where the Free Church had long carried on missionary activity.

The Evangelical Presbyterian Church is a denomination of only thirteen congregations and about seven hundred members. One congregation is in England, where it maintains close relations with the Evangelical Presbyterian Church in England and Wales, the Free Church of Scotland, the Reformed Church in the Netherlands (Liberated), the Orthodox Presbyterian Church in the United States, and the Free Church in Southern Africa. Affiliated with the British Evangelical Council and the International Conference of Reformed Churches, the Evangelical Presbyterian Church in Ireland publishes the *Evangelical Presbyterian.*

The Free Presbyterian Church of Ulster

The youngest of the Irish Presbyterian denominations is the Free Presbyterian Church, which originated as a schism from the Presbyterian Church in Ireland in 1951. Separation came after many fruitless protests against deviations from that church's historic doctrinal position and its increasing ecumenical activities that reflected a serious departure from Reformed theology. Free Presbyterians cite St. Patrick's Day, 1951, as the birth date of their denomination at the village of Crossgar, County Down, Northern Ireland. The Presbytery of Down had denied the leaders of a local evangelistic effort permission to use the hall of Lissara Presbyterian Church, and elders who refused to accept that decision were suspended from their office. This led those elders to consider Presbytery officials enemies of Christ, since they had made such halls available for public entertainment but closed this one to people seeking the salvation of lost souls.

The decision to prohibit the use of the hall at Lissara was due in part to opposition toward Ian Paisley (b. 1926), the invited evangelist from Ravenhill Evangelical Church in Belfast. Mr. Paisley's fervent orthodoxy and militant resistance to theological liberalism made him unacceptable to the ecumenically minded leaders of the Presbyterian Church in Ireland, who tried to thwart his preaching mission. Paisley's congregation at Ravenhill had withdrawn from the major Presbyterian body in 1927, after the denomination refused to discipline J. E. Davey, a theologian teaching at its college, one who boldly espoused doctrines in conflict with Scripture and historic Presbyterian standards.

The controversy surrounding Davey had led to a trial for heresy, but the church court had sustained Davey's position in the body by an overwhelming majority vote. This decision might not have provoked the secession of the Ravenhill congregation had it been a singular incident, but it was only the latest in a series of such cases. In 1924–1925, for example, F. W. O'Neill, a missionary to China with the Presbyterian Church in Ireland, delivered a series of lectures published as *The Quest for God in China*, a work in which he praised Buddhism and Roman Catholicism while ridiculing the Westminster Confession of Faith for its presentation of historic Christianity as the only truly revealed religion. The O'Neill and Davey cases, preceded by others of a similar character, caused a crisis of conscience for orthodox believers, and those at Ravenhill took action in 1927 to protest the defection of their denomination.

When the Presbytery of Down closed the Lissara church hall only ninety minutes before the scheduled preaching mission was to begin, the resistant elders arranged for the meetings to occur in Killyleagh Grange Hall in the town of Crossgar. God greatly blessed Paisley's preaching in that place, as numerous conversions occurred. When the preaching mission concluded, the elders who arranged it, supported by many ardent believers, chose to form a new church, one free from all connections with the Presbyterian Church of Ireland and its ecumenical affiliations. In this way the Free Presbyterian Church came into being at Crossgar in March 1951. Soon Paisley's own congregation voted to join the brethren at Crossgar, and the Ravenhill Evangelical Church became the Ravenhill Free Presbyterian Church, and soon thereafter other groups of orthodox believers expressed interest in forming additional Free Presbyterian congregations. By 1960 seven such local churches were operating in Ulster, and Paisley was the elected moderator of their presbytery.

From its inception, the new denomination demonstrated vigorous opposition to religious liberalism and to Roman Catholicism. In 1966 a public protest outside the meeting of the Presbyterian Church in Ireland

General Assembly led to the arrest of Paisley and two other ministers, as ecclesiastical and government officials collaborated to silence Free Presbyterian criticisms. Although the marchers had obtained police permission for their demonstration, the authorities charged them with unlawful assembly, and those apprehended spent three months in jail. Upon their release a large crowd of supporters greeted the ministers, who soon resumed their preaching. In a short time a surge of zeal across Ulster produced several more Free Presbyterian congregations, and the ministry of that body extended to the Republic of Ireland with the opening of a congregation in Dublin. In Canada, United States, and Australia as well church extension projects were initiated. By the end of the twentieth century, in Ulster alone there were seventy-five congregations with about fourteen thousand members, while another twenty-four congregations were subject to the Ulster Presbytery, but Paisley urged those in North America to form their own governing court. This became a reality in 2005, as the Free Presbyterian Church became a denomination of two presbyteries.

This church subscribes to the historic Westminster Confession of Faith but with a significant modification that allows for both the traditional Reformed view of infant baptism and the Baptist practice of administering the sacrament to none but professing believers. Free Presbyterians abstain from tobacco and alcoholic beverages and disdain contemporary modes of worship deemed to be oriented toward entertainment. The church maintains Whitefield College of the Bible in Northern Ireland and Geneva Reformed Seminary in the United States as the principal schools for educating its ministers. The denomination has no organic connection with other churches. Its publications are *The Revivalist* and *Truth for Youth*. Kenya is the major site of Free Presbyterian foreign missions.

SUGGESTED ADDITIONAL READINGS >>

Bruce, Steve. *God Save Ulster: The Religion and Politics of Paisleyism.* Oxford: Oxford University Press, 1989.

Ford, Alan. *The Protestant Reformation in Ireland, 1590–1641.* Portland, Ore.: Four Courts Presbyterian, 1985.

Gribben, Crawford. *The Irish Puritans.* Darlington, U.K.: Evangelical Press, 2003.

Hamilton, Thomas. *History of Presbyterianism in Ireland.* 2nd ed. Belfast: Ambassador Productions, 1992. Reprint of 1887 edition.

Hogan, Edmund M. *The Irish Missionary Movement: A Historical Survey, 1830–1980.* Dublin: Gill and Macmillan, 1990.

Holmes, Andrew R. *The Shaping of Ulster Presbyterian Belief and Practice, 1770–1840.* Oxford: Oxford University Press, 2006.

Holmes, Finlay. *The Presbyterian Church in Ireland: A Popular History.* Dublin: Columba, 2000.

Lennon, Colm. *The Lords of Dublin in the Age of the Reformation.* Dublin: Irish Academic, 1989.

Moore, Tom. *A History of the First Presbyterian Church Belfast, 1644–1983.* Belfast: First Presbyterian Church, 1983.

Paisley, Rhonda. *Ian Paisley, My Father.* Basingstoke, U.K.: Marshall, Morgan, and Scott, 1988.

Porter, J. L. *The Life and Times of Henry Cooke.* Belfast: Ambassador Publications, 1999. Reprint of 1871 edition.

Thomas, Jack, ed. *Into All the World: A History of the Overseas Work of the Presbyterian Church in Ireland, 1840–1980.* Belfast: Overseas Board of the Presbyterian Church in Ireland, 1990.

Wells, Ronald A. and Brian S. Mawhinney. *Conflict and Christianity in Northern Ireland.* Grand Rapids: Eerdmans, 1975.

NINE

England and Wales

Presbyterian Beginnings in England

Anglican dominance was the pattern of church life in England after passage of the Settlement of 1559, a measure that affirmed the Church of England with episcopal polity. The Presbyterian presence at that time was small, and few records remain. Elizabeth I (r. 1558–1603) insisted upon a *via media,* a broad Protestant church that allowed for some latitude in doctrine and practice, even though its Articles of Religion were staunchly Calvinistic in content. The law mandated the liturgy prescribed in the Book of Common Prayer, and the monarch, as supreme governor, held ultimate authority over the Church of England.

Among the staunchest Protestants, the Elizabethan Settlement was not acceptable because it affirmed Reformed theology on one hand but rejected Presbyterian polity on the other. Whereas some Anglicans considered the form of church government optional, Presbyterians regarded it a divine requirement. Critics of the Church of England included learned theologians who had lived as refugees in Switzerland during the years of Bloody Mary's reign (1553–1558), and while there they had adopted the Reformed view of polity as a scriptural mandate that was not negotiable. The queen's opponents on this issue became known as Puritans, but not all who bore that name subscribed to the Presbyterian doctrine of church government. Elizabeth had no zest for persecuting dissenters, but she insisted upon her own authority over religious matters, a posture that aggravated Puritans in general, and Presbyterians in particular. The Protestant rigorists could not, however, afford to alienate the queen entirely, for she was England's bulwark against any resurgence of Catholicism.

The most prominent champion of Presbyterianism at that time was Thomas Cartwright (1535–1603), a Cambridge University professor whose lectures on the New Testament Acts of the Apostles included rejection of episcopacy and a strong advocacy of Presbyterian polity. Cartwright's bold assertions cost him his position at the university, and soon he left for Geneva, where he joined Beza, Calvin's successor as chief pastor of the Reformed church there. Gradually many Puritans, like Cartwright, became convinced the Church of England could not be further reformed, and they cited the monarch's obstinacy as the principal reason. Those of Presbyterian persuasion were particularly disturbed about the queen's intransigent support for episcopacy. This led them, along with the Independents, to become nonconformists, that is, those who refused to submit to the church established by law in the 1559 Act of Uniformity. Their dispute with the Church of England was ecclesiological, not theological, since almost all Puritans were Calvinists.

In 1572 Presbyterian ministers John Field (1525–1587) and Thomas Wilcox (ca. 1549–1608) prepared *An Admonition for the Reformation of Church Discipline*, a treatise in which they requested termination of prelacy in the Church of England and the adoption of Presbyterianism in its place. The royal government responded by arresting Field and Wilcox and ordered the suppression of their publication. Thomas Cartwright returned from the Continent in time to participate in this controversy.

A Presbytery at Wandsworth

Before 1572 ended, some Puritan dissenters replied to the royal policy by forming a presbytery of sorts at Wandsworth, a suburb of London. This was not a fully developed church court in the Reformed tradition but a segment of the congregation at the local parish, a group that elected elders and then tried to function as a "church within a church" (*ecclesiola in ecclesia*) in order to promote the purification of the church in piety and polity. Soon comparable groups in other areas were following the example of Wandsworth, much to the chagrin of the queen and her bishops, who viewed this development as potentially subversive.

Opposition from the Crown

Even before the appearance of Presbyterian interest at Wandsworth, some Puritan ministers had been meeting in private for mutual edification, exercises they called *prophesying*. Queen Elizabeth suspected these meetings would produce antigovernment agitations, so she ordered Archbishop Edmund Grindal (1519–1583) to suppress them, but Grindal, a prelate of Puritan doctrinal beliefs, respectfully refused. The offended monarch then commanded all bishops throughout England to stop the prophesyings and to threaten imprisonment for any who persisted in the practice. Grindal fell from royal favor and was about to resign when he died in 1583. Three years earlier Parliament had enacted a law forbidding publication of Puritan books that opposed prelacy. The same legislation imposed fines upon people who did not attend services of the established church. The queen's new archbishop of Canterbury was John Whitgift (ca. 1530–1604), an anti-Presbyterian, who had earlier obtained the removal of Cartwright from Cambridge University.

Royal opposition notwithstanding, secret gatherings of Puritan-Presbyterian ministers continued, and out of such assemblies came a Book of Discipline as a basis for organizing sessions and presbyteries in the classical Reformed model. By 1590 about five hundred ministers had subscribed to the Book of Discipline, thereby declaring Presbyterian polity to be a divine mandate. It appeared Presbyterianism was becoming a powerful force in England, one that even the determined and dynamic queen could not thwart. Her policies actually increased the resolve of the Presbyterians, who boldly circulated leaflets known as *Marprelate Tracts* as a means by which to denounce the practice of prelacy, sometimes in crude language.

Queen Elizabeth, a bold, assertive woman, was not easily intimidated or deterred. Her method of combating the Presbyterians was to use the episcopate and Parliament plus a newly created High Commission to thwart her opponents. The commission was a court in which was no jury, and it could impose sentences of fines and imprisonments from which there could be no appeal. The commission decreed execution for a few of the vociferous critics of royal policy, and the Presbyterian movement lost strength in the last years of Elizabeth's reign.

Reigns of James I and Charles I
The accession of James I (r. 1603–1625; James VI in Scotland) produced even greater hostility toward Puritans and Presbyterians. As monarch in Scotland since 1567, James Stuart had maintained severe disdain for Presbyterianism with its insistence on limited government and the independent authority of the church. Once in England he embraced the Anglican establishment heartily and resolved to tolerate no dissent. The Presbyterian cause therefore made little progress in England during his reign. Some recalcitrant Puritans fled to America, while many who remained in England refused to comply with the king's demands.

Charles I (1625–1649) was even more hostile to Puritan-Presbyterian beliefs than his predecessor, for the new ruler despised their doctrine as well as their polity. With Archbishop of Canterbury William Laud, who served him until 1645, Charles strove to impose episcopacy in both of his domains. Defiant Puritan resistance led to civil war.

Puritan Belligerence

Adamant and tactless insistence upon divine-right monarchy produced almost constant friction between the Crown and Parliament during the reigns of the first two Stuart monarchs. Contentions about religion were not the only issues, but to the Puritans they were the foremost concerns. In 1641 several London ministers therefore requested the Houses of Parliament to petition the king to allow a convocation to examine the state of religion in the realm. A bill to accomplish that objective passed in the legislature, but the king rejected it. Parliament then, on its own authority, convened an assembly of learned ministers to consider "the settlement of the government and liturgy of the Church of England; and for the vindicating and clearing of the doctrine of the said church from false aspersions and interpretations." Invited participants were to meet in the chapel of Henry VII at Westminster, and 121 ministers and thirty laymen gathered to plan the further reform of the Anglican Church, although Parliament had given them only a consultative role.

Westminster Assembly (1643–1648)

Deliberations began on June 13, 1643, with the goal of ridding the Church of England of prelacy and achieving purity in doctrine. It quickly became evident, however, that not all Puritans held the same ecclesiology. A few members argued for an Erastian polity. That is, they adhered to the teaching of Thomas Erastus (1524–1583), a Swiss Reformer, who maintained the civil government should have authority over church discipline, for it alone enjoys the God-given right to impose penalties. Although Erastus did not espouse full state control of the church, fear that his view might lead to that caused the Westminster Assembly to reject it. A few other participants favored episcopacy, but that opinion was completely unacceptable to a large majority of those present. The major dispute was Presbyterianism versus Congregationalism, or Independency.

Since the king was already at war with Parliament, his bishops did not attend, although four of them had received invitations to do so. The assembly resolved to seek reform in all three British kingdoms, in two of which, Scotland and Ireland, Presbyterianism flourished already. For five and a half years, meeting at intervals, the body worked for reforms. Most of the members favored the Presbyterian position, but in England it was not to prevail. The assembly was a creation of Parliament, and its conclusions took effect only when Parliament ratified them.

As explained in the chapter on Scotland, the Westminster Assembly at first proposed to revise the Anglican Thirty-Nine Articles of Religion, but after much discussion the commissioners decided to draft new documents as the best way to express the Reformed faith. They abandoned the Book of Common Prayer and adopted their own form of government and the Westminster Confession of Faith and Larger and Shorter Catechisms.

On June 19, 1647, Parliament declared all parishes in England and Wales must submit to Presbyterian polity as agreed upon at the Westminster Assembly. This provided for the creation of presbyteries, synods, and a national assembly. The Presbyterian cause appeared to be at the threshold of triumph, but the strange sequel shows that the assembly performed a work of inestimable and permanent value for Presbyterians in Scotland, Ireland, America, and the world at large, but it had almost no lasting effect in England, the country for which the commissioners designed their actions. A provincial synod did begin work in London in May 1647, but by August 1660 it was no longer operating. A comparable effort in Lancashire enjoyed an even shorter lifespan.

Reasons for Presbyterian Failure

Several factors contributed to Presbyterian failure in England, and political issues were prominent among them. Since the Westminster Assembly was a creation of Parliament, political considerations were bound to be influential. The war with the king's forces did not go well at first, a development that led Parliament to seek aid from the Scots, who in turn required English acceptance of the Solemn League and Covenant as a condition for their support. Six Scots joined the Westminster Assembly but did not vote in its proceedings. Their influence was, nevertheless, decisive in leading that body to draft new doctrinal standards rather than revise the Anglican ones. Few Englishmen were familiar with Presbyterian polity, and England's Parliament did not relish the prospect of a church independent of state control. The Erastians lost in the assembly but won in Parliament. The most important figure in preventing the triumph of Presbyterianism was Oliver

Cromwell (r. 1653–1658), an Independent who rather feared a Presbyterian victory would lead to suppression of the Congregationalists. Independents dominated the Puritan army, with which Cromwell was a hero.

Presbyterians wanted the church to be free from state control, but they expected the state to support the church and to prevent dissenters from undermining its position. Because of this aspiration, they acquired a reputation for being opposed to freedom of religion. From their perspective, the Independents feared they might exchange Arminian tyranny for Calvinist tyranny. When Presbyterians protested the execution of Charles I, Cromwell and other Independents became even more alarmed. Presbyterians were, in general, glad to see the end of the interregnum, a posture that excited further suspicion, and their emphasis upon ecclesiastical discipline led many Englishmen to dislike their polity.

Triumph of Monarchy and Episcopacy

Most Presbyterians welcomed the royal restoration in 1660, perhaps because Charles II (r. 1660–1685) was a Scot and because he had promised to respect freedom of religion. In the Declaration of Breda Charles agreed to implement freedom of religion and to support enactment of a law to protect it. Beyond that, he signed the Solemn League and Covenant.

At first the new monarch appeared to honor his commitment, as he arranged a conference between twelve Anglican bishops and twelve representative Puritan and Presbyterian ministers. It met at the Savoy Palace in 1661 but accomplished little. By the time that meeting occurred, England had elected a strongly monarchist and pro-Anglican House of Commons, while bishops of the Church of England, sitting in the House of Lords, were, for the most part, averse to any compromise of traditional Anglican polity.

Act of Uniformity (1662)

Once Charles II was convinced the temper of the nation had become anti-Puritan, he assumed the posture of an enemy of Puritan interests, as the Act of Uniformity attests. This legislation, which required all ministers to obtain episcopal ordination or vacate their churches, left no uncertainty about the monarch's disposition toward nonconformity in religion. The same law ordered all pastors to use the Book of Common Prayer. About two thousand clerics, most of them Presbyterians, suffered ejection from their pulpits rather than comply with the law. The effect of this enforced uniformity was to eliminate any organized Presbyterian structure in England. Puritans were, at that point, forced out of the Church of England.

Ministers ousted from the establishment sometimes held unapproved religious services, but the Conventicle Act (1664) levied fines and imprisonment on those who did so. The law forbade dissenting ministers to teach school or to reside within five miles of their previous churches. A second Conventicle Act (1670) increased the penalties of the first legislation, but some services continued in secret anyway.

The Glorious Revolution (1688–1689) brought some improvement in the fortunes of England's Puritans, and for a brief time Presbyterians and Congregationalists drew together in cordial cooperation. Disputes about the law and the gospel, contentions that included charges of antinomianism, however, produced a rupture between the two groups near the end of the seventeenth century. Presbyterians were, at that point, disposed to open chapels without seeking to connect them through church courts, a practice that hastened the decline of their own polity. Every pastor in this arrangement operated autonomously with no accountability to any authority, and, as a consequence, the Presbyterian Church of England became weak and drifted into teaching dubious doctrines.

Departures from the Reformed Faith

The rise of Arminianism within the Church of England affected dissenting bodies adversely, a condition that became evident by the opening of the eighteenth century. Arminian soteriology and Socinian theology gained popularity with many intellectuals attracted to a rationalist worldview. As these heresies spread through the churches, personal piety declined and numerical strength waned. In 1715 there were about 550 Presbyterian congregations in England, but by 1772 there were only 302, and many of them were not orthodox.

A major factor in the decline of English Presbyterianism was the abandonment of subscription to the Westminster Confession of Faith. This led some concerned Presbyterians to meet in London in order to assess the reasons for the decline of their denomination, but they did not agree to restore mandatory subscription to the confession. Since Presbyterians no longer had courts above the local sessions, there was no way to discipline teachers of false doctrine, and eventually many Presbyterian congregations became Unitarian and Arminian in doctrine, congregational in polity.

Thus, as J. N. Ogilvie, writes, "under the chilling influences of civil persecution, social ostracism, and spiritual infidelity, Presbyterianism in the eighteenth century drooped, and all but died. Isolated congregations remained throughout the country which were Presbyterian in name, but with a few bright exceptions, they had adopted the Unitarian creed, and the Congregational mode of government."[*]

Resuscitation and Reorganization of Presbyterianism

Early in the nineteenth century a brighter day dawned on the feeble remnant of the Presbyterian Church of England. Several influences were helpful to its revival and growth. In the first place, the great Wesleyan revival had infused a large measure of evangelical fervor into the church life of England. This was felt especially among the dissenting bodies, and the scattered congregations of Presbyterians that were more or less loyal to the faith of the fathers began to strengthen the things that remained and had been ready to die.

In the second place, the revival of evangelical piety in the churches of Scotland, which put an end to the long and blighting reign of Moderatism, contributed to a similar revival in churches in England that were closely united in sympathy with the Presbyterianism of Scotland. In the northern counties of England that bordered on Scotland, there were quite a number of the old English churches that, through all the vicissitudes of intervening years, had maintained the Westminster type of Presbyterianism in its purity, insofar, at least, as their circumstances would permit. They had sent their sons to Scottish universities to be trained for their pulpits, and they had been served by ministers from the Scottish churches.

In the third place there were an increasing number of immigrants from Scotland settling in the great centers of English population. These sometimes formed churches of their own and sometimes cast in their lot with the English survivors. In either case they helped to draw ministers from the Scottish churches.

Survival of English Presbyterianism

As indicated, the revival in which John and Charles Wesley and George Whitefield were prominent produced some resurgence of strength among

---

[*]J. N. Ogilvie, *The Presbyterian Churches: Their Place and Power in Modern Christendom* (Philadelphia: Westminster Press, 1897), 95.

English Presbyterians, who demonstrated a renewal in piety and interest in sound doctrine. As a consequence some previously stagnant congregations realized a revival of spiritual fervor. The Toleration Act (1689) allowed freedom of worship to nonconformists who obtained a license from the civil authorities, but dissenters still had to pay tithes to the Church of England. Toleration did not extend to Roman Catholics or Unitarians, but many of the latter called themselves Presbyterians, as broad toleration in practice occurred while discrimination remained in principle. The Wesleys were able to preach freely because of the new policy, while at the same time evangelistic Scots crossed into England to spread Reformed doctrine. Many such Scotsmen settled in northern England to spread Reformed doctrine, and there Scottish pastors served English congregations. After the Act of Union (1707) united England and Scotland politically, even more Scottish Presbyterians lived and evangelized in northern England, and a modest resurgence of Presbyterianism occurred, one that allowed for the formation of church courts once more. Some Scottish preachers serving in England were from the Secession Church.

Reorganization of the Presbyterian Church of England early in the nineteenth century became evident when, in 1836, a number of congregations holding to the Westminster Confession of Faith formed a synod. When the Free Church of Scotland seceded from the national church in 1843, most of the synod in England supported the secession and severed its connections with the Church of Scotland. A parliamentary enactment in 1844 allowed Unitarian congregations that had once been Presbyterian to retain their properties, if they had held and used them at least twenty-five years.

In 1867 churches with Secession roots in northern England were sufficiently strong and numerous to constitute an English Synod of the United Presbyterian Church of Scotland, and 1876 brought the union of that body with the Synod of the Presbyterian Church of England, a denomination of about fifty thousand members. By the twentieth century the Presbyterian Church of England had about three hundred congregations serving about sixty thousand constituents, but it was once more experiencing decline. In 1890 the synod had adopted a revised confession known as the Articles of Faith, a document that reproduced most, but not all, of the historic Westminster Confession. In 1906, the same synod declared its right to alter its constitution and subordinate doctrinal standards "as duty may require," a rather ambiguous statement that could allow for substantial deviations from historic Reformed theology.

Developments since World War I

The effects of the Great War (1914–1918) upon the Presbyterians of England were very damaging. Many church members perished in combat, and forty-one pastors left their congregations to become military chaplains. The subsequent lack of pastoral leadership caused some local churches to close, as church life in general declined. This weakened condition led leaders of the Presbyterian Church to seek closer relations with other free churches and with the Calvinistic Methodist Church in Wales. When the Great War ended, English Presbyterians were in a poor financial condition, a fact evident in the low salaries many ministers received. In response to critical losses facing their church, Presbyterians in 1922 authorized women to assume offices previously reserved for men.

Despite declining membership and serious financial difficulties, the Presbyterian Church of England managed to maintain its program for ministerial education, an enterprise in which the church enjoyed the services of some noteworthy academic theologians. The denomination's major theological school had been established in London in 1844 but had moved to Cambridge in 1899. Westminster College remained the church's divinity school for many years, until it joined the Chestnut College, an institution of the former Congregational Union, and thereafter served both denominations. Some professors at Westminster College earned international reputations not only for their erudition but for their liberal persuasion as well.

James Oswald Dykes (1835–1912), a native Scot educated at the University of Edinburgh and New College in the United Kingdom and at the universities in Heidelberg and Erlangen in Germany, was principal and professor of theology at Westminster College from 1888–1907 and while there published three books about the kingdom of God plus a work titled *The Divine Worker in Creation and Providence* (1907).

A second scholar of note was John Skinner (1851–1925), Dykes's successor as principal at Westminster College, a man who earned acclaim as an Old Testament specialist, although one who subscribed to higher critical theories about the composition of the Bible's books. Skinner's *Critical and Exegetical Commentary on Genesis* (1910) received wide applause in liberal circles, as did his commentaries on the books of Samuel, Kings, Isaiah, and Ezekiel. *Prophecy and Religion* is his interpretation of Jeremiah.

Another Scotsman who made a major contribution to English Presbyterianism was John Wood Oman (1860–1939), who studied at Edinburgh and then in Germany before becoming a pastor at Paisley, Scotland. From there he moved to England, where, in 1907, he became principal at Westminster College. Oman was author of *The Natural and the Supernatural* and *Concerning the Ministry*.

Herbert H. Farmer (1892–1981), a native Englishman and a graduate of Westminster College, served in a pastoral ministry until 1931 and then moved to the United States to teach at the Hartford Seminary Foundation for four years. He returned to Westminster College to become the successor to Oman as professor of systematic theology. Farmer's first noteworthy publication, *The World and God*, appeared in 1935. It is a work that shows clearly he was not an orthodox Calvinist but rather a philosopher of religion much indebted to the teaching of Immanuel Kant. In 1949 Cambridge University appointed him Norris-Hulse Professor of Divinity, and in that position he promoted his liberal ideas, especially his fondness for exalting religious experience rather than biblical doctrines. A volume of his sermons titled *The Healing Cross* (1938) expressed this preference even before he assumed a position at Cambridge. Farmer was highly influential in English Presbyterian circles, especially because of his role in the education of ministers.

Another distinguished Scot who served English Presbyterians was William Robertson Nicoll (1851–1923), a minister of the Free Church educated at the University of Aberdeen. Nicoll was a skillful editor of religious periodicals as well as major publishing projects such as the *Expositor's Greek New Testament* and the *Expositor's Bible*. He founded the *British Weekly* in 1886 as an organ to advocate Christian social responsibility, and his own books, such as *The Return of the Cross*, *The Church's One Foundation*, and *Reunion in Eternity*, enjoyed wide popularity.

As an organizer and editor of multivolume works, Nicoll enlisted scholars who applied the methods of higher criticism to the Scriptures in order to relate them to literary, scientific, and philosophic trends of the early twentieth century. George Adam Smith, for example, contributed two volumes on Isaiah to the *Expositor's Bible*, while Marcus Dods (1834–1904) wrote a commentary titled *The Gospel of John* for the same series. These and other authors Nicoll employed continued to affirm the divine character of the Bible, even as their concessions to higher criticism weakened confidence in its integrity and therefore its authority as God's Word. Dods, for example, in *Revelation and Inspiration* (1877) and in *The Bible: Its Origins and Nature* (1905) maintained there are numerous errors of detail in Scripture while the overall message is reliable.

While theological education was moving in the direction of liberalism, English Presbyterians conducted overseas missions in Taiwan, Malaya, India, and Hong Kong. Church membership declined, nevertheless, as the twentieth century moved forward. The Second World War brought destruction of some church buildings, including that of Regent Square Presbyterian Church, one of the stronger congregations of the denomination. Several local churches in the area of London dissolved during the decade after the war.

The general weakness of the Presbyterian Church of England and the dispirited outlook of its leaders led to a merger with the Congregational Church in England and Wales. In 1972 almost all remaining Presbyterian congregations in England joined the newly created United Reformed Church. A large majority of Congregational churches did the same, including most of those in Wales. The local churches of strictly Welsh origin, especially ones conducting Welsh language services, remained separate.

By 1971, just before the formation of the United Reformed Church, the Presbyterian Church of England had only about 56,700 communicant members and 303 congregations, while the Congregational Church had about 162,800 members in 2,133 congregations. Perhaps because the Presbyterians were weaker, they were more enthusiastic for the merger than were their new ecclesiastical partners. Only two Presbyterian churches declined to endorse the union. They instead united with the Church of Scotland.

Further evidence of the impoverished condition of English Presbyterianism appeared in 1980, when the Reformed Association of Churches of Christ, a body that rejected infant baptism, a historic distinctive of both Presbyterian and Congregational belief, was received into the United Reformed Church. Thereafter the united denomination recognized both infant and believer's baptism as options for church members. This decision reflected the ecumenical character of the United Reformed Church, in which doctrinal exactitude is not a major concern.

By the end of the twentieth century, the United Reformed Church had 102,500 members in 1,768 congregations. It ordains women as ministers and is a member of the World Alliance of Reformed Churches and the World Council of Churches. For the education of pastors the church relies on British universities, and a monthly publication titled *Reform* is its official organ.

Presbyterianism in Wales

Presbyterianism in Wales for many years bore two distinguishing marks. It was decidedly Welsh and was not Presbyterian—at least not in name. The denominational designation was Calvinistic Methodist Church, but the use of the term *Methodist* primarily related to neither doctrine nor polity but rather to manner of life, much in line with its earlier significance in England. Furthermore, the church originated in those times when the Methodist revival was sweeping the country. *Calvinistic* was added only after the Wesleyans entered Wales.

Chronologically speaking, the Welsh Calvinistic Methodist Church is somewhat of a newcomer to the Presbyterian family in Britain, actually dating as a separate entity from its first ordination of ministers in 1811. Its roots run back to a revival in 1735 to 1736, followed by an association meeting held in January 1743 at which George Whitefield (1714–1770) presided. Long before these events, in 1567, publication of the New Testament in the Welsh language had prepared the way for the furtherance of the gospel in that land. A native version of the entire Bible followed twenty-one years later. During the days of the Commonwealth, on February 22, 1649, Parliament passed a singular Act for the Better Propagation and Preaching of the Gospel in Wales. As was true with regard to certain other statutes enacted by that body, the Anglicans brought intemperate, though not entirely unjustified, indictment against this measure.

For seventy-five years the movement that culminated in the church's organization, like Presbyterianism in Elizabethan England, remained within the bounds of the Anglican communion. The work of Griffith Jones (1683–1761), a minister of the Church of England, proved an unpremeditated prelude to the formation of the Calvinistic Methodist Church. Impressed by the number of persons unable to read, he established what came to be known as Circulating Schools (1730). These took their name from the itineration of the teachers who moved from place to place after a stay of several months in each location. Jones published an annual, *Welsh Piety* (1737–1761), which incorporated an account of their conduct and progress.

Howell Harris (1714–1773), a lay preacher whom the Anglicans declined to ordain, was not only a convert of, but a leading spirit in, the revival of religion that began in 1735. This was likewise true of Daniel

Rowlands (1713–1790), the early Apostle of North Wales, ordained by the Anglicans in that year. Associated in this enterprise were two other ministers, Howell Davies (ca. 1716–1770) and Peter Williams (1722–1796), the latter of whom the Calvinistic Methodists eventually expelled on charges growing out of certain notes appearing in a commentary of the Bible that he published in 1770. The renowned evangelist, George Whitefield, lent his influence to the movement. One of the most widely known of the early Welsh preachers was William Williams (1717–1791) of Pantycelyn, author of the familiar hymn "Guide Me, O Thou Great Jehovah."

Interested participants in the revival formed what they termed "societies," the first of these being established at Wernos in Brecknoshire in May 1737. County societies soon followed in 1740, and an even more comprehensive association convened at Dygoedydd, Carmathernshire, two years later. These groups functioned within the framework of Anglicanism, but that church gave them little if any support or encouragement. At times the societies were subjected to persecution, their members suffering both legal indictment and illegal harassment.

An untimely break between Harris and Rowland, known in Calvinistic Methodist circles as "The Rupture," took place in December 1752. This followed a period in which Harris had repeatedly used expressions indicative of his belief that the first person of the Trinity had suffered in the earthly sufferings of the Savior. Harris discontinued all fellowship with the association, even forming another such body. He established a sort of monastery at Trevecca, spent some time in the militia during the war with France, and became reconciled with Rowlands in 1769.

With the passage of time the need for additional ministers became more evident, a need that the Church of England did not meet. Eventually, in the summer of 1811, the Quarterly Association, the ranking body of this nature within the movement, ordained twenty-one men to the ministry. The association took this action entirely independent of the authorities of the Anglican Church, although Thomas Charles (1755–1814) of Bala, who conducted the services of ordination for the first eight of those thus set apart for the ministry, had formerly served as a curate in that order.

Charles was one of the great leaders in the history of the Calvinistic Methodists and has been repeatedly identified as the organizer of their church. He was this and more. As an effective itinerating preacher, devoting a great part of his effort to North Wales; promoter of traveling schools and Sunday schools; one of the founders of the British and Foreign Bible

Society; and author, editor, publisher, and printer of religious literature, he left his church and a wider circle of Christian people his continuing debtors when he died. He composed a Welsh catechism that went through dozens of editions, and in 1808 issued a four-volume work titled *Geiriadur Ysgrythyrol* (Scriptural dictionary), described by one of his admirers as "next to the Bible, the best book in the Welsh language."

Among other ministers prominent in the affairs of the Calvinistic Methodist Church during its formative years were Thomas Jones (1756–1820) of Denbigh (Thomas Joneses in Wales are like John Smiths in America and are plentiful among the Welsh clergy) and John Elias (1774–1841). Jones was one of eight lay preachers originally ordained to the church's ministry in 1811, an associate of Thomas Charles, and came to occupy a prominent position in the councils of his denomination. John Elias, who was John Jones by birth, assumed the surname of his grandfather in appreciative token of that ancestor's spiritual influence upon him. He was among the powerful preachers of the Calvinistic Methodists. An unswerving Calvinist, he exercised varied gifts of leadership among his brethren for a number of years, especially during the two decades following the death of Thomas Jones.

Ecclesiastical Organization

The assumption of the powers of ordination both necessitated and signaled a formal break with episcopacy, and further organizational development necessarily ensued. Two quarterly associations were formed, one for the north and the other representing the south of Wales. A Calvinistic Confession of Faith, adopted in 1823, consisted of forty-four articles and was patterned after the Westminster Confession. In 1826 a Constitutional Deed followed, and this was registered with the civil authorities.

It had become obvious that if the church proposed to ordain its own ministers, it had to provide facilities for their education. Accordingly, the Connexion, as the body was known, established two theological colleges, one at Bala in 1837, to be adopted by the North Wales Association two years later, and another at Trevecca by the South Wales Association in 1842. In 1905 the latter was transferred to Aberystwyth.

To a Home Mission Society, dating from 1814, the church added foreign missionary endeavors, which were directed toward India, in 1840. It began evangelistic work in Brittany (France) during 1842, selecting this field because of the kinship of the Welsh and the Bretons. Up to this time many of its members had supported the London Missionary Society.

The church in Wales has historically flourished on revivals, and one such season of refreshing took place during 1858 to 1862, in which David Morgan proved an effective preacher. Additions to the Calvinistic Methodist Church within this period are said to have numbered thirty-five thousand. The revivalists held services in many different places, including meetings conducted far underground in the mines of Wales.

The Calvinistic Methodists added a General Assembly to the structure of their church in 1864. This body long exercised much less authority over the regional associations than is usual in such instances, acting chiefly in an advisory capacity. It still falls short of possessing the powers traditionally assigned to such a court.

Lewis Edwards (1809–1887), a student in London and later at the University of Edinburgh and for fifty years principal of what became known as Bala College, is credited with introducing a number of Presbyterian principles into the Calvinistic Methodist Church. His son, Thomas Charles Edwards (1837–1900), succeeded his father at Bala after an interval of several years and added further distinction to the family name in educational circles of the church.

In 1889 Presbyterians of Wales living along the borders met for the first time in what was soon to develop into an annual conference. In 1856 an English-speaking Sunday school had come upon the scene at Aberdare in Wales. This work grew into Trinity Church, which the synod of the Presbyterian Church of England took over in 1875 in rather peremptory fashion, leading to a lengthy controversy. This growing use of the English language gave rise to what came to be known as the "English Causes." Ultimately the church granted legislative powers within its own territory to this group as the Association of the East after the Second World War.

The Forward Movement, inaugurated in 1893 with a view to reaching English-speaking Welshmen, gave a decided impetus to the work of home missions. This led to the erection of numerous halls in Welsh centers that enabled the Connexion to reach many who otherwise would never have come under its influence.

The relatively youthful Evan John Roberts (1878–1951), a former collier and later blacksmith, was the central figure in a revival that visited Wales in 1904 to 1905. Large congregations and great singing were characteristic of services held in this connection, in the course of which thousands of persons came into the church. Song, prayer, testimony, and exhortation largely displaced the formal sermons usually associated with such seasons. Various individuals, including Roberts himself, gave evidence of susceptibility to the influence of the occult and the psychic during these times, but these involvements were generally subordinated to the more important aspects of the movement. In spite of some subsequent retrogression, the Connexion profited substantially from the awakening.

Cylchgrawn Cymdeithas Hanes Eglwys Methodistiaid Calfinaidd Cymru, further identified on its title page as *The Journal of the Historical Society,* was organized. Certain of the *Journal's* articles appear in Welsh, while others are published in English, indicative of the bilingualism of the church as well as that of its circle of readers.

Twentieth-Century Developments

The twentieth century was a time of change. In 1972 an act of Parliament added "Presbyterian Church of Wales" to the Connexion. The original Constitutional Deed of the Church (1826) prescribed that "no alteration of Doctrine to be taught and maintained by the said connexion shall be at any time allowed or even discussed." On July 18, 1933, Royal Assent confirmed a parliamentary act that modified these provisions and authorized the church to act autonomously with regard to spiritual matters. In the following year Parliament passed such legislation as raised the status of the General Assembly to a position coordinate with that of the associations with respect to constitutional affairs.

The Presbyterian Churches of England and Wales entered into an agreement in 1944 whereby ministers of the two bodies were placed in a position of mutual eligibility. This rendered pastoral interchange quite practical and strengthened the ties existing between these neighboring churches.

The church adopted a very brief confession of faith in 1957. This consists of six short paragraphs intended for use in services of worship. It follows the order and echoes the substance of the Apostles' Creed, closing with a statement embodying the answer to the first question of the Westminster Shorter Catechism.

A Short Confession of Our Faith

We believe in God, the Father Almighty, Creator and Ruler of all things.

We believe in Jesus Christ, His Only Begotten Son, our Lord and Savior.

Through His life, His death on the cross, and His resurrection, He conquered sin and death, forgiving our sins and
reconciling us to God.

We believe in the Holy Spirit; through Him Christ dwells in
the believers, sanctifying them in the truth.

We believe in the Church, the Body of Christ and the fellowship of the saints; in the Holy Scriptures, in the ministry of
the Word and the Sacraments.

We believe in the coming of the Kingdom of God, and in the
blessed hope of life eternal through our Lord Jesus Christ.

We believe that the chief end of man is to glorify God and to
enjoy Him forever.

With the beginning of 1958, a scheme for the support of the ministry
became a part of the church's program. Under its provisions each of the
pastors receives an equal salary from the central fund of the denomination.
Individual congregations have the privilege and opportunity of increasing
this compensation through direct remuneration of their own pastors.

The General Assembly of 1962 launched a campaign to secure the sum
of 150,000 pounds for the cause of church extension. A shifting population
had emphasized the need for church buildings in new locations. By 1964
the Connexion was in process of reorganizing its facilities for the preparation of ministers. As a result, it arranged to center all such education in the
theological college at Aberystwyth.

During the late 1960s and early 1970s several ministers withdrew
from the Welsh church in protest against what they considered to be its
laxity in doctrinal matters. Seven of the twenty-eight ministerial students
resigned from the theological college of the church in the spring of 1967
for similar reasons. The action of the General Assembly in designating the
short declaration of 1933 as the church's official standard of faith and order
proved to be a particular point of controversy in this connection, since critics contended that this decision relegated the original confession of 1823
to a place of secondary importance—a "museum piece," was the descriptive
phrase used by one of their number.

In the same context the organization of what came to be known as the
Reformed Presbyterian Church in Wales followed the withdrawal of two
of the smaller Presbyterian congregations of the city of Cardiff in the summer of 1968. These local churches attributed the dissolution of their ties

with the parent church to what they termed "a serious departure from the Scripture principles upon which the founders of this Connexion built," on the part of the Presbyterian Church in Wales.

The church in Wales evidenced the same propensity toward decline in communicants that marked the course of a number of Presbyterian bodies of other lands during the seventies and eighties of the twentieth century, though in this case the downward trend began much earlier. These losses, which have been in part at least attributed to unemployment and to World War II, were of such a drastic nature that by 1974 the church's membership had fallen below the one-hundred-thousand mark for the first time during the century. Twenty years earlier this membership figure had exceeded one hundred and eighty thousand. There was even a greater proportionate decrease in the ministerial forces of the church, with the total of those in pastoral service standing at 288 at the end of the twenty-year period. Whereupon, the General Assembly turned toward the possibility of recruiting and training lay preachers in an effort to supply this lack of ordained leaders. There were those who suggested that such shortage might be overcome through the expedient of ordaining women to the ministry.

Publications of a periodical nature in the Calvinistic Methodist Church of Wales have for many years appeared in the English as well as in the Welsh language. *Trysorfa Ysprydol* (Spiritual treasury) was the title of a very early religious quarterly begun in 1799 by Thomas Charles and Thomas Jones of Denbigh. This periodical ran until 1802 and, upon revival, from 1809 until 1813.

In 1912 the church acquired *Y Traethodydd* (The essayist) by purchase. This theological journal dated back to 1845. *Y Drysorfa* (The treasury) and *Trysorfa y Plant* (Children's treasury), which began publication in 1862, centered their attention upon the work of the church. This was likewise true of the foreign missionary journal, *Newyddion Da* (Good news), published 1881–1885 and 1892–1893.

Y Coleuad (The light), long the official weekly of the Connexion, began as a private venture in 1869 with the promise of support from many churchmen. The denomination arranged for the purchase of this paper in 1912 and first published it in 1914. *Y Cymro* (The Welshman) originated as an independent weekly in the latter year and soon established itself as a real competitor to *Y Goleuad*. Efforts to combine the two, put forth by the church, proved ineffectual. Publication of the Calvinistic Methodist Church's *Y Blwyddiadur* (The year book) dates from 1898.

The church in Wales eventually found itself in want of a foreign-language paper for the benefit of English readers. As early as 1864, *The Treasury* began to fill this need, but closed in 1884. The Connexion provided a subsidy for *The Monthly Tidings* after its entrance into the same field in the following year, and on one occasion (1892) renewed this annual grant with the proviso that the editor would discontinue the acceptance of advertisements extolling the reputed virtues of certain medical preparations of questionable efficacy. In 1893 the church purchased *The Monthly Tidings* and renamed it *The Monthly Treasury*, a title retained until its exit from the scene in 1912.

The Welsh Calvinistic Methodist or Presbyterian Church in Wales is organized in three regional associations, designated as those of the North, South, and East, the latter, as previously noted, representing the English-speaking wing of the Connexion. The General Assembly, which has held annual meetings since 1864 with several exceptions, convenes in the month of June. For some years the Baptist, Congregational, Methodist, and Presbyterian churches in Wales have been engaged in conversations looking toward union.

The Evangelical Presbyterian Church in England and Wales

A serious effort to regain a vigorous Presbyterian ministry in England and Wales began in 1986, when concerned Reformed leaders met in London and formed the Presbyterian Association as a temporary measure with the objective of forming a denomination loyal to the faith expressed in the historic Westminster Standards. Although there were no interested congregations in Wales at that time, the Presbyterian Association in 1995 became the Evangelical Presbyterian Church in England and Wales, an indication of its aspiration to establish local churches in both of those parts of the United Kingdom. From its inception this body has been evangelical and Reformed in doctrine and assertively evangelistic in practice.

The roots of the Evangelical Presbyterian Church extend to the decade of the 1950s, when publications of the Banner of Truth Trust began to circulate throughout Great Britain. A number of Christians in England and Wales gratefully responded to the call for reformation coming from the *Banner of Truth*, a Reformed magazine produced in Edinburgh. A growing number of orthodox books from the same publisher reinforced the call, and pastors who attended Banner of Truth Ministers' Conferences launched an effort to form a confessional and connectional church body. The Presbyterian Association was the first step in that endeavor.

The first church services held as a consequence of the fresh enthusiasm for a Presbyterian presence led to the formation of two congregations that are now components of the Evangelical Presbyterian Church. In 1991 an interim presbytery began to function as an outgrowth of the Presbyterian Association. This consisted of five local churches—Blackburn, Cambridge, Chelmsford, Durham, and Hull, four of which had been constituted since 1986. In 1995 those congregations formed a regular presbytery, and in 2000 two bodies in Cardiff joined them, thereby making the new denomination Welsh as well as English. Both of the congregations in Wales are relatively new church plants.

The Evangelical Presbyterian Church in England and Wales enjoys substantial support from Mission to the World, an arm of the Presbyterian Church in America, and students from this British church have studied at Greenville Presbyterian Theological Seminary in South Carolina.

SUGGESTED ADDITIONAL READINGS >>

Beeke, Joel R. and Randall Pederson, *Meet the Puritans.* Grand Rapids: Reformation Heritage Books, 1986.

Carruthers, S.W. *The Westminster Confession of Faith (1646–47).* Manchester, U.K.: Aikman, 1937.

Collinson, Patrick. *The Religion of Protestants.* Oxford: Clarendon, 1985.

Evans, Eifion. *Daniel Rowland and the Great Awakening in Wales.* Edinburgh: Banner of Truth, 1985.

―――. *The Welsh Revival of 1904.* London: Evangelical Press, 1974.

Gardiner, Samuel Rawson. *The First Two Stuarts and the Puritan Revolt, 1603–1660.* New York: Thomas Y. Crowell, 1970. Reprint of 1834 edition.

Gilbert, A. D. *Religion and Society in Industrial England: Church, Chapel, and Social Change, 1740–1914.* London: Longmans, 1975.

Griffiths, O. M. *Religion and Learning: A Study in English Presbyterian Thought.* Cambridge: Cambridge University Press, 1935.

Henderson, G. D. *Presbyterianism.* Aberdeen, U.K.: University Press, 1954.

Jones, Owen. *Great Preachers of Wales.* Stoke-on-Trent, U.K.: Tentmaker, 1995. Reprint of 1885 edition.

Kenyon, J. P. *The Stuarts.* Glasgow, U.K.: William Collins & Sons, 1958.

Loane, Marcus L. *Makers of Religious Freedom in the Seventeenth Century.* Grand Rapids: Eerdmans, 1961.

Martin, Robert P. *A Guide to the Puritans.* Edinburgh: Banner of Truth, 1977.

Merle d'Aubigne, J. H. *The Protector: A Vindication.* Harrisonburg, Va.: Sprinkle Publications, 1997. Reprint of 1857 edition.

Moorman, J. R. H. *A History of the Church in England.* New York: Morehouse-Barlow, 1959.

Morgan, Derec L. *The Great Awakening in Wales.* Norwich, U.K.: Epworth, 1988.

Morgan, John. *Godly Learning: Puritan Attitudes toward Reason, Learning, and Education, 1560–1640.* Cambridge: Cambridge University Press, 1986.

Norman, E. R. *Church and Society in England, 1770–1970.* Oxford: Clarendon, 1976.

Nuttall, G. F., ed. *Howell Harris, 1714–1773: The Last Enthusiast.* Cardiff: University of Wales Press, 1965.

Ogg, David. *William III.* New York: Collier, 1967.

Overton, J. H. *The Evangelical Revival in the Eighteenth Century.* London: Longmans, Green, 1891.

Paul, Robert S. *The Lord Protector; Religion and Politics in the Life of Oliver Cromwell.* Grand Rapids: Eerdmans, 1955.

Prall, Stuart. *Church and State in Tudor and Stuart England.* Arlington Heights, Ill.: Harlan Davidson, 1993.

Ryken, Leland. *Worldly Saints: The Puritans as They Really Were.* Grand Rapids: Academie Books, 1986.

Selbie, W. B. *Nonconformity: Its Origin and Progress.* London: Thornton Butterworth, 1912.

Smith, David L. *Oliver Cromwell: Politics and Religion in the English Revolution.* Cambridge: Cambridge University Press, 1991.

Stephen, Leslie. *History of English Thought in the Eighteenth Century.* 2 vols. 3rd ed. New York: G. P. Putnam's Sons, 1902.

Tyacke, Nicholas. *Anti-Calvinists: The Rise of English Arminianism ca. 1590–1640.* Oxford: Oxford University Press, 1987.

Walker, D., ed. *A History of the Church in Wales.* Penarth, Wales: Church in Wales Publishers, 1976.

Walzer, Michael. *The Revolution of the Saints.* New York: Anthenaeum, 1969. Reprint of 1965 edition.

Watts, Michael R. *The Dissenters: From the Reformation to the French Revolution.* Oxford: Clarendon, 1978.

TEN

Establishing Presbyterianism
in America

The Puritans who arrived in North America in 1620 and planted Plymouth Colony were independents in their view of church polity, but a larger migration in 1628 brought to Massachusetts settlers who had not yet seceded from the Church of England. Cordial relations between the two early colonies reflected their mutual adherence to Calvinist theology, and gradually there developed both Congregational and Presbyterian forms of church government. In New England Congregationalism became dominant, while Presbyterianism flourished in colonies to the south and west. Although by the opening of the eighteenth century Presbyterians had settled in several areas, there was at that point no Presbyterian church organization.

Colonial Beginnings

As conditions of life became harsh in Ulster, Scots-Irish Presbyterians, weary of being compelled to pay assessments for the Episcopal Church of Ireland and beset by economic hardships, began migrating to America to escape discrimination at home. A major movement of that character began in 1710, and soon thereafter about six thousand Presbyterians per year were sailing to the New World. Those who arrived in Massachusetts, however, soon encountered opposition from Congregationalists when they began erecting their own church building, which a mob destroyed while it was under construction. The earlier cordiality based upon doctrinal agreement no longer prevailed. Presbyterians fared better in Maine and New Hampshire, but eventually most of their churches in those areas became Congregational.

Ulster Scots enjoyed much better success in the Middle Colonies of New York, Pennsylvania, and Delaware, and by 1750 Scots-Irish had become influential in many colonies, especially in Virginia and South Carolina. Many Highland Scots moved to the Carolinas after an uprising in support of the Stuart Pretender to Scotland's throne failed in 1747. Some of the rebels avoided imprisonment at home by leaving for America. Immigration and natural reproduction had, by the end of the eighteenth century, produced about five hundred communities of Scots and Scots-Irish dotting the landscape of the American colonies.

Francis Mackemie

Ascertaining the founding of the first Presbyterian church in America is a difficult, perhaps impossible task. Two rather obscure Presbyterian ministers from England, Francis Douty (ca. 1658–1708) and Matthew Hill, did mission work in Maryland and Virginia at an early date, but information about their labors is scant. While they appear to have been the pioneers, it is customary to hail Francis Mackemie (1658–1708) as the father of Presbyterianism in America. About 1684 he organized a congregation at Rehoboth, Delaware, which has a convincing claim to be the initial Presbyterian church in the American colonies. A less well-attested claim is that of a church at Jamaica, Long Island, which asserted 1672 as the date of its origin.

Mackemie was a Scot born in Donegal, Ulster, who lived during an era of persecution due to Episcopal opposition to the Presbyterian presence in Ireland. Educated at the University of Glasgow, he received ordination from the Presbytery of Laggan, which commissioned him a missionary to America. After preaching in Barbados for a few years, he went to Maryland in 1684 to begin a very successful ministry in the Middle Colonies of British America. His itinerary took Mackemie from Massachusetts to South Carolina. In 1704 he sailed to London, there to enlist other ministers for service in the colonies. His appeals led Presbyterians and Congregationalists to donate funds for the support of missionaries, and John Hampton and George McNish accompanied Mackemie to the New World.

The early Presbyterian preachers encountered stern opposition in some colonies, especially where the Church of England had the status of being the religion established by law, as in New York, Virginia, the Carolinas, and Maryland. The missionaries had to endure persecution from the same church that had driven them and their people from their homes in the Old World. Mackemie and Hampton spent two months in prison in New York for preaching without a license, and although a court acquitted them, the cost of defending their case was very high.

Opposition notwithstanding, Mackemie and his associates persisted in the work of evangelism and church planting, and it appears five churches on the Eastern Shore of Maryland and Delaware owe their origin to these labors. By the end of the eighteenth century, Presbyterian congregations were operating in Virginia, Maryland, New Jersey, Pennsylvania, and New York.

Mackemie was a champion for freedom of religion, perhaps because he was a victim of intolerance. His greatest claim to fame is, however, the formation of the first presbytery in America, which occurred at Philadelphia in 1706. Using the Irish practice as their model, he and six other ministers organized the Presbytery of Philadelphia as an indigenous church court not connected with ecclesiastical bodies in the British Isles. This meant that while Anglicans in America were subject to the bishop of London, Presbyterians ordained their own pastors in the colonies. Presbyterian churches increased in number, and by 1720 there were thirty-seven of them.

The movement of Presbyterians to South Carolina prompted a call to Britain for more ministers, and William Pollock and William Livingstone, Scots educated at Edinburgh, arrived in 1706 after obtaining support from the Presbytery of Dublin and the Synods of Ulster and Glasgow. English and Welsh settlers in America often joined the Scots and Irishmen in Presbyterian congregations, thereby making the first presbytery in America a composite body of nationalities.

In 1716 there occurred a significant denominational development with creation of the Synod of Philadelphia, which embraced the presbyteries of Philadelphia; Snow Hill, Maryland; Newcastle, Delaware; and Long Island, New York. Soon after formation of this synod, two Puritan congregations in New Jersey joined the Presbyterian church. By that time seventeen pastors, twelve from Scotland and Ireland, all firm Calvinists, served the churches in the synod.

The Need for a Doctrinal Standard

As the Presbyterian presence in America grew, leaders of the movement became convinced a statement of doctrine was in order. This happened in part due to challenges to orthodoxy in Scotland and the New Light controversy in Ireland, which began in 1719. In Ulster Pastor John Abernathy led an effort against requiring subscription to the Westminster Standards, and in so doing he proposed that sincerity, not doctrine, be recognized as the primary evidence of faith. As that persuasion gained growing acceptance, the Presbyterian Church in Ireland became involved in much contention, especially as Arminian ideas won adherents and Arian and Socinian beliefs soon followed. Since most Presbyterian preachers in America had come from Scotland or Ireland, churches in the colonies became concerned about issues agitating the British Isles. As early as 1705, the Synod of Ulster had required all candidates for licensure to subscribe to the Westminster Confession of Faith, a condition the Scottish Parliament had imposed in 1693, which is clear evidence that concerns about deviations from Reformed orthodoxy preceded the New Light controversy. That dispute, however, prompted Presbyterians to take further action.

The Adopting Act

The move in America to require subscription began in the Newcastle Presbytery in 1724, and vocal opposition soon threatened to cause a schism. Jonathan Dickinson (1688–1747), for example, resisted imposition of subscription, not because of doctrinal objections, but because he believed the move would not protect orthodoxy and might, in effect, lead entrants into the ministry to lie in order to gain acceptance into their presbyteries. The Synod of Philadelphia approved the Adopting Act (1729) nevertheless and thereby required all candidates for the ministry to accept the Westminster Standards as declarations of sound doctrine in their "essential and necessary articles." This left room for exceptions in matters deemed not essential, but lack of a definition of "essential and necessary" made further controversy almost inevitable.

In 1730 the synod considered the question of definition and allowed exceptions with regard to chapters 20 and 23 of the Westminster Confession in which are statements relating to the role of civil magistrates in the life of the church. Otherwise all candidates for the ministry were expected to subscribe to the Westminster Standards as the official position of the American Presbyterians. In general, response to this action was positive, and the church clearly maintained its orthodoxy at a time when the errors of deism, Socinianism, Arminianism, and various expressions of rationalism were threatening to undermine Christian teaching.

The Great Awakening and Presbyterian Responses

During the eighteenth century an impressive revival of spiritual interest occurred in both Europe and America, and immigrant preachers, as well as those born in the New World, were highly influential in arousing religious fervor. Among the pioneers in this development, Theodore Jacobus Frelinghuysen (1691–1747), a native of Germany, led a vigorous evangelistic effort in the Raritan Valley of New Jersey. An advocate of experimental (i.e., experiential) Calvinism, Frelinghuysen responded to a call for ministers in America, where he emphasized the need for conversion to Christ and a revival of spirituality among believers. Dutch Reformed ministers already serving in New York and New Jersey sometimes resisted the fervent pietism of the newcomer and regarded it as excessively emotional, but he would not be deterred.

After encountering opposition from clerics he offended, Frelinghuysen moved from New York to the Raritan Valley, where his labor met with much success. His theology was strongly Calvinistic, although his evangelistic practice seemed at times to give little attention to the doctrines of grace as proclaimed in the Canons of Dort (1619), the official statement of the church he served. Frelinghuysen boldly denounced evil wherever he found it, and he was relentless in urging people to repentance and faith in Christ. Other revival preachers of that era hailed him for his work and recognized him as a divinely appointed agent of spiritual awakening.

Frelinghuysen sometimes quarreled with church leaders in Amsterdam, so he sought autonomy for the Dutch Reformed Church in America. In 1747 the Classis of Amsterdam granted that request, but by then Frelinghuysen had died.

Among the admirers of Frelinghuysen were George Whitefield (1714–1770), the famous Anglican evangelist in America, and Gilbert Tennent (1703–1764), a Presbyterian from Ulster whose family had migrated to America in 1718. After receiving a master of arts from Yale College in 1725, Tennent served as pastor briefly in Delaware and then moved to New Brunswick, New Jersey, where he met Frelinghuysen, whose zeal for the ministry affected him deeply. Tennent's father, William Sr. (1673–1746), who brought the family to America, was a Presbyterian minister, as was his son William Jr. (1705–1777). At one point, while William Jr. was preparing for his ordination examination, he fell into a coma and appeared to be dead. Soon before the scheduled burial, however, he awoke and continued his ministry. In 1732 he succeeded his deceased brother, John, as pastor in Freehold, New Jersey, where he remained until his own demise.

In addition to his vigorous preaching, Gilbert Tennent participated with his father in the work of ministerial education through the Log College, established at Neshaminy, Pennsylvania, about 1735. Disciples of the Tennents founded the College of New Jersey, which eventually became Princeton University. Graduates of the Log College traveled widely to promote revival, and they excited large throngs of people. While Presbyterians did this, Jonathan Edwards (1703–1758) conducted a similar work among Congregationalists in Massachusetts. Proponents of revival preaching rebuked their critics by accusing them of being spiritually dead, and some revivalists tried to undermine the ministries of pastors who did not support them. It was not unusual for revival preachers to advise parishioners to desert their ministers if they opposed the methods of the Great Awakening. No exponent of revival was more outspoken in such matters than Gilbert Tennent, who castigated the critics in a sermon titled "The Danger of an Unconverted Ministry" (1740).

Old Side–New Side Division

Antagonism between the revivalists and their opponents within Presbyterian circles led to a division in 1741. By then neither faction was willing to work with the other, and it had become impossible to meet peaceably in the courts of the church. Those who espoused the tenets of what they regarded as an awakening became known as New Side Presbyterians, while the traditionalists were labeled Old Side Presbyterians. At a meeting of the Philadelphia Synod in 1741, the Old Side enacted a measure to exclude those members who engaged in what was alleged to be anti-Presbyterian behavior. Since members from the New Side were in the minority, there was little they could do but leave the synod, which they did in the midst of a stormy altercation. Each faction thereafter attacked the other in print, and the New Side's cordiality toward George Whitefield was a prominent issue between them.

The Presbytery of New York tried to mediate this dispute and seemed qualified to do so, since none of its members had participated in the effort to exclude the New Side members from the Synod of Philadelphia. These efforts failed, and in 1745 the Presbytery of New York joined the Presbytery of New Brunswick and created the Synod of New York. The college at Princeton then became the center for the education of New Side ministers, whose zeal continued to enlarge that movement at the expense of its opponents. Two separate Presbyterian churches competed for support, although they claimed to hold identical views of doctrine and polity. One side stood for rigid conservatism in forms of worship and methods of evangelism while the other emphasized experimental piety in worship and permitted wide latitude for emotional expressions.

The Old Side enjoyed support from Scottish and Irish immigrants, particularly in Virginia and the Carolinas, but in New England and the

Middle Colonies the New Side prevailed. The numerical strength of the opposing synods was about equal, but as New Side influences spread to Virginia and the Carolinas, the Old Side there declined.

New Side Successes in the South

The New Side realized a significant gain in the South when believers in Virginia, dissatisfied with the Anglican Church, left it and met privately for worship and Bible study. The colonial governor summoned them to give an account of their actions. Just prior to their audience with the governor, the group had acquired a copy of the Westminster Confession of Faith, which they then presented as their own creed, even though they had barely read it before the meeting. Governor William Gooch, a Scotsman well acquainted with Presbyterianism, informed the dissidents they were Presbyterians and instructed them to refrain from disturbing the peace. Soon after this the little group of Reformed believers enjoyed the preaching of William Robinson (d. 1746), a product of the Log College at Neshaminy, Pennsylvania, who had come from England and was converted while in New Jersey. Ordained by the Presbytery of New Brunswick in 1741, Robinson became an evangelist in Virginia and North Carolina, and while he was in Hanover County, Virginia, he discovered the former Anglicans who had embraced the Westminster Standards. Grateful beneficiaries of Robinson's brief ministry gave him funds that he used to aid Samuel Davies in obtaining an education. Four years later Davies became the first pastor of the infantile Presbyterian congregation in Hanover County.

In addition to serving this little group of Reformed believers, Samuel Davies (1723–1761) became a champion for freedom of religion in Virginia, where the Anglican Church was the established denomination. By contending that the Toleration Act (1689) applied to England's colonies as well as to the kingdom itself, Davies obtained permission to evangelize and organize churches over the protests of Anglican clerics. He then helped to form the Presbytery of Hanover, the first in that colony.

After a preaching tour in the United Kingdom, Davies returned to Virginia in 1755, when Whitefield visited the colony. By the end of that year six New Side congregations were flourishing there. From 1756–1763 the French and Indian War raged in America, and Samuel Davies's vigorous support for the British cause led the governor of Virginia to apply the Toleration Act so Presbyterians and others could enjoy full freedom of worship.

The Synod of Philadelphia in Decline

In the meantime, the Synod of Philadelphia was at a standstill. While rightly protesting against the extremes to which the New Side carried their revival measures, the leaders swung too far to the other extreme. They alienated all those whose hearts were earnestly set on evangelical aggressiveness, and no revivals of any marked power attended their labors. A lack of revivals meant a dearth of candidates for the ministry. The stream of immigration from Scotland and Ireland had well-nigh ceased to flow. Consequently their ministerial force dwindled, instead of increasing. There were accessions, but these did not keep pace with the losses by death. Obviously a church cannot prosper with a constantly diminishing roll of ministers. While, therefore, the Synod of Philadelphia is entitled to credit for a noble testimony against fanaticism, its history is a warning against undue suspicion of revivals.

Reunion of the Synods

While the Old Side Synod of Philadelphia languished and the New Side flourished, there were leaders in both camps who lamented the separation and sought reunion. The Synod of New York led the way in conciliation, as some of the original disputants died and emotions subsided. The year 1758 brought reunion on the basis of the Westminster Standards with an agreement to abide by the polity and discipline of the Westminster Directory for Public Worship. Reformed orthodoxy was to be the hallmark of the reunited church.

Obtaining Educated Ministers

For a long time the Presbyterian church in America obtained ministers from Scottish universities, but eventually graduates of Harvard and Yale began filling Presbyterian pulpits, even though they had studied at Congregational institutions. Although this seemed acceptable since both churches adhered to the same Calvinist theology, William Tennent initiated strictly Presbyterian education with the founding of the Log College, a means to prepare ministers of the New Side persuasion. Three sons of the founder graduated from that college, and they and other graduates exerted strong influence on the development of American Presbyterianism for about a century thereafter. Eventually some graduates of the school in Neshaminy established other Log Colleges, for example, one at Faggs Manor, Pennsylvania, of which Samuel Davies was a product. Other colleges were in

Lancaster County, Pennsylvania, and Nottingham, Maryland. By the end of the eighteenth century almost one hundred schools and colleges were operating under Presbyterian auspices. Although the initial purpose was to prepare ministers, these institutions educated others as well.

Princeton College was the most prominent success of Presbyterian endeavors in higher education. A project of the Synod of New York, it opened in 1746 at Elizabethtown, New Jersey, and moved to Princeton in 1755. The first five presidents of Princeton were revival preachers Jonathan Dickinson (1688–1747), Aaron Burr (1716–1757), Jonathan Edwards (1703–1758), Samuel Davies (1723–1761), and Samuel Finley (1715–1766). This institution espoused the New Side perspective in the tradition of the original Log College.

The development of Princeton and other schools as outgrowths of the Log College relieved American Presbyterians of the necessity of going to Scotland to study or to the Congregational Institutions of Harvard and Yale. Princeton educated not only future clergymen but laymen too, for service to both church and society was the college's mission. The first graduating class (1748) produced five Presbyterian ministers and one lawyer. The attorney Richard Stockton (1730–1781) became a signer of the Declaration of Independence and was very influential in bringing John Witherspoon (1723–1794) to the College of New Jersey (Princeton) as president in 1766.

Church Growth

Toward the end of the seventeenth century, Charleston, South Carolina, became the site of substantial growth for Presbyterianism, as immigrants from Scotland and Ireland and Huguenots from France arrived in that area. By 1730 the increasing numbers of Reformed believers allowed for the formation of a presbytery, one that had no connection with any higher church court. In 1770 that body applied for admission to the Synod of Philadelphia and New York, but for reasons no longer apparent, the synod rejected that application. The Presbytery of South Carolina therefore remained independent until long after the American War for Independence.

In North Carolina Scots situated along Cape Fear River, where James Campbell settled in 1758 and conducted services in both the Gaelic and English tongues. Prior to his arrival, it appears the Scots were without the leadership of a resident minister. In rapid succession three Presbyterian congregations were established in the area, and Campbell remained there until the outbreak of the American Revolution, when he fled. The influx of Scots-Irish settlers right up to the War for Independence led to the founding of additional Presbyterian local churches, although the Anglican Church still predominated in both of the Carolinas.

The reunion of 1758 also promoted significant church growth, some of it due to missions to Indian tribes. New York, New Jersey, and Pennsylvania remained the strongest centers of the American Presbyterian Church, but in the year of reunion the Presbytery of Hanover reorganized itself to incorporate churches of both synods in Virginia and North Carolina. Those in North Carolina obtained dismissal to form the Orange Presbytery in 1770. By 1776 the Presbyterian Church in the New World had about twenty thousand members in about three hundred congregations organized into twelve presbyteries. Membership in the Anglican and Baptist churches was larger, but in the Middle Colonies, Presbyterians were strongest.

Presbyterians and the War for Independence

By the early eighteenth century, the American Presbyterian Church was acting independently of any ecclesiastical authority in Europe, and the enjoyment of religious freedom and independence in several colonies made Presbyterians resentful toward the ones in which a religious establishment discriminated against them and other nonconformists. The Church of England was, in this regard, the chief offender, and dissidents viewed it as the king's church, the monarch of whom they were becoming critical due to what they perceived to be excessive taxation and violations of their chartered rights as his subjects. Large numbers of colonial Americans were of a Scottish background and so had a heritage of suspicion toward England and a deep disdain for authoritarian royal government. One issue in particular aroused the Presbyterians' concern and motivated them toward resistance, and that was the proposal to appoint an Anglican bishop to preside in America, a proposal that excited opposition from Congregationalists and other nonconformists as well.

For several years before American resentment toward British policy erupted in armed resistance, Presbyterians and Congregationalists in particular opposed creation of an Anglican diocese in America because they feared it would lead to a loss of their liberty. The British Parliament had earlier established a Roman Catholic bishopric in Canada, but parishes of the Anglican Church there and in the lower thirteen colonies were still subject to the bishop of London. Nonconforming Protestants in the United Kingdom had at times suffered economic and social discrimination because of policies authorized by Parliament in which the Anglican bishops sat as members of the House of Lords, and it was common to view these prelates as oppressors of non-Anglican Christians. Conscious of the situation in England, Presbyterians in America were vocal in denying Parliament's authority over matters of religion, and wherever Irish Presbyterians settled, anti-English sentiment was pronounced.

Among Presbyterians in America who protested British taxation, John Witherspoon, president of the College of New Jersey, was one of the most influential critics of imperial policy. He eventually became a member of the Continental Congress and a signer of the Declaration of Independence. James Galloway, once speaker of the Pennsylvania Assembly and a fervent loyalist, accused Presbyterians of being the chief agitators for independence from Great Britain, and many Royalist officials agreed.

When the War for Independence began, Presbyterians displayed such enthusiasm for the effort that one loyalist complained the colonies had "run off with a Presbyterian parson." Ministers of the Presbyterian Church, almost without exception, supported the war, often referring to the contract theory of government to justify the rebellion, an idea that resonated well with Scots and Irishmen, some of whom hailed that doctrine as political Calvinism.

Presbyterian laymen comprised entire regiments of the colonial army, especially in Pennsylvania, and many elders in their church became military officers. Generals Morgan and Pickens, for example, who led the troops at the battle of Cowpens, South Carolina, were Presbyterian elders. Like most American dissidents, however, Presbyterians did not at first renounce the monarchy but instead demanded recognition of their rights as British subjects. A synodical resolution in 1775 declared the struggle was a civil war within the British Empire.

The first Presbyterian body to endorse independence for America was the Presbytery of Hanover, Virginia, which declared that political independence was essential for freedom of religion. The first formal political expression of support for independence came in the form of the Mecklenburg Declaration of May 20, 1775, issued in North Carolina with vigorous Scots-Irish participation. It amounted to a repudiation of King George III.

Armstrong, M. W. with L. A. Loetscher and C. A. Anderson. *The Presbyterian-Enterprise*. Philadelphia: Westminster, 1956.

Balmer, Randall and John R. Fitzmier. *The Presbyterians*. Westport, Conn.: Praeger, 1994.

Beeke, Joel R., ed. *Forerunner of the Great Awakening: Sermons by Theodorus Jacobus Frelinghuysen (1691–1747)*. Grand Rapids: Eerdmans, 2000.

Briggs, Charles A. *American Presbyterianism: Its Origins and Early History*. Edinburgh: T. & T. Clark, 1885.

Coalter, Milton J. Jr. *Gilbert Tennent: Son of Thunder*. Westport, Conn.: Greenwood, 1986.

Ford, Henry Jones. *The Scotch-Irish in America*. Hamden, Conn.: Archon Books, 1966.

Fortson, S. Donald, ed. *Colonial Presbyterianism: Old Faith in a New Land*. Eugene, Ore.: Pickwick, 2007.

Gewhr, W. M. *The Great Awakening in Virginia*. Gloucester, Mass.: Peter Smith, 1965. Reprint of 1930 edition.

Hall, David, ed. *The Practice of Confessional Subscription*. Oak Ridge, Tenn.: Covenant Foundation, 1997.

Hart, D. G. and John R. Muether. *Seeking a Better Country: 300 Years of American Presbyterianism*. Phillipsburg, N.J.: P&R, 2006.

Maxon, Charles H. *The Great Awakening in the Middle Colonies*. Gloucester, Mass.: Peter Smith, 1958.

McLoughlin, William G. *Revivals, Awakenings, and Reform*. Chicago: University of Chicago Press, 1978.

Murphy Thomas. *The Presbytery of the Log College*. Philadelphia: Presbyterian Board of Publication, 1889.

Murray, Iain H. *Revival and Revivalism: The Making and Marring of American Evangelicalism*. Edinburgh: Banner of Truth, 1994.

Noll, Mark A. *The Rise of Evangelicalism: The Age of Edwards, Whitefield, and the Wesleys*. Downers Grove, Ill.: InterVarsity, 2003.

Pilcher, George W. *Samuel Davies: Apostle of Dissent in Colonial Virginia*. Knoxville: University of Tennessee Press, 1971.

Schlenter, Boyd S. *The Life and Writings of Francis Makemie*. Montreat, N.C.: Presbyterian Historical Society, 1971.

Smylie, James H. *American Presbyterians: A Pictorial History*. Philadelphia: Presbyterian Historical Society, 1985.

———. *A Brief History of the Presbyterians*. Louisville, Ky.: Geneva, 1996.

Sweet, William Warren. *Revivalism in America*. New York: Charles Scribner's Sons, 1944.

Tait, L. Gordon. *The Piety of John Witherspoon*. Louisville, Ky.: Geneva, 2001.

Thompson, Ernest Trice. *Presbyterianism in the South*. Vol. 1. Richmond, Va.: John Knox, 1973.

Trinterud, Leonard J. *Forming an American Tradition: A Re-examination of Colonial Presbyterianism*. Philadelphia: Westminster, 1949.

Webster, Richard. *A History of the Presbyterian Church in America from Its Origin until the Year 1760*. Philadelphia: Joseph M. Wilson, 1857.

Westerkamp, Marilyn J. *Triumph of the Laity: Scots-Irish Piety and the Great Awakening, 1625–1760*. Oxford: Oxford University Press, 1985.

White, Henry Alexander *Southern Presbyterian Leaders, 1683–1911*. Edinburgh: Banner of Truth, 2000. Reprint of 1911 edition.

ELEVEN

Presbyterians in the Young Republic

A uniquely American Presbyterianism emerged from the War for Independence, even before hostilities ended in 1783, and after the war it became clear that church growth and movements of peoples required some reorganization of the Presbyterian Church. Pastors and elders in distant regions often could not attend synods in Philadelphia or New York, so the situation warranted formation of a national representative body that could convene in various places from year to year. Some church members, however, feared such a body would infringe upon the authority of the presbyteries. The Synod of Philadelphia and New York was not a truly representative convocation since it was composed of all ministers and one elder from each congregation, and those 419 local churches were situated all the way from Georgia to New York. Despite the reservations of some, the movement to create a central court went forward and achieved its goal in 1788.

The First General Assembly

The new church structure in America did not correspond to the Scottish model in which the General Assembly held most of the authority. Instead synods and presbyteries retained much autonomy. To facilitate efficiency, the Synod of Philadelphia and New York agreed to divide into four: Philadelphia, New York and New Jersey, Virginia, and the Carolinas. Each synod then embraced several presbyteries.

At the time of reorganization, the American Presbyterian Church revised the Westminster Standards by eliminating items that reflected the relationship of church and state as it was in Scotland, and it affirmed the separation of the two spheres. Further revisions of the standards or the constitution of the church would thereafter require approval of two-thirds of the presbyteries. With these measures in place, the first General Assembly met in May 1789 at Philadelphia's Second Presbyterian Church.

The Presbyterian-Congregational Plan of Union (1801)

By the end of the War for Independence, the Presbyterian and Congregational churches were the strongest denominations in America. Both were avowedly Calvinistic in doctrine and both desired an educated ministry. It was common for Reformed believers to transfer from one body to the other. Cordial relations and common beliefs seemed to make these denominations natural allies in the work of spreading the gospel, despite their diverse polities. As early as 1791 it became a practice for representatives of each body to attend meetings of the other, that is, the General Assembly of the Presbyterian Church and the General Association of Connecticut, the Congregational assembly. Other Congregational associations in New England eventually made the same arrangement.

The region west of the Allegheny Mountains began to attract settlers late in the eighteenth century, and soon communities of Reformed believers dotted the landscape in Ohio, Kentucky, and Tennessee. In order to serve those areas more effectively, the two Reformed churches resolved to cooperate. They agreed to accept each other's pastors and to preserve whatever form of polity was in place when the ministers arrived on the scene. Some congregations included members who had come from both bodies. Despite some obvious advantages, this would prove to be a precarious experiment for the Presbyterians.

At first the benefits of cooperation in place of competition were impressive, as vigorous evangelism and church growth swelled the ranks of Christians in the western territories. The Presbyterians gained the most, and people began to refer to a Second Great Awakening among the pioneers. Church membership in the region rose from about twenty thousand in 1800 to about 222 thousand in 1837, and Baptists and Methodists also enjoyed great gains in the area.

In order for the Plan of Union to work, the Presbyterians had to modify their traditional ecclesiology so as to allow for the operation of churches in which the membership included Congregationalists. In such cases each local assembly could create a committee to act in place of a session. That committee could then represent the congregation in a presbytery and its members would function as elders, even though they had not been ordained to that office. In 1803 this arrangement was negotiated with the Congregational Convention of Vermont and in 1811 with the Congregational General Association of Massachusetts. Because of these arrangements, a number of Congregational ministers dispatched by their denomination's American Board of

Commissioners became functioning members of presbyteries. Eventually such ministers and committee members from mixed congregations obtained access to the synods and General Assembly of the Presbyterian Church. This was especially the case in Ohio and western New York.

Although it was far from obvious in 1801, the Plan of Union had the potential for diluting the doctrine of the Presbyterian Church, regardless of its theological affinity with the Congregationalists. This was due to departures from Calvinist orthodoxy in New England, of which Presbyterians seem to have been unaware at the time. A distinctive New England Theology, in which Arminian elements were evident, began to appear in Union churches, that is, mixed congregations with pastors from New England. The Plan of Union did not provide adequate means for church discipline, and there was no rigorous enforcement of subscription to the Westminster Confession of Faith. Conservative Presbyterians sometimes complained at the lack of ecclesiastical authority over missions in frontier areas. At times they cited Congregationalists for introducing a liberal theology into Union churches. In 1837 the Presbyterian Church was to abrogate the Plan of Union because of such concerns.

Old School–New School Controversies

When it became clear that Congregational ministers serving Union churches were espousing a New Divinity, that is, an adulteration of historic Calvinism, some orthodox Presbyterians complained. Because they insisted on adherence to the Westminster Standards, they became known thereafter as *Old School* Presbyterians in contrast to the innovators in doctrine labeled *New School* Presbyterians. Old School exponents, in addition to seeking confessional subscription, wanted stricter church control over missionary endeavors. John Witherspoon was a vigorous spokesman for Old School concerns, and Princeton was the intellectual center of that movement.

New School Presbyterians sought loose subscription to the Westminster Standards and broad interdenominational cooperation, and some advocates of these practices were rather receptive to liberal ideas coming from New England. Friction between the opposing schools of thought produced parties, and the Presbyterian Church became a battleground of competing persuasions. Most exponents of Old School beliefs were Scots-Irish Pennsylvanians or those of their background who had migrated to the south or west. The New School drew most of its support from New England, from which it spread across the frontier lands during the era when the Plan of Union was in effect.

Enthusiasts for New School ideas derived inspiration from the writings of Samuel Hopkins (1721–1803), a Congregational theologian from Connecticut, who had studied with Jonathan Edwards and had inherited Edwards's library. Although Hopkins professed to systematize the teaching of his mentor, he altered it substantially by denying the imputation of Adam's sin to his posterity and by rejecting the penal-substitutionary doctrine of the atonement. Hopkins published his views in his *System of Doctrines Contained in Divine Revelation, Explained and Defended*, which appeared in 1793.

Within Presbyterian circles, two of the most fervent adherents to New School ideas were Lyman Beecher (1775–1863) and Albert Barnes (1798–1870), both of whom incurred charges of heresy. Beecher, originally a Congregationalist who became a Presbyterian, was a graduate of Yale, one who assigned little importance to precise doctrine or denominational distinctives. From 1832 to 1842 he was president of Lane Theological Seminary in Cincinnati, a Presbyterian institution. Beecher supported revivalist preaching and called for moral and social reforms, but he did not subscribe to the Westminster Confession of Faith.

Beecher obtained the presidency of Lane Theological Seminary with the support of Joshua L. Wilson, an Old School pastor of note, who came to regret recommending Beecher once his liberalism became evident. Perhaps because Beecher had a reputation for being a strong Trinitarian while in Boston and a fervent evangelist, Wilson was unaware of his unorthodox ideas. Soon after Beecher began his work in Cincinnati, Wilson called on his presbytery to investigate the seminary president's theology. Soon thereafter Wilson charged Beecher with maintaining New School views about original sin and regeneration and with misleading the presbytery by making an insincere subscription to the Westminster Standards. The presbytery, however, exonerated Beecher, as did the synod to which Wilson had appealed. The case reached the General Assembly in 1836, but there it languished, and the dispirited Wilson dropped the matter.

Another prominent figure whose role in the Old School–New School disputes led to a trial for heresy was Albert Barnes (1798–1870), a pastor in Morristown, New Jersey, who moved to Philadelphia in 1830. Soon after Barnes arrived in the Quaker City, Ashbel Green (1762–1848), minister at Second Presbyterian Church there, accused him of espousing Pelagian doctrine. The specific charges included an assertion that human nature is not depraved because of sin, so people have a natural ability to obey God's laws and to embrace Christ without preceding supernatural regeneration. The Presbytery of Philadelphia rejected the charges, but the synod suspended Barnes from the ministry. He then appealed to the General Assembly, in which adherents to New School beliefs held a majority. The assembly reversed the decision of the synod and restored the accused pastor by a vote of 145 to 78.

The basis of the heresy charge against Barnes was a sermon he delivered while in Morristown, one titled "The Way of Salvation," and his book *Notes on Romans,* in both of which he rejected orthodox Reformed teachings about sin and salvation. Barnes admitted disagreements with the Westminster Standards but insisted he was a loyal Presbyterian nevertheless. Like others in the New School movement, he supported revivalist preaching and programs for social reform. A learned scholar educated at Princeton Theological Seminary, he eventually published an eleven-volume commentary, *Notes, Explanatory and Practical, on the New Testament*, and several volumes on books of the Old Testament. When New School elders established Union Theological Seminary in New York City, Barnes was one of its most fervent supporters. He remained at his Philadelphia pastorate until retirement in 1868.

The inability of the orthodox party to remove Beecher, Barnes, and others of their persuasion demonstrated the strength of the New School within the Presbyterian Church and led to a schism in 1837. Although meetings of the General Assembly were almost always in Philadelphia, members of the New School from New York and Ohio attended in greater numbers than those from more conservative, but more distant, areas of the church.

The Division of 1837–1838
In 1837 the Old School made a vigorous effort to obtain control of the General Assembly, and victory seemed to be within reach, as the assembly abrogated the Plan of Union with the Congregationalists and dismissed four synods that were in control of the New School. The synods were Western Reserve, Utica, Geneva, and Genesee, all of them organized while the Plan of Union was in effect.

New School proponents responded to the Old School measure at the General Assembly by convening a meeting in Auburn, New York, which became known as the Auburn Convention. That body denied the validity of the expulsion of the four synods and declared they were still components of the Presbyterian Church. When the General Assembly convened in 1838, representatives of the New School failed to obtain recognition from the Old School moderator in the midst of an uproar. The New School faction then moved to another site in Philadelphia, while the Old School and the New School both claimed to be *the* Presbyterian Church.

The numerical strength of the two parties was roughly equal, with about 126 thousand adherents to the Old School and 106 thousand to the New School. Deep divisions then affected all areas of Presbyterian life, and controversies often preempted evangelism. Baptists and Methodists gained while Presbyterians quarreled, so the growth of their church slowed dramatically, as many Americans of Scots-Irish ancestry joined other denominations, and many presbyteries became divided because of issues agitating unrest.

Further divisions occurred as Congregational churches drifted deeper into liberalism and sometimes disdained all Presbyterians, even those of the New School, whom they came to regard as too conservative. The Congregationalists themselves disavowed the Plan of Union in 1852. Meanwhile the abolition of slavery in the United States became a passionate cause for the New School, and that led to the separation of almost all Presbyterian churches in the South, where congregations formed the United Synod of the Presbyterian Church in 1858.

Resurgence of the Old School

Although divisions damaged both parties, the Old School recovered rather quickly, energized by the conviction that it had preserved the Reformed faith. By 1860 the Old School had grown to about 290 thousand members, and it resolutely rejected New School appeals for reunion, evidence of a profound distrust of liberalism. The coming of the War between the States cost the Old School about seventy thousand southern adherents, and wartime passions distracted Presbyterians from theological issues, as regaining unity became their foremost concern.

In 1862, while war raged, the Old School General Assembly proposed a resumption of fraternal relations, and the New School responded eagerly. To achieve reunion two bodies formed committees to recommend steps to be taken. Although both schools accepted the Westminster Standards in principle, there was strong disagreement about requiring subscription. In the end they affirmed the standards but left controversial matters unresolved.

The merger occurred in 1870 and produced a Presbyterian church of 446 thousand members. To celebrate the reunion the church resolved to raise a thank offering of five million dollars. The response to the appeal produced $7,607,491, evidence of the great enthusiasm for ending the division. By 1904 church membership had risen to almost 1.1 million, and missionary outreach was flourishing. All appeared well for the Presbyterians as the nineteenth century drew to a close, but doctrinal issues that had arisen earlier remained, only temporarily obscured by the prosperity reunion had produced.

Assaults on Reformed Theology: Unitarianism and Universalism

New England, once a Puritan stronghold, gradually became the site of rationalistic attacks upon Christian orthodoxy from which Presbyterians were not immune. Belief in the triune nature of God and the concomitant doctrine of Christ's deity and humanity had often encountered criticism because they appear to contradict the canons of reason. Objections to these historic Christian teachings had a special appeal for intellectuals who despised the doctrine of human depravity as well. Prosperous Bostonians who assumed they were masters of their own destiny and not helpless sinners often found the Episcopal Church more attractive than the plain Congregational meetinghouses, and in 1785 King's Chapel, originally a parish of the Church of England, became the first avowedly Unitarian church in America. Founded in 1688 by action of the colonial governor of Massachusetts, it was at that time the only Anglican (Episcopal) Church in Puritan New England. While James Freeman (1759–1835) led the congregation as pastor, he proposed Unitarian beliefs and convinced the people to excise from their prayer book all references to the Trinity.

The revolt against orthodoxy in general and Calvinism in particular permeated Congregational churches gradually, causing a split into orthodox and liberal factions. Among Congregationalists the leading liberal was Charles Chauncy (1705–1787), pastor at First Church, Boston, who became Unitarian in theology and eventually a Universalist in his view of salvation. He expressed severe disdain for revivalist preaching.

A graduate of Harvard, where his father was president, Chauncy's scholarship assured him a respectful hearing from other intellectuals, so his services attracted many who shared his dislike for traditional Christian emphases. Both in his preaching and in his writing, Chauncy espoused his belief in the unitary nature of God and in the universal salvation of all people. In 1785 he published *The Fall and Its Consequences*, a work he intended as a rebuttal of George Whitefield's ministry. His books *The Benevolence of the Deity* and *The Salvation of All Men*, both issued in 1784, had already provoked a response from Jonathan Edwards.

When Unitarian and Universalist doctrines appeared in their midst, most Congregational pastors chose not to contest the liberalism but to tolerate diversity within their church. Indifference toward doctrine was thus becoming pronounced in Congregational ranks, as orthodoxy receded before the advancing liberalism. The defection from historic Christianity of numerous Congregationalists became evident when Unitarians formed a separate denomination while William Ellery Channing (1780–1842), president of Harvard College, was their leader. By 1825 the American Unitarian Association had 125 local affiliates, many of them former Congregational assemblies.

Channing, another Harvard graduate, was pastor at Federal Street Church, Boston, and a renowned figure in the literary circles of that city. His theology featured a categorical rejection of the Trinity, Christ's substitutionary atonement, and, of course, original sin and human depravity. Although he subscribed to the Unitarian view of the Godhead enthusiastically, Channing often lamented the evidently sterile state of spirituality among adherents of that persuasion. Social reform, especially the abolition of slavery, was his passion.

Universalism as an organized religious movement appeared first in Gloucester, Massachusetts, in 1799, introduced by John Murray (1741–1815), an English immigrant who became a chaplain for American soldiers during the War for Independence. Although he had a Calvinistic heritage, Murray became an Arminian due to the influence of Methodist preacher John Wesley. Murray went to Massachusetts in 1774 and there founded a Universalist church five years later.

Universalists contended that divine goodness precludes eternal punishment for sinners, while Unitarians maintained that sinful humans do not deserve such punishment. The basic agreement between these groups is evident in their man-centered worldview. Lyman Beecher, then a pastor in Boston, resisted the popular anti-Trinitarian teachings and urged revivalism as the proper response to it. His efforts may have retarded the growth of Unitarianism for a while, and his defense of the orthodox doctrine of God made him appear an acceptable candidate for the presidency of Lane

Theological Seminary, a Presbyterian institution, considered previously in this chapter.

Underlying the rise of liberal theology was the influence of scholars whose embrace of rationalism made Calvinistic principles appear repulsive. Among them Samuel Hopkins, once a student of Jonathan Edwards, was a pioneer. His modifications of historic Calvinism were in the direction of a man-centered concept of salvation, and Timothy Dwight (1752–1817), a grandson of Edwards, also encouraged revisions of the Reformed faith.

Dwight was educated at Yale College and ordained in the Congregational church, serving as pastor at Greenfield, Connecticut. In 1795 he became president of Yale, a frequent preacher in the college chapel, and professor of moral philosophy. His reputation for learning enabled his institution to gain an excellent academic standing. Dwight's preaching was fervent and broadly evangelical, for unlike his grandfather, Dwight avoided doctrines about which Christians were divided. Dwight was an able author of poetry as well as theology and a staunch opponent of anti-Christian philosophy. His book *The Triumph of Infidelity* (1788) is an attack upon Voltaire, David Hume, and other skeptics. His own departures from historic Reformed belief appear in *Theology Explained and Defended* (1819), a collection of his sermons and lectures in which he rejected the imputation of Adam's sin to the human race, particular redemption (limited atonement), and the inability of sinners to contribute to their own salvation.

Nathaniel W. Taylor (1786–1818) was another powerful figure whose influence encouraged deviations from the Reformed faith. Taylor graduated from Yale, where he absorbed much influence from the teaching of Dwight, for whom he was a secretary until he received a call to become pastor at First Congregational Church, New Haven, in 1812. Although he was not an evangelist, Taylor's endorsement of revivalist preaching had a substantial effect upon the beliefs and practices of such preachers and their churches. In 1822 he became professor of theology at Yale and in that position defended the revivalists against their critics. In doing so, however, this distinguished scholar, along with his mentor Dwight, became one of the formulators of the New Haven Theology, which appealed to both Congregationalists and New School Presbyterians.

New Haven Theology denied God's absolute sovereignty over creation and scorned the Reformed doctrine of election and thereby aroused opposition from Old School Presbyterians, especially Princeton theologian Charles Hodge. Defenders of the Reformed faith regarded New Haven ideas as Pelagian heresy. Taylor's denial of the substitutionary nature of Christ's death was the most conspicuously offensive feature of his teaching. Many Arminians ignored this aspect of New Haven Theology, perhaps because Dwight and Taylor supported revivalist methods of evangelism, while strict Calvinists opposed them. Due to the influence of the Yale theologians, Congregational churches were often receptive to liberalism, and other denominations followed them. Advocates of the liberal teachings held that their intention was not to subvert, but to preserve the Christian faith by deleting those Calvinistic concepts that many intellectuals found repulsive. In their effort to be doctrinal moderates, Dwight and Taylor failed to convince the Unitarians in theology proper, while their Arminian soteriology alienated the Calvinists.

During disputes about New Haven Theology, Horace Bushnell (1802–1876) entered Yale Divinity School and attended Taylor's lectures. Although he had no affinity for Calvinism, Bushnell found Taylor's theology unattractive, and without making overt attacks upon it, he ignored Reformed doctrine in favor of an Arminian experience-centered religion.

As pastor of North Congregational Church, Hartford, Connecticut, Bushnell advocated an undogmatic conception of Christianity that emphasized the human need to experience the presence of Jesus within, as opposed to formulating precise statements of faith and insisting on subscription to them. He regarded traditional theological studies as speculations always subject to modification. In his view, disputes such as Calvinism versus Arminianism are senseless, since both systems (and others too) contain elements of truth. Bushnell sought an elastic Christianity with room for much latitude in belief. In his book *God in Christ* (1849), he contended the language of religion is always figurative, so dogmatic pronouncements are not appropriate. Christian unity, he thought, could not occur until believers realized the poetic character of religious terms.

Perhaps the most enduringly influential of Bushnell's writings is *Christian Nurture* (1847). In this popular work the author rejected the doctrine of human depravity and argued that children have the natural ability to grow up as Christians and never realize any sense of personal sinfulness. Proper influence could encourage the development of Christian character without the intervention of divine grace. In asserting this belief Bushnell put himself at odds with the revivalists' demand for conversion. His influence helped diminish the importance of dogma and promoted a religion of feelings, which was consistent with the worldview that dominated Europe and America in the romantic Victorian era.

The Cumberland Presbyterian Church

The influence of New England theology and liberalism in general infiltrated Presbyterian ranks and gained acceptance there, especially among intellectuals, who despised the rigors of historic Calvinism. The trend away from orthodoxy was not, however, limited to academic and intellectual circles. In Kentucky there arose a strong dislike for the Reformed emphasis on divine sovereignty and human inability to please God. Frontier revivals were thriving there at the time, often under the leadership of preachers with little formal education. In such circumstances it was easy to regard great religious excitement as evidence of divine approval, and some Presbyterians joined the revivalists enthusiastically. Barton W. Stone (1772–1844) was one.

A pioneer in the Kentucky revivalist movement, Stone was pastor of congregations at Cane Ridge and Concord. At his ordination he had subscribed to the Westminster Standards, but he reserved the right to deviate from them should he find any items that conflicted with the Word of God. He attended revival meetings in Logan County, Kentucky, in 1801 and there witnessed bizarre outbursts of emotion that included apparently uncontrollable gyrations of the body accompanied by loud wailing and profuse weeping. Convinced the Holy Spirit was at work, Stone soon introduced such practices to his congregation at Cane Ridge.

Reports of events at Cane Ridge alarmed leaders of the Presbyterian Synod of Kentucky, which censured Stone. He responded by withdrawing from the synod and forming, in collaboration with other revivalists, the Springfield Presbytery. That body dissolved after only a few months, when the members declared they would no longer be Presbyterians but thereafter *Christians*. Eventually they adopted the practice of baptizing believers only and then by immersion, while they declared baptism a requirement for salvation. In 1830 Stone and most of his followers united with Alexander Campbell (1788–1866) and became known as Disciples of Christ.

Concurrent with the work of Barton Stone, there arose contention within the Cumberland Presbytery of the Presbyterian Church (U.S.A.) due to emotional excesses and departures from Reformed doctrine conspicuous among revival preachers. When adherents to confessional Presbyterianism demanded subscription to the Westminster Standards, a schism occurred. Three pastors of Arminian persuasion responded to suspension from the

ministry by creating the Cumberland Presbyterian Church, which organized in 1810 in Dickson County, Tennessee. The new denomination
radically revised the confession of historic Presbyterianism so as to eliminate divine sovereignty in salvation, which Cumberland Presbyterians
regarded as chiefly a matter of human choice.

The Cumberland Presbyterian Church grew rapidly in frontier areas, and
as it did, the church moved further from the Reformed faith. A Calvinist-
Arminian hybrid, it attracted many adherents through vigorous evangelism.
In 1868 African American leaders within the church expressed a desire to
form an autonomous body of their own, a request the predominantly white
Cumberland Presbyterian Church granted. Details about this amicable
division are lacking, but it is clear the black Cumberland Presbyterians initiated it. They convened a constituting assembly at Henderson, Kentucky,
but poor attendance required them to meet again, this time at Huntsville,
Alabama, but this meeting also drew few people. It was not until 1870
that a sufficient number of black churchmen could gather to complete the
process of founding the Colored Cumberland Presbyterian Church. That
occurred at Murfreesboro, Tennessee, where a white congregation provided
its facilities for the occasion.

In 1880 the original Cumberland Presbyterian Church applied for
membership in the World Association of Reformed Churches, only to be
refused because of its deviations from Reformed theology. That action led
the church to revise its official doctrine to satisfy the World Association.
In 1906 most, but not all, Cumberland Presbyterian congregations merged
with the Presbyterian Church (U.S.A.). The stricter local churches declined
because they perceived the agreements about doctrine were only cosmetic.

Charles Grandison Finney

While Presbyterians were arguing about revivalism and methods of evangelism and trying to repel rising heresies, Charles G. Finney (1792–1875)
became a dynamic church leader whose teachings agitated further contention. A lawyer from Adams, New York, he experienced a conversion in 1821
and was ordained by the Presbytery of St. Lawrence only three years later,
after private study with a pastor in New York State. Soon Finney began
enthusiastic preaching across his home state in the manner of the revivalists
and quickly gained nationwide attention. Some pastors disapproved of his
methods and the emotional outbursts they evoked, but his influence spread

nevertheless into New York City, Philadelphia, and Boston, and eventually he traveled to England to preach.

From 1832 to 1836 Finney was pastor of Second Presbyterian Church in New York City, and while in that position, he published *Lectures on Revivals of Religion* (1835), a work that made him a highly controversial figure. In that book Finney asserted that divine intervention is not essential for revival, for proper techniques can achieve it unaided. A revival, he wrote, "is not a miracle...in any sense. It is a purely philosophical result of the right use of constituted means—as much as any other effect produced by the application of means." Impressive numerical responses to Finney's preaching convinced many Presbyterians to support him.

In 1836 Finney became professor of theology at Oberlin College in Ohio, of which he was president from 1851 to 1866. Soon after moving to Oberlin, he left Presbyterianism to become a Congregationalist. His ideas about doctrine and evangelism became known eventually as the Oberlin Theology.

By the time Finney abandoned Presbyterianism, he had become openly hostile toward the Reformed faith and had developed a belief in perfectionism by which he contended victory over sin is a simple matter of decision to renounce it. In 1841, the Presbytery of Cleveland, Ohio, issued a formal denunciation of the Oberlin Theology and urged local churches not to accept graduates of Oberlin College as pastors.

Finney often misrepresented the Reformed view of divine sovereignty by portraying it as a species of fatalism. In opposition to God's gracious intervention to regenerate lost sinners, he promoted marketing techniques to arouse the emotions of people concerned about salvation. Belief in free will and self-determination were the bases of his evangelism, and when his "new measures" produced numerical results, as in Rochester, New York in 1830–1831, Finney claimed divine approval for his methods. In 1847 he produced *Lectures on Systematic Theology*, an experience-centered justification of his revivalism. Although evangelism was always his foremost concern, Finney had a keen interest in social reform and thus supported the abolition of slavery, education for females, abstinence from alcohol, and observance of the Sabbath. He was a frequent critic of Freemasonry. Opposition from Presbyterians notwithstanding, his evangelistic methods gained wide acceptance and became standard practice among revivalists who espoused semi-Pelagian views of sin and salvation. It is almost impossible to exaggerate Finney's influence upon religion in America.

Alexander, Archibald. *Sketches of the Founder and the Principal Alumni of the Log College.* Philadelphia: Presbyterian Board of Publication, 1851.

Baird, Samuel J. *A History of the New School.* Philadelphia: Claxton, Remsen, and Haffelfinger, 1868.

Boles, John B. *The Great Revival: 1787–1805.* Lexington: University Press of Kentucky, 1972.

Calhoun, David B. *Princeton Seminary.* Vol. 1. Edinburgh: Banner of Truth, 1994.

Cannon, William R. *The Theology of John Wesley.* New York: Abingdon, 1946.

Cheetham, Henry H. *Unitarianism and Universalism: An Illustrated History.* Boston: Beacon, 1962.

Dallimore, Arnold. *George Whitefield.* London: Banner of Truth, 1970.

Hart, D. G. and Mark A. Noll, eds. *Dictionary of the Presbyterian and Reformed Tradition in America.* Downers Grove, Ill.: InterVarsity, 1999.

Hart, D. G. and John R. Muether. *Seeking a Better Country: 300 Years of American Presbyterianism.* Phillipsburg, N.J.: P&R, 2006.

Hoffecker, W. Andrew. *Piety and the Princeton Theologians.* Phillipsburg, N.J.: P&R, 1981.

Jamison, Wallace N. *The United Presbyterian Story.* Pittsburgh: Geneva, 1958.

McGoldrick, James Edward. *Christianity and Its Competitors: New Faces of Old Heresy.* Fearn, Ross-shire, U.K.: Christian Focus, 2006.

Noll, Mark A. *Princeton and the Republic, 1768–1822.* Princeton, N.J.: Princeton University Press, 1989.

Robinson, David. *The Unitarians and the Universalists.* Westport, Conn.: Greenwood, 1985.

Selden, William K. *Princeton Theological Seminary: A Narrative History, 1812–1992.* Princeton, N.J.: Princeton University Press, 1992.

Smith, Edwyn Allen. *The Presbyterian Ministry in American Culture: A Study in Changing Concepts, 1700–1900.* Philadelphia: Westminster, 1962.

Sweet, William Warren. *The Story of Religion in America.* Rev. ed., New York: Harper & Brothers, 1950.

TWELVE

The Southern Presbyterian Church

Antislavery agitation within the Presbyterian church led to severe disagreements. Abolitionists from the North denounced slavery as anti-Christian and thereby provoked strong resentment in the South. Organized opposition to slavery had been occurring for some time even in the Southern states, but vehement attacks by Northern abolitionists caused Southerners to become defensive, which led to the dissolution of some abolitionist movements in that region. The dispute became a quarrel about the constitutional right of the states to decide such matters without interference from the federal government. The election of Abraham Lincoln as president in 1860 convinced most Southerners their rights were in jeopardy, so it was time to sever their bonds with the Federal Union.

Ecclesiastical Effects of Political Tensions
When the General Assembly of the Presbyterian Church (U.S.A.) met in Philadelphia under the control of Old School exponents, it quickly became evident the body was deeply divided because of the political issues disturbing the nation. The occasion called for the greatest prudence and patience, a gentleness, delicacy, and self-control that could hardly be expected from any but saints fully sanctified.

Some members of the General Assembly regarded slavery as sin and secession from the Union as treason, while others believed Scripture sanctions slavery. Southerners in general viewed the defense of states' rights as a patriotic duty mandated by their allegiance to the American Constitution, which did not forbid slavery. There was no common ground between the opposing points of view, and hope of preventing a schism was unrealistic, especially because the War between the States had already begun when the General Assembly convened. Charles Hodge of Princeton Theological Seminary tried to calm irritated tempers by proposing the church not specify to which side its members had to declare their allegiance. The assembly nevertheless resolved to support the Union. The Spring Resolution, named for its author, Gardiner Spring (1785–1873), an influential pastor in New York City, called for full support of the federal government. Since only a few Southerners attended the General Assembly that time, the body adopted Gardiner's proposal by a vote of 156 to 66, after long, contentious debates. This action signified a major departure from the Old School practice of avoiding pronouncements about political matters.

The Presbyterian Church in the Confederate States of America (C.S.A.)

During the summer of 1861, forty-seven Southern presbyteries withdrew from the Presbyterian Church (U.S.A.) in protest against perceived unconstitutional actions of the General Assembly in adopting the Spring Resolution. The Southern churches moved swiftly to create a new national organization within the Confederacy, and the first meeting of their General Assembly was at Augusta, Georgia, in December of that year, at which they elected B. M. Palmer (1818–1902) their moderator. The pastor of First Presbyterian Church, New Orleans, Palmer was a distinguished preacher, an effective churchman, and a staunch supporter of the Confederacy. He was of the traditional persuasion that the church should refrain from political statements and actions, but he regarded slavery as a divinely sanctioned institution and considered Northern military intrusions as acts of aggression against a godly people. He accused some abolitionists of being atheists. Northern opponents of slavery often quoted Palmer as an example of Southern bigotry. Meanwhile the Northern Presbyterian Church (U.S.A.) labeled its Southern counterpart apostate.

The Presbyterian Church (C.S.A.) affirmed the Westminster Standards and issued an *Address to the Churches of Jesus Christ throughout the World* as an effort to justify its separation from the Northern church. James Henley Thornwell (1812–1862), a former president of South Carolina College and later professor of theology at Columbia Theological Seminary, was the principal author of the *Address,* which contended church unity between countries at war with each other was impossible, so Southern Presbyterians must support the national government under which God had placed them. Thornwell, like Palmer, was a champion of Old School orthodoxy, which he expounded in a highly learned manner.

The war (1861–1865) forced the Presbyterian Church (C.S.A.) to move its meetings and offices as fighting devastated the South. The church managed to maintain mission work among African and Native Americans in spite of the war, and it supplied chaplains for the Confederate armies.

Recovery and Reconstitution

Although Presbyterian churches in the South suffered badly during the war, the Southern Presbyterian denomination realized substantial gains even while the conflict raged. In 1864 the United Synod of the Presbyterian Church agreed to merge with the larger body and thereby added 190 congregations and twelve thousand members to it.

The United Synod was a New School body in the South that withdrew from the Presbyterian Church (U.S.A.) when the 1861 General Assembly denounced slavery and demanded support for the federal union. Robert L. Dabney (1820–1898), a renowned professor at Union Theological Seminary in Richmond, Virginia, led the committee that produced the plan of union by which the Southern church and the United Synod joined together.

A further enlargement of the Presbyterian Church (C.S.A.) occurred in Kentucky, where Presbyterians were sharply divided over slavery and other issues that had fractured the Federal Union. The Synod of Kentucky could not remain united, and R. J. Breckenridge (1800–1871), on the faculty of Danville Theological Seminary and a zealot of Old School principles, insisted the synod affirm allegiance to the United States of America. As a consequence a large part of the Synod of Kentucky aligned with the Southern church. In the Carolinas the small Independent Presbyterian Church did the same, as would a presbytery in Maryland in 1867 and the Associate Reformed Presbyterian Church in Alabama the same year. When the Associate Reformed Presbytery in Kentucky aligned with it, the Presbyterian Church in the United States, the name adopted after the War between the States, had acquired 490 congregations and thirty-five thousand members from these mergers.

Although the Southern church gained many adherents in the South and in border states, efforts at reconciliation with the Presbyterian Church (U.S.A.) failed. Northern Presbyterians had accused their Southern brethren of schism, heresy, and blasphemy before and during the recent war, so healing the breach was difficult, and fraternal relations were not restored until 1882. Even then, it was not reunion, but cooperation in some areas of ministry such as foreign missions, publications, and education. In 1904 the Northern church, in a gesture of goodwill, disavowed all charges earlier made against its Southern counterpart.

The Character of the Presbyterian Church in the Southern United States

In the Southern church, adherence to the Westminster Standards was typical, and that included belief in the inerrancy of Scripture. The church excluded women from the eldership and from teaching and leading in public worship. There was a firm decision to avoid involving the church in civil affairs and all political matters, and it continued to insist Scripture does not condemn slavery.

In order to minister to the black population within its area, the Presbyterian Church in the United States (Southern) sought creation of separate congregations for African Americans while providing education for their pastors and subsidizing some of their local churches. Before the war blacks had for a long time attended church with their white masters but were seated in separate sections of the building. Fear of slave revolts after the Nat Turner uprising of 1831 had, however, caused plantation owners to discourage missions to the blacks. Some efforts to evangelize and instruct them continued nevertheless, as the work of Charles Colock Jones (1804–1863) attests.

A Presbyterian minister educated in the North, Jones was pastor at First Presbyterian Church, Savannah, and later a professor of church history at Columbia Theological Seminary. While living in the North he had denounced slavery, but upon returning to the South, he endorsed it. He had deep concern for the spiritual welfare of slaves and therefore devised a program to evangelize them. In a culture where blacks were almost all illiterate, Jones urged education so they could learn to read Scripture. To facilitate this he produced a *Catechism of Scripture, Doctrine, and Practice… for the Oral Instruction of Colored Persons* and a book titled *The Religious Instruction of the Negroes in the United States*. Jones believed education was essential before any slaves would be ready to assume the responsibilities of free people, and he did not promote or expect an early end to slavery as an institution. When abolition did occur, segregation soon followed, sometimes at the instigation of blacks themselves, as in the Colored Cumberland Presbyterian Church.

Following the defeat of the Confederacy, the Southern states endured military occupation and authoritarian policies that the victors imposed. The Southern Presbyterian Church had suffered great losses due to casualties in battle, and many church properties had been damaged or destroyed. Help with the recovery was not, however, long in coming, as Christians in various parts of the country contributed generously. The 1865 General Assembly changed the name of the denomination to the Presbyterian Church in the United States (U.S.).

The year 1896 brought a considerable acquisition of strength to the Southern church when most congregations of the Synod of Kentucky, after withdrawing from the Northern church, affiliated with the Presbyterian Church (U.S.). This occurred because the General Assembly of the Presbyterian Church (U.S.A.) (Northern) resolved it would receive Southern ministers only if they renounced the Confederacy and slavery. Stuart Robinson (1814–1881), a prominent leader in the Louisville Presbytery, composed a formal complaint to the Northern church, much to the irritation of that body and federal officials. About ten thousand Kentucky Presbyterians joined the Southern church as a consequence of the policy affirmed in its Northern counterpart.

Although the Presbyterian Church (U.S.) made some significant gains in membership during and soon after the War between the States, there were losses as well. These were due in part to the departure of some black congregations when missionaries of the Northern church began energetic efforts to enlist freedmen in the South. The Southern church nevertheless continued its work with blacks, and a major endeavor of this sort was creation of the Institute for the Training of Colored Candidates for the Ministry at Tuscaloosa, Alabama, a school often called Tuscaloosa Institute. In 1884 the General Assembly of the Presbyterian Church (U.S.) renamed the school Stillman Institute in honor of its founder, Charles Allen Stillman. It was to become Stillman College in 1948.

Missions and Interchurch Relations

Consonant with the high commitments made in 1861, Southern Presbyterians began mission work in foreign lands in 1866 by taking over the support of Elias B. Inslee (1823–1871) who had previously served under the Old School Presbyterian Church in China. Three additional ministers, Ben Milm (1844–1928), Matthew H. Houston (1841–1905), and John L. Stuart (1840–1913), set out for that Asian land in the autumn of 1868, and the China Mission was well on its way to establishment and service. In December of that same year, these four met for the purpose of organizing themselves as a mission society.

Christina Ronzone (1831–1896) sailed for her native Italy in 1866 in order to engage in educational work under the direction of the Waldensian Church of that country, with support provided by the Executive Committee of Foreign Missions of the Presbyterian Church (U.S.). In succession the assembly opened missions in Colombia, South America (1869), Brazil (1869), Mexico (1874), Greece (1874), Japan (1885), the Congo (1890), Cuba (1899), and Korea (1892). The Committee of Foreign Missions later discontinued efforts in Italy, Colombia, and Greece and transferred its work in Cuba to the care of the Presbyterian Church (U.S.A.).

In 1869 the General Assembly of the Presbyterian Church (U.S.A.) officially recognized the independent existence of the Southern church and in 1870 made overtures looking toward the establishment of fraternal relations and even ventured to suggest eventual reunion. The Southern brethren were ready for neither, and said so in definite language by an assembly vote of eighty-three to seventeen, though they did proceed to appoint a committee for conference with the Presbyterians of the North.

The General Assembly of 1871 elected William Swan Plumer (1802–1880), possessor of the most famous beard in the history of Southern, and perhaps American, Presbyterianism, as its moderator. He thus became the only ex-moderator of either the Old or New School Assembly to be accorded a similar honor by the Southern Church. Plumer had taken a very active part in the proceedings of the eventful assembly of 1837 and presided over the sessions of its meeting of the following year, each of which was so intimately associated with the Old School–New School division of the Presbyterian Church.

A namesake of this venerable patriarch, William Plumer Jacobs (1842–1917), began what was to prove a notable venture in the field of child care in 1875 with the establishment of Thornwell Orphanage at Clinton, South Carolina. It was in connection with the sponsorship of another of the institutions that he founded at Clinton, Presbyterian College, that the evidently exasperated Jacobs felt moved to record the scarcely controvertible conviction, "We had better trust in the Lord than in the Synod of South Carolina."

Not until 1882 did the Northern and Southern assemblies establish fraternal relations between the two churches. In that year each of these high courts voiced certain regrets for past expressions "which may be regarded as reflecting upon, or offensive to" the other. Herrick Johnson (1832–1913), moderator of the Presbyterian Church (U.S.A.) assembly, followed the communication from that body with a telegram explaining that Northern contrition did not pertain to deliverances relative to "loyalty and rebellion." Despite this unexpected and disconcerting rider, the assemblies arranged reciprocal visits by their respective representatives in 1883. By 1887 proposals looking toward organic union entered into the ensuing conversations, but more than six decades were to pass before any action involving constitutional commitments was to take place.

Although the General Assembly of 1874 was not prepared to join in the formation of what came to be known as The Alliance of the Reformed Churches throughout the World Holding the Presbyterian System, the assembly of the following year moved cautiously toward participation. In 1876 the assembly elected a number of delegates to attend the Alliance's 1877 meeting in Edinburgh, and the church thereafter continued to demonstrate a growing concern for this Pan-Presbyterian association.

While James Woodrow expressed the opinion in the course of a five-hour speech before the Synod of South Carolina in 1884 that the truth or falsity of the doctrine of evolution was "a matter of extremely small importance," there were others whose actions clearly indicated their strong disagreement. In 1861 Woodrow, an Englishman by birth though a Scot by heritage, an American by adoption, and a Southerner by conviction, joined the faculty of Columbia Theological Seminary, where he occupied the chair represented by the Perkins Professorship of Natural Science in Connection with Revelation. Twenty-two years later (1883), the board of directors of the seminary, no doubt moved by rumors then current, requested him to publish his views on the subject of evolution, with particular reference to the creation of the body of Adam. The Columbia Alumni Association, aware of this request, selected Woodrow to make the customary annual address before its members in 1884. A delay in the publication of his opinions on the subject in question resulted in this speech, delivered on May 7, 1884, serving as the first formal presentation of the subject of his conclusions on the matter. At this time he expressed the belief that the body of Adam may have been evolved from that of a lower animal, though he held to the creation of the soul of humanity's first parent by a direct act of God.

As a result of this and like statements, a reconstructed board of directors of the seminary removed Woodrow from his chair with the concurrence of the supporting synods and of the General Assembly. The Presbytery of Augusta, of which he was a member, found him not guilty of heresy, but the Synod of Georgia reversed this judgment, and the General Assembly confirmed the synod's action. Woodrow's standing as a minister of the church remained unchanged, however; in 1901 the Synod of South Carolina elected him as its moderator.

By the end of its first quarter of separate existence, the Presbyterian Church (U.S.) listed 150,396 communicants as compared with approximately seventy thousand at its beginning. It should be remembered that some 27,599 of this total had been received through union with other bodies. At the same time, the church embraced 2,236 local congregations and 1,116 ministerial members.

Into the Twentieth Century

The General Assembly broke with precedent in 1893 as it elected ruling elder James W. Lapsley (1835–1901) of Anniston, Alabama, as its moderator. This marked the first time that anyone other than a minister had held this office.

In 1897 the General Assembly celebrated the 250th anniversary of the close of the Westminster Assembly with the delivery of a series of addresses dealing with that famous gathering of the seventeenth-century divines. These speeches subsequently appeared in book form as the *Memorial Volume of the Westminster Assembly, 1647–1897.*

Three prominent Southern Presbyterian ministers, each serving at widely separated places, demonstrated effective concern with as many questions of moment during the nineteenth century. John Leighton Wilson, at that time a representative of the Congregational Mission Board at Cape Palmas on the African coast, was interested in the termination of the trade in slaves. In this connection, he wrote a convincing pamphlet on the subject. Lord Palmerston arranged for the printing of a special edition of ten thousand copies for distribution among numerous persons in England. Soon thereafter the British naval squadron charged with halting this trade was strengthened through the introduction of faster ships, a move vigorously advocated by Wilson in his publication.

Hampden C. Dubose (1845–1910) of the church's China Mission proved an able leader in the fight against the opium traffic in the Far East. Benjamin M. Palmer, the great New Orleans pastor and preacher, administered what might well be termed the coup de grace to the Louisiana Lottery. This was accomplished through an address he delivered on the night of June 25, 1891, in the Grand Opera House of that city.

Almost to the end of the nineteenth century, Union Theological Seminary operated in the Virginia village of Hampden-Sydney, in close proximity to the college of that name. Here, according to Samuel Hall Chester (1851–1940), one of its students, the seminary was subjected to "almost the isolation of a monastery." In 1898, however, an important move was completed when the institution opened its sessions in the city of Richmond. This change of location took place under the guidance of Walter W. Moore (1857–1926), later president of the seminary and probably the leading spirit of the Southern church through the first quarter of the twentieth century.

The distinctive missionary endeavors of Edward Owinga Guerrant (1838–1916) marked the closing years of the old and the opening ones of the new century. Guerrant was a former Confederate soldier of Huguenot ancestry who labored in the mountain regions of Kentucky and several adjoining states. A physician before he entered the ministry, he carried on much of his activity under the auspices of the Soul Winner Society over which he presided. In 1913 the executive committee of Home Missions of the Presbyterian Church (U.S.), reported that the holdings and work of the society had been transferred to its care.

In 1906 the church acquired a summer conference ground in the mountains of North Carolina, known as Montreat, through the interests and exertions of James R. Howerton (1861–1924), at that time pastor of the First Presbyterian Church of Charlotte, North Carolina. Howerton served briefly as president of the Mountain Retreat Association, as the holding corporation of the center was known. In 1911 Robert Campbell Anderson Jr. (1864–1955) left the pastorate to become his delayed successor. Holding the office of president for thirty-six years, he retired in 1947, leaving an institution that had achieved eminence as a denominational center both in America and Britain. He found a capable colleague in his wife (d. 1962), who gave freely of her interest and means toward the up-building of Montreat. In 1916 the Andersons, along with certain associates, established a school for girls that now operates as a coeducational institution under the name of Montreat-Anderson College.

In 1909 the General Assembly, meeting at Savannah, Georgia, engaged in a celebration of the four hundredth anniversary of the birth of John Calvin. Twelve speeches delivered in this connection later appeared in print as *Calvin Memorial Addresses.*

The 1909 General Assembly took action looking toward the consolidation of several of its separate committees and the promotion of the grace of giving across the church. This resulted in the setting up of a permanent Committee on Systematic Beneficence, designed to bring about a more

united effort in appeals for monetary support and to stimulate the benevo-
lences of the Church. Other committees constituted at the same time were
those of Foreign Missions, Home Missions, Christian Education, and
Ministerial Relief, and Publication and Sabbath School Work.

The church celebrated its semicentennial at the 1911 meeting of the
General Assembly, held at Louisville, Kentucky, with appropriate addresses
delivered by three of its ministers, Henry Alexander White (1861–1926),
Theron H. Rice (1867–1922), and Egbert W. Smith (1862–1944). The
published volume that later incorporated these speeches bore the title of
Semi-Centennial Memorial Addresses.

Women's organizations in the congregations of the church in the South
began to take form in the early years of the nineteenth century, while those
on a presbyterial level first emerged in the closing years of that era. The
General Assembly of 1912 sanctioned the structure of a churchwide society
for women that took the name of the Women's Auxiliary of the Presbyterian Church in the United States. This organization was so known until
1949, when the assembly replaced the title of Women's Auxiliary with
that of the Women of the Church. Mrs. W. C. Winsborough (1865–1940)
became superintendent of the Women's Auxiliary in 1912 and continued as
leader of the women until 1929.

The 1923 General Assembly took action toward the formation of the
men of the church in somewhat similar fashion. While some progress was
made in this connection from time to time, the men never responded to the
challenge of a distinct organization as did the women.

With a view to the preparation of religious workers other than ministers, and with the education of women especially in mind, the church began
operation of the General Assembly's Training School for Lay Workers in
1914. Located adjacent to the campus of Union Theological Seminary in
Richmond, Virginia, it has thus been able to draw upon the seminary for
instructors and make use of the library of the older institution, as well as
provide many a minister, or incipient minister, with a wife. In later years
(1959) the name of the Presbyterian School of Christian Education displaced the earlier designation of the institution. The General Assembly of
1915 erected a synod, new not only in name but in concept as well, in that
it followed the general boundaries of the southern Appalachian Mountain region rather than conforming to state lines. The Synod of Appalachia
originally covered portions of Tennessee, North Carolina, and Virginia,
with several churches in Kentucky and West Virginia. Robert F. Campbell

(1858–1947), pastor of the First Church of Asheville, North Carolina, who became prominent as a leader in the formation of the synod, served as its first moderator. The Synod of Appalachia functioned in an effective manner with respect to the progress of Presbyterianism within its borders until its dissolution, over its own protest, with its final meeting held in 1973.

Work among the African Americans was the object of particular attention on the part of the church during 1916. In 1899 Presbyterians had organized an independent synod by the name of Afro-American. Two black presbyteries made up of black constituents, Central Alabama and Ethel, were formed within the Southern Presbyterian Church. In 1916, following conferences with representatives of the Afro-American Synod, the General Assembly made plans for the reorganization of the synod under the auspices of the Presbyterian Church (U.S.). These endeavors resulted in the erection of what came to be known in 1917 as Snedecor Memorial Synod. The synod thereupon took its place as a regular court of that order in the framework of the General Assembly.

During World War I (1917–1918), the church committed its ministry to men in uniform to a body known as the War Work Council. This group, with James I. Vance (1862–1939) as chairman, included fifteen of the denomination's leaders. The council's report to the General Assembly of 1918 indicated that fifteen camp pastors were at work under its auspices.

A series of financial campaigns in the interests of educational institutions occupied the attention of a number of the synods of the church in the years immediately following the war. Marion E. Melvin (1876–1954) effectively supervised much of this activity and subsequently accepted a call of the General Assembly to become secretary of stewardship for the church.

In an effort to promote and coordinate the entire work of the Southern Presbyterian Church, the General Assembly of 1927 formed what came, for obvious reasons, to be known as the Committee of Forty-Four. This replaced the several executive committees that had functioned on the assembly level in previous years. It represented an unusual concentration of power and was not long to endure, for the General Assembly of 1933 dissolved the committee and returned to the plan of administration through its former separate agencies. The concept of the Committee of Forty-Four was dormant, rather than dead, and was to emerge once more in the realm of ecclesiastical organization after the passage of forty years.

In 1926 the church accepted the offer of Samuel Mills Tenney (1871–1939) and the Presbyterian Historical Society of the Synod of Texas, through which it tended its collections of Presbyteriana as a nucleus of a churchwide historical institution. This resulted in the establishment of the Historical Foundation of the Presbyterian and Reformed Churches (1927) at Montreat, North Carolina.

The earlier years of the decade beginning in 1930 brought with them an economic depression that placed severe handicaps on the work of all denominations in the United States, including Southern Presbyterians, and a quite perceptible tendency toward less conservatism in doctrinal matters. This liberalization began to make itself known soon after 1930 and in ten years was becoming increasingly evident in the deliberations of the General Assembly. The death of Walter W. Moore in 1926 might well be considered a turning point with respect to these changes.

Another war followed the Depression. During its course, religious ministry among the armed forces as represented by the Presbyterian Church (U.S.) was under an organization known as the Defense Service Council with Benjamin R. Lacy Jr. (1886–1981), president of Union Theological Seminary, as chairman and Daniel T. Caldwell (1892–1952) as director in the field.

Through regularly prescribed procedures, the church inserted two additional chapters in its confession of faith during 1941–1942. These were titled "Of the Holy Spirit" and "Of the Gospel."

Midcentury and Beyond

The year 1949 was a time of reorganization of the agencies of the church, including the setting up of a general council charged with the overall planning and financing of the denomination's benevolent work. These arrangements called for certain combinations of agencies and alteration of titular designations in several instances. The power exercised by the general council was indicated by the fact that it had virtual control over the formulation of the budget of the various boards and agencies, although these, of course, were officially fixed by the General Assembly.

The dissolution of Snedecor Memorial Synod in 1950 indicated an altered approach to the work of the church among black believers. Following this enactment, the former presbyteries of that synod were, with some changes in names and alignment, incorporated into the regular synods. This plan of organization prevailed until 1964, when the General Assembly took action eliminating black presbyteries and assigning their ministers and churches to other presbyteries of appropriate geographical jurisdiction.

In 1942 a volume titled *Ministerial Directory of the Presbyterian Church, U.S., 1861–1941* made its appearance. Eugene C. Scott (1889–1972), stated clerk of the General Assembly, compiled this treasury of clerical biography, which was issued in revised form a decade later. The book proved to be of exceptional serviceability, and its major usefulness was providing vacant congregations with data on prospective pastors and as an instrument for serious biographical and historical study.

An effort to unite the Presbyterian Church (U.S.A.), the United Presbyterian Church, and the Presbyterian Church (U.S.) failed in 1954–1955 when the presbyteries of the Southern church voted adversely with respect to the proposal, as related in a previous chapter.

Pursuant to the reorganization of 1949, the General Assembly located several boards and agencies of the assembly that had previously operated elsewhere in Atlanta, Georgia. This concentration led to that city becoming in reality the church's year-round capital, with a portion of such activity shifted to Montreat during the conference season of July and August each year. The assembly forces thus settled in Atlanta secured an extensive parcel of centrally located real estate on which they erected a commodious building in keeping with their requirements.

Efforts to celebrate the centennial of the church's organization in 1961 did not generate much enthusiasm. The exercises attendant upon such endeavors proved of only minor efficacy in promoting a constructive recall of the great events of the past. One edifying result of the project, however, was the publication of T. Watson Street's *The Story of Southern Presbyterians*.

After the failure of an earlier effort, the General Assembly of 1963 submitted to the presbyteries a revision of the Form of Government, providing for the ordination of women to offices of the church. Following an affirmative response on the part of a substantial majority of these courts, the 1964 General Assembly took final action making women eligible for ministry, the eldership, and the diaconate. Women sat as commissioners in the 1965 General Assembly.

The General Assembly of 1934 had established a Permanent Committee on Social and Moral Welfare that developed into a Department of Christian Relations in 1946. Deliverances on the matter of race relations and integration in the 1950s signaled the growing concern of the church in the area represented by these actions. Much of the attention of the 1964 General Assembly centered upon the relation of the Southern Presbyterian Church to the blacks, as did that of a considerable portion of its constituency during the ensuing twelve months. The 1965 General Assembly, following the required constitutional approval by the presbyteries, enacted an amendment to the Directory of Worship that reads: "No one shall be excluded from participation in public worship in the Lord's house on the grounds of race, color, or class."

In addition to overseas missions earlier established in China, Brazil, Mexico, Japan, The Congo, and Korea, the church initiated evangelical activities in Portugal (1946), Ecuador (1946), and Iraq (1956). In each of these three fields Southern Presbyterians began their work as cooperative enterprises with other denominations. This was true also of similar endeavors later begun in several other lands. The closing of the mainland of China because of the Communist conquest resulted in a concentration of missionary forces on the island of Taiwan (1949). By 1965 the World Mission representative of the Presbyterian Church (U.S.) had reached a total of 553 agents.

A meeting heralded as a Consultation of Missions took place at Montreat under the direction of the Board of World Missions in the fall of 1962. Numerous workers from the foreign field gathered with those from the home base and engaged in a full discussion of the missionary enterprise. These sessions revealed a growing emphasis upon the social aspects of missions and an increased trend toward the assumption of responsibility on the part of the various national groups for the work in their respective areas.

By the late 1960s it had become clearly evident that there was marked divergence between two wings of the church that may be described as liberals and conservatives. These differences grew out of a conflicting concept of the Scriptures and their place in the convictions and practices of the church, with the liberal element placing strong emphasis upon social action, and the conservatives contending that evangelism ought to be kept to the fore in Christian work. By the end of the decade, the liberals had gained such commanding control of the General Assembly that their policies and programs almost invariably prevailed in that court.

As a result of these differences, a group of Southern Presbyterians began the Reformed Theological Seminary at Jackson, Mississippi, in fall 1966. The establishment of this institution grew out of the dissatisfaction of its founders with theological education in the Presbyterian Church (U.S.). The Reformed Seminary, which has no official connection with the church, emphasizes the doctrine of the inerrancy of the original text of the Bible, the theology of the Westminster Standards, the biblical form of church polity, and the evangelical mission of the church. It has grown rapidly. The academic year of 1975–1976 brought an enrollment of 270 students, with a faculty representing a number of different Presbyterian and Reformed denominations.

In a generally unforeseen demonstration of ecumenical proclivity, the General Assembly of 1966 voted to assume the obligations incidental to full participation in the Consultation on Church Union. Southern Presbyterians had previously attended meetings held in this connection only as observers.

Following a controversy as to whether a three-fourths or a simple majority vote of the presbyteries was required for the enactment of such legislation, the General Assembly of 1968 ruled that union presbyteries and synods with other denominations of like faith and order could be legally created following a favorable vote of one assembly, the concurrence of a majority of the presbyteries, and ratification by the next assembly. A number of union presbyteries, generally in the border areas of the church, were soon functioning after the foregoing procedure had legitimized such courts. The vote of the presbyteries, however, was adverse with respect to union synods.

In 1969 efforts to unite the Presbyterian Church (U.S.) and the Reformed Church in America (Dutch Reformed) fell short of success. The Southern General Assembly acted favorably upon the proposal, as did its constituent presbyteries and the General Synod of the Reformed Church, but it failed to receive the requisite two-thirds vote of the classes of the latter body. This did not deter the 1969 Southern General Assembly from voting for the appointment of a committee to confer with a like representation from the Presbyterian Church (U.S.A.).

In the wake of a period of planning by an ad interim committee, the Assemblies of 1971 and 1972 moved to reduce the number of synods in the church. Upon their formation, certain of these new synods combined the territory of presbyteries within their bounds to enlarge the courts of this gradation.

On the other hand, the real rarity of things new under the sun was exemplified by an act of the 1972 Assembly reviving the shades of the Committee of Forty-Four of an earlier era. This Assembly set up a provisional general executive board of seventy members, to be replaced in 1973 by a permanent board of the same nature and name. The new inclusive body exercised functions previously pertaining to such boards as those of Overseas Missions, National Ministries, Christian Education, and Women's Work. The administration of the affairs of the Board of Annuities and Relief remained unchanged. Also, 1973 marked the appearance of the second and third volumes of Ernest Trice Thompson's *Presbyterians in the South*, thus completing the publication of a work of major importance.

The 1969 General Assembly of the church appointed a special committee and charged it with the work of preparing a contemporary confession of faith. In 1976 this committee submitted such a document to the Assembly, which acted favorably upon the committee's recommendation and transmitted the new confession to the presbyteries for their consideration and action. This Assembly action proposed that the new confession, titled A Declaration of Faith, be adopted as one of ten doctrinal standards of the church, the other nine to include the Westminster Confession of Faith, the Larger Catechism, and the Shorter Catechism. Less than two-thirds of the presbyteries, however, took favorable action upon the Assembly's proposals. Since a vote of three-fourths of these presbyteries was necessary for the making of such a constitutional change, the projected plans failed.

The United Synod

The separate existence of the United Synod was of brief duration. When that synod joined forces with those of the Presbyterian Church in the Confederate States of America in 1864, it had functioned for fewer than seven years.

Even before the adjournment of the New School General Assembly of 1857 at Cleveland, Ohio, fifteen commissioners aligned with the Southern party, in conjunction with two other ministers, issued a letter setting forth the reason for their impending withdrawal from the New School church. This was in the nature of a protest against the actions of the Assembly on the question of slavery. The letter included a proposal to bring together "all Constitutional Presbyterians in the land who are opposed to the agitation with regard to slavery in the General Assembly" and to express the desire to form a nationwide church of such constituents. Richmond, Virginia, was the site for the meeting.

More than 150 delegates representing the Southern contingent of the New School gathered for five days during August 1857. They collectively expressed the opinion that union with the Old School General Assembly would be desirable and made arrangements for a meeting to be held in Knoxville, Tennessee, in the spring of the following year.

The United Synod of the Presbyterian Church (U.S.A.) dated from April 2, 1858, when it was formally organized in Knoxville. It then adopted a declaration of principles along the lines of the letter of the previous year.

At this initial meeting the synod made a proposal for union with the Old School Assembly, then in session at New Orleans, but the latter body rebuffed these advances. The synod made provision for a Domestic and Foreign Missionary Board during this 1858 meeting.

The synod met next at Lynchburg, Virginia, in 1859. Reports submitted at this meeting indicated that the United Synod then consisted of three subordinate synods (Virginia, Tennessee, and Mississippi), fourteen presbyteries, 118 ministers, 187 churches, and 12,125 communicant members.

The court held further meetings at Huntsville, Alabama, in May 1860 and at Richmond in 1861. No meeting took place in 1862 due to the lack of a quorum. The Synod of 1863 appointed a committee to confer with a like representation from the Southern General Assembly with a view to drawing up a basis for union between the two churches. These committees met at Lynchburg on July 24 of that year and found little difficulty in preparing such a document. Robert L. Dabney, chairman of the assembly's committee, facilitated this work by his opening remarks at the first session held by the conferees.

The 1864 General Assembly of the Presbyterian Church in the Confederate States of America took favorable action on union, though basing it upon the existing standards of the two churches rather than the articles submitted by the union committee. Not a single commissioner appeared at Dublin, Virginia, for the 1864 meeting of the United Synod, the war having reached southwest Virginia by that time. The stated clerk then issued a call for a special meeting of the synod to convene at Lynchburg on August 25 of that year. There, on August 26, the commissioners ratified the plans presented for union as already acted upon by the General Assembly. In accord with article 6 of these provisions, the union became effective on that date.

Efforts of the United Synod to achieve union with the Southern Presbyterians were not altogether successful. One of its subordinate synods, that of Tennessee, expressed disapproval of the course of action taken by the United Synod and sought re-entry into the General Assembly of the Presbyterian Church in the United States of America, meaning the New School Assembly. This assembly received the Tennessee Synod at its meeting in 1866, with genuine satisfaction. Herein lies the explanation of the fact that the United Presbyterian Church (U.S.A.) later claimed a considerable constituency in the eastern portion of Tennessee.

The strength of the United Synod lay in Virginia, east Tennessee, and Mississippi, with scattered congregations in several other states. At the time of the union of 1864, it embraced three subordinate synods and a total of thirteen presbyteries.

Two religious weeklies were associated with, and approved by, the United Synod. One of these, the *Christian Observer*, was a refugee from Philadelphia to Richmond during the course of the War between the States. Its editor, Amasa Converse (1795–1872), moderated the final sessions of the United Synod at Knoxville. The *Presbyterian Witness* (1851–1860) of Knoxville, and, for a brief period, of Bristol, Tennessee, also served as an organ of the denomination.

Michael Demetrius Kalopothakes (1825–1911), a native of Greece, represented the synod as an evangelist in that land. The War of 1861–1865 presented serious difficulties for both the church and its missionary in the support and conduct of this work in Greece.

The United Synod passed into the Southern Presbyterian Church and into history.

SUGGESTED ADDITIONAL READINGS >>

Amant, Penrose. *A History of the Presbyterian Church in Louisiana*. Richmond, Va.: Whittet & Shepperson, 1961.

Calhoun, David B. *Cloud of Witnesses: The Story of First Presbyterian Church, Augusta, 1804–2004*. Augusta, General Assembly: First Presbyterian Church, 2004.

———. *The Glory of the Lord Risen upon It: First Presbyterian Church, Columbia, 1795–1995*. Columbia, S.C.: First Presbyterian Church, 1994.

———. *The Splendor of Grace: Independent Presbyterian Church, Savannah, 1755–2005*. Savannah, Ga.: Independent Presbyterian Church, 2005.

Conkin, Paul K. *Cane Ridge: America's Pentecost*. Madison: University of Wisconsin Press, 1990.

Craig, D. I. *A History of the Development of the Presbyterian Church in North Carolina*. Richmond, Va.: Whittet & Shepperson, 1907.

Dabney, Robert L. *A Defense of Virginia*. New York: E. J. Hale & Son, 1867.

Davis, Robert P., et al. *Virginia Presbyterians in American Life: Hanover Presbytery, 1755–1980*. Richmond, Va.: Hanover Presbytery, 1982.

Hart, D. G. and John R. Muether. *Seeking a Better Country: 300 Years of American Presbyterianism*. Phillipsburg, N.J.: P&R, 2006.

Hill, Samuel, ed. *Encyclopedia of Religion in the South*. Macon, Ga.: Mercer University Press, 1984.

Johnson, Thomas Cary. *History of the Southern Presbyterian Church*. New York: Christian Literature Company, 1894.

Jones, F. D. and W. H. Mills. *A History of the Presbyterian Church in South Carolina since 1850*. Columbia: Synod of South Carolina, 1925.

Lacy, Benjamin R. *Revivals in the Midst of the Years*. Richmond, Va.: John Knox, 1945.

Matthews, Harold M. Jr. *Religion in the Old South*. Chicago: University of Chicago Press, 1977.

McDonnold, B. W. *History of the Cumberland Presbyterian Church*. Nashville: Board of Publication, Cumberland Presbyterian Church, 1893.

Nabers, Charles H., ed. *The Southern Presbyterian Pulpit*. New York: Fleming H. Revell, 1928.

Palmer, Benjamin Morgan. *The Life and Letters of James Henley Thornwell*. Reprint, Edinburgh: Banner of Truth, 1974.

Parker, Harold M. Jr. *The United Synod of the South: The Southern New School Presbyterian Church*. Richmond, Va.: John Knox, 1961.

Piepkorn, Arthur C. *Profiles in Belief: Protestantism*. 2 vols. San Francisco: Harper San Francisco, 1978.

Robinson, William Childs. *Columbia Theological Seminary and the Southern Presbyterian Church, 1831–1931*. Atlanta: Dennis Lindsey, 1931.

Smith, Morton H. *A Brief History of Subscription to the Creeds and Confessions with Particular Reference to Presbyterian Churches*. Taylors, S.C.: Greenville Presbyterian Theological Seminary, 2002.

———. *Studies in Southern Presbyterian Theology*. Phillipsburg, N.J.: Presbyterian & Reformed Publishers, 1987. Reprint of 1962 edition.

Stacy, James. *A History of the Presbyterian Church in Georgia*. Elberton, Ga.: Press of the State, 1912.

Street, T. Watson. *The Story of the Southern Presbyterians*. Richmond, Va.: John Knox, 1960.

Thompson, Charles. *The Presbyterians: The Story of the Churches*. New York: Baker & Taylor, 1903.

Thompson, Ernest Trice. *Presbyterian Missions in the Southern United States*. Richmond, Va.: Presbyterian Committee of Publication, 1934.

———. *Presbyterians in the South*. 3 vols. Richmond, Va.: John Knox, 1963–1973.

Thompson, R. E. *A History of the Presbyterian Churches in the United States*. New York: Christian Literature Company, 1895.

Vance, James I., et al. *Pioneer Presbyterianism in Tennessee.* Richmond, Va.: Presbyterian Committee of Publication, 1898.

Vander Velde, Lewis G. *The Presbyterian Churches and the Federal Union, 1861–1869.* Cambridge, Mass.: Harvard University Press, 1932.

Weeks, Lewis B. *Kentucky Presbyterians.* Atlanta: John Knox, 1983.

Wells, John M. *Southern Presbyterian Worthies.* Richmond, Va.: Presbyterian Committee of Publication, 1936.

White, Henry Alexander. *Southern Presbyterian Leaders, 1683–1911.* Edinburgh: Banner of Truth, 2000. Reprint of 1911 edition.

THIRTEEN

Reformed Theology in
Nineteenth-Century America

In 1808 Archibald Alexander (1772–1851), pastor of Pine Street Presbyterian Church, Philadelphia, and moderator of the General Assembly, appealed to that body to establish schools of theology for the education of ministers. The Presbytery of Philadelphia, at the urging of Ashbel Green (1762–1848), minister at Second Presbyterian Church in that city, responded to Alexander's call by asking the next General Assembly to proceed with the implementation of his proposal, and Princeton Theological Seminary became the first in a series of institutions created for the explicit purpose of preparing Presbyterian ministers.

The Founding of Princeton Theological Seminary

Princeton College had for some time educated pastors for the church, but by the early nineteenth century, suspicions had arisen that the teaching there was not entirely orthodox. The number of graduates from that college becoming ministers had been declining, while the older Harvard and Yale Colleges were in the control of Congregationalists, and at Harvard, Unitarian beliefs were in the ascendancy. In 1812 Ashbel Green succeeded Samuel Stanhope Smith (1751–1819) as president of Princeton College and, in the same year, became chairman of the board of directors at the new Princeton Theological Seminary. Archibald Alexander left the Pine Street Church in Philadelphia to become the first professor at the seminary, where he remained until his death. Samuel Miller (1769–1850) and Charles Hodge (1797–1878) soon joined him on the faculty.

The founding of Princeton Seminary marked the birth of staunchly Reformed scholarship on an institutional basis to serve the American Presbyterian Church. The seminary became duly famous, as professors maintained high academic standards while defending Old School principles against the higher criticism of the Bible. Adherence to the Westminster

Standards, including the inerrancy of Scripture, was the hallmark of this confessional institution. Only three students enrolled for the first year of classes, and Alexander taught all subjects. Enrollment rose to five the next year, when Samuel Davies joined the faculty.

Other Seminaries

Additional Presbyterian seminaries developed soon after the opening of Princeton. Auburn Theological Seminary in New York opened in 1818 and Union Theological Seminary in Virginia in 1823. Columbia Theological Seminary in South Carolina began in 1828. Lane Theological Seminary in Ohio began as an Old School institution, but its president, Lyman Beecher, soon led it in the New School direction.

The major alternative to Princeton Seminary in the northeast was Union Theological Seminary in New York City, which opened in 1836, and was, from its inception, for the most part under the control of New School proponents. Although Union Seminary required its professors to subscribe to the Westminster Standards, it stressed existential religion more than doctrinal orthodoxy. Eventually the school abandoned subscription, and its professors clashed with those at Princeton Seminary.

Princeton Theologians

Archibald Alexander

Archibald Alexander (1772–1851) was from Virginia of a Scots-Irish family, and he studied at Liberty Hall Academy, which became Washington and Lee University. He was president of Hampden-Sydney College (1796–1807) and pastor at Pine Street Presbyterian Church, Philadelphia (1807–1812). As moderator of the General Assembly, he promoted the establishment of Princeton Seminary, of which he became president and first professor.

As president of Princeton, Alexander stressed academic excellence and led the institution in defending historic Christianity by compiling evidences in support of the faith and logically refuting its critics, all the while acknowledging the witness of the Holy Spirit was essential to convince unbelievers that Scripture is the Word of God.

When Old School zealots proposed ousting New School exponents from the denomination, Alexander strove to preserve unity, but eventually he became convinced that was not possible. As evidence of his changed attitude, he supported abrogation of the Plan of Union with the

Congregationalists. Deep personal piety characterized his life, matched by excellent scholarship throughout his career.

Samuel Miller

Samuel Miller (1769–1850) was a graduate of the University of Pennsylvania and son of a Presbyterian pastor in Delaware. By the time he became moderator of the General Assembly in 1806, he had acquired a reputation for fine scholarship. One of the founders of Princeton Theological Seminary, Miller joined the faculty as professor of church history and polity in 1813, a position he held until his death in 1850.

An expert on church government, Miller opposed episcopacy and congregationalism in favor of Presbyterian polity with its rule by elders. He was a staunch opponent of New England Theology and a vigorous advocate of Old School principles. His book *Letters Concerning the Constitution and Order of the Christian Ministry* (1807) assured his reputation as a defender of Presbyterianism. When Miller taught church history, he began with the Old Testament church and stressed its continuity with its New Testament successor. As champions of literal creation as revealed in Genesis, Miller and Alexander worked well together.

Charles Hodge

Charles Hodge (1797–1878) began teaching at Princeton in 1822. His many publications, including *The Way of Life* (1841) and his *Systematic Theology* (1873), plus numerous articles in the *Biblical Repertory and Princeton Review,* received wide acclaim. As editor of the seminary's publication, Hodge exerted broad influence throughout Protestant circles in America.

Hodge was born in Philadelphia and graduated from Princeton College in 1815 and from Princeton Seminary in 1819. Except for two years of study in Europe, he spent his entire career at Princeton Seminary, where he taught more than three thousand students. Hodge published commentaries on Romans, Ephesians, and Corinthians. He was moderator of the General Assembly in 1846. In 1874 he assailed the hypothesis of organic evolution with his book *What Is Darwinism?* When a painful hip disorder prevented him from walking, Hodge conducted classes in his own home.

Hodge was among the first American scholars to attend a European university. At Halle he studied Semitic languages and attended lectures at the University of Berlin. Archibald Alexander feared Hodge might imbibe German higher criticism of the Bible, so he wrote to his colleague in

Germany, urging him to remain loyal to Scripture. Hodge not only honored Alexander's request but also became a militant defender of Scripture and the most widely acclaimed theologian in America at that time.

Joseph Addison Alexander

Joseph Addison Alexander (1809–1861) became an assistant to Hodge in 1834. This son of Archibald Alexander was born in Philadelphia, educated at Princeton College, and studied ancient languages in Europe, a discipline he pursued to the point that eventually he mastered forty-five languages. Although learned in higher criticism, he, like Hodge, defended the integrity of Scripture with impressive scholarship. He wrote commentaries on Psalms, Isaiah, Mark, and Acts and produced numerous scholarly articles. His academic productivity was prodigious.

Joseph Addison Alexander was staunchly Reformed in the Westminster tradition, but he was not prominent in church affairs, preferring the life of scholarship to ecclesiastical leadership. Union Theological Seminary in New York offered him a faculty position, but he refused it to go to Princeton, where he established the department of Old Testament Studies. Alexander's elective classes in Arabic, Syriac, and Aramaic produced some outstanding missionary scholars well prepared for service in the Middle East.

Defense of the Faith at Princeton Theological Seminary

Princeton professors were quick to realize the New England Theology of Samuel Hopkins, Nathaniel Taylor, and others subverted the Reformed faith. This was especially apparent with regard to the doctrine of original sin, the denial of which led Archibald Alexander and Hodge to defend that biblical teaching vigorously. The danger of the denial became clear when Charles G. Finney began espousing a Pelagian view of sin and salvation in a persuasive manner that convinced many people. Finney had particular disdain for Princeton Seminary and its Old School Presbyterianism, which he considered unenlightened. In 1831, while at Park Street Church, Boston, Finney preached "Sinners Bound to Change Their Own Hearts," a sermon in which he scorned Calvinism and derided the Westminster Confession of Faith. Hodge accused Finney of nullifying the work of Christ by making salvation merely a matter of human choice.

While Princeton scholars rejected Finney's doctrine and criticized his evangelistic methods, they sought for revival themselves. Archibald Alexander, Hodge, and their faculty colleagues were warmhearted, experimental preachers, and devout men of prayer. Prayer meetings of professors and students were daily occurrences at the seminary in 1831, and numerous conversions took place, as students came to love the God about whom they had been learning in classes. In 1837 Archibald Alexander and Samuel Miller preached at New Brunswick, New Jersey, where hundreds of people professed faith in Christ. Piety and scholarship were then partners at Princeton Seminary.

William Henry Green

Apologetics, the defense of the faith, was a matter of emphatic effort at Princeton, as professors there understood how German higher criticism undermined confidence in the reliability of the Bible. Joseph Addison Alexander led the way in this endeavor, and William Henry Green (1825–1900) soon joined him. Green, a graduate of Lafayette College and Princeton Seminary, joined the faculty as a professor of Old Testament, and he remained in that position for fifty years. He was chairman of the Old Testament committee that produced the American Standard Version of the Bible (1901). His books *The Higher Criticism of the Pentateuch* (1895) and *General Introduction to the Old Testament* (1898) established his reputation as an erudite defender of orthodoxy and made him the major opponent of Charles A. Briggs, controversial higher critic at Union Theological Seminary, New York.

Archibald Alexander Hodge

Princeton theologians perceived that underlying the higher critical approach to Scripture lay an antisupernatural conception of Christianity. Archibald Alexander Hodge (1832–1886), son of Charles Hodge, whom he succeeded in the chair of theology, led the opposition to the naturalist view of the faith. After graduating from Princeton Seminary, A. A. Hodge had gone to India as a missionary, but illness forced him to return. After a term of service as a Presbyterian pastor, he became a professor at Western Theological Seminary, Allegheny, Pennsylvania, from which he moved to Princeton in 1878 and remained until his death.

A firmly confessional scholar, A. A. Hodge expounded the Reformed faith in his *Outlines of Theology* (1878), in which he replied to liberals who approached Scripture with the axioms of a naturalist worldview. Hodge was relentless in insisting on the inerrancy of the Bible. When secularists proposed restricting religion to private life, Hodge argued that God holds nations as well as people accountable for obeying His moral law. Hodge accepted the separation of church and state, but his postmillennial eschatology led him to call for the integration of all areas of national as well as personal life with the Christian faith.

B. B. Warfield

Upon the death of A. A. Hodge, Benjamin Breckinridge Warfield (1851–1921) followed him as professor of theology. He had graduated from Princeton College and Princeton Seminary and had pursued further study in Europe. After a pastoral ministry in Baltimore, Warfield became professor of New Testament at Western Theological Seminary, from which he moved to Princeton in 1887.

A prolific author, Warfield produced hundreds of articles and several books in defense of the Scripture and the Reformed faith. His vigorous apologetic for orthodoxy did not reflect a pugnacious attitude, as Warfield, in the manner of a gentleman scholar, admired others with whom he disagreed and complimented them when they made helpful contributions. His opposition to naturalism was firm, and he resisted efforts in the Christian community to accommodate its ideas. No one was better informed about liberal and radical theologians than he, as with great skill he perceptively showed how critics of Christianity wrote from the perspective of their anti-supernatural worldviews. Some of Warfield's best essays are book reviews in which he examined the works of others in a judiciously fair manner.

Even more than his predecessors at Princeton Seminary, Warfield argued for the rational superiority of Christianity over its critics, and he never shrank from confronting a challenge, as when in 1903 he produced articles in opposition to revising the Westminster Confession of Faith.

Among Warfield's works are *The Lord of Glory* (1907), *The Plan of Salvation* (1915), and *Counterfeit Miracles* (1918). Eventually his major writings were collected and published in ten volumes. So convinced was he of the truth of biblical teaching that he believed Christianity would, in the end, discredit all of its competitors in the arena of debate.*

---

*It is rather incongruous, however, that this champion of biblical doctrine conceded that Adam and Eve might have had animal ancestors. Helpful sketches of the Princeton theologians appear in David B. Calhoun, *Princeton Seminary*, 2 vols. (Edinburgh: Banner of Truth, 1996).

Reformed Education in the American South

Hampden-Sidney College

As early as 1776 the Presbytery of the South established a school for theological education at Hampden-Sidney College, where Samuel Stanhope Smith (1751–1819) was the founding professor. Smith was a graduate of Princeton College and became a popular preacher in Virginia. Smith was not consistently Reformed in his beliefs, as his willingness to accommodate rationalist ideas attests, although he firmly asserted confidence in the authority of the Bible. In 1779 he became professor of moral philosophy at Princeton College.

Liberty Hall Academy

Another early effort to provide theological education in the South led to the founding of Liberty Hall Academy at Lexington, Virginia, in 1776, a school that was to become Washington and Lee University, of which Archibald Alexander was a product. When the Synod of Virginia resolved to create a theological seminary, it tried unsuccessfully to enlist Alexander to lead it.

Union Theological Seminary

In 1812 a full-fledged seminary was established at Hampden-Sydney College, when Moses Hoge, president of the college (1807–1820), became the first professor of theology there. This program for ministerial education became Union Theological Seminary, now in Richmond, Virginia. Hoge was a vigorous Calvinist, and Union Seminary, under his leadership, maintained a staunch allegiance to the Reformed faith.

Columbia Theological Seminary

Presbyterians in South Carolina and Georgia also desired creation of a theological school, but their efforts did not bear fruit until 1831, when Columbia Theological Seminary opened in the capital city of South Carolina. George Howe (1802–1888), one of the first professors, was a graduate of Andover Theological Seminary in Massachusetts and had taught at Dartmouth College. Howe was the most influential person in organizing the curriculum at Columbia, and his use of books by Andover professors brought some New England influences contrary to Reformed orthodoxy at the time the whole Presbyterian Church was agitated by the issues between the Old School and New School factions. Columbia Seminary, however, aligned with Old

School principles, and Howe himself appears to have embraced that position. He remained on the faculty there until 1883 and was a firm adherent to the inerrancy of Scripture. At both Union and Columbia Seminaries strictly confessional teaching was the rule, and the Southern Presbyterian Church enjoyed a steady supply of learned orthodox pastors because of the position of the seminaries.

Reformed Theologians of the American South

James Henley Thornwell

One of the most influential theologians in Southern Presbyterianism was James Henley Thornwell (1812–1862), a native of South Carolina and graduate of South Carolina College summa cum laude in 1831. After a sudden conversion he aspired to become a minister and enrolled at Andover Theological Seminary, but he found the teaching, and especially the academic quality of instruction, deficient, so he moved to Harvard. Thornwell complained about the New School character of the teaching at Andover and the growing acceptance of Unitarian concepts at Harvard, and so in 1834, he returned to South Carolina. Although he intended to enroll at Columbia Seminary, a shortage of ministers led him to accept a pastorate in Lancaster, South Carolina. His examination for licensure before the Presbytery of Harmony impressed that body so well that a professor from Columbia Seminary hailed him as already an accomplished theologian.

After three years of pastoral ministry, James Henley Thornwell became a professor at South Carolina College, first in rhetoric and literature, later as professor of sacred literature and evidences of Christianity. From 1852 to 1856 he was president of South Carolina College, a position he resigned to become professor of theology at Columbia Seminary. Always an active churchman, Thornwell preached often and in 1847 became moderator of the General Assembly of his denomination. He helped to found the Presbyterian Church in the Confederate States in 1861. Death took him when he was but fifty years of age.

As a theologian Thornwell adhered loyally to the Westminster Standards and used Calvin's *Institutes of the Christian Religion* as a textbook in his classes. He had become acquainted with liberal religion as espoused by his predecessor in the presidency of South Carolina College, Thomas Cooper, a man of Unitarian convictions who was known to ridicule orthodox Christian beliefs. Thornwell, on the contrary, was an avowed champion of those very principles, one who quickly established his reputation as a learned apologist for Christianity. As editor of the *Southern Presbyterian Review* and the *Southern Quarterly Review*, he was a highly influential spokesman for biblical faith and practice. Most of his compositions appear now in four volumes of his *Collected Writings*.

As a champion of orthodoxy, Thornwell defended it against all critics, and as a Southerner, he defended the secession of the South from the Union in 1861 and maintained there is a moral basis for slavery. In the matter of church polity, Thornwell argued the case for Presbyterianism as a divine requirement. He affirmed the equality of teaching and ruling elders and contended the church itself is a missionary society and so should not create boards and other agencies to do such work. He stressed the *spirituality* of the church, a principle that viewed such non-scriptural matters as slavery and other political issues as lying outside the church's domain of competence and authority.

Robert Lewis Dabney

Equally important in the history of Southern Presbyterian theology was Robert Lewis Dabney (1820–1898), born in Virginia and educated at Hampden-Sydney College and the University of Virginia, where he earned the master of arts in 1842. He obtained his theological education at Union Seminary in Virginia. From 1847 to 1853 Dabney was a pastor until he joined the faculty of his seminary to teach church history. In 1859 he moved to the chair of systematic theology and established such a reputation for excellence that Princeton Seminary tried unsuccessfully to recruit him.

During the War between the States, Dabney was a chaplain to Confederate soldiers and later became an officer serving with General Stonewall Jackson, but poor health forced him to leave the army. After the war he published a laudatory biography of Jackson. The devastation due to four years of fighting left many Southerners in dire straits, and Dabney was no exception. He farmed just to feed his family. Union Seminary had to reduce its operations during the war and did not regain its full capacity until 1866. Dabney, nevertheless, taught there during the lean postwar years.

Among Dabney's writings are *The Defense of Virginia and the South* (1867); *Sacred Rhetoric*, a work about preaching (1870); and *Systematic and Polemic Theology* (1871). Many of his essays on various topics appear as his *Discussions*, four volumes published in 1897.

In 1883 Dabney moved to Austin, Texas, to teach at the University of Texas, and while there he helped to found Austin Theological Seminary.

Failing health and blindness forced him to retire in 1894. Undeterred by failing health, in 1897 he addressed the General Assembly of the Southern Presbyterian Church with a series of lectures about the historic Westminster Assembly that promulgated the confessional position of the Presbyterian churches.

Dabney was a man of many talents—mental, verbal, and manual—and a deep piety attended his brilliance. An exponent of strict Calvinism, his greatest effectiveness as a preacher was to fellow intellectuals. Poorly educated listeners had difficulty grasping his messages. In seminary classes Dabney made the *Institutio Theologicae Elenticae* of Swiss Reformed theologian Francis Turretin (1623–1687) the primary textbook, as did Alexander and Hodge at Princeton Seminary. Underlying all of Dabney's beliefs was his full submission to the supreme authority of Scripture. He was perhaps the greatest of the great Southern Presbyterian theologians and, like the others, a confident subscriber to the Westminster Confession of Faith.

Benjamin Morgan Palmer
Although Benjamin Morgan Palmer (1818–1902) gained fame principally as a pastor and eloquent preacher, he was a fine theological scholar as well. This native of Charleston, South Carolina, with a Puritan ancestry through New England, experienced the grace of conversion in 1836. In 1838 he graduated from the University of Georgia and then enrolled in Columbia Theological Seminary, after which he served pastorates in Georgia and South Carolina. From 1853 to 1856 he taught church history at his seminary but then returned to the pastoral ministry, serving at First Presbyterian Church, New Orleans. During the War between the States, he was a military chaplain and a popular spokesman for Southern patriotism. Union conquest of New Orleans caused him to flee to Columbia, South Carolina, where he succeeded James Henley Thornwell in the chair of systematic theology. At the end of the war, Palmer returned to New Orleans and resumed his ministry at First Presbyterian Church, where he remained until his death. He was a skillful expositor of the Bible and a vigorous exponent of the Reformed faith, doctrinal preaching being his great interest.

Despite the brevity of his academic career, Palmer was a fine theologian. While teaching at Columbia Seminary, he added the reading of A. A. Hodge's *Outline of Theology* to the works of Calvin and Turretin. Like Thornwell and the Hodges, he subscribed eagerly to the Westminster Standards. He unequivocally opposed Darwinian evolution and theistic efforts to accommodate Christianity to it. His posture on this issue brought Palmer into conflict with James Woodrow (1828–1907), a PhD from the University of Heidelberg, who was proficient in both theology and science. In 1861 Woodrow joined the faculty of Columbia Theological Seminary as professor of natural science in connection with revelation, and in 1869 he became a professor of science at South Carolina College while maintaining his seminary position concurrently. From 1891 to 1897 he was president of South Carolina College.

Although Woodrow was a sincerely pious man and strong supporter of Presbyterian causes, his espousal of theistic evolution made him the center of an intense controversy that led eventually to dismissal from his post at Columbia Seminary, although his presbytery refused to judge him a heretic. In 1886 the General Assembly of the Presbyterian Church (U. S.) affirmed the immediate creation of Adam and Eve, much to the delight of Palmer and other defenders of literal creation. Woodrow remained, nevertheless, a minister of his church in good standing. He was an uncle of Woodrow Wilson, twenty-eighth president of the United States.

Palmer was founder and editor of the *Southern Presbyterian Review*, to which he contributed many articles. His major publications include a defense of infant baptism titled *The Children of Professing Believers* (1835), *The Family Companion or Prayers for Every Morning and Evening* (1848), *The Broken Home or Lessons in Sorrow* (1890), *Theology of Prayer* (1894), and *The Threefold Fellowship and the Threefold Assurance* (1902). A two-volume edition of his sermons appeared in 1876.

John Lafayette Girardeau

Worthy of inclusion in any survey of Southern Presbyterian theologians is John Lafayette Girardeau (1825–1898), a South Carolinian of Huguenot descent reared in a godly home of decidedly Reformed character. A product of Columbia Theological Seminary, Girardeau studied with Thornwell and Palmer, both of whom made a deep and lasting impression upon him. Their fame as theologians has somewhat obscured the contributions of their outstanding pupil, but his work is deserving of attention as much as that of his mentors. Like them, Girardeau combined high scholarship with evangelistic fervor and thereby became one of the finest thinkers and preachers the Southern Presbyterians would ever produce.

Upon graduating from seminary, Girardeau considered foreign mission service, but he settled upon a mission field at home, one every bit as needy as any foreign land. After four years as pastor of two rural churches, he moved to Charleston, South Carolina, where in 1854 he assumed direction of a ministry to African American residents, both slave and free people, under the auspices of Second Presbyterian Church. By the time he arrived there, this ministry had flourished to the point that the congregation was meeting in its own six-hundred-seat building. As Girardeau preached and served this body, the numbers continued to grow, and by 1857 the congregation had erected a building with a capacity to accommodate fifteen hundred worshipers. This was a biracial assembly in which white people were the minority.

Girardeau had the ability to communicate with common people while maintaining his scholarship and satisfying the spiritual needs of both learned and ignorant people. At that time slaves were not permitted to achieve literacy. This pastor to those people instructed them orally and led them to memorize Scripture passages, hymns, and catechism answers. Because he understood the Gullah dialect of Low Country black people, Girardeau was able to relate to them well and so to structure his sermons in a manner they could comprehend. The year 1858 saw particular blessings for Zion Presbyterian Church, as perhaps as many as one hundred conversions occurred, and many more people became church members. Girardeau trained African American leaders to serve small groups within the congregation, thereby to make religious instruction more effective. When the war erupted in 1861, Girardeau became a chaplain to South Carolina soldiers and gained a reputation for compassion shown to Union prisoners as well as Confederate troops. When the war ended, he would have returned to his Charleston congregation, but the Freedman's Bureau would not allow him to do so.

The remarkable work of John L. Girardeau as a pastor notwithstanding, his role as a theologian is equally significant. In 1876 he became a professor of theology at Columbia Seminary, where he remained until failing health forced him to retire in 1895. Like most Christian thinkers of his era, Girardeau espoused Scottish Common Sense Realism as his philosophy and therefore considered revelation and reason as correlative means to understand life and the world, there being no actual conflict between them. Yet, consistent with his Reformed persuasion, he always extolled the supreme authority of Scripture and wrote extensively to expound the sacred text and to defend it against its critics. Regarding philosophy as the handmaiden of theology, Girardeau produced *The Will in Its Theological Relations* (1891), a work that bears the impress of Thornwell's influence.

A splendid scholar and articulate teacher-preacher, Girardeau made a special contribution to theological studies with his insightful examination of the doctrine of adoption, a subject treated in his *Discussions of Theological Questions* (1905). His other publications include *Calvinism and Evangelical Arminianism* (1890) and a volume of his sermons (1907). After the War between the States, he served as moderator of the General Assembly of his church.

Presbyterian Responses to Heresy

Before the end of the nineteenth century, Presbyterians had to deal with serious challenges to the Reformed faith coming from within the Presbyterian Church (U.S.A.) (Northern). Two of the most prominent dissidents were Charles Augustus Briggs (1841–1913) of Union Theological Seminary, New York, and Henry Preserved Smith (1847–1927) of Lane Theological Seminary, Cincinnati, Ohio.

Briggs, a graduate of the University of Virginia and Union Seminary in his native city New York, pursued doctoral studies at the University of Berlin and became expert in ancient languages. Originally employed to teach Hebrew and cognate languages at his seminary, he became the chair of biblical theology in 1890, a position the institution created for him. In the inaugural address he delivered upon assuming that chair, titled "The Authority of Holy Scripture," Briggs denied the inerrancy of the Bible and called for adoption of German higher criticism as the correct approach to the Scriptures. This led the Presbytery of New York to try him for heresy, only to acquit him. The General Assembly of 1891, however, vetoed his appointment to the newly created chair. The General Assembly of 1892 affirmed the inerrancy of Scripture, and the same body the next year suspended Briggs from the ministry of the church. The board of directors at Union Seminary responded to those decisions by severing the institution's connection with the Presbyterian Church. In 1898 the accused heretic joined the Episcopal Church.

Briggs was an acute scholar and a prolific writer. In 1880, before becoming controversial, he became co-editor of the *Presbyterian Review,* a position he shared with Archibald Alexander Hodge, but disputes between them led to termination of that journal in 1889. William Henry Green at Princeton Seminary was the chief antagonist of Briggs. Despite his troubles with the Presbyterians, Briggs achieved great recognition for his learning and became editor of the multivolume *International Critical Commentary* on the

Bible, to which he contributed the work on the Psalms in 1906. Among his other writings are *The Bible, the Church, and Reason* (1892); *Higher Criticism of the Hexateuch* (1893); and the *Hebrew and English Lexicon of the Old Testament* (197), a collaborative work with two other Semitic scholars.

Although Briggs advocated a critical approach to the Bible and denied its inerrancy, his doctrine was, in general, surprisingly conservative, even to the point he criticized some of his faculty colleagues at Union Theological Seminary because they denied the virgin birth of Jesus.

Henry Preserved Smith of Ohio obtained his education at Amherst College, Lane Seminary, and the University of Berlin and became a distinguished scholar in both church history and Hebrew language. In 1877 he joined the faculty at Lane Theological Seminary as professor of Old Testament. He, like Briggs, denied the inerrancy of Scripture, and when Briggs incurred the charge of heresy, Smith defended him. The Presbytery of Cincinnati tried Smith for heresy and suspended him from the ministry in 1892. The next year Smith defended his views in print with the publication of *Inspiration and Inerrancy*. In 1898 he became a professor at Amherst College, from which he moved to Meadville Theological Seminary in Pennsylvania to teach comparative religion. Smith finished his academic career as librarian at New York's Union Theological Seminary, where he served until 1925.

In the field of Old Testament studies, Smith produced *A Critical and Exegetical Commentary on the Books of Samuel* (1899), *Old Testament History* (1903), and *The Religion of Israel* (1914), all of which reflect his liberal view of Scripture. After his dismissal from the Presbyterian ministry, Smith became a Congregationalist.

A few years after Smith's trial, Arthur Cushman McGiffert (1861–1933), a noteworthy church historian once associated with Lane Theological Seminary, incurred an accusation of heresy for his book *A History of Christianity in the Apostolic Age* (1897). By the time that book appeared, McGiffert had moved to Union Theological Seminary, New York. He avoided a trial in the Presbyterian church by withdrawing his membership and becoming a Congregationalist. In 1917 he became president of Union Seminary and in that position led the institution ever farther from its Presbyterian roots. McGiffert's personal beliefs were decidedly liberal and reflect the influence of his German mentors Adolf Harnack (1851–1930) and Albrecht Ritschl (1822–1889). McGiffert's *History of Christian Thought* (1933) remains a useful reference work, nevertheless.

Heresy trials and expulsions from the ministry did not turn the tide against liberalism, and defenders of accused scholars claimed they had been victims of persecution. Slowly but surely, some Presbyterian seminaries embraced liberal ideas, perhaps as a means to acquire acceptance in the broader academic community. Auburn Theological Seminary in New York State and McCormick Theological Seminary in Chicago led the way, while Princeton Theological Seminary, along with Western Theological Seminary and Pittsburgh Theological Seminary, both in Pennsylvania, remained strongholds of orthodoxy. As the twentieth century began, Pennsylvania and New Jersey were the most conservative regions in the Northern Presbyterian Church, while the Southern Presbyterian Church was still overwhelmingly so.

SUGGESTED ADDITIONAL READINGS >>

Beattie, Francis R. *Presbyterian Standards*: *An Exposition of the Westminster Confession of Faith and Catechisms*. Richmond, Va.: Presbyterian Committee of Publication, 1896.

Briggs, Charles A. *Theological Studies.* New York: Charles Scribner's Sons, 1914.

Conser, W. H. *Church and Confession: Conservative Theologians in Germany, England, and America, 1815–1886*. Atlanta: Mercer University Press, 1984.

Dabney, Robert L. *Discussions by Robert L. Dabney*. 4 vols. Edited by C. R. Vaughan. Richmond, Va.: Presbyterian Committee of Publication, 1895.

Danhof, R. J. *Charles Hodge as a Dogmatician.* Goes, Netherlands: Oosterbaan and Le Contre, 1929.

Girardeau, J. L. *Calvinism and Evangelical Arminianism: Compared as to Election, Reprobation, and Related Doctrines*. Columbia, S.C.: W. J. Duffie, 1890.

Hageman, John F. *History of Princeton and Its Institutions*. 2 vols. Philadelphia: J. B. Lippincott, 1879.

Handy, Robert T. *A History of Union Theological Seminary in New York.* New York: Columbia University Press, 1987.

Hays, George P. *Presbyterians: A Popular Narrative of Their Origin, Progress, and Achievements.* New York: J. A. Hill, 1892.

Hodge, Alexander A. *The Life of Charles Hodge.* New York: Charles Scribner's Sons, 1880.

Hoeveler, R. David. *James McCosh and the Scottish Intellectual Tradition.* Princeton, N.J.: Princeton University Press, 1981.

Hoffecker, W. Andrew. *Piety and the Princeton Theologians.* Grand Rapids: Baker, 1981.

Kemeny, P. C. *Princeton in the Nation's Service: Religion Ideals, and Educational Practice, 1868–1928.* Oxford: Oxford University Press, 1998.

Kerr, Hugh T., ed. *Sons and Prophets: Leaders in Protestantism from Princeton Seminary.* Princeton, N.J.: Princeton University Press, 1963.

Loetscher, Lefferts A. *Facing the Enlightenment and Pietism: Archibald Alexander and the Founding of Princeton Theological Seminary.* Westport, Conn.: Greenwood, 1983.

Longfield, Bradley T. *The Presbyterian Controversy—Fundamentalists, Modernists, and Moderates.* Oxford: Oxford University Press, 1989.

Mackintosh, H. R. *Types of Modern Theology: Schleiermacher to Barth.* New York: Charles Scribner's Sons, 1937.

Massa, Mark S. *Charles Augustus Briggs and the Crisis of Historical Criticism.* Philadelphia: Fortress, 1990.

Miller, Samuel Jr. *The Life of Samuel Miller.* Philadelphia: Claxton, Remsen, and Haffelfinger, 1869.

Noll, Mark A. *Princeton and the Republic.* Princeton, N.J.: Princeton University Press, 1989.

———. *The Princeton Theology, 1812–1921.* Grand Rapids: Baker, 1983.

Selden, William K. *Princeton Theological Seminary: A Narrative History, 1812–1992.* Princeton, N.J.: Princeton University Press, 1992.

Thornwell, James Henley. *The Collected Writings of James Henley Thornwell.* Edited by J. B. Adger and J. L. Girardeau. Richmond, Va.: Presbyterian Committee of Publication, 1881–1886.

Welch, Claude. *Protestant Theology in the Nineteenth Century.* 2 vols. New Haven, Conn.: Yale University Press, 1972.

Wells, David F., ed. *Reformed Theology in America: A History of Modern Development.* Grand Rapids: Eerdmans, 1986.

FOURTEEN

Other Reformed Bodies in America

The voyages of Henry Hudson, in the employ of the Dutch East India Company, initiated the creation of Dutch colonies in the New World. Settlements were situated along the Hudson and Delaware Rivers, and by 1626 this enterprise was known as New Netherlands. The pioneers were traders who did not have the services of ordained ministers, but believers met for worship nevertheless. Because of the perceived commercial value of trade in America, a Dutch West India Company came into being in 1621 and gained fame for purchasing Manhattan Island from the natives.

The Dutch Reformed Church

Many of the early settlers in New Netherlands were Protestant refugees fleeing persecution in their homeland during the Eighty Years' War (1568–1648), a struggle in which the Spanish monarchy attempted to subject the Low Countries to rigid royal authority and to impose Catholicism upon the entire populace. The arrival of displaced Protestants greatly enhanced spiritual life in the colonies, as many were fervent Calvinists eager to plant their faith in the New World. Peter Minuit (1589–1638), the first governor, was an earnest believer. The first Reformed pastor to arrive was Jonas Michaelius (b. 1577), who established the first formal church in America with about fifty members. Governor Minuit was an elder in that congregation. Michaelius graduated from the University of Leiden and ministered at home for about twenty years before going to America in 1628. He eagerly sought the conversion of the Indians and was distressed about the poor quality of leadership in the West India Company. In order to obtain reforms in company operations, Michaelius returned to the Netherlands. His efforts, however, did not succeed, and company officials would not allow him to resume work in America. Commercial interests sometimes conflicted with the missionary objective of the Dutch Reformed Church in the colonies.

Zealous missionary work among the Mohawk Indians led, however, to many conversions, while religious dissidents from Massachusetts found refuge in New Amsterdam, where the government maintained a policy of toleration. There was a brief period while Peter Stuyvesant was governor (1647–1664) when Lutherans were not welcome in the Dutch colonies, but the West India Company mandated toleration. When the English took control of New Netherlands in 1664, the Anglican Church became the favored religion, but English King William III (1688–1702), himself a Dutchman, granted the Reformed Church full freedom in the colony that had become New York. The Dutch Reformed Church was subject to the Classis of Amsterdam and remained so for about 150 years. Church services were in the Dutch language as late as 1820.

When the Great Awakening began about 1730, Theodore J. Frelinghuysen (1691–1747), a Reformed pastor in the Raritan Valley of New Jersey, became a prominent revival preacher who exerted great influence upon Gilbert Tennent and Jonathan Dickinson. Frelinghuysen formed an American coetus as a unit of church government, which the Classis of Amsterdam validated, but not for another nine years. The coetus could neither license nor ordain ministers who, until 1754, had to go to Amsterdam to receive such authorization. In that year the Dutch Reformed Church in America organized its own classis, a decision that provoked substantial tension with church leaders in the Netherlands.

John Livingston (1746–1825), a Scotsman who settled in the Netherlands and obtained his education there, went to America to mediate the dispute between factions. His success convinced the Classis of Amsterdam to recognize the autonomy of the Reformed Church in the New World. That status came to maturity when, in 1794, the Dutch Reformed Church in America constituted its General Synod. In 1800 the church created particular synods for New York City and Albany. One for New Brunswick, New Jersey, came into being in 1869. Each congregation was to have a consistory of elders and deacons.

Livingston was the pioneer in Dutch Reformed educational endeavors in America, as pastor and professor tutoring more than one hundred candidates for the ministry. The first Reformed college was at New Brunswick, a school that eventually became Rutgers University. In 1866 Hope College opened in Holland, Michigan. The first theological seminary of the Dutch Reformed Church in America began classes in 1810 at New Brunswick, where it continues to this day.

The doctrinal position of the Dutch Reformed Church was, at the time of its organization in America, one of strict Calvinism as expressed in the historic Three Forms of Unity, and when the Presbyterians became agitated because of Old School–New School disputes, the Reformed Church supported the Old School party. In 1867 the Dutch Reformed Church became the Reformed Church in America. It sent missionaries to China, India, and Japan.

The Christian Reformed Church

A new wave of immigration from the Netherlands between 1840 and 1920 brought a large infusion of Reformed believers, most of them strongly orthodox. At first the new settlers joined the Dutch Reformed Church, but some found that body lax in doctrine and discipline and so formed the Christian Reformed Church, a move that reflected a substantial secession from the national church in the Netherlands, which occurred in 1834. Dutch immigrants who moved to Michigan and Iowa established many Christian Reformed congregations there, and when the Dutch Reformed Church refused to disavow Freemasonry, many more Reformed believers moved to the Christian Reformed Church.

Christian Reformed culture in the New World was at first rather parochial, as believers tried to sustain one another in the faith through systematic catechetical instruction, works of charity, and maintaining their own schools. By about 1880, however, the neo-Calvinism of Abraham Kuyper gained some acceptance, and Christian Reformed believers began efforts to permeate all of society with biblical principles. However, some members feared the movement to the extent that a faction withdrew from the Christian Reformed Church and formed the Protestant Reformed Church in 1925. The schism notwithstanding, the Christian Reformed Church maintained its strict confessional teaching well into the twentieth century, but lapses have occurred in recent decades. Beginning with Synod 1959, the church began to question the inerrancy of the Scriptures, and the way was opened for other changes in faith and practice, including ordination of women to church offices.

The educational endeavors of the Christian Reformed community have been impressive, as Calvin College and Calvin Theological Seminary in Grand Rapids, Michigan, attest. Parent-controlled schools on the elementary and secondary levels have been established wherever members of the denomination have settled, and Dordt College in Iowa; Trinity Christian

College in Illinois; King's University in Edmonton, Alberta; and Redeemer University College in Ancaster, Ontario serve the Christian Reformed constituency without being official church institutions. The denomination has more than a thousand congregations, most of them in the United States but many in Canada as well, with over three hundred thousand members.

The German Reformed Church

Pennsylvania was the first of the colonies in America to receive a considerable number of German settlers, who, at the invitation of Governor William Penn, formed Germantown in 1683. German settlers were not numerous until about 1720, when persecution of Protestants in the Rhineland caused thousands to flee to England, from which many came to America. French king Louis XIV (r. 1643–1715) was the perpetrator of repression in the Rhineland, where he attempted to coerce conformity to his own Catholic religion. Of the refugees to the New World, most went to Pennsylvania, and those who did so brought their German Reformed religion with them, but without the services of pastors. At first Christian schoolteachers provided leadership for the church, but in 1720 John Philip Boehm (1688–1749) arrived, and George Michael Weiss (1697–1762) soon followed.

Boehm was a schoolmaster in Worms, Germany, before emigrating, and at the request of Reformed believers near Philadelphia, he organized the first German Reformed Church in America. When Weis arrived in 1727, he challenged Boehm's lack of formal ordination to the ministry and called him incompetent. Boehm's supporters then appealed to the Classis of Amsterdam to approve his work, and it did so, ordaining him in 1729. German Reformed congregations in America put themselves under the oversight of the Dutch Reformed Church until 1791.

Boehm encountered difficulties and some opposition from other German leaders in Pennsylvania as well, and the situation became particularly tense when Count Nicholas von Zinzendorf (1700–1760), leader of the Moravian Brethren, arrived in Pennsylvania and tried to unite all German residents there into the Moravian Church. Boehm resisted that effort, and with the aid of Classis Amsterdam, he recruited more Reformed pastors to serve his church in America, for he feared the mystical ideas of Zinzendorf.

The formal organization of the German Reformed Church in America was initially Boehm's work. Under his leadership the church approved the Heidelberg Catechism and the Canons of Dort and adopted a confession of his own composition. In 1746 the Synod of Holland sent Michael Schlatter

(1718–1790), a German educated in the Netherlands, to Pennsylvania to improve the organization of the Reformed congregations there. He helped to form a coetus of twelve congregations, each with its own consistory. In time Schlatter organized another thirty churches of his denomination in the Middle Colonies. His successes in America won admiration for his work in Europe, which enabled him on a visit there to collect funds and recruit more ministers for service in the New World. With this financial support, Schlatter established schools for German children in Pennsylvania and elsewhere. His church sought to remain strictly Reformed at a time when a broad form of evangelicalism was becoming popular in America.

In 1793 the German Reformed Church in America adopted a constitution that made it autonomous and no longer subject to the oversight of the Classis of Amsterdam. In order to promote denominational solidarity, the church published a *Weekly Messenger* in the German language. In 1819 it organized regional classes, a measure that proved somewhat disappointing because the one in Ohio declared its independence from the parent body.

To facilitate the preparation of ministers, the German Reformed Church established Franklin College and Mercersburg Theological Seminary, both in Pennsylvania. Although the seminary was not large, it enjoyed the services of some very distinguished scholars, among them, John Williamson Nevin (1803–1886) and Philip Schaff (1819–1893), whose reputations for learning made their institution duly famous. Both Nevin and Schaff disapproved of American revivalism and stressed liturgical worship as part of a developing tradition in Christianity. Their articles in the *Mercersburg Review* expressed their criticism and in the process made them controversial figures.

So influential were these seminary professors that it became a practice to refer to a "Mercersburg Theology" to identify their thinking. In addition to their articles, they produced scholarly books that enjoyed a broad readership. Nevin's *The Anxious Bench* (1843) is an attack on revivalism, while his *Mystical Presence* emphasizes his belief in the real presence of Christ in the Eucharist, the sacrament Nevin made the central feature of worship. Schaff wrote *The Principle of Protestantism* (1844), compiled and edited *Creeds of Christendom* (1877), and produced a massive *History of the Christian Church* (1892), all works of thorough scholarship written in a delightful style, even though the author's native language was German. Schaff founded the American Society of Church History and was its first president.

Critics of the Mercersburg Theology complained that it elevated tradition over Scripture and the sacraments over personal faith. Protests led to the founding of Ursinus College near Philadelphia as an alternative to Mercersburg. This did not, however, indicate a resurgence of orthodoxy. Gradually, specific beliefs of the Reformed faith lost popularity and ecumenical interests took precedence over sound doctrine. The only official confession of the German Reformed Church was the Heidelberg Catechism, which Nevin and Schaff professed to accept. Their ideas nevertheless aroused complaints, and their writings show clearly they were not consistently Reformed.

Small Conservative Churches

In addition to American expressions of major Protestant groups from Europe, a number of small bodies took root in the New World, most of them loyally orthodox in character. One such was the Reformed Presbyterian Church from Scotland, a strict Covenanter body descended from the work of Richard Cameron and Donald Cargill in the seventeenth century. These dissidents in Scotland opposed the settlement of 1688–1689, by which the Crown extended freedom of worship to oppressed minorities. The Covenanters held the government had no right to decide matters of religion, and they insisted on the provisions of the Solemn League and Covenant. Persecution drove many of them to Ireland and from there to America, where they established their first congregation in Lancaster County, Pennsylvania. In the free atmosphere of tolerant Pennsylvania, the Reformed Presbyterians flourished and by 1809 had a functioning synod of congregations. Although grateful for the liberty they enjoyed, these Covenanters avoided involvement with the civil government because the new American republic would not officially recognize the kingship of Jesus Christ, one of their most cherished principles.

Arguments about the proper relationship of believers to the civil authority led to a rupture within the Reformed Presbyterian Church in 1833, when a party known as the General Synod discarded the traditional posture, while the conservative wing known as the Reformed Presbyterian Church in North America maintained it. It became common to refer to the traditionalists as *Old Lights*. This body is strictly confessional and adheres carefully to the regulative principle of worship, which it construes to mandate exclusive psalm-singing as opposed to hymns of human composition. This church was an early opponent of slavery, some of its members participating in the

Underground Railroad. The Reformed Presbyterian Church of North America regularly calls for the adoption of an amendment to the United States Constitution, one to affirm the kingship of Christ. The church operates Geneva College, Beaver Falls, Pennsylvania, and the Reformed Presbyterian Theological Seminary in Pittsburgh. Ottawa Theological Hall serves its congregations in Canada, and the *Covenanter Witness* is the denominational organ. The church has, at various times, conducted foreign missions in Syria, Turkey, China, Japan, and Cyprus. Western Pennsylvania and eastern Kansas are centers of strength for this diminishing denomination.

The Associate Reformed Presbyterian Church is another Scottish denomination transplanted to America. It began as a secession from the Church of Scotland in 1733, as Ebenezer Erskine led a protest against Erastianism. The Associate Presbytery came to the New World through emigration from Scotland and Ireland in the first half of the eighteenth century. By 1753 three ministers had formed the Associate Presbytery of Pennsylvania, and by 1776 church growth led to creation of the Associate Presbytery of New York, which included New England. In 1782 a merger of two presbyteries created the Associate Reformed Presbyterian Church, which was the first union of two denominations in American history. Some northern congregations of the newly united church eventually joined other Presbyterian bodies, but in southeastern United States the Associate Reformed Presbyterian Church grew substantially, and by 1802 it had eight presbyteries bound together in a general synod. Regional factions did, at times, cause some losses that common subscription to the Westminster Standards did not prevent.

In 1836 the Associate Reformed Presbyterians opened Erskine Theological Seminary followed by Erskine College in 1843. The two institutions share a beautiful campus in Due West, South Carolina. By the early twentieth century the church had about twelve thousand members in nine presbyteries. In the next century that figure rose to about thirty-five thousand. Pakistan and Mexico have been the major foreign mission fields of this denomination.

Like the Associate Reformed Presbyterian Church, the United Presbyterian Church of North America originated in Scotland and had roots in secessions from the Church of Scotland. Seceders formed the Associate Synod in 1733 in protest against lay patronage, a practice by which wealthy landowners chose ministers for parishes of the national church. Complaints about the growing influence of rationalism among Church of

Scotland clerics also encouraged some to withdraw from the parent body. In 1782 the Associate Synod joined with older Reformed Presbyterians, a Covenanter group, and thereby organized the Associate Reformed denomination. A number of people from the united church settled in Ulster, and others went to America, especially to Pennsylvania and North and South Carolina. In 1858 the Associate Reformed body merged with the Associate Synod and thus created the United Presbyterian Church of North America, a denomination of fifty-four thousand members.

A very conservative body, this church at first maintained exclusive psalmody and strict adherence to the Westminster Standards, although it adopted a Judicial Testimony that enunciated some principles the Westminster Confession did not include. Among them were a denunciation of slavery and a disapproval of membership in secret societies. Although heavily Scots-Irish in its ethnic character, the United Presbyterian Church gradually became broader in its membership, while immigrants from the British Isles continued to affiliate with it. The missionary outreach of this body was very vigorous, especially in Egypt and India, and new church planting progressed well into the nineteenth century. Church membership reached 130 thousand by 1905. The United Presbyterian Church maintained several colleges plus Pittsburgh Theological Seminary in Pennsylvania and Xenia Theological Seminary in Ohio. Like many others, this denomination gradually relaxed its staunch adherence to Reformed orthodoxy, and it drew closer to the Presbyterian Church (U.S.A.), with which it merged in 1958.

SUGGESTED ADDITIONAL READINGS >>

Balmer, Randall. *A Perfect Babel of Confusion: Dutch Religion and English Culture in the Middle Colonies.* New York: Oxford University Press, 1989.

Bratt, James. *Dutch Calvinism in Modern America.* Grand Rapids: Eerdmans, 1984.

Brouwer, Arie R. *Reformed Church Roots: Thirty-Five Formative Events.* New York: Reformed Church Press, 1977.

De Jong, Gerald T. *The Dutch Reformed Church in the American Colonies.* Grand Rapids: Eerdmans, 1978.

Ford, Henry Jones. *The Scotch-Irish in America.* Hamden, Conn.: Archon Books, 1966.

Glasgow, W. M. *History of the Reformed Presbyterian Church in America.* Baltimore, Md.: Hill & Harvey, 1888.

Hoeflinger, N. C. and R. D. Stuebbe, eds. *History of the Eureka Classis.* Reformed Church in the United States, 1985.

Hutchinson, G. P. *The History behind the Reformed Presbyterian Church, Evangelical Synod.* Cherry Hill, N.J.: Mack, 1974.

Jamison, Wallace N. *The United Presbyterian Story.* Pittsburgh, Pa.: Geneva, 1958.

Thompson, Ernest Trice. *Presbyterianism in the South.* Vol. 2. Richmond, Va.: John Knox, 1973.

FIFTEEN

Presbyterian and Reformed Churches in the British Empire

The first Reformed believers to appear in Canada were Huguenots from France seeking to escape persecution at home, where Louis XIV had deprived them of their freedom of worship. The refugees settled along the St. Lawrence River and in Nova Scotia. In 1713, as a provision of the treaty that ended the War of Spanish Succession, Britain obtained Nova Scotia, where the population was largely Roman Catholic. After several years of trying to pacify the rebellious Catholics, the British government removed them to the distant south and allowed Protestants to replace them. The new settlers came from the United Kingdom and some from the New England colonies in what was soon to become the United States. Perhaps ten thousand Protestants arrived in the first year of settlement, and the growth continued thereafter, making urgent the need for pastors to serve the spiritual needs of the people. In 1763 Britain acquired all of France's Canadian lands and opened them to English-speaking immigrants, most of them Protestants, of whom many were Presbyterians.

Presbyterian and Reformed Churches in Canada

The churches in Scotland were quick to respond to the need for ministers in Canada, and three pastors and two elders formed the first presbytery there in 1786. These initial efforts at establishing a Presbyterian structure were the work of groups that had withdrawn from the Church of Scotland, and the divisions evident in the old country led to the formation of separate Presbyterian bodies in Canada. By 1795 a second presbytery was operating in competition with the first one, but in 1817 those two joined to form the Presbyterian Church of Nova Scotia. The united denomination had by then spread across the Maritime Provinces and counted about forty-two thousand members but had only nineteen pastors to serve the churches, while immigration continued to enlarge the population.

Efforts to provide an adequate educated ministry for the Presbyterian churches encountered much difficulty because the British authorities favored the Anglican Church, which dominated the non-Catholic areas of the country, and laws discriminated against other religious groups. Presbyterians might have sent ministerial candidates for study at King's College, Windsor, Ontario, but that institution required subscription to the Anglican Thirty-Nine Articles of Religion, and the rules of the college forbade participation in non-Anglican services of worship. What was even more inhibiting was that non-Anglican congregations had no right to own property, so there was less freedom of religion in Canada than in the United Kingdom itself. This situation led Presbyterians to join with other nonconformists to seek redress, but the British Parliament was not responsive. In order therefore to combat discrimination in education, Presbyterians opened Queen's College, Kingston, Ontario, in 1842. While this helped their cause considerably, Presbyterians and other dissenters endured unequal treatment from British authorities for some time thereafter.

The influence of the Scottish churches was, of course, pronounced in Canada. In 1825 Scots formed the Glasgow Colonial Society, which sent forth ministers of the Church of Scotland to Canada, where they organized a synod related to the Church of Scotland. When the Disruption of 1843 occurred, almost all congregations in the Synod of Canada supported the Free Church secession, and the synod severed its relations with the established church in Scotland while affirming its loyalty to the Westminster Confession of Faith. Contentions related to church problems in Scotland, however, eventually produced five separate Presbyterian bodies in eastern Canada. Total membership of those bodies reached 110 thousand by 1850. Later reconciliations reduced the number of Presbyterian organizations to two, one in league with the Church of Scotland, the other with the Free Church.

Expansion toward the west took Presbyterians into Ontario, where, to that point, their numbers had been few. Ontario was, however, the most populous province and the center of Protestant strength, and Presbyterian efforts flourished there. The Presbyterian Church in Canada, which supported the Free Church in Scotland, became the strongest body in the country and by 1861 had 150 thousand members, which included 10 percent of the population of Ontario. In that year the major body joined with the United Presbyterian Church, another secessionist body with roots in Scotland. By 1875 almost all Canadian Presbyterians were in one denomination.

The Presbyterian Church in Canada became vigorous in evangelizing settlers to the west of Ontario and new immigrants as well, and it sent missionaries to India and China. The outreach to the Roman Catholics of Quebec was extensive and the results encouraging. Knox College, Toronto, became the most important Presbyterian institution of higher learning in the land. It came into being as an alternative to Queen's College, when the Disruption of 1843 divided the Presbyterians of western Canada (then Ontario), even more than it did in the east. Queen's College remained in league with the Church of Scotland and so was no longer acceptable to those who supported the Free Church secession. The Free Church of Canada constituted itself as a denomination in July 1844, but reunion occurred in 1861. In 1875 this body and the reunited ones in eastern Canada joined at a meeting in Montreal and declared themselves the Presbyterian Church in Canada. Home mission work occupied the reunited church as Canada expanded to the Pacific coast, and the Presbyterians moved that way. The strength acquired through mergers enabled Canadian Presbyterians to accelerate their missionary efforts by expanding into the West Indies, New Hebrides, and Formosa (Taiwan). By the close of the nineteenth century, the church claimed well over two hundred thousand members and appeared to be solidly united and firmly committed to its task. Trying times were, however, just ahead. The steady growth of the Roman Catholic population throughout Canada presented a major challenge at a time when Canadian Presbyterians were becoming divided among themselves because of theological disputes related to the critical approach to Holy Scripture that originated in Europe but had arrived in North America and there caused disruption in all major Protestant denominations, including the Presbyterian Church in Canada.

By the opening of the twentieth century, ecumenical discussions in Canada had become frequent and led to proposals to merge several denominations. The justification advanced for such a move was to facilitate a Protestant ministry to the western provinces without duplications by various denominations. World War I, however, preempted attention, and serious moves toward church unity did not occur until after that conflict. Soon Methodists, Congregationalists, Anglicans, Baptists, and Presbyterians were talking about church union. The Anglicans and Baptists opted to remain outside such a structure, while the Methodists and Congregationalists were eager to join. The Presbyterians were divided over the issue, but most of them supported the scheme, and the United Church of Canada became a reality in 1925. Those Presbyterians who did not enter the United Church met on June 9, 1925, at Knox Presbyterian Church, Toronto, where, under the leadership of David George MacQueen, pastor at First Presbyterian Church, Edmonton, Alberta, they declared they would maintain the continuing General Assembly of the Presbyterian Church in Canada. This party, known as the Continuing Presbyterians until 1939, comprised about 30 percent of Canadian Presbyterians.

Many congregations' refusal to join the United Church impaired the cause of ecumenicity, but the main body of Presbyterians kept control of all the denomination's colleges, some of which soon merged with those of other denominations now within the union. Manitoba College, for example, merged with Wesley College, a former Methodist institution, while Westminster Hall joined with Ryerson College, another Methodist school. It had become clear that loyalty to historic Reformed doctrine had diminished greatly in Presbyterian circles.

Maintenance of a separate Presbyterian denomination after 1925 proved a daunting task, since about 90 percent of the clergymen had joined the United Church. With the theological schools in the control of the new church, Presbyterians faced an acute shortage of educated ministers, and the weakened structure of the church made it difficult to remedy that situation. The specific theological position of the church too was in doubt, since opposition to church union did not necessarily signify adherence to the confessional Reformed faith. In fact, the Presbyterian Church in Canada remained an ecumenically inclined denomination in which doctrinal matters were of secondary importance. Walter W. Bryden (1883–1952) was the leading theological scholar of the church, whose influence made the dialectical theology of Swiss scholar Karl Barth (1886–1968) the most popular view in that body. Bryden, a graduate of Knox College who studied in Europe as well, became a professor of church history at his alma mater and later rose to the position of principal at Knox College. In his book *The Christian's Knowledge of God* (1940), Bryden promoted a mediating position between liberalism and orthodoxy. John T. McNeill (1885–1975) was another church historian of note in the Canadian Presbyterian Church. A specialist in Calvinism, he produced a celebrated *History and Character of Calvinism* (1954) and edited a new translation of Calvin's *Institutes of the Christian Religion* (1960). Like Bryden, this excellent scholar was committed to broad church union rather than to the historic teachings of his own religious heritage, as his book *Unitive Protestantism: The Ecumenical Spirit and Its Persistent Expression* (1964) attests.

By the middle of the twentieth century, the Presbyterian Church was experiencing a distressing decline in membership and attendance. Divisive theological and social issues that confronted all major denominations cost this one dearly, and had it not been for more immigration in the years after World War II, the decline would have been even greater. The church is no longer principally a Scots-Irish body but one broadly inclusive of many ethnic groups. It is a member of the World Alliance of Reformed Churches, the Canadian Council of Churches, and the World Council of Churches. As the twentieth century closed, membership stood at about 236 thousand in about eleven hundred congregations. Knox College and Vancouver School of Theology are its main institutions for ministerial education, while its major publications are *The Presbyterian Record* and a missions periodical, *Message of Glad Tidings*. This church ordains women as pastors and ruling elders.

In addition to the major Presbyterian Church, several other Reformed bodies have established their presence in Canada, some of Dutch background especially. Immigrants from the Netherlands, as they did in the United States, brought the Christian Reformed Church to Canada, and after World War II there was a major influx of new settlers of this persuasion. This denomination, an outgrowth of the older Reformed Church in America, has several Canadian congregations and a regional synod there. The strength of the Christian Reformed Church in Canada is evident in the numerous schools its people have established on all levels of instruction. In higher education The Institute for Christian Studies, Toronto; Redeemer College, Ancaster, Ontario; and King's College, Edmonton, Alberta, serve the Christian Reformed constituency in the Dominion. The United Reformed Church, a staunchly confessional secession from the Christian Reformed Church in 1996, has nearly forty affiliated congregations in Canada. Another denomination with Dutch ancestry is the Canadian and American Reformed Churches, with over fifty local assemblies in Canada and the United States. This church too is strictly Calvinistic in doctrine, adhering to the historic Three Forms of Unity. A comparable body, but one without a strong Dutch connection, is the Reformed Church of Quebec, a denomination of about six congregations closely associated with the conservative Presbyterian Church in America. The Heidelberg Catechism and the Westminster Confession of Faith are its official doctrinal standards.

The Reformed witness in the Dominion of Canada diminished in the twentieth century, as ecumenical efforts, especially formation of the United Church of Canada, preempted the attention of religious leaders. The United Church is by far the largest non-Catholic body in the country, with about three million professing adherents. Attendance in that denomination is much lower than the membership, and the church has assumed the posture of being the most liberal of all such bodies, endorsing homosexuality and tolerating same-sex marriages. Smaller conservative churches maintain their loyalty to historic principles in theology and morality, but in so doing they face increasing hostility from the civil authorities, who espouse the same social agenda as the liberal churches.

The Commonwealth of Australia

Australia, the smallest continent and largest island on the planet, has had a rather unique religious history in that the original settlers from Europe did not go there in a quest for freedom, religious or otherwise. Dutch seamen of the East India Company were the first Europeans to arrive in Australia, but they judged the land of little value and did not establish colonies there. British interest began when Captain James Cook landed at Botany Bay and claimed the land for his monarch in 1770. After the secession of the American colonies from the British Empire, the government of William Pitt decided to use Australia as a penal colony to relieve crowded conditions in British prisons. What became the great city of Sydney began in this way. Even after the government stopped transporting convicts to Australia, the immigrants who went freely were there for commercial and political, not religious, purposes. Australian history, then, has been largely the product of secular influences, with the Christian churches at the periphery of society.

Since British settlement was the determining factor in shaping the contours of Australian culture, it is not surprising that the Anglican Church emerged as the major non-Catholic religious body. As non-British ethnic groups emigrated there, they brought their particular religious traditions with them and thereby encouraged the development of a pluralistic society. The first Protestant efforts to minister in Australia were those of the London Missionary Society, a Congregationalist agency of a Calvinistic character, which began work on the island of Tasmania in 1830. Henry Hopkins (1787–1870), wool merchant and dedicated Christian, succeeded well in trade at Hobart, Tasmania, and was responsible for establishing several churches on the island, all of them independent assemblies in accord with Congregationalist polity. These works were Reformed in doctrine but not in church government. By 1837 they had formed a Congregational Union, and as the nineteenth century progressed, churches of that connection developed in various parts of the country.

Presbyterian ministries in Australia began with the work of John Dunmore Lang (1799–1878), who landed at Sydney in May 1823. This graduate of the University of Glasgow (MA and DD) distinguished himself for scholarship and for evident zeal for the Christian faith. While at university he worshiped in the church where Thomas Chalmers was pastor, so he imbibed much evangelical influence that affected his thinking for the rest of his life, despite later lapses into unethical behavior. At the urging of his brother, who had preceded him, and upon invitation from the governor of New South Wales, Lang sailed for Australia after obtaining ordination by the Presbytery of Irvine in the Church of Scotland. Upon arriving he became a pastor to Scottish settlers.

Lang quickly became convinced Australia was a suitable place for Britons to live, so he began promoting large-scale immigration to his new home. In order to encourage this and to obtain additional ministers to serve with him, he made numerous trips to Britain, there seeking government support for the colony and teachers to staff its much-needed schools. Lang was a skillful journalist, a tireless writer of books, essays, magazine and newspaper articles, and letters to editors. In 1834 he published *An Historical and Statistical Account of New South Wales*, and the next year he founded *The Colonist*, a weekly paper, and other periodicals followed.

As a church leader Lang was very influential but often controversial. He and other ministers established the Presbytery of New South Wales in 1832, and he recruited both Presbyterian and Lutheran pastors for work in the colony. The quality of some of his associates was a cause for concern, as some of them proved unfit for the ministry and more inclined toward excessive drinking than preaching. This led him to seek the ouster of the delinquents and replacement with worthy men, but other ministers were not inclined to take disciplinary action against the offenders. This led Lang to organize a separate church court to deal with the matter, but while he was in the United Kingdom in 1841, that body rejoined the original presbytery to form the Synod of Australia. Upon his return he accepted the authority of this synod, only to renounce it soon thereafter as a synagogue of Satan when some of its members criticized him. At that point he resigned his state stipend because he believed state support of religion was fraught with many dangers for the churches. His congregation at Scots Church, Sydney, was the largest and richest one of the Presbyterian assemblies in the country, so it could well afford to relinquish state support.

In 1843 Lang commenced a political career that lasted until 1869 when he obtained a seat on the legislative council. That gave him a forum in which to expound his belief that Britain should sponsor massive migrations to Australia as a means of relieving poverty in the United Kingdom. He portrayed his new homeland as a place of boundless opportunities for wealth, and he attempted to beguile the colonial governor into granting land to immigrants. In fact, he lured people to go to Australia by promising them free land upon their arrival. Lang's deceitful claims ruined his standing with the Colonial Office and aroused much animosity in Australia. He nevertheless was quite successful in promoting immigration, as several hundred people left the British Isles for the Land Down Under.

Lang was almost always in controversy and had many critics. In 1850 he publicly advocated severing Australia's political ties with Britain by declaring the country a republic. A bogus accusation he leveled against a political opponent led to a conviction for libel and four months in prison. A second offense of that nature brought a six-month sentence, but he served that in relative comfort due to the benevolence of the warden.

Lang's actions as a minster were controversial as well. In 1850 he and ministers he had brought from Britain composed the Synod of New South Wales, after the Presbytery of Australia had deposed him from the ministry and after he obtained reinstatement by action of a civil court. Although a convinced Presbyterian, Lang worked closely with Baptists and Congregationalists, and with them and others he was often a spokesman for the poor and the homeless, who regarded him as their benefactor. He was very successful in achieving his political objectives, such as the end of state financial subsidies to churches, the termination of transporting convicts to Australia, and the introduction of responsible parliamentary government. He sought and secured the separation of Victoria and Queensland into separate colonies. In 1865 the Synod of New South Wales, of which he was the principal organizer, joined a Presbyterian union that brought together both those Presbyterians who had supported the Church of Scotland and those who had endorsed the Free Church after the Disruption of 1843.

As the nineteenth century moved forward, Presbyterians in Australia, like those in Europe and America, became distressed about the ascendancy of higher criticism of Scripture that had spread there from Germany.

Ministers educated in Europe were very likely to have been influenced by the critical scholarship becoming dominant in the universities there, and gradually the same approach to the faith made its debut in domestic theological schools. The popularity of Darwin's view of evolution and growing acceptance of the extreme antiquity of the earth encouraged a decline of confidence in the trustworthiness of the Bible and led some scholars and ministers to question established doctrines of Christianity they deemed incompatible with modern enlightened views.

Perhaps the most notorious case of obvious departures from the faith appeared in the work of Samuel Angus (1881–1943), a native of Ireland educated at Queen's University there and subsequently at Princeton University and Princeton Theological Seminary in America. Angus studied further at the universities in Marburg and Berlin and became an acknowledged authority on German philosophy and theology of the critical school. Despite his very liberal persuasion, Angus became a professor of New Testament and church history at St. Andrew's College, Sydney, in 1914, a position he held until his death. Although his approach to the faith provoked criticisms, most Presbyterians seemed content to allow him to teach them to future ministers, perhaps because his reputation for scholarship made them proud to have his services. Angus and some learned friends actually formed a club of various theologians who nicknamed themselves the "Heretics," so confident were they that their position was unimpeachable. There was, however, a negative reaction, which led to the trial of Angus after he rejected the Trinity, the virgin birth of Jesus, and the divine character of Scripture. The charge originated though, not among his fellow Presbyterians, but from students of other denominations enrolled in his classes. One Presbyterian of strong conviction did, however, request the General Assembly of Australia to examine the teachings of Angus. This did not lead to prosecution for heresy, and near the close of 1932 Robert J. H. McGowan (1870–1953), a former moderator of that assembly and one learned in history and theology, assumed the lead of an effort to rebut Angus's views and to obtain his removal from the ministry. Using the proper judicial procedures, McGowan received approval from the General Assembly of Australia to examine Angus's position. His commission provided abundant evidence of heresy and recommended a trial in the Presbytery of Sydney. In the midst of these proceedings the accused professor produced a book titled *Truth and Tradition* in which he assailed the Reformed faith in general and its conception of God in particular. This publication notwithstanding, the General Assembly New South Wales in

1934 refused to condemn the author and only admonished him to be more cautious in expressing ideas offensive to many in the church. McGowan's further efforts to expel Angus were not successful, perhaps because many Presbyterians had grown indifferent toward doctrine, deeming the peace of the church more important than its confessional posture. In his published autobiography *Alms for Oblivion* (1943), Angus frankly rejected many of the claims of Christianity and thereby verified the charges brought against him.

By the time Angus became a controversial figure in Presbyterian circles, that church was in general lapsing into an attitude of unconcern about its own Reformed heritage and moving toward an ecumenical position in which denominational distinctives mattered little. Other professors at St. Andrews College, like Angus, but not as radical, espoused views incompatible with historic orthodoxy and Presbyterian beliefs. European neo-orthodoxy became a popular teaching during the Second World War and for some time thereafter, as the books of Barth and Brunner commanded considerable attention. These scholars seemed conservative when compared with Angus and other radicals, but they did not signal a return to orthodoxy, despite the apparent significance of the term used to identify the school of thought in which they were pioneers. The "assured results" of higher criticism remained the presupposition of their approach to the Bible.

The church scene in Australia is much like that in Christendom at large in that sectarian divisions are a fact of life. Presbyterians and comparable Reformed bodies have suffered from doctrinal disagreements and disputes about proper procedure, so that numerous denominations have emerged. The Presbyterian Church of Australia is the largest such body, but its membership at the end of the twentieth century was barely forty thousand. Once much larger, this denomination lost 70 percent of its people when the majority in that body adhered to the Uniting Church in Australia, a union with Methodists and Congregationalists effected in 1977. Those who remained in the Presbyterian Church of Australia were, for the most part, the more conservative members. The church prior to the union of 1977 had been becoming increasingly liberal in belief and practice, but after that date a resurgence of orthodoxy occurred that continues now but not without opposition. The church remained in fellowship with the World Alliance of Reformed Churches, but it withdrew from the Australian Council of Churches and the World Council of Churches in 1979 as a protest against liberal theological and political pronouncements and actions by those bodies. It eventually severed its connection with the World Alliance of Reformed Churches for the same reason.

The Presbyterian Church in Australia conducts missionary efforts in New Hebrides, Korea, and India, and it maintains theological colleges in Melbourne, Brisbane, and Sydney. The number of graduates becoming ordained ministers has been increasing substantially, and there are affiliated congregations in all the Australian states. The official publication of this denomination is titled *Australian Presbyterian Living Today*.

A decade before creation of the Uniting Church, while the Presbyterian Church of Australia was still under liberal control, dissident conservatives withdrew to form the Presbyterian Reformed Church of Australia, a dynamic but small body with several congregations and only one presbytery. There were about sixteen meeting places operating with the services of about fifteen ministers. As the twentieth century drew to a close, church membership stood at about seven hundred. Despite its small size, the church maintains John Knox Theological College in Sydney and has a mission work in New Hebrides and an affiliated congregation in Auckland, New Zealand. *The Protestant Review* is its major publication. The Presbyterian Reformed Church is rigorously Calvinistic in teaching, subscribing to the Westminster Standards and opposing ecumenical measures so popular in other churches. Dissension over ecclesiastical discipline has cost this body some members in recent years.

Westminster Presbyterian Church is another conservative body in Australia and one that has received considerable support from the Presbyterian Church in America, a strong evangelical denomination with a vigorous worldwide missionary program. This church originated in conjunction with mission work among aborigines in the mid-1960s, and contacts with American Presbyterians led to support from that source. There are now congregations in Western Australia, Queensland, and New South Wales united in a single presbytery of sixteen local churches and about a thousand members, but attendance is almost twice that figure. The evangelistic church is loyal to the Reformed confessions, and ministerial education programs are underway in Perth and Brisbane.

As indicated, the Disruption of 1843 in the Church of Scotland had repercussions in Australia, and the Presbyterian Church of Eastern Australia is a product of that event. Organized in 1846 by three ministers and one elder who supported the secession of the Free Church of Scotland in 1843, this body affirmed its subscription to the Westminster Confession of

Faith in opposition to the liberalism in Scotland, which most Presbyterian churches in Australia accepted. This church does not allow any substantial exceptions to the Westminster Standards on the part of its officers, and like older Scottish churches, it uses only psalms with no musical accompaniment in services of worship. In 1953 the three congregations of the Free Presbyterian Church of Victoria joined with the Presbyterian Church of Eastern Australia, which now has fifteen local churches and about nine hundred members. This denomination maintains close ties with the Free Church of Scotland and sends some of its theological students to the Free Church College in Edinburgh, while others attend Presbyterian Theological College in Melbourne. The Presbyterian Church of Eastern Australia supports the missions of the Free Church in South Africa, India, and Peru. *The Presbyterian Banner* is its principal journal. The church is active in the International Conference of Reformed Churches.

In addition to Australia's historic contacts with Scottish Presbyterianism, Dutch immigrants have brought their particular expression of the Reformed faith to the land. In the period after the Second World War, large numbers of Dutch people, displaced by the conflict and seeking improved living conditions, arrived, over a hundred thousand of them, by 1966. Most of them were without religious interest and did not affiliate with any church in their adopted homeland. Those who did show such interest affiliated with the Presbyterian Church of Australia and subsequently with the Uniting Church. Those immigrants who had ties with the Reformed Churches of the Netherlands, the denomination of Abraham Kuyper, had been advised by that body to join the Presbyterian Church of Eastern Australia, and some did so, but cultural differences made them uncomfortable and seemed to necessitate creating a distinctly Dutch church of their own, the first such congregation being founded in Tasmania in 1951. Others soon developed in Brisbane, Sydney, Melbourne, and Perth. In this way the Reformed Churches of Australia came into being with the Three Forms of Unity as their confessional basis.

Like the Christian Reformed Church in America, its Australian counterpart emphasizes parental responsibility for the education of children, so a large number of private schools have appeared in communities where church members are numerous. Like Kuyper, prominent leaders in this denomination aspired to create a Christian university, and they began with founding the Reformed Theological College at Geelong. Although operated by the Association for Christian Education, the college serves the

church and enjoys its support without being strictly a denominational institution. Relations with their mother church in the Netherlands were cordial
at first, but a serious dilution of the faith in the Reformed Churches of the
Netherlands led to tensions and frequent disapproval of the Dutch church
because of its membership in the World Council of Churches, its toleration
of homosexuality, and a general decline in fidelity to orthodox Christian
teachings. Relations with the Presbyterian Church of Australia and the
Presbyterian Church of Eastern Australia have been positive. Most of the
growth in church membership has been biological, although an active evangelistic outreach is in progress. Victoria and Tasmania are the sites of the
church's greatest strength, though it has congregations in six states. By the
end of the twentieth century, about ten thousand people claimed affiliation
with this denomination, and attendance at services was over 80 percent.
The Reformed Churches of Australia have close fraternal relations with the
Reformed Churches of New Zealand, both bodies being associated in the
Reformed Ecumenical Council. In the latter part of the twentieth century
the inroad of charismatic influences created tensions within the Reformed
Churches of Australia, as did debates about the role of women in church
offices, both of which issues cost the church some losses in membership.

Another body of Dutch origin and conservative theological posture is
the Free Reformed Churches of Australia created in the early 1950s in
Western Australia. The formation of this body reflects conditions in the
Dutch kingdom, where the Reformed Churches of the Netherlands mandated that its officers subscribe to a peculiar view of infant baptism that
Abraham Kuyper advocated. Whereas the historic Reformed teaching on
this subject regarded infant baptism as a sign and seal of the child's induc-
tion into the covenant community of God's people, Kuyper had maintained
that the church should baptize infants on the supposition they are regenerate until and unless they show evidence to the contrary in later years.
Most of the members of the Reformed Churches of the Netherlands
accepted this view, but a minority opposed presumed regeneration. A division occurred in 1944 that produced the Reformed Churches (Liberated),
composed of about 10 percent of the members in the church from which
they seceded. The learned professor Klaas Schilder (1890–1952) was their
leader. The Free Reformed Churches of Australia oppose Kuyper's position
and uphold the traditional Reformed teaching about infant baptism. The
Presbyterian Church of Eastern Australia has sought fellowship with this

denomination, and discussions have occurred but without concrete results. Both have joined the International Conference of Reformed Churches.

The Free Reformed Churches have close relations with the Canadian Reformed Churches. The Australian church has nine congregations and about thirty-five hundred adherents, some in Tasmania, the rest in Western Australia. Each local assembly maintains a Christian school, and church attendance is almost 100 percent of the membership.

A number of very small Reformed bodies have developed in Australia, almost all of them orthodox in character. A Hungarian Reformed Church, for example, organized in 1973 on the basis of work initiated in 1949 under the auspices of the Presbyterian Church of Victoria. The congregation at Fitzroy voted to refrain from joining the Uniting Church in 1977, thereby becoming a separate body. This church maintained Hungarian language services and placed much emphasis on preserving Hungarian culture, thus limiting its outreach severely. No formal Presbyterian structure has developed, and autonomous congregations function similarly in other parts of the country. A willingness to accommodate laxity in doctrinal matters makes the future of this group as a Reformed witness unlikely.

Koreans too have settled in Australia and established Presbyterian congregations to serve the needs of their particular ethnic constituency. One such group is in fellowship with the Uniting Church, while another is conservative and collaborates with genuinely Reformed ministries. Sectarian divisions among Korean Presbyterians have been common, often due to issues that to outsiders appear rather obscure. As of yet no major Korean denomination has emerged. A Bible Presbyterian Church, with roots in the United States but more closely with Singapore, appeared in 1969 as a fundamentalist, premillennial, militantly anti-ecumenical movement, but it has not prospered, except among Chinese-speaking immigrants who comprise three congregations.

Another Reformed body of a fundamentalist character is the Free Presbyterian Church, connected with the denomination of the same name in Ulster. Only two congregations in Australia have affiliated with this movement, which uses only the King James Version of the Bible and maintains belief in premillennial eschatology while allowing parents the option of baptizing their children soon after birth or permitting them to seek baptism after making a profession of faith. These churches are subject to the Free Presbytery of Ulster.

Although about 50 percent of Australians identify themselves as Protestants while about one-quarter are Roman Catholics and the same number profess to be Anglicans, the Commonwealth is a decidedly secular society. The Reformed witness has not been robust, though a resurgence of historic Calvinism, especially within the Presbyterian Church of Australia, is encouraging.

The Dominion of New Zealand

New Zealand lies about twelve hundred miles from Australia, and each of the major islands, which the settlers named the North and South Islands, is about five hundred miles in length. Although remote from Europe, this country became the site of significant development in the history of the Reformed faith. The famous Captain Cook discovered New Zealand in 1769, but it was not until 1840 that British settlement began. Native chiefs (Maoris) agreed to British sovereignty, and settlement proceeded. A New Zealand Company under the leadership of Edward Gibbon Wakefield (1796–1862), a dynamic but rather unscrupulous entrepreneur, founded a National Colonization Society in 1830 as a means to promote emigration overseas as a way to alleviate the suffering of poor people in the United Kingdom. Wakefield, though head of a private venture, wanted British government support and close supervision of the colonists going abroad. Although the government rejected some of his ideas, emigration went forward.

Presbyterians arrived in the North Island in 1840 as the Scottish part of a settlement at the site of what became the city of Wellington. John MacFarlane (1807–1859) was the first pastor and thus the founder of the Presbyterian Church in New Zealand. Congregationalists, Anglicans, Roman Catholics, and Wesleyans were already there when the Presbyterians arrived. MacFarlane and his people from the Church of Scotland established congregations, but he had to return to Scotland in 1844 due to failing health. Other ministers soon arrived, however, and the work continued. By midcentury some forty thousand Maoris were attending worship in churches of various denominations, and the New Testament was available in their language. Christianity was having a civilizing effect upon a people notorious for violence and cannibalism. The first missionaries had discouraged European settlement for fear it would arouse native animosity and interfere with the work of spreading the gospel. When Europeans came anyway, the missionaries persuaded the native chiefs to accept British sovereignty as the best means to preserve peace and order.

Soon after MacFarlane initiated his ministry as an emissary from the Church of Scotland, effects of the Disruption of 1843 reached New Zealand, and in 1851 some Scots in Wellington appealed to the Free Church of Scotland to send a pastor who would establish a congregation of that connection. John Moir then went to the islands and became minister at what is now St. John's Presbyterian Church in Wellington. The Free Church dispatched pastors to the South Island as well, as when Thomas Burns (1796–1871), nephew of the famous poet Robert Burns, went to Otago to serve the spiritual needs of the Scots there. In 1849 Burns organized a church, and by 1854 the Presbytery of Otago was in operation. Progress was such that a Synod of Otago and Southland came into being in 1866. This growing body of committed Presbyterians quickly realized their responsibility to spread the gospel beyond their adopted homeland and sent Peter Milne and his wife as missionaries to the tribes of the New Hebrides.

While the Free Church was making much progress on the South Island, it continued to build on the work of MacFarlane in the North. David Bruce (1824–1911) led a vigorous church extension across that island, using Auckland's St. Andrew's Church as his base. Although the Church of Scotland was stronger than the Free Church in the North, tensions between the two bodies were not as severe in the colony as in Scotland itself, and there was an attempt as early as 1861 to unite the two. This proved impossible to sustain at that time, but later efforts succeeded. In 1901 the General Assembly of the Presbyterian Church of New Zealand became the supreme court of the united denomination. As this church grew, it sent missionaries to China, India, and Indonesia while maintaining a domestic outreach to the Maoris, whom the church accepted readily and integrated with its European membership. Alexander Don, secretary of foreign missions from 1914 to 1923, was a commanding figure in missionary expansion among Presbyterians.

Theological education for Presbyterian ministerial candidates in New Zealand began after Donald McNaughton Stuart (1819–1894) arrived in 1860 to become pastor of Knox Presbyterian Church, Dunedin. A learned scholar, Stuart helped organize the Theological College of the Presbyterian Church, which began to offer instruction about 1874. This seminary later changed its name to Knox Theological Hall to avoid confusion with Knox College, an institution of arts and sciences.

Although the Presbyterian Church and other denominations sought the conversion of Maoris and welcomed them as church members and officers, relations between Europeans and natives were sometimes hostile. Land disputes led to open warfare intermittently from 1859 to 1871 in some parts of the North Island until British forces crushed the rebels. The discovery of gold on the South Island in 1861 brought fortune hunters who cared little about natives' rights. The Presbyterian Church, in these days of disruption and thereafter, maintained a broad program of social services to aid needy people without regard to their ethnicity. Orphanages, hospitals, homes for elderly people, youth hostels, and homes for unwed mothers became permanent features of the church's social ministry.

In connection with their educational efforts, New Zealand Presbyterians published a number of periodicals through the nineteenth century, and in 1894 the General Assembly designated the *Christian Outlook* the official journal for the entire church. As in Australia, there were efforts to unite several Protestant bodies into a single church. The decade of the 1920s was a time of particular emphasis for this scheme involving Methodists, Congregationalists, Presbyterians, and, for a brief time, Anglicans. These endeavors were not successful, but in 1969 a large number of Congregational churches and ministers aligned with the Presbyterian General Assembly. By that time the influences of secular humanism and liberal theology had permeated most churches, and attendance at services had declined considerably. Perhaps as a reaction to this trend, charismatic assemblies began to appear and acquired a substantial following, while traditional Protestant churches lost members. Had it not been for Polynesian immigrants, the decline of mainline denominations would have been even larger. As Presbyterians assessed their losses, a resurgence of evangelical fervor among young ministers became evident in the last quarter of the twentieth century, but the denomination as a whole appeared uncertain about how to respond to the challenges it faced.

While the Presbyterian Church experienced decline, other expressions of the Reformed faith demonstrated considerable vitality. In the 1940s Dutch immigrants arrived in New Zealand, some of them refugees from Indonesia. Expecting to find churches comparable to those they had known in their previous home, they began attending Presbyterian services but soon learned the doctrines of the Reformed faith no longer comprised the message of that church. In 1951 some Dutch settlers in Auckland agreed to establish a church true to their Calvinist heritage, and they appealed to fellow believers in the Netherlands for a minister. J. W. Deenick answered their call. In rapid order the Reformed Churches of New Zealand took form, a synod being organized in 1953 by congregations in Auckland, Willington, and Christchurch. Soon others were founded in several communities, about twenty local assemblies in all. While still in its infancy, this body initiated a missionary work in Taiwan.

The Reformed Churches of New Zealand adhere to the historic Three Forms of Unity, while approving the Westminster Confession of Faith as well. Presbyterian polity is their form of church government. There are three presbyteries and a General Synod, the latter meeting every three years. Membership at the opening of the twenty-first century was about thirty-five hundred. The Reformed Churches of New Zealand are affiliated with the International Conference of Reformed Churches and maintain fraternal relations with other staunchly Calvinistic bodies in America, Europe, and South Africa.

As liberal theology gained ascendancy in the Presbyterian Church of New Zealand, other alternatives made their debut alongside the Reformed Churches of New Zealand. The Evangelical Presbyterian Church is the result of secession in 1974, as believers in Calvinist teachings sought to preserve their heritage. Thus far they have succeeded in establishing only one congregation in Christchurch. Rather than create a new denomination, this group aligned with the Westminster Presbyterian Church of Australia. It is a zealously evangelistic assembly committed to the historic Reformed faith.

Grace Presbyterian Church of New Zealand came into being soon after the opening of the twenty-first century as a reaction to liberal doctrine and toleration of homosexuality and the ordination of women in the mainline Presbyterian denomination. The new body has nine particular churches and four missions intended to become such. It has cordial relations with the Reformed Churches of New Zealand, the Presbyterian Church of Australia, and the Presbyterian Church in America. The Free Presbyterian Church of Scotland also has three congregations in New Zealand, with an aggregate membership of only about three hundred, and one pastor serves all three groups.

The Union/Republic of South Africa

Located at the southern tip of Africa, this country experienced its introduction to Christianity when Portuguese explorers arrived late in the fifteenth century on their way to Asia. The Portuguese erected some stone crosses and bestowed some Catholic names upon various places, but they did not attempt a permanent settlement at the Cape of Good Hope. As a consequence, the small native population had relatively few contacts with the Europeans. It was not until the Dutch arrived at the Cape in 1652 that Europeans decided to remain there in substantial numbers. Since the Dutch immigrants were Calvinist in religion, their brand of the Reformed faith took root quickly, but there was, at first, no vigorous effort to seek the conversion of the natives. Within a few decades German and French Protestants arrived, some fleeing persecution in their homelands. In France, for example, Louis XIV had revoked the Edict of Nantes (1598), which Henry IV had promulgated to the benefit of his Calvinist subjects.

Jan van Riebeeck (1619–1677) led the original settlers to establish a station for ships of the Dutch East India Company to obtain provisions, and no minister was present in the new colony, so lay leaders cared for the spiritual needs of the community. The Classis of Amsterdam assumed responsibility for approving such leaders until ordained pastors became available. Even though there was no organized missionary outreach to the natives, some Africans did embrace the faith, the first baptism occurring in 1662. The first Dutch minister arrived in 1665, and 1688 brought an influx of French Huguenots, who thereby strengthened the Reformed presence at the Cape. Some German Lutherans also were there, enjoying a rather grudging toleration from Reformed leaders, but the first Lutheran pastor did not settle in the colony until 1780. Missionaries of several denominations began working at the Cape during the era of the Napoleonic Wars in Europe, which ended in 1815.

As the eighteenth century matured, many churches in the Netherlands, because of the popularity of rationalism in the theological schools, began to deviate from Reformed orthodoxy, but almost all in South Africa remained staunch in their allegiance. Perceiving themselves as the Lord's people in a strange land, Reformed believers regarded their faith as spiritual cement binding them together, so they were not inclined to accept alien religious ideas. As the Europeans became a settled community, they expanded their agriculture and became known as *Boers,* the Dutch word for farmers. The relative homogeneity of these people experienced a challenge when Great Britain acquired control of the Cape of Good Hope in 1814, when the Congress of Vienna negotiated treaties ending the wars against Napoleon I and Revolutionary France. British administration had begun earlier, when the United Kingdom, with the agreement of the Dutch authorities Napoleon had ousted, occupied the Cape to prevent the French from seizing it. Britons began migrating to South Africa in 1820, when about four thousand arrived there, but emissaries of the London Missionary Society had been in the country for about twenty years prior to formal British annexation. English-speaking congregations developed alongside the older bodies of Dutch Reformed believers who were speaking Afrikaans, a dialect based on Dutch that contained French and native elements as well.

The original Reformed church in South Africa was the *Nederduitse Gereformeerde Kerk*, related to the state church in the Netherlands. Since there are no English terms that adequately convey the precise distinctions that identify the several Reformed bodies that developed in South Africa, it is necessary to refer to them by their chosen Afrikaans names. The *Nederduitse Gereformeerde Kerk* is still the largest Reformed denomination, but a migration of Boers into the interior of the country in 1837 led to formation of the *Hervormde Kerk*, another Calvinist body, in what became known as the Transvaal Republic. This occurred when Boers at the Cape, resentful toward British policies, left that region to seek an independent political life across the Vaal River. Those who engaged in the Great Trek became heroes in the thinking of most Boers, and their settlements in the Transvaal region brought conflict with black tribes that sometimes exploded into warfare in which the Boers (Afrikaners) displayed impressive courage and fighting ability, as battlefield victories confirmed their belief that God approved their actions.

Presbyterians began to exert considerable influence on the religious development of South Africa when Britain sent Scottish troops of a Calvinist persuasion to the Cape. Although they lacked ministers to serve their spiritual needs, the soldiers formed a Calvinist Society for worship and Bible study. In 1812 George Thom (1789–1842), a missionary on his way to India, stopped in Cape Town, where he met the Scots in need of a pastor. They convinced him to remain, and as a result of that decision, St. Andrew's Church became a regular Presbyterian congregation. When the government recalled the Scottish regiment, however, the church faltered badly. By 1824, however, new Scottish arrivals revived the work and erected a church building. In 1827 John Adamson became the pastor at St. Andrew's Church and remained there until 1841.

Almost from the beginning of their settlement in South Africa, Presbyterians undertook missionary outreach efforts. The Glasgow Missionary Society, an agency of the Church of Scotland, dispatched workers to the Eastern Cape, where they founded Lovedale, a school for the preparation of preachers and church workers trained in various trades as well, so they could support themselves. Originally at the town of Alice, the school moved a short distance and was thereafter situated within the confines of Cape Colony. The founders named the institute in honor of John Love (1757–1825), leader of the Glasgow Missionary Society. The school accepted students from all Christian denominations. Eventually the government of Cape Province assumed operation of Lovedale, which then became the nucleus of the later University of Fort Hare.

The formation of a presbytery for South Africa occurred in 1823, as congregations were established at several sites in the Eastern Cape. An expansion of church planting into the interior and Natal began in 1850, with creation of the Presbyterian Church of Natal, of which Scotsman William Campbell, a minister of the Free Church, became pastor the next year. By that time Presbyterians were enjoying impressive growth in areas of economic development connected with the discovery of diamonds and gold. Churches thus established served both black Africans and white Europeans, most of whom were Scots. By the end of the nineteenth century, the Presbyterians had gained sufficient strength to constitute a General Assembly, which convened in Durban in 1897. This united the presbyteries of Cape Town, Natal, and Transvaal, some congregations connected with the Free Church of Scotland, and two previously independent local assemblies. The united body became known as the Presbyterian Church of Southern Africa, when it embraced congregations outside South Africa proper by reaching into Rhodesia (now Zimbabwe) and Northern Rhodesia (now Zambia). Growth in the twentieth century was steady but not rapid, and the church claimed 180 local congregations and a membership of about ninety thousand communicants, of whom about one-third are blacks. The denomination has become increasingly liberal in the last century and now ordains female pastors and holds membership in the World Council of Churches. Its greatest strength is in urban areas. It has recently made gains among Indians and people of mixed race. Since 1898 a separate Presbyterian Church of Africa, almost entirely black, has enjoyed great growth and now claims over 925 thousand members. It declared itself separate due to a financial dispute with the Free Church of Scotland, and it, like the Presbyterian Church of Southern Africa, is now rather liberal in doctrine, ordains women to all church offices, and maintains ecumenical connections through the World Council of Churches.

Smaller Presbyterian denominations have appeared in South Africa, but unlike their counterparts in other countries, they have not maintained an orthodox theology. The Reformed Presbyterian Church in Southern Africa originated in Scottish mission work but declared its independence in 1923. It is overwhelmingly a black church, though some people of mixed race have joined. Strongest in the Eastern Cape, Natal, and Malawi, it numbers about fifty-two thousand members and is affiliated with the World Alliance of Reformed Churches and the World Council of Churches.

An even smaller denomination is the Evangelical Presbyterian Church, once known as the Tsonga Presbyterian Church because almost all adherents speak that language. Swiss missionaries founded this movement in 1875 in Transvaal to serve people employed in the mining industries. From there the church spread into the Orange Free State and Zululand. It claims about thirty thousand members, accepts infant or believers' baptism, and maintains membership in the World Council of Churches. In 2000 the Presbyterian Church of Southern Africa and the Reformed Presbyterian Church declared they had formed the Uniting Presbyterian Church in Southern Africa.

While the story of Presbyterian development in South Africa is not difficult to relate, that of the Reformed churches with Dutch roots is complex. As indicated already, the Dutch Reformed Church established the first lasting Christian presence in the country, and that body remains the largest denomination there. Geographic relocations of peoples, such as in the great Trek, economic developments such as the discovery of diamonds and gold, and problems associated with race have all affected the Reformed churches profoundly.

Until 1843 the government at the Cape supported the *Nederduitse Gereformeerde Kerk* financially and asserted corresponding control over its affairs, a relationship that continued in part until 1875, when support ended entirely. A law in 1843 prohibited the extension of the approved state church beyond the boundaries of Cape Colony, a measure that led to the formation of autonomous Reformed churches in Cape Colony, Natal, the Orange Free State, and Transvaal. A union of these bodies was not to be achieved until 1962. The *Nederduitse Gereformeerde Kerk* gained independence from its Dutch mother church in 1824, and as it grew, black converts were welcome to worship along with whites. This continued for many years, but eventually some whites complained about sharing a common communion cup with blacks, so a synod in 1857 called for the use of separate cups, even though the races were to worship together. As a concession to white members who raised the issue, the synod allowed for the creation of racial congregations. This in turn led to the formation of what were regarded as mission churches such as the *Nederduitse Gereformeerde Sendings Kerk*, founded in 1880 as an evangelistic outreach to the Coloured People (mixed race) of the Cape. The mother church created a special seminary for the education of pastors to serve the *Sendings Kerk*, and from a humble beginning with only four ministers, this movement grew rapidly and by the end of the twentieth century had well over a million members. Racial segregation (*apartheid*) became the official policy of the Union of South Africa in 1948.

From 1899 to 1902 an Anglo-Boer War convulsed South Africa and ended in the defeat of the Afrikaners after a fierce and heroic resistance to the might of the British Empire. Only with extreme difficulty and resort to some barbarous methods did Britain prevail. In part the cause of the conflict was British refusal to protect the Boers against black tribes and British support of the tribes against the Afrikaners' claims. Several times the government in London had violated promises made to the Afrikaner states in the interior, until the Boers revolted. The discovery of major gold deposits in Transvaal exacerbated Anglo-Boer relations, especially when the Afrikaner administration tried to inhibit Britons from exploiting the situation in order to gain great wealth. As a consequence of defeat the Boers became very hostile toward Britons, but the imperial government, in an enlightened measure of statesmanship, moved quickly to repair the damage of the war and to extend loans to impoverished Afrikaners, who formed their own political party. In 1910, Great Britain allowed elections in South Africa and made the country a self-governing dominion to be known as the Union of South Africa. Louis Botha (1863–1919), a heroic Boer general, became the Union's first prime minister. The Boers had lost the war militarily but had won it politically. These developments were to have lasting consequences for the future of the Reformed churches, which, in general, supported the policy of *apartheid* once it became official. For some time after the war the Reformed churches seemed introverted and took little part in the wider affairs of Reformed and Presbyterian churches around the world. The *Nederduitse Gereformeerde Kerk* did not join the Alliance of Reformed Churches until 1924.

In addition to the *Nederduitse Gereformeerde Kerk*, and the *Hervormde Kerk*, formed by the Trekkers of 1837, a third Reformed denomination appeared in 1859. This was the *Gereformeerde Kerk*, theologically the most conservative of the three bodies. Its teaching portrayed the Afrikaners as a New Israel under divine guidance moving toward the New Jerusalem. Preachers of this church held that black people bear the curse of Noah on his son Ham (Gen. 9:18–24). Perhaps because it had no close ties with the civil government of South Africa, this church, in a strange twist of events, was the first to renounce apartheid, a decision that preceded similar declarations of the other Reformed bodies by about twenty years.

As the second half of the twentieth century progressed, Reformed Christians across South Africa slowly became convinced that apartheid was an unjust social policy, one they could not reconcile with their faith. In 1980 the World Alliance of Reformed Churches, as a means to express disapproval of apartheid, dismissed the major Dutch Reformed Church from membership in that body. Six years later the church officially ended segregation of its congregations and announced people of all races were welcome. Although this has not resulted in full integration, no barriers of policy remain, and many congregations are still uniracial because that is the preference of people in choosing churches.

In addition to the major Reformed denominations, there are several smaller ones which, in some cases, maintain greater allegiance to Calvinist doctrine. The Reformed Church in Africa is one such group. It has about two thousand members, most of them ethnic Indians, although membership is open to all races. Strongly evangelistic, this church concentrates on missions to Muslims and Hindus, most of its members themselves being former Hindus.

As might be expected, reactions to the broadened social policy of church and state in South Africa provoked some reaction, and one consequence of this was the organization of the Afrikaans Protestant Church in 1987, as archconservatives withdrew from the *Nederduitse Gereformeerde Kerk*, protesting that its liberal posture would lead the country into chaos, perhaps into Communism. Some ministers and communicants from other Reformed churches also joined this movement, and by the end of the century it had about fifteen thousand adherents. The Afrikaans Protestant Church does not ordain women, holds strictly to the historic Reformed confessions, and refrains from ecumenical relations with liberal church bodies. A similar but distinct denomination is the *Vrye Gereformeerde Kerke* (Liberated Reformed Churches), a staunchly confessional association that began in 1950 as a result of Dutch immigration. Desiring to maintain their historic faith, this group adheres to the Three Forms of Unity while it conducts vigorous evangelism. Some believers dissatisfied with the drift toward liberal theology in other churches have joined the Liberated Reformed fellowship, which has about a half-dozen congregations and a membership of nearly sixteen hundred.

Its interchurch relations are exclusively with orthodox Reformed bodies in other countries.

The Free Church in Southern Africa originated in the work of Scottish missionaries in 1843 as a ministry to Xhosa-speaking blacks. When most congregations of the Free Church of Scotland reunited with the Church of Scotland in 1900, those that did not declared themselves the continuing Free Church of Scotland, and the South African congregations that remained aloof from the reunion aligned with the dissidents in Scotland whose missionaries still served them. In 1982 the Free Church in Southern Africa assumed autonomy but still receives vital financial support from its Scottish brethren. This denomination claims about four thousand members and is affiliated with the International Conference of Reformed Churches. The Westminster Standards are its official statement of doctrine.

Although the country has endured racial tensions and worldwide criticism, South Africa has been a very fertile field for Christianity. Almost 80 percent of the population professes allegiance to the faith in some form of its expression. Calvinism remains relatively strong but is receding before the advance of theological liberalism and secular humanism. The coming of British evangelicalism blended with Dutch Reformed thinking produced a vibrant Protestantism that continues to exert much influence, perhaps more than in any other African nation. In 1961 South Africa withdrew from the British Commonwealth of Nations, thereby renouncing allegiance to the crown and declaring the country a republic. The end of apartheid brought national elections in which all races participated, so South Africa now has a multiracial government in which blacks are dominant. The Methodist Church of Southern Africa is the largest religious body, and several denominations have formed the South African Council of Churches in an effort to promote unity. Such endeavors have been only slightly successful, as conservative-evangelical churches remain separate from ecumenical measures. In both rural and urban areas church attendance remains relatively high, evidence of Christianity's ongoing influence in national life.

SUGGESTED ADDITIONAL READINGS >>

Bailey, Thomas M. *The Covenant in Canada: Being Four Hundred Years History of the Presbyterian Church in Canada.* Hamilton, Canada: Mac Nab Circle, 1975.

Bardon, R. *The Centenary History of the Presbyterian Church of Queensland.* Brisbane, Australia: General Assembly of the Presbyterian Church of Queensland, 1949.

Bloomberg, Charles. *Christian-Nationalism and the Rise of the Afrikaner Broederbond, 1918–48.* Edited by Saul Dubow. Bloomington: Indiana University Press, 1959.

Bradshaw, F. Maxwell. *Scottish Seceders in Victoria.* Melbourne: Robertson & Mullens, 1947.

Bredekamp, H. and R. Ross, eds. *Missions and Christianity in South African History.* Johannesburg: Witwatersrand University Press, 1995.

Breward, Ian. *A History of the Churches in Australia.* Oxford: Oxford University Press, 2001.

Cameron, James A. *A Centenary History of the Presbyterian Church in New South Wales.* Sydney: Angus & Robertson, 1905.

Clifford, N. Keith. *The Resistance to Church Union in Canada, 1904–1939.* Vancouver, Canada: University of British Columbia Press, 1985.

Davidson, Allan K. *History of the Church and Society in New Zealand.* 2nd ed. Wellington, New Zealand: New Zealand Education for Ministry, 1991.

Davies, Alan. *Infected Christianity: A Study of Modern Racism.* Montreal: McGill-Queen's University Press, 1988.

De Gruchy, J. W. *The Church Struggle in South Africa.* Cape Town: David Philip, 1979.

DeKlerk, Willem. *The Puritans in Africa: A Study of Afrikanerdom.* London: Rex Collins, 1975.

Dickinson, John. *History of the Presbyterian Church of New Zealand.* Dunedin, New Zealand: J. Wilkie, 1911.

Du Plessis, Johannes. *A History of Christian Missions in South Africa.* London: Longmans, Green, 1911.

Elder, J. R. *The History of the Presbyterian Church of New Zealand, 1840–1940.* Christchurch, New Zealand: Presbyterian Book Room, 1940.

Gauvreau, Michael. *The Evangelical Century: College and Creed in English Canada from the Great Revival to the Great Depression.* Montreal: McGill-Queen's University Press, 1991.

Gerstner, Jonathan Neil. *The Thousand Generation Covenant: Dutch Reformed Covenant Theology and Group Identity in Colonial South Africa.* Leiden, Netherlands: Koninklijke Brill, 1991.

Grant, John Webster. *The Church in the Canadian Era.* Rev. ed. Vancouver, Canada: Regent College Publishing, 1998.

Gregg, William. *History of the Presbyterian Church in the Dominion of Canada.* Toronto: Presbyterian Printing and Publishing, 1885.

Handy, Robert T. *A History of the Churches in the United States and Canada.* New York: Oxford University Press, 1984.

Harris, Dorothy with Douglas Hynd and David Millikan, eds. *The Shape of Belief: Christianity in Australia Today.* Homebush, Western Australia: Lancer, 1982.

Hexham, Irving. *The Irony of Apartheid: The Struggle for National Independence of Afrikaner Calvinism against British Imperialism.* Lewiston, N.Y.: Edwin Mellen Press, 1981.

Hofmyr, J. W. and G. J. Pillay, eds. *A Historic Christianity in South Africa.* Praetoria, South Africa: Haum Tertiary, 1994.

Hutchison, Mark. *Iron in Our Blood: The Presbyterian Church in New South Wales.* Sydney: Ferguson, 2001.

Isichei, Elizabeth. *A History of Christianity in Africa from Antiquity to the Present.* London: SPCK, 1995.

Jackson, H. R. *Churches and People in Australia and New Zealand.* Winchester, Mass.: Allen & Unwin, 1987.

Macdonald, Aeneas. *One Hundred Years of Presbyterianism in Victoria.* Melbourne: Robertson & Mullens, 1937.

Mark, Malcolm and Kenneth G. McMillan. *Canadian Presbyterianism in Action, 1761–1961.* Toronto: Synod of Toronto & Kingston, 1961.

McEldowney, Dennis, ed. *Presbyterians in Aotearoa, 1840–1990.* Wellington, New Zealand: Presbyterian Church of New Zealand, 1990.

McKean, John. *The Church in a Special Colony, 1866–1991.* Dunedin, New Zealand: Synod of Otago and Southland, 1994.

McLeod, John M. *History of Presbyterianism on Prince Edward Island.* Chicago: Winona, 1904.

McNeill, John T. *The Presbyterian Church in Canada.* Toronto: General Board of the Presbyterian Church in Canada, 1925.

Miller, R. S., ed. *The Presbyterian Church of Tasmania.* Hobart, Australia: Presbyterian Publications, 1973.

Moffatt, Robert. *Missionary Labours and Scenes in Southern Africa.* New York: Robert Carter, 1843.

Moir, John S. *The Church in the British Era.* Toronto: McGraw-Hill Ryerson, 1972.

———. *Early Presbyterianism in Canada.* Edited by Paul Laverdure. Gravelbourg, Canada: Gravelbooks, 2003.

———. *Enduring Witness: A History of the Presbyterian Church in Canada.* 2nd ed. Toronto: Committee of History, the Presbyterian Church in Canada, 1987.

Moodie, T. Dunbar. *The Rise of Afrikanerdom: Power, Apartheid, and the Afrikaner Civil Religion.* Berkeley: University of California Press, 1975.

Murray, Iain H. *Australian Christian Life from 1788.* Edinburgh: Banner of Truth, 1988.

Nichol, C. and J. A. Veitch. *Religion in New Zealand.* Wellington, New Zealand: Religious Studies Department at Victoria University, 1980.

Noll, Mark A. *A History of Christianity in United States and Canada.* Grand Rapids: Eerdmans, 2001. Reprint of 1992 edition.

Pearson, Keith D. *Understanding the Presbyterian Church.* Melbourne: Joint Board of Christian Education of Australia and New Zealand, 1969.

Piggin, Stewart. *Evangelical Christianity in Australia.* Oxford: Oxford University Press, 1995.

Prozesky, M., ed. *Christianity in South Africa.* Bergulei, South Africa: Southern Publishers, 1990.

Rawlyk, George A., ed. *Amazing Grace: Evangelicalism in Australia, Britain, Canada, and the United States.* Grand Rapids: Baker, 1993.

———, ed. *The Canadian Protestant Experience, 1760–1990.* Montreal: McGill-Queen's University Press, 1990.

Robinson, J. Campbell. *The Free Presbyterian Church of Australia.* Melbourne: Hamer, 1947.

Scrimgeour, R. J. *Some Scots Were Here: A History of the Presbyterian Church in South Australia, 1839–1977.* Adelaide, Australia: Lutheran Publishing House, 1986.

Vanderpyl, Dirk, ed. *Trust and Obey: A History of the Reformed Churches of New Zealand.* Hamilton, New Zealand: Reformed Church Publishing Society, 1994.

Walsh, Henry H. *The Church in the French Era.* Toronto: Ryerson Press, 1966.

Ward, Rowland S. *The Bush Still Burns: The Presbyterian and Reformed Faith in Australia, 1788–1988.* Wantirna, Australia: Globe Press, 1989.

———. *The Free Presbyterian Church of Australia.* Melbourne: Box Hill, 1984.

———. *The Making of an Australian Church: A History of the Presbyterian Church of Eastern Australia.* Ulverstone, Australia: R. S. Ward Publisher, 1978.

———. *Presbyterianism in Tasmania, 1821–1977.* Ulverstone, Australia: R. S. Ward Publisher, 1977.

White, C. A. *The Challenge of the Years.* Sydney: Angus & Robertson, 1951.

Williams, William. *Christianity among the New Zealanders.* Edinburgh: Banner of Truth, 1989. Reprint of 1867 edition.

Presbyterianism in Twentieth-Century United States

As the nineteenth century drew to a close, increasing wealth was becoming a striking feature of life in the United States. Many churches had ornate buildings, and church-related colleges were flourishing, often with large endowments contributed by affluent Protestant churchmen. Ministers were more educated than ever before, and Protestant Americans were becoming a comfortable middle class, a situation that caused many poor people to leave traditional churches, some to join Pentecostal or holiness sects. Tense relations between capital and labor sometimes led to violence, and some clergymen, Presbyterians among them, thought a new approach to social action was in order.

Social Conditions and the Social Gospel

A wholesome concern for the needs of the poor and underprivileged was, of course, entirely consistent with a fervent evangelical faith, but some thinkers proposed a drastic revision of historic Christianity as the best means to resolve what they were calling *Christianity and the Social Crisis,* the title of a book by Walter Rauschenbusch (1861–1918), a Baptist theologian. He and Washington Gladden (1826–1918), a pastor in the same denomination, became leading exponents of the Social Gospel, a call for building the kingdom of God on earth through concerted social action programs involving both the churches and the government. Prominent leaders in many denominations responded affirmatively, and appeals for social outreach began replacing evangelism and biblical exposition in many pulpits, as ministers emphasized meeting material needs more than proclaiming the forgiveness of sins and life in eternity.

The roots of this new doctrine were in the liberal theology of the nineteenth century brought to America from Europe by scholars who had studied in universities where orthodoxy was in disfavor. Presbyterians in the northern United States proved much more receptive to this thinking than did their brethren in the Southern church. Some liberals boldly portrayed the kingdom of God as the fulfillment of their social ideal as the concepts of Rauschenbusch and Gladden permeated Presbyterian circles.

Missionary expansion was another feature of American churches as the nineteenth century closed, and it was not long before the new social conception of the faith regarded missions as primarily humanitarian endeavors to alleviate suffering on earth rather than to prepare lost sinners for salvation in heaven. As denominational officials embraced this idea while their churches drifted away from their confessional standards, they sought to reduce competition among churches by creating interdenominational agencies of cooperation. The Student Volunteer Movement, for example, appeared on many college and university campuses to recruit young people for service in foreign lands, and thousands responded. John R. Mott (1865–1955), a Methodist layman, published *The Evangelization of the World in This Generation* (1900), which excited great zeal, but already disagreements about the definition of the gospel were becoming evident.

While Protestants debated about the Social Gospel, the growth of urban culture greatly affected the outlook of their churches in large eastern cities, once Protestant strongholds that were receiving a major influx of Roman Catholic immigrants. Since many of the new arrivals were poor, churches often initiated extensive social programs in order to remain relevant to the changing times.

Intellectual Challenges to the Faith

By the opening of the twentieth century, Darwinian evolution had gained much acceptance, while its conflict with Scripture aroused much debate. In supposedly Christian colleges and universities, professional educators often replaced ministers as presidents, and businessmen became trustees and administrators who reduced the role of religion in the curricula, as theology gave place to comparative religion. In such matters American institutions were following the lead of European universities.

As prestigious universities embraced the historical-critical approach to the Bible and Christian doctrine, seminaries, eager for academic recognition, did the same, and many so-called professional theologians soon regarded Christianity as only one of several ancient religions and not the product of divine inspiration and intervention into history. They viewed the books of the Bible as expressions of the authors' primitive worldview, which, in their judgment, makes the Scripture unreliable in matters of history, science, and ethics. Protestant scholars, Presbyterians among them, divided sharply over how to respond to attacks on Scripture. Charles Hodge of Princeton Seminary, for example, was adamant in opposition to all concessions to the evolutionary worldview, a perspective he regarded as atheism. Benjamin B. Warfield, of the same faculty, however, maintained *theistic* evolution is not incompatible with the Bible. He and other learned professors thought they could employ the sciences in support of Christianity and thereby make its claims more credible. This was true of W. G. T. Shedd (1820–1894), a professor at New York's Union Theological Seminary, as well. Although he was a staunch and defensive Calvinist, Shedd was willing to adjust the faith so as to allow some concessions to contentions of higher critics. He edited the works of Samuel Taylor Coleridge, whose ideas the liberals found very attractive. Charles Augustus Briggs followed Shedd at Union Seminary and took Shedd's concessions to greater lengths.

As the nineteenth century ended, it was clear orthodox Protestants were losing control of higher education in America. Even theology was not withstanding the demands of skeptics and liberals, so new definitions of the Christian faith appeared and gained considerable popularity.

Modernist Theology

While the twentieth century was still young, Protestants became deeply divided between modernists, who accepted the critical approach to Christianity, and fundamentalists, who opposed it. Each school of thought purported to be preserving the faith from destruction, but the methods one employed contradicted the methods of the other, showing that both could not be right. Modernists eagerly adjusted the claims of the faith so as to accommodate prevailing ideas in the academic community, as the influence of Horace Bushnell (1802–1876) illustrates well. This Congregationalist minister, a Yale graduate, regarded all traditional doctrines and creeds as but poetic expressions of faith rather than literal declarations of truth. A prolific and persuasive author, Bushnell exerted broad influence, even in Presbyterian circles. His books *God in Christ* (1849) and *Christian Nurture* (1847) remain popular among people who share his views, and in the nineteenth and early twentieth centuries enjoyed great acceptance in theological schools. In *The Vicarious Sacrifice* (1866), Bushnell denied the substitutionary atonement of Jesus' death by portraying it as the supreme expression of God's love and a heroic example of selflessness. When some

Presbyterian scholars endorsed such views, their church became embroiled in divisive controversies.

Arthur Cushman McGiffert (1861–1933) was one of the early modernists to become prominent in Presbyterian disputes. A graduate of Union Theological Seminary in New York and a PhD from the University of Marburg, McGiffert taught at Lane Theological Seminary, Cincinnati, until 1893, when he obtained a position at Union Seminary. Publication of his *History of Christianity in the Apostolic Age* (1897) provoked the charge of heresy, because in that work the author contended the teachings of Jesus and Paul are contradictory. He cited Paul as the founder of what became traditional Christianity, and he accused the apostle of distorting the claims of Christ. McGiffert proposed to serve the church by recovering the real teachings of Jesus through the techniques of *scientific history*. This, he held, led him to see Jesus as primarily a social reformer rather than a savior.

Publication of his book aroused such a furor that McGiffert left Presbyterianism to become a Congregationalist. Union Seminary, nevertheless, retained him, and in 1917 he became its president, a position he held until 1926. His ideas reflect his studies in Germany with Adolf von Harnack (1851–1930) and Albrecht Ritschl (1822–1889), leaders of radical theology in Europe. By the end of his career, McGiffert had abandoned Christianity in any recognizable expression. His influence was, however, decisive in making Union Theological Seminary the fountainhead of modernist theology in the United States.

Even more famous than McGiffert in the promotion of modernist beliefs was Harry Emerson Fosdick (1878–1969), who had studied with McGiffert at Union Seminary. Although Fosdick was a Baptist, the Presbytery of New York had approved his appointment as associate pastor at First Presbyterian Church, New York City, in 1918. His exceptional oratorical talent attracted throngs to the services, thereby assuring the popularity of both the church and its preacher. On May 21, 1922, Fosdick preached a sermon titled "Shall the Fundamentalists Win?" Soon this appeared in print, and about 130 thousand pastors received copies. Controversy exploded in many places. The Presbytery of Philadelphia responded with an overture to the General Assembly to require Fosdick to conform to the doctrines of the Westminster Confession of Faith, with Pastor Clarence Macartney of Arch Street Presbyterian Church, Philadelphia, leading the plaintiffs.

In his notorious sermon Fosdick asserted liberal views of Scripture, the virgin birth and substitutionary atonement of Jesus, and the Savior's second coming. He appealed for toleration of diversity on such doctrines that, it is evident, he did not regard as essential to the faith. The next year Fosdick lectured at Yale Divinity School, and his presentations appeared as *The Modern Use of the Bible,* a work in which he advocated the critical approach to Scripture. His boldness in asserting his position reflected his confidence that many Presbyterians would endorse his plea for an inclusive policy of toleration toward diverse belief, which they did. A conservative journal, *The Presbyterian,* responded to Fosdick's sermon with an editorial titled "Shall Unbelief Win?"

The General Assembly of the Presbyterian Church (U.S.A.) in 1923 reaffirmed historic orthodoxy and directed First Presbyterian Church, New York City, to conform to the Westminster Confession of Faith, but the vote to do so was 439 in favor, 359 opposed, clear evidence that liberalism had made deep inroads into the church. The same General Assembly chose as moderator Charles F. Wishart, who favored an inclusive policy and sought to maintain unity by discouraging debates about doctrine. Pastor George Alexander of First Presbyterian Church agreed to abide by the mandate of the General Assembly, but neither he nor the Presbytery of New York did so. On the contrary, that presbytery soon licensed two candidates for the ministry who denied the virgin birth of Jesus. One of them, Henry P. Van Dusen, later obtained ordination and became a professor at Union Theological Seminary.

Fosdick left the Presbyterian church to become pastor of Riverside Church, an affiliate of what is now the American Baptist Churches but was then the Northern Baptist Convention. His radio broadcasts, delivered with great eloquence, spread liberal ideas across the nation.

In addition to the critical approach to Scripture popular among liberal churchmen, the theory of organic evolution agitated much interest in Presbyterian circles. A dramatic court case, the Scopes Trial of 1925, pitted the articulate layman William Jennings Bryan (1860–1925) against the clever lawyer Clarence Darrow in Dayton, Tennessee. Bryan, a former congressman, secretary of state, and a presidential candidate, was deeply concerned about the moral decay he perceived in American society and had been a leader in supporting passage of the Eighteenth Amendment to the United States Constitution, which outlawed alcoholic beverages. Bryan condemned the teaching of evolution as unscientific and detrimental to public morality, and he joined prosecutors of John Scopes, a high school biology instructor teaching the Darwinian hypothesis. Although the court convicted and fined Scopes, the trial produced massive ridicule of Bryan and the fundamentalists for whom, in this case, he was the spokesman. Bryan, however, endured little of the scorn, because he died only five days after the trial.

As unsettling as the Scopes affair was, controversies related to the foreign missions program of the Presbyterian Church (U.S.A.) were even more divisive. The central figure in this dispute was now famous novelist Pearl S. Buck (1892–1973), who spent her childhood in China with her missionary parents. After graduation from Randolph-Macon College in 1914, Pearl Sydenstricker returned to China in 1917 and there married John L. Buck. She taught at Kiangan Mission in Nanking from 1921 to 1931.

Buck became an acclaimed author when, in 1932, she received a Pulitzer Prize for the novel *The Good Earth*. By then it had become clear that she did not adhere to orthodox Christian beliefs, going so far as to criticize the doctrines of the Reformed faith and decrying the efforts of missionaries to seek the conversion of Chinese people of other religions. In 1933 Buck resigned from the Presbyterian Board of Foreign Missions in the midst of furious controversy her pronouncements had ignited, a dispute which eventuated in the division of the church.

Although the General Assembly of the Presbyterian Church (U.S.A.) had rejected Fosdick and had rebuked the Presbytery of New York, that court continued to ordain ministers of modernist persuasion. Even before the Assembly of 1923, Robert Hastings Nichols (1873–1955), a professor at Auburn Theological Seminary in New York, circulated an essay that called for doctrinal license in the church. Although it did not win acceptance at that Assembly, it aroused the liberals to mobilize their supporters, and thirty-three ministers from upstate New York met to plan strategy. Using Nichols's essay as their basis, they produced the Auburn Affirmation, which they "designed to safeguard the unity and liberty of the Presbyterian Church in the United States of America." This document, which became the symbol of Presbyterian liberalism, contended the action of the General Assembly against Fosdick was unconstitutional, and it called for toleration of diverse interpretations of the Westminster Confession and the Scriptures. Signers of the Auburn Affirmation contended there are no actual fundaments of the faith, only theories about Christian beliefs, and so they called for a broad view of religion without definitions of doctrine. When the finished document appeared in print in 1924, it bore 224 signatures and amounted to a manifesto of modernism in opposition to the historic Reformed faith.

By the time the above declaration appeared, the Presbytery of New York had become the most blatantly liberal court in the church, and its most prominent leader was Henry Sloan Coffin (1877–1954), pastor at Madison Avenue Presbyterian Church and a professor of pastoral theology at Union Theological Seminary. Coffin, a vigorous supporter of Fosdick, was acknowledged leader of Presbyterian liberals. Coffin may have acquired some of his skepticism toward orthodoxy from his father, a lawyer who never joined the church because he could not reconcile the conflicting claims of science and religion. Edmund Coffin, nevertheless, attended Fifth Avenue Presbyterian Church regularly. He was legal counsel to Union Seminary during the trial of Charles A. Briggs, a proceeding Henry attended when he was but sixteen years old. The experience left a lasting impression upon young Coffin, who had already expressed his desire to become a minister.

Like other liberals, Coffin rejected the Westminster Standards as antiques and irrelevant to modern needs, yet he attended Fifth Avenue Church while the conservative John Hall was pastor. Hall, a member of the board of directors at Princeton Theological Seminary, was an opponent of those who sought to revise the Westminster Confession, and he rejected higher criticism and the theory of organic evolution.

After graduating from Yale University, Coffin went to Edinburgh to study theology at New College, and while there he discarded whatever orthodox tenets he once held in favor of so-called progressive ideas he hoped American Presbyterians would eventually endorse. While he was in Britain, controversy about the views of McGiffert raged at home. After a few months of study at Marburg, Coffin returned home and finished his education at Union Seminary, graduating in 1900. Ordination and a call into the pastoral ministry soon followed. Most of Coffin's books are collections of his sermons, and prominent among them are *The Creed of Jesus* (1907), *The Ten Commandments* (1915), and *In a Day of Social Rebuilding* (1918). In these and other works Coffin portrayed himself as a liberal evangelical who, by making accommodations to modern culture, was preserving Christianity by making it attractive to enlightened people. Experience, he held, is the foundation of religion and must be the basis for preaching. In his judgment the Bible is the product of evolving religious experience.

Presbyterian Orthodox Theology

The assaults of the modernists did not, of course, go unanswered, as publication of *The Fundamentals: A Testimony to the Truth*, which appeared in 1915, attests. This set of small books was an early effort to reassert Christian super-naturalism by publishing the essays of noteworthy scholars, Presbyterians among them. These books, funded by oilmen Lyman and Milton Stewart of California, contain about a hundred articles that defend basic Christian beliefs. Contributors include Scottish theologian James Orr, Princeton Seminary's Warfield and Charles R. Erdman, Anglican Bishop H. C. G. Moule, Southern Baptist Edgar Y. Mullins, and American dispensationalist C. I. Scofield. Since the authors wrote from differing confessional positions, they had to avoid contentions about doctrine and emphasize agreement about the *fundamentals* of the faith, hence the title of the series. They did this because of their common concern that supernaturalism as a faith and worldview was at stake. Some essays are militant, others moderate in tone. Curtis Lee Laws, a Baptist journalist, seems to have coined the term *fun-damentalists* to identify orthodox believers who sought to defend the faith against those who were assailing it. As the Presbyterian Church (U.S.A.) became increasingly receptive to liberalism, conservatives within it looked outside their own tradition for support and often joined with Baptists to defend the faith.

In the contest against modernism in the Presbyterian Church (U.S.A.), Clarence Macartney (1879–1957) took the lead. This graduate of Princeton Seminary and a distinguished pastor in Paterson, New Jersey; Philadelphia; and Pittsburgh in 1924 became moderator of the General Assembly. He was the most prominent leader of the orthodox party within his church, and when Princeton reorganized in 1929 so as to accommodate liberal teachings, Macartney supported the creation of Westminster Theological Seminary in Philadelphia as a conservative alternative for ministerial education. Charles R. Erdman (1866–1960), a Princeton Seminary professor, led the less militant conservatives and was Macartney's rival for the position of moderator in 1924. By a vote of 464 to 446, Macartney won, after being nominated by William Jennings Bryan. The liberals had supported Erdman because they believed he would be more tolerant toward their doctrinal deviations than the staunchly Calvinistic Macartney. Once the election had occurred, Coffin resolved to resist Macartney, especially because of the latter's opposition to Fosdick.

Macartney came from a Covenanter family, his father being a professor at Geneva College and a minister in the Reformed Presbyterian Church of North America. A strict Reformed believer, he held that the United States must become a Christian nation submissive to Christ as king. Orthodoxy and piety were his heritage, but while he was a student at the University of Wisconsin, he was exposed to anti-Christian ideas that caused him to doubt. Once he resolved those doubts, however, Macartney became a vigorous defender of the Reformed faith. He studied theology with Warfield, Francis Paton, and Robert Dick Wilson, all renowned scholars at Princeton Seminary, which was then a bastion of orthodoxy. Frederick Loetscher, a professor of church history at his seminary, made an especially deep impression upon Macartney, who loved history, as his sermons attest. Upon graduation from seminary, he obtained ordination in the Presbyterian Church (U.S.A.).

At the General Assembly of 1924, Macartney led the conservative majority, but that body took no action against signers of the Auburn Affirmation, a failure that impaired the credibility of the orthodox party and cost it some support. Rather than contest the licensure of Van Dusen, the General Assembly referred the matter to the Synod of New York, and it did not approve a motion that would have required all officers of the denomination and its agencies to subscribe to what were then deemed the fundamentals of the faith. Despite the election of Macartney, the Assembly did little to retard the progress of modernism within the church. Coffin was pleased the Assembly did not condemn Fosdick, whom he urged to join the Presbyterian Church, but Fosdick refused. The controversy he had initiated had, however, only begun.

Like Macartney, Erdman was a key figure in the controversies about modernism, but unlike the assertive pastor, this Princeton professor carefully avoided taking a position that might lead to schism. Erdman regarded himself as fully orthodox and had contributed to *The Fundamentals*. A graduate of Princeton University and Princeton Theological Seminary, Erdman was a son of a New School Presbyterian pastor who associated with Dwight L. Moody. Prior to joining the seminary faculty in 1906, Erdman held pastorates in Philadelphia and Princeton. As professor of practical theology, he remained at the seminary until retirement in 1936.

In 1925 Erdman succeeded Macartney as moderator of the General Assembly at a time when conservatives were poised to demand subscription to historic Reformed theology. Rather than support such a move, he regarded church unity as more important than doctrinal precision and urged a broadly evangelical posture to which a confessional church was an obstacle. Erdman affirmed the inerrancy of Scripture where it teaches about Christ and salvation, but he would not commit himself beyond that point.

When the General Assembly considered requiring subscription from all church officers, he referred the matter to a committee, perhaps in the hope of thereby keeping peace in the church. As moderator Erdman appointed committee chairmen of his own disposition and collaborated with Coffin to avert a schism. Coffin believed correctly the trend in the church was moving in his direction, and he was glad for Erdman's support, however unaware Erdman might have been about the damage to orthodoxy he was abetting. Although the liberals had not yet achieved control of the denomination, aid from conservatives such as Erdman encouraged them to believe success was within reach.

The tensions evident at the General Assembly of 1925 reflected the growing controversy at Princeton Seminary as well, even though it was the traditional citadel of the Reformed faith. John Gresham Machen (1881–1937) became the central figure in the struggle to preserve the seminary's allegiance to orthodoxy, an effort that failed in the end. Machen, after graduation from Johns Hopkins University, earned the MA from Princeton University and the BD from Princeton Seminary before pursuing further studies at Marburg and Goettingen Universities in Germany. Upon his return Machen joined the faculty of his seminary as an instructor in New Testament and became an assistant professor in 1914. Along with Oswald T. Allis, Robert Dick Wilson, William Greene, Geerhardus Vos, and Caspar W. Hodge, he stood for Old School Presbyterianism at a time when that position was losing favor in the church at large. On the other side of a divided faculty were President J. Ross Stevenson and Professors Erdman, Loetscher, John D. Davis, and J. Ritchie Smith, who favored openness toward liberal ideas in order to bring the seminary into the mainstream of theological scholarship.

In 1925 William Brenton Greene announced he would retire as professor of apologetics, and Macartney was in line to succeed him. Although Machen urged Macartney to accept the position, the pastor refused, perhaps because his respected mentor in church history, Loetscher, advised him to remain a pastor. At that point Macartney accepted a call to First Presbyterian Church, Pittsburgh. The seminary board of directors then elected Machen to the chair in apologetics, but that required the approval of the General Assembly. Even if Machen then obtained the position, it would leave the chair of New Testament open and, if a liberal succeeded Machen there, the conservatives would lose a position on the faculty. When the General Assembly convened in 1926, the committee on seminaries proposed creation of a special committee to promote harmony at Princeton Seminary, a proposal Stevenson and Erdman supported. The assembly then postponed action on the appointment of Machen pending the report of the special committee to be presented the following year. In 1927 that committee reported its investigation showed all professors at the seminary were loyal Presbyterians, and it recommended a reorganization of the government of the seminary as a means to relieve strife within the institution and that all faculty appointments be deferred until such reorganization was completed. Stevenson contended there were no serious doctrinal issues at the seminary, and the General Assembly agreed by approving the recommendations of the committee. This decision actually increased the tensions at the seminary, and the General Assembly of 1928 responded by delaying the reorganization and called for another effort to reconcile the factions of the faculty. The Assembly of 1929 rejected an appeal from Machen and enacted the reorganization to the advantage of the liberals.

In addition to his leadership in defending the integrity of his seminary, Machen wrote extensively. His *Origin of Paul's Religion* (1921) and *The Virgin Birth* (1930) are classics in upholding biblical teaching against skeptics, but his most famous and influential work is *Christianity and Liberalism* (1923), in which he argued with compelling logic that liberalism is not a school of Christian thinking but a different religion, one which affirms alien beliefs about God, man, the Bible, salvation, and the church. Even some of his opponents admitted that Machen had made a powerful case for that position.

A founding father of Westminster Theological Seminary in 1929, Machen continued the struggle for doctrinal integrity in the Presbyterian Church (U.S.A.) even after the denomination had rebuffed his efforts at Princeton Seminary. In 1933 he organized the Independent Board for Presbyterian Foreign Missions to provide the local churches with an alternative to the denominational board then under the control of liberals. The General Assembly of 1934 promptly denounced that endeavor and ordered its officers to resign from the Independent Board. When Machen and others refused, the Presbyterian Church (U.S.A.) suspended them from the ministry, an action that led to the formation of the Presbyterian Church of America, now known as the Orthodox Presbyterian Church. Machen died from pneumonia contracted while in North Dakota, where he was promoting the work of the new denomination.

The founding of Westminster Theological Seminary at Philadelphia in 1929 was a landmark in the resurgence of Reformed orthodoxy prompted by the challenges of modernism. As early as 1927 some Princeton professors had discussed the possibility of forming a new seminary, should that become necessary to preserve the historic faith. Oswald Thompson Allis (1880–1973), professor of Old Testament, was especially enthusiastic for the idea, and Machen soon agreed, perhaps because he believed the major battleground between Christianity and secular culture necessarily involved higher education. Macartney also favored this move, and Westminster Seminary opened for classes in September 1929. In addition to Machen and Allis, Robert Dick Wilson (1856–1930) and Cornelius Van Til (1895–1987) left Princeton to assume duties at the new institution. Soon Allan MacRae (1902–1997), Paul Woolley (1902–1984), and R. B. Kuiper (1886–1966) joined them. Machen and Allis made large financial contributions to the seminary, and fifty students enrolled for classes.

By the opening of Westminster Seminary, most other theological schools had begun stressing the study of sociology, psychology, religious education, and philosophy of religion as they passed under the control of liberals. Princeton had long resisted that trend, and Westminster proposed to perpetuate the Princeton tradition with a level of scholarship second to none. Its graduates were to be prepared to defend the faith against all alien ideologies.

Controversy about Foreign Missions

Concurrent with the struggle to preserve Princeton Seminary, Machen and other Reformed believers faced the problem of defections from the faith among Presbyterian foreign missionaries, as the career of Pearl Buck, already cited, illustrates. In this intrachurch conflict, Machen's chief adversary was another professed conservative, Robert E. Speer (1897–1947), a layman and secretary of the Presbyterian Board of Foreign Missions from 1891–1937. Speer had become excited about missions through the influence of Dwight L. Moody and John R. Mott, and in 1926 he published *The Unfinished Task of Foreign Missions,* and he produced entries for *The Fundamentals,* but he did not take a firm position on disputes at Princeton Seminary until he supported the reorganization of 1929, by which time he had become a trustee of that institution.

Always ecumenical in outlook, Speer became a leader in the Federal Council of Churches and the International Missionary Council. He was moderator of the General Assembly in 1927. When conservatives complained because he approved liberals for appointment to missionary posts, Speer blunted their criticism somewhat by the publication of his book *The Finality of Christ* (1933), in which he affirmed the claims of Jesus to be the exclusive Savior of sinners. That affirmation notwithstanding, Speer regarded disputes about doctrine as distractions from the real task of the church, which is to spread the gospel worldwide. The Board of Foreign Missions he served had fifteen members, four of whom had signed the Auburn Affirmation. Robert Speer was never a liberal by conviction, but he befriended liberals such as Coffin and gradually broadened his own beliefs without becoming a modernist. Like many other Presbyterian leaders of that day, he had great fondness for Bushnell's writings, and like Bushnell, he had a low opinion of systematic theology and confessions of faith. The historic debate between Calvinism and Arminianism, for example, did not concern him.

During Speer's tenure at the Board of Foreign Missions, the Protestant community in general became agitated by proposals to alter the entire missionary enterprise in a radical manner. This began in 1930, when John D. Rockefeller Jr. funded a project to study Protestant missions and to make suggestions for improvement. Seven denominations, including the Presbyterian Church (U.S.A.), participated under the leadership of Harvard University philosopher William Ernest Hocking in producing a *Laymen's Inquiry* about Christian work in Asia. This report, based on a fact-finding tour of the mission fields, showed how modernist principles had shaped the committee's recommendations. The report portrayed Christianity as part of an emerging world religion, and it maintained that missionaries should promote understanding and fraternity among religions rather than proclaiming divisive doctrines. Hocking was a liberal Congregationalist, but some of his collaborators were Presbyterians who shared his view that social services should be the primary work of missions.

The Foreign Missions Board of the Presbyterian Church (U.S.A.) responded to *Re-Thinking Missions* with some disdain, and it reaffirmed Speer's belief in the exclusive saviorhood of Christ, but that did not resolve the matter. Pearl Buck hailed the report and urged all mission agencies to adopt its recommendations. She next scorned the doctrines of original sin and the claim Jesus alone is the Savior. The controversy thus engendered led her to resign from the Board of Foreign Missions.

Speer responded to *Re-Thinking Missions* with an article in the *Missionary Review of the World* (January 1933), in which he politely but firmly rejected some features of the report as theologically unacceptable and insisted Christ is the only Savior. Machen was not satisfied with Speer's critique of the report and labeled the document as abominable syncretism. Machen was especially disturbed because Speer had claimed all Presbyterian missionaries were orthodox believers, and he decried the use of money Bible-believers had contributed being awarded to liberals. Macartney also assailed *Re-Thinking Missions*, but Erdman, then president of the Board of Foreign Missions, tried to reassure all concerned that the board would uphold the historic Reformed faith.

In April 1933 the Presbytery of New Brunswick considered Machen's overture relative to the controversy and invited Speer to address that body. When he did so Speer appealed for unity in the church and contended there was no major problem with any missionaries of the church. The Presbytery of New Brunswick did not sustain Machen's overture, but the Presbytery of Philadelphia did, so the matter went to the General Assembly in 1933. By then Pearl Buck had resigned, but that did not mollify the conservatives. The General Assembly approved a majority report from the Committee of Foreign Missions and thereby affirmed confidence in Speer and the board by a huge margin of votes. Machen and other conservatives then announced their intention to create an Independent Board for Presbyterian Foreign Missions, an action Macartney did not support. The Independent Board became a reality only two months after the General Assembly, with Machen as its president.

SUGGESTED ADDITIONAL READINGS >>

Block, Irvin. *The Lives of Pearl Buck: A Tale of China and America.* New York: Thomas Y. Crowell, 1973.

Brown, Arthur J. *One Hundred Years: A History of Foreign Missionary Work of the Presbyterian Church in the USA.* New York: Fleming H. Revell, 1936.

Buck, Pearl S. *My Several Worlds: A Personal Record.* New York: Stein & Day, 1954.

Calhoun, David B. *Princeton Seminary.* Vol. 2. Edinburgh: Banner of Truth, 1996.

Coalter, M. J. with M. J. Mulder and L. B. Weeks, eds. *The Presbyterian Presence.* 7 vols. Louisville, Ky.: Geneva, 1990–1994.

Coffin, Henry Sloan. *The Meaning of the Cross.* New York: Charles Scribner's Sons, 1931.

Cole, Stewart G. *History of Fundamentalism*. New York: Richard R. Smith, 1931.

Dollar, George W. *A History of Fundamentalism in America*. Greenville, S.C.: Bob Jones University Press, 1973.

Dorn, Jacob H. *Washington Gladden: Prophet of the Social Gospel*. Columbus: Ohio State University Press, 1968.

Erdman, Charles R. *Our Missionaries in China*. Philadelphia: Russell & Martien, 1923.

Fosdick, Harry Emerson. *Christianity and Progress*. New York: Fleming H. Revell, 1922.

———. *A Guide to Understanding the Bible*. New York: Harper & Brothers, 1938.

———. *The Modern Use of the Bible*. New York: Macmillan, 1938.

Furniss, Norman T. *The Fundamentalist Controversy, 1918–1931*. New Haven, Conn.: Yale University Press, 1954.

Fry, C. George and John Paul Fry. *Pioneering a Theology of Evolution: Washington Gladden and Pierre Teilhard de Chardin*. Lanham, Md.: University of America Press, 1988.

Hart, D. G. *Defending the Faith: J. Gresham Machen and the Crisis of Conservative Protestantism in Modern America*. Baltimore, Md.: Johns Hopkins University Press, 1994.

Hart, D. G. and John R. Muether. *Seeking a Better Country: 300 Years of American Presbyterianism*. Phillipsburg, N.J.: P&R, 2006.

Hocking, William Ernest, ed. *Re-Thinking Missions*. New York: Harper & Brothers, 1932.

Loetscher, Lefferts A. *The Broadening Church*. Philadelphia: University of Pennsylvania Press, 1957.

Macartney, Clarence E. *The Making of a Minister*. New York: Channel, 1961.

———. *Twelve Great Questions about Christ*. Grand Rapids: Baker, 1956.

Machen, J. Gresham. *Christianity and Liberalism*. Grand Rapids: Eerdmans, 1946. Reprint of 1923 edition.

———. *The Christian View of Man*. Reprint, Edinburgh: Banner of Truth, 1984.

———. *The Virgin Birth of Christ*. London: James Clarke, 1930.

Marsden, George M. *Understanding Fundamentalism and Evangelicalism*. Grand Rapids: Eerdmans, 1991.

McIntire, Carl. *Modern Tower of Babel*. Collingswood, N.J.: Christian Beacon Press, 1949.

———. *Twentieth Century Reformation*. 2nd ed. Collingswood, N.J.: Christian Beacon Press, 1945.

Minus, Paul M. *Walter Rauschenbusch: American Reformer*. New York: Macmillan, 1988.

Nichols, Stephen J. *J. Gresham Machen: A Guided Tour of His Life and Thought.* Phillipsburg, N.J.: P& R, 2004.

Patterson, James A. *Robert E. Speer and the Development of North American Mission Theology.* Cambridge, Mass.: North American Missiology Project, 1998.

Piper, John F. *Robert E. Speer: Prophet of the American Church.* Louisville, Ky.: Geneva, 2000.

Rauschenbusch, Walter. *Christianity and the Social Crisis.* New York: Association Press, 1907.

———. *A Gospel for the Social Awakening.* New York: Association Press, 1906.

Reese, Edward. *The Life and Ministry of Carl McIntire.* Glenwood, Ill.: Fundamental Publishers, 1976.

Roy, Ralph Lord. *Apostles of Discord.* Boston: Beacon, 1953.

Speer, Robert E. *The Church and Missions.* London: James Clarke, 1926.

———. *The Finality of Christ.* Westwood, N.J.: Fleming H. Revell, 1924.

———. *The Principles of Jesus Applied to Some Questions Today.* New York: Fleming H. Revell, 1902.

Stonehouse, Ned B. *J. Gresham Machen: A Biographical Memoir.* Grand Rapids: Eerdmans, 1964.

Sundquist, Scott and Caroline Becker Long. *A History of Presbyterian Missions, 1944–2002.* Louisville, Ky.: Geneva, 2008.

Warfield, Benjamin B. *Counterfeit Miracles.* Unicoi, Tenn.: Trinity Foundation, 2008. Reprint of 1976 edition.

———. *The Inspiration and Authority of the Bible.* Philadelphia: Presbyterian and Reformed, 1948.

———. *The Plan of Salvation.* Rev. ed. Grand Rapids: Eerdmans, 1955.

Wheeler, W. Reginald. *A Man Sent from God: A Biography of Robert E. Speer.* Westwood, N.J.: Fleming H. Revell, 1956.

SEVENTEEN

Scholarship in Defense
of the Faith

The modernist theology that arose in Germany during the nineteenth century did not go unanswered, as orthodox scholars in Europe and America rose to meet the challenge. Ernst Hengstenberg (1802–1869), a professor at the University of Berlin, was foremost among conservatives in upholding the integrity of the Old Testament against the claims of higher critics and in the process produced *The Christology of the Old Testament,* a work even his opponents acknowledged was erudite and impressive. Hengstenberg likewise edited the *Evangelical Church Review*, in which he and other orthodox scholars tried to stem the tide of infidelity in European theological faculties. While this was occurring in Europe, Princeton Theological Seminary led a comparable effort in the United States.

The Challenge of Neo-orthodoxy

Albert Schweitzer

Despite strenuous and learned endeavors to preserve orthodoxy, however, modernism continued its march relentlessly and gained control of most universities and schools of theology, both in the Old World and the New. By the opening of the twentieth century, a potent challenge to the faith appeared in the work of Albert Schweitzer (1875–1965), a physician and a PhD from the University of Strasbourg who went to Equatorial Africa as a medical missionary. In 1906 Schweitzer published *The Quest for the Historical Jesus,* a work in which he rejected the deity of Christ and argued that Jesus misunderstood Himself and misled millions, even though He was an outstanding example of selfless service to others. Schweitzer maintained the New Testament is unreliable, so scholars must seek to find the real Jesus, whose spirit blesses all who follow His example. Schweitzer admitted it might not be possible to find the actual Jesus. His arguments aroused vigorous responses, even from scholars not orthodox but less radical than he.

Karl Barth

Among European theologians who had abandoned orthodoxy, the radicalism of authors such as Schweitzer caused some to rethink their own position, perhaps because they foresaw the destruction of Christianity as a credible worldview, should such ideas prevail. One who reacted in that manner was Karl Barth (1886–1968), who became the most influential theologian in Europe during the era between the World Wars. Born in Basel, he studied at universities in Bern, Berlin, Tuebingen, and Marburg but did not earn a doctoral degree. For twelve years Barth was a pastor in Switzerland, but he found preaching difficult because his liberal education had given him no vital message to proclaim. He became alienated from his former professors when most of them supported Germany at the outbreak of World War I. Disgusted with his mentors and dissatisfied with his own ministry, Barth disavowed the modernists' ethics and their view of Scripture and history. He began assailing the god of modern liberalism and resolved to make a fresh investigation of the Bible without prejudice.

In fall 1916 Barth preached to a congregation of which his friend Edward Thurneysen was pastor. That sermon contained the seeds of all he would eventually develop and proclaim as his own theology. In that address he emphasized the sovereignty and wholly unique character of God and maintained man's knowledge of God comes exclusively from divine revelation, that is, from what he called the *Word of God*. Moreover, he insisted God intends to redeem all creation through Christ. These ideas appeared in a more thorough, systematic expression in a commentary on Romans, which Barth produced in 1919.

As his exposition of Romans attests, Barth had rejected the humanistic ideas of his former professors, and in 1921 he became a professor himself by joining the faculty at the University of Goettingen, a Lutheran school of theology, which employed him in the interest of adding a Calvinist to its teaching staff. While in that position Barth produced five more editions of his commentary, each one reflecting changes in his thinking, but some themes remained constant through his writings.

One concept that did not change was Barth's view of Scripture. He argued that readers of the Bible must divorce themselves from all philosophies in order to understand the message of Scripture. God has revealed Himself only through Jesus Christ, so true theology must be christocentric, a *theology of the Word*. In this way Barth proposed to refute liberal ideas about the self-sufficiency of autonomous human nature. He at the same time dismissed all arguments from natural theology to prove the existence of God. Barth attacked liberal theologians vigorously, yet underlying his teaching was a concession to liberalism nevertheless. He accepted the contentions of higher criticism about the composition and consequent fallibility of the Bible but argued people should attend to its message anyway, because it is the primary *witness* to Christ, the living Word. In his view the Bible contains the Word of God, for God has spoken through it and will continue to do so, despite errors in the text. Such errors do not impair the witness of Scripture. Barth made it clear he regarded some portions of the Bible as myths. The biblical account of creation, for example, is not historical but is revelatory nevertheless, since revelation comes through superhistorical events. Through the power of the Holy Spirit, the Bible *becomes* the Word of God to believers as the Holy Spirit transcends its errors. Revelation came through events, and the Bible is the record of those events. The revelation and the record are not, however, identical.

Another constant theme in Barth's writings is his treatment of the doctrine of election. He accused Augustine and Calvin of regarding God abstractly apart from Christ. To understand God's sovereignty to include the acceptance or rejection of humans in the matter of salvation, Barth contended, is speculation. People may know God only in Christ, who is both the electing God and the elected man, and election is universal, since God's final word to mankind is *yes!* The church must therefore proclaim God has elected everyone, and only Christ is reprobate. Perhaps some people will reject their election in Christ and be lost. If so, that is due to their decisions, not because of a divine decree.

When Hitler came to power in Germany, Barth had to leave for Switzerland. He had helped to form the Confessing Church as a protest against Nazi efforts to reduce the churches to instruments of party propaganda, and from his refuge in Switzerland he wrote *The German Church Struggle,* an account of the ways in which German Christians responded to Hitler's demands.

Emil Brunner

Another Swiss theologian who reacted strongly to the prevailing modernism of his day was Emil Brunner (1889–1965), a doctor of theology from the University of Zurich, who had studied at the University of Berlin and New York's Union Theological Seminary as well. He joined the faculty of theology at Zurich in 1924.

Like Barth, Brunner rejected some tenets of modernism and published his attacks upon them. His writings aroused such interest that English translations spread his ideas quickly to the United Kingdom and the United States. During 1938 to 1939 he lectured as visiting professor at Princeton Theological Seminary and in 1953 to 1954 at the Christian University of Japan. He lectured about psychology and ethics as well as on theological topics.

Although Barth and Brunner shared a strong disdain for conventional liberalism, there was a running debate between them in the 1930s, as they differed about the role of reason in apologetics. Brunner, like Barth, professed to be a theologian of the *Word,* that is, a revelation that transcends human knowledge and reason. He too did not regard the Bible as per se divine revelation. Instead he maintained revelation is dynamic and comes through personal encounter with God, so the content of revelation is not facts or doctrine but apprehension of God Himself. Brunner thought he found errors in the Bible. He, for example, thought there is an irreconcilable conflict in Scripture between the concept of a final judgment and a universal salvation, and he thought the Bible is not a reliable guide to future events. His books *The Mediator* (1927) and *The Divine Imperative* (1932) enjoyed broad popularity, but Barth complained they postulated revelation apart from Christ. It is evident the two scholars disagreed about the matter of natural revelation, which Barth rejected entirely.

Barth and Brunner agreed that God speaks through Scripture, which contains the Word of God without being, in all its parts, the actual Word. Brunner likened Scripture to an old phonograph record now scratched and warped, a record that reproduces a voice but one cluttered with incidental noises because of the condition of the disc. Such noises are the words of men, the human authors of the text, so it is necessary to discern the Word of God through interpretation. Brunner admitted the authors of Scripture claimed divine inspiration for the very words they wrote, but he rejected that claim anyway. In the matter of soteriology, Brunner scorned historic Reformed teaching as blasphemy and asserted that faith is a human quality and precedes regeneration. His view of this matter appears in a book of sermons published in English under the title *The Great Invitation* (1955), which provides a succinct way to view his beliefs in general.

Dietrich Bonhoeffer

Another scholar of repute who became disillusioned with modernism was the German Dietrich Bonhoeffer (1906–1945), who gained fame as an opponent of the Nazis and paid for that with his life. Although his church connection was Lutheran, Bonhoeffer exerted much influence in Reformed circles in Europe and America. Like Barth and Brunner, he rejected the liberalism of his day but maintained the critical approach to Scripture.

A son of a well-known psychiatrist and part of a highly cultured family, Bonhoeffer chose a career in the ministry against the wishes of his parents and prepared academically at the universities in Tuebingen and Berlin, and he spent one year at Union Theological Seminary, New York. In 1930 he began teaching at the University of Berlin and soon became a leader in ecumenical activities. He was among the first German clerics to oppose Hitler.

Perhaps the turmoil and tragedies of his life explain why Bonhoeffer did not compose a systematic statement of his beliefs, instead responding to crises as they arose. Some of his books he wrote while in prison after the Nazis learned of his connection with a plot to overthrow Hitler. Lucidity was not one of Bonhoeffer's assets, and various interpreters have easily found what they desire in his writings. One view regards him as a forerunner of the Death of God theology that enjoyed some popularity in academic circles during the 1960s.

Barth's influence on Bonhoeffer's thinking is evident, both in theological and political matters. Like Barth, he believed all revelation comes through personal encounter with Christ and is not in propositional form, even though that is how the Bible presents it. Bonhoeffer held Christianity must remain relevant to modern culture by adjusting its teachings and demands to an ever-changing world, one he labeled "A World Come of Age." He said modern people could explain the world without divine revelation, and Christians must accept this reality, since it is no longer possible for learned people to remain religious in the traditional sense of that term. He wrote of a *religionless Christianity* that discarded all traditional conceptions about God, and he called for vigorous and selfless social service in Jesus' name, for Christ was *the man for others.*

Although Bonhoeffer thought the time had come to abandon historic beliefs about God, he maintained that humanity still needs Christ as an example to follow. Such proposals led eventually to the rise of a school of *secular* theology that derived some of its inspiration from Bonhoeffer's ideas. He did not, however, in his zeal to excite concern for earthly needs, deny eternity. He, on the contrary, said he expected to go to heaven, there to meet Jesus, who would welcome all who served Him on earth.

Among Bonhoeffer's writings, the one that is least difficult to read is *The Cost of Discipleship* (1937), a powerful indictment of German churches and professing Christians everywhere who presume to possess a faith that is actually not theirs. The theme of this work is the author's denunciation of "cheap grace," by which he meant what, in an American context, could be called "easy believism." Bonhoeffer witnessed churches capitulating to Nazi demands and, in some cases, allowing themselves to become propaganda instruments for a godless state. He therefore denounced presentations of the gospel that lacked a demand for repentance, without which, he affirmed, there is no salvation. Several of his other books are now available in English, but the complexities of his own thinking and his inability to express his ideas clearly have made Bonhoeffer a highly controversial figure. It is evident, nevertheless, that his influence has not buttressed orthodoxy but rather encouraged theological novelties.

It has been customary for several decades to refer to the above theologians as exponents of a school of thought called *neo-orthodoxy*, and those who endorse such teachings have welcomed the work of Barth, Brunner, Bonhoeffer, and others as wholesome reactions against the excesses of the radical liberalism that inflicted immense damage upon Christianity in the nineteenth and early twentieth centuries. A careful and critical reading of these scholars, however, will show their ideas were neither new nor orthodox but, in the end, helped to further the skeptical approach to Scripture that they assumed is unimpeachable.

Rudolf Bultmann

While the works of neo-orthodox theologians were quite influential, they did not signal the end of radical interpretations of Christianity, as the career of Rudolf Bultmann (1884–1976) attests. Like Bonhoeffer, he was a Lutheran whose ideas permeated Reformed circles. A son of a pastor and grandson of a missionary, Bultmann from childhood expressed serious religious interests. He studied philosophy and theology at Tübingen, Marburg, and Berlin and in 1912 became a lecturer in New Testament at the University of Marburg, where he later became a professor and spent the rest of his career. For a while Bultmann shared most of Barth's beliefs, but the influence of philosopher Martin Heidegger (1889–1976), another professor at Marburg, led him to embrace existentialism as a worldview, which he then applied to the study of the New Testament. This led him away from neo-orthodoxy and into the radical-critical school of theology to which he gave new impetus.

Bultmann wrote *The History of the Synoptic Tradition* (1921), an early expression of the direction he was pursuing, but his most influential book did not appear until 1958, when he published *Jesus Christ and Mythology*. He advocated *form criticism*, which assumes the New Testament contains little factual information about Jesus but abounds with expressions of faith from His disciples who composed it and thereby produced mythical accounts. References to miracles are therefore reflections of the primitive worldview of the authors, and whatever historical material does appear in the New Testament is heavily encrusted with myth. The apostle Paul, for example, called Jesus the Son of God because Hellenistic religions abounded with tales of heroes called "sons of god." According to Bultmann, Gnostic myths inspired Paul and the author of the Gospel of John especially, and it is not possible to know much about the real Jesus.

Bultmann's skepticism toward the New Testament was not, of course, unique, but he contended his purpose was to uncover real Christianity and to make it attractive to modern people. Although his own church condemned Bultmann's approach to Scripture, his influence spread broadly, and in reply to his critics, he claimed elimination of its *mythical* forms would benefit Christianity greatly. He believed Jesus died on a cross, and he said humans should embrace the crucified Christ, but they would not do so if the church insisted He had risen from the dead. In Bultmann's view the world is a closed system, so miracles are impossible. Jesus, nevertheless, becomes real to believers through a personal encounter prompted by faith, even though Jesus is dead. The resurrection as a fact does not matter; faith in the resurrection does. Like Bonhoeffer, Bultmann's irrational fideism encouraged the thinking that produced the Death of God theology.

Defenders of the Reformed Faith

Abraham Kuyper and Herman Bavinck

As the challenges of modernism confronted the faith, a few European scholars vigorously defended the integrity of Scripture, and among the early apologists, Abraham Kuyper (1837–1920) and Herman Bavinck (1854–1921) were especially prominent. Both were professors at the Free University of Amsterdam, which Kuyper founded to provide Christian higher education at a time when older universities were espousing secular humanism. The erudition of these scholars and others like them gave the Free University and Protestant orthodoxy an academic credibility badly needed in the intellectual climate of the late nineteenth century. Numerous European and American students chose to study in Amsterdam as an alternative to the secular universities in their homelands.

Geerhardus Vos

In at least one case, a Dutchman went to America for his theological education. This was Geerhardus Vos (1862–1949), who studied at Calvin and Princeton Seminaries before returning to Europe for study at the universities in Berlin and Strasbourg. From the latter he received the PhD. In 1893 Vos became a professor of biblical theology at Princeton Seminary, a position he held until his retirement in 1932. He viewed divine revelation as focused on God's redemptive acts in history, which became the central theme of his teaching and of his book *Biblical Theology* (1948). Vos had produced *The Teaching of Jesus Concerning the Kingdom of God and the Church* in 1903 and *Pauline Eschatology* in 1930. Although distressed by the reorganization of the seminary in 1929, Vos remained on the faculty, a voice affirming the inerrancy of Scripture and upholding the historic principles of the Reformed faith with a level of scholarship second to none.

Louis Berkhof

Louis Berkhof (1872–1957) was another immigrant from the Netherlands who valiantly defended orthodoxy with impressive erudition. Berkhof arrived in the United States in 1882 and graduated from Calvin Theological Seminary, Grand Rapids, in 1900. After additional study at Princeton Seminary, he returned to Calvin Seminary as a professor and was its president from 1931 to 1944. Berkhof greatly appreciated the work of Kuyper in his homeland, and, like Kuyper, he applied the cultural mandate and wrote about social, economic, and cultural issues while urging Christians to develop their own political and social organizations.

When alien teachings due to the inroads of dispensationalism on one hand and higher criticism on the other threatened the doctrinal integrity of the Christian Reformed Church, Berkhof defended historic Reformed theology vigorously. He produced *Reformed Dogmatics* in 1932, a book that became *Systematic Theology* in subsequent editions. It is a masterpiece of lucid writing that covers the whole field of doctrine with all due regard for the historical development of dogmatics through controversies, ancient and modern. His *Manual of Reformed Doctrine* is a condensed version in popular form, one that makes the heart of his work accessible in a nontechnical manner. In these and other books, Berkhof demonstrated deep personal piety matched by thorough scholarship expressed in very readable prose. During his presidency Calvin Theological Seminary was a bastion of the Reformed faith.

Cornelius Van Til

Although he too was born in the Netherlands, Cornelius Van Til (1895–1987) lived eighty-two years in America. Originally a member of the Christian Reformed Church, Van Til studied at Calvin College and Calvin Seminary before going to Princeton Seminary and Princeton University. His Princeton PhD in hand, he spent a brief time as a pastor in the Christian Reformed Church and then joined the faculty of Princeton Seminary to teach apologetics, only to leave that institution to become a founding father of Westminster Theological Seminary along with Machen and others. In 1936 Van Til transferred to the ministry of what is now the Orthodox Presbyterian Church. He taught apologetics at Westminster until he reached eighty years of age.

Van Til's devotion to the orthodox Reformed faith was fervent, so he upheld the tenets of that position as vigorously as any of his predecessors in that discipline. His method was, however, unconventional and therefore aroused some controversy, which continues, even since his demise. He composed a system of defending the claims of Christianity that integrated the traditional rationalist-evidentialist approach of old Princeton with the presuppositional arguments of Kuyper and Bavinck. Van Til insisted God is self-attesting, and all humans reason in a circle, for all begin with assumptions for or against God. Human autonomy is a myth. All human knowledge is analogical to God's knowledge, and apprehension of truth requires self-conscious dependence on God and His revelation. To question the authenticity and authority of the Bible is to claim autonomous superiority to God, which is sin. Like Kuyper before him, Van Til perceived a radical antithesis between Christian and non-Christian thinking because believers and unbelievers begin with opposing assumptions about what is true. Van Til called neo-orthodoxy "New Modernism" because it assumes human autonomy and competence to interpret all of life.

In Van Til's judgment, unbelief is a moral problem related to the unregenerate condition of faithless minds. When such thinkers claim autonomy, they are engaging in rebellion against God. They are wrong in believing facts are neutral and can interpret themselves. God alone is the final interpreter of all facts, and all facts are components of His plan. That means all facts of creation witness for the Creator, so humans are not neutral observers. They are for God or against Him, and their posture in this regard shows whether they are regenerate or unregenerate. Only God has comprehensive, infallible knowledge of all facts, so He alone can interpret them properly. Humans cannot understand even themselves apart from divine revelation.

Van Til set forth his system of apologetics in *Defense of the Faith*, which appeared in 1955 and underwent several revisions. Although that is his best-known book, Van Til's other contributions too are important, especially his analyses and critiques of neo-orthodoxy. *The New Modernism* (1946), *Has Karl Barth Become Orthodox?* (1954), and *Christianity and Barthianism* (1962) are powerful rebuttals of neo-orthodoxy, which he regarded as but another version of liberalism and rejection of God's Word. Van Til was especially distressed by the way neo-orthodox writers used traditional evangelical language to convey ideas incompatible with Scripture and the Reformed confessions.

Gordon Haddon Clark

Gordon Haddon Clark (1902–1986) was another vigorous defender of orthodoxy in the twentieth century, but one whose position brought him into conflict with Van Til's school of thinkers. Born and educated in Philadelphia, where he earned the PhD in philosophy at the University of Pennsylvania, Clark taught at that institution for twelve years (1924–1936) and at the Theological Seminary of the Reformed Episcopal Church, also in his native city. He pursued further study in Paris and joined the faculty of Wheaton College, Illinois, in 1937.

At Wheaton College Clark's presence enhanced the academic reputation of the institution, and many students responded well as he rebutted the claims of modernism and challenged poorly informed fundamentalists in his classes. His vigorous Calvinism, however, offended some students and some fellow professors, whose broad evangelicalism he held in disdain. In 1943 Wheaton College dismissed Gordon Clark, but he soon obtained a position at Butler University, Indianapolis, where he remained twenty-eight years, a period during which he produced a large number of books. Prominent among his works are *Christian Philosophy of Education* (1946), *A Christian View of Men and Things* (1951), and *From Thales to Dewey* (1956). An almost encyclopedic scholar, Clark produced about thirty books and numerous articles on a broad spectrum of topics.

In 1943 Clark received ordination as a teaching elder in the Orthodox Presbyterian Church, but conflict with Van Til, also a minister in that denomination, disrupted his relationship with that body. Always a rigorous logician, Clark insisted that human knowledge is the same as God's knowledge, and he thought Van Til's position was irrational fideism. The details of their dispute are rather arcane and beyond the scope of a book about general Presbyterian history, but it is appropriate to relate that the controversy divided stalwart apologists for the Reformed faith at a time when there was a pressing need for unity. Clark eventually left the Orthodox Presbyterian Church and moved to the Reformed Presbyterian Church, Evangelical Synod, which operates Covenant College, where Clark ended his academic career.

John Murray
In the discipline of systematic theology, one of the strongest and most erudite exponents of orthodoxy was John Murray (1898–1975), who came from the Free Presbyterian Church of Scotland to study at Princeton Theological Seminary with Machen and later joined him on the faculty at Princeton and from there went to Westminster Theological Seminary, where he taught until 1966. He joined the Orthodox Presbyterian Church but remained a British subject and, upon his retirement from Westminster, returned to Scotland and lectured across the United Kingdom. Murray was a keen theological thinker, one who carefully based his expositions of doctrine upon thorough exegesis of Scripture. He applied the insights of Geerhardus Vos acquired through his study at Princeton to his own work as a theologian. He believed Charles Hodge had produced a systematic theology textbook of such quality there was no need to write one of his own. Murray's own books are relatively short in length, a tribute to his skill in stating matters concisely, and all reflect his precise exegesis. *Redemption Accomplished and Applied* (1955), *Principles of Conduct* (1957), *Divorce* (1961), and *Christian Baptism* (1962) are among his contributions. His commentary, *The Epistle to the Romans* (1965), is an outstanding example of his scholarship. Most of his writings have been collected and reproduced in four volumes as *Collected Writings of John Murray* (1983).

Ned B. Stonehouse
Another thorough scholar whose work brought credit to the historic Reformed faith in the last century was Ned B. Stonehouse (1902–1962),

a graduate of Calvin College and Princeton Theological Seminary, who studied at the University of Tuebingen and earned the ThD at the Free University of Amsterdam. A member of the original faculty of Westminster Seminary, Stonehouse helped to organize the Orthodox Presbyterian Church in 1936 and took an active part in denominational life and in the relations of his church with other Reformed bodies. As a New Testament scholar, he made his mark with published studies about the Synoptic Gospels, such works as *The Witness of Matthew and Mark to Christ* (1944), *The Witness of Luke to Christ* (1951), and *The Origin of the Synoptic Gospels* (1963).

Stonehouse, a close friend and associate of Machen, rendered important service in producing *J. Gresham Machen: A Biographical Memoir* in 1954. This is the initial biography of Machen and an insider's account of the struggles Machen endured that led to the formation of the Orthodox Presbyterian Church.

Edward Joseph Young

In the field of Old Testament studies Edward Joseph Young (1907–1968) was one of the most brilliant and productive. Young graduated from Stanford University and began preparation for the ministry at San Francisco Theological Seminary, but liberal teaching there convinced him to move to Westminster Seminary, where he acquired great admiration for Machen and for his own professor of Old Testament, Oswald T. Allis. Young earned a PhD in Semitic studies at the Dropsie College for Hebrew and Cognate Learning in Philadelphia and studied at the University of Leipzig as well.

Always a self-effacing gentleman, Young enjoyed the respect even of scholars who rejected his fervent adherence to biblical orthodoxy. His mastery of about thirty languages assured Young a hearing in almost all circles of Old Testament specialists. His *Introduction to the Old Testament* (1949) long dominated the field as the best work of its kind, not least of all because it answers almost all traditional criticisms in a manner that reflects the author's keen appreciation for those with whom he disagreed. In *Thy Word Is Truth* (1957), Young issued a ringing affirmation of confidence in the Bible as the infallible Word of God, while *The Book of Isaiah* (1972), published after his sudden death, upholds the single authorship of that prophecy and exegetes the text in a masterful way.

Young was a deeply spiritual man and a fervent preacher of God's Word. Active in the Orthodox Presbyterian Church, he was much in demand as a lecturer and preacher in the United States and abroad. Amazing ability as a linguist enabled him to communicate the gospel in various tongues. Many books and articles remain as his legacy to the exposition and defense of the Reformed faith.

Francis A. Schaeffer

One of the most popular and influential spokesmen for orthodoxy in the twentieth century was Francis A. Schaeffer (1912–1984), once an agnostic, who turned to Christ while he was a student at Drexel Institute of Technology in Philadelphia. Soon after his conversion, Schaeffer transferred to Hampden-Sydney College in Virginia and graduated in 1935. He then attended Westminster Seminary but moved to Faith Theological Seminary, Elkins Park, Pennsylvania, where he received the bachelor of divinity in 1938. After ordination in the Bible Presbyterian Church, Schaeffer served pastorates in Pennsylvania and Missouri.

In 1948, together with his wife, Edith, Schaeffer became a missionary to Switzerland as an appointee of the Independent Board for Presbyterian Foreign Missions, and in 1955 the Schaeffers founded L'Abri, a study center that ministered to intellectuals from many nations. Circulation of his books and recorded lectures attracted international attention and drew many people to L'Abri to study with this persuasive advocate for Christianity as a worldview.

Among Schaeffer's books, *The God Who Is There* and *Escape from Reason,* both published in 1968, cite rejection of belief in absolute truth as the major cause for the decline of Western civilization, and the author held G. W. F. Hegel (1770–1831), German dialectical philosopher, primarily responsible for initiating the decline. Schaeffer showed how decadence in theology occurred when theologians allowed secular philosophers to set the academic and intellectual agenda. This has led, he contended, to a decay of morality, as the practices of abortion and euthanasia attest.

As his overall interpretation of Western civilization, Schaeffer presented *How Should We Then Live?* (1976), a book later made into a series of films. In this work he called for a return to Christian principles as proclaimed during the Protestant Reformation, and he warned that social and political collapse leading to the rise of dictatorship would occur if the West failed to change. A return to biblical moral absolutes was the only way to avert such a disaster.

Carl McIntire

One of the most prominent and controversial defenders of Christianity in the last century was Carl McIntire (1906–2002), a 1931 graduate of

Westminster Theological Seminary expelled from the Presbyterian Church (U.S.A.) when he refused to obey the mandate to resign from the Independent Board of Foreign Missions. With Machen, he founded the Orthodox Presbyterian Church, but less than a year later, while he was a pastor in Collingswood, New Jersey, McIntire left that infant denomination to form the Bible Presbyterian Church, a fundamentalist body with only a diluted allegiance to the historic Reformed faith.

In order to provide an alternative to Westminster Seminary, McIntire, together with scholars Allan MacRae (1902–1997) and J. Oliver Buswell (1895–1977), established Faith Theological Seminary. In 1941 he organized the American Council of Christian Churches as a fundamentalist reply to the liberal National Council of Churches, and in 1948 McIntire led in forming the International Council of Christian Churches. For many years his daily radio program, *Twentieth Century Reformation Hour*, and his newspaper, *The Christian Beacon*, were the major organs promoting his brand of militant fundamentalism.

McIntire's complaint against Westminster Theological Seminary and the Orthodox Presbyterian Church pertained mainly to eschatology and the concept of Christian liberty. Like most fundamentalists of the era, McIntire espoused a premillennial view of the return of Christ, a position not necessarily unacceptable at Westminster and in the Orthodox Presbyterian Church. To McIntire and his disciples, however, this was a crucial matter on which there was no room for accommodation of other views, and many who supported McIntire went beyond historic premillennialism and embraced dispensational eschatology. That posture put them at odds with Reformed theology, which has always taught continuity between Israel of the Old Testament and the New Testament Church, a teaching dispensationalists vigorously deny. An article by Westminster professor R. B. Kuiper (1886–1966) on the millennial question so aroused McIntire and his associate MacRae that they were ready to leave the Orthodox Presbyterian Church because of it.

The issue of Christian liberty that caused dissension was the use of alcoholic beverages, which Buswell contended, Scripture forbids. He and the McIntire faction insisted that total abstinence be the policy of the church, but the General Assembly rejected that proposal and settled the matter *sola Scriptura*, thereby upholding the traditional Reformed position, which denounces drunkenness but affirms believers' freedom to drink in moderation.

Another divisive issue that afflicted the new Presbyterian denomination was related to the policies of the Independent Board for Presbyterian Foreign Missions, of which Machen was president. Since they had asserted independence from the Presbyterian Church (U.S.A.), some members of the Independent Board were supporting the development of independent local assemblies unconnected to one another and apart from the authority of any presbytery. One example of the trend in Philadelphia was the withdrawal of Central North Broad Street Presbyterian Church from the liberal denomination and its subsequent declaration that it would never align with any denomination. Under the leadership of Pastor Merril T. MacPherson, this congregation became the Church of the Open Door, a ministry Reformed in doctrine but no longer Presbyterian in polity. Failure to maintain Presbyterian church government made the Independent Board, in practice, a non-Presbyterian mission agency. This controversy and debates about eschatology and Christian liberty led McIntire, Buswell, and MacRae to leave the Orthodox Presbyterian Church and to form the Bible Presbyterian Church, a body that described itself as "Calvinistic, fundamental, premillennial, and evangelistic." McIntire dominated this denomination, which made the Independent Board its missionary arm, even though that agency had no denominational connection. Rigorous separation, personal and ecclesiastical, was the posture of the Bible Presbyterian Church, but there was no faithful application of Presbyterian principles in its government.

In 1954 a group of Bible Presbyterian pastors and elders protested the drift away from historic Reformed polity in general and against McIntire's authoritarian manner in particular. Buswell was among those who parted company with McIntire in 1956 and helped to form the Bible Presbyterian Church, Columbus Synod, which encompassed about 60 percent of the denomination. The remaining 40 percent formed the Bible Presbyterian Church, Collingswood Synod, still under McIntire's leadership. The Columbus Synod then withdrew from both the American and International Council of Christian Churches. The Columbus Synod established Covenant College in 1956 and Covenant Theological Seminary the next year. Francis Schaeffer and now well-known biblical counselor Jay Adams were members of the Columbus Synod, and Adams persuaded that body to accept the amillennial view of eschatology alongside historic premillennialism. In 1961 that synod became the Evangelical Presbyterian Church of North America, General Synod, and thereby gave birth to the Reformed Presbyterian

Church, Evangelical Synod. In 1982 it joined with the Presbyterian Church in America, the history of which is the subject of the next chapter.

SUGGESTED ADDITIONAL READINGS >>

Allis, O. T. *The Five Books of Moses.* Philadelphia: Presbyterian and Reformed, 1943.

———. *The Old Testament: Its Claims and Its Critics.* Grand Rapids: Baker, 1972.

Bavinck, Herman. *Reformed Dogmatics.* 4 vols. Translated by John Vriend. Grand Rapids: Baker Academic, 2003–2008.

Bolick, Gregory G. *Karl Barth and Evangelicalism.* Downers Grove, Ill.: Inter-Varsity, 1980.

Calhoun, David B. *Princeton Seminary.* 2 vols. Edinburgh: Banner of Truth, 1996.

Clark, Gordon H. *God's Hammer: The Bible and Its Critics* 2nd ed. Jefferson, Md.: Trinity Foundation, 1987.

———. *In Defense of Theology.* Milford, Mich.: Mott Media, 1984.

———. *Karl Barth's Theological Method.* Philadelphia: Presbyterian and Reformed, 1963.

———. *Religion, Reason, and Revelation.* Philadelphia: Presbyterian and Reformed, 1961.

Coray, Henry W. J. *Gresham Machen: A Silhouette.* Willow Grove, Pa.: Orthodox Presbyterian Church, 1981.

Humphrey, J. Edward. *Emil Brunner.* Waco, Tex.: Word Books, 1976.

Jewett, Paul K. *Emil Brunner's Concept of Revelation.* London: James Clarke, 1954.

Klooster, Fred H. *The Significance of Barth's Theology.* Grand Rapids: Baker, 1961.

Kuiper, R. B. *To Be or Not to Be Reformed.* Grand Rapids: Zondervan, 1959.

Kuyper, Abraham. *Abraham Kuyper: A Centennial Reader.* Edited by James D. Bratt. Grand Rapids: Eerdmans, 1998.

———. *Lectures on Calvinism.* Grand Rapids: Eerdmans, 1931.

———. *The Work of the Holy Spirit.* Translated by Henry De Vries. Grand Rapids: Eerdmans, 1969. Reprint of 1900 edition.

Machen, J. Gresham. *Christianity and Liberalism.* Grand Rapids: Eerdmans, 1946.

———. *The Origin of Paul's Religion.* New York: Macmillan, 1921.

———. *The Virgin Birth of Christ.* London: James Clarke, 1930.

McGoldrick, James Edward. *God's Renaissance Man: The Life and Work of Abraham Kuyper.* Darlington, U.K.: Evangelical Press, 2000.

Nash, Ronald H. *Christian Faith and Historical Understanding.* Grand Rapids: Zondervan, 1984.

———. *The Word of God and the Mind of Man.* Grand Rapids: Zondervan, 1982.

———. *World Views in Conflict.* Grand Rapids: Zondervan, 1992.

Parkhurst, Lewis Gifford Jr. *Francis Schaeffer: The Man and His Message.* Wheaton, Ill.: Tyndale House, 1985.

Schaeffer, Francis. *Death in the City.* Chicago: InterVarsity, 1969.

———. *Escape from Reason.* London: InterVarsity, 1968.

———. *The God Who Is There.* Downers Grove, Ill.: InterVarsity, 1968.

Van Til, Cornelius. *Christianity in Modern Theology.* Philadelphia: Westminster Theological Seminary, 1955.

———. *The Christian Theory of Knowledge.* Nutley, N.J.: Presbyterian and Reformed, 1969.

———. *The Defense of the Faith.* Rev. ed. Philadelphia: Presbyterian and Reformed, 1963.

———. *The New Modernism.* 3rd ed. Nutley, N.J.: Presbyterian and Reformed, 1973.

Young, Edward J. *An Introduction to the Old Testament.* Grand Rapids: Eerdmans, 1949.

———. *Thy Word Is Truth.* Grand Rapids: Eerdmans, 1957.

EIGHTEEN

Formation of the Presbyterian Church in America

Seminary education at the approved theological schools of the Presbyterian Church (U.S.) had become increasingly liberal by the 1940s, so many pastors received no adequate instruction in the Reformed faith and were neither prepared for nor disposed to defend it against innovations. The same trend occurred concurrently in the Presbyterian Church (U.S.A.), where departures from confessional orthodoxy were even farther advanced. In both the Southern and Northern churches, zeal to maintain the Westminster Standards was obviously declining. The influence of Barthian theology deeply infected Presbyterian seminaries, where professors denied the inerrancy of Scripture and the historic doctrines of grace. In some cases the Social Gospel took precedence over evangelism, and liberal church leaders promoted ecumenical programs incompatible with the Reformed faith. They strove to draw the Presbyterian Church (U.S.) closer to its Northern counterpart and into the National and World Councils of Churches.

Continuing Dilution in the Southern Presbyterian Church

Revisions of the Westminster Confession of Faith occurred in 1939 to eliminate references to the pope as "Antichrist" and to the Church of Rome as a "synagogue of Satan." In 1942 the Southern church added new chapters to the confession in order to clarify its understanding of the Holy Spirit and the gospel, and thereafter a growing eagerness for further revisions became evident. In 1969 the General Assembly appointed a committee to compile a book of historic confessions and to present a modern statement of faith, a task not completed until 1976. When approved by the General Assembly that book included the Apostles' and Nicene Creeds, the Geneva Catechism, the Scots' Confession, the Heidelberg Catechism, the Westminster Standards, the Theological Declaration of Barmen (1934), together with a Contemporary Declaration of Faith. Efforts to secure ratification by three-fourths of the presbyteries failed, perhaps due to reactions against the controversial Confession of 1967, which the Northern church added to its own Book of Confessions. Despite rejection of the proposed new confession, it was obvious most Southern Presbyterian ministers did not adhere to the Westminster Standards, even in their revised form, and additional efforts at revision would be forthcoming.

Liberal ecumenical activities, begun in the late nineteenth century, continued in the twentieth century, especially after the two regional churches restored fraternal relations in 1882. The decision to do this was made necessary by the entry of the Southern church into the World Alliance of Reformed Churches in 1876. In 1912 the Presbyterian Church (U.S.) joined the Federal Council of Churches but withdrew in 1931 and remained outside until 1941, when it returned to membership. The Southern church became part of the National and World Councils of Churches and joined the Consultation on Church Union in 1966.

Parallel to and connected with ecumenical activities, Southern Presbyterians became ever more inclined toward deviations from their historic doctrinal position. In 1961 the General Assembly declared the chapter of the Westminster Confession that deals with predestination and election was inadequate, and its expressions on those doctrines are not essential components of the Reformed faith. In 1971 the General Assembly affirmed there is no actual conflict between biblical teaching and the theory of organic evolution, this despite the actions of four previous assemblies that rejected evolution.

The year 1964 brought the ordination of women in the Southern church. Two years later it denounced capital punishment and in 1970 condoned abortion. In these matters liberals followed the lead of their colleagues in the Presbyterian Church (U.S.A.), with which they desired to merge.

Leading the Southern church even farther away from its foundations was the Fellowship of St. James, a secret organization, the creation of four Virginia clergymen, of whom Ernest Trice Thompson (1894–1985), a renowned historian and professor at Union Theological Seminary, was most prominent. The fellowship admitted to membership only carefully selected liberals and kept its proceedings secret. It appears to have been a liberal "think tank" that encouraged its members to seek positions of influence within the denomination. Some members of the Fellowship of St. James were leaders in the Fellowship of Southern Churchmen, a public body of liberals from several denominations. Parallel to these movements was the

Fellowship of Concern, an open organization within the Southern Presbyterian Church committed to a liberal religious and social agenda, with civil rights its most conspicuous interest.

The liberals' enthusiasm for merger with the Northern Presbyterian Church led them to propose a Plan of Union in 1954, a measure that narrowly failed to obtain the required approval of two-thirds of the presbyteries, but the General Assembly approved increased cooperation with the Presbyterian Church (U.S.A.) and thereby accelerated the momentum toward merger anyway. By 1968 favor toward merger had increased to the point that the General Assembly authorized the formation of union congregations and presbyteries between the two major Presbyterian denominations. The liberals' domination of the church courts made resistance almost impossible, and prosecuting heresy was no longer an option for the conservatives. There were no remaining means to preserve orthodoxy in the Southern church, as subsequent events demonstrated conclusively.

Efforts to Preserve the Reformed Faith

Although valiant attempts to maintain the doctrinal integrity of the Presbyterian Church (U.S.) failed, that was not because the conservatives did not exhaust every means they could find. One such noteworthy endeavor was the founding of the *Southern Presbyterian Journal* as an organ of orthodoxy. L. Nelson Bell, M.D. (1894–1973), a missionary returned from service in China, led the way in this effort, and William Childs Robinson (1897–1982), beloved professor of church history at Columbia Theological Seminary, joined Bell and others in this project. Henry B. Dendy (1895–1981), pastor of Weaverville Presbyterian Church in North Carolina, and G. Aiken Taylor (1920–1984), destined to make his periodical famous, followed him. The supporters of the *Journal* had some reason to be encouraged, since their efforts may have defeated the 1954 Plan of Union.

In addition to the efforts of pastors and professors to defend the faith, laymen made a substantial contribution. Bell led in forming Concerned Presbyterians, a movement of ruling elders, and Kenneth Keyes, a wealthy realtor, contributed much to that organization. Keyes, an elder in Shenandoah Presbyterian Church, Miami, Florida, helped to initiate the mailing of a newsletter to eighty thousand church members in the interest of arousing them to support the attempt to preserve orthodoxy. Liberals denounced all such measures as divisive.

The Presbyterian Evangelistic Fellowship, founded in 1964 by William E. Hill Jr., was another strong conservative voice within the Southern Presbyterian Church. The fellowship held summer conferences that drew large numbers of people to rallies in defense of orthodoxy. Hill and other leaders of the movement rebutted complaints from liberals by affirming doctrinal purity necessary for genuine evangelism. By that time many liberals had come to regard evangelism as a way to *inform* people that, because Christ died for everyone, all would be saved.

Late in 1969 leaders of the several conservative bodies issued a Declaration of Commitment to preserve the Reformed faith and announced, should their efforts fail, they were prepared to leave the denomination. As they looked to the future, they formed the Continuing Church movement, which drew initial support from about 260 sessions representing about seventy thousand church members. Two years later the committed conservatives agreed to a plan for separation from the Southern church, and Paul Settle, pastor of Northside Presbyterian Church, Burlington, North Carolina, became the first full-time executive of Presbyterian Churchmen United. That body led the way in calling for establishment of a Continuing Church to maintain historic Presbyterian beliefs that liberal control of the existing church had put in jeopardy. A number of planning meetings preceded the convocation of the first General Assembly of the National Presbyterian Church at Briarwood Presbyterian Church in Birmingham, Alabama, in December 1973. The new denomination was to be a *continuing* Presbyterian church because it maintained the historic doctrinal position of the Reformed faith as expressed in the Westminster Standards.

Soon the National Presbyterian Church became the Presbyterian Church in America, a change in name to avoid contention with the National Presbyterian congregation in Washington, which did not secede from the Southern church. The new denomination had repudiated modernism-liberalism and had affirmed Reformed orthodoxy *in principle*, but as subsequent developments would show, not all congregations of the continuing body were Reformed in practice. Some were broadly evangelical in character and did not subscribe strictly to the Westminster Standards. Because of this blending of staunch Calvinists with evangelicals reacting against false beliefs, the Presbyterian Church in America, from its inception, suffered from a lack of theological concurrence and from some lack of interest in genuine Presbyterian polity. Some congregations, for example, have given more support to non-Reformed mission agencies than to their own church. In matters of doctrine, disagreements about extrabiblical revelations, the regulative principle in worship, theonomy, the length of the days of creation, and other matters have perplexed the church almost from its beginning in 1973.

Although founded as an act of separation from a liberal denomination, the Presbyterian Church in America has inclined toward ecumenism when such endeavors do not require compromises with unbelief. A major expression of this interest appeared in 1982, when the Reformed Presbyterian Church, Evangelical Synod, united with the Presbyterian Church in America, thereby adding 164 congregations and over twenty thousand members to the church. In addition, Covenant College and Covenant Theological Seminary then became denominational institutions. Distinguished scholars such as Francis Schaeffer, R. Laird Harris, and Will Barker thus became ministers of the united body. The Presbyterian Church in America eventually invited union with the Orthodox Presbyterian Church and the Reformed Presbyterian Church in North America, but both of those bodies declined the offer. The Orthodox Presbyterian Church has, since then, flourished with a vigorous program of church-planting, but the Reformed Presbyterian Church has languished. All of these churches remain members of the North American Presbyterian and Reformed Council, a conservative organization through which they maintain fraternal relations.

The Church Since 1973

Despite some lack of unanimity in doctrine, the Presbyterian Church in America has been a dynamic body that has gained the status of a nationwide denomination and is now the second largest Presbyterian body in the United States. Its missionary outreach is extensive both at home and abroad. Mission to the World is its international agency, while Mission to North America administers domestic expansion. Mission to the World now employs about six hundred missionaries serving in about sixty countries, while Mission to North America has about 250 of its people engaged in such activities as planting new congregations, while some 160 members of the church minister as chaplains, many in the American armed forces, others in various hospitals, prisons, and social agencies. Reformed University Ministries serves the needs of Christians in colleges and universities across the country and vigorously seeks the conversion of unbelievers on the campuses. Ministries of mercy engage many members of the denomination in caring for impoverished families, victims of natural disasters, sick and elderly people, and at Crisis Pregnancy Centers, which offer help to troubled women and girls in order to discourage abortion.

The Presbyterian Church in America does not ordain women as ministers, ruling elders, or deacons, but through its Women in the Church program, it encourages broad active participation in church life where such functions do not require ordained personnel. Great Commission Publications is the denomination's publishing arm, a joint venture with the Orthodox Presbyterian Church. A new magazine, *By Faith,* is now the official publication of the church. The central offices of the denomination are in Lawrenceville, Georgia. About sixteen hundred congregations in the United States and Canada comprise this denomination of about 332 thousand members.

Leaders of the Church

Before concluding this survey of the Presbyterian Church in America, it is in order to relate some information about its most influential leaders, past and present, many of whom have contributed noteworthy public service to the nation as well as to the church.

Morton Howison Smith

In accord with Presbyterian tradition, the Presbyterian Church in America has insisted on a learned ministry, and a number of its theological educators have produced noteworthy works of scholarship. This became evident from the inception of the denomination, the creation of which was, in part, the work of orthodox theologians who resolved to preserve historic Reformed Christianity, which many professors in older seminaries had abandoned. Prominent among such scholars was (and continues to be) Morton Howison Smith (1923–), first stated clerk of the General Assembly and a founding father of Reformed Theological Seminary, Jackson, Mississippi, and Greenville Presbyterian Theological Seminary, Taylors, South Carolina. Educated at Westminster and Columbia Seminaries and the Free University of Amsterdam, from which he received the ThD, Smith is author of *Studies in Southern Presbyterian Theology; How the Gold Is Become Dim; Harmony of the Westminster Confession and Catechisms; Commentary on the PCA Book of Church Order;* and a two-volume *Systematic Theology.* Well past the time when most people think of retirement, Smith remains an active churchman and is professor of Systematic Theology at Greenville Seminary.

Joseph A. Pipa Jr.

Joseph A. Pipa Jr. (1947–), also on the faculty of Greenville Seminary, where he serves as president and professor of historical and systematic theology, is active in denominational affairs on the local and national levels. A respected scholar and vigorous preacher, this former pastor studied with Morton Smith at Reformed Theological Seminary prior to earning the PhD at Westminster Seminary, Philadelphia. Pipa is author of *Root and Branch*, a lucid study of Christology; "William Perkins and the Development of Puritan Preaching"; and *The Lord's Day*, a strong plea for respectful observance of the Christian Sabbath. He has recently authored a commentary on the epistle to the Galatians.

C. Gregg Singer

Closely associated with Morton Smith, first at Belhaven College in Mississippi and later at Greenville Seminary, was C. Gregg Singer (1910–1999), a graduate of Haverford College who earned the PhD at the University of Pennsylvania. This distinguished historian lectured widely on college and university campuses, where he vigorously asserted a biblical interpretation of history. Singer wrote many books, including *A Theological Interpretation of American History; From Rationalism to Irrationality: The Decline of the Western Mind; John Calvin, His Roots and Fruits;* and *South Carolina in the Confederation, 1781–1789*. In addition to his academic productivity, he was a fervent preacher who often filled Presbyterian pulpits as a supply pastor.

Robert L. Reymond

Among theologians who have served in the Presbyterian Church in America, one of the most prominent is Robert L. Reymond (1932–), who earned three degrees at Bob Jones University and undertook postgraduate study at several universities and seminaries. A professor at Covenant Theological Seminary and later at Knox Theological Seminary, Reymond is much in demand as a guest lecturer and preacher, and his publications have been numerous. A keen analyst of modern theology, he was written *A Christian View of Modern Science; Brunner's Dialectical Encounter; Barth's Soteriology; The Justification of Knowledge; A New Systematic Theology of the Christian Faith;* and *The Reformation's Conflict with Rome, Why It Must Continue;* and several more learned works.

R. C. Sproul

Perhaps the best-known theologian of the Presbyterian Church in America is R. C. Sproul (1939–), now president of Ligonier Ministries and pastor of St. Andrews Presbyterian Church, both in Orlando, Florida. A graduate of Pittsburgh Theological Seminary and the Free University of Amsterdam, Sproul is a fervent exponent of Reformed theology and a vigorous defender of orthodoxy who has taught as a resident professor or a special lecturer at Gordon Conwell Theological Seminary, Reformed Theological Seminary, Westminster Theological Seminary (California), and Knox Theological Seminary. A leader of the Council on Biblical Inerrancy, Sproul is well known for his extensive teaching ministry, both in person and through audio and video recordings. His numerous books include *If There Is a God, Why Are There Atheists?*; *In Search of Dignity*; *Classical Apologetics*; *Lifeviews*; *Chosen by God*; *One Holy Passion*; *Pleasing God*; *The Holiness of God*; *The Mystery of the Holy Spirit*; and *Knowing Scripture*. Sproul is general editor of the *New Geneva Study Bible*, subsequently published as the *Reformation Study Bible*.

John M. Frame

Another influential theologian serving with this denomination is John M. Frame (1939–), a graduate of Westminster Theological Seminary and Yale University, who has served on the faculty of his alma mater as well as at Westminster Seminary, California, and Reformed Theological Seminary, Orlando. Frame's many publications include *The Doctrine of the Knowledge of God*; *Apologetics to the Glory of God*; *Cornelius Van Til: An Analysis of His Thought*; and *No Other God: A Response to Open Theism*.

R. Laird Harris

An Old Testament scholar of renown who rendered great service within the Presbyterian Church in America was R. Laird Harris (1911–2008), a longtime professor at Covenant Theological Seminary who graduated from Westminster Seminary and earned the PhD at the Dropsie College for Hebrew and Cognate Learning. Harris lectured in many nations and established his reputation as a precise, methodical scholar through his impressive publications. *The Inspiration and Canonicity of the Bible* is a strong defense of inerrancy and of the self-attesting inspiration and authority of the Bible. In addition he produced *Man, God's Eternal Creation*; *An Introductory Hebrew Grammar*; and the popular *You and Your Bible*. Perhaps Harris's most significant project is the *Theological Wordbook of the Old Testament,* of which he was the general editor. His contributions appear in the *Expositor's Bible Commentary* and the *New Geneva Study Bible* as well.

David B. Calhoun

In addition to a number of biblical and theological scholars, the Presbyterian Church in America has enjoyed the services of some noteworthy church historians. Among them David B. Calhoun (1937–) is perhaps the foremost. Educated at Columbia Bible College and Covenant Theological Seminary, Calhoun earned the PhD at Princeton Theological Seminary, the history of which he related in a two-volume work titled *Princeton Seminary (1812–1929).* More than its title implies, this is a valuable account of Presbyterian history at large in the period covered. *Faith and Learning* is another of his useful contributions, and his histories of prominent local congregations such as First Presbyterian Church, Columbia, South Carolina, and First Presbyterian Church, Augusta, Georgia, plus *A Place for Truth: The Bicentennial James Henly Thornwell Lectures,* have established Calhoun as a scholar of great erudition and an author who communicates well with ordinary readers.

Douglas F. Kelly

Another church historian who has combined thorough research with skill in writing is Douglas F. Kelly (1943–), a professor at Reformed Theological Seminary, Charlotte. After graduating from the University of North Carolina, Kelly obtained the bachelor of divinity at Union Theological Seminary, Richmond, and proceeded to the University of Edinburgh from which he received the PhD. A productive author, he has published a devotional work titled *If God Already Knows, Why Pray?* and has translated *The Sermons of John Calvin on II Samuel.* Also, *Preachers with Power; Four Stalwarts of the South; The Emergence of Liberty in the Modern World; Creation and Change;* and *Carolina Scots* are products of his pen.

Frank J. Smith

Deserving of inclusion in this consideration of church historians is Frank J. Smith (1954–), a graduate of Westminster Seminary, Philadelphia, who earned the PhD at the City University of New York. Although primarily a journalist, Smith rendered great service to the denomination by compiling *The History of the Presbyterian Church in America,* a thorough account of the body from the separation from liberalism in 1973 to the end of the twentieth century. Extensive research and massive documentation mark this reliable account of a young, dynamic church.[*]

Prominent Pastors

D. James Kennedy

Much of the strength of any denomination depends upon the quality of pastors who serve its congregations, and the Presbyterian Church in America has enjoyed the blessing of a large number of learned, godly, and vigorous teaching elders on the local level. Perhaps the most famous of these is D. James Kennedy (1930–2007), founder of Coral Ridge Presbyterian Church, Ft. Lauderdale, Florida, a congregation of about ten thousand members established in 1959, when forty-five people formed a mission station. In only a few years this became the fastest growing church in the denomination, and its influence reached far beyond its own community when Kennedy initiated a radio and later a television ministry. *The Coral Ridge Hour* now reaches most nations of the world.

Kennedy, a graduate of Columbia Theological Seminary and holder of the PhD from New York University, was one of the most zealous evangelists of his era, and his program, Evangelism Explosion, has assisted his own church and numerous others to reach multitudes for Christ. In addition, Kennedy was author of over fifty books and responsible for the organization of Westminster Academy, a school of about thirteen hundred students on the elementary and secondary levels, and Knox Theological Seminary, a distinguished institution committed to orthodox Christianity. He was known and respected as a champion of biblical morality in all areas of life.

Kennedy Smartt

Closely associated with D. James Kennedy in the work of evangelism has been Kennedy Smartt (1924–), one of the founders of the Presbyterian Church in America. James Kennedy credited Smartt with teaching him how to conduct evangelism. Smartt is the author of *I Am Reminded: An Anecdotal History of the PCA*, an account by one who participated in almost all the formative measures that led to separation from the liberal Southern Presbyterian Church and the creation of the successor denomination. His

---

[*]As mentioned in chapter 17, Gordon H. Clark and Francis Schaeffer, who made major contributions to the defense of orthodoxy, were ministers in the Presbyterian Church in America.

book is a lively account of the soul-searching and heart-wrenching events that made separation necessary so believers could remain loyal to Christ. Smartt is a graduate of Davidson College and Columbia Theological Seminary, on whom the Atlanta School of Biblical Studies conferred the doctor of divinity. His pastoral ministry has taken place in Georgia and Virginia, and he has served in administrative positions with Mission to the World and Mission to North America. In 1998 he became moderator of the General Assembly of his church.

James Montgomery Boice

Among the outstanding pastors of this denomination was James Montgomery Boice (1938–2000), who served Philadelphia's Tenth Presbyterian Church for thirty-two years. A scholar of international repute, Boice combined erudition with evangelistic zeal and pastoral compassion, as he led his dynamic congregation in center-city Philadelphia. Through the *Bible Study Hour* he proclaimed the gospel to multitudes, while as a founder of the Alliance of Confessing Evangelicals, he contended for the faith of historic Protestantism. A graduate of Harvard University and Princeton Theological Seminary, he earned the doctor of theology at the University of Basel, where he studied with the renowned neo-orthodox theologian Karl Barth. Boice wrote extensively on theological matters and produced expositional commentaries on many books of the Bible. *Foundations of the Christian Faith*; *The Doctrines of Grace*; *Renewing Your Mind in a Mindless World*; and *Dealing with Bible Problems* are among his most popular works.

J. Ligon Duncan III

J. Ligon Duncan III (1960–) is another scholar-pastor who has served God in this church with distinction. A native of Greenville, South Carolina, where he grew up in a Christian family and attended Second Presbyterian Church, Duncan is from a long line of ruling elders. Educated at Furman University and Covenant Theological Seminary, he obtained the PhD at the University of Edinburgh. Soon after ordination he joined the faculty of Reformed Theological Seminary, Jackson, Mississippi, to teach systematic theology. In 1996 he accepted a call to become senior pastor at First Presbyterian Church, Jackson, while remaining on the faculty of the seminary in an adjunct capacity. He has been very active in denominational affairs at the presbytery level and is the youngest person to be elected moderator of the General Assembly, a post he held in 2004–2005. He is president of the Alliance of Confessing Evangelicals as well.

As a scholar Duncan has maintained keen interest in the doctrinal standards of his church and has become an authority on the Westminster Assembly that produced them. He has edited many works, both historical and contemporary, and contributed chapters to several books and articles to various periodicals. He collaborated with David W. Hall in compiling *The Westminster Assembly: A Guide to Basic Bibliography*, and himself produced *Moses' Law for Modern Government: The Intellectual and Sociological Origins of the Christian Reconstructionist Movement*. Under Duncan's leadership First Presbyterian Church has remained steadfastly loyal to historic Reformed theology while conducting a very active ministry of teaching, evangelism, and missions. It is one of the largest congregations in its denomination, of which it was a founding member.

Paul Settle

Another pastor of much significance in the history of the Presbyterian Church in America is Paul Settle (1935–), an influential leader in Presbyterian Churchmen United and the Continuing Presbyterian Church during the painful period of separation from the liberal parent denomination. Prior to that this graduate of Columbia Theological Seminary had served pastorates in West Virginia and as minister of education in Alabama and Florida. In 1976 he became pastor of Second Presbyterian Church, Greenville, South Carolina, a position he held until 1991. Settle was associate pastor at Park Cities Presbyterian Church, Dallas, from 1993 to 2003, and in 1980 was elected moderator of the General Assembly. A skillful writer, Settle has produced *Studies in the Catechism*; *A Time to Die*; and a beautifully illustrated history of the denomination titled *To God All Praise and Glory*. For several years he conducted a radio ministry through the program *Grace Triumphant*.

Frank M. Barker Jr.

One of the largest congregations in the Presbyterian Church in America is Briarwood Presbyterian Church, Birmingham, Alabama, which was the site of the first General Assembly of the new denomination. From 1960 to 1999 Frank M. Barker Jr. (1932–) was pastor of this very influential ministry. Educated at Auburn University, Columbia Seminary, and Reformed Theological Seminary, this faithful pastor wrote *A Living Hope*; *Encounters with Jesus*; and *First Timothy*. In addition to his pastoral ministry, Barker was a founder of Birmingham Theological Seminary, a graduate institution that has awarded about three hundred master's degrees.

Noteworthy Public Servants

James Danforth Quayle

In addition to an impressive array of theologians and pastors, a number of church members have become highly visible in government service or have held elective office. Perhaps the most prominent of these is James Danforth Quayle (1947–), vice-president of the United States (1989–1993). Prior to occupying the second highest position in the federal government, Quayle was a newspaper editor and a member of the House of Representatives (1977–1981) and the United States Senate (1981–1989). A graduate of DePauw University, he earned a law degree from Indiana University in 1974. An outspoken advocate of biblical principles, particularly in moral matters, Quayle has expressed his faith clearly in his books *Standing Firm: A Vice-Presidential Memoir*, *Worth Fighting For*, and *The American Family: Discovering the Values that Make Us Strong*.

C. Everett Koop, M.D.

Only slightly less well known than Vice-President Quayle is C. Everett Koop, MD (1916–), who served as surgeon general during the administration of President Ronald Reagan. This renowned physician, a ruling elder in Philadelphia's Tenth Presbyterian Church, has been a relentless advocate for Christian morality, a fact evident in his staunch opposition to abortion, infanticide, and terminating the lives of children with birth defects. A skillful pediatric surgeon who has saved the lives of numerous afflicted babies, Koop has argued vigorously for treatment rather than allowing such handicapped children to die. Always concerned with public health, Koop has been an outspoken critic of tobacco producers, whose products he insisted carry warning labels to indicate the health risks users could incur. To express opposition to abortion and infanticide Koop wrote *The Right to Live, the Right to Die*, and he collaborated with Christian apologist Francis Schaeffer in producing the book *Whatever Happened to the Human Race?* Often the object of criticism from secular humanists, Koop refused to compromise his biblical convictions to satisfy the demands for political expediency, a stand that brought him international acclaim. Some thirty-five institutions awarded him honorary degrees.

James DeMint and James Talent

Another member of this denomination who has gained high public office is Jim DeMint (1951–), now the junior senator from South Carolina, a seat he won after serving three terms in the House of Representatives. During his campaign for the Senate, DeMint expressed his position on controversial issues such as abortion and homosexuality freely, to the point he maintained homosexuals should not be permitted to teach in public schools. He thus suffered some political damage and did apologize for giving offense but not for the positions he had affirmed. He defeated his Democrat opponent by almost 10 percent of the vote. He has since established a reputation for being one of the most conservative members of the Senate and a leading critic of wasteful government spending.

James Talent (1956–) of Missouri also served briefly in the Senate, where on the basis of his convictions he supported many of the same positions DeMint advocated. In the election of 2006, however, Talent lost his seat to a Democrat.

Kenneth Ryskamp, William Barker, and Kenneth Bell

In the judicial branch of government members of the Presbyterian Church in America have rendered commendable service to their country. Among them Kenneth L. Ryskamp (1932–), senior judge in the United States District Court for Southern Florida, is a fine example. A graduate of Calvin College and the University of Miami School of Law, Ryskamp received his appointment from President Ronald Reagan. A ruling elder in Granada Presbyterian Church, Coral Gables, Florida, he was moderator of the General Assembly in 1982, which received the Reformed Presbyterian Church, Evangelical Synod, into the Presbyterian Church in America.

Two more members of this denomination who have served as judges are William M. Barker (1941–), and Kenneth B. Bell (1956–). Barker, a ruling elder and long-time Sunday school teacher at First Presbyterian Church, Chattanooga, Tennessee, graduated from the University of Cincinnati College of Law and obtained a seat on the circuit court by appointment of Governor Lamar Alexander and then became a justice on his state's supreme court in 1998. Florida Governor Jeb Bush appointed Bell to the Supreme Court in 2003. This remarkable jurist was an elder in his church in Pensacola before he and his family moved to Tallahassee. He has been president of the board of directors of the Waterfront Rescue Mission and remains an active Presbyterian churchman. Bell received his law degree at Florida State University.

As the twenty-first century moves forward, so does the Presbyterian Church in America through vigorous programs of church-planting and extensive mission work abroad. The church faces challenges from the increasing secularism of American culture and from some recent doctrinal novelties that lie beyond the scope of this study. Constant vigilance will be required if this denomination is to fulfill and maintain its professed purpose to be "True to the Bible and the Reformed Faith and Obedient to the Great Commission of Jesus Christ."

SUGGESTED ADDITIONAL READINGS >>

Balmer, Randall and John R. Fitzmier. *The Presbyterians*. Westport, Conn.: Praeger, 1994.

Lucas, Sean Michael. *On Being Presbyterian*. Phillipsburg, N.J.: P&R, 2006.

Richards, John Edwards. *The Historical Birth of the Presbyterian Church in America*. Liberty Hill, S.C.: Liberty Press, 1987.

Settle, Paul. *To God All Praise and Glory: Under God, Celebrating the Past, Claiming the Future: the Presbyterian Church in America*. Lawrenceville, Ga.: Presbyterian Church in America, Administrative Committee, 1998.

Smartt, Kennedy. *I Am Reminded: An Autobiographical, Anecdotal History of the Presbyterian Church in America*. Chestnut Mountain, Ga.: privately printed, n.d.

Smith, Frank J. *The History of the Presbyterian Church in America*. 2nd ed. Lawrenceville, Ga.: Presbyterian Scholars Press, 1999.

Smith, Morton H. *How Is the Gold Become Dim: The Decline of the Presbyterian Church, United States as Reflected in Its Assembly Actions*. Greenville, S.C.: Southern Presbyterian Press, 1973.

NINETEEN

Other American Reformed and Presbyterian Churches in the Twentieth Century

Theological disagreements within and between various Reformed denominations continued throughout this century, as liberals and conservatives contended for control. This situation was especially evident in the Christian Reformed Church, which endured several secessions as it broadened its outlook and sought to accommodate the trends in American culture. The first such division was the result of disputes about the doctrine of common grace, that is, God's gracious disposition and kindly benevolence toward unbelievers. The doctrine in question appeared in the writings of Dutch theologian Abraham Kuyper, who exerted great influence upon leaders of the Christian Reformed Church.

Protestant Reformed Churches in America

In 1924 rejection of common grace became the basis for the formation of the Protestant Reformed Church, as consistories of three congregations signed an Act of Agreement and adopted the temporary name "Protesting Christian Reformed Churches" under the leadership of Herman Hoeksema (1886–1965), pastor of Eastern Avenue Christian Reformed Church, Grand Rapids, Michigan. Hoeksema had fought the infiltration of dispensational doctrines into Reformed churches and was an occasional critic of Calvin Theological Seminary, of which he was a graduate. When he rejected the doctrine of common grace, the synod of the Christian Reformed Church rebuked him and removed him and two other pastors from its ministry in 1925. This expulsion led to the formation of the Protestant Reformed Church, a denomination committed to the Three Forms of Unity.

The new church quickly established its own seminary and missionary endeavors at home and abroad, plus several Christian elementary schools and one high school. These schools are under parental control, not official denominational institutions. The Reformed Free Publishing Association produces books and literature and *The Standard Bearer*. In the 1950s a number of congregations of this body returned to the Christian Reformed Church due to disputes about the application of saving grace as it relates to faith and repentance. At the end of the twentieth century there were twenty-seven Protestant Reformed congregations with about seven thousand members in a church that supports missionary works in Singapore, New Zealand, Australia, and Great Britain. The denominational seminary publishes a semiannual journal of theology.

United Reformed Churches in North America

The 1980s and 1990s were an especially tumultuous time for the Christian Reformed Church, as conservatives attempted to resist concessions to the higher criticism of the Bible, efforts to open all church offices to women, and growing acceptance of evolution at Calvin College, plus an ambiguous position regarding homosexuality. Dissidents formed the United Reformed Church in 1996. Its confessional standards are the Three Forms of Unity, and it has 112 congregations and nearly twenty-five thousand members in the United States and Canada. It is affiliated with the International Council of Reformed Churches. The United Reformed Churches do not have a denominational seminary or college. Ministers in this denomination attend and have graduated from several different seminaries, including Mid-America Reformed Seminary, Westminster Seminary California, Puritan Reformed Theological Seminary, and Greenville Presbyterian Theological Seminary. Each minister undergoes a rigorous oral examination in front of classis before he can become an ordained minister of the Word and Sacraments. This church supports missionary work in Trinidad, India, and Latin America, and the United Reformed Churches have seventeen church plants in various cities in the United States and Canada, from Washington, D. C., to Kauai, Hawaii, to Prairie, Alberta. *The Trumpet*, a mission newsletter, provides information to the churches about mission work and church plants.

Netherlands Reformed Churches

This conservative Calvinistic denomination has roots in the Netherlands. Its mother denomination in the Netherlands was officially organized in 1907 under the leadership of G. Hendrik Kersten and Nicolaas H. Beversluis. These churches are heavily influenced by the Dutch *Nadere Reformatie* (Dutch Further Reformation) of the seventeenth and early eighteenth centuries, a movement that sought to apply Reformation truths to daily life and experience. Though its ties are close to the Dutch mother church, the NRC is a distinct denomination whose first synod was held in 1910. Since 1975 the NRC have been active in Christian education, and currently its Christian education association includes eleven elementary schools and seven high schools. This small denomination consists of twenty-six North American congregations with ten thousand members. Its mother church in the Netherlands (*Gereformeerde Gemeenten*) consists of 160 congregations and ten thousand members.

Heritage Reformed Congregations

In 1993, the Netherlands Reformed denomination underwent a split over the issue of the preaching of an unconditional offer of grace, and after the consistory of the largest congregation (Grand Rapids, Michigan) was deposed on the supposed ground of schism, the Heritage Reformed Congregations (HRC) were formed. The HRC supports the authentic NRC tradition that adheres to an unconditional offer of grace in gospel proclamation. Under the leadership of Joel R. Beeke, the HRC established the Puritan Reformed Theological Seminary in 1995, which now has students from thirty denominations and twenty countries around the world. Presently the HRC consists of about two thousand members in ten congregations. The denomination is very active in home and foreign missions. While most of the denomination's ministers labor in North America, three presently serve in South Africa and Malawi. Its denominational periodical is *The Banner of Sovereign Grace Truth* and it supports an active publishing program through Reformation Heritage Books. The HRC subscribes to both the Three Forms of Unity and the Westminster Standards, and is a member of the North American Reformed and Presbyterian Council and the International Conference of Reformed Churches.

Reformed Church in the United States

Not related to the Christian Reformed Church and its Dutch heritage is the Reformed Church in the United States, which traces its roots to the arrival of German immigrants in 1725, when they established the German Reformed Church. As that body expanded to the west, it formed congregations in North and South Dakota and Iowa which, in turn, organized a Northwest Synod. In 1934 the German Reformed Church merged with the Evangelical Synod of North America to create the Evangelical and Reformed Church, but the Eureka Classis of the German Reformed

Church chose to remain outside that union, and its twenty-six congregations and fourteen hundred members became the Reformed Church in the United States. Disavowing all claims to be a new denomination, this movement regarded all congregations that had joined the merger as schismatic and portrayed itself as the genuine Reformed church loyal to the Scriptures and the Heidelberg Catechism. While the Evangelical and Reformed Church became increasingly liberal, the Reformed Church in the United States maintained strict orthodoxy. Not until 1940 did this church adopt English as the language for worship.

The Reformed Church in the United States has expanded beyond the area of the Eureka Classis and now has congregations as far apart as California and Pennsylvania, forty-three in all. Its ministers obtain their theological education as a rule at Heidelberg Theological Seminary, Vermillion, South Dakota; New Geneva Theological Seminary, Colorado Springs; Mid-America Reformed Seminary; City Seminary in Sacramento, California; and, by recent approval, at Greenville Presbyterian Theological Seminary. *The Reformed Herald* is this church's major periodical, and it maintains fraternal relations with the Canadian and American Reformed Churches, Orthodox Presbyterian Church, the Reformed Presbyterian Church of North America, the Reformed Churches in the Netherlands (Liberated), and Reformed bodies in Mexico and Zaire. It is a member of the North American Reformed and Presbyterian Council and the International Conference of Reformed Churches.

Free Reformed Churches of North America

A Reformed denomination of more recent origin is the Free Reformed Churches, a body of Dutch ancestry distantly related to the *Afscheiding* of 1834, which produced the *Christelijk Gereformeerde Kerk* (Christian Reformed Church) in the Netherlands, from which immigrants brought their faith to North America after World War II. Most of them settled in the Canadian provinces of Ontario and British Columbia, where they formed the Free Reformed Churches rather than join the Reformed Church in America or the Christian Reformed Church in North America. Eventually congregations in Michigan, New Jersey, and the state of Washington affiliated with this denomination, drawn by its fervent orthodoxy as affirmed in the Three Forms of Unity. Its ministers obtain their education at Puritan Reformed Theological Seminary in Grand Rapids, Michigan.

With twenty-one congregations in the United States and Canada, the Free Reformed Churches sponsor missionary works in Guatemala, and they maintain the *Banner of Truth Radio Broadcast*, while publishing *The Messenger*, the denomination's official magazine. A member of the International Conference of Reformed Churches, this church maintains ties with the *Christelijk Gereformeerde Kerk* (Christian Reformed Church) in the Netherlands.

Reformed Church in America

The Reformed Church in America, the oldest major Protestant denomination in North America, originated in the Dutch colony of New Netherlands as an extension of the Dutch Reformed Church in Europe. After the English seized the Dutch possessions, immigrants from the Netherlands were few, but by then several Dutch congregations were well established in what are now New York and New Jersey. In 1747 the Classis of Amsterdam complied with a request for autonomy from its American congregations. The American War for Independence further detached those congregations from their mother church, and in 1784 the American church founded its own seminary in Brooklyn but moved to New Brunswick, New Jersey, in 1810. Theodore Frelinghuysen, famous revival preacher in the Great Awakening, was the primary figure in creating the first theological seminary in the New World.

By the time the seminary moved to New Jersey, people of various nationalities had joined the church, a development that necessitated conducting services in the English language. A fresh wave of arrivals from the Netherlands about the middle of the nineteenth century, however, infused the church with more cultural influence from Europe, especially because Dutch pastors accompanied their parishioners, to whom they continued to minister in their native tongue. Many of the newly arrived believers moved to the Midwest—to Holland, Michigan, and Pella, Iowa, especially. Albertus van Raalte (1811–1876) led the migration to Michigan, while Hendrik Scholte (1805–1868) took a group to Iowa. Both settlements eventually joined the Dutch Reformed Church, which, in 1867, became the Reformed Church in America. Slowly English became the medium of worship and instruction in churches and schools.

The Three Forms of Unity have, from its inception, been the official doctrinal statements of the Reformed Church in America, but in the twentieth century the church relaxed its demand for strict subscription as it entered into ecumenical relations and became more liberal. Two theological schools, New Brunswick Theological Seminary in New Jersey and Western Theological Seminary in Michigan, and Hope College in Holland, Michigan, and Central and Northwestern Colleges in Iowa are this denomination's institutes of higher education.

The Reformed Church in America is a member of the National and World Council of Churches as well as the World Alliance of Reformed Churches. It reports about one thousand churches in the United States and Canada with close to 200 thousand confessing members. The church ordains women to all offices, and *RCA Today* is its official publication. Missionaries labor in Canada and eleven other nations. The church's most famous missionary is Samuel Zwemer (1867–1952), who invested many years evangelizing Arabs in the region around the Persian Gulf and in Egypt. In 1929 Zwemer became professor of missions and the history of religions at Princeton Theological Seminary. An expert on Islam, he wrote *The Cross above the Crescent*; *Islam: A Challenge to the Faith*; and *The Origin of Religion*.

Conservative Presbyterian Bodies

Korean American Presbyterian Church

Dynamic growth of Presbyterianism in Korea has exerted considerable influence upon the formation of Korean congregations in America, as the founding of the Korean-American Presbyterian Church in 1978 attests. By 1996 this body had nineteen presbyteries and was supporting twenty missionaries abroad. The total membership was about thirty-three thousand and growing steadily, as church extension reached into Canada, Central and South America, and Germany. Strictly confessional, this denomination refrains from ordaining women, maintains close relations with the Orthodox Presbyterian Church, and is a member of the North American Presbyterian and Reformed Council. The church operates the International Reformed University and Seminary in California.

Associate Reformed Presbyterian Church

Another conservative movement of note in America is the Associate Reformed Presbyterian Church, a denomination with roots in Scottish Secessionist and Covenanter history. This church appeared in North America in the eighteenth century but experienced most of its growth in the next two centuries. Like the Covenanters, this body adopted the Westminster Standards and sang only psalms until synodical action in 1946 allowed the use of hymns. Portions of the church joined the United Presbyterians, but those that did not preserved their own denomination with its strength in the southeastern United States, although there are congregations elsewhere, including a few in Canada.

While the Associate Reformed Presbyterian Church is traditional in its confessional position, it does ordain female deacons but not elders. Organized into ten presbyteries, this body maintains Erskine College and Erskine Theological Seminary in Due West, South Carolina, and is an affiliate of the North American Presbyterian and Reformed Council.

Evangelical Presbyterian Church

Recent developments led to the formation of the Evangelical Presbyterian Church in 1981, when twelve congregations left the Presbyterian Church (U.S.A.) and the Presbyterian Church (U.S.) in protest against theological liberalism. The founders of the new body intended to maintain historic Reformed doctrines while allowing for new teachings they deemed to be scriptural. The church affirms the Westminster Confession of Faith plus a supplementary statement known as Essentials of the Faith, which allows for the ordination of women and the practice of charismatic gifts of the Holy Spirit other Reformed churches regard as no longer in effect.

The Evangelical Presbyterian Church has enjoyed considerable growth in its brief history, and by the early twenty-first century it had about seventy thousand members and supported approximately sixty foreign missionaries, not all of them serving with denominational agencies. In 1987 a number of congregations in Argentina adhered to this church. Due to a vigorous program of planting new congregations, about two hundred local assemblies are linked together in Presbyterian polity.

Allowing for the ordination of females, the practice of Pentecostal gifts, and loose subscription to the Westminster Standards excludes this denomination from membership in the North American Presbyterian and Reformed Council, but it is active in the National Association of Evangelicals and the generally liberal World Alliance of Reformed Churches. The Evangelical Presbyterians maintain close relations with the Christian Reformed Church of North America and with charismatic Presbyterians in Puerto Rico.

Free Presbyterian Church

A much smaller Reformed denomination is the Free Presbyterian Church in North America, which began in 1976 while it was still part of its mother church in Northern Ireland. In 2004 the North American congregations formed their own presbytery, which now has local assemblies in twelve American states and four Canadian provinces. Although rigorously Calvinistic, the Free Presbyterian Church allows for diversity in the matter of infant and believer's baptism and accommodates various views of eschatology. Geneva Reformed Seminary in Greenville, South Carolina, is the denomination's school for educating ministers. The church forbids drinking alcoholic beverages and uses only the King James Version of the Bible, although it does not denigrate the value of other translations. Free Presbyterian missionaries labor in Kenya and Mexico, and *Let the Bible Speak* is the name of this church's radio broadcast. Lifeline Publications is also a tract ministry of this church.

The Korean Presbyterian Church in America
Although conservative churches with Korean constituencies have shown impressive growth in America, one liberal body merits attention. It is the Korean Church in America, founded in 1976 through the union of three immigrant presbyteries that had been affiliated with the Presbyterian Church of Korea. As of the end of the twentieth century, some 275 local bodies had aligned with this church, some in Canada and a few in Latin America. Approximately twenty-nine thousand people hold membership in this affiliate of the World Alliance of Reformed Churches. This denomination ordains women and in general espouses an inclusive doctrinal position similar to that of the Presbyterian Church (U.S.A.), with which it has close relations.

SUGGESTED ADDITIONAL READINGS »

Beeke, Joel R. *The Heritage Reformed Congregations.* Grand Rapids: Reformation Heritage Books, 2007.

Benedetto, Robert with Darrell L. Guder and Donald K. McKim. *Historical Dictionary of Reformed Churches.* Lanham, Md.: Scarecrow Press, 1999.

Bratt, James D. *Dutch Calvinism in Modern America.* Grand Rapids: Eerdmans, 1984.

Gritters, Barry. *The Family: Foundations Are Shaking.* Hudsonville, Mich.: Protestant Reformed Church, 1988.

Hanko, Herman. *For Thy Truth's Sake.* Grandville, Mich.: Reformed Free Publishing Association, 2000.

Hart, D. G. and Mark A. Noll, eds. *Dictionary of the Presbyterian and Reformed Tradition in America.* Downers Grove, Ill.: InterVarsity, 1999.

Lathan, Robert. *History of the Associate Reformed Presbyterian Synod of the South to Which Is Prefixed A History of the Associate Presbyterian and Reformed Presbyterian Churches.* Harrisburg, Pa.: privately printed, 1882.

Mead, Frank S. with Samuel S. Hill and Craig D. Atwood. *Handbook of Denominations in the United States.* 12th ed. Nashville: Abingdon Press, 2005.

Melton, J. Gordon, ed. *Encyclopedia of American Religions.* Vol. 1. Tarrytown, N.Y.: Triumph Books, 1991.

Osterhaven, M. Eugene. *The Spirit of the Reformed Tradition.* Grand Rapids: Eerdmans, 1971.

Protestant Reformed Church. *Our Goodly Heritage Preserved: 75 Years, 1925–2000. The Protestant Reformed Churches in America.* Grandville, Mich.: Protestant Reformed Churches in America, 2000.

Synod of the Associate Reformed Presbyterian Church. *The Centennial History of the Associate Reformed Presbyterian Church, 1803–1903.* Charleston, S.C.: Walker, Evans, and Cogswell, 1905.

VandenBerge, Peter M., ed. *Historical Dictionary of the Reformed Church in America, 1628–1978.* Grand Rapids: Eerdmans, 1978.

Ware, Lowry and James W. Gettys. *The Second Century: A History of the Associate Reformed Presbyterians, 1882–1982.* Greenville, S.C.: Associate Reformed Presbyterian Center, 1995.

TWENTY

The Reformed Faith in Mexico and Central America

Roman Catholicism was the initial form of Christianity introduced into Latin America, that region south of the United States in which Spanish is the major language, although Portuguese prevails in Brazil, and some of the Caribbean islands use French, Dutch, or English. Following in the wake of Columbus, Spaniards explored and settled large areas of the New World and brought their Catholic religion with them. Despite exploitation and brutality toward the natives, many Indians adhered to the new religion, in some cases because of forced conversions. Spaniards from the Iberian Peninsula dominated the colonies in America until *criollos*, whites born in the New World, rebelled in collaboration with *mestizos*, products of Spanish-Indian unions, and seized authority in various colonies. By the end of the eighteenth century, movements toward independence from the European powers were forming across the region and by 1825 almost all of Spanish and Portuguese America had gained independence.

The Roman Catholic Church in Latin America was conservative to the point that the Inquisition had operated with the support of ruling authorities in the era prior to independence. While Franciscan, Dominican, and Jesuit religious orders spread the doctrines of Rome, educated some of the natives, and ministered to their material needs, their church nevertheless supported colonial regimes engaged in exploitation of both indigenous peoples and slaves imported from Africa. When conversions to Catholicism occurred, they were often the result of mass baptisms of people with little understanding of the faith they professed to embrace. Sometimes the missionaries adapted Catholic teachings so as to incorporate native traditions and beliefs wherever possible as a means to make the new religion attractive and to ease pagans into it. The result was a blending of Christian and pagan ideas that left the converts poorly informed and unable to distinguish clearly between inherited superstitions (Indian or African) and the new religion they had adopted only formally.

No nation in Europe resisted the Protestant Reformation more militantly than did Spain, so her colonies in the New World did not welcome Protestant efforts to evangelize there. The political and social revolutions that ended European rule, however, damaged the Roman Church by depriving it of the support it had long received from colonial administrations. Many officials who assumed control of the new governments viewed the Catholic Church as an obstacle to progress, and an anticlerical attitude was pronounced among them. Like its mother in Spain, the Roman Church in Latin America had become stagnant and reactionary, poorly equipped to withstand challenges from outside the region in the form of radical philosophies from Europe and Protestant competition coming from the United States. Nowhere was this more evident than in Mexico.

Mexico

In 1810 Mexico declared independence from Spain and in 1822 proclaimed itself a republic, but not until the 1870s did the country achieve political stability. The long years after Mexico gained self-rule were full of turbulence, and it was during this time the first Protestant effort in Mexico occurred in 1826, when the American Bible Society began distributing the Scriptures. From 1846 to 1848 Mexico and the United States fought over disputed borderlands, during which conflict Protestants intensified the distribution of Bibles. Although the Mexican government did not allow Protestant missionaries to enter the country, Melinda Rankin (1811–1888), working with the nondenominational American and Foreign Christian Union, opened a school at Brownsville, Texas, where Mexicans could study and learn gospel truth. She entered Mexico in 1855 and built a school at Monterrey. Eventually Rankin placed that work under the auspices of the American Board of Commissioners for Foreign Missions, an arm of the Congregational Church, which began its own mission in Mexico in 1872.

Presbyterians entered Mexico in the 1870s, with both the Presbyterian Church (U.S.A.) (Northern) and the Presbyterian Church (U.S.) (Southern) dispatching missionaries only a few months apart and the Associate Reformed Presbyterians following soon thereafter. Some independent Protestant congregations agreed to become Presbyterians. Until 1901 the Northern and Southern Presbyterian churches maintained individual missions, but in 1901 they merged to form the Synod of Mexico, a national autonomous church body. This was evidence of substantial growth in a brief period of time. To facilitate the preparation of native pastors, the

Presbyterian Theological Seminary opened at Mexico City in 1882 and in 1901 became an institution of the National Presbyterian Church in Mexico which, at that time, had about fifty-five hundred members in seventy-three organized congregations and numerous preaching stations. The National Presbyterian Church is now the second largest non-Catholic religious body in the country, only the Assemblies of God being more numerous. By the end of the twentieth century, the National Presbyterian Church claimed 1.2 million adherents in forty-eight hundred local churches and is a member of the World Alliance of Reformed Churches. Neither this church nor any other Presbyterian denomination in Mexico ordains women. Medical and educational efforts on all levels of instruction have been Presbyterian ministries in Mexico almost from the beginning of mission work there, and Bible translation into various dialects has been in progress since the early twentieth century.

As the fruit of Associate Reformed Presbyterian work from the United States, the Associate Reformed Presbyterian Church of Mexico maintains a ministry in the northeast part of the country and has recently expanded into Mexico City and Guadalajara. In 1891 some missionaries opened a school, the Instituto Juarez, named in honor of Mexican president Benito Juarez from 1861–1872, who led resistance to French occupation of the country during the era of the American War between the States, when the United States could not enforce the Monroe Doctrine against European interventions into the Western Hemisphere.

At the end of the twentieth century, the Associate Reformed Presbyterian Church of Mexico claimed 2,365 members in sixty-three congregations arranged into five presbyteries. The Westminster Standards assert the church's doctrinal position, while its theological school operates in Tampico. This denomination became autonomous in 1964.

In 1959 the Christian Reformed Church in North America initiated mission work in Mexico and focused upon migrant workers who had returned to their homeland after periods of employment in the United States. This was a joint endeavor in collaboration with the Presbyterian Reformed Church of Mexico, a body formed when some congregations withdrew from the National Presbyterian Church. The relationship with the Christian Reformed Church proved tenuous, however, as some pastors and elders soon severed their ties with the missionaries from the United States. The two presbyteries that retained the connection with the Christian Reformed Church took the name Presbyterian Reformed Church of

Mexico, while the others were known as the Independent Presbyterian Church. Recent reports show that the Presbyterian Reformed Church is the larger body with about twenty-six thousand members, while the Independent Church has only about one-tenth that many. The larger denomination operates John Calvin Theological Seminary, but the smaller church is more rigorous in affirming historic Reformed theology.

Central America

Across most of Latin America Protestantism made substantial gains in the second half of the twentieth century, while attendance at Roman Catholic services declined, even though a large majority of people in the region affirm that religion in principle. Protestant growth has occurred in almost all Latin states and has embraced both urban and rural populations. This development is not due entirely to reactions against Catholicism but is often because of the attraction of Pentecostal teachings in which both Protestants and Catholics engage, but which enjoy more prominence among Protestants. To some extent the Pentecostal beliefs and practices correspond to features of the indigenous religions of the region, which may explain why native Indian peoples have shown the greatest interest in Protestant Pentecostal churches that allow more innovations in worship practices than does the Roman Church.

Roman Catholicism arrived in Central America when Spanish explorers established their country's rule in the region. Most states therefore still have Catholic majorities, but Belize, the former British Honduras, has a slight Protestant majority. Presbyterian and Reformed missionary efforts in Central America have not thus far produced impressive numerical results. In Panama, for example, there are no organized Reformed churches, while in Nicaragua there is but a tiny work of the Christian Reformed Church and some charitable ministries of Presbyterian origin.

For a long time Catholic domination in political affairs kept Protestant missions out of the region, and even after the coming of independence, persecution of religious nonconformity was common. When missionary work became practical in the nineteenth century, Presbyterian and Reformed churches were slow to respond, so Reformed believers in Central America are few.

Belize

Even in Belize the Anglican Church is the major non-Roman Catholic denomination, while the Presbyterian Church of Belize has only about five hundred members. The Presbyterian effort began as an outreach of the Free Church of Scotland about 1850, but in 1905 the little body in British Honduras affiliated with the Church of Scotland. Presbyterianism in Belize has experienced little growth, and there is much uncertainty about doctrine, a great deal of that due to inadequate supply of ministers well educated in the Reformed faith. Not until 1958 did the Presbyterian Church extend its ministry to native Indians, and since then it had grown only slightly and now has eight congregations associated with the National Presbyterian Church, a body that ordains women and maintains close relations with the generally liberal Presbyterian Church (U.S.A.).

Costa Rica

The constitution of this former Spanish colony recognizes Catholicism as the official religion but allows freedom to all. Farmers and merchants from Europe and North America introduced Protestantism in the mid-nineteenth century, and nondenominational mission agencies such as the Central American Mission and the Latin American Mission sent workers there, Presbyterians among them. The Central American Mission was a creation of Congregationalist Bible interpreter Cyrus I. Scofield (1843–1921), famous editor of the *Scofield Reference Bible*, who organized the mission when it became clear no major denomination was prepared to move into Cost Rica. The first appointees of this mission were Presbyterians William McConnell and his wife, who arrived at San José in 1891. The Latin American Mission entered Costa Rica in 1921, and again, a Presbyterian, Angel Archilla Cabrera from Puerto Rico, led the way. In 1924 Latin American Mission personnel founded the Biblical Seminary of Latin America, which has prepared numerous missionaries for work throughout the region.

Although Reformed believers have served with these nondenominational agencies, only in recent years have Presbyterian church bodies begun to emerge in Costa Rica. Energetic Presbyterians from South Korea have established several congregations, and the Christian Reformed Church in North America has maintained a work there since 1982. Beginning in San José, the Christian Reformed ministry has extended its reach to the Pacific coast, and five Reformed congregations are now associated in a national consistory. Like its North American patron, this church ordains women.

In 1994, the *Confraternidad Latinoamericana de Iglesias Reformadas* (Latin American Fellowship of Reformed Churches), or CLIR, was founded to provide a forum for fellowship and joint ministry among

Reformed and Presbyterian churches. Bill Green has worked as executive secretary of CLIR since 1997, and Nick Lamme began working with him in 2009. Although CLIR's headquarters are in Costa Rica, the association extends to denominations in many countries of Latin America. Member churches must subscribe to one of the historic Reformed confessions of faith, and they work together to project their unity by holding international conferences, sponsoring seminary exchanges of professors, and supporting church planting in Latin American countries that do not have a Reformed gospel witness. Through Editorial CLIR, a publishing house, gospel-centered literature is provided for the churches, both through translation from English and original works written by Reformed scholars and pastors from Latin America. CLIR also facilitates the training of future church leaders. Both the Orthodox Presbyterian Church and the United Reformed Churches support the ministry of CLIR.

June Gallman (1961–), an appointee of the Presbyterian Evangelistic Fellowship in the United States who studied at Greenville Presbyterian Theological Seminary, has for several years been conducting a ministry to female prisoners and their families. This is both an evangelistic and a social outreach to women addicted to drugs and incarcerated for a variety of drug-related crimes. A halfway house for released prisoners is a vital part of this endeavor. A local congregation of Reformed believers has developed in connection with the prison ministry. It now enjoys support from the PCA Mission to the World.

El Salvador

After three centuries of Spanish rule, the smallest of the Central American countries became independent in 1839. Roman Catholicism is still the majority religion, although the Central American Mission initiated work there near the end of the nineteenth century. The Assemblies of God followed soon, and today the Pentecostals have the largest following among the nation's Protestant population, which is about 22 percent of the whole. The constitution of 1871 recognizes Catholicism as the official faith, but it allows full freedom to others.

Protestantism arrived in El Salvador during an era when the Liberal Party governed and restricted the privileges of the Roman Church. The Central American Mission remains in the country as a denomination in its own right with about 175 local congregations. The presence of a Reformed witness is of recent date, and only two such bodies maintain ministries in

El Salvador. The Christian Reformed Church is a product of missionaries from the church of that name in North America, who assisted in forming the national denomination in 1978. Internal dissensions led, however, to two secessions that produced separate ecclesiastical bodies. The Reformed Church of El Salvador, begun in 1979, is now much larger than its parent denomination and claims thirty-three hundred members in six congregations. It endorses the Westminster Confession and other Reformed standards but has broad ecumenical relations. A member of the World Alliance of Reformed Churches, it relies upon the University of San Salvador, a Lutheran institution, for the education of its pastors. The Christian and Reformed Church is the second secessionist body, and it, like the denomination it left, is very small and exerts but little influence in the country.

Guatemala

Four centuries of rather repressive Spanish rule ended with the securing of independence for Guatemala in 1839. The native Indian population remains the majority, and Catholicism is the religious profession of about 70 percent of the people. The Spaniards imposed their religion on the land, which may explain why most of the natives have had only a meager understanding of Catholic doctrine and why allegiance to Rome has been largely formal rather than a matter of conviction. The country's constitution guarantees freedom of religion, so when in 1958 the Roman Church gained the right to teach religion in public schools, Protestants received the same concession.

The first Protestant missionaries to Guatemala went there at the invitation of the country's president, Don Justo Rufino Barrios (1835–1885), a liberal who resented political pressure from the Catholic clergy and viewed Protestantism as a means to thwart it. Barrios asked the Presbyterian Board of Foreign Missions in New York to send workers, and John C. Hill and his wife responded in 1882, thereby initiating the Presbyterian presence in the land.

From the pioneer labors of the Hill family, a National Evangelical Presbyterian Church of Guatemala arose and became a vibrant religious movement that founded schools and hospitals and promoted translation of the Bible into native dialects. The American Hospital in the capital city became renowned for the quality of health care, while the Mann Center and the Quiche Bible Institute provided Christian education for Indians. Through collaboration with the Central American Mission and W. Cameron Townsend (1896–1982), who became founder of Wycliffe

Bible Translators, the Presbyterian mission helped to produce the New Testament in the Cakchiqud Indian language. Additional translations followed, as did creation of Mayan Bible schools for Indians of that tribe.

The National Evangelical Presbyterian Church of Guatemala was the first denomination in Central America to gain self-government, which occurred in 1962, when the mission from the United States integrated with the native presbyteries. This church has enjoyed substantial growth, especially among Mayans. Although it initially concentrated its efforts in the cities and ministered to the middle classes, the church eventually reached out to all classes, and its largest synod is now one of indigenous peoples.

By the end of the twentieth century, the National Church had about twenty-five thousand members in 155 congregations. It endorses the Westminster Standards but does not require strict subscription from its officers. Like the Presbyterian Church (U.S.A.), with which it has fraternal relations, the National Evangelical Presbyterian Church ordains women and maintains membership in the World Alliance of Reformed Churches. The Evangelical Presbyterian Seminary is its theological school.

Disputes about doctrine and ecumenical relations have produced one major and a few minor secessions from the National Church. In 1993 the Presbyterian Synod of Southwest Guatemala withdrew from the National Church and soon faced a civil suit over contested church properties. The dissident body led in organizing the Federation of Latin American Reformed Churches, a conservative body that protested the policies of its liberal counterpart. The new synod claims sixty-seven hundred members and adheres to the Westminster Confession but ordains women as elders and deacons, but not as ministers.

The Bethlehem Bible Presbyterian Church, with about a thousand members in five local assemblies, is another conservative separatist group, and it does not ordain women, while the even smaller Independent Presbyterian Church shuns ecumenical connections but seeks cooperation with other bodies committed to biblical practices. This rather fundamentalist church is a member of the International Council of Christian Churches and maintains close relations with the Independent Board for Presbyterian Foreign Missions in the United States.

Honduras

As in other countries of this region, the Central American Mission has done the most to plant the Protestant faith in Honduras, and that agency operates a de facto denomination in a predominantly Catholic nation. In contrast to other Latin American states, most Honduran Protestants are not Pentecostals. Anglicans from Belize introduced the Protestant faith, and several North American bodies sent missions. The Evangelical and Reformed Church (now the United Church of Christ) dispatched its agents to Honduras in 1921 to labor in the northwest part of the country where, to evangelism, they added educational and medical ministries. The local churches that developed from these efforts formed the Synod of Honduras as a national body that eventually became the Evangelical and Reformed Church of Honduras. Today it has close relations with the very liberal United Church of Christ, ordains females, and emphasizes the social responsibilities of the faith more than doctrine and evangelism. The total membership is about fifteen thousand in forty-five congregations and numerous preaching stations.

The Christian Reformed Church in Honduras began as a project of a small group of believers in the Evangelical and Reformed Church who moved to Tegucigalpa in 1962 and asked aid from the Christian Reformed Church in North America. Two missionaries from that body arrived in 1972, and from that modest beginning several Reformed congregations were established. By 1990 there were eighteen local assemblies and about sixteen hundred members organized into a national synod, and a theological school was educating future ministers. Like its North American patron, the Christian Reformed Church affirms the Three Forms of Unity as its statement of doctrine, and it ordains women. It now has cordial relations with the Evangelical and Reformed Church of Honduras.

In addition to the above bodies, there is the Presbyterian Church of Honduras, a denomination formed by Reformed believers who moved there from Guatemala in 1960. With support from the Presbyterians in their homeland, they planted churches and engaged in social projects such as founding hospitals, schools, clinics, and drug treatment centers. More conservative than other Reformed denominations in Honduras, this church affirms the Westminster Confession and the Heidelberg Catechism and does not ordain women officers. Aggregate membership is about seven hundred people in seven congregations.

Although Pentecostal Protestants are most numerous across Central America, Presbyterian and Reformed efforts there continue. There is no substantial Reformed presence in Panama, but the Christian Reformed Church in North America has a very small work in Nicaragua, where approximately two hundred people identify with that body. This mission originated as a charitable endeavor when a devastating earthquake struck Nicaragua in 1972. Progress in church-building has been very slow for the Christian Reformed Church, while the Assemblies of God and the Central American Mission have enjoyed more success.

SUGGESTED ADDITIONAL READINGS »

Barrett, David B., ed. *World Christian Encyclopedia*. Oxford: Oxford University Press, 1982.

Bauswein, Jean-Jacques and Lukas Vischer. *The Reformed Family Worldwide: A Survey*. Grand Rapids: Eerdmans, 1999.

Benedetto, Robert and Darrell L. Guder and Donald K. McKim. *Historical Dictionary of Reformed Churches*. Lanham, Md.: Scarecrow Press, 1999.

Fahlbusch, Erwin, et al., eds. *The Encyclopedia of Christianity*. 5 vols. Grand Rapids: Eerdmans, 2008.

Glover, Robert H. and J. Herbert Kane. *The Progress of World-Wide Missions*. Rev. ed. New York: Harper & Row, 1960.

Moreau, A. Scott, et al., eds. *Evangelical Dictionary of World Missions*. Grand Rapids: Baker, 2000.

TWENTY-ONE

The Caribbean Basin

Most peoples of this region affirm allegiance to some form of Christianity, although there is a significant Hindu community in Guyana and Trinidad-Tobago. Roman Catholicism and several expressions of Protestantism are evident, and in the case of Haiti, voodoo subsists along with Catholicism, as many people participate in both forms of worship.

Cuba

A possession of Spain until the Spanish-American War brought independence in 1899, Cuba has suffered under dictatorial governments ever since and currently remains subject to the Marxist regime of Fidel Castro, who led a popular revolt against the previous authoritarian ruler in 1958. Soviet influence and Communist ideology were paramount until the Soviet Union disintegrated in 1989. Roman Catholicism has been the dominant religion since the Spaniards occupied the country in the sixteenth century, and a majority of Cubans continues to profess Catholicism despite decades of Communist rule. Some people, however, practice African cults brought to the country by slaves during the era of colonial rule. Catholicism ceased to be the state religion when Cuba became independent, and the constitutions of 1904 and 1940 affirmed freedom of religion, which Castro's regime promised to maintain.

For a brief time in the eighteenth century Great Britain ruled much of Cuba but returned it to Spain in 1763 in exchange for Florida. During the period of the British presence Anglicans arrived, and slowly other Protestants appeared and began distributing Bibles in the Spanish tongue and seeking converts through commercial contacts. Spanish authorities then did not allow missionaries in the land. A law in 1855 prohibited further distribution of Bibles, but the practice continued covertly. Few natives, however, responded positively to Protestant appeals.

Although a few American Protestant churches initiated missionary efforts despite the opposition of Spanish authorities, only after the war in 1898 did such endeavors become pronounced. Southern Baptists were among the first, and others soon followed, the Protestant Episcopal Church enjoying noteworthy success. After some unofficial contacts before independence, both the Northern and Southern Presbyterians entered Cuba about the opening of the twentieth century, although the Presbyterian Reformed Church in Canada traces its mission to 1890, when Evaristo Collazo went there from Florida and obtained Presbyterian ordination as a pastor. From this beginning a Reformed mission developed into a church. In 1918 the Northern and Southern Presbyterians combined their works into a single enterprise, which they named the Presbyterian Church of Havana, an affiliate of the Presbyterian Church (U.S.A.).

In 1967, due in part to anti-United States sentiments encouraged by Castro's government, the Presbyterian Reformed Church in Cuba declared itself independent and separate from any American denomination. By then the Cuban church had become involved in ecumenical ventures with other Protestant groups at home and had adopted a Cuban confession as a supplement to the Westminster Standards and other historic Reformed documents. This church had lost its schools and some properties after Castro seized power, but it continued to function nevertheless with about fifteen thousand members in fifty-nine congregations. It now ordains women and is a member of the World Alliance of Reformed Churches and the World Council of Churches.

The Christian Reformed Church in Cuba is another denomination, one that originated because of the zeal of Bessie Vander Valk, a member of the Christian Reformed congregation in Patterson, New Jersey, who in 1940 went to Cuba to work with the Cuban Evangelical Association. She married a native pastor, Vicente Izquierdo, and together they spread the gospel, supported by contributions from individuals within the Christian Reformed Church in her homeland. In 1958 that denomination made their ministry an official outreach of the church.

The Castro revolt forced the Izquierdos to leave Cuba in 1960, but the Christian Reformed Church there has grown anyway, and, at the opening of the twenty-first century, it claimed about twelve hundred adherents in twelve congregations. Unlike its North American patron, this body does not ordain women, even though it maintains fraternal relations with its mother church.

Guyana

The first Presbyterians to settle in Guyana came from Scotland as planters in 1766. When their descendants helped to organize the Presbyterian Mission Society in 1860, the focus of attention was the conversion of Asian Indian laborers, an effort Canadian Presbyterians supported generously. Even before that, however, Reformed believers had resolved to create a denomination that became the Presbyterian Church of Guyana. From its inception that body conducted vigorous evangelistic work among slaves and warmly welcomed converts from among them into its congregations. Most remaining Dutch Christians joined this church. Soon after the abolition of slavery, the Presbyterian Church of Guyana became a functioning presbytery of the Church of Scotland. It remained so until 1967, when it became independent. The church claims fifty-six hundred members in twenty-five congregations and is a member of the World Alliance of Reformed Churches.

A second Presbyterian body in Guyana is directly the product of Canadian missionaries. The Guyana Presbyterian Church traces its origin to the arrival of John Morton (1839–1912) in 1880, a Canadian minister who had earlier served in Trinidad. Morton then urged Canadian Presbyterians to make Guyana their mission field, and soon other ministers answered the call and proceeded to concentrate on seeking the conversion of Asian Indians working on sugar plantations. By 1930, several organized congregations were flourishing, but not until 1945 did they form a presbytery. They at first called themselves the Canadian Presbyterian Church in Guyana but in 1961 changed that to the Guyana Presbyterian Church. The socialist government of Guyana, after it obtained independence in 1966, seized the schools this church had established. The Guyana Presbyterian Church is a denomination of about twenty-five hundred members in forty-four local churches. It conducts services in both the English and Hindi languages. An affiliate of the World Alliance of Reformed Churches, it affirms the historic doctrinal standards of the Reformed faith but ordains women. This church opened its own theological college in 1998.

Jamaica and the Cayman Islands

These islands are predominantly Protestant in religion, but the Reformed witness there is weak. Spain ruled until 1655, when Britain took control and allowed Presbyterians to settle there and to initiate evangelism. In 1800 the Scottish Missionary Society sent three workers to Jamaica to seek converts among slaves working in the sugarcane fields. When the British

Parliament abolished slavery in 1834, about 300 thousand people gained freedom, and a large number of professions of faith followed, a development that led to the organization of numerous local churches. In 1836 some of those congregations formed the Jamaican Missionary Presbytery and created a Presbyterian Academy to educate native pastors. By 1848 the Presbyterians were sufficiently strong to establish their own synod, and soon thereafter they began sending missionaries of their own to Nigeria and the Gold Coast of Africa. The Presbyterian Church of Nigeria was a fruit of this endeavor. At the same time the Presbyterian Church of Jamaica dispatched evangelists to northwest India, while at home it was seeking the conversion of Indian laborers who had replaced some of the former slaves.

Parallel with the promising growth of Presbyterianism was the corresponding ministry of the London Missionary Society, in which the Congregationalists were dominant. Missionaries of this agency planted churches in the islands, and by 1877 a Congregational Union of Jamaica was in operation, supported by Congregational churches in the United Kingdom. Gradually the Presbyterian and Congregational churches grew closer together, and 1965 brought a merger as the United Church of Jamaica and Grand Cayman, which has become a rather liberal body without a confessional position and closely connected with the ecumenical movement through the World Council of Churches. About twenty thousand people identify with the United Church, a body of some two hundred congregations that ordains women and concentrates on social ministries.

A serious effort to regain a strong Reformed witness in these islands began in 1962, when the Protestant Reformed Churches in the United States responded to a plea from a concerned congregation in England and sent missionaries to this region. To the dismay of the Protestant Reformed workers, however, the churches that accepted their aid were not really disposed toward the Reformed faith but had roots in Arminian-Wesleyan holiness doctrines. The ministry that began well soon foundered, as most of the holiness assemblies renounced Calvinistic teachings, and by the close of the twentieth century, only 125 people still held membership in the Protestant Reformed Church of Jamaica, while the American denomination that had initiated the mission abandoned it.

Netherlands Antilles and Aruba

Although the Dutch West India Company established commercial operations on the islands of Curacao, Bonaire, Aruba, St. Maarten, Saba, and

St. Eustatius in the sixteenth and seventeenth centuries, the European Christians did not win many natives to their faith. Spanish explorers and missionaries had preceded the Dutch, and efforts to supplant Roman Catholicism were not successful. The Dutch Reformed Church initiated missionary work in these islands in 1635, but for the most part that was a ministry to Europeans, and eventually Anglicans and Methodists appeared as competitors for the rather feeble Reformed movement.

Near the opening of the nineteenth century, the Reformed congregations in Curacao, Bonaire, and Aruba merged to form what became the Protestant Church of the Netherlands Antilles, and by then the Reformed presence on the other islands had almost disappeared. At the beginning of the twenty-first century only 2 percent of the islanders affirmed any version of Protestantism, while a huge majority aligned with Catholicism.

After World War II immigrants from Holland brought the Reformed Church in the Netherlands (Liberated) to Curacao to serve the spiritual needs of settlers and to conduct evangelism among the populace as a whole. The predominantly Dutch character of the church and its liturgy, however, impaired communication with others, so progress was slow, and as of 1999, there was only one congregation of 135 people there. It adheres closely to the Three Forms of Unity and maintains relations with its mother church.

Trinidad and Tobago

Since Spaniards were the first Europeans to arrive in these islands, they quickly implanted Catholicism, but Great Britain obtained control in 1797, and Anglicans arrived in substantial numbers. The Anglican Church is still the largest non-Roman Catholic denomination, having about 15 percent of the population in its membership.

The Presbyterian presence in Trinidad and Tobago originated in the nineteenth century, when Scottish settlers arrived and formed a Trinidad Presbyterian Association and sought ministers from their homeland to serve their spiritual needs. Missionaries from the Secession Church then went to Port-of-Spain in 1836 and there founded a Presbyterian church. Ten years later some Portuguese Protestants moved from Madeira to Port-of-Spain and joined the Presbyterian congregation already functioning there.

After Britain abolished slavery in 1834, planters in these islands, like those elsewhere in the Caribbean region, employed Asian Indians as agricultural workers, and most of them were Hindus, people whose descendants now account for about 30 percent of the population. Efforts to evangelize the Hindus began in earnest when John Morton (1839–1912), a Canadian Presbyterian, initiated that work in 1867, and other missionaries followed soon. The Canadians preached on plantations and founded schools as well as churches. In 1892 they opened St. Andrew's Theological College, where one of the students, Lal Bihaii, a converted Hindu, greatly assisted the spread of the faith among his fellow Indians. One year before the theological school commenced classes, the Scottish and Canadian congregations merged into a single presbytery. Church growth allowed for creation of a synod by 1961.

Despite some encouraging developments, however, the Reformed faith has not prospered in Trinidad and Tobago. For a long time the Church of Scotland supplied pastors, but as that body became more liberal, there was a corresponding decline in fervor for evangelism, while ministers educated in Scotland displayed little interest in historic Reformed theology. Pentecostal Christians, alive with enthusiasm, have taken many members from the Presbyterian Church. In 1967 the Presbyterian Church in Trinidad became independent from the Canadian church. About forty thousand people of these islands identify themselves as Presbyterians, and conversions from Hinduism are rare. Muslims too are present in the land, and they, like the Hindus, maintain their own schools and thereby obstruct Christian influence through education.

Puerto Rico and the Dominican Republic

Catholicism arrived in Puerto Rico with the appearance of Christopher Columbus, and that religion continues to command the allegiance of most of the people. Early efforts to introduce Protestantism during periods of Dutch and English enterprise brought no lasting results, and Spanish policy forbade non-Roman Catholic religious activities. Not until 1868 did Spain allow some freedom of religion in Puerto Rico, and the Protestant Episcopal Church from the United States was the first to establish its presence in the colony.

Puerto Rico passed to the control of the United States as a consequence of the Spanish-American War (1898), and soon thereafter several Protestant denominations dispatched missionaries to the islands, the Methodists and the Seventh-Day Adventists being the most vigorous. When the Pentecostal Church of God began working there in 1916, it quickly gained converts and proceeded to become the largest non-Catholic religious movement in the land.

Reformed ministries in Puerto Rico began in earnest in 1900, when the Home Mission Board of the Presbyterian Church (U.S.A.) entered the area and found an indigenous group of believers eager to support a Reformed church. Working in the western part of the land, missionaries established medical clinics under the leadership of Grace Atkins, M.D., and by 1904 a hospital was in operation, one that gradually became renowned as the Presbyterian Hospital of San Juan. Rather than compete with other Protestant denominations, the Presbyterians cooperated in educational efforts that included a college at San German.

The first organized Presbyterian congregations in Puerto Rico were the work of missionaries J. M. Greene (1842–1921) and Milton E. Caldwell (1850–1907), who went there in 1899. Early successes allowed for formation of a presbytery by 1902, but there would be no synod until 1973. The Presbyterian church that resulted from these developments was not large, and by the year 2000, it had only eighty-three hundred members. It is a liberal ecumenical body, a synod of the Presbyterian Church (U.S.A.).

A more conservative group is the Christian Reformed Church in Puerto Rico, which has only a few congregations and a membership of about three hundred. It does not ordain women. Three native pastors and one missionary care for the flock while seeking to evangelize, especially through distribution of Christian literature under the imprint *Sola Scriptura*. Although numerically small, this Christian Reformed Church is zealous and forward looking, as the enrollment of thirty ministerial students in its theological school attests.

The Christian Reformed Church has enjoyed much greater success in the Dominican Republic, a nation that occupies about two-thirds of the island of Hispaniola, the first Spanish colony in the New World. The brutal policies of the colonial rulers eliminated the indigenous population quickly after the Spaniards arrived in 1493. In the seventeenth century France took that part of the island that is now Haiti, and in 1795 Spain formally ceded that territory to France. A revolt of Dominican Creoles in 1808 restored Spanish rule in that part of the island, but further exploitation led to the ouster of the Spaniards and a declaration of independence for the Dominican Republic in 1821. Early in the twentieth century the country fell under the rule of gangsters who stole tax revenues and left the Republic unable to pay its debts to European powers, which threatened to foreclose on the state. The United States then invoked the Monroe Doctrine and assumed control of the Dominican government and its revenues. An audit of Dominican finances showed 90 percent of every dollar collected in taxes had disappeared, and no one would account for the losses. Not until 1924 did the Dominican Republic once more govern itself.

Because of its Spanish and French heritage, this country has a large majority of Catholics, with only 11 percent of the people claiming a Protestant persuasion. Free Methodists from the United States organized the first Protestant mission there, and the Protestant Episcopal Church soon followed. Pentecostal groups also initiated work, as did several nondenominational evangelical missions. There was no serious effort to implant the Reformed faith in the Dominican Republic until the 1970s, when the Christian Reformed Church in North America took the lead.

Reformed believers in Puerto Rico received inquiries from people in the Dominican Republic who had become interested in Calvinistic doctrines about which they had learned through radio broadcasts. The Christian Reformed Church then dispatched Ray Brink and Neal Hegeman and their wives as its missionaries to the Republic, where they did most of their work among Haitians who had crossed the border to take jobs in agriculture. Church services for those people were in Creole, but eventually Spanish-speaking congregations were formed to minister to native Dominicans. In 1990 the two language groups agreed to form separate classes of the Christian Reformed Church in the Dominican Republic, and at the end of that century the church claimed some ten thousand adherents in eighty-eight local congregations and numerous preaching stations. The Three Forms of Unity comprise the official doctrinal standard, and the church maintains membership in the Reformed Ecumenical Council.

Haiti

Long a base for French pirates in the Caribbean Sea, Haiti is the western part of the island of Hispaniola. In 1664 the French West India Company seized this territory from the Spaniards, and France ruled it ineptly and oppressively until 1795, when a revolt secured independence. In 1804 the country declared itself a republic after one of the few successful slave revolts in history. Most Haitians are descendants of black Africans imported as slaves to replace the indigenous Indians who were decimated by disease to which they had no previous exposure.

Because of their African heritage, most Haitians practice voodoo in conjunction with Roman Catholicism and fail to see any serious tensions between the two religions. Only an educated minority speaks French, while the illiterate majority converses in Creole. Haiti's experience with self-government has been through a long era of incompetent and often criminal mismanagement that has left it the poorest country in the Western Hemisphere. As in the Dominican Republic, the United States has intervened more than once (as recently as 1994) to restore order and to stop massive violence.

The prevalence of voodoo has produced a bizarre and untraditional form of Catholicism, and Protestant mission efforts have encountered much difficulty in Haiti, ever since some Wesleyans arrived there in 1816, only to experience persecution that forced them to withdraw. In the 1820s, however, the government of Haiti invited black people from the United States to settle there, and those who did so brought their Protestant faith with them. Baptist missionaries from the United States and the United Kingdom also brought their beliefs, as did agents of the Protestant Episcopal Church who arrived in 1861. The Baptists have been the most successful in gaining converts, although other denominations also have made considerable progress, and about 20 percent of Haiti's people now espouse some expression of Protestantism.

In 1986 the Christian Reformed Church in North America entered Haiti as an extension of its work in the Dominican Republic. Two Dominican pastors, Obelto Cheribin and Emilio Martinez, went to Haiti to promote theological education for Protestants of the country. The John Calvin Institute of Port-au-Prince is the fruit of their endeavor, as is a Christian Reformed congregation in that city. In 1991 the government of the Dominican Republic repatriated about seventy thousand Haitians, some of whom had embraced the Christian Reformed Church in the land where they had been working. This led to the formal organization of that church in Haiti, as about 1,250 people professed that religion and joined the church. The North American parent denomination and its World Relief Committee have worked together to meet both the spiritual and material needs of impoverished believers in this very poor nation. By the year 2000 twenty-six local assemblies and three preaching stations comprised the Christian Reformed Church in Haiti. Like its North American patron, this body ordains women and affirms the Three Forms of Unity as its confessional statement.

Presbyterians too have recently established a Reformed witness in Haiti, principally through the work of Charles Amicy (1960–), a native Haitian converted from Catholicism and educated at Greenville Presbyterian Theological Seminary, from which he graduated in 1995. Since returning to Haiti, this remarkable evangelist has helped to establish the Reformed faith in his region through planting five Presbyterian congregations with an aggregate membership of about nine hundred. This growing church operates four Christian schools, a pharmacy, and a medical clinic, and is on the verge of forming a presbytery. In 2007 Octavius Defils (1968–), another former Catholic, one with a voodoo background, graduated from the same seminary and returned to his homeland to assist in the work of the church there. These exceptional pastors often experience opposition from enemies of the gospel, and thievery, threats, and various forms of violence confront them often. They receive support from the Presbyterian Church in America through its Mission to the World, and individual congregations such as Second Presbyterian Church, Greenville, South Carolina, and Independent Presbyterian Church, Atlanta, Georgia, have been especially generous with financial support and by sending short-term missions to Haiti to assist this growing church. Recent accusations of moral and financial corruption against Charles Amicy have caused some contributors to withdraw support for his ministry. Octavius Defils, however, continues to receive assistance from Presbyterian sources in the United States.

SUGGESTED ADDITIONAL READINGS >>

Brereton, Bridget. *A History of Modern Trinidad, 1783–1962*. Kingston, Jamaica: privately printed, 1981.

Dussel, Enrique. *The Church in Latin America, 1492–1992*. Maryknoll, N.Y.: Orbis Books, 1992.

Gonzalez, Justo L. *The Development of Christianity in the Latin Caribbean*. Grand Rapids: Eerdmans, 1969.

Hageman, A. L. and P. E. Wheaton, eds. *Religion in Cuba Today*. New York: Association Press, 1971.

McGavran, D. A. *Church Growth in Jamaica*. Lucknow, India: Lucknow, 1962.

Rogozinski, Jan. *A Brief History of the Caribbean*. 6th ed. Princeton, N.J.: Recording for the Blind, 2003.

Simpson, G. E. *Religious Cults of the Caribbean*. 3rd ed. Rio Piedras, Puerto Rico: Institute for Caribbean Studies, 1980.

TWENTY-TWO

South America

The first Protestant attempt to evangelize in South America occurred in Brazil, when about three hundred French Reformed believers known as Huguenots arrived in 1555 on an island off the coast. They went to the New World with the encouragement of Admiral Gaspard de Coligny (1519–1572) and King Henry II (r. 1547–1559) and erected Fort Coligny and founded a colony under the supervision of Nicolas Durand de Villegaignon (ca. 1510–1571), who then appealed to John Calvin to send ministers to serve the spiritual needs of the settlers. Soon two Reformed pastors, Pierre Rechier (d. 1580) and Guillaume Charretier (d. 1601), reached Brazil in May 1557, along with another two hundred Protestants. Although Admiral Coligny would soon become the heroic leader of persecuted Protestants in France, Villegaignon rather quickly professed Catholicism and initiated repression of Huguenots in the colony. He may have done so to ingratiate himself with Portuguese authorities, whose king had asserted sovereignty over the land. Forcibly expelled from the island, the Reformed believers sailed for France on a barely seaworthy vessel with inadequate provisions. Some of them starved during the voyage, while others survived by eating rats and mice and even leather from their luggage and shoes. Meanwhile the colony itself languished, and Villegaignon left for France late in 1558. This first effort to establish a Reformed presence in South America had failed. A few Protestants who had fled to the mainland tried to evangelize the natives, but Portuguese officials persecuted them.

A second attempt at planting the Reformed faith in Brazil occurred in 1624, when the Netherlands took control of a portion of the Atlantic coast and ruled it for thirty years. Pastors from the Dutch Reformed Church proclaimed the gospel to both colonists and natives. When the Portuguese regained that territory, however, the Protestant mission had to cease its work, and there would not be another such endeavor for about two centuries.

Active Protestant Missions in Brazil

Previous repressions notwithstanding, by the second half of the nineteenth century, several Protestant missions from North America were active in Brazil. They were able to function there because the nation had been independent since 1822, and the new monarchy implemented a liberal policy of toleration toward religious diversity. Methodists, Baptists, Anglicans, and others were already engaged in Brazil when Robert Kalley, M.D., a Scotsman of Reformed conviction but without Presbyterian endorsement, arrived in Rio de Janeiro in 1855, after previous missionary service in Madeira. Kalley's medical ministry made him acceptable and enabled him to withstand Catholic opposition and occasional violence against his facility. The doctor remained at his post until 1875, supported for the most part by Congregational churches in the United Kingdom.

About the same time Kalley was serving the spiritual and health needs of Brazilians, James C. Fletcher (1823–1901) was engaging in evangelism in Rio de Janeiro and its environs, and he too was a Reformed believer without the support of a Presbyterian church. The first official Presbyterian missionary in Brazil was Ashbel Green Simonton (1853–1867), an Old School believer from the United States educated at Princeton Theological Seminary, where a sermon by theologian Charles Hodge convinced him to dedicate himself to service abroad. Simonton arrived in August 1859 and quickly demonstrated great zeal and energy in church planting, thereby providing a solid foundation for Presbyterian growth in the future. In 1860 Alexander L. Blackford (1829–1890) and his wife joined Simonton and assisted the acceleration of planting new congregations. Before long additional missionaries from both the Northern and Southern Presbyterian churches in the United States followed, and the Presbyterian Church of Brazil, by the end of the nineteenth century, had become the strongest Protestant body in the nation, with the city of San Paulo as the center of its strength.

Once well settled in Brazil, Presbyterians established many schools on all levels of instruction, and their Mackenzie Institute became a renowned university with thousands of students enrolled. In 1888 the Northern and Southern Presbyterian missions united to create a single Presbyterian Church of Brazil. Several excellent clinics and hospitals plus a publishing house further strengthened the Presbyterian presence, the progress of which Roman Catholic opposition was unable to thwart.

Late in the nineteenth century, theological disputes related to the rising tide of liberalism caused divisions among Brazilian Presbyterians, one of the first such issues being the church's position regarding Freemasonry. The failure of the church to reject this movement as incompatible with the Christian faith led Pastor Eduardo Carlos Pereira (1856–1923) to organize a secession that formed the Independent Presbyterian Church of Brazil in 1903, a denomination that soon gained many adherents across the country and claimed a membership of over one hundred thousand by the year 2000. Although this church affirms the Westminster Confession of Faith, it ordains female ministers, whereas the older Presbyterian Church of Brazil, now almost 500 thousand strong, endorses the same Reformed doctrinal standard but does not ordain women. Both denominations are members of the World Alliance of Reformed Churches.

Fragmentation among Presbyterians in Brazil continued through the next century, as in 1940, eleven congregations left the Independent Presbyterian Church to form the Conservative Presbyterian Church. Although this body has fewer than five thousand members, it has recently demonstrated impressive vitality in creating its own seminary and organizing a synod. It maintains close relations with the Presbyterian Church in America, another conservative and growing denomination. A Fundamentalist Presbyterian Church came into being in 1956 in northeastern Brazil, once more a product of doctrinal disputes. With about two thousand members, this group has its own synod and cooperates with other fundamentalist organizations such as the International Council of Christian Churches.

Pentecostal influences too have agitated disagreements among Brazilian Presbyterians as creation of the Renewed Presbyterian Church attests. Contrary to orthodox Reformed theology, which contends the miraculous gifts of the Holy Spirit ceased at the completion of the New Testament revelation, some members of the Independent Presbyterian Church accepted Pentecostal teaching about extrabiblical revelation and founded a denomination of their own in 1968, as did a second group in 1972. Merger of these two produced a single Renewed Church, which, as of 1999, claimed fifty-seven thousand members. Rather than affirm the Westminster Standards, which insist upon the sole authority of Scripture, this church endorses the Apostles' Creed and espouses distinctively Pentecostal doctrines while retaining Presbyterian polity. It does not ordain women. The church has about 270 congregations and operates its own publishing house and two schools for ministerial education.

The refusal of the original Presbyterian Church of Brazil to ordain women aroused complaints that led to formation of the United Presbyterian

Church of Brazil in 1978. This liberal, ecumenical denomination of about fifty-two hundred members in eighty congregations is an affiliate of the World Alliance of Reformed Churches and the World Council of Churches. It professes to endorse almost all the historic Reformed confessions but seems to attach little importance to their contents.

In addition to the bodies already cited, there are several ethnic churches in Brazil that seek to serve immigrants who have Reformed connections. There are at least three Korean churches with an aggregate membership of forty-two hundred, all of which, in principal, affirm the Westminster Standards. They all minister in Korean language services but differ among themselves about the proper role for women in the offices of the church. All have close relations with the Presbyterian Church of Korea. One Japanese, one Taiwanese, one Canadian, and two Dutch bodies, all of them quite small, likewise espouse the Reformed faith in Brazil.

The current state of the Presbyterian Church (U.S.A.), with its policy of ordaining women ministers and its refusal to condemn homosexuality as sin, has had profound effects upon its interchurch relations with Presbyterians in Brazil. Strained relations between the major Reformed denomination in America and the Presbyterian Church of Brazil became evident as early as 1973, when the Brazilian church complained that Presbyterian missionaries from the United States were teaching so-called liberation theology, which portrayed Jesus as the emancipator of economically impoverished peoples rather than the Savior from sin. This led to a severing of ties between the Brazilians and the Northern Presbyterian church in America. When the Northern and Southern churches merged, the Brazilian church cut its ties with the newly united denomination. All efforts to restore relations have failed, and a resurgence of Reformed theology in Brazil has widened the gap. Brazilian scholars have been translating the works of such distinguished Reformed theologians as John Calvin, B. B. Warfield, Charles Hodge, and J. Gresham Machen, and pastors have shown considerable receptivity to these authors, their Calvinistic forefathers. When the Supreme Council of the Presbyterian Church of Brazil considered a motion to restore relations with the Presbyterian Church (U.S.A.), that assembly defeated the measure by a vote of eight hundred to eight.

Brazilian Presbyterians have within their ranks some excellent academic theologians educated in the United States, Europe, and South Africa, many of them staunchly orthodox in their subscription to the Reformed faith. As influential leaders in the Presbyterian Church of Brazil, they have retarded

moves toward liberalism and so maintained their denomination's adherence
to the Westminster Confession of Faith. Although Pentecostal churches
have made the greatest gains in recent years, Brazilian Presbyterians too
have grown, often at the expense of the Roman Church, which has been
losing thousands of members each year.

In addition to church bodies in Brazil that bear the name Presbyterian,
there are others that practice that form of polity and espouse Calvinist
doctrine, at least in general. Among them are the Evangelical Reformed
Churches of Brazil, originally a Dutch immigrant church brought to Brazil
in 1911. After a period of uncertainty about their precise doctrinal identity,
the settlers established a relationship with the Reformed Church in America and the Reformed Churches in the Netherlands. The first organized
congregations of this body did not appear until 1933, when it took the
name Reformed Evangelical Church in Brazil but later changed its name
to the one now in use. This denomination reported about twenty-seven
hundred members at the end of the last century; it affirms the Westminster
Standards plus the Belgic Confession and the Heidelberg Catechism. The
church, nevertheless, ordains female elders and deacons but not pastors. It
is a member of the World Alliance of Reformed Churches and has close
relations with the Reformed Churches in the Netherlands. A Reformed
Church of Brazil, planted by Canadian Calvinists in the 1970s, has some
two hundred members, while the Reformed Church of Colombo, related
to the Reformed Churches (Liberated) in the Netherlands, has but one
congregation and fewer than one hundred members.

Argentina

In contrast with the impressive growth of the Reformed faith in Brazil,
the Presbyterian story in South America's second largest nation is dis-
heartening. Discovered by the Spaniards in 1516, this country remained
under colonial rule until 1816. It did not attain to political stability until
the adoption of a constitution in 1853, and Buenos Aires, the largest city,
did not submit to the authority of a national government until 1880. For
most of the nineteenth century the land was in turmoil, and the dominant
Roman Catholic Church lost credibility due to the generally poor quality
of its clerics and overall neglect of its members. Into this situation in 1820
stepped James Thomson (1788–1854), a dynamic Scottish Baptist serving
with the British and Foreign Bible Society, who traveled widely in Latin
America distributing the Scriptures and establishing schools. In the midst

of Argentina's political turbulence, the Roman Church could not resist the advent of Protestantism effectively, as many liberals resented that church and therefore favored an alternative version of Christianity. The national government so appreciated Thomson's work in education that it conferred honorary citizenship upon him, as did Chile.

The first major effort to establish a Protestant church in Argentina was the work of Methodists from the United States, who arrived in 1836. Scottish Presbyterians and Anglicans had appeared a decade earlier, but as chaplains to minister to English-speaking people only. It was not until 1886 that immigrants from Holland founded the Reformed Churches in Argentina, and so exponents of historic Calvinism had a rather late start in their mission to Argentina.

One of the earlier Protestant groups to appear in this country was the Evangelical Waldensian Church established by settlers from Italy in 1860. Although the Waldenses had a historical connection with the Reformed faith since William Farel, a coworker with John Calvin, introduced them to Protestant doctrines, they were no longer committed to that system of belief, although they did practice a semi-Presbyterian polity. The Waldenses soon spread into Uruguay, where they now enjoy a stronger position than they do in Argentina.

Like their Italian counterparts, German immigrants too settled in Argentina, where they founded the Evangelical Church of the River Plate in 1843. This was something of a hybrid with Reformed and Lutheran elements evident, a phenomenon that reflected concurrent church union moves in Germany. The growth of this German language ministry was slow, retarded perhaps by the church's public identity as the Evangelical German Synod, the name in use until 1965, when the current name was adopted.

In its present form the Evangelical Church of the River Plate reports about forty-five thousand members in sixty congregations. It affirms both Martin Luther's Small Catechism and the Heidelberg Catechism, thereby reflecting the composite character of the church. It holds membership in the World Alliance of Reformed Churches and the Lutheran World Federation as well as the World Council of Churches. It does ordain women and is, in general, a liberal expression of Protestantism.

As indicated above, Scottish Presbyterians arrived in Argentina in 1829. The Church of Scotland supported this ministry to English-speaking people at first but eventually terminated that aid. Not until 1986 did St. Andrew's Presbyterian Church, as this body became known, initiate an outreach to

Spanish-speaking Argentines. Eventually this group obtained support from the Evangelical Presbyterian denomination in the United States. St. Andrew's Presbyterian Church subscribes to the Westminster Confession of Faith, but like its American patron, it ordains women. Some two thousand people hold membership in this body, the affiliations of which are confined to Latin American organizations.

As are many other nations, Argentina is the site of Korean missionary endeavors. By the end of the twentieth century three Korean denominations were engaged there. They reported an aggregate membership of about five thousand. All three churches profess allegiance to the Westminster Standards and other Reformed documents. The Central Presbyterian Church of Buenos Aires is the largest of these bodies and is a presbytery of the Korean Presbyterian Church of America.

American Presbyterians' involvement in Argentina extends to 1853, but like earlier Scottish efforts, did not prosper, and by 1859, the American project had ceased. Meanwhile the St. Andrew's Presbyterian Church experienced serious internal dissensions and suffered from an exodus of Scottish-Argentines from the country. This church addressed its problems by seeking additional ecumenical connections, a step that has often been a last resort for failing denominations.

In 1985 Pastor Antonio Gomez, with support from the Evangelical Presbyterian Church in the United States, established the Argentine Presbyterian Church in Rosario, a movement that soon became self-sustaining, although it still has only a few hundred adherents and one congregation. Espousing the Westminster Standards and the Canons of Dort, this church nevertheless seeks ecumenical relations of a broadly evangelical character and ordains women as elders and deacons.

While Presbyterian and Reformed churches in Argentina have languished, Pentecostals have flourished and now outnumber all other Protestant bodies combined.

Chile

Soon after Ferdinand Magellan (1480–1521) discovered the southern tip of South America, Spain claimed the region and so ruled Chile until 1810 and imported Catholicism, with which 77 percent of the people still identify, but often in an only nominal way. As in Argentina, James Thomson was a pioneer in introducing the Protestant faith. He arrived in 1821 as an agent of the British and Foreign Bible Society and to promote the Lancaster System of education then popular in the United Kingdom. Thomson did not remain in Chile long, even though there was considerable receptivity toward his efforts in education. David Trumbull (1819–1889) was the first resident Protestant missionary, an emissary of the Congregational mission society, who settled at Valparaiso in 1845 and invested over twenty-five years of service in the country. In 1873 Trumbull's mission agency transferred its work in Chile to the Presbyterian Church (U.S.A.), and he immediately joined the Presbyterian mission.

The Chilean government did not allow Protestants to evangelize the Catholic population, so Trumbull at first concentrated his ministry on seamen visiting the port of Valparaiso, and in 1847 he obtained permission to open a church for English-speaking Protestants, a move that led to erection of an edifice that became a Presbyterian church officially in 1873. Translation of Scripture and Christian literature into Spanish was a major emphasis of this mission, a project that progressed in the face of Catholic opposition. Gradually the Presbyterians spread across much of Chile, but their numbers have never been large. Organization of a presbytery occurred in 1883.

By 1889, when David Trumbull died, several Presbyterian missionaries were active in Chile, and the Presbyterian Church of Chile was functioning as a member of the Synod of New York. During the twentieth century, however, disagreements between missionaries and native church leaders became intense, related to some extent to the modernist-fundamentalist controversies in the United States. This led in 1944 to a division in which some conservative pastors and elders formed the National Presbyterian Church, an evangelistic body that quickly initiated church planting, especially as dissidents left the older denomination and sought to form new congregations. This division was only the beginning of what became a pattern of schisms, as some members of the National Presbyterian Church concluded that it too was no longer orthodox. In 1960 people of that conviction founded the Fundamentalist National Presbyterian Church and affiliated with the International Council of Christian Churches, of which Bible Presbyterian Pastor Carl McIntire of Collingswood, New Jersey, was the leader. The remaining National Presbyterian Church, denying any departure from orthodoxy, established relations with the Presbyterian Church in America and with the Reformed Churches in the Netherlands.

During the era of schisms, the original Presbyterian body continued to experience dissension within its own ranks, as its leaders quarreled about doctrine and procedures, and the Presbyterian Church (U.S.A.) began reducing its presence in Chile. In 1964 the Presbyterian Church of Chile declared itself independent. The liberal faction within that denomination, however, restored relations with the Presbyterian Church (U.S.A.) in 1972 by constituting itself as the Evangelical Presbyterian Church and joined the World Alliance of Reformed Churches and the Latin American Council of Churches. In the 1980s the Presbyterian Church in America decided to focus the work of its mission in Chile on planting new congregations, and so its missionaries left the National Presbyterian Church to the natives and initiated a vigorous and successful church extension program.

By the opening of the twentieth century, the Presbyterian Church of Chile had about nineteen hundred members in twenty-five congregations, refrained from ordaining females as pastors but allowed them to be elders and deacons, and held membership in the World Alliance of Reformed Churches while affirming the historic Reformed confessions. The National Presbyterian Church was only slightly smaller, with fourteen hundred members in twenty-five congregations and the same official position on doctrine but did not ordain women officers. Two theological institutes provided education for ministers and church workers. The National Fundamentalist Presbyterian Church reported some five hundred members, while the liberal Evangelical Presbyterian Church had about six hundred. The five relatively new congregations connected with the mission of the Presbyterian Church in America are still small, but the one in Santiago has about two hundred adherents, and one of the other four is now well organized and recognized as a particular Presbyterian church.

Toward the end of the last century Presbyterians from Korea arrived in Chile, and three churches of this nationality now minister there. In 1982 the Presbyterian Church in Korea-Tong Hap sent Lim Soon-Sam initially to be pastor to Koreans living in Chile, but Lim quickly extended his outreach by cooperating with the National Presbyterian Church to seek converts among native Chileans. He was instrumental in establishing five local assemblies in the area of Santiago, and at his urging, the church in Korea dispatched more missionaries, thereby accelerating the work and taking it beyond the environs of the capital city. In conjunction with the National Presbyterian Church, these Korean pastors organized the Christian Presbyterian Church of Chile, a body inclusive of both Koreans and Chileans. The Korean missionaries and the natives together formed a presbytery that has twelve congregations and about seven hundred members. The church does not ordain women, and it espouses the Westminster Confession, the

Heidelberg Catechism, and other Reformed documents. It maintains close relations with its parent church in Korea and with the Presbyterian Church (U.S.A.). A separate Korean Presbyterian Church of Chile has only one congregation of approximately four hundred members, almost all of them ethnic Koreans, and it is connected to the Presbyterian Church in America. The smallest Korean Presbyterian body is a Pentecostal assembly known as the Korean United Church in Chile. Established by missionaries, it has only about 350 members and is closely related to the Korean American Presbyterian Church. Even though Pentecostal practices are popular in Chile, this church has not grown significantly.

Uruguay and Paraguay

The advent of Protestantism in Uruguay was due to a migration of Italian Waldenses that began in 1856, when Jean Pierre Planchon, a young adherent to that faith, landed at Montevideo. After finding employment and concluding the country was a suitable place to live, Planchon urged his fellow Waldenses to follow him to Uruguay, and about seventy of them did so the next year. This initial migration led to others, and soon Waldenses were settled not only in Uruguay but in Argentina, Paraguay, and Brazil as well.

The immigrants soon established the Evangelical Waldensian Church of the River Plate as a South American extension of their parent church in Italy. Economic hardships in Italy and the memory of recent persecutions at the hands of the Catholic Church prompted this exodus to the New World. The first pastor for these Waldenses did not arrive until 1860, but within a few years their strength was sufficient to create in Buenos Aires a Union Theological Seminary as a joint project with Methodists from the United States who had arrived in Uruguay in 1839.

Once settled in Uruguay, the Waldenses founded a number of schools and eventually a lyceum which gained government approval as a preparatory school for students who aspired to attend a university. Parallel with these endeavors was a vigorous publishing ministry with several periodicals in print at various times.

To their good fortune, by the time the Waldenses situated in Uruguay, the Roman Catholic Church there had been declining for some time, and the nation was on its way to becoming the most secular society in South America. Political turbulence followed the securing of independence in 1825. At first the new republic acknowledged Catholicism as the official religion but allowed freedom for other faiths, but the involvement of the

Roman clergy in partisan politics led to separation of church and state in 1918. By then only about 25 percent of the people were attending Catholic services, and even that number declined thereafter. An anticlerical party known as the *Colorados* gradually imposed restrictions upon the Roman Church, even prior to depriving it of its status as the official faith. In contrast with its fortunes in some other Latin states, the Catholic Church in Uruguay has not been powerful, and its first bishop did not take up residence there until 1878. It became customary to refer to Christmas as Family Day and to Holy Week as Tourist Week. Religious conviction is not a prominent feature of life in Uruguay.

In spite of the strongly secular atmosphere in the country, a few Protestant churches of a somewhat Reformed character have taken root in Uruguay, with the Waldenses leading the way. Their church in 1999 reported a membership of 13,700 in twenty-five congregations, but some of them are in Argentina. All church offices are open to women, and the polity approximates that of Presbyterian churches in other lands. In addition to the ancient ecumenical creeds, this church affirms the Waldensian Confession of 1655. Historic Reformed theology, however, appears to receive little emphasis, and the Waldensians' closest interchurch relations are with the Methodists in their own country and in Argentina, although there is some connection with the Presbyterian Church (U.S.A.) as well. The Waldensian Evangelical Church of the River Plate is a member of the World Alliance of Reformed Churches and the World Council of Churches.

The only other identifiable Reformed body in Uruguay is the Reformed Evangelical Uruguayan-Hungarian Church, which immigrants from Hungary planted in 1919. There was some increase in this community when believers fled from Soviet oppression after the Hungarian revolt in 1956. This church, however, is very small and shows no signs of vitality.

The development of a Reformed witness in Paraguay is only slightly more encouraging than that in Uruguay. Independent since 1811, Paraguay began its life as a nation with the prospect of rapid growth, but conflicts leading to wars with its neighbors were costly and retarded political and economic progress. As in most Latin states, Roman Catholicism is the major religion, but few Paraguayans are fervent for that faith. Methodists and Disciples of Christ from the United States initiated missions there late in the nineteenth century, but the Methodists left in 1918, after arranging for the Disciples to assume full responsibility for that work. As the next century progressed, several Protestant denominations appeared, but

Presbyterian and Reformed efforts are of recent origin, the first being a mission from the Presbyterian Church of Brazil in 1970. Not until 1984 were native Paraguayan pastors ready to provide leadership. The Presbyterian Church in Paraguay, which has developed as a consequence of the Brazilian initiative, has produced only five local assemblies and barely two hundred church members. Like its Brazilian parent denomination, this body affirms the Westminster Standards and refrains from ordaining females.

A more promising phenomenon is the Reformed Presbyterian Church-Korean Mission in Paraguay, begun in 1975 as a ministry to ethnic Koreans who had settled in Asuncion, the capital city. As the Korean community grew, some individual congregations united to form a mission connected to the Korean Presbyterian Church of America through that denomination's South American Presbytery. The Korean Reformed Presbyterian Church quickly extended its outreach to Spanish-speaking peoples and therefore cooperated with the National Presbyterian Church of Chile in establishing a seminary in which the language of instruction was to be Spanish. The Reformed Presbyterian Church had about twenty-five hundred in two congregations and twenty-one preaching stations at the end of the last century. The Westminster Confession of Faith is the church's official statement of doctrine, and it does not ordain women.

The Korean United Church began in 1965 as the work of immigrants of a Calvinistic persuasion, but its polity is only semi-Presbyterian. With only a few more than seven hundred adherents in one congregation at the end of the twentieth century, this body ministers in both Korean and Spanish and is an autonomous body without evident interchurch connections. It does not ordain female officers.

In addition to the Brazilian and Korean missions to Paraguay, there is an effort begun by Taiwanese believers in 1978. Chou Shen Chong, a Taiwanese pastor in Brazil, led in forming a congregation of Presbyterians of his own ethnicity in Asuncion. Although this is a ministry in Spanish as well as Chinese, and the church conducts substantial works of charity, growth has been very slow, and barely one hundred people held membership as of 1999, and no resident pastor was then on the scene. The Westminster Confession and the Heidelberg Catechism are its doctrinal statements, and the church maintains close relations with the Presbyterian Church of Taiwan. It does ordain women as church officers. In general Christianity has not prospered in Uruguay and Paraguay, and the Reformed churches, being late arrivals, have yet to demonstrate much influence in this predominantly secular culture.

Bolivia

A country with a large Indian minority, Bolivia was a Spanish possession until 1825, when it gained independence through the dynamic efforts of Simon Bolivar (1783–1830), who led a revolt against the colonial rulers. Independence was, however, a mixed blessing, as uprising followed uprising and kept the country in turmoil. The first Protestant approach to Bolivia was the work of Methodist evangelist and later bishop William Taylor (1821–1902), who founded a mission station at Antofagasta in 1878. That site, however, soon passed to the rule of Chile, which left no access to Bolivia at that time. Not until 1901 did the Methodists establish a lasting mission in Bolivia and then in La Paz. Baptists from Canada also arrived in the country, as did several nondenominational missions in the first half of the twentieth century, while Reformed churches in America and Europe directed their missionary outreach elsewhere. As a consequence it was late in the 1970s before Presbyterians arrived in Bolivia, and then it was Koreans and Brazilians that took the lead. By the year 2000 several presbyteries were in operation, as seven Reformed bodies were conducting their ministries. These missions are related to the Presbyterian Church of Korea-Tong Hap, the Korean Presbyterian Church of America, and the Presbyterian Church of Brazil.

Founded in 1986, the Korean Presbyterian Mission in Santa Cruz de la Sierra II is the largest of these movements. At the end of the twentieth century it had five thousand members. It does not ordain women, and it maintains two schools. The Westminster Standards comprise its doctrinal position. The first congregation of this same connection is the Korean Presbyterian Mission in Santa Cruz de la Sierra I, and it reported fifteen hundred members in 1999. The issue of ordaining females has caused dissension among Korean Presbyterians in Bolivia, but as of the end of the last century, most churches refrained from the practice.

A Brazilian contribution to the development of a Reformed witness in Bolivia came through Pastor Joao Carlos de Paula Mota, whom the Presbyterian Church of Brazil sent there to work in Couhabana. With the assistance of additional workers from his homeland, Mota was able to expand that ministry to several more cities, although this Presbyterian Church of Bolivia reported only two congregations in 1999. The Presbyterian

Church in America has recently adopted Bolivia as one of its mission fields and now has one missionary family working there.

Peru

Once the center of a vast Inca Empire, Peru became a Spanish possession when Francisco Pizarro (1470–1541) led his brutal *conquistadores* in subduing the Indians, thereby initiating a long era of exploitation that did not end until a war of rebellion secured independence in 1821. The end of repressive Spanish rule did not, however, terminate the country's troubles, as political factions pursued their objectives with great violence.

The Spaniards brought the Roman Catholic Church, to which most Peruvians still adhere, although Protestant churches have made impressive gains since the government granted full freedom of religion, a measure enacted into law in 1915. Prior to that Catholicism was the official faith, and competing religions were illegal. Catholic clerics taught religion in public schools, and the state subsidized the Roman Church financially. Since relatively few natives became priests or nuns, clerics came from Spain and France to serve in Peru. Some of the priests brought discredit upon their own church by greedily enriching themselves at the expense of their parishioners. Some younger native priests, on the other hand, displayed a liberal attitude unusual for that era, and when James Thomson appeared as a representative of the British and Foreign Bible Society, they encouraged distribution of the Scriptures. As he did elsewhere, Thomson impressed the civil authorities with his proposals for education, but he remained in the country only two years. He did establish some schools nevertheless while, at the same time, spreading Protestant teachings through the ongoing circulation of the Scriptures. There were, however, few converts during his sojourn there. The American Bible Society continued that work after Thomson left for Central America and another missionary endeavor.

Methodists from the United States were the first Protestants to establish a lasting ministry in Peru. William Taylor once more was instrumental in the outreach of his church. He appeared in Peru in 1877, but when he departed to assume a bishopric in Africa, the Methodist mission declined and eventually went defunct, only to be revived in 1891.

Another Protestant pioneer in Peru was Francisco G. Penzotti (1851–1925), a Waldense from Uruguay who endured persecution at the hands of Catholic zealots. His conversion had been due to Methodist influence, and he did not proclaim distinctively Reformed doctrines despite the Calvinistic heritage of his church in Italy. Much of Penzotti's ministry involved distribution of the Scriptures in conjunction with the American Bible Society.

The introduction of a Reformed witness in Peru was the work of John Ritchie (1878–1952), a Scottish Presbyterian serving with the Regions beyond Missionary Union. This zealous, dynamic Calvinist cooperated with the American Bible Society and became involved in the struggle for freedom of religion in Peru. He helped to form the Evangelical Church of Peru in 1922 and was a leader in the creation of the National Evangelical Council of Peru in 1940. A productive author, Ritchie published several periodicals and a book titled *Indigenous Church Principles in Theory and Practice*, a significant contribution to missiology.

The Free Church of Scotland entered Peru in 1912, where its personnel founded the College of St. Andrew in Lima, an institution that quickly acquired a reputation for academic excellence. John A. Mackay (1889–1983) was the first principal of the college and later became president of Princeton Theological Seminary. The Free Church established several congregations at various points in the capital city.

Due to the labors of Scots and Americans, two Presbyterian churches have developed in Peru alongside the older Evangelical Church, which remains the largest of the Reformed denominations in the land, with a membership of over twenty thousand. This body maintains a generally Presbyterian polity and endorses the Westminster Confession while maintaining fraternal relations with the other two Reformed churches. It does not ordain women as ministers or elders but does permit them to serve as deacons. The Evangelical Church of Peru, although officially Calvinistic, cooperates with the Christian Missionary Alliance from the United States, which is, for the most part, an Arminian mission.

The two newer Reformed bodies are the Evangelical Presbyterian Church of Peru and the National Presbyterian Church, which, in 1995, merged to become the Evangelical Presbyterian and Reformed Church in Peru. The first of the two uniting bodies had been a product of missionaries of the Free Church of Scotland, of which John A. Mackay was a leading scholar. This group erected its first church building in 1936 and held its first General Assembly in 1963. It had five presbyteries and about three thousand members at the time of the merger. Spanish was the sole language of its ministries.

The work of the National Presbyterian Church had begun in 1936 under the leadership of American missionary Alonzo Hitchcock, who began evangelizing in the area of Ayocucho. Soon a team of translators was rendering Scripture into the Indian Quechua language. By 1963 this church had some eight thousand members organized into eleven presbyteries and was conducting services in both Spanish and Quechua.

The combining of these two denominations produced a church of approximately fifteen thousand members and 136 congregations at the end of the last century. The united church adopted the historic Reformed confessions and now maintains close relations with the Free Church of Scotland and some Reformed bodies in the Netherlands. It is a member of the Evangelical Council of Peru.

The prospect for substantial growth of the Reformed faith in Peru appears promising. The Presbyterian Church in America has made that nation one of its primary mission fields and has sent a large and growing number of its agents there through Mission to the World, the foreign mission arm of that denomination. Civil authorities in several locales have welcomed the missionaries, especially those engaged in educational and medical services.

Ecuador

As in some other Latin American states, James Thomson of the British and Foreign Bible Society was the Protestant pioneer in Ecuador, arriving there in 1824 to distribute Bibles. Among eager recipients of the Scriptures were residents of a monastery who purchased twenty-five copies. Never one to remain in an area for long, Thomson proceeded to Colombia, and no other Protestant missionaries appeared to reside in the country until 1896. The Gospel Missionary Union at that point sent its agents even though they expected a hostile reception due to Catholic opposition. To their advantage, however, a political revolution reduced that probability shortly before they arrived. Soon the Christian and Missionary Alliance from the United States entered Ecuador, this time to labor among Indians in Quito and Montecristi, but fierce opposition forced the missionaries to work as inconspicuously as possible, and converts for some time were few. The interdenominational ministry of radio station HCJB, the Voice of the Andes, which began broadcasting in 1931, however, became a major influence in Colombia as well as in Ecuador, where it remains in Quito.

The initial effort to implant a Reformed ministry in Ecuador was a joint enterprise of the Presbyterian Church (U.S.A.), the Presbyterian Church (U.S.), and the United Brethren in conjunction with the Evangelical Waldensian Church of the River Plate in Brazil. This organization, known as the United Andean Mission, began operations near Quito in 1946 with works in evangelism, education, agriculture, and health care. In 1965 these ministries passed to the United Evangelical Church of Ecuador, which the missionaries from North America and Brazil had created. This was the first national Protestant church in the country, a composite body inclusive of congregations from Presbyterian, Methodist, Brethren, and United Church of Christ connections.

The United Evangelical Church, with about fifteen hundred members and fifteen congregations in 1999, had become a hybrid in polity, for congregational elements subsisted along with a synodal structure. The Apostles' Creed is the church's only statement of faith. This body maintains close relations with the United Methodist Church and the Presbyterian Church (U.S.A.) and is a member of the World Alliance of Reformed Churches. This decidedly liberal denomination has opened all church offices to women, and despite its Reformed roots, does not affirm historic Calvinism.

The only genuinely Presbyterian movement in Ecuador at the beginning of this century was the Reformed Presbyterian Church of Ecuador, which began in 1991 through Mission to the World, which now has four missionary families on that field. A presbytery in Quito has five congregations, and a second one is in the process of formation in Guayaquil at the time of this writing. Like the Presbyterian Church in America, its patron, this church affirms the Westminster Standards and does not ordain female officers.

Colombia

Colombia was subject to Spanish rule until 1819 when it, along with Panama, Venezuela, and Ecuador, gained independence through the leadership of Simon Bolivar. The new state of Greater Colombia did not, however, endure, and by 1903 all the constituent members had separated from it. During and after colonial domination, the Roman Catholic Church enjoyed government support, and opposition to Protestants was intense and often violent. Persecutions brought death to evangelicals, and destruction of their property was common. Even after the enactment of laws to protect nonconformists, persecution continued, and civil authorities often ignored it. When moderate conservatives held political power in the republic, they imposed some restrictions on the Roman Church that worked to the advantage of Protestants, and from 1849–1880, an era of liberal government, additional reduction of that church's privileges occurred, as the state decreed freedom of religion. The Catholic Church remained hostile nevertheless, and the public in general supported the posture of the dominant church. In 1902 Colombia signed an agreement with the Vatican by which the state gave lands to that church and promised annual financial subsidies.

After James Thomson appeared in Colombia in 1825, a Catholic backlash soon terminated what seemed to be a promising beginning for Protestantism. The next such effort was a Presbyterian initiative by Henry B. Pratt (1832–1912) in 1856. This graduate of Princeton Theological Seminary, who was a skillful linguist, represented the Presbyterian Church (U.S.A.). Pratt soon put his talent to work by producing a new translation of the Bible into Spanish, which appeared in 1893. The first organized Presbyterian congregation in Colombia became a reality in 1861, but conversions were few for the first twenty years of this ministry. Pratt went home to the United States for a period but returned with his wife. By then his denomination and the Southern Presbyterian Church had invested additional personnel and funds, and the work began to grow. Several excellent schools in Bogotá and Barranquilla attest the effectiveness of this endeavor. In 1888 the Southern Presbyterian Church awarded its assets in Columbia to its northern counterpart. Not until 1957 did the mission become the Presbyterian Church of Colombia, although three native presbyteries had been operating long before. In 1982 Colombian Presbyterians collaborated with those in Venezuela and Ecuador to create a theological seminary to serve the churches in those nations.

Toward the end of the last century, the Presbyterian Church of Colombia experienced much dissension that led to a division of the church into two synods. Due in part to ecclesiastical politics, this contention produced two bodies that did not renounce each other but chose to operate autonomously while remaining parts of a single church. The separation involved dividing church assets by common agreement, and since the two groups could not work together harmoniously, they agreed to disagree. One faction became the Presbyterian Synod, and in 1999 it reported about forty-five hundred members in thirty-five congregations, while the other party declared itself the Reformed Synod, a body of some fifty-seven hundred members in fifteen congregations. Both synods ordain female ministers, and both endorse the Westminster Confession, at least in principal. The two synods are members of the World Council of Churches.

The Cumberland Presbyterian Church from the United States sent a mission to Colombia in 1929, a ministry that has grown to thirty-two local churches and about forty-three hundred members. Most of the local assemblies are in the state of Caldas. Like its North American patron, the Cumberland Presbyterian Church in Colombia affirms the historic Reformed theological documents rather loosely and assigns more importance to the Cumberland modification of the Reformed faith in the direction of Arminian beliefs, so this church is Presbyterian in polity but not Reformed in doctrine.

In addition to those churches that are self-consciously Presbyterian in identity, there are other Reformed bodies, one of which is the Evangelical Reformed Church of Colombia, a ministry of Korean origin that began in 1987 when Pastor Kim Wui-Dong arrived in Bogotá, where he helped to establish several congregations and a theological seminary. At first the Koreans worked with the Reformed Synod but eventually opted for separate identity.

Through much of the 1950s, Colombia was the scene of social and political disorder, which included violence perpetrated against missionaries, but especially against native Protestants. Over two hundred of Colombia's schools were forced to close, many churches and chapels fell victim to arson, and murder of evangelicals was frequent. By the end of 1957, however, a change in civil government and a somewhat conciliatory attitude on the part of the Catholic hierarchy brought relief. In the years 1960 to 1966, the Protestant population almost doubled. Vatican Council II brought further improvements when, in 1965, the Roman Church began referring to Protestants as "separated brethren" rather than heretics. There has been no overt persecution of non-Catholics in Colombia since then, although discrimination against them has been common. In 1973 the hierarchs of the Roman Church endorsed a government policy to recognize freedom of religion for all citizens of the nation.

Venezuela

Credit for liberating Venezuela from Spanish rule belongs to Simon Bolivar, creator of the state of Greater Colombia, of which Venezuela was a component until that structure fragmented. José de San Martín (1778–1850), who led forces fighting for independence in the southern part of South America, assisted Bolivar in the liberation and creation of a Venezuelan republic, even though San Martin favored monarchical regimes for the new Latin states. By 1824 the rebels had prevailed against the Spaniards.

Bolivar regarded the Roman Catholic Church as a force for social stability, although he had no personal affection for its teachings. As Latin peoples became increasingly unruly after obtaining independence, his conviction about the social utility of the Catholic religion grew stronger, so the new Venezuelan government continued state patronage of the Roman Church. The state did, however, impose restrictions upon the clergy and sought to prevent foreign priests from serving in the country. While Antonio Guzman Blanco (1829–1899) ruled as a military dictator in the period 1870 to 1889, the government closed Catholic schools and seminaries and ordered that priests obtain their education in the theology department of the state university. General acceptance of these measures shows the declining influence of the church in the national life, although Catholicism regained a bit of its lost stature after Blanco had to leave the presidency due to a revolt. Foreign priests and nuns were again allowed to work in Venezuela and seminaries reopened, but the overall status of the Catholic Church was weak. Because some of the foreign clerics were Spanish, they were often viewed as enemies of independence and therefore subjected to abuse, even violence. Even after legislation to protect foreign clerics was in place, Catholic missionaries did not regain the influence they had exerted during the era of colonial rule.

The declining position of the Roman Catholic Church in Venezuela made the country somewhat receptive to other expressions of Christianity. The first Protestant undertaking there was the work of Christian Missions in Many Lands, an arm of the Church of the Brethren in the United States, which began in 1883 in Caracas. The Presbyterian Church (U.S.A.) entered the country in 1897, when Theodore and Julia Pond, who had served twenty-five years in Syria and a period in Colombia, moved to Caracas. Their mission began as a response to previous evangelism by Emilio Sylva Bryant, a Spaniard adopted by an English family in Venezuela. Converted as a child, Bryant arrived in the capital city when he was eighteen years old, and he immediately began seeking the salvation of his neighbors. Although he died from tuberculosis at age twenty-four, he had by then gathered a number of converts who in turn became founders of the first Presbyterian congregation in Caracas.

The Ponds were the only Presbyterian missionaries there until 1912, when others arrived. They had enjoyed an enthusiastic reception from Heraclio Osuna, who had been a Presbyterian elder in Colombia. Osuna and his wife had already opened a Christian school, an academy that eventually became the International College of Caracas. Theodore Pond, soon after arriving, became the leader of the Protestant congregation in the capital city, and in 1912 that body organized formally as the Presbyterian Church of Venezuela.

The early growth of the Reformed faith in this country notwithstanding, progress was so slow that a presbytery did not come into being until 1946. At that point additional church planting spread the ministry well beyond Caracas. By 1970, however, the growing popularity of Pentecostalism had taken many adherents from Presbyterian ranks, and conflicts about doctrine related to the appearance of liberation theology caused further departures. The Presbyterian Church of Venezuela lost half of its members and many pastors. In 1983 El Redentor (The Redeemer), the original Presbyterian congregation, divided as controversies continued with devastating consequences. By the end of the twentieth century the Presbyterian Church had fewer than a thousand members and only twenty congregations. This church remains in a much diminished condition and maintains a generally liberal theological posture as a member of various ecumenical organizations, while it ordains women to all offices. Subscription to historic Reformed confessions appears to be only nominal.

El Redentor, the first and largest Presbyterian congregation, withdrew from the Presbyterian Church of Venezuela in 1983 and became a Pentecostal church. There is, however, a staunchly confessional Reformed Faith Church in Barquisimento founded in 1984 by Pastor Cesar Rodriguez, but it had only about two hundred members. This body zealously affirms the Westminster Standards and other traditional Reformed statements, refrains from ordaining women, and maintains close relations with the Reformed Churches (Liberated) in the Netherlands.

SUGGESTED ADDITIONAL READINGS >>

Browning, W. E. *The River Plate Republics: A Survey of Religious, Economic, and Social Conditions in Argentina, Paraguay and Uruguay.* London: World Dominion, 1928.

Dussel, E. *The Church in Latin America, 1492–1992.* London: Burns and Oates, 1992.

Enns, A. W. *Man, Milieu, and Mission in Argentina.* Grand Rapids: Eerdmans, 1971.

Ewell, Judith. *Venezuela: A Century of Change.* Stanford, Calif.: Stanford University Press, 1984.

Goff, J. E. *The Persecution of Protestant Christians in Colombia, 1948–58.* Cuernavaca, Mexico: CIDOC, 1968.

Hamilton, K. E. *Church Growth in the High Andes.* Lucknow, India: Lucknow, 1962.

Kessler, J. B. A. *A Study of the Older Protestant Missions and Churches in Peru and Chile.* Goes, Netherlands: Oosterbaan and Le Contre, 1967.

Klaiber, J. L. *Religion and Revolution in Peru, 1824–1976.* Leiden, Netherlands: E. J. Brill, 1979.

Kragnes, Earl N. *The Evangelical Church in the River Plate Republics.* New York: International Missionary Council, 1943.

Mecham, J. Lloyd. *Church and State in Latin America.* Chapel Hill: University of North Carolina Press, 1966.

Nickerson, R. Andrew and Charles J. Kolinski. *Historical Dictionary of Paraguay.* Metuchen, N.J.: Scarecrow Press, 1993.

Phillips, C. A. *A History of the Presbyterian Church in Venezuela.* Caracas, Venezuela: Presbyterian Mission Press, 1958.

Pierson, Paul E. *A Younger Church in Search of Maturity: Presbyterianism in Brazil from 1910–1959.* San Antonio, Tex.: Trinity University Press, 1974.

Read, W. R. *New Patterns of Church Growth in Brazil.* Grand Rapids: Eerdmans, 1965.

Read, W. R. and F. A. Ineson, eds. *Brazil 1980: The Protestant Handbook.* Monrovia, La.: MARC, 1983.

Wagner, C. P. *The Protestant Movement in Bolivia.* South Pasadena, Calif.: William Carey Library, 1970.

Wheeler, W. Reginald and Webster E. Browning. *Modern Missions on the Spanish Main.* Philadelphia: Westminster Press, 1925.

Williams, E. *Followers of the New Faith: Culture, Change, and the Rise of Protestantism in Brazil and Chile.* Nashville: Vanderbilt University Press, 1967.

TWENTY-THREE

Arab North Africa

Although North Africa was once part of the Roman Empire and the site of a prominent Christian presence, centuries of contention about doctrine and rivalries among ecclesiastical leaders brought a decadence that left the churches there unable to withstand the advances of Islam. Today, as a consequence of Muslim conquests, Christianity barely survives, and efforts of Reformed missions have produced little lasting fruit. From Morocco in the west to Egypt in the east, churches are few and the Christian witness feeble, although approximately 10 percent of Egyptians still identify themselves as disciples of Christ, at least in some formal way. Over 90 percent of North Africans are Muslims.

Egypt

Proximity to Palestine brought numerous Jews to Egypt in pre-Christian centuries, and Alexandria in particular became a center of Jewish culture and scholarship. The message of Jesus arrived there in the first century, as Christians implemented their Lord's command to carry the gospel throughout the earth. The New Testament and ancient historical documents indicate the apostles were engaged in this endeavor, and one tradition identifies John Mark as founder of the church in Egypt. Acts 18:24 to 26 cites Apollos as an Alexandrian Jew, and just as that city had been noteworthy in Jewish history, it became a center for Christian scholarship, as the association of such church leaders as Tertullian, Cyprian, and Augustine of Hippo attests.

From its appearance in this country, the Christian faith made its most significant gains among the Greek-speaking parts of the population, although others embraced it as well. Once the church was well established, it sent missions to Libya, Ethiopia, and elsewhere in the region. In this way the Coptic Orthodox Church developed as the major expression of Christianity in this area of northeast Africa.

The Coptic Church became involved in some of the christological disputes of the early centuries, and the Greek Orthodox Church condemned its position as heresy. Such controversies weakened the Christian community in a land where pagan superstitions were still pronounced, and the Copts unintentionally allowed some pagan beliefs to become parts of their doctrine. When Islam arrived in Egypt, the church there was in no position to defend itself vigorously, and large numbers of its members accepted the teachings of Muhammad. Roman Catholic missionaries brought their church to this country in the seventeenth century, and some of those bodies remain, but only a fraction of 1 percent of the population is Catholic. The Coptic Church, however, despite its unorthodox teaching about the person and work of Christ and badly diminished condition, has survived, and now about 9 percent of the people profess that religion. The various Protestant communities together account for less than 1 percent.

The Moravians were the pioneer Protestant missionaries in Egypt, but their work failed. The Anglican Church Mission Society initiated its mission in 1818 but cooperated with the Copts in the hope of converting Muslims and Jews. The Anglicans withdrew in 1862 but returned in the 1880s, after Great Britain had secured political dominance in the land. The initial Reformed effort to evangelize Egyptians was the work of the United Presbyterian Church of North America, which entered in 1854, and some churches that owe their origin to that endeavor remain. The oldest and largest Protestant denomination is the Evangelical Church of Egypt—Synod of the Nile. Long a mission of the United Presbyterian Church, it became independent in 1958. Almost all the converts who adhered to this mission were former Copts, very few were Muslims. The United Presbyterian mission spread broadly across Egypt and established several schools and colleges as well as an extensive medical ministry. By the end of the nineteenth century, the Presbyterians were strong enough to open a seminary in Cairo, a development achieved through funds collected from native church members. Gradually the American missionaries placed themselves under the direction of the Evangelical Church and assumed the role of fraternal associates. One of their number, Dr. Charles Roger Watson (1873–1948), became founder of the American University in Cairo.

The Evangelical Church suffered substantial losses when, in 1882, the Christian (Plymouth) Brethren convinced several thousand believers to join their movement, one entirely under native leadership and featuring dispensational interpretation of the Bible incompatible with the Reformed faith. Although this secession injured the Evangelical Church badly, that body still had about three hundred thousand members by the year 2000. It maintains membership in the World Alliance of Reformed Churches and the World Council of Churches and fraternal relations with the Presbyterian Church (U.S.A.). It does not ordain women.

A very small Armenian Protestant community supports the Armenian Evangelical Church, which had but one congregation with approximately five hundred members. The Anglican Church claims some ten thousand adherents. The government of Egypt affirms freedom of religion in principal, but Islam is politically powerful and radical Muslims have in recent years shown increasing strength, as they seek to make the Sharia rules of their religion the law of the land. The Muslim Brotherhood is the most prominent such organization, and though it officially disavows violence, zealots within its membership have engaged in terrorist tactics to impose their faith on all Egyptians.

The Maghreb

The Arab countries of Libya, Tunisia, Algeria, and Morocco comprise the geographical region known as the Maghreb, where Arab conquests in the seventh century imposed Islam upon Berber tribes and almost effaced any traces of a Christian presence. As a consequence of centuries of Muslim rule and resentment against later European domination, there are no organized churches in Libya and only tiny Christian communities in the other Maghreb nations.

Tunisia was once an important center of Christianity, but the Arabs relentlessly repressed the church until, by the twelfth century, it had ceased to exist there. Late in the sixteenth century the country passed under the control of the Turks, who maintained the Muslim dominance. In 1881, however, France occupied Tunisia and patronized Roman Catholic missions, which had been striving for some time to gain a following. Only a few natives embraced Catholicism, so support for the Roman Church came almost entirely from European settlers. In 1957 Tunisia gained independence, and its new government soon stripped the church of its privileges, confiscated most of its properties, and encouraged Europeans to leave the country. Only five Catholic churches remained open.

Protestant missions to Tunisia began in 1829, when the London Society for Promoting Christianity among the Jews sent its agents there to seek converts among descendants of Jewish refugees expelled from Spain in 1492. Some Jews, but very few Muslims, responded favorably. The non-denominational North Africa Mission initiated its ministry in 1882, with distribution of Bibles as its major emphasis. French Protestants residing in Tunisia by then had their own Reformed church, but it had little influence on the natives. No Protestant effort proved successful in this country, and at the end of the last century, the Reformed Church in Tunisia, with about one hundred members in a single congregation, was the sole representative of organized Protestantism in the nation. That body subscribes to historic Calvinism as expressed in the Heidelberg Catechism, and it relies on the Reformed Theological Seminary of Jackson, Mississippi, for the education of its ministers.

Algeria, like Tunisia, had been subject to the Romans, Vandals, Arabs, and Turks before it became a French possession in 1830. The North Africa Mission was the first Protestant agency to evangelize there, and it enjoyed some success among Berber Kabyley peoples into whose language its missionaries translated the Bible. Meanwhile Bible societies from several nations distributed the Scriptures in Arabic across the land.

During the era of French dominance, several Protestant missions became engaged in Algeria, and the French Reformed Church was the most prominent among them. Most of its ministries were, however, for the benefit of European settlers. The French government did not regard Algeria as a colony but a department (state) of metropolitan France, and more Europeans situated there than in any Arab land. By the end of the nineteenth century, thousands of French Algerians had grown up there as natives, and their presence bred resentment among the Arabs, even though the government made provisions for them to become full citizens of France. After World War II Algeria exploded in an anti-French rebellion that led to protracted civil war, political independence, and the expulsion or exodus of at least 70 percent of the Algerians of European ethnicity. This greatly reduced the Christian presence in the country.

Once the Arabs were in control of Algeria, they urged churches and missions to leave, and today a small Roman Catholic community remains alongside the Protestant Church of Algeria, a remnant of the Reformed church that once had an extensive mission there. Only about five hundred people identify with this ecumenical body, which has no firm confessional basis. Eight tiny congregations comprise the Protestant Church, which has affiliated with the World Alliance of Reformed Churches and the World Council of Churches.

The history of Morocco closely resembles that of Algeria, although the European presence there was never as prominent. The Roman Empire annexed Morocco in the first Christian century, and Christianity there became well established in the latter part of Roman rule. Muslim invaders conquered the country in the seventh century, as Arabs imposed their authority upon the older Berber populace. As in other parts of North Africa, the church in Morocco almost collapsed when confronted by militant Islam. In the nineteenth century France and Spain intruded into the country, and by the beginning of World War I, they had divided it between them. France granted independence to her section in 1956, and Spain followed suit twenty years later, in both cases after violent demonstrations of nationalism proved too strong to suppress.

Although Islam dominated Morocco from the seventh century, the monarch there was tolerant toward Jews who fled from Spain to avoid forced conversion to Catholicism during the reign of Ferdinand and Isabella, who styled themselves the Catholic sovereigns of Spain. As a consequence of this receptivity, a substantial Jewish community developed in Morocco, which explains why the first Protestant mission effort there was an undertaking of the London Society for Promoting Christianity among the Jews initiated in 1875. The North Africa Mission arrived seven years later. The Southern Morocco Mission, a Scottish ministry, began working there in 1888, and other Protestant agencies followed. English Presbyterians dispatched the Central Morocco Mission, the first systematic effort to plant a specifically Reformed witness in the land. The French Reformed Church also invested considerable resources, but for the most part to provide spiritual care for people of French nationality.

When Morocco became independent, the French Reformed Church agreed to recognize the autonomy of its mission, which then became the Evangelical Church in Morocco, the only organized body there professing the Reformed faith. At the end of the last century, that church reported a membership of sixteen hundred in six congregations bound together in a Presbyterian polity and affirming the same confession as the Reformed Church of France. It does not ordain women, is a member of the World Alliance of Reformed Churches and the World Council of Churches, and maintains close relations with its parent church in France. There are some other Protestant churches in Morocco, the aggregate membership of which is about the same as that of the Evangelical Church. Roman Catholicism and Eastern Orthodoxy too are present in this Muslim country, which is more tolerant than most, although radicals aspire to impose Sharia there as elsewhere. The government does not allow foreign missionaries to work in the country, and the Evangelical Church subsists by refraining from evangelism among Muslims.

SUGGESTED ADDITIONAL READINGS >>

Abun-Nasr, Jamil M. *History of the Maghrib in the Islamic Period.* Cambridge: Cambridge University Press, 1987.

Ageron, Charles R. *Modern Algeria: A History from 1830 to the Present.* Translated by Michael Bett. London: Hurst, 1991.

Aroian, Lois A. and Richard P. Mitchell. *The Modern Middle East and North Africa.* New York: Macmillan, 1984.

Bailey, Betty Jane and J. Martin Bailey. *Who Are the Christians in the Middle East?* Grand Rapids: Eerdmans, 2003.

Betts, Robert B. *Christians in the Arab East.* Athens, Greece: Lycabettus Press, 1975.

Cooley, J. K. Baal. *Christ and Mohammed: Religion and Revolution in North Africa.* New York: Holt, Rinehart, and Winston, 1965.

Cragg, Kenneth. *The Arab Christian: A History in the Middle East.* Louisville, Ky.: Westminster/John Knox, 1991.

Gilsenan, M. *Saint and Sufi in Modern Egypt.* Oxford: Oxford University Press, 1973.

Holme, L. R. *The Extinction of the Churches in North Africa.* New York: Burt Franklin, 1969.

Horner, Norman A. *A Guide to the Christian Churches in the Middle East.* Elkhart, Ind.: Mission Focus, 1989.

Meinhardus, O. F. A. *Christian Egypt, Ancient and Modern.* 2nd ed. Cairo: American University Press, 1965.

Perkins, K. J. *A History of Modern Tunisia.* Cambridge: Cambridge University Press, 2004.

St. John, Ronald B. *Historical Dictionary of Libya.* Metuchen, N.J.: Scarecrow Press, 1991.

Wessels, Antoine. *Christians in the Middle East.* Translated by John Medendorp and Henry Jansen. Kampen, Netherlands: Kok Pharos, 1995.

Wright, John L. *Libya: A Modern History.* Baltimore, Md.: Johns Hopkins Press, 1982.

TWENTY-FOUR

Africa below the Sahara Desert

Since the desert forms a natural barrier between northern and southern Africa, it is a convenient place to distinguish the two parts of the continent, which are as different culturally as they are geographically. North Africa is part of the Mediterranean world and the Arab portion thereof, whereas most of the region south of the Sahara is populated by black people who speak a variety of languages and have lived for most of their history in tribal societies. As Muslim traders from the north and from across the Red Sea penetrated this region, they brought their religion with them and won some converts, especially along the east coast and in Sudan. Most Africans, however, remained in a primitive stage of religious development animistic in character.

Christianity arrived in this part of Africa in the fifteenth century in connection with Portuguese explorations, but Catholicism reached only the coastal areas, and when Portuguese power declined in the seventeenth and eighteenth centuries, the Catholic presence diminished. To their shame, the Portuguese and other Europeans, as well as the Arabs, were interested in this region chiefly as a source from which to obtain slaves, sometimes called "black gold." Africans eagerly sold captives taken in tribal wars, and slave traders transported them to auction blocks in the New World and in islands off the coast of Africa. The black Africans' introduction to Christianity was anything but uplifting, but, nevertheless, multitudes of them eventually embraced the faith even while in servitude.

Although many professing Christians saw no conflict between their faith and the exploitation of slaves, by the opening of the nineteenth century an antislavery movement was beginning to organize, especially in Great Britain. There, evangelical believers, allied with Quakers and secular humanitarians, obtained abolition of the slave trade in 1807 and of the institution itself in 1834. The United States followed suit in the 1860s with a series of laws and constitutional amendments. Other slave-trading nations also ceased the traffic in human beings, but more slowly and with more reluctance. This was especially so in the Arab states across the Red Sea.

Abolition of the slave trade outside of Africa did not eliminate the practice of slavery within that continent, for tribal wars continued, and prisoners often became victims of forced servitude to the victors. When missionaries, Catholic and Protestant, arrived in Africa, they sometimes petitioned their governments at home to intervene in order to stop the barbarities Africans were perpetrating against one another. This appeal and the great commercial opportunities exploration and settlement presented led Europeans to seize large portions of the continent, and before the nineteenth century ended, almost all of Africa was under foreign rule. Catholicism, as a consequence of this penetration, became strongest in areas subject to French, Portuguese, Belgian, and, to a degree, German authority, while Protestantism prevailed in British-ruled regions and, to a lesser extent, in the German colonies. Missionaries from the United States, some Catholic but most Protestant, also appeared in Africa. Since chapter 15 of this book tells the story of Reformed Christianity in South Africa, that nation will not be part of the following accounts.

The spread of Christianity in central and southern Africa was the work of European, American, and white South African churches, and Great Britain sent more missionaries in the nineteenth century than any other country. The lands of east Africa provide a suitable place to begin this study.

Sudan

To the south of Egypt, where the desert gives way to vegetation, lies Sudan, populated by Arabs in the north and black Africans in the south. Long an unruly country where tribal rivalries agitated violent conflicts, Sudan was once subject to British rule in a structure called Anglo-Egyptian Sudan and because of that arrangement came into contact with Western ideas. The primitive southern part of Sudan was the scene of great unrest generated by resentment toward the more prosperous north. Warfare between Arabs and black Africans has been frequent, and in recent years contention between Muslims and Christians has further exacerbated the situation. Today Christians often endure severe persecution at the hands of Muslims, whom the government does not restrain.

The great missionary surge of the nineteenth century did not reach Sudan until 1890, when the Anglican Church Missionary Society arrived there. In 1901 agents of the United Presbyterian Church of North America introduced the Reformed faith in the region. The government of Anglo-Egyptian Sudan did not, at that time, allow missionaries to work in the north, perhaps for fear of provoking Muslim uprisings, so the Presbyterians labored in the south in the province of Upper Nile. The Evangelical Church of Egypt meanwhile was operating in the north as the Presbytery of Sudan, but that was not a foreign intrusion comparable to the Americans' effort in the south. A Sudan Presbyterian Evangelical Church continues in that region today.

When the Anglican and Presbyterian missions began in Sudan, most peoples of the south were still pagans, although there was a small Coptic community. The two Christian missions worked well together, especially in educational endeavors, but ordination of a native pastor did not take place until 1942. By then northern Sudan had opened somewhat to Christian mission schools, although the government wanted the churches to serve only their own constituents and to refrain from evangelizing Muslims. It seems the government was eager to obtain the educational benefits the missions offered but did not desire the success of Christianity as such. A United Presbyterian Church developed in the north nevertheless, but separate from its southern counterpart. Anglo-Egyptian Sudan disbanded in 1956, as the country gained independence but under a corrupt, repressive regime, and soon the new nation exploded in civil war. This was due in part to Muslim domination of the state and the failure to protect the rights of the Christian and pagan minorities in the south. The era of independence has been one of recurrent violent conflicts and broken agreements. In 1983 the government announced it would impose Sharia law upon the nation. Domestic warfare continues to the present, and the Presbyterian Church has had to divide into one presbytery in the government-controlled area and another in rebel-held territory. The suffering of Christians has been extensive and intensive and has included even crucifixions of believers. Church growth, however, has continued despite the persecution.

In addition to the work initiated by the United Presbyterian Church, Reformed believers in Australia and New Zealand invested their resources in the Sudanese Church of Christ, which began in 1913 as a ministry of the Sudan United Mission. This became an independent church in 1962 and has withstood persecution and efforts to impose Arab culture. Although the constitution of 1973 in Sudan affirms toleration of all religions, non-Muslims have been subject to frequent repressions, even while the government made occasional concessions to the churches.

There are now three church bodies that affirm a Reformed posture at least in principal, the largest by far being the Presbyterian Church of Sudan, which has about 450 thousand members in 320 congregations and 230 preaching stations united in two presbyteries. The Heidelberg Catechism and the Westminster Confession of Faith are its official doctrinal statements. A member of the World Council of Churches and the World Alliance of Reformed Churches, the Presbyterian Church of Sudan has fraternal relations with liberal denominations such as the Presbyterian Church (U.S.A.), the Reformed Church in America, and the Presbyterian Church of Ireland.

Somewhat isolated in the northern part of the country is the Presbyterian Evangelical Church of eight thousand members in twenty-four congregations and many more preaching points. More conservative than the larger Presbyterian Church of Sudan, this denomination adheres to the Westminster Standards and does not ordain female officers. It operates Nile Theological College in Khartoum. The Sudanese Church of Christ, founded in 1913, is Reformed in polity and historically a product of Presbyterian missions, but its doctrinal position is broadly evangelical, and it does not subscribe to any of the traditional Reformed confessions. This denomination of about twelve thousand members in sixty congregations and numerous preaching stations ordains women as deacons but not as pastors or elders. In conjunction with the very similar Sudan Interior Church, it operates Gideon Bible School in the capital city. The sister denomination, the Sudan Interior Church, has thirty thousand members in one hundred congregations, and it too ordains women as deacons but not as pastors or elders. This body does not have a distinctively Reformed doctrinal basis, but it does operate with a Presbyterian form of polity. Trinity Presbyterian Church of the Sudan is the other Reformed body, with some seventeen thousand members in 233 congregations and several mission stations. The Westminster Confession is its official theological statement. Located in northern Sudan and Upper Nile Province, this church subsists independent of other bodies but has loose relations with the Presbyterian Church (U.S.A.).

All Christian churches in Sudan face an entrenched and militant Muslim majority that regards them as infidels, while it aspires to impose the religion of the Koran and the Sharia upon them. Persecution is a constant threat confronting believers in Christ, many of whom have perished in the recurrent religious warfare that wracks the land. What effect the

2011 creation of an independent Southern Sudan will have upon Christians remains to be seen.

Ethiopia

Between Sudan and the Red Sea lies the Republic of Ethiopia, known as Abyssinia as well. Until 1974 this was a monarchy, the emperor of which claimed to be a descendant of King Solomon and the Queen of Sheba. Haile Selassie (1930–1974) aspired to lead his primitive nation into the modern world and did much to stimulate diplomatic and commercial contacts with Western nations. He professed Christianity and was loyal to the Coptic Church but receptive to Protestant missions as well. A rather benevolent autocrat, he failed to keep his regime free of corruption, and his own army overthrew him in 1974.

Shortly before the Second World War, Benito Mussolini provoked border incidents to justify invading Ethiopia from the Italian colonies on the Horn of Africa, and Haile Selassie fled to England. British imperial forces, however, many from South Africa, defeated the Italians easily and restored the emperor in 1941. Since the declaration of a republic, this country has become the site of a growing contest between Muslims in the eastern and northwestern sectors and Christians who occupy most of the rest of the land. The population as a whole is about evenly divided between Muslims and Christians, and many others remain pagans.

Christianity came to Ethiopia in the fourth century through the work of an obscure figure named Frumentius, a Syrian, whom Athanasius, patriarch of Alexandria, appointed bishop there. The Ethiopian (Coptic) Orthodox Church cites the year 332 as the date of its foundation. When Islam became a world power in the seventh century, that church faced a deadly menace, but it withstood the onslaught then and another in the sixteenth century. The Coptic Church holds to a heretical doctrine that maintains Jesus Christ has but one nature, and so he is not fully God and man. The church's canon of Scripture conforms to neither the Catholic nor the Protestant model, and many elements of regional superstitions have become features of Coptic practice. Knowledge of the decadent condition of that church led some Anglicans to go to Ethiopia in the nineteenth century with the hope of reforming it, but those efforts failed.

In point of time the first Protestant mission to Ethiopia came from the Swedish Evangelical National Missionary Society in 1865, and because of its achievements, Lutheranism would gain a substantial following. Today the Ethiopian Evangelical Church-Mekane Jesus is the largest Lutheran body. Agents of the United Presbyterian Church in North America landed in Ethiopia in 1919, after the government appealed for aid in combating an influenza epidemic that swept through the earth after World War I. Dr. Thomas Alexander Lambie (1885–1954), then serving in Sudan, answered the call from Ethiopia and helped to establish the George Memorial Hospital in Addis Ababa, and soon numerous clinics and schools were operating under Presbyterian auspices in various places. The Italian aggressors seized the hospital and some other church properties and tried to impose Catholicism and papal authority during the period of fascist occupation (1935–1941). After the defeat of the Italians, the Ethiopian government took control of George Memorial Hospital but continued to employ mission personnel to operate it.

Lambie and other missionaries had to leave Ethiopia when Mussolini's forces took control, and during their absence native believers formed the Evangelical Church Bethel in 1940. This body became independent in 1947 as a Presbyterian church in its own right, and it joined the World Alliance of Reformed Churches in 1970.

After the British victory over the Italians, various Protestant groups in Ethiopia initiated efforts to achieve a form of church union, and in 1959 the Ethiopian Evangelical Church-Mekane Jesus came into being with encouragement from Swedish missionaries and native leaders. This brought churches of Lutheran and Reformed character together in a single body, but one that recognizes the distinctive heritage of each component. Since the Lutherans were more numerous, the united church reflects their dominance. The Bethel Church (Presbyterian) operates in three synods, while the Lutherans maintain seven others. This arrangement has worked well, and both wings of the denomination have grown in recent years. The Bethel synods have about 415 thousand members, while the Lutherans number about 1.5 million. The church as a whole has almost thirty-eight hundred local assemblies and many mission extensions. It has close relations with both the Presbyterian Church (U.S.A.) and the Evangelical Lutheran Church in America. It holds membership in the World Council of Churches and the Lutheran World Federation. One seminary and several Bible institutes provide education for ministers and church workers.

Beside the fairly well-established Ethiopian Evangelical Church, Reformed missionaries from the United States have been working in remote areas under difficult circumstances. Agents of the Reformed Church in America, the Orthodox Presbyterian Church, the Presbyterian Church in America, the Christian Reformed Church, and two Dutch denominations are laboring in this country, and the Presbyterian Church in America has made a major investment of personnel and resources there through its Mission to the World. The Reformed Presbyterian churches in Scotland and Ireland have a joint mission there as well.

The experience of missionaries from the Orthodox Presbyterian Church illustrates the dangers foreign evangelists have encountered in Ethiopia. The Eritrean Liberation Front, a rebel movement of Marxist character, in 1974 murdered a Dutch nurse working with the Orthodox Presbyterian mission and held another, Deborah Dortzbach, captive for twenty-seven days. Mrs. Dortzbach described her ordeal in a book titled *Kidnapped*. The Orthodox Presbyterians had been operating a substantial medical ministry along with vigorous evangelism, but the Ethiopian army seized its hospital, and violence the government failed to suppress forced the missionaries to flee from the country in 1976. In 1977 Marxist guerillas seized the national government and brought Soviet and Cuban soldiers into the country as a means to impose their dictatorship. They declared Ethiopia an atheistic state and began cruel repression of all church bodies, but the churches withstood the persecution and emerged stronger because of it. A counterrevolution in 1991 overthrew the Communist regime and restored freedom of religion. While turmoil raged, Pentecostals made great gains, and the Full Gospel Church is now the largest indigenous Christian body in Ethiopia.

Eritrea

Located immediately north of Ethiopia, just above the Horn of Africa, lies the small country of Eritrea, which the Kingdom of Italy annexed in 1893. In World War II Britain took this area and held it as a United Nations Trust Territory until the country received autonomy as a province of Ethiopia in 1952. When Ethiopia declared Eritrea an integral part of its empire, armed rebellions quickly led to brutal warfare that did not end until the rebels secured national independence in 1993.

The population of Eritrea is about evenly divided between Muslims in the north and professing Christians in the south, most of whom adhere to the Eritrean Orthodox Church, once a part of the Coptic Church of Ethiopia. There is a small Roman Catholic community and an even smaller Protestant presence, perhaps 2 percent of the nation. As in Ethiopia, the Lutherans were pioneer missionaries here, as the Swedish Evangelical

National Missionary Society undertook evangelistic, medical, and educational ministries that included extensive translation work. Mussolini tried to thwart this mission, perhaps because it was non-Italian, and the Waldenses then continued the Protestant effort until the Lutherans could return after the defeat of fascist forces in that part of Africa. The Waldenses then withdrew, leaving the Lutheran mission in charge, and about twenty thousand Eritreans identify themselves as Lutheran Christians.

After the Second World War, missionaries of the Orthodox Presbyterian Church from the United States entered Eritrea and established a Reformed ministry in the land. These evangelists engaged in translation of the Bible and Christian literature while seeking the conversion of pagans, Muslims, and Copts.

The era of independence has not been a peaceful one for Eritrea. The Eritrean Liberation Front led the secession from Ethiopia, but that struggle left the country devastated. By the end of the twentieth century, a Popular Front for Democracy and Justice had emerged as the dominant political party in an unstable nation that suffered from internal discord concurrent with hostility from Ethiopia and Sudan. Once in power this party became fearful of both radical Islamists and evangelistic Christians, and so it has ruled in an authoritarian manner while ignoring constitutional provisions for basic civil rights. The government still recognizes only the Eritrean Orthodox Church, the Roman Catholic Church, and the Lutheran Church. Adherents to other bodies are subject to persecution if they practice their faith in public. A costly war with Ethiopia in 1998 hurt the country badly and led the regime to become even more repressive toward all dissenters, political and religious. Lengthy prison terms and even torture of nonconforming Christians have occurred, and the United States Department of State lists Eritrea as a country Americans would do well to avoid.

Kenya

South of Ethiopia, east of Uganda, with the Indian Ocean on its southeast coast, is Kenya. Once a British protectorate, it became a Crown Colony in 1905. This country attracted a substantial number of European settlers who brought their particular forms of Christianity with them. The first to do so were Roman Catholic Portuguese whose Augustinian friars established a small mission that hostile Muslims destroyed in 1631. Protestants arrived in 1844, when the Church Missionary Society sent J. Ludwig Krapf (1810–1881), who drafted a plan to create a series of mission stations across Africa.

Eventually this became a reality, but not through the work of the Church Missionary Society exclusively. His own illness following the deaths of his wife and child forced Krapf to leave Africa in 1853, but by then John Rebmann (1820–1876), who had arrived in 1844, was ready to lead the work, and soon the outreach spread to various parts of Kenya. British Methodists too began mission work near Mombasa in 1862, while the Church of Scotland assumed responsibility for the mission the British East Africa Company had endowed in 1891.

Although successes of the Church Missionary Society produced a major Anglican presence in Kenya, Reformed missions prospered as well, as the decision of the Church of Scotland to make the East Africa Mission its own attests. Thomas Watson (d. 1900) had led that endeavor until his death. Numerous missions from the United Kingdom and the United States launched evangelistic, medical, educational, and agricultural endeavors leading to an attempt to form a united Protestant church, but that failed, and the effort ended in 1972. Several councils of churches have been formed, however, and the nondenominational Africa Inland Mission, an American project formed in 1895, gradually became the largest Protestant body in the land, in effect, a denomination in its own right.

The major Reformed denomination in Kenya is the Presbyterian Church of East Africa, which claims over three million members in more than a thousand congregations. This work began as a mission that the Church of Scotland adopted in 1901. Progress was slow at first, and by 1913, fewer than a hundred people had joined this church. There was no organized polity until 1920 and no ordinations of native pastors until 1926. Lack of numerical gains did not, however, immobilize this ministry, and gradually it grew into a well-developed denomination that extended beyond the borders of Kenya. The decades of the 1950s and 1960s were a period of dynamic growth, as the church became independent of foreign authority. The Presbyterian Church of East Africa, after gaining autonomy, maintained fraternal relations with the Church of Scotland, the Presbyterian Church (U.S.A.), the Presbyterian Church of Ireland, the Presbyterian Church of Canada, and other denominations. It became a member of the World Alliance of Reformed Churches and the World Council of Churches.

As the twentieth century ended, relations between the Presbyterian Church of East Africa and other members of the World Alliance of Reformed Churches became strained, especially over the issue of homosexuality. In a manner similar to reactions of conservative Anglican parishes in

Africa, this Presbyterian body protested the acceptance of homosexuality in European and American churches. For sixty years relations with the Presbyterian Church (U.S.A.) had been very close, but they deteriorated as the American denomination's leaders remained firm in their acceptance of what African Christians regard as a sinful practice. Soon after Anglican bishops in Africa rejected support from the Episcopal Church in the United States to protest its consecration of a homosexual prelate, the Presbyterian Church of East Africa decided to sever its ties with its American patron, thereby forfeiting financial support from the Presbyterian Church (U.S.A.).

In 2004, when Dr. David M. Githi, moderator of the Presbyterian Church of East Africa, went to Richmond, Virginia, to address the General Assembly of the Presbyterian Church (U.S.A.), he encountered an unfriendly, even discourteous reception. Snubbed by American church leaders and criticized for immature thinking about a crucial social issue, Githi asked Susan Andrews, moderator of that General Assembly, to extend her proffered apology to a letter of repentance to the church in Africa. This occurred shortly after Andrews had preached to the assembly in favor of homosexual relations. Some conservatives present on that occasion complimented Githi for his courageous stand for biblical morality and promised their support for his church. Commissioners from the National Capital Presbytery, with which the church in East Africa had already broken relations, tried to pacify the African leader, but to no avail. Conservatives connected with the Confessing Church, an evangelical movement within their denomination, initiated efforts to raise financial support for their brethren in Africa but apart from usual denominational channels.

The Presbyterian Church of East Africa, at this time, appears to be reconsidering its ecumenical relations, although it remains a member of the World Alliance of Reformed Churches and the World Council of Churches. It does ordain women officers while affirming the Westminster Confession nevertheless. The church operates many schools and clinics, a teachers' college, and a pastoral institute for the preparation of ministers.

The Reformed Church of East Africa is another Presbyterian body of note, one that made its debut in 1944 when Pastor and Mrs. B. B. Eybers arrived in Eldoret to serve the Dutch Reformed community there. An informal ministry had existed there prior to their arrival, one maintained by South African farmers who had settled there. The Eybers ministered at Plateau Mission Station from 1944 to1960, as they prepared native pastors and evangelists, founded schools, and produced a hymnal and books for

Sunday school teachers. When the Eybers retired, sixteen congregations were operating with native pastors and over three hundred members. In 1961 the Netherlands Reformed Church in Holland assumed responsibility for this mission, and in 1963 the congregations formed a synod known as the Reformed Church of East Africa. Missionaries from the Netherlands then conducted evangelistic, medical, educational, and literature translation endeavors. By 1976 membership had grown to more than four thousand, with Africans assuming an ever-growing responsibility for church affairs.

By the end of the last century, the Reformed Church of East Africa had 205 local assemblies and a membership of approximately 110 thousand. It is a member of the fundamentalist International Council of Christian Churches. Its candidates for the ministry study at Faith College of the Bible and Mwingi Bible School.

In 1961 the Reformed Presbyterian Church, Evangelical Synod, an American denomination of orthodox character, began mission work in Kenya. As this work progressed, the African Evangelical Presbyterian Church developed with one presbytery in which three Kenyan pastors were leaders. The arrival of more missionaries from the United States enabled this church to undertake an urban ministry in Nairobi that featured planting congregations in the metropolitan area of the rapidly growing capital city. By 1974 some two thousand people regularly attended services in the twenty-three local churches of this body. Vigorous evangelism had been a characteristic of this movement from its inception.

Much of the impressive growth of the mission and the African Evangelical Presbyterian Church was due in part to the labors of Pastor and Mrs. Saunders Campbell, who led some churches formerly connected with the Independent Board for Presbyterian Foreign Missions to participate in establishing the new denomination. Campbell planted Community Presbyterian Church in Nairobi in 1973, and soon other church plants were taking root in that city and several others. The African Evangelical Presbyterian Church rather quickly became sufficiently strong to send its native missionaries to other towns and cities. As the twentieth century ended, some ten thousand held membership in this body. As is the case with almost all Reformed churches of an orthodox character, this one does not ordain females. It holds staunchly to the Westminster Standards and cooperates with the Orthodox Presbyterian Church, the Presbyterian Church in America, and one Korean denomination. Grace Bible College and Trinity Bible Institute are its schools.

The Bible Christian Faith Church is a small Reformed body that originated as an offshoot of the African Inland Mission, as ten congregations separated from that mission and looked for support from the Free Presbyterian Church of Ulster, which has sent a few missionaries to assist the work in Kenya. About six hundred members meet in six assemblies and affirm the Westminster Confession as their statement of doctrine. This group enjoys close fellowship with the Independent Presbyterian Church of East Africa, and it is a member of the World Christian Fundamentalist Congress. Reformed denominations continue to show much interest in Kenya, and the Presbyterian Church in America now has several of its agents serving there.

Uganda

Located between Kenya and Congo, Uganda, once a series of tribal monarchies, became a British protectorate in 1894 and did not gain independence until 1962. The country has a diverse African population with a substantial Muslim minority. Christianity has enjoyed more success there than in most other African states, and today 83 percent of the people profess some expression of that faith. Thirty-three percent identify with Catholicism, 25 percent with the Anglican Church, 8 percent with other Protestant bodies, while 16 percent are Muslim, and the rest still pagans.

Henry M. Stanley (1841–1904), an explorer who became a Christian under the influence of the famous David Livingstone, continued Livingstone's work, and in 1874 Stanley entered Uganda and convinced a tribal king there to accept missionaries. The Church Missionary Society responded, with Alexander Mackay (1849–1890) leading the way. This dedicated Scotsman, his family, and his coworkers suffered badly from tropical diseases and from persecution due to native resistance, some of it agitated by Catholic priests. Mackay died after fourteen years of continuous service in Africa, never returning to Scotland.

Despite the hardships Church Missionary Society personnel encountered, they persevered, and the Church of England sent bishops to administer the mission, and by 1904, sixty-two thousand Ugandans had professed the Christian faith. The African Inland Mission and other Christian groups participated in the evangelization of Uganda, but the Presbyterians did not enter that field until the 1970s, and the Presbyterian Church in Uganda did not take form until 1979.

The Presbyterian work began through the efforts of Kefa Sempangi, a native pastor educated in the United States. The first church building of the new body was erected in 1980. This young denomination, much to its misfortune, suffered a schism in 1989 that produced the Reformed Presbyterian Church. In 1999 the Presbyterian Church in Uganda reported about forty-one hundred members in twelve congregations. The church adheres to the Westminster Confession and does not ordain women. Its ministers, as a rule, obtain their education at Westminster Theological College, which opened in 1996, although some attend the African Bible College, which has campuses in Liberia and Malawi as well as in Uganda. Church planting and evangelism have been the priority for the Presbyterian Church in Uganda, and missionaries from the Orthodox Presbyterian Church and the Presbyterian Church in America are currently serving in the country. In 2003 a division within the Presbyterian Church in Uganda led to the formation of the Orthodox Presbyterian Church there, and American missionaries Anthony and Kathleen Curto and Philip and Meredith Proctor have served that church well. The Reformed Church in the United States sent Thomas B. Mayville to Uganda in 2007 to assist with theological education.

Another Reformed movement of note in Uganda is the Evangelical Free Church, organized in 1986. It has enjoyed rapid growth, and at the end of the last century had approximately twenty thousand members. It too subscribes to the Westminster Standards and refrains from ordaining females. The Free Church Christian College is its educational institution.

The Reformed Presbyterian Church in Uganda, the result of a schism in 1989, organized the next year, after attempts at reconciliation with the Presbyterian Church in Uganda failed. This body of some five thousand members in twelve congregations has its center of strength in Kampala. Like its parent, the Reformed Presbyterian Church affirms the Westminster Standards but subscribes to the Three Forms of Unity from the Dutch Reformed tradition as well. This church operates the Reformed Theological College and holds membership in the Reformed Ecumenical Council and the World Alliance of Reformed Churches. Unlike the church from which it withdrew, this one does not ordain women officers.

A denomination in close fellowship with its American patron of the same name is the Christian Reformed Church in Eastern Africa, which originated in Kenya in 1992 and spread into Uganda. Very much like the Christian Reformed Church in North America, this body of four thousand people in eighty local assemblies affirms the Dutch doctrinal standards. It is an affiliate of the Reformed Ecumenical Council, and it maintains the

Christian Reformed Bible College for the preparation of church workers. Church offices are open to women.

Rwanda

The small, densely populated Republic of Rwanda lies between Lake Tanganyika and Lake Victoria, with Uganda on its northern border. It became part of German East Africa late in the nineteenth century but passed to Belgian control after the defeat of Germany in the First World War. Roman Catholic missionaries called the White Fathers preceded the first Protestants, and the Church of Rome was rather well established there by 1900. The effective parish organization of the White Fathers and a network of fine schools enabled the Catholics to gain a large following, and today about 300 thousand Rwandans profess that religion. Lutherans with the German Bethel Mission arrived in 1907, and other Protestants followed, the Church Missionary Society among them. The Anglican effort was quite successful in its evangelistic, educational, and medical ministries.

After World War I the Belgians required the Germans to leave Rwanda, and the Protestant Missionary Society, an arm of the Reformed Church in Belgium, assumed responsibility for the Bethel Mission. This in turn led eventually to the formation of a Presbyterian body that would gain independence in 1959 as the Presbyterian Church in Rwanda. This denomination continued the ministries the Germans had initiated and added some of its own.

Rwanda experienced brutal turmoil in the nature of tribal wars after the country became independent prematurely in 1962. Thousands fell victims to massacres, but the churches endured through the chaos despite their losses. The Presbyterian Church in Rwanda is the only substantial Reformed body in the land, and though it maintains Presbyterian polity, it lacks any evident commitment to the doctrines of the Reformation, the Apostles' Creed being its only statement of faith. At the beginning of the present century the church claimed 120 thousand members gathered in seventy-four local assemblies. The church ordains women and supports a theological school that has no confessional basis. The Presbyterian Church in Rwanda is a member of the World Council of Churches and the World Alliance of Reformed Churches.

Republic of the Congo

Perhaps because of its secluded location in central Africa, Republic of the Congo (not to be confused with the neighboring Democratic Republic of the Congo) escaped the attention of the European colonial powers until

Henry M. Stanley explored there. While Otto von Bismarck (1815–1898) was chancellor of the German Empire, the nations asserting claims to parts of Africa met at the Congress of Berlin in 1884, where they recognized Leopold II, king of the Belgians (r. 1865–1909) as sovereign over the Congo Free State, a private enterprise in which the Belgian monarch was a major investor. In 1908 the Belgian Parliament required the king to relinquish his colony to the state, and it then became Belgian Congo. During the era of colonial rule, the Belgians did little to prepare the people for self-government, so when independence became a reality in 1960, the country exploded in tribal violence exacerbated by a Communist faction inspired by the Soviet Union and Red China. Dictatorship was the pattern of government for many years after independence, and tribal animosities continued to provoke warfare in the country.

Since Belgium is a predominantly Roman Catholic country, its king and government patronized Catholic missions there, although Protestants from the United Kingdom were the pioneers in planting Christianity. When they witnessed exploitation of the natives, the missionaries exposed it, but colonial administrators did little to correct conditions, which included forced labor. The Belgians in general resented the presence of Protestant missions and tried to thwart them in favor of Catholic efforts.

Southern Presbyterians from the United States entered Congo in 1891 to work among people of the Baluba tribe, and William Morrison (1867–1918) reduced the tribal language to writing and translated the Bible and other Christian literature. Successes in this endeavor led the Presbyterians to invest heavily, and Congo became the largest mission field of the Southern Presbyterian denomination. By 1957, 175 missionaries were there serving seventy thousand professing believers, the ancestors of whom had been, in many cases, slaves. It is worth noting that the Presbyterian mission, from its inception, included both black and white Americans eager to serve together.

Presbyterians joined eventually with other Protestants in an effort to form a Church of Christ in the Congo, a move motivated by mission personnel who had imbibed liberal theology and inclined toward ecumenical relations at the cost of confessional fidelity. While Joseph Mobutu Sese Seko was dictator of the Congo (1965–1997), he encouraged ecumenical movements to form a united church he intended to dominate. When that became evident, ecumenical leaders, both missionaries and natives, began criticizing the regime, sometimes at great risk. During the era of authoritarian rule, the government changed the name of the country to Zaire,

and a Reformed Conference of Zaire came into being in 1988 to promote interchurch cooperation. Several Presbyterian groups participated in
this organization, which in 1997 adopted the name Reformed Alliance of
Congo-Kinshasa.

Since the overthrow of Mobutu, the Presbyterian Community in the
Congo has developed the largest association of Reformed believers in the
country. It originated as the Southern Presbyterian Mission in 1891, but
between 1960 and 1970 disagreements related to ethnic-tribal tensions split
this movement into three separate denominations. This led eventually to the
formation of the Reformed Alliance as a means to restore some measure of
unity, and the divisions notwithstanding, the Presbyterian Community still
has over 1,250,000 adherents in 525 congregations. It affirms the Westminster Confession, at least in principal, but its relations are with liberal bodies
such as the Presbyterian Church (U.S.A.), the World Council of Churches,
and the World Alliance of Reformed Churches. The Presbyterian Community maintains a theological school in Kasai and engages in extensive social
and medical ministries. It ordains women for all church offices.

The two secessions from the Presbyterian Community produced the
Presbyterian Community of Eastern Kasai and the Reformed Community
of Presbyterians. The first of these offshoots reports twenty-seven thousand members and, like its parent, ordains females, holds membership in
the Reformed Alliance of Congo-Kinshasa and the World Alliance of
Reformed Churches, and operates many medical clinics and its own pastoral institute for the education of ministers. This church has not officially
adopted the Westminster Standards.

The Reformed Community of Presbyterians is a Pentecostal group
with its own confession, one that emphasizes the gifts of the Holy Spirit
presumed to be in effect now as in the apostolic age. It is affiliated with the
World Alliance of Reformed Churches, but it demonstrates little interest
in historic Calvinist theology. Its membership is about 11,200 people in
twenty-one local churches.

In 1955 missionaries in Leopoldville organized the Presbyterian Community of Kinshasa to serve the urban populace of the capital city. This was
an ecumenically oriented endeavor, but its efforts to promote church unity
were shaken by divisions that produced a schism of Pentecostals in 1964.
The Presbyterian Community of Kinshasa has maintained its ecumenical
posture and a generally liberal theology with an emphasis on social services
through health clinics and schools. Approximately sixty-seven thousand

people identify with this denomination, a member of the World Alliance of Reformed Churches, in fellowship with the Presbyterian Church (U.S.A.).

Another ministry focused on urban centers in Congo is the Protestant Community of Shaba, begun in 1953 through the work of Belgian Protestants. From its beginning this church embraced people of various Protestant connections, but its polity is Presbyterian, and it adheres officially to the Heidelberg Catechism as its statement of faith. Some eighteen thousand people are in this church, but membership has been declining for several years. Educational work is its major ministry. This church ordains women and is an affiliate of the World Alliance of Reformed Churches.

In 1978, in response to interest generated by the radio program *Reformed Perspectives*, Pastor A. R. Kayayan began a ministry that led to formation of the Confessing Reformed Church in Congo, a denomination twenty-four thousand strong. With support from the Dutch Reformed Church in South Africa and the Christian Reformed Church in North America, augmented later by aid from the Reformed Church in the United States, this body gained government recognition in 1991. More conservative than other Reformed movements in Congo, this one affirms the historic documents of the Dutch Reformed tradition, especially the Three Forms of Unity, and refrains from ordaining women. In addition to its patrons in North America and South Africa, this church has close relations with the Reformed Churches (Liberated) in the Netherlands, and it relies on the theological school of the International Council of Reformed Churches for the education of its ministers.

Malawi

This nation on the shores of Lake Malawi is densely populated, but 75 percent of its people speak the same tribal language, while the use of English is becoming more common all the time. David Livingstone toured Malawi in the mid-nineteenth century and there witnessed the brutalities of the slave trade, which aroused him to appeal for British missionaries and merchants to evangelize and civilize the region. The Church of England was the first to respond to Livingstone's appeal, as it established a mission there in 1861. In 1875 the Free Church of Scotland sent missionaries to the northern part of the country, while the Church of Scotland did likewise in the south. The year 1889 brought agents of the Dutch Reformed Church in South Africa to central Malawi. These efforts of three Reformed churches produced the Church of Central Africa, Presbyterian, as synods of the existing missions agreed, in 1924, to create a united denomination. By that time Malawi had been a British protectorate for thirty-three years. Missionaries were critical of colonial officials at times, even though the government encouraged and assisted the extension of education and health care. One complaint was that the colonial administration had made no provisions for higher education in the country. After World War II agitation for the end of British rule became pronounced, and church leaders were among vocal proponents of independence, which became a reality in 1964. Malawi's first president, Kamuzu Banda (d. 1997), was a Presbyterian elder, and today about 20 percent of Malawans are members of the Presbyterian Church.

Aside from a schism that led in 1933 to formation of the Blackman's Church of Africa, Presbyterian, the Church of Central Africa, Presbyterian is the only Reformed denomination in the country. It operates as a General Synod for three member synods, each of which retains much autonomy and conducts its own ministries without resort to a higher church court. Cooperation among component synods is unsystematic and irregular, although they jointly support a theological school. All Reformed missionaries working in Malawi were, at the end of the last century, members of the national church, and some hold offices within it but receive their income from sending churches.

The Church of Central Africa, Presbyterian, has been vigorous in evangelism and missions of its own and is almost self-supporting. Its agents have labored in Mozambique, and its radio broadcasts and literature distribution have reached across central Africa. This church has continued the work of the Dutch Reformed mission to the Muslims of the land, a work prompted in the nineteenth century by Arab involvement in the slave trade. Overcoming illiteracy is a major objective, one that has progressed well. Church growth too has been encouraging.

At the end of the twentieth century the Church of Central Africa, Presbyterian claimed almost eight hundred thousand members in over five hundred congregations. It does not ordain women as ministers but allows them to serve as elders and deacons. The official doctrinal position of the church features acceptance of almost all historic Reformed confessions and catechisms. This body is an affiliate of the World Alliance of Reformed Churches, the Reformed Ecumenical Council, the World Council of Churches, and regional ecumenical organizations. It maintains close relations with the Church of Scotland. Membership in extradenominational associations is a decision each of the three synods makes for itself, and the pattern is not uniform.

The Blackman's Church of Africa, Presbyterian, seceded from the original Presbyterian church in 1933, when Pastor Yesaya Zerenje Mwase protested some policies and practices of the missionaries and some matters pertaining to church discipline. In 2000 this rather obscure movement had about five hundred members in three congregations.

Malawi, in a general sense, may be the most Christian country in Africa, at least in regard to the percentage of people who claim church affiliation. Protestants as a whole comprise 52 percent of the population, while 11 percent are Roman Catholic. Seventeen percent are Muslims, and 20 percent practice some form of indigenous religion. The Reformed Church in America maintains a mission in Malawi at present, and the African Bible College campus there provides education from a Reformed perspective.

Zambia

In the middle of south central Africa sits the very poor country of Zambia, once known as Northern Rhodesia. The British South Africa Company of Cecil Rhodes (1863–1902) administered this territory until Great Britain declared it a protectorate in 1924. Zambia's principal resource is copper, and the fluctuating level of world demand for that metal has largely determined the country's economic health, so when demand is low, severe consequences ensue for Zambia.

Christianity arrived in the region near the close of the nineteenth century, as the Paris Mission, the London Missionary Society, and the Presbyterians, in that order, sent their personnel. Soon Roman Catholic White Fathers and the Dutch Reformed Church in South Africa too were engaged. Others followed as the twentieth century began.

David Livingstone appeared in Zambia in 1851, but early attempts to plant the faith there were not successful. Not until 1877, when the Paris Evangelical Society arrived, did Protestants establish their presence in Zambia. The London Missionary Society, with which Livingstone was serving, followed in 1883 and enjoyed considerable success in the copper mining area. Political independence came to the country in 1964 and with it a change of name from Northern Rhodesia to Zambia.

The Reformed mission began in this country as a Presbyterian enterprise in 1894, a work enhanced by the arrival of Dutch Reformed missionaries from South Africa five years later. Although there is now a

United Church of Zambia with almost a million members, that body is not Reformed, even though the Church of Scotland contributed to one of the missions that composed it in 1965. The Methodists were especially influential in the movement for a United Church, and it resembles the loose theology of that tradition much more than the confessional posture of Reformed churches.

The Church of Central Africa, Presbyterian-Synod of Zambia, closely related to the denomination of the same name in Malawi, is a body that owes its origin to one of the synods in Malawi that sent its people across the border into Northern Rhodesia. As in Malawi, a United Church of Rhodesia (Zambia) did develop, but a number of somewhat remote congregations in the eastern part of the country retained their separate identity as a Presbyterian church of twenty thousand adherents in twenty-nine congregations. This body affirms the Scots Confession, the Belgic Confession, the Westminster Confession, and other historic Reformed symbols and is a member of the Reformed Ecumenical Council. It operates Justo Mwale Theological College.

The largest historically Reformed denomination in Zambia is the Reformed Church in Zambia, founded in 1898 by a native evangelist who convinced a powerful tribal chief to invite the Dutch Reformed Church to send missionaries from South Africa. Numerous conversions led to dynamic church growth under the missionaries' supervision. Only slowly did natives gain authority in this church, and not until 1966 did it become autonomous. Tensions with the Dutch Reformed Church due to South Africa's policy of apartheid strained relations between the Reformed Church in Zambia and its South African patron and caused them to be suspended in 1991.

The Reformed Church in Zambia in 1999 reported a membership of five hundred thousand in 145 congregations and hundreds of preaching stations. The Heidelberg Catechism and the Canons of Dort express in principle the church's official position on doctrine, while it maintains membership in the World Council of Churches nevertheless. This church now has close relations with the post-apartheid Dutch Reformed Church in South Africa, the Reformed Churches of the Netherlands, and the World Alliance of Reformed Churches. Women do not serve in its pastoral ministries but do hold office as elders and deacons.

In 1991, when Frederick Chiluba became president of Zambia, he put the prestige of his office behind efforts to spread Christianity throughout his nation. Placing a Bible in every home was one of the president's announced objectives, and believers were especially glad when, in 1995, Chiluba declared Zambia a Christian country.

Zimbabwe

Southeast of Zambia lies Zimbabwe, a landlocked country that has borders with Mozambique, South Africa, Botswana, and Malawi, as well as Zambia itself. Endowed with considerable mineral resources, especially chromium, this country has the potential for great economic development, but political dictatorship and Marxist economic policies have been retarding growth ever since the government of Robert Mugabe came to power in 1987.

Portuguese Jesuits were the first missionaries to this region, but their efforts were not successful, and not until the latter part of the nineteenth century did Christianity make substantial gains. Roman Catholic missionaries returned in 1879, and today their church is the largest one in Zimbabwe, with approximately 12 percent of the population in its membership. The various Protestant groups together, however, include about 4 percent of the people. The initial Protestant mission was the work of Robert Moffat (1795–1883), a Scottish agent of the London Missionary Society, who arrived at Cape Town, South Africa, in 1816. Moffat's work had long-lasting consequences, for it inspired David Livingstone to go to Africa.

In 1829 Moffat visited the Matabeland area of what was to become Southern Rhodesia (now Zimbabwe), but a settled mission was not established there until 1859. For thirty years the London Missionary Society was the only Protestant ministry that endured in that country, and the numerical results of the missionaries' labor were discouraging. The situation changed for the better, however, when, in 1889, the British South Africa Company, a creation of Cecil Rhodes, obtained the right to occupy and administer the territory to become Rhodesia under a charter from the British government. The South Africa Company made large grants of land to Christian organizations willing to work in the country, and the Church of England responded quickly, as did the Methodists soon thereafter.

The next effort came in 1891 from the Dutch Reformed Church in South Africa, which invested heavily in this enterprise, as its station named Morning Star employed the largest Protestant mission staff in the land. In 1923 Great Britain declared Southern Rhodesia a Crown Colony, thereby ending the rule of the South Africa Company. Independence came in 1965, when the government of Prime Minister Ian Smith (1919–) renounced British authority after lengthy disputes about the racial composition of the colonial administration and assembly. Rhodesia by then had a mixed government in which whites and blacks qualified as voters and for government positions on an equal basis. Marxists responded to the Smith regime with guerilla warfare in which Robert Mugabe, the current dictator-president, was a leader. By 1980 Mugabe was in power and proceeded to impose a one-party state and a Communist-style economic program that has brought his country increasing impoverishment, which he has persistently blamed on the diminishing white minority.

In spite of the dismal political and economic condition of Zimbabwe, there is a rather strong Christian presence in the land, and Reformed churches have developed effective programs that began in the colonial era and continue to the present. The Reformed Church in Zimbabwe is an example. Begun in 1891 as a mission of the Cape Synod of the Dutch Reformed Church, this denomination reported eighty thousand members at the end of the last century. The church has local assemblies and preaching stations in several parts of the nation to minister to various tribal identities. The Reformed Church in Zimbabwe affirms the Dutch Reformed statements of doctrine and holds membership in the Reformed Ecumenical Council and the World Alliance of Reformed Churches as well as the World Council of Churches. Murray Theological College at the Morning Star station provides education for pastors, and schools on lower levels teach a broad spectrum of subjects to others. Hospitals and health clinics are significant social agencies of this denomination.

Another product of South African missions in Zimbabwe is the Dutch Reformed Synod of Central Africa, begun in 1895 north of the Limpopo River, a region that proved fertile ground for church growth. The congregations in that area united in 1957 to form the Synod of Central Africa, and in 1962 that body joined with churches south of the river to create a General Synod, autonomous and self-supporting. Affiliated with the World Alliance of Reformed Churches and the Reformed Ecumenical Council, this denomination of only twenty-six hundred members in sixteen assemblies ordains women to all offices while subscribing officially to the Three Forms of Unity. For the education of its ministers the church relies on the Stellenbosch University.

The Presbyterian Church of Southern Africa is still another consequence of South Africa's contributions to the Christian development of Zimbabwe. Bulawayo in 1896 was the birthplace of the first Presbyterian Church in the country, and a second formed at Harare seven years later.

Education has been a major emphasis of this body since its beginning, as its several fine secondary schools attest. Two presbyteries operate as divisions of this denomination in Zimbabwe, while the General Assembly has its offices in Johannesburg. The Presbyterian Church of Southern Africa accepts the Westminster Confession and a statement adopted in 1890 by the Presbyterian Church of England. In fellowship with the World Alliance of Reformed Churches and the World Council of Churches, this movement has about nine thousand members in eighteen congregations and several preaching stations. Its ministerial candidates, as a rule, study at the United Theological College in Harare or at universities in South Africa.

The Church of Central Africa, Presbyterian-Harare Synod also has a ministry in Zimbabwe, one initiated to serve the spiritual needs of migrant workers from Malawi who went to Zimbabwe for employment in agriculture or mining, beginning in 1912. Since the migrants were unfamiliar with the language of Rhodesia, the Church of Central Africa sent pastors to care for them. Others came from South Africa for the same purpose. The Harare Synod is now one of five connected with that denomination. Its membership in Zimbabwe is almost twelve thousand, and this synod does not ordain women to any church offices. The Heidelberg Catechism and the Canons of Dort are its formal statements of faith, and the synod enjoys close relations with the Dutch Reformed Church in South Africa and the Reformed Churches in the Netherlands. It is an affiliate of the World Alliance of Reformed Churches, the Reformed Ecumenical Council, and the World Council of Churches.

Although the regime of Robert Mugabe is authoritarian, racist, and Marxist in policy, it has allowed the churches of Zimbabwe considerable freedom, so the tradition of church-state collaboration in educational and social services continues. Most of the churches have, however, to some extent, absorbed pagan elements from pre-Christian African culture. The Christian faith is therefore in a rather diluted form, and reports of numerical growth, while impressive, might be misleading.

Mozambique

Situated on the east coast of southern Africa along the Indian Ocean, this former Portuguese colony first received some knowledge of Christianity through Dominican friars in the sixteenth century. For almost five hundred years Mozambique was subject to a colonial rule that was in general inept and at worst exploitative. The Portuguese did little to prepare the people for self-government, and when independence came in 1975, it was under a Marxist regime. Between 1975 and 1992 the country endured a destructive civil war as anti-Communists resisted the ruling faction.

Although Roman Catholic missionaries had begun their work in the sixteenth century, they made slow progress in converting the natives, as only the coastal area proved receptive to the new religion. Later Catholic efforts languished also until near the end of the nineteenth century, when they began to prosper. Protestants arrived in that same century, not Europeans, but natives converted from paganism through contacts with missionaries in adjacent countries. For a long time, Portuguese officials resisted Protestant missions in the colony, but other European powers present in Africa pressured Portugal to open the territory to their personnel. This was a provision of agreements among colonial nations reached in 1885. The first exponents of the Reformed faith to enter Mozambique came from Switzerland, and others followed from Scotland, South Africa, and the United States.

The Swiss Mission in South Africa worked with people forced by warfare to flee from Mozambique into the Transvaal Republic. Converts won under these circumstances eventually transmitted the gospel message to their relatives at home. English Methodists had preceded the Swiss by about fifty years, but their mission failed, as did one under the auspices of the American Board of Commissioners for Foreign Missions. American Methodists did, however, succeed later through the dynamic leadership of Bishop William Taylor, a missionary-statesman of amazing energy, who traveled the world for his church and ended his career in Africa, when illness forced him to retire in 1898.

The Presbyterian Church of Mozambique is a product of the Swiss mission and the labor of Paul Berthoud (1847–1930) in particular. This dedicated Reformed believer had served in a tribal region of South Africa where his family endured opposition from the Boers as well as diseases to which his wife and five children succumbed. Berthoud entered Mozambique in 1887 after Josef Mhalamhala, a native evangelist, had been preaching there for some time. At first the Presbyterian Church worked only in the south, but its presence is now evident throughout the country. This denomination became self-governing in 1948, but during the period of turbulence subsequent to independence, its people suffered much, especially when the Marxist government launched an antireligion policy in 1977. Many believers lost their jobs, homes, even their lives, while thousands fled the country as refugees.

Persecution did not destroy the Presbyterian Church, which now has about a hundred thousand members in 350 congregations bound together by Presbyterian polity and adherence to the Heidelberg Catechism, at least in a formal way. This denomination is an affiliate of the World Council of Churches and the World Alliance of Reformed Churches and regards itself as a partner with the Presbyterian Church (U.S.A.), which has missionaries serving with it in Mozambique. Education and social services are the major emphases in this arrangement. Like its American supporter, the Presbyterian Church of Mozambique ordains women to all of its offices.

The Evangelical Church of Christ in Mozambique owes its origin to Scottish Presbyterian missionaries who went there in 1876 to explore the area around Lake Nyama. Native Christians living in Malawi encouraged the missionaries to enter their homeland. It was not until 1912, however, that the Presbyterians were able to establish a settled mission station that, the next year, became the Scottish Presbyterian Church, later renamed as the Evangelical Mission of Nauela. It is now the Evangelical Church of Christ in Mozambique.

The Scottish missionaries remained at this post only until 1933 and then relinquished it to agents of the Church of the Brethren, who maintained it five years and then transferred it to the nondenominational South Africa General Mission. The colonial administration closed this ministry in 1959 as part of its anti-Protestant measures to restrict the churches. By 1969 the situation had improved, and the Evangelical Church revived, but as a Congregational-Baptist movement, as it remains. This denomination of about forty thousand people does not subscribe to any Reformed confessions, but it holds membership in the World Alliance of Reformed Churches nevertheless. Reformed in heritage, this body is no longer so in principle or in practice.

A denomination that does affirm Presbyterian polity and the Three Forms of Unity is the Reformed Church in Mozambique, which functions in two synods. The first bears the name of the denomination, and the second adds Mphatso Synod to it. Each synod has approximately thirty thousand members. Neither ordains females as pastors or elders. Although the synods enjoy great autonomy, they are almost identical in doctrine, and both are affiliates of the Reformed Ecumenical Council. They support a theological school jointly and conduct extensive health-care ministries. While these synods are self-governing, missionaries from the United States continue to labor there, as, for example, the Reformed Church in America, which has two families on that field.

Botswana

Immediately north of South Africa, between Namibia and Zimbabwe, is the Republic of Botswana, a landlocked nation of 1.5 million people living in a country that is mostly desert. Mining operations in diamonds, copper, and coal are its major economic activities.

Several strong tribal monarchies once controlled this land, but in the nineteenth century it became the British protectorate of Bechuanaland, when the leading tribal king asked for aid to thwart Boers from South Africa who had been encroaching on the territory. In 1885 Great Britain made the region south of the Molopo River a Crown Colony but left the rest of Bechuanaland a protectorate.

The introduction of Christianity into this region was the work of Robert Moffat and David Livingstone, agents of the London Missionary Society, and by 1857 the entire Bible had been translated into the native Setswana tongue, thanks to the efforts of workers in the London Mission. The conversion of Prince Khama Boikano in 1862 was a milestone in the Christian history of his country. From 1872 to 1923 he was king of his tribe and in that position promoted Christianity vigorously. A large number of his subjects followed their monarch's example and were baptized. To his credit, Khama then ruled on the basis of Christian principles as he perceived them, with the result that his policies greatly diminished pagan influences. His rule, however, led to the creation of a state church, an arrangement that is always harmful in that it encourages a civil religion in which formal adherence to the church becomes a political duty. In 1890, when London Mission Society personnel challenged his authority, the king expelled the missionaries and declared himself head of the church.

In addition to the London Society, German Lutheran and Dutch Reformed missions established their presence in what is now Botswana, in both cases as extensions of existing ministries in South Africa. In 1863 the Cape Synod of the Dutch Reformed Church dispatched a mission to the Bagkgatla tribe and thereby began the work that would lead to formation of the Dutch Reformed Church in Botswana, which eventually became a multi-ethnic denomination of some fifty-four hundred people in ten congregations. Henri Gonin, a Swiss missionary, led this evangelistic approach to the Bagkgatla people then living near Rustenburg, South Africa, and when in 1870 that tribe moved into Botswana, South African missionaries followed and established social, educational, and medical works while seeking more converts. Not until 1979 did the Dutch Reformed Church in Botswana become autonomous. This body affirms the Three Forms of Unity, is a member of the Reformed Ecumenical Council, and maintains close relations with its mother church in South Africa. It is affiliated with the World Alliance of Reformed Churches as well, and it ordains women to all church offices.

Lesotho

Entirely surrounded by South Africa is the tiny kingdom of Lesotho, once known as Basutoland, which became a British Crown Colony in 1868 when the dominant tribal chief appealed to Queen Victoria (r. 1837–1901) for protection against Boers who aspired to annex this area to Cape Colony. This relationship with the British Crown continued until 1966 when the kingdom of Lesotho became an independent state.

The assertion of British authority brought not only protection from the Boers but internal stability to an often unruly land. The first Christian missionaries, representatives of the Paris Evangelical Missionary Society, had entered Basutoland in 1833 and enjoyed a royal welcome from King Moshoeshoe I (1786–1870). Soon, however, tribal wars forced the suspension of missionary work, but the coming of British officials allowed it to resume, and the Lesotho Evangelical Church developed as a consequence. In 1887 that body opened a theological school to prepare native pastors, and by 1898 church growth necessitated formation of a synod. Competition from Catholic and Anglican missions weakened the Evangelical Church somewhat in the twentieth century.

Political independence came to Lesotho in 1966, but as in other African countries, self-rule has been a mixed blessing. When in 1970 the prime minister suspended the constitution and imposed his own dictatorship, the evangelical church supported resistance to his rule and endured persecution as a consequence. The country did not achieve a duly elected government until 1993, a development that permitted the exiled King Moshoeshoe II to return. To the disadvantage of the church, political divisions in Lesotho produced contentions among Christians, and the church remains in a rather unstable condition even now.

The Evangelical Church of Lesotho is Presbyterian in polity and officially Reformed in theology, as its endorsement of the Heidelberg Catechism indicates. It is, however, in general, a liberal-ecumenical denomination in fellowship with the World Council of Churches and the World Alliance of Reformed Churches. About 211 thousand people hold membership, but attendance is poor, a fact attested by the existence of only fifty-six congregations. The church ordains women. Although a vast majority of the people of Lesotho professes some version of Christianity, the Reformed segment is declining, while almost 44 percent of the populace now identify with Roman Catholicism, this in spite of continuing support from Reformed churches in South Africa and Presbyterian churches in the United States and Canada.

Swaziland

Swaziland, a constitutional monarchy near South Africa's border with Mozambique, is southern Africa's smallest sovereign state, one in which 80 percent of the people profess Christianity. The Swazis coalesced into a single people in order to protect themselves from aggressive Zulus. The Boer government of the Transvaal Republic administered this region for part of the nineteenth century, but defeat in the Anglo-Boer War (1899–1902) required it to relinquish control to Great Britain, which then governed it as a protectorate until 1968. Although economically dependent on South Africa, Swaziland has valuable resources in diamonds and coal. Only since 1993 has the country had a duly elected government.

American Methodists were the first to evangelize the Swazis, arriving there in the 1880s as an extension of their mission in South Africa. Nondenominational agencies such as the South Africa General Mission and the Evangelical Alliance Mission followed, but only one very small Reformed ministry has developed. It is the Swaziland Reformed Church, composed of four congregations and fewer than six hundred adherents. This is a product of South African mission work begun in 1946 by the Dutch Reformed Church. Until 1991 this body was a synod of that church but in that year became independent. The Swaziland Reformed Church subscribes to the Three Forms of Unity and does not ordain females as pastors or elders, but does permit them to be deacons. Other than membership in the Swaziland Council of Churches, this body appears to have no broader ecumenical relations.

Namibia

South of Angola, west of Botswana, and northwest of South Africa is Namibia, once known as Southwest Africa. Sparsely populated across a desert terrain with few cities and little water, this is a generally inhospitable region. The country does, however, have extensive mineral resources such as diamonds, uranium, tin, and tungsten, as well as some gold, silver, and natural gas. Most of Namibia's 1.7 million people live in the north and most of them in urban centers.

Although Portuguese explorers discovered this country in the fifteenth century and the Dutch and the English followed, the Europeans found nothing to attract them to settle there. In 1824, however, the Rhenish Mission Society from Germany sent its agents to evangelize the natives, but tribal warfare prompted the government of the German state involved to offer the territory to Great Britain in exchange for protection of the mission and its converts. The British government agreed to annex only the area around Walvis Bay, which left the rest of Southwest Africa in an unstable condition and Christians there without protection. Germany itself was not a nation-state until 1871, and her imperial chancellor and architect of national unity Otto von Bismarck was reluctant to allow his new German Empire to become involved in overseas colonial enterprises that might lead to international conflicts. By 1884 he nevertheless succumbed to pressures from nationalists eager to make Germany a global power. In that year Germany declared a protectorate over Southwest Africa. When German settlers arrived in growing numbers, the Khoikhoi people attacked them and thereby provoked a devastating German retaliation. The discovery of diamonds in 1908 brought more settlers. In World War I South African forces defeated the German defenders, and after that war the League of Nations made the region a mandate to be governed by South Africa. Following the Second World War South Africa petitioned the United Nations to allow it to annex this territory, but the world body refused.

The Lutheran mission in Southwest Africa proved quite successful, and today over four hundred thousand people identify with the Lutheran Church. Reformed missions in Namibia are of much more recent origin and are the work of evangelists from the Dutch Reformed Church of South Africa. The progress of the Reformed faith has been slow, even when its exponents agreed not to compete with the well-established Lutheran churches. The largest such body there is the Dutch Reformed Church in Namibia, which began in the 1880s but could not establish a functioning congregation until 1898. This denomination, at the end of the last century, reported forty-six local assemblies and about twenty-six thousand members. Although autonomous, it depends heavily upon the Dutch Reformed

Church of South Africa, of which it is a synod. The Namibian church affirms the Three Forms of Unity while ordaining females to all church offices. Its ministries reach beyond the towns and cities to primitive Bushmen, with whom it began working in 1961.

Only about one-quarter of the size of the Dutch Reformed Church in Namibia is the Uniting Reformed Church of Southern Africa, another product of South African missions. Although this body had only three congregations at the time, it formed a synod in 1975, and by 1987 three synods were in operation, all working together as the Evangelical Reformed Church in Africa. A fourth synod emerged in 1995, the year in which all the synods concerned agreed to join the Uniting Reformed Church of Southern Africa, which older Reformed believers had created in South Africa the previous year.

In 1999, the Uniting Church had about sixty-nine hundred members and thirty-one congregations in Namibia. Its Caprivi Synod does ordain women, but the others do not. The Three Forms of Unity are the official statement of faith, and the church is an affiliate of the Reformed Ecumenical Council. This denomination maintains the Evangelical Theological Seminary for the education of pastors.

Some Reformed believers who once lived in Angola moved to Namibia in 1929 and quickly organized three local churches in their new homeland. Eventually this body became the Reformed Churches in Namibia and soon initiated evangelism among Bushmen in their own country and in Botswana. Translation of the Bible into the tribal language of the Bushmen was a major project of this mission, one completed within the last few years. Almost two thousand people have aligned with this church of only fourteen congregations. The Reformed Churches in Namibia do not ordain women, and they operate as a regional synod of the Reformed Churches in South Africa. The historic Dutch confessions are the official statements of doctrine.

Two other Reformed movements in South Africa have small constituencies in Namibia, and by the opening of the present century, some sixty-two thousand people were affiliated with the several churches professing the Reformed faith. Church planting, education, and health care are major concerns for all of these bodies, and financial support from South Africa remains crucial for the progress of their ministries.

Angola

On the west coast of southern Africa lies the People's Republic of Angola, a nation of about thirteen million people which was subject to Portuguese colonial rule until 1975. The explorers who discovered this country in 1483 introduced Roman Catholicism, and at first the new religion prospered, but Portuguese involvement in the slave trade alienated the natives. Despite official Portuguese support, the Catholic mission did not regain strength until late in the nineteenth century. Protestant missionaries arrived in 1878, British Baptists as the vanguard, and others soon followed. The colonial administration, of course, favored Catholicism, and other missions sometimes experienced opposition.

When in the 1960s various native movements launched a war for independence, the government closed many Protestant churches and expelled foreign missionaries because of its belief that the foreigners supported the anti-Portuguese rebels. When independence became a reality in 1975, the country became a battleground in the Cold War between the Soviet bloc and Western nations under the leadership of the United States. At one point Cuban forces went to Angola as Soviet surrogates, and South Africa intervened to oppose them. The Marxists won the first national elections, which occurred in 1988, but the anti-Communists refused to accept the results, and warfare continued until 1995.

Through the turbulence the churches of Angola grew quickly, some Reformed bodies among them. The largest of these denominations is the Evangelical Congregational Church in Angola, which, in spite of its name, practices Presbyterian polity and affirms the Heidelberg Catechism as its confession of faith. This church owes its origin to the work of the American Board of Commissioners for Foreign Missions, which began evangelizing in the highlands in 1880. After the declaration of independence, a large portion of the church's members sided with the Marxist movement, as the church became divided over political allegiance. In 1996 the two factions reunited, and by 2000, the church had about 250 thousand members. The Evangelical Congregational Church ordains women to all offices, and it maintains broadly ecumenical relations with other churches in Africa while holding membership in the World Council of Churches.

The Evangelical Reformed Church of Angola began as an Anglican mission in 1922 and then organized as an indigenous church. During the period of anti-Portuguese rebellion, this church endured much persecution at the hands of colonial officials, and many of its members fled into exile.

The movement assumed its present name officially in 1977, two years after independence. Spread across most of the country, the Evangelical Reformed Church has its center of strength in eastern Angola. The Helvetic Confession and the Heidelberg Catechism express its official doctrinal position, and approximately two hundred thousand adherents meet in 452 congregations. Females are eligible for all offices in this ecumenically oriented denomination affiliated with the World Alliance of Reformed Churches, the World Council of Churches, and some African interdenominational agencies. There is a Bible institute and a seminary for the preparation of church workers.

There are two overtly Presbyterian bodies in this nation, the larger one being the Presbyterian Church of Angola, with a membership of only seventy-six hundred in twenty-eight local assemblies. It originated as a schism from the Evangelical Reformed Church in 1984, when a pastor of that church advocated polygamy. Since the coming of peace to Angola due to a ceasefire agreement in 2002, the Presbyterian Church there has enjoyed a partnership with the Presbyterian Church (U.S.A.), which supports the African denomination financially, and membership in the Angolan Presbyterian Church has been growing. Unlike its American patron, this body does not ordain women, and it appears to be more serious about its commitment to Reformed theology than its partner. The Westminster Confession is its standard, and other than its connection with the Presbyterian Church (U.S.A.), it does not have broad ecumenical relations.

The Independent Presbyterian Church in Angola, founded in 1991, is a creation of exiles from the country that fled into Zaire during the civil war. Upon their return they resolved to form a church of their own rather than affiliate with an existing one. Only about one thousand people adhere to this denomination of four local churches. While the polity is Presbyterian, the Independent Church makes no official commitment to any historic Reformed confession, and it ordains women as elders and deacons.

Democratic Republic of the Congo

Once part of French Equatorial Africa, this troubled nation of West Africa first encountered Christianity through Portuguese missionaries who landed there in 1491. Italian Capuchin friars came later in large numbers, but Catholicism's association with the slave trade undermined its credibility with the natives, while the Africans' tendency to blend Catholic teachings with concepts in their traditional cults hindered the mission. For a time

Portuguese officials required foreigners to leave the country, and not until 1883 did Catholic missionaries return. Suppression of the slave trade in the nineteenth century weakened the tribal network that had supplied the Portuguese with captives for sale, and the collapse of the native kingdoms engaged in slavery injured Portuguese commerce badly.

In 1875 French explorer Pierre Savorgnan de Brazza (1852–1905) initiated his expedition into central Africa and in 1880 made a treaty with the chief of the Tio tribe by which that part of Africa became a French protectorate. Additional agreements with other tribes led to a declaration of the French Congo, which, in 1905, became part of French Equatorial Africa. Brazzaville, named in honor of the explorer, became the capital of this territory, which France ruled until, in 1960, it granted independence to its colony. Self-rule did not proceed smoothly, and Congo's government changed hands several times due to revolts and assassinations. Marxists were conspicuous participants in these struggles, as were military dictators.

Protestant mission work in the former French Congo began in 1909, when the Mission Covenant Church of Sweden sent its agents there, a project soon augmented by workers from Covenant Churches in Norway and Finland. The fruit of their labor is the Evangelical Church of the Congo, formed in 1961 as an independent body after many years in mission status. This church is organized along the lines of Presbyterian polity but affirms no confession other than the Apostles' Creed. It practices believer's baptism exclusively and so is not Reformed in doctrine. In recent years this denomination of 136 thousand adherents has become increasingly ecumenical, even to the point of cooperating with the Roman Catholic Church. A member of the World Council of Churches and the World Alliance of Reformed Churches, the Evangelical Church maintains close relations with its parent bodies in Scandinavia. Continuing tribal and ethnic conflicts have impaired the unity of this church and thereby hindered its work.

Nigeria

The most populous country in Africa is the Republic of Nigeria, situated to the south and west of Niger, west of Cameroon, and east of Benin on the Gulf of Guinea. This land of over one hundred million people was, until 1960, Great Britain's foremost colony in Africa. The official language is English, but there are about five hundred native tongues. Numerous tribal entities, each with its own culture, have made Nigeria a very diverse country. Islam was present there long before Christianity, and about half of the people now are Muslims, while some 40 percent profess Christianity. The rest are animists.

As early as the sixteenth century Britain had commercial contacts that expanded over time and led to declarations of a protectorate over various areas. In 1909 Nigeria became a British Crown Colony. Protestantism came to Nigeria when former Christian slaves from Sierra Leone asked for missionaries to teach them the Bible, and the Wesleyan Missionary Society and the Church Missionary Society, both from the United Kingdom, sent workers in 1842. In 1846 the United Free Church of Scotland initiated Reformed efforts when freed slaves from Jamaica and missionaries from Scotland arrived at Calabar and established a dynamic evangelistic endeavor that enjoyed support from churches in Scotland. Among the Christians who labored in the Calabar Mission, none contributed more than Mary Slessor (1848–1915), a devout Presbyterian who invested almost forty years in this part of Africa after working for some time in the Queen Street Mission in Aberdeen, a ministry to alcoholics and other derelicts. When she learned of the death of David Livingstone, Slessor resolved to join the Calabar Mission, at which she taught and subsequently engaged in pioneer evangelism and medical work. Her vibrant faith made such an impression on Nigerian chiefs that they sometimes asked her to mediate tribal conflicts. Often she traveled where no white people had gone before. She founded schools and taught Africans basic skills to help them earn a living. Slessor adopted several African children and lived in the style of the natives, often heedless about her own health and safety.

The Presbyterian Church of Nigeria is, in large part, the product of the Calabar Mission in general and of Mary Slessor in particular. Autonomous since 1954, this denomination has about 125 thousand members in 645 congregations. Its official statement of doctrine is the Westminster Confession of Faith. This church ordains women to all its offices, and it operates the Presbyterian Theological College for the education of ministers and church workers.

A second Reformed body of note in Nigeria is the Qua Iboe Church, so called because it began in an area near the Qua Iboe River in 1887. A European merchant had been promoting Christianity in this region by holding meetings in which he preached to the natives. At his request H. Grattan Guiness (1835–1910) of London, who had assisted in the creation of a mission in the Congo, appealed to students at his Bible institute to volunteer for service in Nigeria, and Samuel A. Bill (1864–1942) from

Ulster agreed to go. The Qua Iboe Mission he established became an effective means for spreading the gospel through preparing native pastors who in turn founded local churches.

At the end of the twentieth century, the Qua Iboe Church reported eighty thousand members meeting in approximately one thousand congregations. It does not ordain women, observes Presbyterian polity, and operates a Bible school, a church training center, and Samuel Bill Theological College. The church has adopted its own statement of faith, one generally Reformed in content.

An American denomination that has invested heavily in Nigeria, the Christian Reformed Church, began its work there when Johanna Veenstra (1894–1933) went there in 1920. This tireless and dedicated Christian from Paterson, New Jersey, daughter of a Christian Reformed minister, served with the Sudan United Mission, a nondenominational organization focused on combating Muslim influence in Africa. Conversions were few, but Veenstra was relentless in her work, often traveling by motorcycle, as she witnessed for Christ in remote places. Her medical ministry was especially effective. Reports Veenstra sent to Christian Reformed congregations in America aroused great concern for Nigeria, and in 1949 her denomination made its World Missions agency an autonomous part of the Sudan United Mission. The amazing receptivity of Nigerians to the gospel caused the Christian Reformed Church to send more missionaries there, and eventually that country became the church's largest mission field. The formal organization of the Christian Reformed Church of Nigeria occurred in 1951. Now about 160 thousand strong, the church has a weekly attendance in excess of two hundred thousand in seventy congregations. It does not ordain females, and its official doctrinal position includes adherence to both the Three Forms of Unity and the Westminster Confession. This church maintains close relations with its North American patron, and it operates Smith Memorial Bible College and Johanna Veenstra Seminary, a school named in honor of the great missionary pioneer.

The Dutch Reformed Church in South Africa also has, since 1911, done extensive missionary work in Nigeria. Among the Tiv people this has led to the creation of the Church of Christ in the Sudan among the Tiv. "Sudan," in this case, is not a geographic term but one that identifies the native black African character of the church membership. In 1960 the Dutch Reformed Church transferred its operations in Nigeria to the World Missions of the Christian Reformed Church in North America. This occurred because the apartheid policy in South Africa aroused opposition to Christian workers from that nation, and the new government of independent Nigeria required all South African missionary personnel to leave the country. The Church of Christ in the Sudan is a self-governing body operating with Presbyterian polity, and since 1985, it has done so without financial aid from the Christian Reformed denomination in America. This church of about nine hundred thousand people subscribes to the historic Dutch Reformed standards and is a member of the Reformed Ecumenical Council and the World Alliance of Reformed Churches. Reformed Theological College and a Bible school are its institutions of higher learning, and it has many high schools and elementary schools as well as hospitals and health clinics.

The Evangelical Reformed Church of Christ owes its origin to the work of the Sudan United Mission's South African branch. Begun in 1916, it is today the largest Reformed denomination in Nigeria, as about 1.5 million people identify with it. This church espouses all the historic Reformed-Presbyterian doctrinal standards, at least in principle, although it ordains women and holds membership in the World Council of Churches. Its other ecclesiastical connections are with the Reformed Ecumenical Council and the World Alliance of Reformed Churches. A pastors' college and a theological seminary provide academic preparation for its ministers. The Evangelical Reformed Church of Christ has close relations with the Reformed Church in the Netherlands and is affiliated with several African ecumenical organizations.

Another sizeable denomination is the Reformed Church of Christ in Nigeria, a movement that originated in 1973 as a schism from the Christian Reformed Church in Nigeria. Most adherents to this body of some five hundred thousand belong to a single tribe. This church, which does not ordain females, subscribes to all the major Reformed confessions and is a member of the Reformed Ecumenical Council and the World Alliance of Reformed Churches while maintaining fraternal relations with the Christian Reformed Church in North America. Veenstra Bible College and Seminary are its principal schools of higher learning, and extensive social services are conspicuous parts of its ministry.

In 1970 the Netherlands Reformed Congregations began a work in Nigeria in conjunction with the Sudan United Mission. In 1988 the local assemblies together formed the Nigerian Reformed Church, a denomination that, at the end of the last century, reported a membership of twenty-five hundred in five congregations and many more preaching stations bound together in a single classis (presbytery). Staunchly orthodox, the Nigerian Reformed Church affirms the Three Forms of Unity and refrains from ordaining women while enjoying close relations with the Netherlands Reformed Congregations in Holland and North America. The Nigeria Reformed Theological College prepares its candidates for the ministry.

Ghana

On the Gulf of Guinea, west of Togo and east of the Ivory Coast, is the Republic of Ghana, long known as the Gold Coast because Portuguese explorers found that precious metal there near the end of the fifteenth century. Dutch and English merchants conducted trade there too, as did the French, Germans, and Swedes to a lesser extent. Early efforts to promote Christianity in connection with European commerce accomplished little, however, because of the foreigners' involvement in the slave trade. The Moravians made a serious effort to establish a mission early in the eighteenth century, but disease took a heavy toll among them and effectively nullified their work. In 1828 the Basel Mission, an organization rooted in German pietism, sent evangelists who survived the hostile climate but only with aid from Jamaican Christians freed from slavery that landed in the Gold Coast and were able to withstand the conditions there to which whites often succumbed.

In 1847 the Bremen Mission, an arm of the German Reformed Church, opened a station in Ghana to minister to the Ewe tribe, an endeavor that has endured as the Evangelical Presbyterian Church, Ghana. Great Britain established a Crown Colony over the Gold Coast in 1874 and protectorates over the ancient kingdom of Ashanti and some northern lands in 1901. The entire country continued under British rule until 1957, when it became independent.

The various missions active in Ghana helped to educate natives who became political figures influential in leading the country toward self-government. Independence, however, brought an initial loss of stability, as political and military factions contended for control. Long before independence the German and Swiss missionaries left, due to the fighting in World War I, and after that conflict, the Untied Free Church of Scotland assumed responsibility for the ministries of the Basel and Bremen missions. With the encouragement of the Scots, the natives developed their own control over church affairs, and today two vigorous Presbyterian bodies are functioning, which, in recent years, have experienced impressive growth.

The Presbyterian Church of Ghana originated as the Basel Mission of the Gold Coast but changed its name to the Scottish Mission Church after the First World War, and then to the Presbyterian Church of the Gold Coast in 1926. This dynamic movement, now with almost five hundred thousand adherents, is one of the most prominent Protestant churches in the country. Its thirteen presbyteries encompass the whole nation, and its social service ministries extend to education, health care, and agriculture as adjuncts to evangelism. Ecumenically oriented, the Presbyterian Church of Ghana is an affiliate of the World Alliance of Reformed Churches and the World Council of Churches and ordains women. The church has a substantial and sometimes troublesome charismatic component. It does not subscribe officially to the traditional Reformed confessions, a sign it is Presbyterian in polity but not uniformly so in doctrine.

The second Reformed body in this West African nation is the Evangelical Presbyterian Church, Ghana, a product, as indicated, of German missions from Bremen. When World War I began, those missionaries had two ministries within the British territory and seven more in the neighboring German colony of Togoland. Defeat in 1918 brought the loss of all Germany's colonies, and Great Britain obtained control of western Togo. The dominant Ewe tribe lived in both the Gold Coast and the newly acquired part of Togo, and the church leaders resolved to have one synod for the whole region. Scottish missionaries soon began evangelizing in Togo, and successes eventually led to a division into two closely related synods, a move in the interest of administrative efficiency.

The Evangelical Presbyterian Church, Ghana, suffered a schism in 1954 due to disputes about languages to be used in services of worship and polygamy, long an accepted custom in that part of Africa. By 1964, however, the factions reached agreement, and most of the seceding congregations returned to their mother church. The prominence and assertiveness of charismatic believers brought further tensions and produced another division, as a considerable minority withdrew to form its own church in 1991.

The Evangelical Presbyterian Church reported almost 145 thousand members in 748 congregations. Women are eligible for ordination to all offices, and the denomination affirms only the Apostles' Creed. It, like its larger counterpart, is Presbyterian in polity but not definitely Reformed in theology. This church, despite its lack of subscription to the historic confessions, holds membership in the World Alliance of Reformed Churches. It operates Trinity College, Legon, for the education of ministers in conjunction with the Presbyterian Church of Ghana and the Methodist and Anglican Churches. The broad character of this denomination is evident in its affiliation with the World Council of Churches.

Ghana remains a point of focus for American and European missions, as the Presbyterian Church (U.S.A.) and the Church of Scotland continue to have personnel on that field.

Liberia

Established in 1822 as a refuge for freed slaves from the United States, this small republic on the western shore of Africa just above the Ivory Coast has not been a fruitful field for the planting of Reformed churches. Perhaps one-third of the people profess some version of Christian belief, but there is only a single organized Presbyterian church in the land, even though the first Presbyterian missionary sent out from the United States went there in 1833. In that same year Methodists and Congregationalists from America initiated work in Liberia.

From the outset mission work in this land was extremely difficult, as disease took a huge toll, and casualties among Presbyterian personnel were especially high. For a while the Presbyterian Church (U.S.A.) sent only black Americans to Liberia because of the presumption they could withstand the illnesses to which so many whites had fallen victim. That proved to be an error. Presbyterians from America continued to go to Liberia in spite of the danger until 1890, when the American denomination closed that field. By that time twelve Presbyterian congregations were operating there.

In addition to the rigors of an unhealthful climate, Liberia has suffered from severe internal discord. The freed slaves from America did not mix well with the indigenous population, and entrusting a poorly prepared people with the responsibilities of self-government was a capital mistake. This became patently clear during the last two decades of the twentieth century, when civil war ravaged the land and caused the death of over 150 thousand people and the displacement of hundreds of thousands more. The conflicts destroyed much of the economy and left Liberia in chaos. The churches, of course, did not escape the devastation. To add to the tensions that wrack this little country, Muslims from Egypt and Pakistan have, since the 1950s, been propagating their beliefs in an already divided nation.

The Presbytery of Liberia became autonomous in 1928, and in 1980 it affiliated with the Cumberland Presbyterian Church in the United States, a denomination that categorically rejects the Westminster Standards and the Reformed teaching about soteriology. As of 1999 about three thousand Liberians identified themselves as Presbyterians, but their church, while Presbyterian in polity, rejects the historic Reformed faith and subscribes to only the Apostles' Creed and the Nicene Creed. The Presbytery of Liberia, a member of the World Alliance of Reformed Churches and the World Council of Churches, ordains females to all church offices.

Although the Presbytery of Liberia does not espouse historic Calvinistic theology, missionaries from the Christian Reformed Church in North America, the Associate Reformed Presbyterian Church, and the Presbyterian Church in America labor there in the interest of establishing a genuine Reformed witness. The Christian Reformed Church began its work there in 1975 in conjunction with some indigenous churches of the Bassa people. In 1983 the Christian Reformed mission joined forces with the Associate Reformed Presbyterians to evangelize Muslims, most of them in the Cape Mount region, but some in Monrovia, the capital city. As of the year 2000, almost half the population of Liberia practiced one or another of the many African traditional cults.

Burkina Faso

North of Ghana and south of Mali lies the nation of Burkina Faso, long a part of French West Africa and once known as Upper Volta. Although most of its people are Muslims, Christianity has made rapid and impressive gains, especially among the Mossi people and more recently among the Burkinabe. Protestant missions from the United States entered this country in 1921, with the Assemblies of God leading the way and the Christian and Missionary Alliance close behind. These and other agencies, for the most part charismatics, have spread across the land, and at this time about 20 percent of the populace professes allegiance to some form of Christian belief. The Reformed presence in Burkina Faso is confined, however, to one church body that began in 1977. Some thirty-three hundred supporters adhere to the Reformed Evangelical Church of Burkina Faso, a denomination with thirty congregations, most of them in the northern part of the land, united in a single synod that espouses the ancient creeds plus the Heidelberg Catechism. A member of the World Alliance of Reformed Churches, this body ordains women. Its growth has not been comparable to that of other Protestant groups in the country, which has been politically independent since 1960 but repeatedly subject to military rule.

Cameroon

Although the Reformed faith is relatively weak in West Africa, the situation in the United Republic of Cameroon, where several Presbyterian groups are present, is something of an exception. North of Gabon and south and east of Nigeria, Portuguese explorers discovered Cameroon in 1472, and soon a plantation economy and the slave trade were thriving, until Dutch slavers seized the area in the seventeenth century. In 1807 Great Britain not only abolished the slave trade in its own territories but resolved to stop it everywhere within British reach. Royal Navy vessels patrolled the coast and interdicted ships of other powers engaged in slavery while British settlers moved on the coast. In 1884, however, German colonial officials convinced native chiefs to accept a protectorate that remained in effect until the dismemberment of the German Empire in World War I. The Paris Peace Conference of 1919 divided Cameroon between Britain and France as mandate powers, an arrangement that continued until 1961, when the country gained independence.

Protestant Christianity came to Cameroon in 1842 when the London Baptist Missionary Society began a work there that led to publication of the Bible in the native tongue, a project completed in 1872. During the period of German administration, however, British missionaries were not welcome, and the Baptists left. The Basel Mission then assumed responsibility for that work, but sometimes encountered resistance from converts won through the Baptists' efforts. Many indigenous people remained Baptists and organized their own churches rather than accept the paedobaptist theology of the Reformed mission. The Basel Mission, nevertheless, expanded its ministry, but the outcome of the war in 1918 required its agents to leave the country, an absence that continued until 1925.

Although British and German missionaries were more numerous, Presbyterians from America also entered this land, the first effort occurring in 1850 when the Presbyterian Board of Foreign Missions sent workers to the island of Corisco. This station provided a base from which evangelists entered Cameroon. The Bulu people responded enthusiastically, and soon Presbyterian churches were thriving in the area. Soon after the Second World War, native ecclesiastical leaders began seeking control over their churches, and by 1957 the Presbyterian Church in Cameroon had become an autonomous denomination. Its roots were in the Basel Mission, and American Presbyterians too concurred with the change to African administration of the schools, clinics, and agricultural stations long under the mission's authority.

At the end of the twentieth century, the Presbyterian Church in Cameroon had about three hundred thousand members in around three hundred congregations and several hundred preaching points bound together in a synodal structure but affirming only the Apostles' Creed and the Nicene Creed as statements of doctrine. A member of the World Alliance of Reformed Churches and the World Council of Churches, this church ordains females and operates its own seminary at Kumba.

With over one million members, the Evangelical Church of Cameroon is the largest denomination there that operates under Presbyterian polity. It grew out of the work of the English Baptists, the Basel Mission, and the Paris Mission, and so has been doctrinally composite for most of its history. Autonomous since 1957, this body maintains over seven hundred local churches. It subscribes to the Apostles' Creed but not to any distinctively Reformed confession, although it has close relations with Reformed churches in the Netherlands and Germany. It is an affiliate of the World Council of Churches and several ecumenical organizations in Africa. The Evangelical Church ordains women, has a wide outreach through literature, and operates a theological school at Ndongue.

An ecclesiastical body in which American missionaries have had a profound influence is the Presbyterian Church of Cameroon, which began as a mission of the Presbyterian Church (U.S.A.) in 1875, as mentioned above. By agreement with German colonial officials, the Americans opened schools in which the German language was the vehicle of instruction, although the missionaries translated the Bible and Christian literature into the native tongues as well. In 1920 the Basel Mission transferred its operations to the American Presbyterians, and thereafter many new mission stations were established, as Christianity grew rapidly. As of 1997 five synods were functioning to administer affairs in a denomination of over 600 thousand people in about five hundred congregations. In addition to the ancient creeds, this body subscribes officially to the Westminster Confession and the Heidelberg Catechism. It has close relations with the Presbyterian Church (U.S.A.) while holding membership in the World Alliance of Reformed Churches and the World Council of Churches.

In 1967 a schism within the Presbyterian Church of Cameroon led to formation of the Orthodox Presbyterian Church of Cameroon. The issues provoking the secession pertained to the ecumenical connections of the parent denomination and its generally liberal posture toward historic doctrines of the faith. Pastor Jean Andjongo organized a band of ministers and elders who withdrew during the General Assembly of the Presbyterian Church and formed the Orthodox Presbyterian Church. When the Presbyterian Church of Cameroon began seizing properties held by seceding congregations, the Orthodox Presbyterian Church appealed to a civil court, which led to bitter quarrels and false accusations, even to the arrest of church members who had resorted to fraud to win their case. The dishonest faction drew support from the International Council of Christian Churches and fundamentalists in the United States. By 1970, however, the turmoil subsided, and the government of Cameroon registered the Orthodox Presbyterian Church as a recognized religious body. Thereafter that denomination grew rapidly and by the year 2000, it had more than a hundred thousand members and two hundred local assemblies organized into three synods. The Westminster Confession of Faith is this church's statement of doctrine. Although the Orthodox Presbyterian Church ordains women as elders and deacons, it does not permit them to be ministers. The denomination remains a member of the International Council of Christian Churches.

Africa below the Sahara Desert has experienced a remarkable advance of Christianity in recent years, even in the face of militant opposition and persecution from Muslims. In several countries the Reformed faith is growing, and American churches of that persuasion continue to invest heavily across the continent. Even within some non-Presbyterian denominations there has been a surge of interest in Reformed theology, a development especially noteworthy among Anglicans, many of whom have become openly critical of their worldwide communion because of its doctrinal liberalism and approval of sexual practices Scripture condemns. The appearance of missionaries from South Korea too has enlivened the Reformed witness on the formerly Dark Continent.

Ade Ajayi, Jacob F. *Christian Missions in Nigeria, 1841–91*. Evanston, Ill.: Northwestern University Press, 1965.

Anderson, William B. *The Church in East Africa*. Dodoma, Tanganyika: Central Tanganyika, 1977.

Baeta, C. G., ed. *Christianity in Tropical Africa*. Oxford: Oxford University Press, 1968.

Bobb, F. S., ed. *Historical Dictionary of the Democratic Republic of Congo*. Lanham, Md.: Scarecrow Press, 1999.

Crummey, Donald. *Priests and Politicians: Protestant and Catholic Missions in Orthodox Ethiopia, 1830–1898*. Oxford: Clarendon, 1972.

Dortzbach, Karl and Debbie. *Kidnapped*. New York: Harper and Row, 1975.

Falk, Peter. *The Growth of the Church in Africa*. Grand Rapids: Zondervan, 1979.

Hallencreutz, C. F. and A. M. Moyo, eds. *Church and State in Zimbabwe*. Gweru, Zimbabwe: Mambo, 1988.

Hastings, Adrian. *The Church in Zimbabwe, 1450–1950*. Oxford: Clarendon, 1994.

———. *History of African Christianity, 1950–1975*. Cambridge: Cambridge University Press, 1979.

Henkel, Reinhard. *Christian Missions in Africa*. Berlin: D. Reimer Verlag, 1989.

Holt, Peter. *A Modern History of the Sudan*. London: Weidenfeld and Nicolson, 1961.

Holt, Peter and Michael W. Daly. *A History of the Sudan from the Coming of Islam to the Present*. 4th ed. London: Longmans, 1988.

Irvine, Cecilia, ed. *The Church of Christ in Zaire: A Handbook of Protestant Missions and Communities, 1878–1978*. Indianapolis: Division of Overseas Missions, Christian Church, 1978.

Isichei, Elizabeth. *A History of Christianity in Africa*. Grand Rapids: Eerdmans, 1995.

Kalu, Ogbu, ed. *The History of Christianity in West Africa*. London: Longman, 1980.

Latourette, Kenneth S. *A History of the Expansion of Christianity*. Vol. 5. New York: Harper and Brothers, 1943.

Lobban, R., et.al. *Historical Dictionary of the Sudan*. 3rd ed. Lanham, Md.: Scarecrow Press, 2002.

Markowitz, Marvin D. *Cross and the Sword; The Political Role of Christian Missions in the Belgian Congo, 1908–1960*. Stanford, Calif.: Stanford University Press, 1973.

Matsebula, J. S. M. *A History of Swaziland*. 2nd ed. Cape Town, South Africa: Longmans, 1976.

McCullum, Hugh. *The Angels Have Left Us: The Rwanda Tragedy and the Churches*. Geneva: World Council of Churches, 1995.

Meyer, Gabriel and James Nicholls. *War and Faith in Sudan*. Grand Rapids: Eerdmans, 2005.

Oliver, Roland. *The Missionary Factor in East Africa*. 2nd ed. London: Longman, 1970.

Ranger, T. O. and John Wellu, eds. *Themes in the Christian History of Central Africa*. Berkeley: University of California Press, 1975.

Sanneh, Lamin O. *West African Christianity: The Religious Impact*. London: Orbis, 1983.

Shaw, Mark. *The Kingdom of God in Africa: A Short History of African Christianity*. Grand Rapids: Baker, 1996.

Vantini, Giovanni. *Christianity in the Sudan*. Bologna, Italy: EMI, 1981.

Weller, John C. and Jane Linden. *Mainstream Christianity to 1980 in Malawi, Zambia, and Zimbabwe*. Gweru, Zimbabwe: Mambo, 1984.

Werner, R., et al. *Day of Devastation, Day of Contentment: The History of the Sudan across 2000 Years*. Nairobi, Kenya: Paulines, 2000.

Zeleza, P. T., ed. *Encyclopedia of Twentieth Century African History*. London: Routledge, 2003.

.

TWENTY-FIVE

Reformed Churches in the Middle East

Although much of this region was once part of the Roman-Byzantine Empire, Islam predominates throughout the area, and only Lebanon has a substantial Christian population. The Ottoman Turks controlled a large part of the Middle East until defeat in World War I caused the demise of their empire, and Great Britain and France obtained League of Nations mandates in 1919. European administration did not, however, bring a large influx of Christian settlers, so in most Middle Eastern countries the Christian presence is minimal and Reformed churches few or not present at all. Cyprus, Turkey, Saudi Arabia, Jordan, Qatar, the United Arab Emirates, Yemen, and South Yemen are almost devoid of Reformed believers, while small churches minister, often under difficult circumstances, in Lebanon, Syria, Iraq, Iran, and Israel.

Lebanon and Syria

About 1819 the American Board of Commissioners for Foreign Missions sent Congregational and Presbyterian missionaries to the region now the site of the independent nations of Lebanon and Syria but then part of the Ottoman Empire. This joint endeavor lasted until 1870, when, by mutual agreement, the Presbyterians assumed responsibility for the work in Syria and Lebanon, while the Congregationalists would minister in Turkey. In this region it soon became customary to identify the missionaries and their adherents as evangelicals, and the churches they maintained assumed that label rather than denominational designations common in America. Turkish authorities permitted the teaching of Christianity and the erection of church buildings, and soon an Arabic translation of the Bible was available.

In 1920 France announced she would grant autonomy to her mandates, but this was only limited self-government, and Lebanon and Syria did not become truly independent until 1946. The missions and local churches had in 1920, however, created one synod for the congregations in those two countries. The Protestants (Evangelicals) throughout the period since 1819, of course, competed with other religious bodies connected with Roman Catholicism, Eastern Orthodoxy, and Islam.

The Presbyterian mission in Syria and Lebanon surrendered all its operations to native control in 1959, but local church leaders were, in some cases, unable to discharge the responsibilities entailed in the operation of a hospital and several schools, so the state took control of those facilities.

Within this area have long been a substantial number of ethnic Armenians, some of whom espouse the Protestant faith. The Union of Armenian Evangelical Churches in the Near East (the former geographical designation for this area), in operation since 1846, originated as a split from the Armenian Orthodox Church, first in Istanbul. Turkish atrocities against Armenians and deportations after the First World War forced the Armenians to relocate to Syria and Lebanon, and the Union they had created became a significant religious body, especially in Lebanon. At the end of the last century, this denomination of twenty-three congregations had about ten thousand members and was ordaining females as deacons and elders but not as pastors. The polity of this body is generally Presbyterian, and it is affiliated with the World Alliance of Reformed Churches, as well as regional ecumenical agencies. The Union does not, however, subscribe to any distinctively Reformed confession. The Near East School of Theology provides education for ministerial candidates of this church, as it does for some other denominations involved in the support and administration of the institution.

From a confessional perspective, the National Evangelical Union of Lebanon is officially Reformed, as its adoption of the Heidelberg Catechism and other Calvinistic statements attests. Approximately twenty-eight hundred people affirm allegiance to this denomination, which began as the Evangelical Church of Beirut. Several local churches in the 1960s agreed to form a federation, and the present National Evangelical Union is the product of their concurrence. The Presbyterian roots of this movement reach to the original project of the American Board of Commissioners, to which the Presbyterians became heirs in 1870. In the 1950s, however, native church leaders opted for congregational polity, and the National Evangelical Union functioned thereafter under that form of church government. The congregations that preferred the Presbyterian system then created the National Evangelical Synod of Syria and Lebanon, a body of about sixty congregations officially committed to Reformed theology as expressed in the Heidelberg Catechism and to Presbyterian polity.

Almost all projects of American and European missions passed to the control of the National Evangelical Synod in 1959. In recent years this denomination has lost members because of emigration from this very troubled region, and as of 1999, it had eight thousand members in thirty-six congregations. The synod espouses several confessions of the Reformed tradition in principle but does not require subscription from its officers. In fellowship with the World Alliance of Reformed Churches and the World Council of Churches and several regional ecumenical bodies, social services are prominent features of this rather liberal denomination.

Israel

Even though Christianity was born in Palestine, only 2 percent of the present residents of the state of Israel profess some expression of the faith, and only 3 percent of that figure are Protestants. The Eastern Orthodox and Roman Catholic Churches are the largest Christian bodies in this officially Jewish nation. Protestants arrived in what was then Palestine, a part of the Turkish Empire, in the nineteenth century, as Lutherans and Anglicans began missions in 1842. The Free Church of Scotland followed in 1885, but early enthusiasm for evangelism diminished in the twentieth century as the increasingly liberal churches sought accommodation with the Jews and the American and European governments in general supported the aspirations of the Jews over those of Arab residents. During the period of its League of Nations mandate, Great Britain administered this territory in a manner favorable to Jewish interests, and in 1948 Israel became an internationally recognized nation, to the dismay of its Arab residents and neighbors, many Christians among them.

The re-creation of a sovereign Jewish state led many Christians in the United States and some in Europe to regard this development as a fulfillment of biblical prophecies, a sign of the impending end of history and the return of Christ, a view very few Reformed believers endorse. Arab Christians, driven from their homeland by the Jewish occupation, of course, deny the prophetic significance of the current Israel. Some Reformed denominations in the Netherlands have missions in Israel but concentrate on ministries to the Christian population, since Israeli law forbids them to seek the conversion of Jews. Even native-born Israeli Christians have encountered violent opposition from Jewish zealots who resent the presence of their churches. A few Reformed bodies maintain ministries nevertheless, but their influence is slight.

St. Andrew's Scots Memorial Church, with only forty members in two congregations, is part of the Church of Scotland. One parish is in Jerusalem and the other in Tiberius, where several Protestant groups use the buildings. Like its Scottish patron, this church ordains women to all offices while maintaining broadly ecumenical relations through the World Council of Churches and the World Alliance of Reformed Churches, although the Westminster Confession remains its official statement of faith.

Another tiny, but in this case, orthodox Reformed body is the Baraka Bible Presbyterian Church, which began in 1946 when Thomas Lambie, M.D. came from the United States with his wife to establish a clinic near Bethlehem, a work that soon expanded into a church of Christian Arabs. An affiliate of the International Council of Christian Churches, this congregation of fifty members refrains from ordaining women while adhering to the Westminster Standards and operating under the rule of elders in typical Presbyterian fashion. Its closest interchurch relations are with Baptists who share this Presbyterian church's allegiance to historic Protestant doctrines.

It appears the largest generally Reformed church in Israel is a Baptist congregation in Rishon LeTsion organized in 1978 under the leadership of Pastor Baruch Maoz, a native Israeli Christian. This assembly of over two hundred people meets on Saturdays, and, despite contrary laws, seeks the conversion of Jews as well as Arabs and immigrants from foreign lands, especially from Russia. This church is staunchly Reformed in theology, except for its rejection of infant baptism. Since its polity is congregational, it would not appear in the present study were it not the most vibrant expression of Reformed doctrine and evangelism in the nation. The church operates as Grace and Truth Christian Congregation. It receives support from several Reformed and Calvinistic Baptist churches in America.

Iraq and Iran

Only slightly larger than in Israel is the Reformed presence in the Persian Gulf nations Iraq and Iran, in both of which Muslims are the overwhelming majority. Iraq, once known as Mesopotamia, was home to about one million professing Christians prior to the United States-led invasion that overthrew the repressive regime of Saddam Hussein in 2003. A large majority of these Christians identified with one or another of the Eastern Rites connected with the Church of Rome.

Christianity appeared in Iraq in the first century, but theological disputes about Christology in the fourth century led most believers there to adopt the Nestorian doctrine, which Christendom at large rejected. Islam entered the country in the seventh century and gradually became a powerful force. Latin missionaries initiated work in Iraq during the thirteenth century, and current Catholic bodies in Iraq owe their existence to those endeavors. Protestants sent their agents in 1820, when British missionaries arrived. In 1850 the American Board of Commissioners for Foreign Missions began work in Mosul, while the Church Mission Society founded a station in 1882, and the Reformed Church and the Presbyterian Churches (U.S.A.) and (U.S.) also entered the country. The several Reformed bodies engaged worked together and eventually formed the United Mission, a ministry that made impressive gains in education but little progress in evangelism. In several cases local Reformed churches enjoyed the pastoral leadership of Egyptian ministers. Because of the educational work of the Reformed missions, many Iraqi Christians rose to prominence in society, even into government positions, after the country became independent of Great Britain in 1924.

Although Reformed denominations invested heavily in Iraq, the results were disappointing. The congregations established often tended toward independency rather than Presbyterian polity, and the number of converts was small. When Saddam Hussein's forces invaded Kuwait in 1991, his country entered an era of instability related to the reproach his aggression provoked throughout the world. Large numbers of Iraqis left their homeland, and Christians were disproportionately numerous among the emigrants. This, of course, weakened the churches, including those of a Reformed character. After the First Gulf War (1991), Iraq became a pariah among nations, and conditions for Christians remaining there worsened, as radical Muslims have launched violent attacks against people whose faith put them at odds with the terrorists. The current state of the Reformed faith in Iraq, like the future of the nation, remains unclear, and the future for Christians of any affiliation remains precarious.

Iran too has had a hostile relationship with the United States and other Western nations since its Islamic Revolution in 1979. At one time, however, Christian missionaries enjoyed great freedom, and Muslims were rather receptive to the gospel. Henry Martyn (1781–1812), the pioneer Protestant missionary, went there in 1811 after a term of service as an Anglican chaplain in India. A man of extraordinary talent as a linguist, he rendered the New Testament into the Persian language while evangelizing Muslims concurrently. Martyn's courage and devotion inspired others to go to Iran, among them members of the Church Mission Society and Presbyterians from the United States. In 1843 agents of the American Board of Commissioners for Foreign Missions arrived in the country, and the Presbyterian Board of Foreign Missions followed. In 1870 the Congregational society transferred its operations to the Presbyterians at a time when about three thousand converts were supporting the mission. Many of those believers had been adherents to the Nestorian Church, which has been present in old Persia since the third century.

By 1870 the Church Missionary Society and the Presbyterian Church (U.S.A.) were the major Christian groups working in the land, the former in the south, and the latter in the north. Education and health care were prominent ministries of both missions, adjuncts to the primary work of evangelism. At one point almost one hundred missionaries served with the Presbyterian effort, and because of their labors, the Evangelical Church of Iran came into being. This body, composed of three language groups, meets separately within the structure of one denomination.

Political developments have had lasting consequences for the Christians in Iran, as, for example, when Riza Shah Pahlavi (1878–1944), a military leader, assumed the rule in 1940. In an effort to modernize the country in the manner of Western nations, his government tried to reverse traditional Muslim conservatism but seized the mission schools as well. A coup in 1941 overthrew Riza Shah Pahlavi, and the new regime assumed a decidedly anti-British posture. As a result the Church Mission Society suffered badly until 1955, when fear of the Soviet Union led Iran to ally with Great Britain in the Baghdad Pact. The Islamic Revolution of 1979, however, brought the current anti-Western theocrats to power, and Iran began imposing Sharia law upon its own people while trying to export its revolution to other nations.

The Evangelical Church of Iran barely survived the tumult of the revolution and its aftermath, even though the laws of the state guarantee the rights of minority religions. This church, which functions with Presbyterian polity, has only about thirty-one hundred members and forty-one congregations. Although it does not endorse any Reformed confession officially, it is a member of the World Alliance of Reformed Churches in addition to some regional ecumenical organizations.

Ninety percent of Iranians are Muslims, and most of them adhere to the Shiite sect, although Sunnis account for about 35 percent of the whole. Almost all professing Christians come from non-Persian elements of society. The authoritarian character of the religious officials who hold the real power in Iran keeps the small Christian minority in fear of repression at anytime. Under 1 percent of the people profess any form of Christianity, but conversions since 1979 have been surprisingly numerous, even though defectors from Islam face persecution.

Although the Middle East was the cradle of civilization and the cradle of Christianity, Islam now dominates both the religious and the political culture of the region. From a human standpoint, therefore, the prospects for Christianity in general and the Reformed faith in particular do not appear promising.

SUGGESTED ADDITIONAL READINGS »

Bailey, Betty Jane and J. Martin Bailey. *Who Are the Christians in the Middle East?* Grand Rapids: Eerdmans, 2003.

Colbi, S. P. *Christianity in the Holy Land.* Tel Aviv: Am Hassefer, 1969.

Deeb-Kandis, Afaf, ed. *Christianity: Its History in the Middle East.* Beirut: Middle East Council of Churches, 2005.

Elder, John. *History of the Iran Mission.* Tehran: Literature Committee of the Church Council of Iran, 1960.

———. *The Presbyterian Church in Iran.* New York: United Presbyterian Church, n. d.

Greene, J. Milton. *Historical Sketch of the Mission in Persia.* Philadelphia: Women's Foreign Mission Society of the Presbyterian Church, 1881.

Horner, Norman A. *A Guide to Christian Churches in the Middle East.* Elkhart, Ind.: Mission Focus Publications, 1989.

———. *A Handbook of the Christian Community in Iran.* Tehran: United Presbyterian Commission in Iran, 1970.

———. *Rediscovering Christianity Where It Began: A Survey of Contemporary Churches in the Middle East and Ethiopia.* Beirut: Near East Council of Churches, 1974.

Moffett, Samuel H. *A History of Christianity in Asia.* San Francisco: Harper San Francisco, 1992.

Presbyterian Church (U.S.A.). *A Century of Mission Work in Iran, 1834–1934.* Beirut: Presbyterian Church Iran Mission, American Press, 1936.

Waterfield, Robin E. *Christians in Persia.* London: Allen and Unwin, 1973.

Wilson, J. Christy. *Apostle to Islam: A Biography of Samuel Zwemer.* Grand Rapids: Baker, 1962.

TWENTY-SIX

Reformed Developments on the Indian Subcontinent

An ancient and rather credible tradition holds the apostle Thomas brought Christianity to this region in the first century, that he founded seven congregations, and died as a martyr in Madras. As the story goes, Thomas found Jewish settlements on the Malabar Coast of India and began his evangelism there. Later he contacted people of the native religions, among whom he won many converts, and people of various churches still identity themselves as St. Thomas Christians.

Mission Efforts in India

Roman Catholic missionaries appeared in India when Portuguese traders arrived in the sixteenth century, and Catholic evangelists attempted to establish papal authority over the older churches but did not succeed. Protestants initiated mission work in 1706, when Lutherans from Denmark and Germany began translating the Bible and assailing the traditional Hindu caste system. These agents of the Danish-Halle Mission and others labored in south India through much of the eighteenth century, but their early successes could not be sustained, and their work stagnated. In 1793, however, William Carey (1761–1834), an appointee of the Particular Baptist Society for Propagating the Gospel among the Heathen, a Calvinistic organization of British origin, initiated a great renewal of Christian activity in the land. He resided at Serampore, a Danish settlement, because areas under the rule of the British East India Company did not accept missionaries, a policy in effect until 1813. A linguist of phenomenal ability, the self-educated Carey translated the Scriptures into many native dialects, and through the Serampore Press, he distributed Bibles and Christian literature broadly while relentlessly pursuing the conversion of the Indians. While preaching Christ, Carey and other missionaries decried brutal Hindu practices such as human sacrifice and the burning of widows in the funeral fires of their husbands.

The challenge presented by the multitudes of India, like the lure of the millions of China, moved a number of Presbyterian churches of Britain and America to select that land as a field for evangelism. The Church of Scotland was the first of these to establish a mission in India, as Alexander Duff (1806–1878) reached its shores in 1830, bearing a commission from that mother church. Like the great apostle Paul, he had become intimately acquainted with the perils of waters and the dangers of the deep, twice suffering shipwreck on the outward voyage. He experienced further and recurring difficulties in retaining his Indian post due to attacks of illness to which he was subjected.

Duff occupies a place in the forefront of modern missionaries. As a Christian educator he insisted that the Bible be read in every classroom and used as a basis of study, "distinctly, avowedly, and exclusively for religious exercises." He held that the teaching of Western science and literature to Eastern students should be done through the medium of the English language. He was intent upon reaching the upper classes of society. Duff helped to found *The Calcutta Review* and edited that influential journal during its earlier years.

The Free Church of Scotland, to which he adhered at the time of the Disruption of 1843, elected him moderator of its General Assembly in 1851 and again in 1873. More than once he left India under the compulsion of ill health, spending several years during the 1830s in his homeland. In the course of a later stay in Scotland, he delivered five addresses at the 1850 meeting of the Free Church Assembly, addresses marked by a felicitous combination of eloquence and conviction. After his final return home, he devoted himself to the promotion of the missionary cause, closing a sustained career with eleven years of service as professor of evangelical theology in New College at Edinburgh.

Even before Duff's coming, Presbyterian and Reformed endeavors for the conversion of India came from two organizations especially dedicated to that work. The Netherlands Missionary Society sent two ministers, J. Kindlinger and A. F. Lacroix, who settled in the Calcutta area in 1820. Two additional ones followed in 1822. Five years later, the society deeded the operation thus established to the London Missionary Society following the incursion of the English in 1824.

Donald Mitchell (1792–1823) was the first ordained minister of the Church of Scotland to enter India as a missionary. There his career was brief, as he arrived in January of 1823 and died of fever on November 29 of the same year. Mitchell's Indian ministry was under the auspices of the Edinburgh, or Scottish, Missionary Society, which commissioned several other workers for India before the Church of Scotland officially assumed responsibility for such work in 1824 and dispatched Duff six years later.

The scholarly John Wilson (1804–1875), who came to Bombay in 1829 as a representative of the Edinburgh Society, was among those involved in the transfer by the society of its work to the Church of Scotland in 1835, and he entered the Free Church following its formation in 1843. He is best known for his contribution to the field of education. His approach was of a somewhat different nature from that of Alexander Duff, in that he stressed the use of the vernacular and directed much attention to the lower classes of society.

A third Scot whose ministry was almost exclusively education was John Anderson (1805–1855), who came to Madras on February 22, 1837. His work with the girls and young women and with those of the various castes of society was notable. Madras Christian College developed from the activities in which he engaged in that east-coast city.

The Presbyterians from the United States began to arrive sometime after the Scots. Following four-and-a-half months on a slow-sailing ship, John C. Lowrie (1808–1900) and William Reed (1802–1834), together with their wives, came to Calcutta in October 1833 with commissions from the Western Missionary Society of the Presbyterian Church (U.S.A.), but their collective ministry proved to be of brief duration. Mrs. Lowrie died in the year of their landing. After leaving for home in the following year on account of illness, Reed died on shipboard and was buried at sea.

Lowrie, after consideration and consultation, moved to the north of India and established a mission at Ladonia in a region that became a center of considerable Presbyterian work. The organization of a presbytery of that name testified to early progress, as such a court was set up in 1837. In the meantime, John Newton (1810–1891) and Charles W. Foreman (1821–1894), along with their wives, had reached this section known as the Punjab and settled in its capital city of Lahore, now in the present Pakistan.

In 1835 the Associate Reformed Church commissioned James McEwen (1801–1845) for service in India. Here it was proposed that he work in affiliation with the mission of the Western Missionary Society. He and his wife arrived and settled at Allahabad, but McEwen's illness led to their relatively early return to the United States in 1838. Following his departure, this enterprise reverted in its entirety to the care of the Presbyterian Church (U.S.A.).

James R. Campbell (1800–1862) and his wife, of the General Synod of the Reformed Presbyterian Church in America, established themselves at Saharanpur, in northwest India, in 1836. The Presbytery of Saharanpur, formed in 1841, withdrew to independence in 1869, with a portion returning to the Reformed Presbyterians.

Immediately after the union of the General Synod of the Presbyterian Church in Ireland and the Associates in 1840, the resultant General Assembly planned, in accord with moves already underway, to establish a mission across the seas. In consequence of this resolution, James Glasgow (1805–1890), a physician, and Alexander Kerr (1812–1841), with their wives, set out for India in the course of the same year. They began work on the west coast of the country, north of Bombay, locating on the peninsula of Kathiawar. Being forced to move more than once, the mission ultimately centered on Surat. In 1843 the Presbytery of Kathiawar developed from the work of this group.

A particularly successful mission in the eastern province of Assam followed the entry of the Calvinistic Methodist Church of Wales into that portion of India in 1840. In 1897 this church added a station in the Lushi Hills of Southern Assam to its mission.

Soon after its formation in 1843, the Free Church of Scotland found a staff of workers at its disposal on the Indian field. This was because the Church of Scotland's missionaries, with only one exception, shifted their allegiance to the newly formed body. Since the properties of the missions were retained by the Church of Scotland, it was necessary that the new quarters and equipment be provided by the Free Church. This was promptly done, and the recently formed organization constituted, or reconstituted, the three presbyteries of Calcutta, Bombay, and Madras in 1843.

In 1819 John Scudder, M.D. (1792–1855), of the Dutch Reformed Church of North America, came to Ceylon as a representative of the American Board of Commissioners for Foreign Missions, but finally settled at Madras. In 1854 three of his missionary sons formed the Arcot-Classis of the Dutch Reformed Church, and in 1857 the American Board transferred its work in that area to the Reformed Church. Dr. Ida Scudder (1870–1960), a granddaughter of the original John Scudder, founded the Missionary Medical College for Women (1918) at Vellore, which since 1942 has been known as the Christian Medical College for Women, later as just the Christian Medical College.

Andrew Gordon (1828–1887) of the Associate Presbyterian Church of North America, along with his family, set out from the United States in fall 1854, settling at Sialkot in the Punjab and now in Pakistan. Here he laid the foundation of one of the outstanding Presbyterian missions in what was for a long time a part of India. Ephraim H. Stevenson (1820–1879) and Robert A. Hill (1820–1902), with their wives, came as reinforcements in 1855. The Associate Presbytery of Sialkot appeared in 1856 as a result of their combined endeavors, with the Synod of the Punjab following in 1893 as a court of the United Presbyterian Church. This synod entered the United Presbyterian Church (U.S.A.) upon its formation in 1957, but returned to independence (1961) upon its dismissal from that body.

George Stevenson (1817–1886), a minister of the Free Church of Scotland, was the first evangelist sent out from Canada by Presbyterians. In 1857 he went to Bancoorah, in the province of Bengal, as a missionary of the Presbyterian Church of Canada. The Sepoy Mutiny of that year, however, brought an untimely end to his service after he and his wife had lived on the field for only a few months. Presbyterians from Canada did not resume formal work in India until 1875.

The Indian, or Sepoy, Mutiny of 1857 came as an insurrection of native troops against the British army and authorities. Missions and missionaries of several areas suffered severely and tragically from the indiscriminate intrusion and attacks of the Sepoys (Indian soldiers in the army) upon foreigners.

Thomas Hunter (1827–1857), a minister of the Church of Scotland who was located at Sialkot, and his wife and child were slain by the insurgents. Members of the Futtegurh Mission of the Presbyterian Church (U.S.A.) were victims of the attackers as they sought refuge at Allagabad through flight down the Ganges River. This group was made up of four ministerial missionaries: David E. Campbell (b. 1825), John E. Freeman (b. 1809), Albert O. Johnston (b. 1833), and Robert McMullin (b. 1832), together with their wives and two children of the Campbells. These ten persons were slain on the parade grounds at Cawnpore on June 13, 1857. A number of native Christians also were among those who died at the hands of the rebels. An important outgrowth of the mutiny was the transfer of power in India from the East India Company to the British government.

The United Presbyterian Church of Scotland began overseas work in central India in 1859 with the dispatch of Thomas B. Steele (d. 1860) and Williamson Shoolbred. The former died before he ever actually reached the field, while his companion labored for thirty-six years in the United

Presbyterian Rajputana Mission. In 1862, in the northeast region of India, the Presbyterians of England joined the evangelical forces in Bengal with Calcutta-born Behari La Singh (1821–1874), a former student of Alexander Duff and a member of the Free Church's mission, as its representative.

George Anderson and his wife entered India near the close of 1871, having been sent out by the United Secession Church of Scotland. This youthful minister had acquainted himself with the elements of medical practice and had studied the Hindistu language before his departure from Edinburgh. The Seoni Mission in central India, established in this connection, entered into affiliation with the Church of Scotland following the union of that body and the Original Secession Church in 1956.

By 1875 representatives of the different Presbyterian churches at work in India had concluded that some type of general organization was desirable in the interest of conference and cooperation. In that year, accordingly, they formed the Presbyterian Alliance of India.

William J. Porteus (1884–1969), a physician who had visited India in 1908 to select a suitable site for a station to be manned by the Presbyterian Church of New Zealand, returned to that Asian land in 1909 with his bride. After a period of special preparation for the Indian field, he began work at Shahabad in the north of that country in the year following. Reinforcements came from New Zealand in 1910, and in 1911 he transferred his work to Jagadhri, this town having been chosen as headquarters of the New Zealand Mission. Porteus and his wife retired to New Zealand in 1926.

The Associate Reformed Presbyterian Synod of the South became increasingly concerned with missions in what was later to become Pakistan in 1906, as Minnie Rebecca Alexander began service with the United Presbyterians in that section of India. In 1910 the Associate Reformed Presbyterians sent out A. J. Ranson (1871–1960), a minister of that church, with his wife (1879–1950), to establish a mission in the name of that denomination. This soon led to the formation of the Presbytery of Montgomery (1911) and in 1964 to the constitution of a national synod, subordinate to the General Synod in the homeland.

Another group of Presbyterian constituency in Pakistan of more recent origin (1968) was formed under the sponsorship of Carl McIntire of the Bible Presbyterian Church of the United States. This church has displayed considerable strength and influence and has made heavy inroads into the United Presbyterians.

A distinctive phase of missionary endeavor in India was the *zenana* work, carried on by women missionaries. This was directed toward the once secluded women of that land living in the *zenana,* that portion of a dwelling set apart for their residence.

A single physician is said to have treated a million patients during his labors with the West Indian Mission of the Presbyterian Church (U.S.A.) in 1897. He was knighted by King George V in 1928, the year in which he retired from the field. His center of operations was at Miraj, located 275 miles to the southeast of Bombay. Here one of India's great medical centers developed, including a hospital, medical college, nurses' training school, dispensary, and leper sanitarium. Miraj became the focal point of six other hospitals connected with the West India Mission.

The response of Christian churches of the world to the demonstrated need for medical ministries in India was encouraging. Numerous hospitals of lesser renown than Miraj were established over those areas of the country in which various missions were operating, and these, in addition to many dispensaries, served in the cure of the sick and afflicted and in the evangelistic outreach of the missions.

A survey of the institutions in Pakistan aligned with the United Presbyterian Church of North America on the eve of its union with the Presbyterian Church (U.S.A.) reveals much of the nature and varied aspects of Indian missions in general. These organizations, under the sponsorship of the United Presbyterians or conducted jointly with other bodies, included the Boys' High School at Rawalpindi (1856), Gujranwala Theological Seminary (1877), the Girls' Boarding School at Hajipur (1879), the Memorial Hospital at Sialkot (1888), Gordon College at Rawalpindi (1893), Kinnaird College for Women at Lahore (1913), the Union Bible Training Center at Rawalpindi (1939), and a vacation resort for missionaries near Murree, obtained in 1948.

The twentieth century was barely under way when a series of church unions began in India. These were to continue across the years with an ever-increasing inclusiveness. The United Church of South India emerged in 1902 as the congregations of the newly formed United Free Church of Scotland joined those of the Arcot Mission of the Reformed Church of America.

On December 16, 1904, the Presbyterian Church of India became an organizational reality. This grew out of a merger of the United Church of South India and the Indian constituents of the Presbyterian churches of Scotland, England, Ireland, Canada, and the United States. The thirty-three presbyteries of the body thus brought into being embraced a total of 332 congregations, which enrolled 22,167 communicants. The Presbyterian constituency began to show a striking increase about this time, rising from 42,799 to 164,069 between the government census of 1901 and that of 1911. In 1921 the Presbyterian Church of India added fifty-three thousand to its inclusive membership with the reception of the Assam community of the Welsh Calvinistic Methodist Church.

In 1908 connections of the United Free Church of Scotland, the Reformed Church of America, the London Missionary Society, and the American Board of Commissioners for Foreign Missions formed the South India United Church. To this a group from the Basel Mission adhered in 1919. The South India United Church, the Methodists, and the Anglicans united in 1947 under the name of the Church of South India. In this instance, as in other mergers involving the Anglicans, the resultant body bore evident and unmistakable marks of episcopacy. The union leading to and the results thereof have drawn high praise on the one hand, and caustic criticism on the other, especially from Reformed believers who saw church union schemes as defections from their historic faith.

The independence achieved in 1947 by India and Pakistan as separate nations reflected itself in the subsequent history of the church in these two countries, and the year 1970 was an eventful one with respect to church union in each of them. On November 1 the Anglicans, Methodists, and portions of the Presbyterians affected a union whereby they organized the Church of Pakistan, despite the fact that the largest of the Protestant denominations, the United Presbyterian Church, along with the Associate Reformed constituency, did not participate in the union. The Synod of the Punjab, which grew out of the mission of the original United Presbyterian Church of North America, became independent of association with the United Presbyterian Church (U.S.A.) in 1961. As the United Presbyterian Church of Pakistan, this synod numbered almost sixty thousand communicants at the time, and included East Pakistan, the present Bangladesh.

On November 29, 1970, a comprehensive union took place among the Protestant churches of India. On that day the Council of the Baptist Churches, the Church of the Brethren, the Disciples of Christ, the Church of India (Anglican), the Methodist Church under the British and Australian Conferences, and the United Church of Northern India, which was made up in part of Presbyterian elements, combined as the Church of North India. This organization embraced almost 600 thousand persons at its beginning; more than a quarter of a million of these people were communicant members.

The products of mergers in India are now some large denominations affiliated with the World Alliance of Reformed Churches but not, in some cases, exponents of historic Reformed theology. Such, for example, is the Church of South India. With over two million members in nine thousand congregations bound together in a modified Presbyterian polity, this body does not subscribe to any traditional Reformed confession, and it ordains women to all church offices. This member of the World Council of Churches became something of a model for ecumenical unions across doctrinal and ecclesiological lines. The Church of North India, more than one million strong, is almost identical in structure and beliefs with its counterpart in the south.

Concentrated in the northeastern part of the country, the Presbyterian Church of India owes its origin to Welsh missionaries who initiated their work in 1841. At the end of the last century this body had some eight hundred thousand members in twenty-nine hundred local assemblies. While this Presbyterian denomination endorses the Westminster Confession formally, its close relations are with liberal bodies that shun confessional commitments. It is a member of the World Alliance of Reformed Churches and is in fraternal contact with the Presbyterian Church (U.S.A.) and liberal bodies in various nations.

Although India has become a showcase for ecumenical successes without regard for doctrinal differences, the historic Reformed faith continues to maintain its witness in the land. The Free Church of Central India, a body of barely five hundred members, remains loyal to the Westminster Standards, refrains from ordaining women, and has close relations with orthodox Reformed churches in several countries. It is an affiliate of the International Council of Reformed Churches. The Reformed Presbyterian Church of India is the product of a merger between the Bible Presbyterian Church and the Reformed Presbyterian Church, which produced a denomination of about three thousand members in five local churches. This body subscribes to the Heidelberg Catechism and the Westminster Confession and does not ordain females. It too is a member of the International Council of Reformed Churches.

Another orthodox denomination is the Reformed Presbyterian Church, Northeast India, which traces its origin to American missionary James R. Campbell, who served with the Presbyterian mission in Mizoram and

Manipur. This church of about forty-three hundred members assumed its present name and structure in 1979. It adheres loyally to the Westminster Standards while holding membership in both the World Alliance of Reformed Churches and the International Council of Reformed Churches. The church operates a seminary and several schools and orphanages.

While the condition of the Reformed faith in India is distressing, several denominations in Europe and North America continue to invest their resources there, often by patronizing native pastors rather than sending foreign missionaries. Dutch, American, Canadian, Scottish, and Swedish churches remain engaged in this country where Hindu versus Muslim animosity sometimes places Christians in dangerous situations. Persecution at the hands of both non-Christian religions is a constant threat.

Pakistan and Bangladesh

In 1947 Great Britain partitioned India in a measure of desperation after two centuries of failure to achieve peace between Hindus and Muslims. This created the nation of Pakistan, which British authorities hoped would satisfy Muslim nationalists determined to be free from Hindu domination. Were this scheme to succeed, it would require the relocation of millions of people, and to facilitate that Britain divided Indian territory so Pakistanis would have eastern and western sectors with India between them. This unrealistic program of resettlement failed because millions of Indian people refused to move. East Pakistan, the poorer, more primitive part of the new republic, resented domination by the western sector and in 1971 declared independence as Bangladesh, so three separate nations emerged from the dissolution of British India. In Pakistan and Bangladesh Islam is the dominant faith, although 16 percent of Bangladeshis and 2 percent of Pakistanis are Hindus. Christians constitute small minorities in all these states.

For over three hundred years (1526–1857), Muslims ruled most of India under the Mughal Dynasty, but the British gradually extended their commerce, as the East India Company made treaties with native princes and gained political authority to protect its trade. The Sepoy Mutiny of 1857 (previously considered in this chapter), however, convinced the British government to assume direct rule with the objective of preparing India for self-government as a dominion of the British Empire. Although that did not occur, the era of British rule brought many missionaries to the land, much to the dismay of Muslims in particular. Since Islam was always a minority religion in India, forward-looking adherents to that faith aspired to gain a nation of their own, and in 1930 their leader, Muhammad Iqbal (1877–1938), proposed creation of such a state in northwest India. He and later Muhammad Ali Jinnah (1876–1948), leader of the Muslim League, demanded an end to British rule and formation of an independent Pakistan, which became a reality in 1947.

At the end of the twentieth century, the Islamic Republic of Pakistan was home to over one million confessing Christians, 55 percent of them Protestants. Some of them are descendants of believers converted while the country was still part of British India, but many more had become Christians due to vigorous mission work that began at the time of national independence. The vast majority of conversions have occurred among the Hindu minority, very few from among the Muslims. Three substantial Reformed churches have developed in Pakistan, all of them originating before the partition of India.

The Presbyterian Church of Pakistan began as a mission of the United Presbyterian Church of North America in 1834, and by 1859 a presbytery was operating at Sialkot; by 1893 a Synod of the Punjab had been formed. This body in 1961 became the autonomous United Presbyterian Church of Pakistan. A second Reformed endeavor had begun in 1855 in Lahore. The two bodies united in 1993 to create the present Presbyterian Church of Pakistan, a denomination of approximately 400 thousand people in two hundred congregations. This church endorses the Westminster Confession and the Heidelberg Catechism in principle, but does not require subscription from its officers. A member of the World Council of Churches and the World Alliance of Reformed Churches, the Presbyterian Church of Pakistan maintains broad ecumenical relations that extend to the Church of Pakistan, various charismatic groups, and the Salvation Army. It does not ordain women officers. Its seminary at Gujranwala provides education for ministerial students.

The Church of Scotland entered northwest India in 1856, and the Sialkot Diocese of the Church of Pakistan traces its beginning to that event. This movement was once a presbytery of the United (Presbyterian) Church in North India and Pakistan, but in 1970 Lutherans, Anglicans, Methodists, and Presbyterians formed a union known as the Church of Pakistan, so the former Presbyterian work became a division of the united church. The Sialkot Diocese still affirms the Heidelberg and Westminster Catechisms officially and has close relations with the Church of Scotland while maintaining membership in the World Alliance of Reformed Churches and the

World Council of Churches. Murray College is its theological institution. About forty thousand adherents support this denomination, which ordains females as elders and deacons but not as ministers.

The third Reformed ministry of note in this country is the Pakistan Synod of the Associate Reformed Presbyterian Church, a conservative American denomination that sent its first missionaries to India in 1906. Beginning in 1911 those workers founded churches among the Chuhras, a people consigned by the Hindu caste system to the status of untouchables. The missionaries expanded their ministry of evangelism to include health care and education for the most unfortunate segment of India's population. The present Pakistani cities of Karachi and Multan are sites of vigorous activity for this church, which affirms the Westminster Standards, operates in four presbyteries, and has about 150 thousand members.

Although Islamic radicals have become violent in recent years, the law in Pakistan assures freedom of religion, even though Islam is the faith of the state. The growing influence of Islamists has, however, led the government to restrict evangelistic activities, and Christians are now in a precarious position as the political situation becomes increasingly unstable.

Bangladesh

The dubious distinction of being perhaps the poorest nation on earth belongs to Bangladesh, long part of British India, then East Pakistan, and, since 1971, an independent People's Republic. Independence has brought neither prosperity nor stability to this country of 135 million people, 85 percent of whom are Muslims. Christians number only half of 1 percent of the population, and most of them are Baptists.

Roman Catholicism arrived with Portuguese explorers in the sixteenth century but was not well organized there until 1886, when the first bishopric was established. Protestant mission work began in 1793 under the influence of William Carey's work with the Particular Baptist Society. Anglicans and Presbyterians arrived in the nineteenth century, although the Church of England chaplains ministered to personnel of the East India Company as early as the seventeenth century. In 1817 evangelists from the Church of Scotland mission in Calcutta went east to Rajshahi, where they founded a hospital still in operation. Tribal peoples, more than the majority Bengalis, proved receptive to the gospel, and one such tribe is now about 30 percent Christian. In 1924 the Presbyterian churches united with the Congregationalists and became part of the United Church of North

India. In 1979 a broader union created the Church of Pakistan, but the separation of East from West Pakistan necessitated changing the name to the Church of Bangladesh. One consequence of these ecumenical arrangements was almost to extinguish any significant features of the Reformed faith since the Church of Bangladesh affirms no confession other than the Apostles' Creed and the Nicene Creed and does not maintain genuine Presbyterian polity. This denomination of only 12,500 members, an affiliate of the World Council of Churches, concentrates on social service ministries more than evangelism.

Two other church bodies in Bangladesh have retained the name *Presbyterian* as well as the polity that term implies. The Hill Tracts Presbyterian Church and the Sylhet Presbyterian Synod do not, however, subscribe to any historic Reformed confession. Although neither church ordains women, both are ecumenical in character, and both owe their origin to Welsh missionaries, who began working in that part of India early in the twentieth century. The Hill Tracts Presbyterian Church reported only about twenty-three hundred members and twenty-six congregations, while the Sylhet Synod had some fifty-five hundred people in eighty-seven local churches. Neither denomination is distinctively Reformed in its teachings.

Sri Lanka

About sixty miles southeast of India in the Bay of Bengal lies the Republic of Sri Lanka, formerly Ceylon, and successively under Portuguese, Dutch, and British rule prior to independence gained in 1948. The major religion of this densely populated island is Buddhism, and professing Christians, most of them Roman Catholics, account for only 8 percent of the whole. The Reformed faith arrived when the Dutch seized this territory from the Portuguese in the seventeenth century. When Great Britain took control in the nineteenth century, the government allowed full freedom of religion, and several Protestant missions began working on the island. Particular Baptists, following advice from William Carey, went there and gained a substantial following, as did the Anglicans of the Church Missionary Society, but Catholicism too acquired many adherents, due to the British policy of toleration.

During the era when the Netherlands ruled Ceylon, the Dutch Reformed Church enjoyed the support of colonial officials, but that era ended in 1796 when the British appeared, although they did not secure their domination until 1815. The Church of Scotland sent agents to Ceylon in 1842 to minister to the growing Scottish settlement, and that led to formation of St. Andrew's Church in Colombo and a second congregation in Kandy. The Presbytery of Ceylon came into being as a creation of these two local churches, and soon the Dutch Reformed Church joined that body. In 1952, however, doctrinal disputes shattered that presbytery, and two congregations formed the Presbytery of Lanka to take its place. Ecumenical efforts comparable to those on the Indian mainland have not prospered in Sri Lanka, and ethnic rivalries between the majority Singhalese and the minority Tamils led to civil war in 1983, the effects of which remain and continue to endanger the peace and stability of the country. The churches have, at times, been caught in the crosscurrents of political strife.

The Dutch Reformed Church remains the strongest Protestant denomination of a Calvinistic character in the nation, although its membership is barely fifty-two hundred people who worship in twenty-five congregations. The church adheres to the Three Forms of Unity of the Dutch Reformation as well as the Westminster Confession of Faith. It does not ordain females and has close relations with the Christian Reformed Church in North America, the Dutch Reformed Church in South Africa, and the Reformed Church of Australia. The Dutch Reformed Church in Sri Lanka is an affiliate of both the Reformed Ecumenical Council and the World Alliance of Reformed Churches. It operates its own theological seminary and a Bible institute, and in recent years its home mission projects have planted several new local churches.

St. Andrew's Church in Colombo is now but a single congregation of ninety members. It too affirms the Westminster Confession in principle, but it is more broadly ecumenical in its relations than is the Dutch Reformed Church, as its membership in the World Council of Churches attests. It receives some support from the Church of Scotland.

The Presbytery of Lanka, with a membership of only five hundred in three congregations, observes a traditional Reformed polity and endorses the Westminster Standards. It too has fraternal relations with the Church of Scotland and the World Alliance of Reformed Churches. This body does not ordain women.

The condition of the Reformed witness on the Indian subcontinent and Sri Lanka is generally stagnant, and in areas where Islam is dominant, Christians of all affiliations are in increasing danger of persecution.

Butler, Howard T. *The Life and Work of Henry Martyn.* Madras: Christian Literature Society, 1921.

Duff, Alexander. *The Church of Scotland's India Mission.* Edinburgh: J. Johnstone, 1835.

———. *India and India Missions.* Edinburgh: J. Johnstone, 1839.

———. *India and Its Evangelization.* London: YMCA Press, 1851.

Duff, W. P. *Memoirs of Alexander Duff.* London: Nisbet, 1890.

Farquar, J. N. *Modern Religious Movements in India.* London: Macmillan, 1929.

Firth, C. B. *An Introduction to Indian Church History.* Madras: Christian Literature Society, 1961.

Laird, Michael A. *Missionaries and Education in Bengal, 1793–1837.* London: Clarendon, 1972.

Padwick, Constance. *Henry Martyn: Confessor of the Faith.* Rev. ed. London: InterVarsity, 1953.

Smith, George. *The Life of Alexander Duff.* 2 vols. London: Hodder and Stoughton, 1879.

United Presbyterian Church. *A Century for Christ in India and Pakistan, 1855–1955.* Lahore, Pakistan: United Presbyterian Church, 1958.

Vemmelund, L. *The Christian Minority in the Northwest Frontier Province of Pakistan.* Rawalpindi: Christian Study Center, 1973.

Zacharia, Mathai. *The Indian Church: Identity and Fulfillment.* Madras: Christian Literature Society, 1971.

TWENTY-SEVEN

Reformed Churches on the Peninsula of Indochina

Situated in Southeast Asia are the nations of Myanmar, Thailand, Cambodia, Laos, and Vietnam, a region often called Indo-China. Although the Reformed presence is not prominent there, Reformed missionaries have labored in the area, and some churches now function as fruits of their endeavors.

Myanmar

Known as the Socialist Republic of the Union of Burma until 1989, this nation situated on the Bay of Bengal is overwhelmingly Buddhist, Christians accounting for barely 5 percent of the population. Portuguese traders accompanied by Franciscan friars introduced Roman Catholicism in the sixteenth century, but few conversions occurred. Protestant missions began with the arrival of English Baptists from India at the urging of William Carey early in the nineteenth century. That project did not prosper, but Baptists from the United States soon continued that effort with impressive successes. The renowned Adoniram Judson (1788–1855), left for India as a Congregationalist but had become a Baptist by the time he arrived there. He and his companions inspired Baptists in America to adopt their ministry and thereby gave rise to the American Baptist Foreign Mission Society. The British East India Company would not allow the missionaries to remain, so they moved to Burma, where they baptized their first convert in 1819. Judson translated the Bible into Burmese and began work on an English-Burmese dictionary but did not live to complete it.

Baptist evangelistic efforts were quite successful among tribes in the hill country, especially the Karens, and Burma became the most productive mission field in which American Baptists were engaged. Anglicans and Methodists also enjoyed some success, especially after Great Britain imposed its rule on the country in 1834, a dominion that continued until independence in 1947.

Within the Protestant community in Myanmar the Reformed churches comprise a tiny but growing minority and are most active in the hill country, especially in the state of Chin. In 1907 Reformed missionaries from Great Britain initiated work among the Mara people in northeast Burma, and a church developed there near the border with India. When Great Britain granted independence to both of those countries, the church, which had congregations on both sides of the border, divided into two denominations, the Mara Evangelical Church being on the Burmese side. This body reported a membership of seventeen thousand people in ninety-six congregations organized in a Presbyterian polity and holding membership in the World Alliance of Reformed Churches. This church ordains women as deacons and elders and affirms the ancient creeds of Christendom but does not subscribe to any historic Reformed confession.

A smaller but more energetic body is the Independent Church of Myanmar, established in 1938 in the state of Chin. Although plagued by internal disputes, this denomination was able to regain unity in 1979 and has since then enjoyed substantial growth. It now has local assemblies in several parts of the nation. About five thousand people hold membership in the Independent Church, an affiliate of the World Alliance of Reformed Churches and a subscriber to the Westminster Confession of Faith. The church does not ordain women, and despite the term *Independent* in its name, operates with Presbyterian polity.

The largest Reformed denomination in Myanmar is the Presbyterian Church of Myanmar, founded by immigrants who began arriving from India in the Upper Chindwin region in 1914. At first these believers accepted teachers from Baptist and Methodist missions, but they eventually resolved to maintain their own distinctively Reformed doctrine and so created a formal Presbyterian church in 1956. Fellow Reformed Christians in India assisted these Presbyterians by sending a pastor to lead them, and by 1962 their church had about five thousand members and was planting congregations in various parts of Burma.

By the close of the last century, the Presbyterian Church of Myanmar had grown to some thirty thousand adherents bound together by Presbyterian polity in 256 congregations but subscribing to only the Apostles' Creed and the Nicene Creed. A member of the World Alliance of Reformed Churches, this body has broad ecumenical relations with churches around the world, but it does not ordain females. Tahan Theological College provides education for its ministerial students.

Four small denominations in Myanmar espouse historic Reformed theology through their subscription to the confessions of that heritage, and the Christian Reformed Church of Myanmar, which reported a constituency of about five thousand, is numerically the strongest of them. Chan Thleng, once a minister in the Presbyterian Church of Myanmar, founded the United Christian Church in 1985, but after a period of study at Calvin Theological Seminary in Grand Rapids, Michigan, he returned to his homeland and convinced his followers to adopt the name Christian Reformed Church. An ethnic Matu, Chan Thleng translated the New Testament into the language of his people, a project he completed in 1991. Some fifty local assemblies now comprise the Christian Reformed Church, a body that affirms the Three Forms of Unity and functions governmentally with the consistorial system typical of Reformed churches in Europe and North America. It holds membership in the Reformed Ecumenical Council and does not ordain women. The church's closest relations are with the Evangelical Presbyterian Church in Myanmar. The Christian Reformed Church in North America provides some financial support for the educational ministries of this church.

In 1983 believers dissatisfied with the teachings in several other churches formed the Evangelical Presbyterian Church in Myanmar as an orthodox Reformed denomination resolved to withstand the perceived liberalism in their former connections. Pastor Robert Thawn Luai organized this protest against the ecumenical and charismatic tendencies in other bodies. Most of the forty-nine congregations of the Evangelical Presbyterian Church are in the state of Chin. This church holds staunchly to the Westminster Standards as its doctrinal position and refrains from ordaining females to church offices. About one thousand adherents support its ministries.

The Presbyterian Church in America, through its Mission to the World, has been instrumental in promoting the Reformed Presbyterian Church of Myanmar, which came into being in 1995, when Tial Hlei Thanga, a teacher, led in the formation of another firmly Reformed denomination. After study at Reformed Theological Seminary, Jackson, Mississippi, Thanga obtained ordination in the Presbyterian Church in America, and with some support from that body, returned to his homeland as a church planter. The Reformed Presbyterian Church he served became self-supporting in a short time, as people of the Calvinistic persuasion left other churches to align with the new denomination. By the year 2000 some fourteen hundred people identified with the Reformed Presbyterian Church, a body unequivocally committed to historic Presbyterian doctrine and polity. This denomination, an affiliate of the International Council of Christian Churches, urges its ministerial candidates to study in Jackson, Mississippi.

Nationalism and socialism have been major factors in shaping government politics toward religion in Myanmar. In 1961 Buddhism became the state religion, but the law extended protection to other beliefs as well. The imposition of military rule in 1962, however, quickly ended the privileged status of Buddhism and declared all faiths equal before the law. All religious bodies had to register with the state, which then seized Christian schools and hospitals and expelled foreign missionaries in 1966. Thereafter the government interfered little in the affairs of native churches, which, devoid of missionary support, were left to their own resources. In recent years resurgent Buddhism has produced strong resentment against military rule, and the future for Christian churches, should Buddhism regain its former status, is not clear.

Thailand

Between Myanmar on the north and west and Laos and Cambodia on the east lies the kingdom of Thailand, a constitutional monarchy in which military leaders have often exerted decisive political authority. Long known as Siam, this country first encountered Christian influence through Portuguese missionaries who arrived in 1498. The progress of Catholicism since then has been very slow and that of Protestantism only a little greater. The Netherlands Missionary Society and the London Missionary Society introduced the Reformed faith beginning in 1828. At present only about 1 percent of the sixty-nine million people profess any expression of Christianity. Resistance to Western culture, often perceived to be decadent and domineering, has been pronounced and accounts for the slow growth of a foreign religion. Baptists and Presbyterians from the United States made major evangelistic efforts in the nineteenth and twentieth centuries, but the results were disappointing, as most Thais view Buddhism as their national religious heritage. Thousands of Buddhist temples and monasteries dot the landscape, and the government has, in general, encouraged the practice of Buddhism as an expression of patriotism.

Protestant missions in Siam began well, as Karl F. A. Gutzlaff (1803–1851) and his wife, who arrived in 1828, initiated the translation of the Bible into Siamese and followed that with the production of a dictionary and a grammar in that tongue. The American Board of Commissioners for Foreign Missions, in response to a plea from Gutzlaff, sent the first American missionary to Siam in 1831, and Baptist agents appeared soon thereafter. The Presbyterian Board of Foreign Missions dispatched its personnel to Siam in 1840, as William P. Buell and his wife arrived in Bankok. The Congregational mission terminated its work after eighteen years without a convert, and the Baptists did the same soon thereafter, leaving the Presbyterians alone on that field.

The Presbyterian experience in this country was filled with hardships, as hostile government officials and Buddhist monks inflamed the populace against the missionaries. Converts often endured persecution, and prospects for success in church planting seemed remote until the death of the antiforeign king brought a more liberal monarch to the throne, one who ended the repression and, to a degree, welcomed the missionaries, especially when they performed valuable social services in education and health care. Prince's Royal College, McGilvary Theological Seminary, McCormick Hospital, and McKean Leprosy Colony all became esteemed institutions that enjoyed acceptance, but still converts to Christ were relatively few, although somewhat numerous in the northern part of Siam.

In 1934, after several Protestant denominations had undertaken work in the country, congregations connected with the Presbyterian mission organized the Church of Christ in Thailand as a body under native control. By 1957 the Presbyterians had relinquished all mission properties to the native church to which foreign missionaries then became subject. During World War II Japanese forces occupied Thailand and forbade Christian work, but after the war several Protestant bodies sent personnel there.

The Church of Christ in Thailand, from its formation, was an ecumenical structure that embraced various Protestant traditions, Baptists and Disciples of Christ being the most prominent partners with the Presbyterians. The union church adopted Presbyterian polity but did not embrace Reformed theology. At the end of the twentieth century this denomination of about sixty-nine thousand members espoused only the Apostles' Creed. It is an affiliate of the World Council of Churches and the World Alliance of Reformed Churches, ordains women, and in general emphasizes social services more than evangelism. An Evangelical Fellowship of Thailand, some twenty-five thousand strong, is much more evangelistic in character, but it too is not Reformed in doctrine.

Cambodia, Laos, and Vietnam

These countries of Indo-China were subject to French rule until they gained independence after World War II. Roman Catholic efforts to convert the natives of this region began in the sixteenth century and, in Vietnam, enjoyed some success, much less in Cambodia and Laos.

In Cambodia, during the era of Communist domination under the Khmer Rouge and its brutal leader Pol Pot, a period that extended from 1975 to 1979, over a million people perished in massacres, and Roman Catholic and Protestant churches were closed and missionaries expelled. The most prominent Protestant effort to evangelize this country was the work of the Christian and Missionary Alliance, but from a numerical perspective, the mission enjoyed little success. A tiny Presbyterian Church of Cambodia remains, but data about it are scant. An estimated ten thousand Cambodians identify with the several denominations there since the restoration of non-Communist civilian rule under Prince Norodom Sihanouk.

Christianity did not reach Laos until late in the nineteenth century, with Roman Catholics leading the way into one of the least accessible nations of Asia. As in Cambodia, the Christian and Missionary Alliance made the strongest effort to implant the Protestant faith in Laos, although Presbyterian missionary Daniel McGilvary (1828–1911) from the United States initiated evangelistic work there in 1872. The first organized Protestant churches in this land were the work of Swiss missionaries in 1902. In 1928 the believers who had joined with the Swiss mission aligned with the Christian and Missionary Alliance. The Communist regime, which came to power after World War II, oppressed Christians, and many of them fled. Not until 1982, after the Red rule ended, did the remaining Protestants in the northern and southern parts of the country form the Lao Evangelical Church, a hybrid denomination of about forty thousand members, which combined elements of Presbyterian and Congregational polity. This church does not hold to any Reformed confession of faith, the Apostles' Creed being its only official statement of doctrine. Some Laotian refugees who fled to the United States formed the Lao Presbyterian Church through the patronage of the Presbyterian Church (U.S.A.).

Franciscan and Jesuit agents from the Philippines brought Catholicism to Vietnam in the sixteenth and seventeenth centuries, and perhaps 10 percent of the people there now profess that religion. French rule began in 1867, when the Europeans imposed a puppet government on the long-divided country. Protracted guerilla warfare under the leadership of the

Communist Ho Chi Minh and the failed efforts of the United States to intervene on behalf of the anti-Communist government of South Vietnam led to a national union under a Red regime in 1976.

As in most of Indo-China, Protestantism came to Vietnam in large part due to the work of the Christian and Missionary Alliance. An Evangelical church is the fruit of that effort, but the native denomination is neither Presbyterian in polity nor Reformed in doctrine.

SUGGESTED ADDITIONAL READINGS >>

Blanford, C. E. *Chinese Churches in Thailand.* Bankok: Suribyan, 1975.

Bray, E. B., ed. *Mission Directory of Thailand, Cambodia, and Laos.* Bangkok: Newasia, 1972.

Chandler, David. *A History of Cambodia.* Boulder, Colo.: Westview Press, 2008.

Gutzlaff, Carl F. *Journal of Three Journeys along the Coast of China in 1831, 1832, and 1833.* London: Desert Island, 1834.

Heffey, J. C. *By Life, By Death.* Grand Rapids: Zondervan, 1969.

Hoke, Donald E. *The Church in Asia.* Chicago: Moody, 1986.

McGilvary, Daniel. *A Half Century among the Siamese and the Lao.* New York: Fleming H. Revell, 1912.

McLeish, Alexander. *Christian Progress in Burma.* London: World Dominion Press, 1932.

Ponchaud, Francois. *The Cathedral of the Rice Paddy: 450 Years of the Church in Cambodia.* Paris: Le Sarment, 1990.

Reimer, R. E., ed. *Protestant Directory of Churches, Missions, and Organizations in South Vietnam.* Saigon: Office of Missionary Information, 1973.

Smith, Alex G. *Siamese Gold: A History of Church Growth in Thailand.* Bangkok: Overseas Missionary Fellowship Publishers, 1982.

United Presbyterian Church. *Vietnam: The Christian, the Gospel, and the Church.* Philadelphia: United Presbyterian Church, 1967.

Von der Mehden, F. R. *Religion and Nationalism in Southeast Asia.* Madison: University of Wisconsin Press, 1963.

Welles, K. E. *History of Protestant Work in Thailand.* Bangkok: Church of Christ in Thailand, 1958.

TWENTY-EIGHT

Elsewhere in Southeast Asia

Beyond Indo-China, the Reformed faith has established its presence in several island nations of Southeast Asia. These include Malaysia, Singapore, the Philippines, and, especially, Indonesia.

Malaysia

Once a British protectorate, the state of Malaysia, which became independent in 1957, lies south of Indo-China and consists of a large peninsular area and Sarawak and Sabah, parts of North Borneo. When Great Britain granted independence, it included Singapore in the confederation, but that former Crown Colony withdrew in 1965 in favor of its own independence. The cultural composition of this country is diverse, with Malay, Chinese, and Indian peoples on the peninsula and indigenous tribes in North Borneo. On the mainland only about 2 percent of the people profess Christianity, but in Sarawak 29 percent and in Sabah 27 percent do so. Muslims and Buddhists also are numerous in both parts of the nation. As a concession intended to keep order, Britain, for some time, recognized Islam as the major faith and forbade missionaries from entering the land.

Roman Catholicism first appeared in Malaya in the sixteenth century, the work of Portuguese traders and priests who accompanied them. Francis Xavier (1506–1552), a Jesuit, invested three years there, so Catholicism enjoyed an opportunity to establish its presence in Malaya long before Protestants arrived in 1641, when the Dutch seized this area. The new Europeans did not, at that point, initiate vigorous mission work, so the Reformed faith gained few native converts. The London Missionary Society entered the country at Penang and Singapore in 1815, but the emphasis of its agents was to prepare native Chinese residing there to take the gospel to their homeland, which was then closed to missionaries. In 1842 Great

Britain obtained a treaty that allowed Christians to work in China, and the London Missionary Society moved most of its operations there.

Anglicans appeared in Malaya in 1848 and English Presbyterians in 1851. By the time the Presbyterians arrived, a considerable number of Scots had settled in the country and had been pleading for ministers from the United Kingdom to serve their spiritual needs. The respondents, however, went beyond caring for the Scots and initiated evangelism among the populace, especially those of Chinese descent. The Presbyterian Chapel on Prinsep Street, Singapore, soon became the center of this dynamic mission.

As more ethnic Chinese arrived in Malaya, English Presbyterian missionaries continued to respond to the call, and church planting succeeded to the point that a presbytery was formed, and by 1901 a synod was functioning. While the ministry to Chinese Malays prospered, English-speaking congregations developed in Kuala Lumpur and Ipoh.

World War II disrupted Christian mission work in Malaya because Japanese forces occupied the country. Soon after the war, however, missionaries returned, and when the Communist regime in mainland China expelled foreign Christians in 1949, some missionaries moved to Malaya to augment the Christian presence there. By 1962 a Chinese Presbyterian Synod had three presbyteries, and by 1967 in Singapore alone there were thirteen Presbyterian congregations and fifteen elsewhere in Malaya. The English-speaking congregations had, in 1958, obtained independence from the Presbyterian Church of England, and in 1971 that body joined the Chinese Synod. When Singapore opted for political independence in 1965, the Presbyterian Synod divided into two, one for the new state, and the other for Malaysia. The Presbyterian Church in Malaysia, at the end of the twentieth century, had about seven thousand adherents in 105 congregations. It is an ecumenical denomination related to the World Alliance of Reformed Churches and the Reformed Ecumenical Council along with regional interchurch organizations. This church ordains women to all offices and subscribes to the Apostles' Creed and its own Presbyterian constitution. Trinity Theological College is its main educational institution.

In addition to Presbyterian efforts, the Basel Mission and the Australian Borneo Evangelical Mission have been active in Malaysia, but the congregations they have organized do not subscribe to the Reformed faith, although those connected with the Basel Christian Church practice a loose form of Presbyterian polity while holding membership nevertheless in the Lutheran World Federation. The same is true of the Protestant Church in

Sabah, while the Evangelical Assembly of Borneo, a ministry of Australian origin, is Pentecostal.

Islam is the official religion in Malaysia, and the head of state is protector of that faith. The law does, however, recognize the rights of other beliefs, including the Christian minority, which is substantial in various parts of the land. How well that arrangement will continue is uncertain, as radical Muslims aspire to impose their own laws on the entire country.

The Republic of Singapore

Within Singapore three Reformed churches maintain ministries to a fraction of the municipal population. The Presbyterian Church in Singapore, a denomination of nine thousand people in twenty-eight local congregations, is the largest of these bodies. Organized as a synod separate from that in Malaysia in 1975, this movement has enjoyed a substantial growth since assuming independent status. Its two presbyteries are distinguished by the languages they employ, Chinese and English. The church ordains women while operating within traditional Presbyterian polity and subscribes, at least in principle, to the Westminster Confession of Faith. Social service ministries receive much emphasis, as this church's schools and health care facilities attest. Trinity Theological College and Singapore Bible College educate pastors and church workers. This body is an affiliate of the World Alliance of Reformed Churches.

The Life Bible Presbyterian Church, with some thirteen hundred adherents meeting in six assemblies, is a conservative secession from the Presbyterian Church in Singapore in the 1950s. The International Council of Christian Churches, under the leadership of American pastor Carl McIntire, persuaded native pastor Timothy Tow Siang Hui to lead an exodus in protest against his denomination's failure to preserve historic Reformed doctrine and its support for the liberal World Council of Churches and its leftist political pronouncements. This led to creation of the Life Bible Presbyterian Church in 1955. Within a year this movement organized the Presbytery of Singapore and Malaysia, and soon church planting bore fruit sufficient to enable the new denomination to extend its influence to Australia, Indonesia, Saipan, Thailand, Burma, and as far away as Africa and Canada.

The prosperity of the Bible Presbyterian Church did not, however, last long. Doctrinal disputes arose, especially some pertaining to charismatic practices, and in 1988 the denomination disbanded, and separate congregations continued to function without the traditional Presbyterian structure. All of them remain committed to the Westminster Standards.

The tiny Evangelical Reformed Church in Singapore also affirms the historic Calvinistic doctrines by espousing the Three Forms of Unity in the Dutch tradition. With only two local assemblies and about 350 members, this body maintains close relations with the Protestant Reformed Churches in the United States.

The Republic of Indonesia

This nation of over two hundred million people, living on some three thousand islands between the Southeast Asian mainland and Australia, is home to a Muslim majority of 87 percent and a Christian minority of 10 percent. Hinduism and Buddhism brought from India together account for 3 percent. Portuguese traders arrived on Malacca in 1511 and once had flourishing trading posts, which they lost to the Dutch in the next century. Gradually all of the country passed to Dutch rule despite strong native opposition. Until 1949 this area was the Dutch East Indies, of which Batavia, the present-day Jakarta, was the capital.

During the era of the Portuguese presence, Roman Catholicism gained a following in parts of the archipelago, and Catholic minorities remain prominent in East Timor and Flores, where Portuguese culture continues to be influential. The Dutch East India Company both prohibited Catholicism in its territories and restricted Protestant missions so as to protect commerce, its priority. This policy notwithstanding, Reformed missionaries accomplished the translation of the Bible into Malay, the trade language, in 1733. The city of Batavia was the center of the Reformed faith where a church council administered ecclesiastical affairs without the traditional synodal structure. Colonial officials exerted great influence in the churches, and only Europeans held pastoral positions. By the opening of the nineteenth century, about fifty-five thousand people identified themselves as Reformed believers.

During the era of the French Revolution (1789–1815), the Netherlands was subject to Napoleonic rule for some time, and in 1799 the subservient Dutch government assumed control of the East India Company and imposed freedom of religion in the colonies. This allowed Roman Catholic missions to return to Indonesia, beginning in 1808. Under French Revolutionary influence, the Dutch government claimed to be neutral in matters of religion, although it continued to support the Dutch Reformed Church as the national religious establishment. The state did not, however, patronize foreign missions, which then became the work of independent bodies such as the Netherlands Missionary Society, which sent pastors to Java and eastern Indonesia, from which they extended the scope of their missions. Other Reformed agencies also dispatched personnel to the East Indies. The Reformed Churches of the Netherlands, an orthodox denomination under the leadership of Abraham Kuyper (1837–1920), were especially vigorous in evangelizing the islands in the area of Java and Sumba.

Until the twentieth century, Europeans alone held pastoral positions, although native teachers became effective unordained evangelists. The formation of theological seminaries changed that, as well-educated Indonesians became available to serve the churches. Beginning in 1927, several Protestant churches gained autonomy, while ethnic differences determined the character of regional ecclesiastical bodies. By 1951 the various Protestant churches claimed 1.7 million members.

When the Japanese occupied the East Indies in 1942, they tried to use the churches as instruments of propaganda, but at the same time they alienated Christians by seizing their schools and hospitals. Deprived of support from foreign sources, the churches in the Indies had to become self-governing and self-sufficient, a development that proved, in the long run, to be beneficial. After World War II Christians in these islands took an active part in the growing nationalist movement and became champions for freedom of religion. By the time Indonesia gained independence in 1949, several Reformed denominations, most of them ethnic-regional bodies, were flourishing. Not all of these churches subscribed to historic Calvinist theology any longer, but several continued to do so. Such churches were operating as independent bodies in which foreign missionaries were associated workers, no longer ecclesiastical officials. Some Christian universities and more seminaries opened in various parts of the country, and the number of converts grew substantially, particularly among primitive tribal peoples. Although other Protestant denominations labored in these islands, the Reformed churches continued to be the largest aggregate body of Christians there. Muslims have at times sought to retard the growth of Christianity by proposing legislation to prohibit seeking converts who already profess a religion, and the national government maintains a Ministry of Religion over which the director is always a Muslim. As the last century ended, clashes between Christians and Muslims increased, especially because many Muslims who attended Christian schools embraced the faith of their teachers. Followers of Muhammad in the Indies often decry Christianity as a Dutch religion, while disciples of Jesus fear a coming imposition of Islam as the state religion. Violence has included destruction of church buildings, most of them on the island of Java.

Professing Christians in Indonesia are involved in the same difficulties that divide their coreligionists in other lands. Liberal-ecumenicals and traditional evangelicals compete for followers, and the pattern of church life reflects these tensions, especially as they occur in the Netherlands. Although a royal decree of 1820 required the several church bodies in the archipelago to combine into the Protestant Church of the Indies, in the twentieth century many congregations joined regional denominations separate from the royal establishment. These bodies as a rule maintain a Reformed identity but do not espouse any historic Calvinistic confession.

A second type of ecclesiastical arrangement somewhat common in Indonesia features a minimal confessional position combined with Presbyterian church government and participation in broad interchurch organizations. Only about 6 percent of Protestants in Indonesia identify with churches committed to traditional Calvinism as affirmed in the Three Forms of Unity. These bodies, which do not ordain women, use psalms rather than hymns in worship, and they make evangelism their priority while in principle rejecting doctrinal deviations from their historic confessions. Almost fifty denominations now correspond to this description, but only the more prominent ones appear in this survey.

The Protestant Church of Nias

The Rhenish Mission Society established its work on the island of Nias in 1865, and although progress was slow at first, the years 1915 to 1920 brought many conversions, and thereafter church planting moved ahead steadily. The churches involved formed a synod in 1936, but schisms injured the church badly, some of the contention being due to social factors, but competition from Roman Catholics and Seventh Day Adventists also proved costly. The Protestant Church of Nias survived, nevertheless, and at the opening of the present century claimed over 325 thousand members.

Organized in a Presbyterian manner, this body, ecumenical in character, is active in health care, education, and social ministries. It ordains females and professes adherence to the ancient creeds of Christianity and both the Heidelberg Catechism and Martin Luther's Small Catechism. A member of the World Council of Churches and regional interchurch agencies, the Protestant Church faces growing opposition from the rising tide of Muslim militancy.

The Karo Batak Protestant Church

Agents of the Netherlands Missionary Society introduced Christianity to the Karoese people of northern Sumatra in 1890, but native resistance retarded the growth of this endeavor for many years. The church became independent of European authority in 1941, and beginning about 1950 its evangelism enjoyed much success despite Muslim opposition. In part this success was due to the church's accommodation to native culture in the pattern of worship, a concession Dutch missionaries had discouraged. In 1979 this church adopted a confession of its own devising, but it affirms the Heidelberg Catechism as well, while operating with Presbyterian polity with approximately 225 thousand adherents in three hundred congregations. An affiliate of the World Council of Churches, the World Alliance of Reformed Churches, and regional ecumenical bodies, this church has opened all of its offices to women. Its closest relations abroad are with the Dutch Reformed Church in Europe and the Evangelical Lutheran Church in the United States. Social services, more than evangelism, are the focus of its concern.

The Evangelical Church in Irian Jaya

On the coast of northwest Irian, German missionaries introduced the Reformed faith in 1855, and soon Dutch Christians arrived to augment that effort. Initial progress was slow, and many missionaries perished without seeing fruit for their labor. The natives were deeply attached to their pagan ways, and headhunting was a tradition among them. Early in the twentieth century, however, conversions became frequent, and the mission prospered until the imposition of Japanese rule in the Second World War. Missionary I. S. Kijne, who spent the period 1923 to 1956 in Irian, was especially effective in evangelism and in preparing native teachers to spread the gospel, but the mission endured cruel persecution at the hands of the Japanese, as many native Christians as well as foreign missionaries experienced imprisonment, even death. After the war the church in Irian regained strength and was able to form a synod in 1956. In 1963 most Dutch missionaries evacuated under pressure from the national government, which had recently secured authority over the area.

Once Irian submitted to the government of the republic, migrants from other parts of Indonesia began arriving in growing numbers and brought

Islam with them and thereby posed a major challenge to the Evangelical Church in Irian Jaya. Missionaries who worked among tribes in the interior were often dissatisfied with this church because of its perceived liberal theology, especially its failure to adopt any historic Protestant confession of faith.

By the year 2000, the Evangelical Church claimed about 650 thousand members in almost nineteen hundred congregations connected in the traditional Dutch form of polity. This denomination ordains females and holds membership in the World Council of Churches and the World Alliance of Reformed Churches. It operates an extensive network of social agencies, especially schools and hospitals, and has a theological seminary of its own.

The Christian Churches of Java

Another denomination with a Reformed heritage is the Christian Churches of Java, a body of over two hundred thousand adherents organized in a semi-Presbyterian government but without commitment to any traditional Calvinist confession. Its theology is liberal, and its focus is on social services.

Originally an indigenous movement, the Christian Churches of Java became an organized body in the nineteenth century when Dutch missionaries gained leadership within it. Efforts to orient congregations away from native traditions in the direction of Western Christianity aroused some opposition and led people to withdraw from this church, but the denomination, in general, accepted European leadership and adopted the typical Dutch form of polity with Europeans in most positions of authority. World War II, however, required changes that placed natives in most of those positions. Missionaries returned after the war but only as assistants with no authority over Indonesian church leaders. When the first synod of the church convened in 1931, only seventy-five hundred people held church membership, but by the beginning of the twenty-first century, it had grown to the present number. Like most other Indonesian denominations, this one is an affiliate of the World Council of Churches, and it is a member of the World Alliance of Reformed Churches and the Reformed Ecumenical Council as well. All its offices are open to both genders.

The East Java Christian Church

Almost identical in development and character with the Christian Churches of Java is the denomination known as the East Java Christian Church, which originated as a movement among Javanese people and later became part of the Dutch Reformed mission. It assumed independent status in 1931, the year of its first synodal meeting. This mainly rural body lacks a confessional commitment but operates with Presbyterian government. An ecumenical church, it belongs to the World Council of Churches and the World Alliance of Reformed Churches while maintaining close relations with the Presbyterian Church (U.S.A.) and liberal denominations in the Netherlands. Health care and education are prominent features of this 150 thousand-member denomination with 118 affiliated local assemblies in which women are eligible for ordination. Tensions between Christians and Muslims led to violence in 1995 to 1996, which inflicted much damage on church properties and caused injuries and death for some church members.

The Christian Church of Sumba

A somewhat confessional body is the Christian Church of Sumba, which subscribes in principle to the Heidelberg Catechism and is affiliated with the Reformed Ecumenical Council and the World Alliance of Reformed Churches. Orthodox Calvinists from the Netherlands dispatched missionaries to this island in 1881, and in 1892 the newly formed Reformed Churches in the Netherlands accepted responsibility for that mission. Hostility between the two major ethnic peoples of Sumba retarded church growth, but by the opening of World War I, progress was becoming evident among the Sumbanese. Unordained native preachers assisted with evangelism, and when the Japanese occupied the area, leadership in the congregations became the responsibility of the natives exclusively. After World War II, the Sumbanese declared their church independent, and missionaries from Europe functioned thereafter in advisory and supportive roles. This denomination cooperates with the Reformed Churches in the Netherlands, from which it receives some support. Like its Dutch partner, the Christian Church of Sumba has become increasingly liberal, emphasizing social services more than evangelism, while ordaining women. Adherents numbering 173 thousand meet in seventy-two congregations bound together in Presbyterian polity.

The Christian Evangelical Church in Minahasa

A substantial denomination with Reformed roots is the Christian Evangelical Church in Minahasa, an area in which Portuguese traders introduced Christianity in the sixteenth century but where Dutch Protestants superseded the earlier efforts. In the second half of the nineteenth century, the Dutch mission enjoyed much success, as large numbers of natives embraced the faith and Indonesian lay preachers spread the gospel to the central and western islands.

The Christian Evangelical Church did not become autonomous until 1927, and even then Dutch ministers continued to lead the church. This body survived during the Second World War by appeasing the Japanese authorities, but the civil war of 1958 to 1961 and the rise of the Communist Party wreaked havoc, especially because the church issued a public rejection of Marxism. After that menace diminished, the church adjusted to the growing materialism of the era by emphasizing social ministries such as health care and education. It now maintains numerous schools, hospitals, and clinics. Church membership stood at 633 thousand in 1999. This denomination ordains women and does not subscribe to any distinctively Reformed statement of faith. It is a member of the World Council of Churches and the World Alliance of Reformed Churches.

The Christian Evangelical Church in Timor

Even larger than its counterpart in Manahasa is the Christian Evangelical Church in Timor, which boasts of 850 thousand adherents in fifteen hundred local assemblies. This body also operates with Presbyterian polity but does not endorse Reformed theology. Under Dutch colonial rule Protestantism spread slowly in Timor, and a policy of general toleration allowed the earlier Catholic community to continue and flourish. Not until 1900 did Protestantism make substantial gains through the efforts of both Dutch missionaries and local workers. From that point, with some periods of stagnation, the movement went forward, especially during the decade of the 1960s. By then Pentecostal influences were prompting church growth, but in a non-Reformed direction. One effect of this development was a decline of interest in doctrine, which led eventually to orienting the church toward theological liberalism in which meeting social needs preempted efforts to seek the salvation of lost people. The Christian Evangelical Church in Timor became an ecumenical body connected to the World Council of Churches and the World Alliance of Reformed Churches. It has its closest relations abroad with the state church in the Netherlands, the Presbyterian Church of Ireland, and the United Church of Christ in the United States, all decidedly liberal denominations.

The Protestant Church in the Moluccas

This church too has historic connections with the Reformed faith. The Protestant Church in the Moluccas traces its origin to 1605, when the Dutch expelled the Portuguese and the Roman Catholic clerics who had introduced that religion in these islands. Dutch pastors proclaimed the gospel and the distinctive principles of Calvinism and translated the Heidelberg Catechism and the New Testament into the native language by 1668. A complete vernacular Bible became available in 1733. Local lay preachers of limited learning assisted Dutch ministers in evangelism, often by reading to gathered natives sermons those pastors had composed.

As the nineteenth century progressed, Christians in the Moluccas became missionaries to other parts of Indonesia. In the south, Moluccas and Irian mission work was especially successful, as native congregations prospered in conjunction with both Indonesian preachers and Dutch pastors serving with the Netherlands Missionary Society. In 1935 the Protestant Church in the Moluccas became autonomous, but World War II brought intense suffering upon this denomination, as the Japanese killed many church leaders. After the war, rebellion against the government of Indonesia inflicted further damage, but by about 1960 a recovery was becoming evident.

By the end of the twentieth century, this Protestant Church was well organized in the Presbyterian pattern and had over 450 thousand members in almost eight hundred local assemblies. In addition to the ecumenical creeds of antiquity, this church affirms the Testimony of the Reformation, a statement of its own composition. A member of the World Council of Churches and the World Alliance of Reformed Churches, this denomination promotes broad interchurch relations while emphasizing social programs through health care and education rather than evangelism.

Confessional Reformed Churches

Although most Protestant bodies with Reformed roots in Indonesia have become liberal-ecumenical denominations, some orthodox Calvinists continue to maintain a witness there, although they are not numerous. One such is the Reformed Churches in Indonesia-Irian Jaya, with a membership of four thousand. This movement originated in 1956, when Reformed believers in Canada and the Netherlands dispatched missionaries to southeast Irian. Conversions did not come quickly, but by 1970 several congregations had been established, and a synod came into being in 1988. Today about sixty local churches are affiliated with this denomination, and a theological school provides education for its ministers. The Three Forms of Unity express the doctrinal commitment of this church, which holds membership in the International Council of Reformed Churches.

A second confessional movement is the Reformed Churches in Indonesia-Nustenggara Timur, which began in 1881 on the island of Sumba as a Dutch mission. In the second half of the last century, when doctrinal dissensions became pronounced among Reformed believers in the Netherlands, those disputes caused comparable divisions in Indonesia, and this church was one of those deeply affected. At the end of that century, this body of forty-two hundred members was operating with a synodal structure while subscribing to the Three Forms of Unity and the Westminster Confession of Faith and enjoying close relations with the conservative Free Reformed Churches in the Netherlands and the Free Reformed Church of Australia. Evangelism and social service ministries subsist in balance within this denomination, one that does not ordain females. The very similar Reformed Churches in Indonesia-Kalimantan Barat, with three thousand adherents, also maintains a staunchly confessional posture as expressed in its allegiance to the Canons of Dort and the Heidelberg Catechism. The Reformed Evangelical Church is another Calvinistic communion, but one of recent origin which, at the end of the last century, did not yet have a well-organized structure. Extensive publishing of Reformed literature is a major emphasis, as is assertive evangelism, particularly among educated people. Several theological seminaries in the United States assist this church by providing education for its future ministers.

The Calvinistic heritage of Indonesian Protestantism notwithstanding, the churches of that tradition have, in general, avoided the use of conventional denominational labels, and most of them no longer emphasize the distinctive principles on which they were founded. Theological liberalism is about as pronounced in the archipelago as in the Netherlands itself, as only a few small churches uphold the Reformation heritage. While more than sixteen million Indonesians identify themselves as Protestants, active adherents to the Reformed faith account for only a fraction of that number.

The Republic of the Philippines

A nation of over eight hundred inhabited islands stretching from Borneo in the south to Taiwan in the north, this country has the largest number of professing Christians in Asia. About 80 percent of the people identify with Catholicism, 9 percent with various expressions of Protestantism, and 5 percent with Islam. Malays comprise the dominant ethnic group, and numerous languages are in use, although a substantial majority speaks English.

Ferdinand Magellan (1480–1521) discovered these islands in 1521 and claimed them for Spain, which then sent armed forces to impose its rule, a domination that continued until 1898, when the United States defeated Spain and established its own authority over the country. Because the Spaniards ruled the Philippines for three centuries, Roman Catholicism is still the major religion there. The formal introduction of Protestantism occurred in conjunction with the American occupation. Japanese imperial rule ended in the defeat of Japan, and in 1946 the United States granted independence to the Philippines. The constitution of the republic, from the start, provided for separation of church and state and full freedom of religion.

Protestant mission work in the islands began informally even while Spain ruled the region. This occurred when merchants distributed copies of the New Testament and a Dominican friar who received one was so impressed with its message that he began calling for reforms in his church and suffered deposition from the priesthood for doing so. The British and Foreign Bible Society sponsored translation projects that made the Scriptures available in several native tongues, and slowly Protestant groups began forming, even before the United States gained control. The first Protestant missionaries from America, upon their arrival, found about four hundred Filipinos professing that faith. Presbyterians were some of the first to dispatch personnel to these islands, James B. Rodgers (1865–1944) being the pioneer, who arrived in 1899 after being transferred from the Presbyterian mission in Brazil. Eager for Protestant success, Rodgers encouraged other denominations to send missionaries, and the Methodists and United Brethren responded readily. Rodgers helped to establish Union Theological Seminary in Manila and to create the United Evangelical Church in 1929. He remained in the country until his death. The work Rodgers initiated grew steadily and became one of the largest mission fields of the Presbyterian Church (U.S.A.).

Perhaps because Rodgers had an ecumenical perspective on Christianity, the Presbyterian mission in the Philippines did not assume the posture of a full commitment to the Reformed faith, and in 1948 it, through the United Evangelical Church, joined with several other bodies to form the United Church of Christ, a broad, inclusive structure lacking any clear subscription to historical Calvinism. This denomination of almost one million members in 1999 reported seventeen hundred congregations. The United Church ordains females and emphasizes education and health care. It is an affiliate of the World Council of Churches, the World Alliance of

Reformed Churches, and the Reformed Ecumenical Council, and engages regularly in domestic ecumenical affairs.

A smaller but comparable body is the United Evangelical Church formed in 1932 by independent congregations from various Protestant traditions, including Presbyterian and Reformed. Prior to organizing as a denomination, the constituent churches had all severed their ties with foreign missions. About thirty thousand people hold membership in the United Evangelical Church, and its seventy-two congregations are bound together in Presbyterian polity but without commitment to any Reformed confession. In addition to ecumenical relations at home, this body is a member of the World Alliance of Reformed Churches, and it cooperates with the larger United Church of Christ in maintaining Union Theological Seminary.

In contrast to the nominal allegiance to the Reformed faith in the two denominations cited, the Christian Reformed Church, with five thousand adherents, subscribes to the Heidelberg Catechism and the Canons of Dort and, since 1983, has been governed in a synodal structure comparable to that of Reformed bodies in Europe and North America. This denomination is the fruit of mission work undertaken by the Christian Reformed Church in North America begun in 1961. By the end of the last century there were thirty-seven affiliated congregations. This church ordains women as deacons but not as pastors or elders. It is a member of the Reformed Ecumenical Council and supports the evangelical-conservative Asian Theological Seminary in Manila rather than the liberal Union Theological Seminary there. A Bible college also provides education for church workers. Church planting, literature, and radio broadcasting are major ministries of the Christian Reformed Church.

As in some other nations, Presbyterians from Korea have been active in the Philippine Islands. This began in 1974, when Pastor Choi Chan-Young appeared there to distribute Bibles. Three years later Kim Hwal-Young, who left Vietnam in the wake of the Communist victory there, initiated an effort to revitalize the Presbyterian Church, which had become part of the United Church in 1948. This led to the formation of the Evangelical Presbyterian Mission and the creation of a Presbyterian denomination, one served by a substantial number of Korean pastors. Organization of a Reformed seminary soon followed, and in 1987 the General Assembly of the Presbyterian Church in the Philippines convened for the first time. In spite of some tensions and defections early in its existence, this body endured, as Presbyterians in Korea and the United States gave support.

Missionaries from the Orthodox Presbyterian Church in America were especially active in this development alongside their Korean comrades and native believers.

By the end of the twentieth century, the Presbyterian Church in the Philippines had about five thousand members worshiping in 145 congregations organized in traditional Presbyterian polity and subscribing to the Westminster Confession of Faith. This church does not ordain women to any of its offices. It maintains close fellowship with the Christian Reformed Church, and evangelism is its major emphasis. Missionaries from the Presbyterian Church in America became active supporters of this denomination toward the end of the last century, and a considerable number of them continue to labor in the islands.

As the twenty-first century unfolds, Christians of all connections face a troubling future, as the Muslim minority (only 5 percent of the whole) has demonstrated receptivity to radical terrorist influences, and violence against disciples of Jesus has occurred.

SUGGESTED ADDITIONAL READINGS >>

Aritonang, Jan S. *Mission Schools in Batakland, Indonesia, 1861–1940.* Leiden, Netherlands: E. J. Brill, 1994.

Brown, Colin. *A Short History of Indonesia.* Crows Nest, New South Wales: Allen and Unwin, 2003.

Campbell-Nelson, John. *Indonesia in Shadow and Light.* New York: Friendship Press, 1998.

Clymer, Kenton J. *Protestant Missionaries in the Philippines, 1898–1916.* Urbana: University of Illinois Press, 1986.

Cooley, Frank L. *The Growing Seed: The Christian Church in Indonesia.* Jakarta: Christian Publishing House, 1972.

———. *Indonesia: Church and Society.* New York: Friendship Press, 1968.

Deats, Richard L. *Nationalism and Christianity in the Philippines.* Dallas: Southern Methodist University Press, 1967.

Gowing, Peter G. *Islands under the Cross: The Story of the Church in the Philippines.* Manila: National Council of Churches in the Philippines, 1967.

Hinton, Keith. *Growing Churches Singapore Style.* Singapore: Overseas Missionary Fellowship, 1985.

Hunt, Robert A. with K. H. Lee and John Roxborough, eds. *Christianity in Malaysia*. Petaling Jaya, Malaysia: Pelanduk, 1992.

Koentjaraningrat, R. M. *Introduction to the Peoples and Culture of Indonesia and Malaysia*. Menlo Park, Calif.: Cummings, 1986.

Pedersen, Paul B. *Batak Blood and Protestant Soul*. Grand Rapids: Eerdmans, 1970.

Roxborough, John. *A Bibliography of Christianity in Malaysia*. Kuala Lumpur: Catholic Research Center, 1990.

———. *A Short Introduction to Malaysian Church History*. Rev. ed. Kuala Lumpur: Catholic Research Center, 1989.

Rush, James R. *The Philippine Church*. Hanover, N.H.: Universities Field Staff International, 1985.

Sitoy, T. Valentino. *Comity and Unity: Ardent Aspirations of Six Decades of Protestantism in the Philippines (1901–1966)*. Quezon City, Philippines: National Council of Churches in the Philippines, 1989.

Sng, Bobby E. K. *In His Good Time: The Story of the Church in Singapore, 1819–1978*. Singapore: Graduate Christian Fellowship, 1980.

Sunquist, Scott W. *A Dictionary of Asian Christianity*. Grand Rapids: Eerdmans, 2001.

Thomas, M. M. and M. Abel. *Religion, State, and Ideologies in East Asia*. Bangalore, India: East Asia Christian Conference, 1975.

Tuggy, Arthur L. *The Philippine Church Growth in a Changing Society*. Grand Rapids: Eerdmans, 1971.

Van Akkeren, Phillip. *Sri and Christ: The Story of the Indigenous Church in East Java*. London: Lutterworth Press, 1970.

Zainu'ddin, A. G. *A Short History of Indonesia*. New York: Praeger, 1970.

TWENTY-NINE

Mainland China

There are references to Christianity in China as early as the fourth century, but the first substantial evidences come from the seventh century, when Nestorian missionaries from Syria and Persia appeared in Xian, where Emperor Tai Tsung (r. 626–649) received them cordially and allowed them freedom to minister to his subjects. By then the Nestorian Church had separated from the Catholic and Orthodox Churches to the West because of disputes about the relationship of the deity and humanity in the person of Christ, and the Council of Ephesus (431) had condemned the Nestorian view as heresy.

Whatever their doctrinal errors entailed, Nestorian missionaries translated portions of the Scripture and Christian literature into Chinese, and several thousand conversions occurred. In the mid-ninth century, however, a reactionary emperor launched a persecution that forced Christians to retreat to the northern edge of China, thereby forfeiting gains they had made in some large cities. Thereafter Nestorian influence declined almost to the point of disappearing. The discovery of a marble tablet dated 781, nevertheless, remains to attest their presence.

The next effort to bring Christianity to China occurred late in the thirteenth century, when John de Monte Corvino (1246–1328), an Italian Franciscan, went to China from India. By then the Mongols had gained control there, and the emperor welcomed the Catholic missionary. Before long the Roman Church claimed to have some six thousand adherents in China, but Catholicism did not become well established there until near the end of the sixteenth century, when the Jesuit Matteo Ricci (1552–1610) arrived in Macao, a Portuguese enclave on the southern coast. Ricci eventually traveled to the imperial capital at Peking, where his knowledge of geography, mathematics, and astronomy astounded government officials, who permitted him to promulgate his beliefs freely. A prince of the imperial family was one of his converts. At Ricci's urging, additional Catholic missionaries went to China, where they enjoyed much success. It is rather ironic that Ricci and his companions disguised themselves as Buddhist monks when they journeyed to Peking.

The Protestant Era

Presbyterians were the first Protestants to enter China, and Robert Morrison (1782–1834), an appointee of the London Missionary Society who arrived in 1807, was the pioneer. This Englishman of Scottish ancestry from childhood demonstrated great intelligence, a studious manner, and a strong Christian faith. While in England he studied Chinese in connection with his academic preparation for the gospel ministry. Despite discouragements from relatives, Morrison sailed for China on an American vessel because the East India Company refused to transport him. Entering through the port of Canton, he soon encountered opposition from Chinese officials in Macao, from Jesuits already engaged there, and from hostile British merchants. By 1809, however, his amazing mastery of the Chinese language convinced the East India Company to employ him as a translator. With that support Morrison proceeded to produce an English-Chinese dictionary, a hymnbook, numerous gospel tracts, and a Chinese Bible. Although he labored twenty-seven years in China, converts were very few, and the first baptism occurred only after seven years of ministry. Morrison, nevertheless, laid a foundation on which Protestant missionaries would build, and his translation of the Scriptures stands as a testimony to his monumental contribution to the cause of Christ in China.

Karl F. A. Gutzlaff was another early emissary of Christ in China. This German Lutheran served with the Netherlands Missionary Society alongside Reformed colleagues in Indonesia before becoming an independent missionary there and in Thailand and before going to China in 1831. Like Morrison, he concentrated on translation work and labored to prepare native evangelists. Perhaps Gutzlaff's greatest contribution was his influence on J. Hudson Taylor (1832–1905), founder of the great China Inland Mission, a nondenominational society that, by Taylor's death, reported some 125 thousand church members in the country.

Although Morrison was Presbyterian, no organized Reformed mission appeared in China until 1842, when agents of the Reformed Church in America established a station in Amoy. The year 1844 brought missionaries of the Presbyterian Church (U.S.A.) to Ningpo, from which their work spread across northern China. Presbyterians in England sent workers to Swatow in 1847, and the Presbyterian Church (U.S.) (Southern) established its presence at Jiangsu and Zhejiang that same year. In rapid order thereafter Presbyterians from Canada, Scotland, New Zealand, and Korea joined their brethren in this enterprise.

William C. Burns (1815–1868), the first, and in some respects the greatest missionary sent out by the Presbyterian Church of England and one who profoundly influenced the life of Hudson Taylor, sailed for that land in 1847. Burns, who adopted the manner of dress and living of the Chinese, contributed to the piety of the church by producing a Chinese version of *Pilgrim's Progress,* and to its worship through his translation and publication of volumes of hymns. He traveled about China almost incessantly during his twenty-one years of residence there.

In 1854 the American Board of Commissioners for Foreign Missions transferred its Amoy station, founded by David Abeel twelve years before, to the custody of the Dutch Reformed Church. Another American-based denomination, the Southern Presbyterian Church, acquired representation in China in 1867 after Elias B. Inslee (1822–1871) had severed his connection with the Presbyterian Church (U.S.A.) and later joined the Southerners.

Hugh Waddell (d. 1902) and physician Joseph M. Hunter and his wife brought the Presbyterian Church in Ireland into the picture in 1869, as they began what was to prove a fruitful ministry in Manchuria. In 1872 John Ross (1842–1915) of the United Presbyterian Church of Scotland entered the same general region. The Church of Scotland was late in reaching China, but in 1878 George Cockburn (1853–1898), in company with three lay workers, laid the foundations of a mission at Ichang, one of the treaty ports opened during the preceding year. Andrew I. Robb and Isaac T. E. Burney and their wives reached Canton in December 1895 as founders of the China Mission of the Reformed Presbyterian Church of North America.

Physician G. T. Logan and his wife left the United States for China in September 1897, thereby adding the Cumberland Presbyterian Church to the number of those at work in that country. New Zealand Presbyterians entered in 1901 and established their New Zealand Presbyterian Village Mission, after settling in the vicinity of Canton. Fellow denominationalists from Australia made the northward trip to China in 1941 but never chose to set up a mission of their own, preferring to lend their efforts in support of other such establishments.

In November 1920 a physician and minister and former worker among the American Indians, Lee S. Huizenga (1881–1945), and his wife and children, with ordained ministers John C. De Korne and Harry A. Dykstra and their wives, disembarked from the ship *China* at Shanghai. This marked the entrance of the Christian Reformed Church (America) into the field. The party later settled in the North Kiangsu area in the vicinity of the field of the Presbyterian Church (U.S.).

During the years of their missionary endeavors, Presbyterians seemed to indicate an affinity for the Chinese, and that people may well have responded in like spirit. After comments relative to the attitude of Occidentals to those of the Orient, Kenneth Scott Latourette remarked:

> It may be, moreover, that the prominence of Presbyterians in China was partly to be attributed to the congeniality of the Chinese village and family structure to the Presbyterian type of organization. It is clear that in 1914 Presbyterians of various churches had more missionaries and communicants in China than any other confessional group of Protestants. Only the un-denominational China Inland Mission exceeded them in numbers of missionaries. Even it did not begin to equal them in Chinese membership.

Missionaries to China at times resorted to the use of tents in the course of their itinerant ministry. Illustrative of this type of evangelism was that of George A. Hudson (1894–1982) of the Southern Presbyterian Mission. Often entering cities or towns where the name of Jesus was practically unknown, he erected the tent that he carried from place to place and spoke for four nights in presenting the claims of the gospel. The speaker devoted the first evening to an introduction to the Christian message and the three succeeding ones to sermons on the doctrine of God, the doctrine of sin, and the doctrine of salvation before striking his tent and moving on to another community.

By 1900 eleven Reformed missions were engaged in the Celestial Empire, as China was then known. In 1906 eight of them created a Council of Presbyterian Churches with a view toward unifying their efforts, a movement that led to formation of a General Assembly in 1922, by which time the new denomination had seventy-seven thousand members and twenty-five presbyteries. At the insistence of native delegates, this body discarded the traditional denominational label and declared itself the Church of Christ in China, perhaps as a gesture to include non-Reformed churches at a later time.

The Church of Christ in China adopted Presbyterian polity in large measure, but it allowed particular synods to decide matters such as the subjects and mode of baptism and qualifications for ordination to the ministry. Rather than affirm the Westminster Standards, this body produced its own statement of beliefs, so from its inception, the Church of Christ in China did not commit itself to historic Reformed theology.

The Japanese occupation of much of China, which continued through the Second World War, forced this church to divide its operations between *Free* and *Occupied* China. When the Communists gained control after that war, the church held its last general assembly in 1948. The dream of uniting all Chinese Protestants within the Church of Christ ended abruptly.

Although in the twentieth century the Church of Christ became the largest denomination in the land, works begun in the previous century, some of them confessionally Reformed, continued. Among those who had been responsible for planting such bodies, perhaps none was more significant than John L. Nevius (1829–1893), a missionary statesman best remembered for his influence in Korea. This graduate of Princeton Theological Seminary and his wife sailed for China in 1853, where, in an amazingly short time, he became a fluent preacher in the native tongue. An itinerant evangelist and teacher, Nevius ministered to a network of congregations in which he promoted self-support, local autonomy, and self-propagation, principles that became known as the Nevius Plan for Missions. He stressed instruction of native pastors and teachers to lead the churches in their efforts to seek the salvation of lost people. More in Korea than in China, Presbyterians implemented his proposals, and a vibrant, healthy Reformed movement developed there, a tribute to the wisdom of his methods.

Medical missions also occupied the attention of American Presbyterians in the nineteenth century, as the work of Dr. John G. Kerr (1824–1901) attests. Kerr invested forty-seven years at the Canton Hospital, where he treated patients and trained physicians and surgeons. Sun Yat-sen (1867–1925), who would become the first president of China, was one of Dr. Kerr's students. An author and translator of medical books, this skillful practitioner of health care was a fervent evangelist as well, for the salvation of the lost was always his first concern.

Some Presbyterian missionaries gained such respect in China that the imperial government employed them in educational and diplomatic roles. W. A. P. Martin (1827–1916) was one such figure. This graduate of Indiana State University and the Presbyterian seminary in that same state served in China from 1850 to 1868. His skill as a translator led the United States legation in China to enlist Martin's aid in concluding a major treaty with the Chinese Empire, and he often advised imperial officials on matters pertaining to international relations. To assist such diplomats Martin rendered Wheaton's *Elements of International Law* into their language, and the grateful emperor made him president of the Imperial University in Peking. Always zealous to promote the cause of Christ, Martin wrote *Evidences of Christianity*, a treatise on apologetics in Chinese, a book that later appeared in Japanese as well.

The cordiality shown toward noteworthy missionaries does not mean there was no opposition to Christianity in China. During the Tai Ping Rebellion (1850–1864) a pseudo-Christian political movement attempted to overthrow the Manchu government, and for a while it appeared to be succeeding, with its leader, Hung Hsui-chuan (1814–1864), declaring himself emperor of Tai Ping (Great Peace). In the end this effort failed, but the gullibility of some missionaries who thought the rebellion would bring a new day of opportunity for Christianity in the empire injured the credibility of their religion in the eyes of many natives. The long struggle had caused millions of deaths, and the failure of the missionaries to disavow the movement cost them dearly.

Soon after the suppression of the Tai Ping Rebellion, E. B. Inslee and his wife, agents of the Southern Presbyterian Church in the United States, returned to China, from which they had fled to avoid the violence. They settled at Hangchow, a city badly damaged during the fighting. There they established the first formal mission station of their denomination in China, and soon a dozen more such stations were operating, as converts came to Christ in growing numbers.

Although the Tai Ping Rebellion caused huge casualties and brought some discredit upon the Christian movement, the Boxer Rebellion of 1900 was, for the missionaries themselves, even more damaging, for it brought death to hundreds of their number. Nicknamed the Boxers, this antiforeign and anti-Manchu uprising was in large part the work of the Society of Righteous Harmonious Fists, a revolutionary movement resolved to overthrow the corrupt, ineffective imperial regime that had been unable to prevent exploitation and frequent intrusions into China. This nationalist opposition vowed to rid the country of all "foreign devils." Missionaries, especially those in remote interior areas, were very vulnerable, and many scores of them perished at the hands of the Boxers. Even children of missionaries were victims of the killers. The number of native believers killed is impossible to ascertain. Adherents to the Reformed faith, of course, did not escape. As intense as the suffering was, however, the heroic sacrifices of staunch believers impressed many Chinese to embrace the Christian faith. Then, the several foreign powers that helped suppress the uprising insisted the imperial government keep the country open to Western influence, and that meant full freedom for missionary work. The decade after 1900 saw more conversions than the entire previous century, and by 1915 there were 220 thousand professing Protestants in the land. By 1926 over eight thousand missionaries were present in China, more than in any other nation. The Reformed Presbyterian Church, the German Reformed Church in the United States, along with the Northern and Southern Presbyterian Churches, were all involved.

Korean Presbyterians too had been active in China beginning in the second half of the nineteenth century, when a considerable number of Koreans settled in the northeast part of the empire. Presbyterian missionaries from Korea and some from Canada worked among the immigrants, and newly founded congregations operated in conjunction with presbyteries in Korea itself. In 1921 a separate presbytery came into being, but the Japanese conquerors compelled all denominations to join what became known as the Korean Church of Christ in Manchuria. World War II inflicted such damage that only a few enclaves of Koreans remained in that area by the end of that conflict. The Communist era brought further suffering, but in 1992 the People's Republic of China and the Republic of Korea established diplomatic relations that allowed Korean churches to resume their ministries in Manchuria.

The imposition of Communist rule in 1949 had forced all churches in China to cut their ties with foreign missions, while the government expelled the missionary personnel. All churches had to merge into a single body subject to government supervision. The Cultural Revolution (1966–1976), a time of extreme measures to enforce obedience to the Red ideology, inflicted great hardships upon Christians, but after that period of repression the state again allowed registered churches to function. In spite of the brutality of the Cultural Revolution, the churches grew, and at present there is evidence that the number of practicing Christians in Red China is in the millions, although reliable statistics are not available.

One consequence of the upheavals Christians have endured in China is the practical disappearance of traditional denominations, including

Presbyterian and Reformed churches. A China Christian Council, formed in 1980, embraces most, but not all, Protestant churches in the nation. This is an ecumenical movement to produce a single church. The council is an affiliate of the World Council of Churches.

Hong Kong

From 1842 to 1997 Hong Kong was a British Crown Colony under terms of a treaty imposed upon the feeble Manchu government after a British victory in the First Opium War (1839–1842). Although the behavior of British merchants in importing an addictive drug was reprehensible and the policy of their government imperious, one benefit ensued for China—an open door for Christian missions in the colony. Large numbers of Protestants from Europe, Asia, and America appeared in Hong Kong as evangelists, church planters, and educators. Their endeavors explain why today Christian schools abound in this territory from which missionaries went to other parts of the country. The city itself early became a printing center where translators produced several versions of the Chinese Bible for distribution across the land. After the Communists seized control of the mainland in 1949, the British colony became even more important as a base from which to spread the Christian faith into other regions, regardless of the official atheism and repressive policies of the Red regime. Thousands of conversions occurred in Hong Kong during the nineteenth and twentieth centuries, and Presbyterian and Reformed missions were conspicuously involved.

Beginning in 1848, the Basel Mission maintained a ministry in Hong Kong, but that work languished until English Presbyterians arrived in 1856 and soon thereafter asked the London Missionary Society to dispatch workers. The Hong Kong Swatow Christian Church is the fruit of those endeavors. In 1999 it reported about sixty-five hundred members in ten congregations and several preaching stations. This church operates under Presbyterian polity, but the Apostles' Creed is its only doctrinal standard. Women are eligible for ordination. The Man Lam Christian Church also has Reformed roots and current connections with the Reformed Church in America. A member of the ecumenical Hong Kong Council of the Church of Christ in China, this denomination has only fifteen hundred members in three local assemblies. It ordains women and does not officially endorse any historic Reformed confession. The Chinese Christian Church of Amoy is another tiny denomination with Presbyterian government but without subscription to Reformed theology. This church of only about seven hundred members is the product of settlers who moved to the colony after the Communists took control of Fujian. The date of its formal organization was 1958.

The only Protestant church in Hong Kong that has both a Reformed heritage and a substantial membership is the Church of Christ in China, Hong Kong Council, an interdenominational body of some twenty-five thousand members in forty-four congregations. Although a member of the World Alliance of Reformed Churches, this church, like those mentioned above, is not distinctively Reformed in doctrine. It operates a theological school as a division of the Chinese University of Hong Kong and maintains a network of elementary and secondary schools also.

Only two ecclesiastical bodies in Hong Kong profess overtly to be Presbyterian. They are called the Cumberland Presbyterian Church, an American missionary outreach by a denomination of the same name in the United States. Beginning late in the nineteenth century, missionaries from America labored in Canton province, but because of the Communist victory, the mission moved to Hong Kong and Portuguese Macao, where it formed a presbytery. The Cumberland Presbyterian Church, at the end of the last century, had only 780 members and eight congregations. It does ordain females to all offices and does not espouse Calvinist doctrine.

The Hong Kong Chinese Presbyterian Church is the other body that operates under the Presbyterian banner, but it has only about 160 members. Christians fleeing from Guangdong province founded this church in 1948. It does not make a formal subscription to Reformed theology.

Since Great Britain returned Hong Kong to China in 1997, the Red regime has been, in general, more tolerant of Christians there than in the rest of the country. The future for the churches in the former colony appears stable at present, but the Reformed faith is not prominent. The Presbyterian Church in America has one missionary family there.

SUGGESTED ADDITIONAL READINGS >>

Brown, G. Thompson. *Earthen Vessels and Transcendent Power: American Presbyterians in China, 1837–1952.* Maryknoll, N.Y.: Orbis Books, 1967.

Bush, R. C. *Religion in Communist China.* New York: Abingdon Press, 1972.

Cary-Elwes, Columbia. *China and the Cross: A Survey of Missionary History.* New York: P. J. Kennedy and Sons, 1956.

Choo, J., ed. *The China Handbook*. Hong Kong: Chinese Church Research Center, 1989.

Covell, Ralph R. *Confucius, the Buddha, and Christ: A History of the Gospel in Chinese*. Maryknoll, N.Y.: Orbis Books, 1986.

———. *A. P. Martin: Pioneer of Progress in China*. Washington, D.C.: Christian University Press, 1978.

De Jong, Gerald F. *The Reformed Church in China, 1842–1951*. Grand Rapids: Eerdmans, 1992.

Hunter, Alan and K. K. Chan. *Protestantism in Contemporary China*. Cambridge: Cambridge University Press, 1993.

Johnston, J. *China and Formosa: The Story of the Mission of the Presbyterian Church of England*. London: Hazell, Watson, and Viney, 1897.

Jones, Francis P. *The Church in Communist China*. New York: Friendship Press, 1962.

Latourette, Kenneth S. *A History of Christian Missions in China*. New York: Macmillan, 1929.

Lyall, Leslie T. *Come Wind, Come Weather: The Present Experience of the Church in China*. Chicago: Moody, 1960.

MacInnis, Donald E. *Religion in China Today*. Maryknoll, N.Y.: Orbis Books, 1989.

———. *Religion, Policy, and Practice in Communist China: A Documentary History*. London: Hodder and Stoughton, 1972.

Moffett, Samuel H. *A History of Christianity in Asia*. San Francisco: Harper San Francisco, 1992.

Nevius, Helen S. Coan. *The Life of John Livingston Nevius*. New York: Fleming H. Revell, 1895.

Nevius, John L. *Christ and the Chinese*. New York: Harper and Brothers, 1869.

———. *The Planting and Development of Missionary Churches*. 4th ed. Nutley, N.J.: P&R, 1973. Reprint of 1958 edition.

Outerbridge, Leonard M. *The Lost Churches of China*. Philadelphia: Westminster Press, 1952.

Overmyer, Daniel J. *Religion in China Today*. Cambridge: Cambridge University Press, 2003.

Patterson, George N. *Christianity in Communist China*. Waco, Tex.: Word Books, 1969.

Pollock, John C. *A Foreign Devil in China: The Story of Dr. Nelson L. Bell, an American Surgeon in China*. Minneapolis: World Wide Publications, 1971.

Spence, Jonathan D. *To Change China: Western Advisors in China, 1620–1960*. New York: Penguin Books, 1980.

Stuart, John L. *Fifty Years in China*. New York: Random House, 1954.

Townsend, William *Robert Morrison: The Pioneer of Chinese Missions*. London: S. W. Partridge, 1890.

Varg, Paul A. *Missionaries, Chinese, and Diplomats*. Princeton, N.J.: Princeton University Press, 1958.

Whyte, Bob. *Unfinished Encounter: China and Christianity*. London: Collins Fount Paperbacks, 1988.

Wylie, Alexander. *Memorials of Protestant Missionaries to the Chinese*. Shanghai: American Presbyterian Mission Press, 1867.

THIRTY

The Republic of China-Taiwan

In contrast to the situation in mainland China, the Reformed faith is prominent and vigorous in the Republic of China, now confined to Taiwan and some lesser islands that the Communists have been unable to acquire.

Portuguese explorers discovered Taiwan in 1590, and impressed with its beauty, they called it Formosa, but they did not settle there. In 1626 Dutch and Spanish merchants established enclaves on the island, but soon the Dutch seized the Spanish holdings for themselves. The natives then were Malay-Polynesians, not Chinese. With the encouragement of the Dutch East India Company, Reformed missionaries from the Netherlands arrived soon after the company had secured control. During the period of Dutch occupation (1626–1662), the Reformed church flourished and may have had as many as six thousand communicants, Europeans and natives combined. In 1661, however, an invasion of Chinese ended Dutch rule and increased the population of Taiwan substantially by the influx of ethnic Chinese. In 1683 the Manchu Dynasty incorporated the island into the province of Fukien, a status that continued until 1886, when Taiwan became a province in its own right. The Japanese took the area in 1894, when they defeated China in a brief war. It reverted to China after the defeat of Japan in World War II.

When the Manchus seized Taiwan in 1683, they expelled the missionaries and persecuted local Christians so brutally that almost no Christian presence was discernable when Presbyterian missionaries arrived in the nineteenth century. Medical missions were prominent in the early days of the Presbyterian effort, as the work of Dr. James Maxwell (1857–1921) attests. This Englishman was an effective evangelist-preacher as well as a skillful physician who directed a large hospital. Leslie Mackay (1844–1901), a Canadian Presbyterian, though not formally educated in the healing arts, learned enough dentistry to treat thousands of people needing such care.

Mackay was especially adept at church planting and so became the founder of the Presbyterian Church in northern Taiwan. By 1912 progress in that endeavor allowed for creation of a synod. A General Assembly, however, did not come into being until 1951. When the mainland fell to the Communists, many missionaries moved to Taiwan. When, in 1970, the World Council of Churches supported the admission of Red China to the United Nations, the Presbyterian Church in Taiwan withdrew from that council. By then that church had over seventy-five thousand members.

By the end of the last century, fewer than 5 percent of Taiwan's people were professing the Christian faith, although most that did so were of the evangelical persuasion. The Reformed faith is the largest expression of Protestantism in the Republic of China, and the Presbyterian Church in Taiwan is the largest Protestant denomination. It now has over 225 thousand adherents in 1,183 congregations. This church is an outgrowth of the work initiated in the nineteenth century by James Maxwell and Leslie Mackay.

During the era of Japanese control, the Presbyterian Church learned to operate autonomously after foreign missionaries left in the 1930s. This church has emphasized the use of the Taiwanese language rather than Mandarin Chinese, although it conducts its ministries in several dialects. Often the Presbyterian Church has defended civil liberties when authoritarian government officials have imposed repressive policies on the populace. Although this denomination is generally ecumenical in its relations, it has not stressed social services at the expense of evangelism but maintains both emphases in balance. Church pronouncements about the political sovereignty of Taiwan have at times brought angry rejoinders from the government, but such resolutions have continued nevertheless, as the church supports the independence of the island rather than the government's claim to be the legitimate authority over all of China.

The Presbyterian Church in Taiwan officially endorses the historic Reformed symbols, including the Heidelberg Catechism and the Westminster Confession of Faith, and it holds membership in the World Alliance of Reformed Churches. It ordains women to all church offices, operates several hospitals, and maintains a number of schools, including a Bible College and a theological seminary. This vigorous denomination has a plan to send two hundred missionaries to other countries in the near future.

More conservative than the Presbyterian Church in Taiwan are several smaller churches, some with ties to missions from the United States. The Reformed Presbyterian Church of Taiwan is one such body. In 1999 this denomination reported having eighteen congregations and about one thousand members. With aid from missionaries of the Presbyterian Church in America, this body operates the Reformed Theological Seminary in the capital city, Taipei. It subscribes to the Heidelberg Catechism and the Westminster Confession, does not ordain females, and conducts most of its services in Mandarin Chinese. Most of its local churches are in northern Taiwan, but church planters are active elsewhere in the country.

The Reformed Presbyterian Church and other conservative groups rely upon Christ College, Taipei, for the education of their people. This institution opened in 1959, when American Presbyterian missionary Dr. James R. Graham (1898–1982) founded this Christian college of liberal arts. In 1975 the Presbyterian Church in America, through its Mission to the World, adopted Christ College as one of its ministries, as Taiwan in general became a major mission field of that denomination. With about 850 undergraduates, this institution welcomes both believers and non-Christians, all of whom receive instruction in the gospel and a Christian perspective on all academic disciplines. By the time they graduate, about two-thirds of the students profess faith in Christ. The college thus performs both an educational and an evangelistic function and is a major instrument in spreading Christian influence across the land.

Missionaries from South Korea have been active in Taiwan, and there are about a dozen local Presbyterian churches operating under their direction. These conservative congregations embrace the Westminster Standards, refrain from ordaining women, and are known collectively as the Presbyterian Church of Korea-Taiwan Mission.

The Christian Reformed Church in North America entered the Republic of China in 1952 to undertake church planting, assisted by radio and literature evangelism. In 1971, upon formation of the Reformed Presbyterian Church of Taiwan, the Christian Reformed mission began cooperating with that body, especially helping in the education of its leaders. There has developed, however, a distinctively Christian Reformed Church in Taiwan, but as of the year 2000, it had only four congregations and about three hundred members. It does not ordain female officers and adheres to the Westminster Standards and the Heidelberg Catechism.

In addition to formally organized Presbyterian denominations, there are some single congregations that practice government by elders on the local level but without connections to one another. There is, for example, one local assembly in Taiwan that corresponds to that description and owes its origin to a mission from New Zealand. This New Zealand Presbyterian Church is staunchly confessional in espousing the Westminster Standards, but its membership in 1999 stood at only fifty people.

Reformed churches outside the Republic of China continue to invest in that country. As indicated, the Presbyterian Church in America is heavily engaged, but the Presbyterian Church (U.S.A.), the Reformed Church in America, the Presbyterian Church of Canada, the Evangelical Presbyterian Church (United States), and the Church of Scotland also are involved. So long as this country remains free from Communist rule, the doors should remain open, presenting Reformed churches with great opportunities to spread the Christian faith.

SUGGESTED ADDITIONAL READINGS >>

China Evangelical Fellowship. *Church Directory of the Republic of China.* Taipei: China Fellowship, 1969.

Clart, Philip and Charles B. Jones, eds. *Religion in Modern Taiwan.* Honolulu: University of Hawaii Press, 2003.

Gates, Alan F. *Christianity and Animism in Taiwan.* San Francisco: Chinese Materials Center, 1979.

Johnston, J. *China and Formosa: The Story of the Mission of the Presbyterian Church of England.* London: Hazell, Watson, and Viney, 1897.

Rubenstein, M. A. *The Protestant Community in Modern Taiwan.* Armonk, N.Y.: M. E. Sharpe, 1991.

Swanson, Allen J. *The Church in Taiwan: Profile 1980.* South Pasadena, Calif.: William Carey Library, 1981.

———. *Taiwan: Mainline Versus Independent Church Growth: A Study in Contrasts.* South Pasadena, Calif.: William Carey Library, 1970.

Vicedom, George F. *Faith That Moves Mountains: A Study of the Tribal Church in Taiwan.* Taipei: China Post, 1967.

THIRTY-ONE

The Republic
of Korea

Situated on the east coast of Asia, the Korean peninsula extends into the Yellow Sea on the west and the Sea of Japan on the east. Long called the *Hermit Nation* because of its relative isolation from the outside world, this country came to the attention of the great powers after the Japanese, in 1876, forced Korea to establish commercial and diplomatic relations with their own empire. Soon China, United States, Great Britain, and other states did likewise. When the Japanese defeated China in 1895, they became the dominant power in Korea, which they annexed officially in 1910 and ruled until the end of World War II.

Soviet forces occupied northern Korea in 1945, while those of the United States took control in the south. Although these victors over Japan declared their intention to create a united and independent Korea, the Soviets instead installed a puppet regime in their sector, an action that led the United States, through the United Nations, to establish the Republic of Korea in the south after free elections there. That division at the 38th parallel remains despite war between the two Koreas from 1950 to 1953.

Buddhism has a large following in Korea, although its strength has diminished in the face of Communist repression in the north and the rapid advance of Christianity in the south. The initial contact with Christianity occurred late in the eighteenth century, when Roman Catholic missionaries met Korean diplomats in Peking and a few conversions occurred. Those who embraced Catholicism then took it to their homeland, where it enjoyed considerable success. Beginning in 1835 Catholic missionaries appeared but soon encountered strong opposition from Buddhist monks who inflamed mobs to attack the missionaries and their converts. The persecution may have brought death to as many as ten thousand people. For some time thereafter Koreans feared Christianity per se as a foreign religion unsuited to their culture.

Protestant Missions

The arrival of Protestant missions came after a period of about fifteen years, during which native Koreans, converted in Manchuria through the witness of Scottish Presbyterians, spread the gospel and distributed New Testaments translated into Korean with their aid. John Ross (1842–1915), serving in Mukden, Manchuria, led the project to render the Scriptures into Korean and to send agents there to circulate them. As a consequence of these endeavors, when Protestant missionaries arrived in the country, they found communities of believers eager for their ministries.

When the United States and the Kingdom of Korea established relations in 1884, American missionaries were permitted to labor on the peninsula. That same year the Presbyterian Church (U.S.A.) sent Horace N. Allen, M.D. to that nation. His medical skills so impressed the royal court that other Christians from America enjoyed a hearty reception. Later Allen became a diplomat for his government in Korea, and the valuable connections he established in that position enabled him to obtain advantages for missionaries of various denominations.

Horace G. Underwood (1854–1916), a graduate of the Reformed Theological Seminary in New Jersey, landed at Inchon in 1885 to do the work of an evangelist. He organized an orphanage and the first Protestant church on Korean soil while promoting literacy and translating Christian material into the Korean tongue. When the Presbyterian Church convened its first General Assembly in 1912, Underwood became its moderator. In 1915 he established Chosun Christian College, where he was president until his death. His son succeeded to the presidency, and members of the Underwood family continue to serve in Korea. The early successes of Allen and Underwood prompted more Presbyterians to go to Korea, and before the end of the nineteenth century, missionaries from Reformed churches in Australia and Canada joined their American colleagues on that field.

One of the most important factors in the impressive gains Christianity made in Korea was the missions' adoption of the Nevius Plan mentioned in chapter 29, "Mainland China." Nevius visited Korea in 1890, before the Presbyterian mission was a decade old. His proposal for self-sustaining churches and maximum involvement of native believers in positions of leadership proved to be the formula for success, as Korean believers, from the inception of their Presbyterian Church, learned to accept responsibility for their own affairs and to undergird their labors with fervent prayers, for which they became duly famous. The exciting story of Korean Christianity in its formative years appears in Underwood's book, *The Call of Korea* (1908).

Although the Presbyterian Church (U.S.A.) led the way evangelizing in Korea, other Reformed denominations soon joined that effort. Australian Presbyterians arrived in 1890 and others from Canada in 1898. For the most part these missions supported the Presbyterian seminary at Pyong Yang, which graduated its first class in 1907, the same year in which the churches formed their first presbytery and sent forth their first missionaries.

Creation of the Pyong Yang Seminary was the work of pioneer missionary Samuel A. Moffett (1864–1939), an emissary of the Presbyterian Church (U.S.A.), who became renowned as an educator in Korea. He first administered the boys' school that Horace Underwood had founded, and after that he organized hundreds of elementary schools as well as an academy that developed into the first Christian college in the country. In 1907 Moffett became pastor of Central Presbyterian Church in Pyong Yang and the same year became moderator of the General Assembly. Moffett's opposition to the Japanese demand that Christians worship at Shinto shrines as a demonstration of their loyalty to the empire led the authorities to expel him in 1936.

To their credit, Korean Presbyterians did not sacrifice evangelistic fervor for social action but accepted both ministries as divinely mandated obligations. Bible study was a major emphasis among them from the start, and that led them into extensive educational endeavors. Local churches sponsored a large number of elementary schools, and almost all of them obtained needed financing from Koreans themselves. By 1938 the large city of Pyongyang had about four hundred Presbyterian congregations with about twenty thousand members, and that was during the time of Japanese control, when the government was sometimes hostile to Christians and tried to compel their attendance at Shinto shrines. When some believers complied with that demand, others resolutely refused and suffered imprisonment, even death, rather than deny Christ. In 1943, after expelling the missionaries, the Japanese rulers required all Presbyterian churches to join the Chosun Presbyterian Church in Japan. After World War II Korean Presbyterians debated about the responses church members had made to the Japanese demand, and disagreements led to schisms among the churches. In 1919, during a period of especially intense pressure to bow at Shinto shrines, the Presbyterians had lost many pastors who suffered for their faith, and many laymen who had joined them in defiance of the imperial authorities.

The Soviet occupation of North Korea led in 1950 to war between that state and the Republic of Korea in the south. Millions of refugees, Presbyterians among them, fled from Communist territory, and all of Korea became a battleground on which the losses inflicted on churches were staggering. Since then North Korea has remained a closed society, so reliable information about the plight of Christians there is difficult to obtain. South Korea, on the contrary, has developed as a constitutional state with a thriving economy based in international trade. Freedom of religion guaranteed by law has allowed churches to minister unhindered, and the Reformed faith remains the persuasion of most Protestants there. There is, however, little unity among adherents to Presbyterianism, as the existence of almost one hundred individual Presbyterian church bodies attests.

Proliferation of Denominations

Although the Reformed faith has flourished in Korea more than in any other Asian country, its development has been punctuated with controversies and divisions. This troubling situation has been due in part to the appearance of liberal theology from Europe and North America, especially in the areas where Canadian Presbyterians were influential. The Canadians at first proved more receptive to liberal ideas than were their colleagues from the United States, but eventually those ideas spread across the land and agitated intense disputes among missionaries and native church leaders. Since debates about historic doctrines and the trustworthiness of Scripture occurred in the midst of contention about dealing with church members who had capitulated to Japanese demands for worship at Shinto shrines, the churches in Korea could hardly avoid schisms. Collision between churchmen loyal to the World Council of Churches and those resolved to maintain orthodoxy became particularly pronounced when the International Council of Christian Churches under the leadership of Carl McIntire from the United States entered the contest. No Presbyterian body in the country could remain aloof in this struggle. Since the number of those churches is so large, this survey will deal only with the more prominent denominations involved, all of which hold officially to the Westminster Standards, and when compared with major denominations in other countries, seem quite conservative.

The Presbyterian Church in Korea (KoShin), one of the larger Reformed bodies, has about 365 thousand members in over thirteen hundred congregations. This church is a creation of people who had opposed Shinto worship during the Japanese occupation, a resistance that led to imprisonment of many church leaders. After the Second World War, believers of this persuasion asked the presbyteries to discipline pastors who had complied with the Japanese requirement. When the General Assembly refused to do this, three ministers who had been incarcerated led a schism that eventually produced the KoShin denomination, but that body divided over other issues. By the end of 1999 the Presbyterian Church (KoShin) reported thirty presbyteries that do not ordain women. A member of the International Council of Reformed Churches, this denomination operates KoShin University in Pusan, which provides theological education for its ministerial candidates.

The Korean Reformed Presbyterian Church (Ko RyuPa) is a schism from KoShin due to disputes about theological education. This very conservative body has close relations with comparable churches in Japan, the Netherlands, and the United States. Its Reformed Theological Seminary in Seoul is rigorously orthodox, and its graduates serve in some five hundred local churches. The denomination as a whole has about eighty thousand members. It refrains from ordaining women and subscribes to the Westminster Confession of Faith.

The Presbyterian Church in the Republic of Korea (KiJang, PROK) developed out of controversies at Chosun Seminary, an institution receptive to some liberal ideas. Departures from historic Calvinism at the Chosun school led one professor and fifty-one students to withdraw and form a rival seminary in 1947. Efforts to reunite the competing institutions failed, and the liberal group formed the Presbyterian Church in the Republic of Korea, a denomination which has become one of the more liberal Reformed bodies in the country. An affiliate of the World Council of Churches and the World Alliance of Reformed Churches plus domestic ecumenical agencies, this church ordains females and emphasizes social ministries among its 325 thousand adherents who worship in approximately eight hundred congregations. The KiJang adopted its own confession in 1987 without officially discarding the Westminster Standards.

The Presbyterian Church of Korea (TongHap) is, in large part, the remaining portion of Korea's original Presbyterian Church, and after numerous secessions, it still has over two million members and about fifty-nine hundred local assemblies. After suffering considerable losses due to disagreements about ecumenical relations, the TongHap body aligned with the World Council of Churches and assumed a rather liberal policy toward doctrinal diversity and acceptance of women's ordination. The Westminster Standards remain among the theological symbols of this church, but subscription is very loose. TongHap is a member of the World Alliance of Reformed Churches.

The second large sector of the original Presbyterian Church in Korea is the present Presbyterian Church of Korea (HapDong), a conservative body that opposed membership in the World Council of Churches. HapDong's staunch orthodoxy withstood a serious challenge when some professors at ChongShin Seminary endorsed the higher criticism of the Pentateuch. When the General Assembly censured that seminary, it withdrew from the denomination and became a private university. Despite this and additional secessions, HapDong has remained strong and is now the largest Reformed denomination in Korea. Well over two million people adhere to this church of over five thousand congregations. Women are not eligible for ordination to church offices, and the Westminster Confession is the official doctrinal statement.

Although much smaller than HapDong and TongHap, the Presbyterian Church of Korea (DaeShin I) is an influential denomination of 140 thousand members. The origin of this body extends to 1948, when three pastors began conducting classes to prepare candidates for the ministry, an endeavor that led to the creation of DaeHan Seminary, around which this denomination developed.

In 1960 Carl McIntire, through the International Council of Christian Churches, obtained funds to establish the Bible Presbyterian Church to be closely allied to DaeHan Seminary, but rivalries among leaders of the Bible Presbyterian Church caused secessions early in the life of that body. In 1972, after numerous disputes, DaeShin I emerged as the major successor to the Bible Presbyterian Church, but the new denomination no longer espoused the fundamentalist views of McIntire. DaeShin I joined the World Alliance of Reformed Churches and has participated in ecumenical affairs the Bible Presbyterians would have disavowed. DaeShin I is now a growing movement of almost twelve hundred congregations that do not ordain women officers. The church has its own theological school. A faction that opposed these measures withdrew and became DaeShin II, but in 1999 it reported only fifteen thousand adherents.

Another Korean denomination with roots in the work of the International Council of Christian Churches is the Presbyterian Church of Korea (BubTong), founded in 1971. When Carl McIntire toured South Korea in 1974, he stressed the anti-Christian character of Communism and called Christians there to oppose the World Council of Churches for its alleged sympathy toward various Marxist movements. He urged Christians to support the rather authoritarian government of President Park Jung-Hee, much to the consternation of both political and religious liberals. BubTong assumed a firm anti-Communist posture and supported the policies of the International Council of Christian Churches. This body, at the end of the last century, had about thirty-four thousand members in 230 congregations bound together in Presbyterian polity while adhering to the Westminster Confession.

Two Reformed denominations of substantial size continue to uphold traditional Reformed theology. The Presbyterian Church in Korea (Hap-Dong BoSu I), with two hundred thousand members, is an affiliate of the International Council of Christian Churches, while the HapDong BoSu II, with almost seven hundred thousand adherents, is not related to either the World Council of Churches or the International Council or any other such organization. The larger of these bodies is a vigorous orthodox movement with nine seminaries and ten Bible institutes, all committed to the Westminster Standards.

The general refusal of Presbyterian churches in Korea to ordain women has led to the formation of organizations for which that is a specified objective. Hence there is a Women Pastors Presbyterian Church known to Koreans as YuMok, established in 1983 by female church leaders dissatisfied with the lack of support for such ministries in the church at large. The constituting group even established its own seminary despite the small size of its following—only fifteen thousand in 103 congregations. Like male-administered denominations, this one too has endured divisions, some of the contention being due to the dominant role of Park Jeong-Ho. When her own General Assembly removed her as moderator, she established the Korean Women Pastors Presbyterian Union (Yun-HapyerMok), which at the end of the last century reported fifty-four hundred members in 125 congregations. Both of these groups practice Presbyterian polity, and Park Jeong-Ho was moderator of the second one as of 1999. The Westminster Confession is, at least in principle, the doctrinal standard of both feminist church bodies.

In contrast with the rather liberal denominations already described, there are many conservative and fundamentalist Presbyterian groups in South Korea. The Korean Christian Fundamentalist Assembly is one such development. It grew out of a seminary established in 1972 by a missionary from the United States with assistance from evangelist-educator Bob Jones of

Greenville, South Carolina, and Pastor Ian Paisley of the Free Presbyterian Church in Northern Ireland. The Fundamentalist Assembly came into being in 1987 as a church with Presbyterian polity and subscription to the Westminster Standards. By the year 2000, it claimed over eighteen thousand members meeting in 116 local churches. A much larger comparable body is the Fundamentalist Presbyterian General Assembly (GunBon-Fundamentalist II), founded in 1983 by a native pastor educated in the United States at Bob Jones University. Pastor Yum Haeng-Soo eventually embraced Reformed theology and discarded the dispensational doctrine he had studied at his university. The church he established seeks to combat secularism by resisting the movement to make concessions to culture, which many denominations appear eager to do. This body in 2000 had almost seventy thousand members worshiping in 216 congregations committed to the Westminster Standards.

Not all conservative Presbyterians in South Korea have engaged in secessions. Some, on the contrary, have promoted unity among bodies already united in theology. The Korean Presbyterian Church (YeJang), formed in 1981 through a merger of three small denominations, now has approximately 350 thousand adherents and 425 congregations involved in vigorous mission work at home and abroad. An affiliate of the International Council of Christian Churches, this body operates its own seminary, denies ordination to women, and subscribes heartily to the Westminster Confession.

Many other conservative Presbyterian bodies are active in South Korea, some with only a few hundred members, but others with a membership as large as 310 thousand. The fragmented condition of the Reformed community has not stifled church growth, and many of the denominations have extensive missionary outreaches to distant parts of the world. If, in their present divided condition, Korean Presbyterians have achieved so much, one wonders what might be accomplished were they united in principle and practice.

SUGGESTED ADDITIONAL READINGS >>

Belke, Thomas J. *Juche: A Christian Study of North Korea's State Religion.* Bartlesville, Okla.: Living Sacrifice Books, 1999.

Brown, George T. *Mission to Korea.* Richmond, Va.: Board of World Mission, Presbyterian Church, United States, 1962.

Campbell, Arch. *The Christ of the Korean Heart.* Columbus, Ohio: Falco, 1954.

Clark, Allen D. *A History of the Church in Korea.* Seoul: Christian Literature Society of Korea, 1971.

————. *Protestant Missionaries in Korea, 1893–1983.* Seoul: Christian Literature Society of Korea, 1987.

Clark, D. N. *Christianity in Modern Korea,* Lanham, Md.: University Press of America, 1986.

Hoke, Donald, ed. *The Church in Asia.* Chicago: Moody, 1975.

Hong, H. S., et al., eds. *Korean Struggles for Christ.* Seoul: Christian Literature Society of Korea, 1966.

Hunt, Everett N. Jr. *Protestant Pioneers in Korea.* Maryknoll, N.Y.: Orbis Books, 1980.

Huntley, Martha. *To Start a Work: The Foundations of Protestant Missions in Korea, 1884–1919.* Seoul: Presbyterian Church of Korea, 1987.

Kang, W. J. *Christ and Caesar in Modern Korea.* Albany: State University of New York Press, 1997.

Kim, In Soo. *Protestants and the Formation of Modern Korean Nationalism.* New York: Peter Lang, 1996.

Kim, John T. *Protestant Church Growth in Korea.* Seoul: Dae-shin Theological Seminary, 1998.

Lee, Sang Hyun. *Korean-American Ministry: A Resource Book.* Louisville, Ky.: General Assembly of the Presbyterian Church (U.S.A.), 1993.

Moffett, S. H. *The Christians of Korea.* New York: Friendship Press, 1962.

Oberdorfer, Don. *The Two Koreas: A Contemporary History.* Reading, Mass.: Addison-Wesley, 1997.

Paik, George L. *History of Protestant Missions in Korea, 1832–1910.* Seoul: Yonsei University Press, 1970.

Palmer, S. J. *Korea and Christianity.* Seoul: Hollym Corporation, 1967.

Rhodes, Harry A., ed. *History of the Korean Mission.* Philadelphia: Presbyterian Church (U.S.A.), 1935.

Rhodes, Harry A. and Archibald Campbell. *History of the Korean Mission.* 2 vols. New York: Commission on Ecumenical Mission and Relations, United Presbyterian Church (U.S.A.), 1965.

Ro, B. R. and M. L. Nelson, eds. *Korean Church Growth Explosion.* Seoul: Word of Life Press, 1983.

Shearer, Roy E. *Wildfire: Church Growth in Korea.* Grand Rapids: Eerdmans, 1966.

Underwood, Horace. *The Call of Korea.* New York: Fleming H. Revell, 1908.

THIRTY-TWO

The Empire of Japan

Now a modern, prosperous nation of over 127 million people, this country of some seven thousand islands appears to have had no exposure to Christian teaching until the sixteenth century. There is a possibility that Nestorians from China entered Japan in the thirteenth century, but no substantial evidence remains to validate that supposition. It is clear, however, that Francis Xavier led Jesuits on such a mission that arrived in 1549. Those Roman Catholics found a feudal society in which clan warfare raged in the absence of strong central government, even though the emperor was, in principle, sovereign over the whole land.

According to tradition, Jimmu Tenno, the first emperor, was a son of the sun goddess, so the country became known as the Land of the Rising Sun. The alleged divinity of the monarch did not, however, provide a basis for national unity, as clans competed for land and laborers. Chinese influences carried to Japan via Korea brought both civilization and the Buddhist religion to these islands in the sixth century. The indigenous Shinto cult rather quickly adjusted to subsisting side-by-side with the imported religion, and many people practiced both, a phenomenon that continues to the present and poses a major difficulty for Christian missions that proclaim Jesus as the exclusive savior. Modifications of Buddhism due to the Japanese habit of syncretism have caused some continental Buddhists to regard the Japanese versions as heresies.

Shinto (the Way of the Gods) features the worship of nature and ancestors, and thousands of Shinto temples adorn the landscape. When state Shinto was the official religion, all Japanese people were included within the cult, even though their personal devotion may have been performed at one or more of the numerous Buddhist shrines. Both of the dominant religions are sufficiently elastic to accommodate great variety in belief and practice, so vast multitudes patronize both without any awareness of conflict between them. When asked to identify their religion, a huge majority of people claim Buddhism, although secularism and naturalism have, in recent decades, made religious professions a mere formality for many Japanese.

Roman Catholic Missions

Portuguese traders first entered Japan about 1543, when their ship sailed into an island port south of Kyushu after being driven there by stormy seas. They enjoyed a ready welcome and were able to repair their vessel and sell their goods for silver. Reports from these merchants led their church to dispatch a mission of three Jesuits under Francis Xavier's leadership. He was a Spaniard educated at the University of Paris along with Ignatius Loyola (ca. 1495–1556), founder of the Society of Jesus. Francis had served in India, where Loyola had sent him at the request of Portugal's monarch John III (r. 1521–1557) and in the East Indies before going to Japan. The impressive Catholic successes in the period 1549–1639 have led some authors to refer to it as "Japan's Christian Century." By the end of the sixteenth century, about three hundred thousand baptisms had occurred, although Xavier's personal ministry in the land extended to only two years. Dominican and Franciscan friars soon followed the Jesuits and so enlarged the Catholic mission.

The early cordiality of clan leaders did not long endure, and 1587 brought a decree from the shogun (military dictator), Toyotomi Hideyoshi (1536–1598), ordering all missionaries to leave the country, and in 1614, when Tokugawa Ieyasu (1542–1616) was dictator, the government outlawed Christianity. Protracted persecution brought death to thousands of Catholics and almost effaced their religion from the land. These events were due in part to unsatisfactory commercial relations with Portuguese and Spanish traders and the offensive behavior of some missionaries. Japan closed her doors to foreigners, except for the Dutch, who had access to but one port once per year. Surviving Catholics thereafter maintained precarious clandestine existence for the next two centuries and were known as *Kakure Kirishtan* (hidden Christians). A massacre occurred in 1638.

Protestant Missions

Although Japan had adopted a policy of isolation from the Western world, the privileges the Dutch enjoyed there allowed a tiny stream of outside influence to reach the country. Western nations did not, however, attempt to regain access to Japan until the nineteenth century, and the first Protestant approaches produced no tangible results. The renowned German missionary Karl F. A. Gutzlaff, in 1832, visited the Ryukyu Islands, south of Japan, and distributed some Christian literature in the Chinese language, and five years later missionaries aboard an American vessel tried to visit Japan, but officials there refused to allow the ship to dock.

About the time the American missionaries failed to gain access to Japan, a native naval officer found a copy of the New Testament in Dutch floating in the bay at Nagasaki, and after finding a translator, he obtained a complete Bible in Chinese. Meanwhile associates of Gutzlaff, with the aid of some Japanese émigrés, translated several biblical books into the Japanese tongue, evidence that Protestants intended to reach the island at their first opportunity.

Opening the doors of Japan became a matter of great interest to Western governments because of the potential for profitable trade and because sometimes their ships needed havens to which they could retreat in stormy weather. At times the Japanese had imprisoned, even enslaved, shipwrecked seamen, so the United States took the lead in dealing with the shogun's government by sending a squadron of warships to Tokyo Bay in 1853. Commodore Matthew C. Perry (1749–1858) presented a request for diplomatic and commercial relations, which became a reality in a treaty concluded in 1854. This event demonstrated the inability of the dictator's regime to maintain the policy of isolation in the face of pressure from a modern naval power, and the agreement soon followed, allowing missionaries to enter the empire.

As a consequence of Perry's success, Townsend Harris (1804–1878) became United States Consul-General to Japan. A man of strong Christian convictions and exceptional diplomatic skill, Harris negotiated a more advantageous treaty, one that allowed Americans to reside in Japan while being exempt from that country's harsh, even inhumane, laws. In 1858 the Japanese agreed to permit the circulation of foreign literature, and missionaries of the Protestant Episcopal Church in America began distributing Christian materials in 1859. Presbyterians followed the Episcopalians only a few months later, when Dr. James C. Hepburn (1815–1911) and his wife, agents of the Presbyterian Church (U.S.A.), landed at Kanagawa. A skillful physician, Hepburn cared for the physical needs of natives while seeking their conversion to Christ. As he gained a mastery of the Japanese language, he translated portions of Scripture. Mrs. Hepburn focused her attention on the needs of Japanese ladies and so gained recognition as the pioneer educator of females in that land. The Hepburns had served in China before going to Japan, so they had some familiarity with oriental languages. Hepburn gained fame by producing a Japanese-English dictionary and a Bible dictionary in the native tongue. Together these intrepid ambassadors for Christ invested thirty-three years in their ministries to the Land of the Rising Sun.

By the end of 1859, Samuel R. Brown (1810–1880) and his wife had arrived in Yokohama, dispatched there by the Dutch Reformed Church in America. They concentrated on education and translation work, as they had done previously in China. Guido H. F. Verbeck (1830–1898) accompanied the Browns as an agent of the same denomination. Verbeck began his ministry teaching English, using the Bible as a reader. He did not gain any converts until 1866, but his work as an educator brought Verbeck great admiration and influence to the point that he helped to establish the Imperial University of Japan. In 1873, in part because of his work, the government rescinded the ban against Christianity in force since the decree of 1614. For several years Verbeck conducted classes for Buddhist priests, even though their interest was to gather information they could use against Christianity.

In 1861 James C. Ballagh (1832–1920) and his wife went to Japan under the sponsorship of the Dutch Reformed Church, the first in a line of missionaries from that American family to serve in that country. Ballagh established the first Protestant church in Japan, a congregation of only eleven people. Despite this humble beginning, Ballagh's tireless zeal and sterling character inspired others to go to this mission field, where he conducted evangelism in a former Buddhist temple while facing much opposition from clan leaders who hated the foreigners and their religion. The government, at that time, still prohibited the people from embracing Christianity, and placards warning against conversion were on display. The need to learn English, however, drove public officials to employ Ballagh and other missionaries to teach it to the children of nobles. This experience improved the missionaries' knowledge of Japanese and thereby facilitated their ministry of evangelism and Bible translation.

As the empire of Japan became acquainted with the modern world, a reaction against all things Western appeared among zealots of the old order, and in 1863, the movement to expel all foreigners reached a pinnacle, as assaults upon missionaries became frequent. Some Christians took refuge in the American consulate. These events occurred at a time when the traditional feudal order was collapsing, and forward-looking leaders were forging a new Japan. In 1868 the Meiji Restoration transformed the country into a modern state with a strong central government within a constitutional monarchy. Feudalism was gone, and Christianity appeared to be one of the beneficiaries of the change, especially when the imperial government, in 1873, revoked the ban on the foreign religion. Soon, however, the architects of modern Japan began promoting state Shinto as the religion and political philosophy appropriate for subjects of the divine emperor. The impressive growth of the churches continued, but by the 1930s, authoritarian rule was stressing that national identity required adherence to the state cult. Only by accommodating themselves to the demands of nationalism could the churches avoid repression. Most Christians therefore strove to show that their faith in no way impaired their patriotism. Reformed believers often were caught in conflict between their allegiance to the King of Kings and their loyalty to the emperor of Japan, a nation increasingly involved in military conquests of its neighbors.

Reformed Churches in Japan

As the labors of missionaries bore fruit, the work of Reformed believers allowed for the formation of the United Church of Christ in Japan, which became a reality in 1877. The Presbyterian mission from the United States joined with that of the Dutch Reformed Church and the recently arrived United Presbyterian Church mission from Scotland to form a single denomination that the Reformed Church in the United States and the Presbyterian Church (U.S.) (Southern) joined soon thereafter. The United Church was an autonomous body that adopted the confessions of the three original constituents, but in 1890 it discarded the term "united" and with it the traditional documents of the Reformed faith. Thereafter the Apostles' Creed alone was to be its doctrinal standard. This Church of Christ became Japan's largest Protestant denomination.

In 1941, when the country was practically subject to military rule, the imperial government required all Protestant bodies to combine as the United Church of Christ (Kyodan), and thirty-four denominations complied. Soon after World War II, however, many churches left the Kyodan to resume self-government. Thereafter several new Reformed denominations came into being. The ecumenical-liberal character of the Kyodan was unacceptable to staunch Reformed believers, both natives and missionaries. The Kyodan nevertheless remained the strongest church, one which, in 1999, reported 205 thousand members in 1,721 congregations. A member of the World Council of Churches and domestic ecumenical agencies, the body ordains women and maintains Tokyo Union Theological Seminary, while operating with a modified Presbyterian polity.

In 1951 thirty-nine congregations withdrew from the Kyodan and formed the Church of Christ in Japan, which, at the end of the last century, had 13,500 members in 174 local assemblies. This church subscribes to the Apostles' Creed, to which it has added a confession of its own composition. It ordains females and employs Presbyterian government while operating its own seminary. The Church of Christ in Japan is an affiliate of the World Alliance of Reformed Churches.

Another denomination formed after the Second World War as a secession from the Kyodan is the Reformed Church in Japan, a body of some nine thousand adherents in 217 local assemblies. It does not ordain females, and the Westminster Standards constitute its affirmation of faith. This church's closest relations are with the Christian Reformed Church in North America, which sent missionaries to aid its Asian partner in the early days of the Japanese church's formation. The Reformed Church in Japan, a dynamic and growing movement, holds membership in the Reformed Ecumenical Council and maintains a seminary in Kobe.

The Presbyterian Church in Japan is the product of a merger of two Reformed bodies in 1956. Eager to preserve historic Calvinism, the Presbyterian Church adheres to the Westminster Standards, refrains from ordaining women, and supports theological schools that espouse its own position on doctrine. Approximately twenty-eight hundred people are members in this denomination of forty-six congregations. An affiliate of the Japanese Evangelical Alliance, this body has no official connections with Reformed churches outside Japan.

Comparable to the Presbyterian Church is the much smaller Biblical Church, a denomination subscribing to the Westminster and the Helvetic Confessions of Faith. Barely one thousand Christians adhere to this conservative church, which does not ordain women to serve in its nineteen congregations. The slightly larger Cumberland Presbyterian Church, originally an American mission, maintains Presbyterian polity, but like its mother church, it does not espouse Reformed theology.

Although the Reformed faith has a very small constituency in Japan, churches of that persuasion in the United States and South Korea are involved in ongoing efforts to evangelize the Land of the Rising Sun. The Reformed Presbyterian Church of North America moved its mission from China to Japan after the Communist government forced foreigners to leave the mainland in 1950, while, as indicated, the Christian Reformed Church in North America assists the Reformed Church in Japan, especially in education and church planting. The Orthodox Presbyterian Church also has missionaries who work with the Reformed Church in Japan in church planting, and one such missionary teaches at the Reformed seminary in Kobe. Several agents of the Reformed Church in America labor in Japan, and for the Presbyterian Church in America, the Land of the Rising Sun is a major field in which about forty missionaries are engaged.

The confessional churches involved in missions to Japan face a daunting task, especially because their insistence on the finality and exclusivity of Jesus Christ as the only savior conflicts with the deeply rooted syncretism that pervades the culture. The liberal-ecumenical missions are more flexible and accommodating, and their emphasis upon social services does not arouse the opposition often encountered by the evangelistic efforts orthodox Reformed Christians regard as indispensable. Some of Japan's most influential native theologians and church leaders became enamored of the dialectical theology of German authors such as Karl Barth and Emil Brunner, advocates of what they call evangelical Christianity. Their interpretation of the faith is, however, far removed from historic Reformed beliefs. Tokyo Union Theological Seminary has been a major generator of this view and some even more radical in their departure from orthodoxy.

SUGGESTED ADDITIONAL READINGS »

Boxer, Charles R. *The Christian Century in Japan, 1549–1650.* Berkeley: University of California Press, 1951.

Cary, Otis. *A History of Christianity in Japan.* Rutland, Vt.: C. E. Tuttle, 1976.

Drummond, Richard H. *A History of Christianity in Japan.* Grand Rapids: Eerdmans, 1971.

Fujita, Neil S. *Japan's Encounter with Christianity.* New York: Paulist Press, 1991.

Germany, Charles H. *Protestant Theologies in Modern Japan.* New York: Friendship Press, 1967.

Iglehart, Charles W. *A Century of Protestant Christianity in Japan.* Rutland, Vt.: C. E. Tuttle, 1959.

Kun Sam Lee. *The Christian Confrontation with Shinto Nationalism.* Philadelphia: Presbyterian and Reformed, 1966.

Mizugaki Kiyoshi. *100 Years of Evangelism in Japan.* Translated by J. A. McAlpine. Columbus, Ga.: Quill Publications, 1986.

Phillips, James M. *From the Rising of the Sun: Christians and Society in Contemporary Japan.* Maryknoll, N.Y.: Orbis Books, 1981.

Tames, Richard and Michael L. Hadley. *Japan's Christian Century.* Amersham, U.K.: Hutton, 1973.

Young, John M. L. *Two Empires in Japan.* Philadelphia: Presbyterian and Reformed, 1961.

THIRTY-THREE

Lesser Pacific Islands

Having given attention to the major island groups in the Pacific Ocean, it is appropriate at this point to consider some of the smaller ones of Oceania, that is, Micronesia, Melanesia, and Polynesia. Some thirty main groups and many smaller ones lie in that part of the world, and only a relatively few have substantial Reformed ministries.

Republic of Vanautu

Long known as the New Hebrides, this group of Melanesian Islands is about eleven hundred miles east of Australia. Although the Portuguese found it earlier, this area first excited European interest in the eighteenth century, when Captain James Cook (1728–1779) explored that region from 1768 to 1778. His reports aroused much interest and led explorers, whalers, and merchants to visit the islands, often to exploit the very primitive natives. Unscrupulous Europeans reveled in the gross immorality of the pagan culture and introduced rum and firearms, which worsened the carnage of the frequent tribal wars. At times the traders placed sick Europeans among the tribesmen to infect them with measles, to which they had no immunity. Seizing the land and making the residents indentured servants were the major interests of the first Britons on the scene.

As reports about conditions in the New Hebrides reached Great Britain, Christians there became concerned to take the gospel to the people and terminate the terrible abuses to which other Britons were subjecting them. The London Missionary Society was the initial instrument to accomplish that goal. John Geddie (1815–1872), a Presbyterian from Canada but born in Scotland, founded the New Hebrides Mission as an outreach of the London Missionary Society supported by the Presbyterian Synod of Nova Scotia's commitment to Polynesia. Geddie established a station on the island of Aneitum and there introduced an alphabet and, in an amazingly short time, began preaching in the local language. By 1863 the New Testament was available in the dialect of Aneitum.

Although Geddie had to contend with tropical diseases, opposition from traders who resented his interference with their evil business, and competition from French Catholic missionaries, he persisted, and the mission extended Christian influence across the island and from there spread elsewhere. Soon other Canadian Presbyterians joined him. Tenderhearted toward natives, Geddie opposed the use of force against them, even when they committed atrocities. Due to his appeals Presbyterians in Australia also began supporting the mission. Eventually someone erected a sign on one island, a table with this inscription: "When he landed in 1848, there were no Christians here; when he left in 1872, there were no heathen."

More famous than Geddie is John G. Paton (1824–1907), an agent of Scotland's Reformed Presbyterian Church, who arrived in the New Hebrides in 1848 and quickly began reporting the brutalities he witnessed, those perpetrated by Europeans, those committed as reprisals by injured islanders, and those that occurred in tribal conflicts, as the victors often ate the flesh of their foes. Paton denounced the recruitment of laborers for work abroad as slavery, a practice Great Britain had abolished throughout her empire in 1834. He estimated seventy-thousand people had been carried away from their homeland for labor elsewhere.

Despite horrible living conditions and almost constant danger, Paton persevered, even after the deaths of his wife and son. In 1862 he went to Australia, where he promoted his mission, and later he traveled to New Zealand and Scotland for the same purpose. In 1866, with seven new missionaries, Paton returned to the New Hebrides and settled on Aniwa, where he enjoyed much evangelistic success. After 1881 he traveled to the United States and Canada to raise funds for his mission, and after his death, members of his family continued to serve in the islands he loved, and as late as 1970, some of his relatives were still ministering there.

Due to the work of Geddie, Paton, and other pioneers, a marvelous transformation of the culture occurred in the New Hebrides. Peoples who had been polytheists, idolaters, and cannibals became devoted Christians. Motivated by faith in God's sovereignty and concern for lost sinners, these missionaries of the Reformed faith planted churches that remain as monuments to the courage and sacrificial character of their founders. Today about fifty-seven thousand islanders adhere to the Presbyterian Church, an ecumenical denomination connected with the World Council of Churches and the World Alliance of Reformed Churches.

New Caledonia

In addition to their achievements in the New Hebrides, missionaries of the Reformed persuasion established a Christian presence in New Caledonia, an island group south and west of the Vanautu. Long under French rule, this was a penal colony for much of the nineteenth century, and descendants of prisoners still reside there. Christians came to Maré, one of a cluster known as the Loyalty Islands, after British explorers discovered this region in 1774. French settlers arrived in 1853 and began mining nickel and cobalt.

Even before Frenchmen appeared, Christians from other islands went there to proclaim the gospel, some of them Protestants from Tonga. Catholic missionaries initiated their work in 1851 and Protestants from Great Britain the next year, when the London Missionary Society sent its people there. When French colonial policy and opposition from the Catholics made the work of the London Missionary Society difficult, in 1897 that organization asked the Paris Evangelical Missionary Society to assume responsibility for that field. Two churches with Reformed roots remain in these islands, but neither any longer espouses the doctrinal position of the original missionaries.

The Evangelical Church in New Caledonia and the Loyalty Islands, which became autonomous in 1962, operates with a Presbyterian form of polity in governing seventy-two congregations in which some thirty thousand people worship. Although this church subscribes officially to the Helvetic Confession and the Heidelberg Catechism, it ordains females to all of its offices and holds membership in such ecumenical organizations as the World Alliance of Reformed Churches and the World Council of Churches while engaging in collaborative efforts with the Roman Catholic Church.

In 1957 the Free Evangelical Church came into being due to a secession from the Evangelical Church which occurred, in part, because of disagreements about political and social issues. This denomination of approximately two thousand members does not ordain women, but its only doctrinal standards are the Apostles' Creed and the Nicene Creed. Since 1992 the church has been in discussion about reunion with the body from which it withdrew. Today a majority of professing Christians in these islands are Roman Catholics.

Cook Islands

The Cook Islands in the south Pacific, a self-governing dependency of New Zealand, received the Christian faith through the work of the London Missionary Society in 1821, when Christians from Tahiti went there. In 1888 Great Britain claimed a protectorate over the islands named in honor of explorer Captain James Cook. John Williams (1796–1839) of the London Missionary Society, who traveled to and evangelized in many parts of the Pacific, had promoted Christianity in the Cook Islands with much success, so that pagan practices ceased in a relatively short time, and large numbers of natives embraced the faith.

Through the work of London Missionary Society personnel, the Cook Islands Christian Church was organized as a Presbyterian body now closely related to the Presbyterian Church in New Zealand. About eleven thousand adherents (two-thirds of the population) worship in thirty-four congregations of a denomination affiliated with the World Council of Churches. The Apostles' Creed and the Nicene Creed are the only doctrinal symbols of this body, which operates Tacamoa Theological College for the education of its ministers.

French Polynesia is another area in which Reformed Christians have made a substantial investment. These 118 islands, of which Tahiti is the largest, stretch over a huge part of the Pacific Ocean. Spanish explorer Ferdinand Magellan discovered them in 1521, but not until 1767 did Great Britain take control of Tahiti. The next year France asserted its claim.

Agents of the London Missionary Society arrived in 1797, and in 1815 the native king embraced Christianity and urged his subjects to do so, and most of them complied readily. Roman Catholic missionaries appeared in 1834, but the native government resisted them. Not until 1842 did Catholics obtain permission to work in the islands, and even then the native regime agreed only because of threats of French military action. France secured its protectorate that same year, and in 1880 it annexed Tahiti and several other islands. In 1958 the French government offered independence, but a large majority of islanders rejected it. Polynesia therefore became an overseas French territory with full autonomy.

Two Protestant churches remain in the territory as fruits of Reformed missionary endeavors. The Evangelical Church of French Polynesia is a denomination of about ninety-five thousand members and eighty-one congregations united within Presbyterian polity while holding membership in the World Alliance of Reformed Churches and the World Council of

Churches and espousing the Apostles' Creed as its sole doctrinal statement. The church ordains women, operates two theological schools, and emphasizes social services through education and health care more than evangelism.

A minor schism in 1940 led to formation of the Independent Church of French Polynesia, a movement that abandoned Presbyterian polity in favor of local church autonomy. At the end of the last century only one congregation of about a hundred people worshiped under this name. Several other tiny churches of Protestant character function in this country, but they employ congregational government and make no formal subscription to any historic Reformed confession.

Western Samoa, composed of eight islands eighteen hundred miles northeast of New Zealand, was the site of great international tensions among Germany, Great Britain, and the United States that eventuated in German annexation in 1899. In World War I troops from New Zealand occupied this territory, and it remained under New Zealand's administration until 1962, when it gained independence.

Protestant Christianity came to Western Samoa through the work of the London Missionary Society, which sent believers from Tahiti and the Cook Islands. Once the mission was established and education was available for evangelists, islanders from this territory carried the gospel to other places in the Pacific Ocean.

The London Missionary Society Church developed as the first Christian body in the islands, and in 1962, that denomination changed its name to the Congregational Christian Church in Western Samoa, a movement that reported over seventy thousand members in 1999. The term *congregational* does not describe this church accurately, for it operates with a form of polity closely comparable to Presbyterianism, and the doctrinal standards of this body include the Westminster Confession of Faith. Although a member of the World Council of Churches and local ecumenical agencies, the Congregational Christian Church does not ordain women. Malua Theological College is its major educational institution.

Across the vast reaches of the Pacific Ocean there are other Reformed ministries, but they are very small and at present do not show signs of great vitality and hence do not appear in this survey.

Cromarty, Jim. *Food for Cannibals: The Story of John G. Paton.* Darlington, U.K.: Evangelical Press, 2004.

Garrett, John. *To Live Among the Stars.* Geneva: World Council of Churches, Institute of Pacific Studies, 1982.

Gilson, Richard. *The Cook Islands, 1820–1950.* Wellington, N.Z.: Victoria University Press, 1980.

Langridge, A. K. and F. H. L. Paton. *John G. Paton: Later Years and Farewell.* London: Hodder and Stoughton, 1910.

Latourette, Kenneth S. *A History of the Expansion of Christianity.* Vol. 5. New York: Harper and Brothers, 1943.

Lawson, J. Gilchrist. *Famous Missionaries: Portraits and Biographies.* Grand Rapids: Zondervan, 1945.

Miller, R. S., ed. *Misi Gete: John Geddie, Pioneer Missionary to the New Hebrides.* Launceston, Australia: Presbyterian Church of Tasmania, 1975.

Neil, Stephen. *A History of Christian Missions.* New York: Penguin Books, 1964.

Paton, James, ed. *The Story of Dr. John G. Paton's Thirty Years with South Sea Cannibals.* Rev. by A. K. Langridge. New York: George H. Doran, 1923.

Thiessen, John Caldwell. *A Survey of World Missions.* Chicago: InterVarsity, 1955.

THIRTY-FOUR

Conclusion

In the providence of God, the Reformed faith has spread to every inhabited continent of the earth, and the number of local churches and denominational bodies operating with Presbyterian polity is large. In some countries, such as South Korea, numerical growth has been impressive, but in others declining membership has been a lamentable fact of ecclesiastical life. In many cases, as this study has shown, subscription to Presbyterian polity does not necessarily indicate adherence to historic Reformed theology. Many denominations affiliated with the World Alliance of Reformed Churches maintain the Presbyterian form of church government and subscribe, in principle, to one or more of the historic Reformed confessions of faith and catechisms. This subscription is, however, in some cases, theoretical rather than actual, as the absence of any means to enforce compliance attests. It is evident therefore that not all Presbyterian churches are Reformed in theology, and some congregations that do embrace historic Calvinism do not endorse Presbyterian polity. A growing number of independent churches and Reformed Baptist congregations fit this description. Many such bodies operate with rule by elders but do not recognize the authority of any higher church court such as a presbytery or a synod.

Although the twentieth century has witnessed numerous departures from historic Presbyterian-Reformed doctrine and procedures, there are causes for encouragement nevertheless. The popularity of Reformed literature, for example, appears to be growing steadily, as the success of publishing houses such as the Banner of Truth Trust, P&R (Presbyterian and Reformed) Publishers, Evangelical Press, Christian Focus Publications, Reformation Heritage Books, and others shows. John Calvin's writings continue to receive much attention from Bible students along with those of modern exponents of Reformed scholarship. Enrollment in confessional schools of theology has grown substantially in recent years, and church-planting by denominations loyal to the Reformed faith is moving ahead steadily, while membership and attendance in liberal bodies declines. This development has been especially apparent in the United States, where the Presbyterian Church in America, the Orthodox Presbyterian Church, and the United Reformed Churches have been very vigorous. In South Korea, South America, and Africa comparable efforts are bearing much fruit. Europe, the birthplace of the Reformation, long the scene of declining churches, is now a mission field on which Reformed churches have focused attention and invested resources. The Evangelical Presbyterian Church in England and Wales is one such endeavor.

Another evidence of Presbyterian-Reformed vitality is the growing number of orthodox congregations leaving denominations that no longer, in large part, adhere to the faith of their founders. The formation of the Presbyterian Church in America in 1973 is one particularly impressive example. The Presbyterian Church of Brazil is another. This large denomination no longer maintains ecumenical relations with the Presbyterian Church (U.S.A.) and has initiated such contacts with the conservative Presbyterian Church in America.

The historical Calvinist confidence in the sovereignty of God remains strong. Convinced the divine program for the ages cannot fail, Reformed believers look to the future optimistically, as they pray for revival, and labor to fulfill their Savior's commission to proclaim His gospel through the world in preparation for His glorious return to earth to claim His rightful dominion over all things.

Index

Argentina, 383–85
Argentine Presbyterian Church, 385
Arianism, 157, 161–62, 199–200
Armenian Evangelical Church (Egypt), 403
Arminianism, 28, 29, 62–64, 65–66, 116,
   158, 181, 199, 200, 213, 219–20
Arminius, Jacob, 62–63
Aruba, 372–73
Asian Theological Seminary, 498
Assemblies of God, 361, 364, 368, 446
Associated Presbyterian Churches of Scot-
   land, 139
Associate Presbytery of Scotland, 128, 158
Associate Presbytery of Sialkot, 465
Associate Reformed Presbyterian Church,
   267, 354–55, 360, 361, 446, 463
Association of Non-Subscribing Presbyte-
   rians, 163
Athanasius, 411
atheism, 47
Atkins, Grace, 375
Auburn Affirmation, 304, 307, 311
Auburn Convention, 215
Auburn Theological Seminary, 246, 259, 304
Augsburg Confession of Faith, 5
Augustine, 26, 62, 109, 143, 317, 401
Austin Theological Seminary, 253
Australia, 276–85
Australian Council of Churches, 280
Austria, 81

Baillie, Robert, 120
Ballagh, James C., 530
Banda, Kamuzu, 424
Bangladesh, 468, 470, 472–73
Banner of Truth Trust, 194, 541
Baraka Bible Presbyterian Church, 456
Barker, Frank M., Jr., 344–45
Barker, Will, 337
Barker, William M., 346
Barmen Declaration, 26, 92, 93
Barnes, Albert, 214–15
Barrios, Don Justo Rufino, 365
Barth, Karl, 25–27, 50, 73, 92, 274, 280,
   316–17, 319, 320, 333, 533
Basel, 24
Basel Mission, 443–44, 447–49, 486
Battle of Flodden Field, 105
Battle of the Boyne River, 155

Bavinck, Herman, 72–73, 321–22, 323
Beaton, David Cardinal, 108–9, 113
Beaton, Donald, 134
Beaton, James, 108
Beecher, Lyman, 214, 218, 246
Beeke, Joel R., 351
Belfast Academical Institution, 161, 163
Belfast Society, 157
Belgic Confession, 59, 60, 62, 63, 68
Belgium, 102–3
Belize, 362–63
Bell, Kenneth B., 346–47
Bell, L. Nelson, 335
Berkhof, Louis, 322–23
Berkouwer, Gerrit Cornelis, 73–74
Berthoud, Paul, 430
Bethel Mission, 420
Bethlehem Bible Presbyterian Church
   (Guatemala), 366
Beversluis, Nicolaas H., 350
Beza, Theodore, 21–22, 23, 38, 120, 176
Bible Christian Faith Church (Kenya), 418
Bible Presbyterian Church, 328–29
   Collingwood and Columbus Synods, 329
Bible Presbyterian Church (Australia), 284
Biblical Seminary of Latin America, 363
biblical theology, 322
Bihaii, Lal, 374
Bilderdijk, Willem, 67–68
Bill, Samuel A., 440
Birmingham Theological Seminary, 345
Bismarck, Otto von, 421, 435
Blackford, Alexander L., 380
Blackman's Church of Africa, Presbyterian,
   424, 425
Black Oath, 149
Blanco, Antonio Guzman, 398
Board of World Missions (Southern Pres-
   byterian Church), 238
Boegner, Marc, 50
Boehm, John Philip, 264
Boers, 289
Bohemia, 78–79
Bohemian Brethren, 79
Boice, James Montgomery, 343
Bolivar, Simon, 391, 395, 397
Bolivia, 391–92
Bonaire, 372–73
Bonhoeffer, Dietrich, 318–20, 321

Book of Common Prayer, 116–17, 152, 179, 180
Book of Confessions, 334
Book of Discipline (Church of Scotland), 111, 114
Book of Discipline (England), 177
Borneo Evangelical Mission, 486
Boru, Brian, 145
Boston, Thomas, 129
Botha, Louis, 293
Bothwell, James, 110
Botswana, 432–33
Boxer Rebellion, 506
Brazil, 379, 380–83
Brazza, Pierre Savorgnan de, 439
Breckenridge, R. J., 227
Bremen Mission, 443–44
Brice, Edward, 148
Briggs, Charles A., 249, 257–58, 301, 305
Brink, Ray, 376
British and Foreign Bible Society, 98, 102, 383, 385, 392, 394, 497
British East Africa Company, 415
British East India Company, 461, 470, 472, 477
British Empire, 276, 293, 470
British Evangelical Council, 170
British South Africa Company, 427
Brown, Alexander, 161
Brown, John, 135
Brown, Samuel R., 530
Bruce, David, 286
Bruce, William, 163
Brunner, Emil, 25, 26–28, 73, 280, 317–18, 319, 320, 533
Bryant, Emilio Sylva, 398
Bryan, William Jennings, 303–4, 306
Bryden, Walter W., 274
Bucer, Martin, 7, 11
Buck, Pearl S., 304, 310–12
Buddhism, 480, 485, 517, 527
Buell, William P., 481
Bultmann, Rudolf, 320–21
Burkina Faso, 446–47
Burma. See Myanmar
Burney, Isaac T. E., 503
Burns, Thomas, 286
Burns, William C., 503
Burr, Aaron, 205

Bushnell, Horace, 220, 301
Buswell, J. Oliver, 328, 329

Cabrera, Archilla, 363
Calabar Mission, 440
Calas, Jean, 45–46
Caldwell, Daniel T., 236
Caldwell, Milton E., 375
Calhoun, David B., 341
Calvin College, 263, 350
Calvinistic Methodist Church in Wales, 184
Calvin, John, 7–8, 12–22, 23, 24, 26, 35, 36, 38, 59, 109, 113, 120, 254, 317, 379, 382
Calvin Theological Seminary, 263, 322–23, 349
Cambodia, 482
Cameron, Richard, 124, 126, 266
Cameroon, 447–49
Campbell, Alexander, 221
Campbell, David E., 465
Campbell, James, 205
Campbell, James R., 464, 469
Campbell, Robert F., 234
Campbell, Saunders, 417
Campbell, William, 291
Canada, 271–76
Canadian and American and Reformed Churches, 275
Canadian Council of Churches, 275
Canadian Reformed Churches, 72
Candlish, Robert, 133
Cane Ridge revival, 221
Canons of Dort, 63, 68, 201, 264
Cape Synod of the Dutch Reformed Church, 428, 432
Carey, William, 131, 461, 472, 473, 477
Cargill, Donald, 266
Caribbean Basin, 369–78
Cartwright, Thomas, 175–76, 177
Castro, Fidel, 369–70
Catherine de Medici, 36, 37–38, 39
Catholics. See Roman Catholics
Cayman Islands, 371–72
Celestine I, Pope, 143
Celtic Christianity, 143
Central America, 362–68
Central American Mission, 363, 364, 365, 366, 368
Central College (Pella, IA), 354

Tokyo Union Theological Seminary, 532, 533
Toleration Act (1689), 183, 203
Tone, Theodore Wolfe, 159
Townsend, W. Cameron, 365
Tow, Timothy Siang Hui, 487
Transylvania, 82–83, 87
Travers, Walter, 148
Treaty of Westphalia, 102
Trinidad, 373–74
Trinidad Presbyterian Association, 373–74
Trinity Christian College, 263–64
Trinity Presbyterian Church of the Sudan, 410
Trinity Theological College (Singapore), 486, 487
Trumbell, David, 386
Tsonga Presbyterian Church, 292
Tulchan Bishops, 112
Tunisia, 403–4
Turner, Nat, 228
Turretin, Francis, 254
Tuscaloosa Institute, 229
Twisse, William, 119–20
Tyndale, William, 106

Uganda, 418–20
Uitenbogaert, Johannes, 62–63
Ulster, 149, 155, 197
Underwood, Horace G., 518–19
Union of Armenian Evangelical Churches in the Near East, 454
Union of Evangelical Churches of Belgium, 102–3
Union of Free Evangelical Churches of France, 48
Union of Reformed Churches, 50
Union of the Evangelical Free Churches, 50
Union Theological Seminary (Buenos Aires), 388
Union Theological Seminary (Manila), 497, 498
Union Theological Seminary in New York City, 215, 246, 249, 257, 305
Union Theological Seminary in Virginia, 232–33, 234, 246, 251
Unitarianism, 161–62, 163, 183, 217
United Andean Mission, 395
United Brethren, 78–79
United Christian Church (Myanmar), 479

United Church of Canada, 274, 276
United Church of Christ, 367
United Church of Christ (Kyodan), 531–32
United Church of Christ (Philippines), 497–98
United Church of Jamaica and Grand Cayman, 372
United Church of Northern India, 468
United Church of North India, 472–73
United Church of South India, 467
United Church of Zambia, 426
United Evangelical Church (Philippines), 497, 498
United Evangelical Church of Czech Brethren, 86
United Evangelical Church of Ecuador, 395
United Free Church Continuing, 139
United Free Church of Scotland, 135–36, 443
United Irishmen, 159–60
United Kingdom of Great Britain, 127
United Mission (Iraq), 457
United Presbyterian Church (Scotland), 135
United Presbyterian Church in North America, 402
United Presbyterian Church of Brazil, 381–82
United Presbyterian Church of North America, 267–68, 409, 412
United Presbyterian Church of Pakistan, 468
United Presbyterian Rajputana Mission, 465–66
United Protestant Church of Belgium, 103
United Reformed Church (England), 186
United Reformed Churches in North America, 275, 350, 542
United Reformed Church of Southern Africa, 436
United Secession Church, 135
United Synod of the Presbyterian Church, 227, 240–42
Uniting Church in Australia, 280, 282, 284
Uniting Presbyterian Church in Southern Africa, 292
Universalism, 218
University of Edinburgh, 129, 130
University of Franeker, 62
University of Groningen, 69
University of Leyden, 61–62, 69, 70, 72
University of Texas, 253